MALT WHISKY YEARBOOK 2021

www.maltwhiskyyearbook.com

First published in Great Britain in 2021 by
MagDig Media Limited

ISBN 978-0-9576553-8-6

MagDig Media Limited
1 Brassey Road
Old Potts Way, Shrewsbury
Shropshire SY3 7FA
ENGLAND

E-mail: info@maltwhiskyyearbook.com
www.maltwhiskyyearbook.com

Contents

Introduction

This is the seventeenth edition of the Malt Whisky Yearbook and the second I´ve written and edited during the pandemic and I feel more optimistic this time than last year. I realise we are not through it yet but many of us seem to have found solutions how to cope with some of the negative consequences. If we haven´t been able to engage in physical meetings at tastings and whisky shows, there´s been no shortage of opportunities to raise a dram and look one another in the eye thanks to zoom and other tools. Still, I for one can´t wait to start travelling to distilleries again. The smell and the heat of washbacks and pot stills at work and the peaceful moments in damp, dunnage warehouse sniffing around the casks – nothing beats that!

Meanwhile there are still books to be written (and read) and one of the really fun parts of working with this year´s edition was to portrait seven outstanding persons who challenged the norm in their respective countries by making something for the first time, at least in modern days, namely malt whisky. You can call them innovators, entrepreneurs or risk takers – in this book I refer to them as Trailblazers of Malt Whisky!

And as usual, my excellent team of whisky writers have excelled themselves this year and have contributed with some fascinating articles:

We are all looking for flavours in our dram. Ian Wisniewski explains how different varieties of roasted malt can give the whisky a new and exciting profile.

The Excise Act of 1823 was not just a way of securing taxes for the crown. Scrutinising the text, Charles MacLean and Arthur Motley found a detailed blueprint of how to make Scotch whisky.

Prediction of future sales is important for any business and even more so for whisky producers. Joel Harrison explains why it is sometimes a guessing game and sometimes a science.

The pandemic has changed our social behaviour and we are now more prone to support local businesses. Neil Ridley thinks here is an opportunity for local heroes around the world.

If you think whisky production abides by the same rules where ever it´s made – think again. Gavin D Smith will guide you through whisky legislation around the world.

The Japanese whisky industry is changing. A new set of regulations is being implemented and foreign investments are pouring in. Stefan Van Eycken has all the latest news.

In Malt Whisky Yearbook 2022 you will also find the unique, detailed and much appreciated section on Scottish malt whisky distilleries. It has been thoroughly revised and updated, not just in text, but also including numerous, new pictures, new distilleries and tasting notes for all the core brands. The chapter on distilleries from the rest of the world has been expanded. You will also find a list of more than 150 of the best whisky shops in the world with their full details and suggestions on where to find more information on the internet. The Whisky Year That Was provides a summary of all the significant events during the year. Finally, the very latest statistics gives you all the answers to your questions on production and consumption.

Thank you for buying Malt Whisky Yearbook 2022. I hope that you will have many enjoyable moments reading it and I can assure you that I will be back with a new, updated edition next year.

Malt Whisky Yearbook 2023 will be published in October 2022.
If you need any of the previous sixteen volumes of Malt Whisky Yearbook,
some of them are available for purchase (in limited numbers) from the website
www.maltwhiskyyearbook.com

Acknowledgements

First of all I wish to thank the writers who have shared their great specialist knowledge on the subject in a brilliant and entertaining way – Stefan van Eycken, Joel Harrison, Charles MacLean, Neil Ridley, Gavin D. Smith and Ian Wisniewski.

A special thanks goes to Gavin who put in a lot of effort nosing, tasting and writing notes for more than 100 different whiskies.

I am also deeply grateful to Philippe Jugé for his valuable input on French distilleries.

The following persons have also made important photographic or editorial contributions and I am grateful to all of them:

Iain Allan, Alasdair Anderson, Russel Anderson, Lukas Andrlik, Alexander Atha, Duncan Baldwin, Dana Baran, Adam Barber, Emma Battat, Alistair Baxter, Graham Bowie, Lauren Braithwaite, Ross Bremner, Keith Brian, Andrew Brown, Gordon Bruce, Mark Brunton, Neil Bulloch, Pär Caldenby, George Campbell, Petra Caspolin, Ian Chang, Ashok Chokalingam, David Clark, Joe Clark, Suzanne Clark, Francis Conlon, Zack Crowe, Victoria Currie, Ewa Czernecka, Magnus Dandanell, Dawn Davies, Alasdair Day, Paul Dempsey, Scott Dickson, Alex Driver, Frances Dupuy, Lukasz Dynowiak, Michael Elliot, Sebastian Eriksen, Simon Erlanger, Graham Eunson, David Ferguson, Andy Fiske, Robert Fleming, John Fordyce, Callum Fraser, Kathrin Furst, Calum Gee, Archie Gillies, Colin Gordon, Jonas Gram, Ewan Gunn, Gary Haggart, Andy Hannah, Soichiro Harada, Wendy Harries Jones, Steve Hawley, Erik Hirschfeld, Paul Hooper, Fraser Hughes, Robbie Hughes, Jill Inglis, Rakshit Jagdale, Sandy Jamieson, Bart Joosten, Julie Jordan, Jenny Karlsson, Davin de Kergommeaux, Samuli Korhonen, Mohan Krishna, Andrew Laing, Mark Lancaster, Emily Lineham, David Livingstone, Allan Logan, Graham Logan, Ian Logan, Alistair Longwell, Barry Macaffer, Iain McAlister, Tommy Macarthur, Brian MacAulay, Gemma McColl, Alan McConnochie, Alistair McDonald, John MacDonald, Laura MacDonald, Mhairi McDonald, Christy McFarlane, Sandy Macintyre, Sarah, McKeeman, Connal Mackenzie, John MacKenzie, Jaclyn McKie, Paul Mclean, Ian McWilliam, Graham Manson, Neil Mathieson, Kwanele Mdluli, Santiago Mignone, Gary Mills, Molly Minter, Carol More, Scott Morrison, Cristina Munoz, Neil Murphy, Sietse Offringa, Ben O´Gorman, Edel O´Keeffe, Graham Omand, Joe O´Sullivan, Gemma Paterson, Hannah Peebles, Sean Phillips, Colin Poppy, Simon Proud, Eleanor Quigley, Struan Grant Ralph, Joanne Reavley, Ian Renwick, David Roussier, Mariella Salerno, Colette Savage, Lila Serenelli, Andrew Shand, Greig Stables, Jennifer Tait, Stephanie Talbot, Claire Tesh, Eddie Thom, Annabel Thomas, Kirsty Thomson, Laura Thomson, Roselyn Thomson, Ruth Thomson, Kaitlyn Tsai, Barbara Turing, David Turner, Sandrine Tyrbas de Chamberet, Andrew Ure, Andrew Waite, Stewart Walker, Ranald Watson, Thuli Weerasena, Weidong Wei, Iain Weir, Ronald Whiteford, Anthony Wills, Jamie Winfield, Kristoffer Wittström, Josh Wong, Allison Young, Derek Younie and David Zibell.

Finally, to my wife Pernilla and our daughter Alice, thank you for your patience and your love and to Vilda, in sweet memory, our labrador who was my faithful companion in the office for more than fourteen years.

Ingvar Ronde
Editor
Malt Whisky Yearbook

Photo: Westland Distillery

Roasted Malt
– the route to new flavours

by Ian Wisniewski

The flavour of a whisky is a combination of several
steps during production and maturation. The cask has often been hailed
as the supreme supplier of taste. Fermentation and the distilling regime
play their parts as well. Rarely though, the barley gets any votes.
It is high time to add malting into the equation.

Is it destiny when different routes lead people to the same destination ? I believe it is, and present my evidence.

The young Bill Lumsden had a quest: finding the perfect cup of coffee in Edinburgh. This prompted an interest in the influence roasting has on the flavour of coffee beans. When appointed distillery manager at Glenmorangie in 1995, Bill acquired a coffee roaster and began experimenting, not with coffee beans but malted barley. Brian Kinsman's appreciation of ale led him to learn about the role of different malts when brewing Stout and Porter. Joining William Grant & Sons in 1997, Brian applied his knowledge to malt whisky.

You see ? The same compass guided them to a place where they could explore the flavours that malt whisky can gain from highly kilned and roasted malts.

The starting point for both options is malted barley. Malting begins by steeping barley in water to prompt germination. This 'activates' enzymes, and 'liberates' starches from the cell walls that had incarcerated them within the grain. Further development is prevented by drying the malt using a kiln. Air is conducted to the malt at controlled temperatures to avoid damaging enzymes, which are heat sensitive. Once warm air has driven moisture from the surface of the barley, kilning reaches the 'break point' (around 38 degrees centigrade) when heat begins drawing moisture from within the grain. Enzymes are less likely to be damaged by heat after the break point, and the temperature is increased to around 78 degrees centigrade.

The resulting malted barley has biscuit, cereal, malty notes, and can include 'background' phenolics (even though unpeated). This stems from guiaiacol, a phenolic compound produced by heat breaking down lignin (plant material within the grain). Guiaiacol is the simplest, but most aroma-active phenolic compound, releasing smokey notes.

This flavour profile can be developed further by kilning longer or roasting the malt. Heat initially breaks down starches into sugars, primarily glucose (a single unit), with lower levels of maltose (two linked units of glucose) and maltotriose (three linked glucose units). Applying heat to sugar creates caramelisation, while heat also prompts interaction between sugar and amino acids, resulting in Maillard reaction.

Flavours produced by Maillard reaction are big and acrid, such as bitter dark chocolate, cacao and coffee. Caramelisation generally produces sweeter notes, such as creme brulee, but also coffee, chocolate and acrid notes, which are examples of the crossover between caramelisation and Maillard reaction. Highly kilned malts include Vienna, Munich and Imperial.

"Each grade of highly kilned malt is a case of taking the temperature higher and kilning for longer, with the temperature rising to around 110 degrees centigrade. Vienna produces wort with quite a dry flavour. Munich is even drier with a biscuity-like flavour," says Steven Rowley, Operations Director, Simpsons Malt.

Roasted malt is produced in a roasting drum fitted with small raised paddles, angled to point in two different directions. As the drum rotates paddles spread the grain, ensuring it falls evenly through the internal space.

There are two types of roasted malt, which both have a different starting point. Crystal malt uses green malt (ie. unkilned) which has a moisture level of around 45%. Roasted malt utilises malted barley (ie. kilned) with around 4.5% moisture.

The production regime also varies. Crystal malt is produced by applying heat to the exterior of the roasting drum, causing moisture to evaporate from the husk, while instigating changes within. Moisture evaporating from the husk remains trapped within the drum, and malt is 'stewed' rather than roasted. Moisture is subsequently released from the drum by opening air flaps, one at the front and another at the rear of the roaster.

"Stewing the grain causes a gelatinisation process in the endosperm of each corn of green malt. Applying heat then dries the moisture from the grain and crystallises the gelatinised starch," says Ian Slater, Plant Manager, Bairds Malt, Pencaitland.

The resulting caramelisation produces creme brûlée, toffee, muscovado sugar sweetness and subtle coffee notes.

"The longer heat is applied the more caramelisation occurs, delivering pleasant dried fruit notes of fig, dates and prunes; along with delicate hints of strawberry jam, mango, chocolate and freshly roasted coffee," adds Dave Watson, Production Director, French and Jupps.

Different grades of roasting

Malt is roasted by conducting hot air into the drum. Entering through the flap at the rear of the roaster, hot air meets the malt while passing through the drum, then exits through the flap at the front. Air is heated by burning a flame, and adjusting the flame size regulates the temperature of the air.

"A roaster is automated to a point, but the traditional process still requires a dedicated, hands on operator, who has learnt his trade through months of training. The operator carefully manages the burner setting, taking repeated samples from the roasting drum to check for even development," says Dave Watson.

Different grades of roasted malt begin with Amber, Brown and Chocolate, with Black and Roasted the ultimate, experiencing up to 200 degrees centigrade in a two hour process.

"Different time/temperature formulas result in different flavours, you can get more/less characteristics and play tunes. Fruityness including dried fruit, raisins, sultanas, Christmas cake, can be dialled up or down," says Steven Rowley.

The grade most requested by distillers is chocolate malt.

"The strong colour and intense flavours are formed by Maillard reactions. We start roasting at 75 degrees centigrade for 30 minutes, then increase the temperature to 180-190 degrees centigrade for about 75 minutes. Then we close the air flaps and don't apply any additional heat, residual heat in the drum takes the temperature up to 210-215 degrees centigrade," says Dave Watson.

At the end of roasting the temperature is reduced to 40 degrees centigrade, and the malt doused with cold water to prevent further roasting. This water evaporates, leaving grain with a moisture level of 2-2.5%, ensuring a shelf life of one year in steel storage bins.

Roasted malts are produced from Winter barley (sown in Autumn, harvested the following Summer/Autumn) while highly kilned malts are Spring barley (sown in Spring, harvested Summer/Autumn). Spring barley, having been malted, is standard for distilling malt whisky.

"Winter varieties are more suitable for roasting as the corns and particularly the husks are more robust and withstand higher temperatures better. Spring barley has a less robust husk that can also be looser,

Roasted malt is produced using special roasting drums

Photo: Roddy Mackay
(courtesy of Bairds Malt)

and the grain size is a bit smaller," says Ian Slater.

Another vital factor is that longer kilning and roasting reduce the level of enzymes (which help convert starch into sugars during mashing), and also of starch (initially converting into sugars then alcohol during fermentation).

"Highly kilned malts still have some enzymic potential, but lose around 5-6% fermentability. Among roasted malts a small amount of enzymes remain in Amber but none in brown or chocolate," says Steven Rowley.

Consequently, malted barley is the majority shareholder in the mash bill.

"It's a constant balance of fermentability and flavour, with roasted malt used for flavour, and malted barley the dominant provider of enzymes," says Brian Kinsman, Master Blender, William Grant & Sons.

Only a few distilleries have utilised highly kilned and roasted malts, with a limited number of releases including The Balvenie Roasted Malt in 2006, while chocolate malt featured in Glenmorangie Signet (2016), with Glenmorangie distilling roasted malt for a few weeks annually. Torabhaig also conducts experimental production runs each October-November.

At Westland in the USA it's continuous rather than occasional production, with highly kilned and roasted malts distilled since Westland was operational in 2011. But then Master Distiller and Co-Founder Matt Hofmann considered this the obvious thing to do.

"When I came into the world of whisky I couldn't understand why the flavour potential of barley wasn't being discussed. We use 20 different varieties of barley, and mix and match these with different kilning and roasting levels. We also use one barley variety in five different formats, pale malt, Munich, 'Extra Special' malt, Brown and Pale Chocolate," says Matt Hofmann.

Similarly, one recipe distilled at Torabhaig in 2019 combined Crystal malt, Brown malt and lightly peated malted barley. In 2020 black malt was combined with heavily peated malt (137.9 ppm) to create depth of flavour and extend the phenolics from the peated malt.

Since the start in 2011, Matt Hofmann of Westland Distillery in Seattle has been using roasted malt

An initial, vital decision is the proportion of malted barley.

"My first idea was 50/50, but when I spoke to some brewers they said the flavour would be too much, the first batches were 30% and even that was too high, as it gave an overpowering flavour," says Dr Bill Lumsden, Glenmorangie's Director of Distilling, Whisky Creation & Whisky Stocks.

Additional flavours are created during fermentation, with the range of notes dependent on the choice of yeast, and length of fermentation.

"Fermenting roasted malt produced a highly flavourful wash, essentially a bolder version of Balvenie with more intense cereal and caramelised notes. We used the same amount of yeast and the usual fermentation time," says Brian Kinsman.

Maintaining the usual regime enables direct comparisons with equivalent malts distilled only from malted barley (we love to compare and contrast). Altering the usual regime offers other possibilities, and as different yeasts promote particular flavour profiles, yeast can be matched to specific malts.

At Torabhaig unpeated malted barley and Imperial malt, which has honeyed notes, was partnered with a brewer's yeast from Norway, Kveik, which contributed fruitiness. The union between them created another element, fruity boiled sweets.

Lower yield with roasting

Fermentation also entails entails another vital purpose, with yeast metabolising sugars and emitting residue in the form of alcohol. As highly kilned and roasted malts contain mere traces of residual sugars yeast experiences disappointment rather than the expected feast. Yeast depends on sugars derived from malted barley to satisfy its hunger, while distillers depend on malted barley for the yield of alcohol.

"Some of our malts represent 50% less yield. Yeast can digest up to malto-triose, but can't eat caramelised sugars. Maillard reaction leaves some of the sugar in the malt no longer fermentable," says Matt Hofmann.

For distillers, chocolate malt is one of the most popular of the different grades of roasted malt

That's a significant price to pay, but the benefits are evident.

"Roasted malts make a big impression on the new make spirit, even when accounting for just 20% (or if you're going for an individual roasted malt such as Pale Chocolate, which is indeed 4%) of the mash bill," says Matt Hofmann.

Roasted malts offer plenty of flavours to choose from, with the spirit cut being the editing stage.

"Pear drop and banana come through first, then chocolate notes appear, followed by coffee. We cut to feints when slightly leathery notes come over, but by then the chocolate and coffee notes have finished," says David Fitt, Chief Whisky Maker, English Whisky Co, which has distilled parcels of Crystal and Chocolate malt with malted barley since 2012.

The spirit cut provides another opportunity to maintain the usual regime, or to innovate.

"We kept the same spirit cut so that it was as much of a controlled experiment as possible. The new make spirit had elevated vanilla sweetness, and in-tensified cereal notes, making it a bolder version of the usual new make spirit," says Brian Kinsman.

At Torabhaig in 2019 a mash bill comprising chocolate malt with unpeated malted barley produced a lot of bitter, dark chocolate notes in the foreshots which resulted in the usual spirit cut being brought forward in order to capture them, with very aromatic coffee notes following.

"Chocolate malt is the most popular choice for distillers, though it gives acrid, bitter cocoa, biscuity, malty, black coffee. It also comes across as acrid and bitter in the wort, and in the new make spirit, so it's all about the interaction with other flavours during maturation," says Graham Manson, Commercial Sales Manager, Bairds Malt.

This means finding, and filling casks that provide flavours which can balance such expressive notes.

"Roasted malt gives bitter cocoa, so we fill the spirit into new American oak barrels which give a nice vanilla that provides balance. Roasted malts also give more maltyness, and to balance this we seek a certain integration. Hazelnut notes from roasted malt come together with caramel from new American oak, which creates Nutella," says Matt Hofmann.

Matching casks to the spirit can also mean selecting less active casks.

"New make spirit from chocolate malt initially seems flatter than our regular new make, as roasted malts act as an overcoat masking the lighter elements. This is why it was initially aged in second fill Bourbon barrels, to minimise wood influence. After three years we see how it is developing, and can then re-rack into more active casks, including first fill Bourbon, virgin oak, Port and Madeira," says Neil Mathieson, Whiskymaker, Torabhaig.

The role of the cask can also be optimised by the filling strength.

"We fill at 55% abv into new American oak, as at this filling strength the spirit extracts more wood sugars and less oak, otherwise too much oak influence would mask the influence of using roasted malt," says Matt Hofmann.

Filling a cask automatically instigates complex reactions between the new make spirit and the cask, with flavour compounds extracted from the cask at the greatest rate within the first three years.

"We also fill virgin casks, which are American oak with a medium char, and these have a massive and rapid impact, bringing chocolate and coffee notes more to the fore," says David Fitt.

For master blenders it's a case of keep calm (for years) and carry on sampling.

"After 8 years of ageing in virgin casks the chocolate and coffee notes are still massively there, but it's too early to say whether these notes will continue to be so prominent, or whether other flavours derived from the cask will increase to the point where they start to mask them," says David Fitt.

Exactly. How does a master blender decide when a cask has peaked ? Not easily, that's for sure.

"Maturing whisky goes through cycles, at 3-6 years it can be fantastic, you leave it until 8 years and it can seem not so good, but better again at 10-12 years. There are low points and high points, but no guarantees. It's not a science, you just have to wait and see," says Andrew Nelstrop, Founder, English Whisky Co.

The cask, and time, influence a malt's development, but the final flavour is determined by a master blender.

"The first batch of spirit distilled from chocolate malt was 12 years old in 2007, and was too intense to bottle on its own. The final recipe for Signet included a fairly substantial amount of chocolate malt, blended with several other styles including the classic Glenmorangie aged in Bourbon barrels, new charred oak, Sherry casks and longer aged malts," says Dr Bill Lumsden.

Early examples of single malts using roasted malt in the mashbill

Roasted malt is an innovative way of adding new flavours to single malts

Photo: Roddy Mackay
(courtesy of Bairds Malt)

When tasting an innovative expression we expect (demand even !) a different experience. But we also look for a family resemblance.

"Much of the new make spirit distilled from roasted malt was filled into Bourbon barrels. There are subtle developmental differences compared to the regular 10 year old, it was like an exceptionally good, rich and honeyed version, with quite a roasted and intense cereal note," says Brian Kinsman.

Bottling The Balvenie Roasted Malt at 14 years wasn't the end of that parcel. The remaining casks continued maturing, and were bottled as The Balvenie Stories 26 year old in 2019.

"The 26 year old was significantly more intense, almost syrupy, with the influence of the Bourbon barrel definitely dominating and the roasted malt adding intensity. But it's still Balvenie, with the characteristic honey notes recognisable," says Brian Kinsman.

Distilleries which have already been exploring highly kilned and roasted malts are all set to continue experimenting, and will (hopefully) be joined by others.

"We've only tried roasted malt so far, but are definitely looking at highly kilned malts. We experiment in the lab first which is never a perfect simulation, milling is a coffee grinder, then mashing and fermentation, with a small copper pot still producing a spirit cut of 200 ml. But at least this gives a sense of the potential, which is assessed by my team and the distillery manager, and whether we go ahead is a collective decision," says Brian Kinsman.

I very much hope the collective decision will be 'Yes. Let's do it.'

Ian Wisniewski is a freelance drinks writer focusing on spirits, particularly Scotch whisky. He contributes to various publications including Whisky Magazine and is the author of eleven books, the latest being The Whisky Dictionary published in September, 2019. He regularly visits distilleries in Scotland, in order to learn more about the production process, which is of particular interest to him.

Picture of Ian Wisniewski courtesy of Finlandia vodka

ANNO QUARTO

GEORGII IV. REGIS.

* *

C A P. XCIV.

An Act to grant certain Duties of Excise upon Spirits distilled from Corn or Grain in *Scotland* and *Ireland*, and upon Licences for Stills for making such Spirits; and to provide for the better collecting and securing such Duties, and for the warehousing of such Spirits without Payment of Duty.   [18th *July* 1823.]

WHEREAS it is expedient that the Duties on Spirits distilled from Corn or Grain in *Scotland* and *Ireland* should be made equal, and that the Regulations for the Collection of the said Duties, and for the Distillation and Manufacture of such Spirits, and for the warehousing of such Spirits without Payment of Duty, should be assimilated in *Scotland* and *Ireland*: May it therefore please Your Majesty that it may be enacted; and be it enacted by the King's most Excellent Majesty, by and with the Advice and Consent of the Lords Spiritual and Temporal, and Commons, in this present Parliament assembled, and by the Authority of the same, That from and after the Commencement of this Act so much and such Parts of the several Acts herein-after mentioned, and of all and every other Acts and Act in force immediately before the Commencement of this Act, for granting any Duty on Wash or Spirits made or distilled from Corn or Grain in *Scotland* and *Ireland* respectively, or upon Licences for keeping of Stills for making such Spirits, or for regulating the Distillation of such Spirits, as relate

Existing Laws for granting Duties on Spirits, and regulating the Trade of Distillers of Spirits in

14 N   or

The 1823 Excise Act

A blueprint of Scotch whisky making

by Charles MacLean and Arthur Motley

The famous Excise Act of 1823 put an end
to illicit distilling and whisky smuggling in Scotland.
Its significance however was even larger. The document describes
in great detail how whisky should be made and to this day
the process remains largely the same.

Readers of *The Malt Whisky Yearbook* will know that the 1823 Excise Act laid the foundations of the modern Scotch whisky industry by "positively encouraging the legal industry in the hope that many small distilleries would be established throughout Scotland". [1]

It is most common to hear commentators state that it made legal whisky production 'profitable', but many who were encouraged to set up business legally went bust soon after, so this is a simplified view. Rather, as the presenters of the first *Liquid Antiquarian* podcast[2] state: "[The Act] provides a detailed blue-print of how a distillery should be constructed and how the spirit should be distilled… a fundamental re-drawing of what whisky is and what it would become".

Before we consider the Act in detail, it is worth looking at its context and background.

Immediately following the declaration of war with the nascent French Republic in 1793 duties on Lowland whisky were trebled, to £9 per gallon of still capacity per annum. By 1803 it had been hiked to £162. Although licensed distilleries above the Highland Line were somewhat better off, rising from £1-10s to £6 -10s per gallon, only 8% of the total quantity of spirit legally distilled in Scotland was made in the Highlands. Moreover, traditional sources of income (crofting, cattle-droving, fishing) were badly affected by the war.

The larger Lowland distillers developed techniques of rapid distillation – shallow stills with broad bases and tall heads, in conjunction with stronger washes, capable of being charged and discharged "almost twenty-two times in an hour"[3]. Distilling at such a rate makes for a harsh, impure distillate, fit only to be rectified and compounded into gin, which much of it was.

Inevitably, illicit distilling increased dramatically. As a minister in Ross-shire wrote: "Distilling is almost the only method of converting our victual into cash for payment of rents and servants; and what may be called our staple commodity"[4]. Another minister remarked: "When I was a boy in Brechin…Everybody, with a few exceptions, drank what was in reality illicit whisky – far superior than that made under the eye of the Excise – lords and lairds, members of Parliament and ministers of the Gospel, and everybody else"[5]. In his memoirs, Ian Macdonald, a retired excise officer with no affection for 'free traders' wrote: "To the smuggler, no stigma was attached on account of his employment; on the contrary, it was considered rather an honourable occupation, as exhibiting an intrepidity and art that acquired for their possessor a distinction in the minds of his companions"[6].

Lord Liverpool's government was bereft of ideas how to combat the problem. The Excise Act 1814 fixed the minimum still capacity in the Highlands at 500 gallons, which was in effect a total ban on licensed distilling: such stills would consume more grain and more fuel than was available in even the most fertile Highland district. A move by the Scottish Excise Board to allow for smaller stills in the Highlands and to remove the inhibition on Highland distillers selling their product in the Lowlands was blocked in the Court of Session by the Lowland distillers. The smugglers had a hey-day.

"The extent of illicit distillation depended in a great measure on the amount of duty, and the nature of the Excise regulations", Ian Macdonald writes. "The smuggler's gain was in direct proportion to the amount of the spirit duty; the higher the duty the greater the gain and the stronger the temptation… The authorities of the time, regardless of the feelings and habits of the people, imposed restrictions which were injudicious, vexatious and injurious; which not only rendered it impracticable for the legal distiller to engage profitably in honest business, but actually encouraged the illicit distiller… Under the operation of the still license [1787-1814], the legal distiller, in his endeavours to increase production, sacrificed the quality of his spirits, until the illicit distiller commanded the market by supplying whisky superior in quality and flavour"[7].

Following the defeat of Napoleon in 1815, the British economy moved rapidly into depression and unemployment, exacerbated by return of thousands of de-mobilised servicemen. Starvation and despair were endemic. Landowners were becoming increasingly nervous: if smugglers could bring the Excise laws into disrepute, all laws might be brought into disrepute and anarchy would hold sway. Together with the maltsters and the few Highland licensed distillers they pressed the new chairman of the Scottish Excise Board, Woodbine Parish, to reduce duty (in order to combat the smugglers), reduce the required still size (to encourage more distillers to become licensed) and to allow weaker washes (to improve the quality of the spirit.

The result was The Small Stills Act 1816, which abolished the Highland Line, allowed stills of no less than 40 gallons capacity throughout Scotland and reduced spirits duty 8/4d (next year it was further reduced to 5/6d. The number of licensed distilleries in the Highlands trebled (to 36), and following an Amending Act in 1818 which at last allowed weaker washes, rose to 57. Many of these new licensed distillers felt a deep sense of betrayal when duty was raised again. On behalf of the Commissioners for Supply for the County of Argyle held in May 1821 Lord John Campbell stated "the late malt duty has been the sole occasion of the almost total cessation of all distillation by the small still system which has lately taken place in the county". Some immediately felt unable to continue in business, "many of whom had embarked on this enterprise under the belief that the duties were to remain at the level formerly"[8].

Widespread smuggling did not disappear therefore, and Justices of the Peace still tended to be lenient; in 1819 more than a quarter of the 4,201 cases heard in magistrates' courts were dismissed. Next year the 4th Duke of Gordon (1743-1827) drew the attention of the Government in the House of Lords to the problem. He advocated an extension of the policies introduced by the Acts of 1816 and 1818, and promised that Highland landowners would actively put down illicit distilling, evicting tenants who were convicted. This led to the appointment of a Royal Commission of Inquiry into the Revenue, chaired by Thomas Wallace, vice-president of the Board of Trade, and also to the Illicit Distillation (Scotland) Act 1822, which raised dramatically the level of penalties and fined landowners who condoned illicit distilling.

The Excise Act 1823 which followed was based on the findings of the Wallace Commission – complementing the 'stern measures' of the above Acts by positively encouraging the legal industry, in the hope that many small distilleries would be established in Scotland and Ireland. Although its 50 pages and 137 sections make for an insufferably dry read, it is a remarkable exercise in the tightening of potential loopholes.

The aims of the Act can broadly be put into three categories: incentives for legal commerce, specific

Following the Napoleonic Wars, England landed in a depression and taxation of whisky was one way to remedy the situation

equipment sanctioned by the Crown, and the control of how the spirit is produced, stored and transported. In effect, it was a 'carrot and stick' measure, with many more opportunities to be legally hit by the 'stick'.

The incentives for legal commerce over illicit went beyond the relatively modest £10 per license to distill (Section III). There was a drawback on spirits exported of 3p per gallon of malt spirit (IV), spirit could be stored free of duty until home consumption (III), and licenses could pass to heirs (CXXVI). This does not mean the many who set up shop as entered distillers succeeded. Many went bankrupt or gave up within a few years, since the illicit distillers did not disappear overnight and remained as competition, and there was considerable capital expense in setting up an approved distillery.

Whisky distillation from A to Z

The Excise Act specifies in great detail how a distillery should be built, and how the liquid should flow from process to process. The 40 gallon minimum (XI) is well reported in histories of whisky, but it is rarely noted just how precisely the Act describes the nature and number of chargers, low wines receivers and feints receivers, the stills, and the pipes connecting all of these utensils (XX). There is a description of how the liquid should flow around this equipment (XXL) and the level of detail extends to the nature of fastenings, cocks, and the colour that most pipes must be painted. Visitors to distilleries still in existence will recognize most of the features as entirely familiar and consistent across many sites. The organization of a post-1823 distillery and many of the features specified aim to create a closed system with regular opportunities for measurement, thereby minimizing the possibility of a crooked distiller cheating the Excise. Significantly, this set up also reduces flexibility and narrows the possible ways in which whisky could be distilled after 1823 - much equipment and many techniques would have become instantly redundant or illegal. Just as the makers of shovels were said to have struck it rich during a goldrush, it must have been a good time for makers of cocks, fasteners and pipes. We can only wonder how many treasured and ancient stills would have been now useless, despite having been part of the family for many years.

Illicit distilling as Sir Edwin Landseer saw it in his famous painting "The Highland Whisky Still"

Reduced taxation would be worth little to the compliant distiller competing in a market against producers who avoided the payment of duties. Many of the clauses in the Excise Act focus on the license holding distiller, and attempt to create a more tightly controlled system of production, with corresponding fines. Distillers taking out licenses should expect close contact with the Exciseman, to the extent that if you lived more than one mile from a market town, you would have to provide lodging on site (section XIV). Whether the Exciseman was your new neighbour or a frequent visitor, you would have to give six days notice before intending to brew (XLII, fine for breach £200), 12 hours notice before moving wash into the stills (LII, £200 fine), furnish said officer with a ladder and lights (CV, fine £100) and allow him to search your distillery, house or any nearby houses (CVIII, fine £50). Brewing and distilling could not take place at the same time (XLI, fine £500). This was a new and closer level of control which extended to constant measurement, recording keeping and declaration.

For example, gravity of wort (XLVII, fine excess against declaration £200) and wash (XLIX, fine £200) were closely watched along with the ultimate output and strength of spirits as the amount of excise levied depended on the gravity of wash (LVI), volume and strength of the low wines (LVII) and the volume and strength of the final spirit (LVIII). Although the romantic notion persists of the distiller's art having been perfected illegally by the smuggler, we should consider how this rigorous and enforced record keeping would have refined technique and scientific understanding over the subsequent decades.

Much thought was put into the flow of ingredients into a distillery and the storage and movement spirit from it. Only grain could be distilled (XVII, fined £200 and all alcohol seized), distilleries could not be located near brewers or rectifiers (XIII), any moveable casks containing spirit must be painted with declared contents (XXXII, all spirit seized), and no spirit could be transported in casks of less than 9 gallons (CXX, fine £200). Any movement of malt into or spirit from a distillery would be logged and approved.

Maturation benefited

Although the new ability to store spirit under government supervision without immediate payment of tax was an incentive, there is an unintended benefit for the future: maturation. We know of no references to widespread commercial maturation by distillers before this time, and none immediately afterwards. However, since a level of cost is delayed warehouses would begin to be filled, and as business fluctuated it is reasonable to assume that significant volumes would remain unsold during the following years. Some customers would surely have noticed that older stock was different and begun to demand it, and by the 1860s Charles Tovey was writing: "No Spirit can pay better for bonding than Whisky… Nothing tends more to increase the reputation of a spirit merchant than supplying good and well-matured Spirit"[9].

The success of the Excise Act might be measured by how many failed revisions to levels of duty and laws of distillation came before it, and how few came after it, but it was not a smooth path for many of those that took the step of registering a distillery. George Smith himself – the Glenlivet poster boy for this period – had to be bailed out by his landlord and sponsor, the Duke of Gordon.

By the mid-1820s, there were also vociferous complaints from Irish distillers, who accused Scottish distillers of widespread duty fraud centering on the malt drawback. Certainly, reports that Scottish spirit was being sold in Dublin significantly cheaper than Irish whiskey are curious, given that much of the grain for whisky making was travelling in the opposite direction. These arguments continued in Parliament and in newspapers until the early 1830s, when a new Act to audit the Customs and Excise Revenues of Scotland was passed (August 1832).

There does not appear to be a corresponding Act for Ireland's revenue office, and exports of mixed mash whisky exported from Scotland to Ireland dropped by roughly 60% between 1831 and 1833. Although it is impossible to prove wrong-doing nearly 200 years later, you can see why the Irish distillers had their suspicions that the malt drawback was being abused. Indeed, it is interesting to note that although the Excise Act covers Ireland, it seems to have been conceived and written with Scotland in mind. The Commissions leading up to the legislation almost entirely take evidence and discuss the Scottish experience. Although mixed mashbill whisky was also made in Scotland, the malt drawback itself immediately disadvantaged the Irish distillers who more commonly favoured mixed grain distillations, and arguably their legal spirit did not suffer from quite such a bad reputation as their Scottish counterparts. Government reports suggesting Scottish distillers almost immediately switched to mixed mashbill after 1823 are curious to say the least and contradict our cheerful tales of malt whisky distiller's success being inevitable due to superior flavour.

The 1823 act fixed the ingredients, equipment and broad method of Scotch whisky distillation as we know it. What came before this date may have been very different to what runs off stills today, but what came after this legislation is likely to have been similar. It is an attractive notion to give the credit for the improvement to noble farmers and gentleman distillers such as George Smith of Glenlivet, but there is every chance that His Majesty's Excise fixed the blueprint of single malt whisky in Scotland.

Charles MacLean has been writing about Scotch whisky since 1981, and has published eighteen books on the subject. He was made a Keeper of the Quaich in 1992, elevated to Master in 2009, in 2012 won the I.W.S.C.'s 'Outstanding Achievement Award', in 2016 was inducted into the Whisky Hall of Fame and in 2019 was named 'International Ambassador of the Year' at the Spirit of Speyside Festival. In 2021 he was honoured by H.M. The Queen with an M.B.E. "For services to Scotch whisky, UK exports and charity".

Arthur Motley has been a professional whisky buyer for over 20 years. He began as cask buyer at SMWS before he moved onto Royal Mile Whiskies where he is now a director. In 2020 he launched the youTube channel 'The Liquid Antiquarian' with Dave Broom, which shared original research of primary sources on a range of drinks. To their surprise, they already claim to have made some significant discoveries that revise their view of certain accepted histories.

[1]) *The Making of Scotch Whisky* – Michael S. Moss and John R. Hume (Edinburgh, 1981)

[2]) *Liquid Antiquarian, 'Scotch Whisky; The Excise Act 1823', October 26th 2020* – Dave Broom and Arthur Motley

[3]) *Report to the Lords Commissioners of the Treasury*, 1799

[4]) *Statistical Account of Scotland 1791-99*. Rev. David Dunoon's entry for Killearnan Parish

[5]) *The Autobiography of Thomas Guthrie* (1803-73)

[6]) *Smuggling in the Highlands* – Ian Macdonald (Stirling, 1914)

[7]) *Smuggling in the Highlands* – op.cit.

[8]) *Malt Duties In Scotland*, House of Commons Report (1914)

[9]) *British and Foreign Spirits* – Charles Tovey (London, 1864)

Back to the Future

by Joel Harrison

The forecasting for future sales of whisky
has become a science for the bigger companies. Yet there is
a wider tale of learning from past mistakes to understand the future,
with the big producers better understanding their stock models,
and new, smaller producers playing more of
an old-school guessing game.

Take a trip to Scotland and you'll find a country shaped by the sea. Aside from a 96 mile land border with England, the rest of Scotland's near-12,000 mile frontier is with the ocean, and it is the crashing of waves, the rise and fall of the tides, that has shaped every part of its coastline, as well as the country's numerous islands and archipelagos. This ebb and flow has hewn an elemental and rugged, yet spellbindingly beautiful land. If it wasn't for these harsh waves, there wouldn't be such dramatic beauty.

It is no surprise then, that the country's most famous produce, Scotch whisky, has been forged from the ever-changing tides of fashion, politics and acts of god. Be it a world war, prohibition or a global pandemic, both supply and demand have often been at the whim of world events; a problem that needs to be addressed when your product must be produced a minimum of three years in advance.

The history of Scotch is littered with examples of great institutions that have caught a critical cold when the winds of change blew hard and harsh, and in an industry that has to be proactive in forecasting the future, the result was often purely reactive.

Convalmore – one of many distilleries that was forced to close in the mid 1980s

In the 1920s, forty distilleries closed as the chill from a mix of huge over-supply, coupled with Prohibition, took its toll. Mercifully, this period was followed by a 'baby boom' in distilling, with twenty-two new sites opening between 1957 and 1976. Yet by the late 1970s demand had once again waned, and warehouses were stacked with whisky that couldn't be sold. Twenty Scotch distilleries closed their gates in the 1980s, including the now storied names of Port Ellen and Brora, and seven more fell to the same fate in the early 1990s; in the same period, just two new distilleries opened.

Today, we are in a new age of Scotch with thirty new distilleries having opened between 2000 and 2018. By 2022, it is expected that at least another twenty will be producing spirit. On top of this, there have been sizable expansions at some of the legacy distilleries such as Glenlivet, Glenfiddich and Mac-allan, and a doubling of production at some of the smaller players like Ardbeg. Oh, and let's not forget the resurrection of some famous names such as the reopening of Brora in 2021, with Port Ellen and Rosebank to follow.

All this represents a big step-change for the production of malt Scotch spirit, with total capacity across the country up from 377,430,000 litres of alcohol in 2016 to nearly 405,000,000 in 2020 (or the equivalent of 28 Glengoyne-size malt distilleries opening up in the space of just four years).

Compare this to the figures published in the 2013 edition of the Malt Whisky Yearbook, which shows total malt distilling capacity across Scotland's distilleries at 319,205,000, we see growth of nearly 30% in capacity over seven years. Quite the remarkable figure, especially when contextualised against the closures of the early 1980s and 1990s.

However, these figures represent capacity. Anyone who has had the joy of going to a lower league football match will happily tell you that soccer stadia are rarely full, let alone even near capacity most of the time. The same is true with whisky distilleries. Just because there is a capacity, it does not mean these figures are being reached when it comes to production.

"Capacity does not mean the distillery is always producing that amount of spirit," the hugely experienced Alan Winchester, Master Distiller of The Glenlivet, once told me.

"Think of the capacity of a distillery like the top speed of a car", he continued. "You rarely, if ever, hit the top speed. Mostly you're humming along at a pleasant rate".

And The Glenlivet distillery is a prime example of the confidence in the future of malt whisky, expanding production capacity from 10.5 million litres in 2013, growing to 21 million litres today, a fact

In his book Dr. Nick Morgan describes the plummeting demand of Scotch in the 1980s as a "perfect storm of circumstance"

not lost on Sandy Hyslop, the Director of Blending & Inventory at Chivas Brothers, owners of The Glenlivet.

"Forecasting is far, far more accurate than when I first started in the industry back in the 1980s", Hyslop notes.

"Back then, the sales director would have had a look and sketched something out and just set a target and forecast. Now, we speak to people all over the world, engaging the marketing directors in each market, which gives us a steer on what they can sell, as well as a buy-in from them on the commitment to future sales."

"Is it always accurate? No, but there are always opportunities to fine-tune it, and it is better to have the stock in the bag than not. Our stock is not managed to the exact glass, to the exact day, as we use a spectrum of ages in our products,", he continues.

"I'm looking at the forecast for the whole lifecycle of our brands, so I'm looking at how much of The Glenlivet 12 we are going to need from now until 12 years out for that, and this includes looking at things like Royal Salute 21 year old. All this forms part of our filling plan, which impacts how many casks we buy, and how many warehouses we build; it is all very complicated, and like 3-dimensional chess", Hyslop notes.

History tells a story

However, history shows us that all is not what it seems, when it comes to growth and industry positivity. Whisky historian, writer and consultant Dr. Nick Morgan, formerly of Diageo and author of the landmark book The Long Stride, which focuses on the history of Johnnie Walker, and with it much of the social and economic history of Scotch itself, is well placed to track the major milestone events within the development of the Scotch whisky category that culminates in today's approach to forecasting and market intelligence.

"Today, the teams who research and forecast future demand take into account a whole range of data-points to try and predict where markets will go in terms of consumption of what you might term 'luxury products' and within that, Scotch whisky," Dr. Morgan notes.

"It is quite astonishing, the complexity of the models they put together, looking at long forecasts going out into the future. But then there is the unknown. You are always at the mercy of the unforeseen, the acts of god", he says.

Looking back at the trajectory of Scotch whisky's growth, Morgan focuses on some key events which have impacted the demand for whisky around the world.

According to Diageo Master Blender Craig Wilson there is more planning for high end single malts today than a couple of decades ago

"Things like the Spanish influenza; the World Wars; the Great Depression; trying to find your way through that is tricky, but a brand like [Johnnie] Walker, with the exception of these world events, was always planning for growth, always struggling to keep up with demand. The question was never about having too much stock, but about having enough", says Morgan.

Evidenced in his book The Long Stride, Morgan writes about the reaction to the plummeting demand of the early 1980s, along with other company economics as a 'perfect storm of circumstance' and the resulting whisky loch (a term, according to Morgan, coined by the Aberdeen Press and Journal in the early 1980s) 'ready to burst its banks'.

However, these seismic world events and economic pressures, which are seemingly catastrophic in the moment for Scotch can very much have a rose-tinted hue. Brora is just one example of this, where casks were left to mature for much longer than they normally would have done, with the result being a col-lection of exceptional casks which would otherwise have been blended away at a much younger age.

Today, there is a steady stream of releases that owe a debt to the over-production and under-sold era of the late 1970s and early 1980s, a time when the big distillers would have been focused on, as Morgan tells me, 'ageing for 5 to 8 years for standard blends and then the big 12 [years old for more deluxe blends]'.

2021 alone has seen official releases from Brora, Talisker, Port Ellen, Rosebank, Littlemill, Loch Lomond, Bowmore, Highland Park and others, not to mention those released by independent bottlers, of whisky drawn from casks filled in the mid-1970s and early 1980s, little or none of which was designed for long ageing.

These rare expressions, which highlight how important the super and ultra premium end of Scotch whisky has become to the business, would not have existed if the business had not seen a contraction in demand towards the end of the last century; a crisis that left behind it a series of gems, casks which have been lucky enough to outlive their peers, which would have been blended away at a much earlier age, while also developing so brilliantly in cask, leaving us with a rich liquid legacy to enjoy today, and no doubt onward into the next couple of decades, too.

With demand for these rare casks rising, the industry has adjusted its understanding not only of making more consistent spirit, but knowing how this will mature into old age. In the future, the rare and aged single malt category will not be fuelled by accidental casks, but those that have been designed for long ageing.

Someone who is at the sharp end of this, is Craig Wilson, Master Blender at Diageo, who says that some expressions are indeed born out of experimentation, over deliberate design.

"You saw an example of this a few years ago in the Special Releases, with a Cragganmore which was smoky, done in the style of Talisker, and this was phenomenally well received as a one-off," he says.

"There is a lot more experimentation going on behind the scenes, mostly to feed our blends, and occasionally we do find some gems for these special one-off releases."

"The big thing that has changed over the last few decades is that whisky would have been designed purely to support blends, and any single malt activity would have been happy accidents out of the back of that, whereas now we are very much planning for future high end releases and even core variants now", Wilson says.

"When we are filling casks now, it is about hedging our bets and putting in a buffer so we have options 15 – 20 years down the line. You can see that now in something like Lagavulin, where we are doing some interesting things, and we are able to create a multi-year pipeline of interesting variants".

Forward thinking

Some of the more wily distillers in the mid-1900s had put in place a strategy of long ageing. One of the forefathers of this practice was the family behind The Macallan distillery, who invested heavily in sherry casks, and needed to create a longer-game focus on demand for their single malt due to the success of their 18 year old expression.

"The Macallan was highly regarded as a great top dressing malt in blends," notes Ken Grier, the former Chairman of The Macallan Distillers Ltd and now owner of De-Still Creative, specialist advisors for luxury brands and the spirits industry.

"The Macallan 18 year old was a phenomenon, really. It allowed us to continue the legacy of long maturation started by the Shiach family who really understood the idea that Macallan produced a robust spirit, one that would stand up to lengthy maturation in sherry oak", Grier says.

"Building on that concept, we started to look at a backward view on demand, starting with looking at the idea of ageing for 30 years, and working back from there, taking into account that not all casks would make it to the ages we were aiming for".

In order to prepare whisky for long ageing, investment in wood is a major key. "Paying eight to ten times more than other distillers for high quality sherry casks allowed for that," notes Grier.

"No one else in single malt was investing as much in long maturation as we were, and this was born from our long-term view on extra-aged stocks, and the demand we believed would be, and now is, there for whiskies of great age".

These endeavours are not cheap, however. It is expensive for distillers to have whisky maturing in warehouses, slumbering away. Far better in bottle, being sold and consumed. A cask in a warehouse is cash in stasis. But the gamble is that some whisky will mature on to be exceptionally old, exceptionally rare, exceptionally expensive and, of course, exceptionally profitable.

This is the gamble that the new raft of smaller, independent distillers will have to navigate. Any business is cash hungry, and none more than those who need to be constantly feeding a stock of maturing whisky, and the more you distil, the more casks are required to hold that whisky, and the more warehouse space required to hold those casks.

"There is a huge amount of up front costs to make malt whisky. It is not just about buying barley and distilling spirit, all of which costs money. The spirit has to be stored, and buying casks and building or renting warehouse space is costly" notes David Robertson, former Master Distiller at The Macallan, and co-founder of the small Holyrood distillery which boasts a capacity of just 250,00 litres a year.

In a unique position to be able to compare and contrast the approach to forecasting and cashflow of the big brands versus small, independent distilleries, Robertson says, "The acute challenge facing a small and start up operation is to lay down enough, but not too much, for future sales. But how much is enough, and not too much, nor too little? Now that is impossible", he muses.

"What most new distillers may not appreciate

Holyrood - one of the latest distilleries to open in Scotland

until too late is how expensive every litre of new make spirit is to produce, and then the wide range of storage costs in the form of wood. Ex-bourbon barrels come in at £100, all the way up to a first fill oloroso sherry hogs head at £700 or more each. This is a phenomenal investment!"

Sandy Hyslop from Chivas Brothers agrees. "Growth is not just about whisky, about new make spirit," he says. "It is about casks, warehouses, people to manage it, lorry drivers, forklifts and such. When marketing tell me they're going to grow a brand at 5% year-on-year, I tell them we are going to need to build two warehouses a year for that. That's eight warehouses over four years", he notes.

"There is a massive investment for the business every time a single percentage is added on to sales forecasts. You're either committed to driving volume up or you're not, as it is a much bigger scenario than people think".

Exposure to risks

As someone who was previously party to the forecast of a major distilling company while at Edring-

ton, does Robertson feel over exposed to the winds of change in drinking fashions, economic downturns or acts of god in his new position as a small scale independent distiller?

"Not really," he says. "For us it is about producing small amount of quality whisky, and selling it when it is ready in line with our business planning and adjusted for how we see the market shifting. Yes, this leads to us forecasting and endless modelling of cash flow, but we believe that if you make good enough whisky, then the rest will fall into place and from what we have seen with new distillers both in Scotland and overseas, there seems to be robust demand for whisky that is distinctive, differentiated and distilled with a real story to tell".

"The news kids on the block," continues Robertson, "can sell well made, special releases of unusual mash bills bylaws looking at heritage varieties, inclusion of speciality malts, and giving consideration to brewers, wine and other novel yeasts; all before we even get to the debate on wood".

In a way, Scotch is now playing the realm of beer, or gin, where there are some huge operators, with major brands, yet also a raft of smaller craft producers, happily making a living selling interesting, unique and local products and can support a raft of smaller producers. However, it is those in the middle that Robertson is most worried about.

"There are some larger new distillers who are announcing 1 or 2 million litre capacity operations who must, by being of this size and capacity, have ambitions to supply the trade and or/do blends themselves", he says.

"I, for one, would be more nervous about this. Yes, they will gain some economies of scale and have a lower cost of production, but can they develop a powerful enough story around spirit creation that will entice the whisky consuming public to buy their offer versus the established distillers/brands", Robertson notes.

Agreeing with this is Harry Taylor, co-founder of Wolfburn distillery. Based in Thurso, the distillery started producing spirit in 2013. When asked if he worries about the sheer volume of mature whisky that will be available for bottling in the next few years across the category as a whole, he notes that, "one of my favourite expressions is by Field Marshall Viscount Slim who said, 'People who worry don't matter. And people who matter don't worry'".

"We can only control what we can control, which is our own product and our own production levels. Of course, we are affected by any change to the industry, but I firmly believe that a good product, correctly priced, will always sell to some degree,

The owners of Wolfburn distillery firmly believe that there will always be a place in the market for a good product at a good price

irrespective of what other people in the industry are doing", Taylor notes.

Does Taylor believe that the smaller raft of indie distillers could be over-exposed to a down-turn in global demand for malt whisky?

"Put simply: yes", he says. "Many of the new start-ups are vulnerable because they lack cashflow and other resources, so rely on things like crowd-funding for finance. Is that sustainable? Only time will tell."

So here we are, at the dawn of a new age of malt distilling in Scotland, an unpreceded time of new distillery builds, coupled with the reopening and revival of some of those previously closed.

One wonders what the workers who locked the gates of distilleries such as Port Ellen, Rosebank and Brora, for what they believed to be the final time in the early 1980s and 1990s, would make of their rein-statement and the host of new distillery openings, especially given that these closures would have been based on forecasts showing a rather gloomy future for Scotch.

I'm sure these workers would be pleased to see the industry in such a vibrant place, if not one that feels as if a two-tier system of those who might, given a downturn in demand, struggle to survive, and those who would continue to thrive, as their forecasting, stock modelling and cash flow ensures they stay open.

Like the crashing waves onto Scotland's shores result in such a beautiful landscape, so the whisky industry is forged by the crashing waves of demand upon its shores shaping its future and showing off the rugged, difficult path of the past.

Joel Harrison is an award winning author, communicator and industry consultant, whose work has been published in over 20 countries, across 16 different languages. His writing work can be seen in publications such as The Wall Street Journal India and The Daily Telegraph in the UK. Harrison also appears regularly on British television across a number of shows as a whisky specialist. He sits as a judge for the International Wine and Spirits Competition (IWSC) where today he holds the role of a Trophy Judge and Chairman across Scotch whisky and other spirits. In 2013 Harrison was made a Keeper of the Quaich.

Annabel Thomas, founder of Nc'Nean distillery, foraging local plants for her range of spirits

Community Spirit
where localism is the key

by Neil Ridley

As society cautiously re-enters a post-Pandemic world,
are we witnessing a new appreciation for 'Localism' within whisky?
If so, does this also mean that the stage is potentially set for
– rather ironically – a major global opportunity
for our new local heroes?

Time for a confession. For the first time in my 15-year career as a drinks writer and commentator, I feel somewhat lost for words. Not that I don't have anything to say: but put simply, the future which once seemed so sparkling clear is, for me, shrouded in a fog of uneasiness and wild speculation.

Like so many of us working in UK hospitality, I'm deeply frustrated; angry even at our inability to act decisively over Covid and I haven't managed to fully embrace the spirit of post-Pandemic optimism, which we probably all really need right now. The evasive and somewhat arbitrary nature of lockdown restrictions and lack of vision regarding returning to a life of global travel has left me with little trust or positivity as 2021 draws to a close. Right now, the only boarders I feel are confidently within my grasp are the earthy ones in my garden, which are currently full of weeds and massively in need of tidying up.

However, one thing which I hold onto dearly is the spirit of Localism which we have seen flourish within our communities over the last 18 months. Like anything precious though, this needs to be nurtured and preserved at all costs, because despite travel restrictions opening up, the caution and fear of Covid will unfortunately remain in all our lives for many more years yet.

Localism may affect us all in different ways, but for me, it has really meant trying to gain a greater understanding and an appreciation of the drinks community on my doorstep: the breweries and distilleries I have perhaps overlooked, simply because they are almost 'too close'. Like many of my global counterparts, not being able to travel (even to Scotland, which is obviously part of the British Isles, yet has still been relatively out-of-bounds to me,) has made me refocus on the drinks produced within a much smaller radius: I have a new-found fondness for those who aim to pioneer new techniques, focus on local ingredients/raw materials and support local communities through employment or other benevolent activities- and it's been a rewarding journey.

The owners of Copper Rivet distillery in Kent have a business model baseed on 3Ps – Pride, Provenance and Place

So what does Localism mean to the whisky community? Particularly those distillers who subscribe to what I mention above.

"The idea of drink local and thinking globally precisely captures our approach to business development," explains Stephen Russell, founder of the Copper Rivet distillery in Chatham, Kent, (and arguably those closest whisky distillery to where I live, excluding London.)

The distillery opened back in 2016, releasing its first 'Masthouse' single malt during the middle of the Pandemic in June 2020. "In a globalised world, with global brands and multinationals, conglomerate brand owners have the ability to create instant international 'successes'. Often those products fade quickly and are repackaged or replaced by the 'next big thing'. Maybe this is because they have leapfrogged one or two jumps in what should be a natural development in the growth of a brand – who knows?"

"By necessity, we have always had what we call our '3Ps': Pride, Provenance, Place'" he continues. "In contrast to mega brands, we felt that we needed to build slowly, anchoring our products in the local community, building a local following, formed not just from their pride in a local business doing something special, but because they love what we produce – as well as what the drinks represent."

"For me, the 'Drink Local' concept is about connecting customers to products and brands through real people and real stories," thinks Jane Overeem, owner of the eponymously titled Overeem distillery in Hobart, Tasmania, originally founded by her father, Casey back in 2005. "Consumers are becoming more and more inquisitive and selective with what they want, and as a producer, authenticity to our customers is paramount. Quality is a must, but communicating a genuine story that is engaging, journey inspiring, and importantly, honest, is what we do at Overeem."

Back in the UK, Annabel Thomas, founder of Nc'Nean in the Western Highlands, one of Scotland's brightest new whisky distilleries, has a slightly different take on Localism. "I think people really value drinks that have a clear sense of place, but don't necessarily ONLY want to consume local-to-them drinks," she points out. "Especially given we are still so restricted on travel, I think people are

To Alex Munch, co-founder of Stauning distillery, terroir means using the ingredients that are particularly good in your region

using food and drink from around the world to 'feel' like they are getting a change even if they can't go anywhere: Aperol Spritz in Cornwall or Mexican food in London etc. Having said that, I think the restriction on travel has also generated a renewed sense of appreciation for what your own country has to offer – we have certainly seen more local tourists coming to Scotland than we would normally."

I'm interested to see the ways in which 'Localism' has been put to good use by our distillers and whether they feel such things will resonate outside of the local community, once people are able to travel more freely again. From the outside perspective, Nc'Nean has been making waves in the Scotch industry for focusing on a more organic, 'Localised' approach to whisky making. I ask Annabel if there's anything specific which is resonating best with its consumers.

"Our ethos is really focused on two things: making spirits in as sustainable a way as possible, and making interesting, creative spirits. I think sustainability is something that has been growing in importance to consumers for decades, but has really only become truly a broad issue recently and

has been exacerbated by the Pandemic. In a recent consumer survey we did (of our own customers,) 65% of our consumers said they actively seek out sustainably/eco-conscious brands. Localism is part of that – using what we have at hand to create the best and most sustainable whisky we can – so we use local wood chip to power our boiler, feed the draff to the local cows and source 100% Scottish (organic) barley."

Leave no flavours behind

I pose a similar question to Alex Munch, co-founder of the pioneering Danish distillery, Stauning.

Would you say the distillery's biggest asset globally is its locality? And with that in mind, what do you think 'terroir and sense of place' means to consumers who have never visited or have any physical access to the distillery?

"Our biggest asset is not what we do, but how we think differently," he points out. "As there is no traditional way of making whisky in Denmark, we had the opportunity to reintroduce abandoned ways of distilling for more flavour. 'Leave no flavours behind' is one of our internal guidelines. You only have a few windows to design a whisky and we want to get the most out of it, even when it's a pain-in-the-ass process of 24 small pot stills, with 24 individual heat settings and cut-point timings," he smiles. "We remind ourselves that we are not here to do 'easy' but to do 'good'."

"However, I have a complicated relationship to the word 'terroir'", he continues. "For 99 out of a 100 whiskies, it's just marketing bullshit and not detectable in an unbranded blind test. I like the true meaning of it, where you use the ingredients that are particularly good in your region, such as the different varieties of rye we can experiment with, grown by two farmers who are just ten minutes away. But to be true to the terroir, comes at a price: the complexity of floor malting, which few do, because it's very troublesome and the yield is lower. It is disproportionally satisfying to know that we have nothing to hide and that we don't take any shortcuts in this regard."

To many readers of the Yearbook, it'll come as no secret that Bruichladdich has long subscribed to the importance of Localism: from the perceived terroir in the barley it uses, to promoting the unique identity of Islay on a global scale, so i'm keen to find out how the past 18 months have been for Christy McFarlane, Global Brand Manager at the distillery.

"For some time now, more and more people are putting an emphasis on eating and drinking locally but it has taken the Pandemic to really action that in the eyes of many, particularly when it comes to fresh produce," she believes. "Our community has come together to buy veg boxes, eat locally caught seafood and prioritises buying from local shops. Maybe it's because we weren't able to fill up our cars at mainland supermarkets, or that we had a bit more disposable income to spend on independent shops, but it would be great for this movement to last as the

"People buy people: they don´t just buy a product" says Dawn Davies from Speciality Drinks

restrictions lift and international audiences return to Islay," she tells me.

"In terms of whisky, we've seen social distancing mean there are smaller physical groups meeting up, but deeper connections being made," she continues. "Virtually, we've seen whisky drinkers join online and meet others who share a passion for our spirits. It will be interesting to see how we manage to keep those connections as the world recovers. Will people have the same appetite for online tastings that are certainly more sustainable, or will they want to return to in-person tastings and drinking in bars and restaurants? Hopefully it's a hybrid of both and we all find a good balance that works."

If any positives can be taken from our time during the Pandemic it is that Localism has, by and large, been embraced by the wider consumer - and clearly - as detailed by the distillers, been a key aspect in helping to promote brands amongst the local community.

David Vitale, owner of Starward distillery in Melbourne

However, can some of these virtues be turned into a wider and more international asset as the world begins to open up again and perhaps places a rene-wed interest - or - excuse the pun - a thirst to Drink Global? One person right at the centre of any po-tential change in consumer drinking trends is Dawn Davies, Head Buyer for Speciality Drinks: home to the globally renowned Whisky Exchange retail website. Given the recent difficulties the world has faced from the commercial, logistical perspective of Covid, I ask her how the search for new whiskies has been affected.

"Everything is taking so much longer at the moment so you really have to plan when you are getting stocks in and also manage the expectations from the brands that you are importing as it is not a quick turnaround," she points out. "For example, I have been waiting over a week for just a quote from a haulier – I need that quote just to work out pricing. A shipment from Japan that was meant to leave in February is still stuck there and the pricing has

tripled to ship. Shipping pricing, plus more 'Covid and import taxes' have driven pricing up again: something that you have to manage and work around with new suppliers."

"However there is an upside," she continues. "As things start to relax, there is much more interest and demand from the UK for new whiskies from around the globe. We brought three new American whiskies in over Covid, a Danish one and we have a Kiwi and an Aussie brand on the water at the moment."

So what do you look for in a new world whisky these days? Is it desirable to have a unique, 'locali-sed' element to it, to be successful?

"I am looking, as always, first for quality of product, but I want something with a real sense of self but that is still balanced and has personality," she explains. "People buy people: they don't just buy product, so any brand or product that makes the customer feel connected to the faces behind or in front of the business will win hearts and minds. They want to go and tell their friends that they visited the distillery or they met the people behind the brands if they do they will be loyal. People are wanting more traceability in their products so I think the risk for brands is those that are not actually producing local but just saying it is a local product because they live there. The customer is now much more savvy than they were a year ago, so brands beware!"

The future of localism

When considering a global viewpoint, it would be remiss of me not to touch on the US and its recent commercial struggles for Scotch single malt in particular. A 25% tariff imposed two years ago by the Trump Administration meant that Scotch exports are down by over £600m, with a future five-year suspension of the tariffs only recently negotiated with the new Administration.

Rather conversely, has the situation been of benefit to the global appeal of other single malts from around the world? I asked for a few thoughts from David Vitale, owner of Melbourne's Starward distillery, currently enjoying a real degree of success Stateside and in Europe - and a man in possession of a rather unique take on the situation, given that he's an Aussie currently residing in Seattle.

"I think there's a fair share of Scotch whisky drinkers in the US who have explored the world of modern whiskies, but to say they were doing that because tariffs made Scotch more expensive is only part of the story," he thinks. "The New World cate-gory is an exciting segment and I think if you are a lover of whisky spelt both ways, you'll be interested in whiskies like Starward."

Even though Annabel Thomas of Nc´Nean has her eyes set of international expansion she says "local is definitely first".

Starward makes a distinctly Australian whisky, but with a modern, innovative feel. How does localism and authenticity work for you and why do you think the rest of the world has resonated so well towards it?

"The things that people love about Starward in Melbourne, are the same reasons people across the world love it," reckons David. "As much as I think my home town is the foodie capital of the world, the reality is that there are lots of cities that share our obsession for flavour and approachability and excellence in all types of food and drinks. So even though Starward is Melbourne born and bred, I think it belongs in all great foodie cities in the world."

Staying in the US for a second, I began to think about those distilleries ploughing their own furrow in the world of American single malt who truly embrace a distinct Localism. Could they potentially make waves in international markets too, stepping out of the shadow of the more traditional American whiskey? Mark Gillespie, the founder of Whisky-cast certainly thinks so.

"Westland in Seattle has been amazing with its focus on locally-grown barley and working with area farmers to escape the commodity system of grain supplies. There are also good 'grain-to-glass' distillers who grow their own grain, then turn it into their own whiskey, such as Frey Ranch in Nevada and Jeptha Creed in Kentucky. Those are just a few, but there are many small locally-oriented distillers out there doing amazing things."

So what lessons can the business learn from the past 18 months of Pandemic, when it comes to growing new products: perhaps locally, then domestically, then finally platforming them on a global scale? It's a question I pose to Richard Bates, Senior Director of Consumer Strategy and Innovation at Beam Suntory: home to the likes of Laphroaig, Bowmore and an extensive portfolio of both Japanese and American whiskies.

"In many ways, 'local' has always been part of the global appeal of Scotch, and Scotch has long been one of the leaders in building appeal based on local provenance," he explains. "So in my opinion, the immediate market for a new Scotch is not local, it is among a global community of whisky explorers," he continues. "The challenge is understanding how to reach this geographically diverse audience. I think one key lesson the business has learned [over the pandemic] is about the enhanced role of digital —and it's something we must fully embrace beyond just e-commerce, but also as a medium to engage consumers and build support for our brands and category as a whole."

"Drinking local is going to remain critical for smaller distillers," thinks Mark Gillespie, "as more consumers now want to support "local" food and drink producers where they can see how those products are being produced. If I were starting a distillery today, I'd focus on the local/domestic market exclusively and not worry about international markets. Given the issues the pandemic has highlighted with global logistics along with tariffs and other politically sensitive issues, it makes more sense for a startup distiller to focus locally and avoid the risk of losing business because of things they have no control over."

"We have never aspired to be a local-only business from a sales point of view," points out Nc'Nean's Annabel Thomas, "but local is definitely first and we love working with Scottish hospitality and retail. Whisky has always been global and if anything, we are having to go more slowly in our international expansion than potential distributors would like. We really want to focus on a few markets and make sure we work with our partners there to establish the brand and help educate consumers about who we are. And that would be my advice for smaller / growing businesses: don't try to do too much at once and spread yourself too thin – do a few countries well."

So what does the future look like for New World whisky? Is localism a concept which is here to stay and can it become the foundation for building a more global reputation? I leave the final words to Alex Munch at Stauning and with Stephen Russell: back where we first began our Local/Global journey in Chatham, Kent.

"Look, as a new world whisky maker, you need to earn the right to be taken seriously," believes Alex. "You are not born with a 200-year-old legacy to stand on. I like making New World whisky, because it keeps us on our toes. The world does not need yet another distillery making the same whisky, or copying others where ever it is from. The world is full of wonderful whisky already, we are here to offer a choice and an opportunity to taste our philosophy and the result of our efforts. Feel free to love it or hate it," he laughs. "As long as our drinkers have a strong opinion about our products, I am happy."

"In short, the focus we've put on building a community following probably helped us survive the Pandemic, concedes Stephen. "And we have certainly redoubled our efforts in building it: the truth is that there are plenty of Kent's 750,000 working age adults who've yet to enjoy our spirits, so we've a lot of work to do!"

Yes, our immediate future may be uncertain. However, in times of uncertainty, we look to the things that comfort us the most: our family, our friends and, as we have experienced over the last 18 months, a resurgence of true Community Spirit. It's here where I draw the most positivity moving forward; especially from those whisky makers finally getting back to putting their heart and soul into creating something, which truly reflects a sense of place and a locality.

Long may it continue. As Dorothy once famously said: 'There's no place like home.'

Neil writes about whisky and other fine spirits for a number of publications globally, including The Daily and Sunday Telegraph. He is a Keeper Of The Quaich and a Liveryman in the Worshipful Company Of Distillers. Neil regularly presents a drinks feature on the popular TV food and drink show, Channel Four Sunday Brunch. His first book, (written with Gavin D. Smith) 'Let Me Tell You About Whisky' was published in 2013 and since then, he has co-authored five further books including 'Distilled', with Joel Harrison, which is now printed in 14 languages. His latest book, The World Atlas Of Gin has been shortlisted for the prestigious Tales Of The Cocktail Spirited award.

What Is Whisky?

by Gavin D Smith

The question may seem uncomplicated
but finding an answer has occupied authorities around the world
for decades and still does. And they rarely come to the same conclusion.
To put it simple – it all depends on where it is produced and where it is sold.
Gavin D Smith is here to guide us through whisky legislation.

"Law is order, and good law is good order."
Greek philosopher Aristotle

'What is Whisky?' was the term popularly applied to the series of discussions and deliberations that took place in Great Britain during the early years of the 20th century as entrenched pot still distillers battled with the blended whisky lobby to determine just what could be labelled 'whisk(e)y. Ultimately, a 'Royal Commission on Whiskey [sic] and Other Potable Spirits' was established in 1908 to examine the issue and it concluded in its report of July 1909:

'...that "Whiskey" is a spirit obtained by distillation from a wash saccharified by the diastase of malt, that "Scotch Whiskey" is whiskey, as above defined distilled in Scotland.'

No compulsory maturation period was stipulated, and no minimum percentage of malt required in a blend was specified. It was a complete victory for the blenders and patent still distillers.

That definition has informed everything that has followed, including the current EU regulations which state that:

"(a) Whisky or whiskey is a spirit drink produced exclusively by:

(i) distillation of a mash made from malted cereals

with or without whole grains of other cereals, which has been:

– saccharified by the diastase of the malt contained therein, with or without other natural enzymes,

– fermented by the action of yeast;

(ii) one or more distillations at less than 94,8 % vol., so that the distillate has an aroma and taste derived from the raw materials used,

(iii) maturation of the final distillate for at least three years in wooden casks not exceeding 700 litres capacity.

The final distillate, to which only water and plain caramel (for colouring) may be added, retains its colour, aroma and taste derived from the production process referred to in points (i), (ii) and (iii).

(b) The minimum alcoholic strength by volume of whisky or whiskey shall be 40 %.

(c) No addition of alcohol…diluted or not, shall take place.

(d) Whisky or whiskey shall not be sweetened or flavoured, nor contain any additives other than plain caramel used for colouring."

Additionally, both Scottish and Irish whisk(e)y benefit from Geographical Indication (GI) status, with the relevant legislation noting "For the purpose of this Regulation a geographical indication shall be an indication which identifies a spirit drink as originating in the territory of a country, or a region or locality in that territory, where a given quality, reputation or other characteristic of that spirit drink is essentially attributable to its geographical origin."

At this point, it should be stressed that the following is not intended to be a definitive description of all regulations relating to global whisk(e)y production. Rather, it is an attempt to highlight some of the key similarities and differences between legislation in a number of significant whisk(e)y-distilling countries.

Scotland

The Scotch Whisky Regulations 2009 broadly follow the EEC definitions of 'whisky,' above, with the added provisos that it must be produced and matured in Scotland, and matured in 'oak,' rather than 'wood.'

Additionally,

"Single Malt Scotch Whisky" means a Scotch Whisky that has been distilled in one or more batches –

(a) at a single distillery;

(b) from water and malted barley without the ad-

dition of any other cereals; and

(c) in pot stills;

"Single Grain Scotch Whisky" means a Scotch Whisky that has been distilled at a single distillery except –

(a) Single Malt Scotch Whisky; or

(b) a Blended Scotch Whisky;

"Blended Malt Scotch Whisky" means a blend of two or more Single Malt Scotch Whiskies that have been distilled at more than one distillery.

"Blended Grain Scotch Whisky" means a blend of two or more Single Grain Scotch Whiskies that have been distilled at more than one distillery.

"Blended Scotch Whisky" means a blend of one or more Single Malt Scotch Whiskies with one or more Single Grain Scotch Whiskies.

The body charged with policing these regulations is the Scotch Whisky Association (SWA) and at times it does come into conflict with producers and bottlers. Back in 2005, Compass Box borrowed a technique from the French wine industry and inserted new oak staves into used casks, which were employed to age whiskies for the firm's Spice Tree whisky.

The SWA objected to this practice, but Compass Box circumvented the issue by using heavily toasted French oak cask heads for future versions of Spice Tree – a practice which was not opposed by the SWA.

The specification of 'oak' rather than just 'wood,' also causes occasional frustrations, with a number of high-profile figures in the Scotch whisky industry stating that they would like the opportunity to finish whiskies in different wood types, such as cherry, walnut, elm and ash.

Compass Box founder John Glaser declares that "We ought to be able to evolve tradition. Why can't we use other wood types apart from oak, provided we use high-quality casks?

"Should you be able to augment casks with additional staves? I think so. It's about interpretation. I would also like to have the ability to use larger casks. The law states that the maximum capacity of a cask should be 700 litres. It seems arbitrary? Why 700? I'd like to be able to mature whisky in smaller casks initially and then vat them into a bigger cask for a time. It would be interesting."

Glaser concludes, however, that "I think the existing laws give a reasonable amount of latitude for producers. The Scotch Whisky Association interprets that law. There is so much we can already do to shape whisky – there's actually a lot more flexibility than people often realise."

On some occasions over the years, John Glaser from Compass Box and the SWA haven´t seen eye to eye

A greater degree of flexibility regarding cask usage was introduced in 2019, with the SWA announcing that casks which previously held gave spirits such as tequila or mezcal, or fruit spirit such as calvados could be used for Scotch whisky maturation, and the first Scotch finished in tequila casks was Buchanan's Two Souls, which appeared later that year.

Another issue relating to Scotch whisky legislation concerns 'transparency,' with Compass Box being informed by the SWA in 2016 that it had broken the law by revealing the precise recipes for two of its whiskies, Flaming Heart and This Is Not A Luxury Whisky.

Compass Box had revealed the ages of component whiskies, but the law only allows the age of the youngest component to be declared on labelling and packaging. Compass Box was joined in its fight for greater transparency by Bruichladdich, which proceeded to offer information relating to whisky 'recipes' on its website, with consumers entering the bottle batch code on the relevant product page to see a list of component casks.

Ireland

Across the Irish Sea, Irish malt whiskey, Irish grain whiskey and Irish blended whiskey all follow rela-tively parallel definitions to those of their Scottish counterparts, but it is in with 'pot still whiskey' that Ireland offers something quite different.

Previously widely known as 'pure pot still whis-key,' since 2014, the official definition has referred to 'single pot still whiskey.' According to the 'Technical File' that defines aspects of Irish whiskey, "Pot Still Irish Whiskey/Irish Pot Still Whiskey is defined as a spirit distilled from a mash of a combination of malted barley, unmalted barley and other unmalted cereals. The mash must contain a minimum of 30% malted barley and a minimum of 30% unmalted barley and be:

a) saccharified by the diastase of malt contained therein, with or without other natural enzymes.

b) fermented by the action of yeast.

c) distilled in pot stills in such manner that the distillate has an aroma and taste derived from the materials used.

"Brewing involves preparation of a mash from a proportional mix of malted and unmalted barley with up to 5% of other cereals such as oats and rye added if required. The traditional practice is to triple distil Pot Still Irish Whiskey/Irish Pot Still Whiskey although this practice is not exclusive and double distillation may also be employed."

Not all Irish distillers are happy with this definition of single pot still whiskey, however, maintaining that it was developed principally by industry leaders Irish Distillers as it suited their existing styles of spirit, and that the inclusion of a maximum five per cent of "other cereals" is at odds with historical models.

Two dissenting voices in the single pot still whiskey debate are Brendan Carty of Killowen distillery in County Down and Peter Mulryan, who operates Blackwater Distillery in County Waterford. Mulryan declares that "In all my 19 years of research I have never yet seen a single historic mashbill for Pot Still Irish that is compliant with that definition. Not one. So, what we are left with is a Technical File defining a category of Irish Whiskey that never existed."

He explains that during his research he has come across mashbills for pot still Irish whiskey that include the use of up to 70 per cent oats, rye and wheat, and he notes that "We have been laying down non-compliant pot still now since 2019 – we have done some single malt, but not a lot. We will be able to sell it as 'Irish whisky,' as although it doesn't comply with the definition 'single pot still' it does qualify as an 'Irish Whiskey'.

"However, both the Irish Whiskey Association and the Irish Whiskey Guild (small producers) are both canvassing their members on an update of the 2014 Technical File, so we are hopeful that the shameful file can be updated."

Apart from the 'single pot still' classification, Irish whiskey legislation differs from that of Scotland in terms of maturation, with a specification that whiskey is matured "…for at least three years in wooden casks, such as oak, not exceeding 700 litres capacity."

The key term here is 'such as oak, and Irish distillers have been experimenting with a number of other wood types. Most notably, Irish Distillers' Method & Madness range has seen single pot still whiskeys finished in chestnut, wild cherry and mulberry casks.

USA

On the other side of the Atlantic, laws relating to whisk(e)y in the USA are set out in Title 27 of the U.S. Code of Federal Regulations, in which the spelling 'whisky' is used throughout.

The Regulations state that "'Bourbon whisky,' 'rye whisky,' 'wheat whisky,' 'malt whisky,' or 'rye malt whisky' is whisky produced at not exceeding 160° proof [80%abv] from a fermented mash of not less than 51 percent corn, rye, wheat, malted barley, or malted rye grain, respectively, and stored at not more than 125° proof [62.5%abv] in charred new oak con-tainers; and also includes mixtures of such whiskies of the same type.

"'Corn whisky' is whisky produced at not exceeding 160° proof [80%abv] from a fermented mash of not less than 80 percent corn grain, and if stored in oak containers stored at not more than 125° proof [62.5%abv] in used or uncharred new oak containers and not subjected in any manner to treatment with charred wood; and also includes mixtures of such whisky."

No minimum period of maturation is specified for corn whisky, and if any of the above variants of whisky are aged for two or more years, they may be labelled as 'Straight.' While Bourbon has no geographical limitations within the USA, 'Tennessee Whiskey' may only be distilled within that state, and, like Bourbon, must be made from a mash of at least 51% corn and stored at not more than 125° proof [62.5%] in charred new oak containers. The 'Lincoln County' process of charcoal filtration often associated with Tennessee Whiskey is not a legal requirement.

Additional categories are Light Whiskey, which has to be distilled above 80%abv and may be matured in uncharred or used oak casks, Blended Whiskey, which has to comprise at least 20% straight whiskey

Bourbon can be made anywhere in the USA

The legal mashbill for an Irish single pot still whiskey is still being debated

or blend of straight whiskeys, while the remainder can be non-straight whiskey, neutral spirits, or a mix of the two. Finally, Spirit Whiskey is defined as containing a minimum five percent whiskey, mixed with neutral spirits.

Interestingly, the regulations also state that "Whisky" is an alcoholic distillate from a fermented mash of grain produced at less than 190° proof {95%abv] in such manner that the distillate possesses the taste, aroma, and characteristics generally attributed to whisky…*and also includes mixtures of such distillates for which no specific standards of identity are prescribed.*" [the author's italics]

This would seem to allow a significant amount of room for manoeuvre among distillers, and Liza Weisstuch, a New York-based journalist who specialises in whisky and travel, notes that "While there are rules defining Bourbon and [American] rye and Tennessee Whiskey and bottled in bond and the rest, distillers can really do whatever they please, as long as they call it by a different name. So, in essence, nobody's 'breaking' any rules. If anything, they're making new ones. It's the wild west in terms of production/ageing. A producer just has to follow the rules in labelling."

Canada

Government of Canada Food and Drug Regulations decree that:

"Canadian Whisky, Canadian Rye Whisky or Rye Whisky

(a) shall

(i) be a potable alcoholic distillate, or a mixture of potable alcoholic distillates, obtained from a mash of cereal grain or cereal grain products saccharified by the diastase of malt or by other enzymes and fermented by the action of yeast or a mixture of yeast and other micro-organisms,

(ii) be aged in small wood for not less than three years,

(iii) possess the aroma, taste and character generally attributed to Canadian whisky,

(iv) be manufactured in accordance with the requirements of the Excise Act and the regulations made thereunder,

(v) be mashed, distilled and aged in Canada, and

(vi) contain not less than 40% alcohol by volume; and

(b) may contain caramel and flavouring.

The vast majority of Indian whiskies contain neutral spirits made from fermented molasses

Comparing Canadian blended whisky with that from the USA, leading Canadian whisky writer and commentator Davin de Kergommeaux notes that while the USA permits the inclusion of up to 80% neutral spirits, no neutral spirits are allowed in Canadian blends. Furthermore, a maximum of 2.5% flavouring is permissible in US blends, while up to 9.09% of "mature spirit or wine" is allowed in Canadian blends.

This is often referred to as the '9.09% rule,' and de Kergommeaux notes that it "…gives a favourable US tax rate and is mostly used for high-volume whiskeys."

'Flavouring' is defined in the regulations as "…any spirit or wine, domestic or imported," though the spirit or wine in question must be at least two years old, ruling out neutral spirit, but there is nothing to prevent a Canadian distiller adding up to 9.09% of US Bourbon or French Cognac and still labelling the resulting lend as 'Canadian whisky.'

The '9.09% rule' only applies to whisky sold outside Canada, and whisky destined for domestic consumption may contain higher levels of 'flavouring.' It is also interesting to note that Canadian whisky may be labelled 'Canadian rye whisky' even if no rye grain is included in the cereal mash.

Australia

According to The Australian Distillers Association Inc, "In Australia it is law that whisky, brandy and rum must be stored in wood for no less than 2 years. It is also law that place of product claims and advertising claims must not be misleading or deceptive."

Australia's whisky regulations were put under the spotlight in 2020 when the Tasmanian-based Lark Distilling Co launched The Lark Wolf Release 2020. This comprised single malt whisky made in the company's Nant distillery, which it had acquired in 2016, but it was packaged under the Lark brand. Additionally, the front label of the bottle only carried the words 'From our Bothwell Distillery,' making no mention that this was where Nant single malt was produced.

The detailed text does make clear the connection, but there was a feeling among commentators that this could be seen as misleading labelling, and something that would not be allowed under Scotch whisky legislation, which specifies that a distillery name may only be used in reference to a whisky that has been wholly produced there.

However, as Andrew Derbidge, the director and cellarmaster of The Scotch Malt Whisky Society in Australia wrote at the time on his www.whisky-andwisdom.com website, "We aren't in Scotland, and we don't have an equivalent industry body to the SWA. The Australian Distillers Association was established in 2004, but it's not a body that necessarily sets rules and regulations. In truth, the Australian whisky industry does not have a set of rules or even guidelines to govern what we name and call our whiskies, so in a sense – no liquor industry rules have been broken."

Nonetheless, back in 1906 the Spirits Act did lay down definitions of both malt and blended whiskies, at a time when Australia was the fourth-largest whisky-producer in the world. The Spirits Act included the interesting stipulation that blended whisky "must consist of not less than twenty-five per cent of pure malt whisky which has been separately distilled by a pot still or similar process." When the aforementioned 'What is Whisky?' case in the UK was settled three years later, the Scottish and Irish malt distillers did not even have the consolation of blends being required to contain a mandatory percentage of malt spirit.

Japan

One might expect definitions relating to Japanese whisky to be very clear and unambiguous, but anyone who has bought a bottle labelled 'Japanese whisky' only to discover it comprises a mix of Scotch and Canadian whisky could tell you otherwise. 'Japanese whisky' merely had to be bottled in Japan to qualify for that misleading description.

As Japanese whisky has gained increasing international sales and kudos during recent years, the more responsible producers and bottlers in the Japanese whisky industry have unsurprisingly become uneasy about the lax way in which their product is defined, and the potential reputational damage for prestigious and truly legitimate brands that might result.

Consequently, from April 2021, members of The Japanese Spirits & Liqueurs Makers Association (JSLMA) are adhering to a new set of regulations and labelling standards.

Essentially, the regulations state that in order to be labelled as 'Japanese whisky,' only malt and other cereal grains may be used, all processing and bottling must take place in Japan, and distillate has to be matured in 'wooden' casks for a minimum of three years. The term 'wooden' gives Japanese producers the same freedom to experiment with non-oak timber that many of their global competitors enjoy.

India

Although there have been concerns about Japanese whisky regulations, overall, there is a broad consensus among whisky-producing nations about just what 'whisky' is, and certainly the requirement that it is produced from grain.

One country that has become infamous for playing fast and loose with even this basic consensus is India, where a very large part of the 'whisky' market comprises Indian-made foreign liquor (IMFL), often blends based on neutral spirits distilled from fermented molasses, and with no requirement for maturation.

This type of Indian 'whisky' has long attracted the ire of the Scotch Whisky Association and similar bodies as it does not even come close to conforming to EU definitions of whisky and is relatively cheap to produce, providing an apparently appealing alternative to whisky made within more conventional regulations.

The most recent legislation relating to Indian whisky comes in the Food Safety and Standards (Alcoholic Beverages) Regulations, 2018. There it is stated that:

"Whisky is an alcoholic beverage made by distilling the fermented extract of malted cereal grains such as corn, rye, barley, or using neutral grain spirit or rectified grain spirit, or neutral spirit of agricultural origin, or their mixture. Whisky may also be of the following types;

Malt or grain whisky: Malt or grain whisky is a distillate obtained from fermented mash of malted or unmalted cereals or a mixture of both with characteristic aroma and taste. It may also be of the following types;

(i) Single malt whisky: Single malt whisky is a distillate obtained from fermented mash that uses one particular malted grain or malted barley, distilled in pot still only, and produced from a single distillery.

(ii) Blended malt whisky or blended grain whisky: Blended malt or grain whisky shall be a mixture of at least 2% from barley malt or grain whisky, with neutral or rectified spirit."

Some Indian whisky producers would like to see regulations tightened, with Ashok Chokalingam, Head of International Operations for Amrut Distilleries, producers of malt whisky and IMFL, noting that "In India we have an upper limit of 50% abv on the whisky bottling strength and we cannot sell cask strength whiskies. As you can see from the regulations, the blended whisky definition is still loose and there is room for our IMFL. I would say it is a step forward for sure compared to what it was and I am hopeful this will go for further review and revision in the near future."

Whatever the regulations in place, wherever whisky is made, let us give Aristotle the last, as well as the first, words. "Quality is not an act, it is a habit."

Gavin D Smith is one of Scotland's leading whisky writers and Contributing Editor Scotland for Whisky Magazine. He regularly undertakes writing commissions for leading drinks companies and produces articles for a wide range of publications, including Whisky Magazine, Whisky Magazine & Fine Spirits – France, Whisky Etc, Whisky Advocate, Whiskeria, The Keeper, Irish Whiskey Magazine, Unfiltered and Whisky Quarterly.

He is the author and co-author of some 30 books, and recent publications include The Microdistillers' Handbook, Ardbeg: Heavenly Peated and World of Whisky (with David Wishart and Neil Ridley).

高峰
KOJI-FERMENTED
TAKAMINE
WHISKEY
8 YEARS OLD
PRODUCT OF JAPAN
40% ALC. / VOL. (80 PROOF)

Japanese Whisky Rules

– or not quite?

by Stefan Van Eycken

Japanese whisky can compete with the top single malts of the world. The lack of rules and regulations though, sometimes leave the consumer in doubt what is actually in the bottle. A new standard set by some of the top producers seeks to eliminate the confusion.

For the past few years, the news coming from the Japanese whisky front has hardly been new at all: more craft malt distilleries established left and right, less whisky to go around, most Japanese whisky releases highly limited and strictly allocated, the most in-demand ones available by ballot only, and astronomic prices at auctions. This year the noise coming out of Japan was a different one, though. The big story of the year was the establishment of a standard for 'Japanese whisky'.

In previous editions of the Malt Whisky Yearbook, we have spotlighted some of the 'darker' areas of Japanese whisky production: the widespread practice of importing malt and grain whisky in bulk from abroad and then using said liquid – with or without further aging and/or blending with domestically produced whisky – in products presented as 'Japanese whisky', as well as the reclassification of spirits that started their life as shochu or awamori as 'Japanese grain whisky' in the U.S.

Aware that the reputation of the Japanese whisky category at large was at risk of being tarnished by

Suntory is one of the producers in the Japan Spirits & Liqueurs Makers Association (JSLMA)

the practices highlighted above, a working group was set up in 2016 within the Japan Spirits & Liqueurs Makers Association (JSLMA) consisting of the three largest producers (Suntory, Nikka, Kirin) as well as the two leading craft distillers (Venture Whisky and Hombo Shuzo). The goal was to try and come up with a standard for 'Japanese whisky'. It's a small miracle the parties involved managed to come to an agreement. Debates were held until early 2021, and then in February – to the delight of many – the announcement was made that a standard had been established that would go into effect on 1 April 2021.

The standard specifies that, in terms of raw ingredients, malted grains must always be used (other cereal grains can be used as well but malted grains must be part of the mashbill) in conjunction with water extracted in Japan. Mashing, fermentation and distillation must be carried out at a distillery in Japan with the alcohol content after distillation not exceeding 95%abv. Maturation must take place in Japan, in wooden casks (note: not necessarily oak) not exceeding a capacity of 700 litres for at least 3 years. Bottling must take place in Japan at an abv of no less than 40%.

With further restrictions in place regarding labeling and the use of certain words that are considered evocative of 'Japan', the new standard was greeted by whisky enthusiasts at home and abroad as the dawn of a new era of absolute transparency. As usual, however, the reality is slightly more complex. First of all, this standard is not law but a standard self-imposed by companies who are part of the JSLMA. The definition of whisky by Japan's National Tax Agency remains unchanged and is unlikely to change in the near future. Further caveats are that there is currently no approval process and no penalties and that there is a transitional period until 31 March 2024, so we are not quite out of the woodwork yet. Another big loophole is that, for companies that are members of the JSLMA, disclosure that a whisky doesn't meet the standards of 'Japanese whisky' must be made in at least one of the following ways: on the bottle label, on the company's website, or in response to a customer inquiry. We'll repeat that: in one of those three ways.

That the standard will lead to changes on the Japanese whisky scene is clear already. Many producers are making efforts to align products in their portfolio with the newly established standard. An example is

Yasato distillery is working with different grain bills

Sakurao Brewery & Distillery (formerly Chugoku Juzo), which started using bulk imported whisky in the 1980s and managed to establish a presence on the 'Japanese whisky' shelves of liquor retailers around the world over the past decade with their Togouchi brand – most certainly not 'Japanese whisky' under the new standard. The company plans to phase out the use of bulk import whisky by 2023 and make all its whiskies JSLMA-standard compliant by then. To make this possible, the company is planning to invest 100 million yen in the summer of 2021 to expand their Sakurao distillery. Many other Japanese whisky producers that have been reliant on whisky imported in bulk from abroad are making similar moves and/or shifting towards transparency and an unambiguous presentation of products that will continue to make use of bulk import whisky.

Grain whisky is growing

An area that we will see emerging and developing over the next few years will be that of craft grain distilling. For all but the three major players on the Japanese whisky scene, the lack of access to domestically-produced grain whisky is the biggest obstacle to releasing Japanese blended whiskies (as defined by the JSLMA-standard). For most Japanese craft distillers, releasing an entry level blended whisky is the only way to have a permanently available product on the shelves, e.g. Ichiro's Malt & Grain (White Label), and to guarantee steady sales. Until further notice, the only option is to import grain whisky in bulk from Scotland, the U.S. or Canada and blend it with in-house produced malt whisky (and/or other malt whisky imported from abroad).

The buzz about an imminent standard for Japanese whisky has been in the air for the past few years and producers left and right have been trying to address the non-availability of domestically-produced grain whisky in their own way. Several craft whisky distilleries have, over the past couple of years, been producing grain whisky in relatively small volumes. Kiuchi Shuzo has been experimenting with various grainbills at their Nukada distillery and at their larger Yasato distillery. Sakurao Brewery & Distillery has been producing grain whisky in their hybrid still and Komasa Jozo has added grain whisky making facilities to their Hioki distillery, which is used for shochu as well as gin production. These are all examples of

Jokichi Takamine perfected the use of koji, mainly used for shochu production, to make also whisky

fairly limited production and none of it has made it to market yet. Speaking to key industry figures in Japan, it's becoming clear though, that in the years to come, we will see a number of dedicated 'craft grain distilleries' emerging – especially, it seems, on Hokkaido, the northernmost of the four main islands of Japan. Rumors are the most-awarded Japanese craft producer is preparing to set up a grain distillery there, and Kenten Jitsugyo (who own Akkeshi distillery) "have plans" to do the same. Meanwhile, the Hokkaido Research Organization has recently announced a project to use locally-grown corn for the production of grain whisky at the currently under-construction Maoi distillery on the island. A few other parties also seem to be gearing up to enter the Japanese grain whisky market, albeit elsewhere in Japan. It will take half a decade or more for these efforts to shake up the Japanese blended whisky game, but it's a development that is to be welcomed and it will be interesting, from a technical point of view, to see what sort of production methods Japanese grain whisky makers will adopt and/or develop.

Clearly, the JSLMA-standard was set up with the aim of encouraging transparency and making life harder for charlatans and the enterprise deserves to be applauded for that reason alone, but some have questioned whether a standard largely modeled after foreign whisky standards is a perfect fit for the Japanese whisky culture. Blending using imported components has long been part of Japanese whisky-making practice and since 1953, there has been no minimum-maturation period specified in the Liquor Tax Law. (There still isn't. To reiterate, the standards discussed here are not law.) Under the current standard, however, the largest selling blends 'made in Japan' by the biggest whisky producers and sold there domestically are not 'Japanese whiskies'. Imagine Johnnie Walker or Ballantine's not being Scotch whiskies. Whether the largest whisky producers in Japan will move to make changes to the composition of their top-selling blends – again: top-selling in Japan – to make them compliant with the JSLMA standard remains to be seen. Not that there is a need to do so, as the labels on these blends don't mention

'Japanese whisky' and therefore don't violate the standard, but for members of the JSLMA not stating that a whisky is compliant with the standard is akin to admitting that it isn't.

The new standard also closes the door on shochu and awamori producers, as their licenses expressly prohibit them from using malted grains, which is now a requirement for 'Japanese whisky' under the JSLMA standard. However, it's worth pointing out that most shochu makers are not members of the JSLMA – they have an association of their own – and are therefore not bound by the new whisky standards. Some voices have questioned though, whether the use of koji[1] does not constitute a culturally meaningful method of producing whisky in Japan. There is certainly a historical precedent: in the early 1890s, the Japanese scientist Jokichi Takamine developed a method to make whisky using koji in Peoria, Illinois for The Whiskey Trust.

The birth of koji whisky

Jokichi Takamine was born on 3 November 1854. After studying western science and chemistry all over Japan, he moved to the UK, where he studied industrial engineering at Glasgow University (and elsewhere in the UK) between 1880 and 1883. To put this in perspective, we are talking 35 years before Masataka Taketsuru arrived in Glasgow. Takamine's journey is a fascinating one but for our purposes, we'll fast forward to 1890, when he moved to Chicago and established the Takamine Ferment Co. Takamine patented the process of using koji in the US and several European countries and, in 1891, he started working for the Illinois Whiskey Trust which was the largest spirits maker in the US at the time, owning 65 distilleries nationwide and being responsible for 80% of all spirits produced in America. While working for the Whiskey Trust, Takamine fine-tuned his 'Takamine Process', using koji to make whisky. Because koji amylase breaks down starch into glucose, it is a more efficient way to make whisky than using malted grains. In essence, it sidesteps the need for malting. A few weeks into production using the Takamine process, the Manhattan Distillery in Peoria burned down in mysterious circumstances. In early 1895, the rebuilt distillery was closed, production ceased and the new owners reverted to malting. What happened to the whiskey made using Takamine's koji process is anyone's guess, but whisky production in America and elsewhere might have been very different if circumstances, some say the maltsters, hadn't conspired against the use of koji.

[1] steamed grains that have been inoculated with the *Aspergillus oryzae* mold, used to convert starches into sugars (e.g. in the production of sake, shochu, soy sauce, miso, etc.)

Takamine went on to greatness in the field of medicine. He isolated adrenaline in 1900 and died a wealthy man in New York in 1922, but at least one producer in Japan has tried to revive the Takamine process to produce whisky. The Shinozaki distillery in Fukuoka has been laying down stock for the past decade. They have a legitimate barrel management program with over 2,000 casks maturing in their warehouses and a master blender on staff, so it's not at all like some shochu distilleries where they have a few casks forgotten in a dark corner of the distillery. A recently released 8 year old is available in the US under the Takamine brand, the family trust having given permission to use the name. Because of the use of koji in the production process, this is not considered whisky in Japan and it doesn't meet the JSLMA-standard of 'Japanese whisky'.

Unhappy to see good quality, barrel-aged koji-fermented distilled spirits painted as 'outlaws', advocates in the US have sought to give them a category of their own: 'koji whisky'. Two recent releases by the American independent bottler Single Cask Nation have used this nomenclature. They are not 'whisky' in Japan, and they are not considered 'Japanese whisky' by the JSLMA-standard, but they are 'whisky' in the US and the use of koji has been an integral part of Japanese culture for the past 1,300 years so one would be hard pressed to argue against it being a culturally meaningful practice in Japan.

Standards, by their very nature, seek to draw a line in the sand, but it's worth keeping in mind that even with the noblest of intentions, standards can sometimes exclude historically grown and, in some cases, meaningful alternative practices. It seems undeniable that we are heading towards a real renaissance of Japanese whisky – the signs are everywhere – but it is to be hoped that healthy ongoing debates on what does and what does not constitute 'Japanese whisky' will remain an integral part of that renaissance.

A new wind is blowing

Ahead of the 100th anniversary of whisky-making in Japan in 2023 or 2024 (depending on whether one considers the establishment of Yamazaki distillery or the actual beginning of whisky production there as the starting point), it seems like a new wind is blowing through the Japanese whisky landscape. Whisky-making in Japan has always been heavily patterned after whisky production in Scotland (and to a lesser extent, the U.S. and Canada), but after almost a century of Japanese whisky makers leaving the country to learn the ropes abroad and bringing home "the fire", we are now starting to see the beginnings of an influx of foreign talent – financial,

Site of the future Komoro Distillery with founder Koji Shimaoka (right) and Master Distiller Ian Chang

technical or both – on the Japanese whisky scene.

Located in Akashi, near Kobe, in Hyogo prefecture, the Kaikyo Distillery is the result of a collaboration between the Yonezawa family, who have been brewing in the area since 1856 and distilling (mainly shochu) since 1918, and Mossburn Disitllers, the company behind the recent success stories of Torabhaig Distillery as well as the Reivers Distillery. In the build-up to the 100th anniversary of spirit production, the Yonezawa family decided to team up with Mossburn Distillers with the aim of producing a single malt whisky. "A lot of effort has gone into completing our sister distillery in Kobe," Neil Matheson of Mossburn Distillers relates, "where we now have a brand new distilling hall with Forsyths twin pots and a separate mash house and ageing cellar. The co-operation between the two teams [in Japan and in Scotland] is great to see and we have been able to spread our advisory team over all three projects as they grow up."

In spite of the enormous demand for Japanese whisky worldwide, the team decided to keep the Kaikyo operation relatively small.

"We decided to stick to a 'craft' base," Matheson

explains, "and we will probably make no more than 200,000 litres of pure alcohol there but I would like to experiment with some rice whiskies and shochu as well."

Kaikyo Distillery got its whisky-production license in 2017 and has launched a range of whiskies under the Hatozaki brand – which contain malt and grain whisky components imported from Scotland and America – while the in-house produced spirit is maturing.

Another project where foreign talent will be playing an integral role in the creation of a new Japanese single malt whisky – to an extent not seen before on the Japanese whisky scene – is the multi-distillery project envisaged by Karuizawa Distillers. This will bring back distilling to the Karuizawa area after the much-lamented loss of the iconic Karuizawa Distillery, which was mothballed in 2000 and demolished in 2015.

Whilst the long-term vision of the newly established Karuizawa Distillers company is to establish several distilleries in the Karuizawa area, the main focus at the moment is on getting the first one – Komoro Distillery, located in the town of the same name – up and running. The project is the brainchild of Koji Shimaoka, who worked in investment banking for over 20 years before moving into the hotel business in Karuizawa. Shimaoka used to stop by the old Karuizawa distillery occasionally and, after its demise, was keen to bring whisky distilling back to the area. It took him 5 years to find a suitable location to build a new distillery. Good things come to those who wait, they say, and on 30 December 2019, Shimaoka managed to get hold of a piece of land in the city of Komoro that ticked all the boxes.

While the site may be somewhat reminiscent of "an iconic Scottish distillery site," in the words of Shimaoka, his vision was far from "copycat". His approach to assembling a team was anything but typical – for Japan, that is. Rather than send some local youngsters to another Japanese distillery (usually Ichiro's) for a week or two, or to Scotland, he decided to "look for the best" abroad and bring those people in right from the start so that they could shape the project from inception to production and all the way through maturation, product development, marketing and education. In April 2020, Shimaoka brought Ian Chang, formerly of Kavalan, on board. Chang didn't need much arm-twisting. "After 16 years of making whisky in a subtropical climate," he comments, "I felt ready for a new challenge in a brand new environment."

The distillery set-up will be a small mashtun, 5 wooden washbacks (Douglas fir, made in Japan) as well as 5 stainless steel washbacks, and one pair of stills made by Forsyths. The two warehouses will be of a hybrid-type: palletized in the middle but dunnage around the sides and with an earthen floor. Warehouse 1 will have a VIP lounge for the use of an exclusive membership club with a view over the casks and beyond to the forest around the distillery. The forest will also be sponsored and looked after by Karuizawa Distillers, in order to create a very natural and environmentally friendly place for activities such as forest bathing, strolls, meditation and self-realization. Casks will be mainly ex-sherry, but there are also plans to use some mizunara as well as non-oak wood (which is allowed for the maturation of whisky in Japan). It's still very early days, but it's clear that Ian Chang will be in his element in his new playground. Speaking in early 2021, he mentioned the possibility of looking into experimenting with yeast to bring out a hint of violet in the new-make spirit at Komoro Distillery, in reference to the symbol of the city, the *Viola mandshurica*.

Shimaoka's vision for Komoro Distillery also includes a whisky academy, for which he has brought in Eddie and Amanda Ludlow of The Whisky Lounge. This may not sound like a big deal compared with distillery programs in Scotland and the U.S., for example but with most distilleries in Japan closed to the public and the only 'academy' sort of experience having been suspended (Nikka's 'My Whisky Zukuri' program, which was in Japanese-only and extremely hard to get into anyway), Karuizawa Distillers' plans for a whisky academy are bound to attract lots of fans, domestically as well as internationally. The company also plans to take the academy around the world for pop-ups and master classes in various cities. The ground-breaking ceremony took place on 27 July 2021 and the project has since been designated by the Komoro city council as a "Regional Future Leading Company"

With rumors floating around of other foreign parties looking to establish distilleries in Japan in the near future, it is clear that this trend is anything but a fad. It will be interesting to see if and how these foreign parties will be contributing to the developing Japanese whisky landscape in novel ways as we enter the second century of whisky production in Japan.

Stefan Van Eycken grew up in Belgium and Scotland and moved to Japan in 2000. He was editor of Nonjatta until 2016 when the site was discontinued, and is also the man behind the ongoing series of rare bottlings of Japanese whisky known as the 'Ghost Series' and the bi-annual charity event 'Spirits for Small Change'. He is regional editor (Japan) for Whisky Magazine UK, and a regular contributor to Whisky Magazine Japan and France. His book "Whisky Rising: The Definitive Guide to the Finest Whiskies and Distillers from Japan" is available in English, Chinese and Japanese.

Malt distilleries

Including the subsections:
Scottish distilleries | New distilleries | Closed distilleries
Distilleries around the globe

Explanations

Owner: Name of the owning company, sometimes with the parent company within brackets.

Region/district: There are five protected whisky regions or localities in Scotland today; Highlands, Lowlands, Speyside, Islay and Campbeltown. Where useful we mention a location within a region e.g. Orkney, Northern Highlands etc.

Founded: The year in which the distillery was founded is usually considered as when construction began. The year is rarely the same year in which the distillery was licensed.

Status: The status of the distillery's production. Active, mothballed (temporarily closed), closed (but most of the equipment still present), dismantled (the equipment is gone but part of or all of the buildings remain even if they are used for other purposes) and demolished.

Visitor centre: The letters (vc) after status indicate that the distillery has a visitor centre. Many distilleries accept visitors despite not having a visitor centre. It can be worthwhile making an enquiry.

Address: The distillery´s address.

Tel: This is generally to the visitor centre, but can also be to the main office.

Website: The distillery's (or in some cases the owner's) website.

Capacity: The current production capacity expressed in litres of pure alcohol (LPA).

History: The chronology focuses on the official history of the distillery and independent bottlings are only listed in exceptional cases.

Tasting notes: For all the Scottish distilleries that are not permanently closed we present tasting notes of what, in most cases, can be called the core expression (mainly their best selling 10 or 12 year old).

We have tried to provide notes for official bottlings but in those cases where we have not been able to obtain them, we have turned to independent bottlers.

The whiskies have been tasted either by Gavin D Smith (GS), a well-known whisky authority and author of 20 books on the subject or by Ingvar Ronde (IR). All notes have been prepared especially for Malt Whisky Yearbook 2022.

Aberfeldy

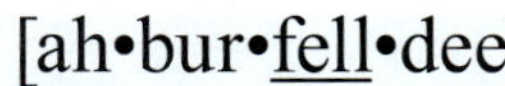

[ah•bur•<u>fell</u>•dee]

Owner: John Dewar & Sons (Bacardi)	**Region/district:** Southern Highlands
Founded: **Status:** 1896 Active (vc)	**Capacity:** 3 400 000 litres

Address: Aberfeldy, Perthshire PH15 2EB

Website: aberfeldy.com	**Tel:** 01887 822010 (vc)

The red squirrels at Aberfeldy are famous and visitors to the distillery stand a good chance of seeing these charming animals. However, recent observations in the area of the invasive grey squirrel can pose a threat to this native Scottish species.

Spreading from the south, the larger grey, American cousin can easily outcompete the red for food and habitat and grey squirrels sometimes also carry the squirrel pox virus which is lethal to the red. Another animal very much in focus at Aberfeldy is the beaver. They have frequently been seen loafing around in the cooling dam, but lately increased beaver activity has forced the distillery staff to protect the surrounding trees from damage by the animals.

The equipment consists of a 7.3 ton stainless steel, full lauter mash tun, eight washbacks made of larch and three made of stainless steel with an average fermentation time of 72 hours, and four stills. During 2020, the staff lost two extra months of production due to the pandemic but for 2021 the plan is to revert back to the usual seven-day week with 23 mashes which equates to 3.4 million litres of alcohol. In 2015 a biomass boiler was installed and in 2021 the redundant heavy fuel boiler will be converted to an LPG (Liquified Petroleum Gas) boiler as a back-up.

Aberfeldy malt has been the backbone of the Dewar's blend for more than a century but following a relaunch in 2014 sales, of the single malt has increased substantially to 1,5 million bottles yearly. The core range consists of **12, 16** and **21 years old**. For the duty free market there are two widely available expressions; a **16 year old** and a **21 year old** both of them finished for up to 12 months in Madeira casks (ex-Bual and ex-Malvasia Malmsey respectively). Another range aimed at selected airports around the world is the Exceptional Cask Series. Recent limited releases include an **18 year old** finished in red wine casks from Côte Rôtie and there is also a **40 year old** which can be hand-filled at the distillery or ordered through their website.

History:

1896 John and Tommy Dewar embark on the construction of the distillery, a stone's throw from the old Pitilie distillery which was active from 1825 to 1867. Their objective is to produce a single malt for their blended whisky - White Label.

1898 Production starts in November.

1917 The distillery closes.

1919 The distillery re-opens.

1925 Distillers Company Limited (DCL) takes over.

1972 Reconstruction takes place, the floor maltings is closed and the two stills are increased to four.

1991 The first official bottling is a 15 year old in the Flora & Fauna series.

1998 Bacardi buys John Dewar & Sons from Diageo at a price of £1,150 million.

2000 A visitor centre opens and a 25 year old is released.

2005 A 21 year old is launched in October, replacing the 25 year old.

2009 Two 18 year old single casks are released.

2010 A 19 year old single cask, exclusive to France, is released.

2011 A 14 year old single cask is released.

2014 The whole range is revamped and an 18 year old for duty free is released.

2015 A 16 year old is released.

2018 A 16 year old and a 21 year old madeira finish are released for duty free.

2020 A limited 15 year old finished in Pomerol casks is released.

2021 A limited 18 year old finished in Côte Rôtie casks is released.

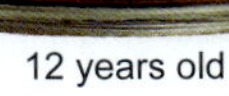

12 years old

Tasting notes Aberfeldy 12 years old:

GS – Sweet, with honeycombs, breakfast cereal and stewed fruits on the nose. Inviting and warming. Mouth-coating and full-bodied on the palate. Sweet, malty, balanced and elegant. The finish is long and complex, becoming progressively more spicy and drying.

Aberlour

[ah•bur•lower]

Owner: **Region/district:**
Chivas Brothers Ltd   Speyside
(Pernod Ricard)

Founded: **Status:**   **Capacity:**
1879   Active (vc)   3 800 000 litres

Address: Aberlour, Banffshire AB38 9PJ

Website: **Tel:**
aberlour.com   01340 881249

Aberlour distillery was acquired more than 25 years before Pernod Ricard took over Glenlivet, the current flagship malt in the company´s portfolio. They put a lot of effort into the Aberlour brand and it soon became the most sold single malt in France.

At least since the 1980s it has held a Top 10 spot among most sold single malts of the world. Lately though the sales figures have dropped. The top year for Aberlour was in 2016 when 4,3 million bottles were sold. Three years later sales had dropped by 35% to only 2,8 million bottles and the brand went from 6th place to 10th on the sales list of single malts. It is hard to say what the reason behind this is. One assumption would be that total malt exports to France, the most important market for the brand, had dropped. But, on the contrary, during the same period malts to France increased by 3%. Recent investments in the distillery however suggest that the owners are optimistic. There are even discussions, although nothing has been confirmed, about doubling the capacity by installing another eight stills and 16 washbacks.

Currently, the distillery is equipped with a 12 ton semi-lauter mash tun, six stainless steel washbacks and two pairs of large and wide stills in a spacious still room. To achieve the desired character of the newmake, which is fruity, the operators run a very slow distillation.

The core range includes **12, 16** and **18 year olds** – all matured in a combination of ex-bourbon and ex-sherry casks. Another core expression is **Casg Annamh** which is bourbon/oloroso matured. A new addition in January 2021 was a **14 year old**. Finally there is **Aberlour a'bunadh**, bottled at cask strength and matured in ex-oloroso casks. Available in the American market is **a'bunadh Alba** matured in American oak. For select markets **12 year old** non chill-filtered, **15 year old Select Cask Reserve** and **White Oak Millennium 2004** are available. A **12 year old Sherry Cask** and a **15 year old Double Cask** are travel retail exclusives. Recent limited releases in the Aberlour Cellar Collection include a **39** and a **44 year old**.

History:

1879 The local banker James Fleming founds the distillery.

1892 The distillery is sold to Robert Thorne & Sons Ltd who expands it.

1896 A fire rages and almost totally destroys the distillery. The architect Charles Doig is called in to design the new facilities.

1921 Robert Thorne & Sons Ltd sells Aberlour to a brewery, W. H. Holt & Sons.

1945 S. Campbell & Sons Ltd buys the distillery.

1962 Aberlour terminates floor malting.

1973 Number of stills are increased from two to four.

1974 Pernod Ricard buys Campbell Distilleries.

2000 Aberlour a´bunadh is launched.

2001 Pernod Ricard buys Chivas Brothers and merges Chivas Brothers and Campbell Distilleries under the brand Chivas Brothers.

2002 A new, modernized visitor centre is inaugurated in August.

2008 The 18 year old is also introduced outside France.

2013 Aberlour 2001 White Oak is released.

2014 White Oak Millenium 2004 is released.

2018 Casg Annamh is released.

2019 A´bunadh Alba is released.

2021 A 14 year old is released.

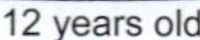

12 years old

Tasting notes Aberlour 12 year old:

GS – The nose offers brown sugar, honey and sherry, with a hint of grapefruit citrus. The palate is sweet, with buttery caramel, maple syrup and eating apples. Liquorice, peppery oak and mild smoke in the finish.

Allt-a-Bhainne

[alt a•vain]

Owner:	Region/district:
Chivas Brothers Ltd (Pernod Ricard)	Speyside

Founded:	Status:	Capacity:
1975	Active	4 200 000 litres

Address: Glenrinnes, Dufftown, Banffshire AB55 4DB

Website:	Tel:
-	01542 783200

The foundation of Allt-a-Bhainne in 1975 was initiated by a Canadian spirits company which would have a huge impact on the Scotch whisky industry for more than 50 years – namely Seagrams.

Founded in the mid 1800s, the Seagram family built a successful company, not least during prohibition in the 1920s when the neighbour to the south, America, was more or less dry, at least officially. In the 1940s the majority owner Sam Bronfman started to take an interest in Scotch whisky. His bid on Robertson & Baxter (later to become Highland Distillers/Edrington) was turned down and instead he successfully bought Chivas Brothers which at this time was a broker and blender without any distilleries. Bronfman decided to turn Chivas Regal into a mega brand and over the years added distilleries (Strathisla, Glenlivet, Glen Grant, Aberlour) to the portfolio and constructed not only Allt-a-Bhainne but also Braeval. Seagram's influence diminished when the second and third generations of the Bronfman family took over. Seagram's Spirits & Wine was acquired by Diageo and Pernod Ricard in 2001 which divided the distinguished company between them.

The equipment consists of a 9 ton lauter mash tun, eight stainless steel washbacks with a fermentation time of 48-50 hours and two pairs of stills. The distillery is currently working seven days a week with 25 mashes resulting in 4 million litres of alcohol.

Allt-a-Bhainne single malt has been an important part of the Scotch blend The 100 Pipers for many years. The brand, which sells around 18 million bottles per year, has its biggest markets in Asia. The smoky, note in the whisky comes from the fact that Allt-a-Bhainne for a number of years have been distilling peated whisky for part of the year. Usually it constitutes 30-50% of the total production and has a phenol specification in the barley between 10 and 20ppm.

Official bottlings are few. A lightly peated **Allt-a-Bhainne NAS** was launched in 2018 and there is also a **15 year old cask strength** distilled in 2005 in the Distillery Reserve Collection, available at all Chivas' visitor centres.

History:

1975 The distillery is founded by Chivas Brothers, a subsidiary of Seagrams, in order to secure malt whisky for its blended whiskies. The total cost amounts to £2.7 million.

1989 Production has doubled.

2001 Pernod Ricard takes over Chivas Brothers from Seagrams.

2002 Mothballed in October.

2005 Production restarts in May.

2018 An official, lightly peated bottling is released.

Allt-a-Bhainne NAS

Tasting notes Allt-a-Bhainne NAS:

IR – Subtle smokiness is mixed with butterscotch, honey, apples and a touch of pepper. Sweet peat on the palate, oranges, ginger, melon, more pepper and vanilla.

Ardbeg

[ard•<u>beg</u>]

Owner:
The Glenmorangie Co
(Moët Hennessy)

Region/district:
Islay

Founded: 1815
Status: Active (vc)
Capacity: 2 100 000 litres

Address: Port Ellen, Islay, Argyll PA42 7EA

Website:
ardbeg.com

Tel:
01496 302244 (vc)

For such a highly profiled and popular single malt brand, the core range of Ardbeg was surprisingly small just a little more than a decade ago. In fact there were only two expressions – the new 10 year old and Uigeadail.

There is a good explanation for this though. When Glenmorangie assumed ownership in 1997 there was an inconsistency in stock both in terms of quality and quantity from certain years. There was no production 1982-1989 and only two months per year from 1989 to 1996. Some casks from the 60s and 70s, very little from the 80s, plenty from 1990 but then less and less up to 1996 were included in the purchase. One of Bill Lumsden' s (the master blender) first actions was to survey the market for casks of Ardbeg and buy whatever could be found from, e g, Allied, Diageo and William Grant. Today there are six core bottlings and every year limited expressions find their way to thirsty fans.

For many years, the Ardbeg crew did everything they could to produce as much as possible with the current equipment and without compromising the quality of the spirit. But an increase of the capacity was required to fulfill demands and in spring 2019 a completely new still house was built and two more stills added. Then enter the covid pandemic and the commissioning was delayed. Today the equipment consists of a 5 ton stainless steel semi lauter mash tun and eight washbacks (with an intention to increase with another three) made of Oregon pine with a fermentation time of 60 hours. Furthermore, there are two pairs of stills with the spirit stills being fitted with purifiers to help create the special fruity character of the spirit. They started to use the new stills in March 2021 and the plan is now to do 22 mashes per week for the rest of the year which would mean around 1,7 million litres of alcohol.

The core range, all of them non-chill filtered, consists of the **10 year old**, a mix of first and re-fill bourbon casks, **Uigeadail,** a marriage of bourbon and sherry casks and bottled at cask strength, **Corryvreckan**, also a cask strength and a combination of bourbon casks and new French oak, **An Oa**, a vatting of whiskies matured in several types of casks that have been married together for a minimum of three months in three huge vats (14,000 and 30,000 litres respectively) and the **5 year old Wee Beastie**, matured in a combination of bourbon and oloroso casks. A sixth member appeared in January 2021 when a **25 year old** was launched.

Recent limited bottlings include the rye cask matured **Arrrrrrr-dbeg** which was released in spring 2021 in honour of retiring distillery manager Mickey Heads. In July 2021 an **8 year old** matured entirely in ex-sherry was presented to the Committee members for "evaluation" and it was later followed by batch 3 of **Traigh Bhan**, this time a 21 year old. The Ardbeg Day expression for 2021 was **Scorch** which had been matured in heavily charred casks. As usual it was released first at cask strength and later bottled at 46%.

History:

1794 First record of a distillery at Ardbeg. It was founded by Alexander Stewart.

1798 The MacDougalls, later to become licensees of Ardbeg, are active on the site through Duncan MacDougall.

1815 The current distillery is founded by John MacDougall, son of Duncan MacDougall.

1853 Alexander MacDougall, John's son, dies and sisters Margaret and Flora MacDougall, assisted by Colin Hay, continue the running of the distillery. Colin Hay takes over the licence when the sisters die.

1888 Colin Elliot Hay and Alexander Wilson Gray Buchanan renew their license.

1900 Colin Hay's son takes over the license.

1959 Ardbeg Distillery Ltd is founded.

1973 Hiram Walker and Distillers Company Ltd jointly purchase the distillery for £300,000 through Ardbeg Distillery Trust.

1977 Hiram Walker assumes single control of the distillery. Ardbeg closes its maltings.

1979 Kildalton, a less peated malt, is produced over a number of years.

1981 The distillery closes in March.

1987 Allied Lyons takes over Hiram Walker and thereby Ardbeg.

1989 Production is restored. All malt is taken from Port Ellen.

1996 The distillery closes in July.

History continued:

1997 Glenmorangie plc buys the distillery for £7 million. Ardbeg 17 years old and Provenance are launched

1998 A new visitor centre opens.

2000 Ardbeg 10 years is introduced and the Ardbeg Committee is launched.

2001 Lord of the Isles 25 years and Ardbeg 1977 are launched.

2002 Ardbeg Committee Reserve and Ardbeg 1974 are launched.

2003 Uigeadail is launched.

2004 Very Young Ardbeg (6 years) and a limited edition of Ardbeg Kildalton are launched.

2005 Serendipity is launched.

2006 Ardbeg 1965 and Still Young are launched. Almost There (9 years old) and Airigh Nam Beist are released.

2007 Ardbeg Mor, a 10 year old in 4.5 litre bottles is released.

2008 The new 10 year old, Corryvreckan, Rennaissance, Blasda and Mor II are released.

2009 Supernova is released, the peatiest expression from Ardbeg ever.

2010 Rollercoaster and Supernova 2010 are released.

2011 Ardbeg Alligator is released.

2012 Ardbeg Day and Galileo are released.

2013 Ardbog is released.

2014 Auriverdes and Kildalton are released.

2015 Perpetuum and Supernova 2015 are released.

2016 Dark Cove and a Twenty Something 21 year old are relased.

2017 An Oa, Kelpie and Twenty Something 23 year old are released.

2018 Grooves and Twenty Something 22 year old are released.

2019 Drum and Traigh Bhan are released.

2020 Blaaack, Wee Beastie and Traigh Bhan batch 2 are released.

2021 An 8 year old, a 25 year old, Arrrrrrrdbeg, Scorch and Traigh Bhan batch 3 are released.

Tasting notes Ardbeg 10 year old:

GS – Quite sweet on the nose, with soft peat, carbolic soap and Arbroath smokies. Burning peats and dried fruit, followed by sweeter notes of malt and a touch of liquorice in the mouth. Extremely long and smoky in the finish, with a fine balance of cereal sweetness and dry peat notes.

8 years old

25 years old

Traigh Bhan Batch 3

An Oa

Wee Beastie

Scorch

10 years old

Uigeadail

Corryvreckan

Ardmore

[ard•moor]

Owner: Beam Suntory

Region/district: Highland

Founded: 1898

Status: Active

Capacity: 4 725 000 litres

Address: Kennethmont, Aberdeenshire AB54 4NH

Website: ardmorewhisky.com

Tel: 01464 831213

Some people confuse a distillery's capacity with what they actually produce but that obviously depends on what the producer think they will be able to sell within the next 5-10 years. But there are other pitfalls when discussing production capacity.

The capacity figure is not just related to size and numbers of the equipment (mash tun, washbacks and stills). It very much depends on how you conduct your mashing, fermentation and distillation and that, in turn, is based on the spirit character you are looking for. One recent example is Ardmore which has had a capacity of 5,5 million litres of alcohol for many years now. In this edition we have changed it to just over 4,7 million. The reason is twofold; a couple of years ago, the distillery moved towards a clearer wort which increases the risk of foaming in the washbacks. They had to be filled lower and the mash was changed from 12,5 tons to 12 tons. The other reason for a lower capacity is that the fermentation time when they make the unpeated Ardlair, was increased to 70 hours.

Traditionally, Ardmore has been the only distillery in the region consistently producing peated whisky with a phenol specification of the barley at 12-14 ppm. The earthy Highland peat is locally sourced from St Fergus. Since the foundation in 1898 the whisky has also been an important part of Teachers, the famous blended Scotch which last year sold 17 million bottles

The distillery is equipped with a 12 ton, cast iron, semi-lauter mash tun, 14 Douglas fir washbacks (four large and ten smaller ones) with a fermentation time of 55 hours for Ardmore and 70 hours for Ardlair, as well as four pairs of stills. At the moment, Ardmore is working a seven-day week with 23 mashes per week resulting in 4.5 million litres of alcohol. Around 55% is the peated Ardmore and the rest is Ardlair which is used for blending purposes only.

The core range of Ardmore single malt is made up of **Legacy**, a mix of 80% peated and 20% unpeated malt, and a **12 year old Port Finish**. **Tradition** and **Triple Wood** are eclusive to travel retail. Limited releases in the last few years include a **20 year old,** and a **30 year old**.

History:

1898 Adam Teacher, son of William Teacher, starts the construction of Ardmore Distillery which eventually becomes William Teacher & Sons' first distillery. Adam Teacher passes away before it is completed.

1955 Stills are increased from two to four.

1974 Another four stills are added, increasing the total to eight.

1976 Allied Breweries takes over William Teacher & Sons and thereby also Ardmore. The own maltings (Saladin box) is terminated.

1999 A 12 year old is released to commemorate the distillery's 100th anniversary. A 21 year old is launched in a limited edition.

2002 Ardmore is one of the last distilleries to abandon direct heating (by coal) of the stills in favour of indirect heating through steam.

2005 Jim Beam Brands becomes new owner when it takes over some 20 spirits and wine brands from Allied Domecq for five billion dollars.

2007 Ardmore Traditional Cask is launched.

2008 A 25 and a 30 year old are launched.

2014 Beam and Suntory merge. Legacy is released.

2015 Traditional is re-launched as Tradition and a Triple Wood and a 12 year old port finish are released.

2017 A 20 year old, double matured is released.

2018 A 30 year old is released.

Legacy

Tasting notes Ardmore Legacy:

GS – Vanilla, caramel and sweet peat smoke on the nose, while on the palate vanilla and honey contrast with quite dry peat notes, plus ginger and dark berries. The finish is medium to long, spicy, with persistently drying smoke.

Trailblazers of Malt Whisky

Neelakanta Jagdale
Amrut, India

Let's set the stage here. India is, not least due to British influence for many years, considered a brown spirit market (rum, brandy and whisky). Today, India is the world's largest producer of whisky with eight of the Top 10 brands. On the other hand, few drops of Indian whisky find its way to the rest of the world due to the fact that in many markets it doesn't meet the standards of what a whisky should be made of, namely cereals. The main volume of Indian whisky is made from molasses derived from sugar canes. So how did an Indian whisky brand like Amrut become so popular around the world?

In 1948, one year after the end of British rule in India, Radhakrishna Rao Jagdale started Amrut. In the beginning the company bought spirits from other producers, bottled it under their own name and sold it mainly to the Indian army. In 1955 they invested in their own equipment and started to distil rum. Not surprisingly as India grows an abundance of sugar cane which, when turned into molasses, becomes a key ingredient in rum. Brandy from grapes was added to the portfolio in 1975 and in 1979, Amrut started to produce malt whisky but only to be a part of their Indian blended whisky MaQintosh.

At that time, the second generation of Jagdale had entered the company. Neelakanta, the son of Radhakrishna, graduated as a Bachelor of Science from Bangalore University in May 1972. Today, one option following graduation would have been to explore the world for a year while reflecting on what to do in the future. Not so for Neelakanta - or Neel as he is fondly remembered by whisky enthusiasts all over the world. His father granted him two weeks av leave before he joined the family company in June at the age of 19. Only four years later, when he was 23, his father died and he found himself managing a company of considerable size. Business continued to grow and while there was no market for single malt whisky in the country at the time, the company continued to supply the Indian army with whisky made from malted grain and sugar cane. Then in 1995, the market changed dramatically. New blended whiskies, containing just a few percent of malt whisky, appeared on the scene while Amrut´s MaQintosh had 30% single malt in the recipe. The new contenders could of course be sold at a much lower price and Amrut suddenly found themselves with stocks of single malt but no customers. At this time Neel started contemplating the idea of launching an Indian single malt whisky.

For inspiration, he looked at Japanese producers struggling to make the perfect copy of a Scotch single malt. He soon realized that this procedure wasn't the way forward he was looking for. If he should make an Indian single malt, it had to stand on its own two legs. At that time, Neel´s son Rakshit had finished his bachelor studies and was working by his father's side. When he decided to go to Newcastle University in 2001 to take his masters degree, Neel gave him an assignment; explore the market for Indian single malt in the UK.

This was, of course, entering the lion's den. Similar to exporting sand to the Sahara. Neel had prepared hundreds of miniatures of Amrut single malt that he sent to his son. Rakshit, together with his co-student Ashok Chokalingam (today Head of Distilling at Amrut), started travelling around bars and restaurants in northern England and Scotland presenting the unusual whisky. In general, they were well received and when Rakshit came back to India after finishing his studies, his report encouraged Neelakanta to pursue his plan. In August 2004, the first Amrut single malt was launched in Café India in Glasgow. But this was not going to be a smooth ride by any means. The idea to have Indian restaurants across the UK as their showcase window towards the consumers didn't work out so well and soon the owners looked across the Channel for other markets. The Netherlands and France, as well as Sweden, were amongst the first to cherish the new Indian single malt. But Neel was still set on being recognized for his whisky in the UK and continued his efforts together with his son and the rest of the team.

Following an unsuccessful meeting with a possible distributor in London in 2006, Neel together with Rakshit and Ashok, found themselves in Tavistock Square next to the statue of Gandhi. Looking at the father of modern India, Neel realized that if the Mahatma could overcome so many hardships then surely he would be able to launch an Indian single malt world-wide.

Another defining moment in the history of Amrut and Neel Jagdale was in 2010 when Jim Murray named Amrut Fusion as the third best single malt whisky in the world in his Whisky Bible. At this time, Amrut had become the talk of the town amongst whisky enthusiasts in Europe but surprisingly it had not yet been released in India. When speaking to Rakshit Jagdale, he describes it as if they were almost forced to launch it in their home market. Indian whisky lovers were complaining they had to go abroad to find the Amrut that everyone was talking about. From there on Amrut became a well known brand with an ever expanding range of new and exciting bottlings including peated, triple distilled, rye and grain whiskies. The brand has also paved the way for other whisky producers from India, for example Paul John and Rampur.

I had the pleasure of meeting Neel Jagdale at the distillery on the outskirts of Bangalore in spring 2016. We had lunch and then a stroll around the distillery. I remember being surprised to see a seemingly inefficient bottling line with at least 30 women hand filling the bottles. I mentioned to Neelakanta that, obviously, here were some opportunities to improve efficiency by installing a fully automated bottling equipment. His response stuck to me. "If I didn't employ these women, they would have a hard time finding a job to help support their families". Neel Jagdale´s engagement in the community didn't stop at that. Both Rakshit and his sister were talented swimmers and their father was anxious to support their interest. In 1984 he started supporting the local swimming pool and became the president for Karnataka Swimming Association. Since then, 150 000 children have learned to swim and the arena has also fostered several Olympian swimmers.

Neelakanta Jagdale passed away in 2019 at the early age of 66. Not only did he leave a legacy of creating the first global malt whisky from India. He also proved to be an entrepreneur with a social conscience.

Auchentoshan

[ock•en•tosh•an]

Owner:	**Region/district:**
Beam Suntory	Lowlands

Founded:	**Status:**	**Capacity:**
1823	Active (vc)	2 500 000 litres

Address: Dalmuir, Clydebank, Glasgow G81 4SJ

Website:	**Tel:**
auchentoshan.com	01389 878561

Auchentoshan single malt has built some of its reputation on being the only distillery in Scotland that practices triple distillation for the entire production and the effect that this has on the flavour profile. It has obviously been a winning concept.

A decade ago, Auchentoshan could be found in spot 24 on the sales list for single malts. Ten years later it is in 17th place thanks to a 320% increase in volumes. Last year it sold an impressive 1,8 million bottles which means it is quickly closing in on the number two single malt in the Beam Suntory portfolio – Bowmore.

In March 1941, the German Luftwaffe made a major attack towards the shipyards and munition factories in Clydebank. The carpet bombing also affected Auchentoshan. Three warehouses of whisky, corresponding to more than a million litres, were destroyed. One of the bomb craters is today a dam from where much of its cooling water for the distillation is sourced.

The equipment consists of a semi-lauter mash tun with a 6.8 ton mash charge, four Oregon Pine washbacks and three made of stainless steel. There are three stills; wash still (17,500 litres), intermediate still (8,200 litres) and spirit still (11,500 litres). From 2021, the distillery has moved to a seven day production which means they will be completing 18 mashes per week which interprets to around 2,3 million litres of alcohol in the year. Due to the new 7-day week all fermentations are now 52 hours.

The core range consists of **American Oak**, without age statement, **12 years, Three Woods, 18 years** and **21 years**. The duty free range is made up of **Blood Oak**, matured in a combination of bourbon and red wine casks and two new expressions launched in autumn 2019; **American Oak Reserve** matured in first fill bourbon and **Dark Oak** which is a vatting of whiskies matured in ex-bourbon, PX and oloroso casks. A limited **29 years old 1988 Vintage** finished in PX casks appeared in early 2019 and this was followed later that year by a bottling, matured in ex-bourbon and **finished in sauvignon blanc barriques**.

History:

1817 First mention of the distillery Duntocher, which may be identical to Auchentoshan.

1823 The distillery is founded by John Bulloch.

1823 The distillery is sold to Alexander Filshie.

1878 C.H. Curtis & Co. takes over.

1903 The distillery is purchased by John Maclachlan.

1941 The distillery is severely damaged by a German bomb raid.

1960 Maclachlans Ltd is purchased by the brewery J. & R. Tennent Brewers.

1969 Auchentoshan is bought by Eadie Cairns Ltd who starts major modernizations.

1984 Stanley P. Morrison, eventually becoming Morrison Bowmore, becomes new owner.

1994 Suntory buys Morrison Bowmore.

2002 Auchentoshan Three Wood is launched.

2004 More than a £1 million is spent on a new, refurbished visitor centre. The oldest Auchentoshan ever, 42 years, is released.

2006 Auchentoshan 18 year old is released.

2007 A 50 year old, the oldest ever Auchentoshan to be bottled, was released.

2008 New packaging as well as new expressions - Classic, 18 year old and 1988.

2010 Two vintages, 1977 and 1998, are released.

2011 Two vintages, 1975 and 1999, and Valinch are released.

2012 Six new expressions are launched for the Duty Free market.

2013 Virgin Oak is released.

2014 American Oak replaces Classic.

2015 Blood Oak and Noble Oak are released for duty free.

2017 Bartender´s Malt is launched.

2018 Bartender´s Malt 2 and 1988 PX Cask are released.

2019 American Oak Reserve and Dark Oak are released for the travel retail market.

12 years old

Tasting notes Auchentoshan 12 year old:

IR – Green and herbal on the nose with notes of pine needles, citrus and fresh oak. Quite dry on the palate with spicy notes coming through (nutmeg, clove and bay leaf) as well as vanilla and roasted nuts and sunflower seeds.

Auchroisk

[ar•thrusk]

Owner: Diageo

Region/district: Speyside

Founded: 1974

Status: Active

Capacity 5 900 000 litres

Address: Mulben, Banffshire AB55 6XS

Website: malts.com

Tel: 01542 885000

In the early 1970s, International Distillers & Vintners, were in need of more production capacity to fulfill the needs for single malt to support their blend J&B which had become a huge success, not least in America.

The company already owned three distilleries (Knockando, Glen Spey and Strathmill) but they were all rather small. Auchroisk on the other hand would be able to produce more than the three combined. At a cost corresponding to £55m in today's worth, not only a distillery was built but also warehouses and blending facilities.

The style of the Auchroisk new make has changed over the years depending on what was needed for the blends. For a long time now though it can be characterised as nutty/malty. This flavour is achieved through a combination of a quick mash and cloudy wort together with short fermentations.

The equipment consists of a 12 ton stainless steel semi-lauter mash tun, eight stainless steel washbacks with a fermentation time of 53 hours and four pairs of stills. The washbacks are large (holding 50,000 litres each) and one washback can serve all four wash stills which hold 12,700 litres each. Auchroisk is working 24/7 with 24 mashes per week, producing 5.8 million litres of alcohol per year.

The first official bottling of Auchroisk appeared already in 1978 but it wasn't until 1986 that it became widely available and under the name Singleton. That particular name is now reserved for another three distilleries in the Diageo range – Dufftown, Glendullan and Glen Ord. The Auchroisk Singleton was a 12 year old starting in bourbon barrels and spending the final two years in ex-sherrry casks which makes it one of the first examples of finishing. In 2001, it was replaced by a **10 year old** Auchroisk in the Flora & Fauna range and this is still the only official bottling. The most recent limited bottling was a **47 year old** in the Prima & Ultima range in September 2021. Bottled at 48,7% it was in fact the first cask ever filled at the distillery back in 1974!

History:

1972 Building of the distillery commences by Justerini & Brooks (which, together with W. A. Gilbey, make up the group IDV) in order to produce blending whisky. In February the same year IDV is purchased by the brewery Watney Mann which, in July, merges into Grand Metropolitan.

1974 The distillery is completed and production begins.

1978 The first bottling appears.

1986 From this year the malt is sold under the name Singleton.

1997 Grand Metropolitan and Guinness merge into the conglomerate Diageo. Simultaneously, the subsidiaries United Distillers (to Guinness) and International Distillers & Vintners (to Grand Metropolitan) form the new company United Distillers & Vintners (UDV).

2001 The name Singleton is abandoned and the whisky is now marketed under the name of Auchroisk in the Flora & Fauna series.

2003 A 28 year old from 1974, the distillery's first year, is launched in the Rare Malt series.

2010 A Manager´s Choice single cask and a limited 20 year old are released.

2012 A 30 year old from 1982 is released.

2016 A 25 year old from 1990 is released.

2021 A 47 year old Prima & Ultima from 1974 is launched.

47 years old
Prima & Ultima

Tasting notes Auchroisk 10 year old:

GS – Malt and spice on the light nose, with developing nuts and floral notes. Quite voluptuous on the palate, with fresh fruit and milk chocolate. Raisins in the finish.

Aultmore

[ault•moor]

Owner:		Region/district:
John Dewar & Sons (Bacardi)		Speyside

Founded:	Status:	Capacity:
1896	Active	3 200 000 litres

Address: Keith, Banffshire AB55 6QY

Website:	Tel:
aultmore.com	01542 881800

When, in 1998, Bacardi took over the Dewar's portfolio, including the world famous blend and four malt whisky distilleries, they were more or less new to the single malt business.

Admittedly they had five years earlier bought the Macduff distillery and the up and coming Lawsons blend but the following decade, focus remained on rum, obviously, and blended Scotch. It wasn't until around 2010 when single malts had become a hot spot for whisky producers that the company had a serious discussion about turning their five single malts into designated brands of their own. One of them was Aultmore which at the time occasionally could be found as a 12 year old. Finally in 2014/2015, under the name The Last Great Malts, all five were blessed with a core range and new packaging.

A lot work went into identifying the history and the provenance of each of the five malts. During the 20th century, locals and fishermen from Buckie, which is situated some 10 kilometres to the north of Aultmore on Moray Firth, asked for "a nip of the Buckie Rd" at inns and pubs along the road. That was the secret name for Aultmore single malt and the same words are now embossed at the bottom of the Aultmore bottle.

Aultmore was completely rebuilt in the beginning of the 1970s and nothing is left of the old buildings from 1896. The distillery is equipped with a 10 ton Steinecker full lauter mash tun, six washbacks made of larch with a minimum fermentation time of 56 hours and two pairs of stills. Since 2008 production has been running seven-days a week, which for 2021 means 16 mashes per week and just over 3 million litres of alcohol.

The core range includes a **12 year old** and an **18 year old**. A **21 year old** that was released for travel retail and the US market has now become part of the core range while the 25 year old, released a few years back, has been discontinued. On top of that there are some very limited but regular releases for the travel retail market in the **Exceptional Cask Series**.

History:

1896 Alexander Edward, owner of Benrinnes and co-founder of Craigellachie Distillery, builds Aultmore.

1897 Production starts.

1898 Production is doubled; the company Oban & Aultmore Glenlivet Distilleries Ltd manages Aultmore.

1923 Alexander Edward sells Aultmore for £20,000 to John Dewar & Sons.

1925 Dewar's becomes part of Distillers Company Limited (DCL).

1930 The administration is transferred to Scottish Malt Distillers (SMD).

1971 The stills are increased from two to four.

1991 United Distillers launches a 12-year old Aultmore in the Flora & Fauna series.

1996 A 21 year old cask strength is marketed as a Rare Malt.

1998 Diageo sells Dewar's and Bombay Gin to Bacardi for £1,150 million.

2004 A new official 12 year old bottling is launched

2014 Three new expressions are released – 12, 25 and 21 year old for duty free.

2015 An 18 year old is released.

2019 Three 22 year old single casks with different second maturations are released for duty free.

2021 A 21 year old is added to the core range.

12 years old

Aultmore 12 years old:

GS – A nose of peaches and lemonade, freshly-mown grass, linseed and milky coffee. Very fruity on the palate, mildly herbal, with toffee and light spices. The finish is medium in length, with lingering spices, fudge, and finally more milky coffee.

Balblair

[bal•blair]

Owner: **Region/district:**
Inver House Distillers   Northern Highlands
(Thai Beverages plc)

Founded: **Status:**   **Capacity:**
1790   Active (vc)   1 800 000 litres

Address: Edderton, Tain, Ross-shire IV19 1LB

Website: **Tel:**
balblair.com   01862 821273

It is now ten years since Balblair opened up a visitor centre and in 2019 some 10,000 people visited it. Although that number is considerably less than some of the bigger distilleries', the owners are probably happy for it.

The intention with the centre was never to attract hundreds of coaches every week. Instead the elegant and contemporary design and the comprehensive tours were aimed at whisky enthusiasts. And to be honest, it takes a dedicated whisky fan to come here. Even though it sits only ten kilometres away from the highly pro-filed Glenmorangie, its location feels far more remote than many other distilleries'. It takes one hour from Inverness to get here but the surroundings are beautiful with the Dornoch Firth just a stone's throw from the distillery. Judging from official records, Balblair is the fourth oldest distillery in Scotland still in produc-tion. Actually, there are some facts pointing to 1749 as a possible start for the distillery. In all honesty though, it should be said that the distillery buildings that we see today are of a later date (1872) when the distillery was rebuilt and moved half a mile to the north.

Balblair is equipped with a stainless steel, 4.4 ton semi lauter mash tun, six Oregon pine washbacks and one pair of stills. The distillery recently went from a five-day week to a seven-day week and the plan for 2021 is to make 19 mashes per week, which means a target of 1.5 million litres for the full year. It also entails that fermentation time is now 60 hours instead of mixing short (60 hours) and long (90 hours) fermentations.

In 2019, the distillery abandoned their tradition of releasing vintage single malts and the core range now consists of **12 year old** matured in ex-bourbon and double-fired American oak, the **15 year old** matured in ex-bourbon casks followed by time in Spanish oak sherry butts, the **18 year old** with the same maturation as the previous and the **25 year old** which starts in ex-bourbon casks and is finished in ex-oloroso sherry casks. All except the 18 year old are also available in travel retail with the addition of a **17 year old** finished in first fill sherry butts.

History:

1790 The distillery is founded by James McKeddy.

1790 John Ross takes over

1836 John Ross dies and his son Andrew Ross takes over with the help of his sons.

1872 The distillery is moved to the present location.

1873 Andrew Ross dies and his son James takes over.

1894 Alexander Cowan takes over and rebuilds the distillery

1911 Cowan is forced to cease payments and the distillery closes.

1941 The distillery is put up for sale.

1948 Robert Cumming buys Balblair for £48,000.

1949 Production restarts.

1970 Cumming sells Balblair to Hiram Walker.

1988 Allied Distillers becomes the new owner through the merger between Hiram Walker and Allied Vintners.

1996 The distillery is sold to Inver House Distillers.

2000 Balblair Elements and the first version of Balblair 33 years are launched.

2001 Thai company Pacific Spirits (part of the Great Oriole Group) takes over Inver House.

2004 Balblair 38 years is launched.

2005 12 year old Peaty Cask, 1979 (26 years) and 1970 (35 years) are launched.

2006 International Beverage Holdings acquires Pacific Spirits UK.

2007 Three new vintages replace the former range.

2008 Vintage 1975 and 1965 are released.

2009 Vintage 1991 and 1990 are released.

2011 Vintage 1995 and 1993 are released.

2012 Vintage 1975, 2001 and 2002 are released. A visitor centre is opened.

2013 Vintage 1983, 1990 and 2003 are released.

2014 Vintage 1999 and 2004 are released for duty free.

2016 Vintage 2005 is released.

2019 A new range with age statements is launched.

12 years old

Tasting notes Balblair 12 year old:

IR – Sugary and malty on the nose with herbal and earthy notes coming through. Rich, creamy and sweet on the palate, grilled corn cobs, caramel, honey and some bitter, oaky notes.

Balmenach

[bal•men•ack]

Owner:
Inver House Distillers
(Thai Beverages plc)

Region/district:
Speyside

Founded: **Status:**
1824   Active

Capacity:
2 900 000 litres

Address: Cromdale, Moray PH26 3PF

Website:
inverhouse.com

Tel:
01479 872569

Balmenach lies nicely tucked in at the foot of the Cromdale Hills on the southern outskirts of Speyside. Until recently, few people had any reason for taking the detour from the A95 to see the distillery.

In 2016 however, a visitor centre was opened but not to promote the single malt. Instead guests were taken on a gin tour! In 2009, the distillery started to produce Caorunn gin which is now one of the top super-premium gins in the UK. On the whisky side, Balmenach is still the only of the five distilleries owned by Inver House that isn't blessed with an official bottling. One might say it's a victim of its own success of being a malt that can do wonders in a blend. They produce old school whisky in the same way as Benrinnes and Mortlach. A long fermentation, a quick distillation in small stills and condensing the spirit vapours using worm tubs results in a meaty and heavy newmake which, after a long maturation, adds a lot of character to a blend, not least to the owner's brand Hankey Bannister.

To get a fascinating eye-witness description of Balmenach, the book Scotch by Sir Robert Bruce Lockhart is recommended. Sir Robert was a famous writer and diplomat, deeply involved in both World Wars, and his great-grandfather James Macgregor founded the distillery.

Balmenach is equipped with an eight ton stainless steel semi-lauter mash tun, six washbacks made of Douglas fir (two of them replaced in 2021) and with a 5-day production there are 7 short fermentations (56 hours) and 7 long (90-100 hours). Finally there are three pairs of stills connected to worm tubs. The production plan for 2021 is to do 14 mashes per week which translates to 2 million litres of alcohol. A new biogas plant was recently installed at Balmenach to handle whisky bi-products such as pot ale and spent lees.

There used to be a 12 year old from the previous owners but the last time an official bottling of Balmenach turned up was in 2002 when a 25 year old was launched to celebrate the Queen's Golden Jubilee. Aberko though, has been working with the distillery for a long time and has released Balmenach under the name Deerstalker.

History:

1824 The distillery is licensed to James MacGregor who operated a small farm distillery by the name of Balminoch.

1897 Balmenach Glenlivet Distillery Company is founded.

1922 The MacGregor family sells to a consortium consisting of MacDonald Green, Peter Dawson and James Watson.

1925 The consortium becomes part of Distillers Company Limited (DCL).

1930 Production is transferred to Scottish Malt Distillers (SMD).

1962 The number of stills is increased to six.

1964 Floor maltings replaced with Saladin box.

1992 The first official bottling is a 12 year old.

1993 The distillery is mothballed in May.

1997 Inver House Distillers buys Balmenach from United Distillers.

1998 Production recommences.

2001 Thai company Pacific Spirits takes over Inver House at the price of £56 million. The new owner launches a 27 and a 28 year old.

2002 To commemorate the Queen's Golden Jubilee a 25-year old Balmenach is launched.

2006 International Beverage Holdings acquires Pacific Spirits UK.

2009 Gin production commences.

Tasting notes Deerstalker 12 years old:

IR – The nose is sweet and fruity, with green garden notes and sweet liquorice coming through. Sweet, fruity barley on the palate with notes of honey, custard, apricots, peaches and slightly bitter notes from the oak.

Deerstalker 12 years old

Balvenie

[bal•ven•ee]

Owner:
William Grant & Sons

Region/district:
Speyside

Founded: **Status:**
1892   Active (vc)

Capacity:
7 000 000 litres

Address: Dufftown, Keith, Banffshire AB55 4DH

Website:
thebalvenie.com

Tel:
01340 820373

The Balvenie is one of the top single malts in the world in terms of sales volumes. Currently it can be found in place number six with nearly five million bottles sold in a year.

Since 2015, the volumes have increased by 50% and the brand is slowly but surely getting closer to Glenmorangie, whose sales figures have been more or less stable the last five years. If this trend continues The Balvenie may be the new number five in a few years from now. The distillery is one of few where you can follow every step of the production on site. They have their own floor maltings producing 15% of their needs and there is also a coppersmith and a cooperage on site.

The distillery is equipped with an 11.8 ton full lauter mash tun, nine wooden and five stainless steel washbacks with a fermentation time of 68 hours, five wash stills and six spirit stills. For 2021, the production plan is 30 mashes per week and 7 million litres of alcohol. The main part is unpeated but each year one week of production comes from peated barley (20-40 ppm).

The core range consists of **Doublewood 12, Doublewood 17, Caribbean Cask 14,** three **Single Barrel (12 years First Fill, 15 years Sherry Cask, 21 years Traditional Oak), Portwood 21, 25** (new since July 2021), **30** and **40 years old.** Recent limited releases include batch 8 of **Tun 1509,** chapter five of **The Balvenie DCS Compendium** and the third release of **50 year old Marriage 0614.** A new, limited range named The Balvenie Stories was launched in 2019 with the 12 year old **The Sweet Toast of American Oak,** the 14 year old **A Week of Peat** and a 26 year old called **A Day of Dark Barley.** A fourth expression, **The Edge of Burnhead Wood** 19 years old, was added in spring 2020, made from barley grown on the estate. In 2021 two more stories were added; **The Second Red Rose 21 years** and **The Tale of the Dog 1974.** For duty free, the previous Triple Cask range has been replaced by **The Creation of a Classic, The Week of Peat 19 years, The Tale of the Dog 1978,** a **15 year old Madeira Cask** and an **18 year old PX Cask.**

History:

1892   William Grant rebuilds Balvenie New House to Balvenie Distillery.

1893   The first distillation takes place in May.

1957   The two stills are increased by another two.

1965   Two new stills are installed.

1971   Another two stills are installed and eight stills are now running.

1973   The first official bottling appears.

1982   Founder's Reserve is launched.

1996   Two vintage bottlings and a Port wood finish are launched.

2001   The Balvenie Islay Cask is released.

2002   A 50 year old is released.

2005   A 14 year old rum finish is released.

2006   The Balvenie New Wood 17 years old, Roasted Malt 14 years old and Portwood 1993 are released.

2007   Vintage Cask 1974 and Sherry Oak 17 years old are released.

2008   Signature, Vintage 1976, Balvenie Rose and Rum Cask 17 year old are released.

2009   Vintage 1978, 17 year old Madeira finish, 14 year old rum finish and Golden Cask 14 years old are released.

2010   A 40 year old, Peated Cask and Carribean Cask are released.

2011   Second batch of Tun 1401 is released.

2012   A 50 year old and Doublewood 17 years old are released.

2013   Triple Cask 12, 16 and 25 years are launched for duty free.

2014   Single Barrel 15 and 25 years, Tun 1509 and two new 50 year olds are launched.

2015   The Balvenie DCS Compendium is launched.

2016   A 21 year old madeira finish is released.

2017   The Balvenie Peat Week 2002 and Peated Triple Cask are released.

2018   A limited 25 year old is relased.

2019   The Balvenie Stories is launched.

2020   A 21 year old is released together with a fourth instalment in the Balvenie Stories series.

2021   The Second Red Rose, The Tale of the Dog and a 25 year old are released.

Tasting notes Balvenie Doublewood 12 years:

GS – Nuts and spicy malt on the nose, full-bodied, with soft fruit, vanilla, sherry and a hint of peat. Dry and spicy in a luxurious, lengthy finish.

Doublewood 12 years old

Ben Nevis

[ben nev•iss]

Owner:
Ben Nevis Distillery Ltd
(Nikka, Asahi Breweries)

Region/district:
Western Highlands

Founded: 1825

Status: Active (vc)

Capacity: 2 000 000 litres

Address: Lochy Bridge, Fort William PH33 6TJ

Website: bennevisdistillery.com

Tel: 01397 702476

History:

1825 The distillery is founded by 'Long' John McDonald.

1856 Long John dies and his son Donald P. McDonald takes over.

1878 Demand is so great that another distillery, Nevis Distillery, is built nearby.

1908 Both distilleries merge into one.

1941 D. P. McDonald & Sons sells the distillery to Ben Nevis Distillery Ltd headed by the Canadian millionaire Joseph W. Hobbs.

1955 Hobbs installs a Coffey still which makes it possible to produce both grain and malt whisky.

1964 Joseph Hobbs dies.

1978 Production is stopped.

1981 Joseph Hobbs Jr sells the distillery back to Long John Distillers and Whitbread.

1984 After restoration and reconstruction totalling £2 million, Ben Nevis opens up again.

1986 The distillery closes again.

1989 Whitbread sells the distillery to Nikka Whisky Distilling Company Ltd.

1990 The distillery opens up again.

1991 A visitor centre is inaugurated.

1996 Ben Nevis 10 years old is launched.

2006 A 13 year old port finish is released.

2010 A 25 year old is released.

2011 McDonald´s Traditional Ben Nevis is released.

2014 Forgotten Bottlings are introduced.

2015 A 40 year old "Blended at Birth" single blend is released.

2018 Ben Nevis 10 years old Batch No. 1 is released.

2021 The design of the 10 year bottle is revamped and Coire Leis is released.

One of the finest representatives of Scotch whisky, Colin Ross, passed away in April 2021 at the age of 73. To many people he personified Ben Nevis single malt but his 54 year long career included several other distilleries.

He started as a trainee manager at Strathisla in 1965 and spent the next six years in Keith. In 1983 he became distillery manager for Ben Nevis and except for a two year spell at Laphroaig, he dedicated his working life to the distillery in Fort William. In a modest yet passionate manner he put Ben Nevis single malt on the map for whisky enthusiasts all over the world to enjoy. In 2015 he was inducted into the whisky Hall of Fame and in autumn 2019 he retired from Ben Nevis. That however did not mean he was ready to leave the whisky business. Six months before his death he was working on plans for a distillery in Western Scotland together with his son Aaron.

During three decades towards the end of the 1800s there were three working distilleries in Fort William. Two of them, Ben Nevis and its sister distillery Nevis, were of such a magnitude that their joint production far exceeded distilleries such as Macallan and Glenlivet. The reason for this can be ascribed to the success of the blend Dew of Ben Nevis, which was introduced by the legendary distillery owner, "Long" John MacDonald.

Ben Nevis is equipped with a nine ton full lauter mash tun made of stainless steel, six stainless steel washbacks and two made of Oregon pine with a 48 hour fermentation as well as two pairs of stills. The plan for 2021 is to make 13 mashes per week and 2 million litres of alcohol. Around 50,000 litres of this will be heavily peated (40ppm in the barley).

The **10 year old** was relaunched with a new design in August 2021. There is also the peated **MacDonald's Traditional Ben Nevis** as well as the recently launched **Coire Leis** without age statement. Very old versions of Ben Nevis have occurred and three vintages from **1966**, **1967** and **1968** were released in Taiwan in 2019.

10 years old

Tasting notes Ben Nevis 10 years old:

GS – The nose is initially quite green, with developing nutty, orange notes. Coffee, brittle toffee and peat are present on the slightly oily palate, along with chewy oak, which persists to the finish, together with more coffee and a hint of dark chocolate.

Benriach

[ben•<u>ree</u>•ack]

Owner:	**Region/district:**
BenRiach Distillery Company (Brown Forman)	Speyside
Founded: **Status:**	**Capacity:**
1897 Active (vc)	2 800 000 litres

Address: Longmorn, Elgin, Morayshire IV30 8SJ

Website:	**Tel:**
benriachdistillery.com	01343 862888

Visitors to Speyside are sooner or later bound to drive the A941 between Elgin and Rothes. It is the artery that connects many of the area´s distilleries. One of these, BenRiach, is situated adjacent to the road and is impossible to miss.

The perfect spot for a visitor centre it would seem, but not much happened in that respect since Billy Walker and his business partners took over in 2004. However, after a few years a tiny shop was opened and it became possible to book a tour in advance if one was lucky. However since May 2021 a proper visitor centre in place offering both tours, tastings and the possibility to purchase BenRiach single malt.

In 2013, the owners resurrected the malting floors that had been closed in 1998. Even though it is only used sporadically very few distilleries in Scotland still practise this time-consuming method. It was more or less obvious from the start that the small volumes distilled from their own malt would be used for special bottlings and in autumn 2021 it was time for the first expression – BenRiach Malting Season First Edition.

BenRiach is equipped with a 5.8 ton traditional cast iron mash tun with a stainless steel shell, eight washbacks made of stainless steel with short (55 hours) and long fermentations (+100 hours) and two pairs of stills. Recent production plans have been 1,8 million litres of pure alcohol which includes peated spirit at 35ppm as well as 15,000 litres of triple-distilled spirit.

The new core range, launched in 2020, consists of **The Original Ten, The Smoky Ten, The Twelve, The Smoky Twelve, The Twenty One, The Twenty Five** and **The Thirty**. Exclusive to the travel retail segment is the recently revamped range including **Triple Distilled Ten, Quarter Cask** and **Smoky Quarter Cask**. Every year a batch of single casks bottled at cask strength is launched under the name **Cask Edition Collection**. The latest appeared in March 2021. Finally, there is the aforementioned, limited **BenRiach Malting Season First Edition** as well as **Smoke Season** bottled at 52,8%.

History:

1897 John Duff & Co founds the distillery.

1900 The distillery is closed.

1965 The distillery is reopened by the new owner, The Glenlivet Distillers Ltd.

1972 Production of peated Benriach starts.

1978 Seagram Distillers takes over.

1985 The number of stills is increased to four.

1998 The maltings is decommissioned.

2002 The distillery is mothballed in October.

2004 Intra Trading, buys Benriach together with the former Director at Burn Stewart, Billy Walker.

2004 Standard, Curiositas and 12, 16 and 20 year olds are released.

2005 Four different vintages are released.

2006 Sixteen new releases, i.a. a 25 year old, a 30 year old and 8 different vintages.

2007 A 40 year old and three new heavily peated expressions are released.

2008 Peated Madeira finish, a 15 year old Sauternes finish and nine single casks are released.

2009 Two wood finishes (Moscatel and Gaja Barolo) and nine single casks are released.

2010 Triple distilled Horizons and heavily peated Solstice are released.

2011 A 45 year old and 12 vintages are released.

2012 Septendecim 17 years is released.

2013 Vestige 46 years is released. The maltings are working again.

2015 Dunder, Albariza, Latada and a 10 year old are released.

2016 Brown Forman buys the company for £285m. BenRiach cask strength and Peated Quarter Cask are launched.

2017 10 year old Triple Distilled and Peated Cask Strength are released.

2018 A 12 and a 21 year old, Temporis 21 years and Authenticus 30 years are released.

2019 Batch 16 of the Cask Bottlings is released.

2020 The entire core range is relaunched with seven new expressions.

2021 Malting Season First Edition is launched.

Tasting notes BenRiach The Twelve:

IR – Fresh on the nose with notes of furniture polish, eucalyptus, tropical fruits, honey and brown sugar. A dry start on the palate is followed by raisins soaked in port, baked apples with vanilla, chocolate, cinnamon and almonds.

The Twelve

Benrinnes

[ben rin•ess]

Owner:
Diageo

Region/district:
Speyside

Founded: 1826

Status: Active

Capacity: 3 500 000 litres

Address: Aberlour, Banffshire AB38 9NN

Website:
malts.com

Tel:
01340 872600

When distilleries around Scotland closed their own floor maltings during the first half of the 20th century, most of them went straight on to buying directly from commercial maltsters, but not Benrinnes.

In 1964 they installed a so called Saladin box, named after Charles Saladin who invented it in the 1890s. A Saladin box is a long concrete box with revolving rakes. The barley is steeped and turned by the rakes and air circulates through perforated floors to keep the temperature under control. To dry, the green malt goes into a kiln, which is very different to traditional ones. It is simply a large, self-filling and self-emptying box with air blowing through it. Benrinnes closed their maltings in 1984 and until 2011, Tamdhu was the only remaining distillery using a Saladin box. Now, also that is gone but perhaps it won't be that long until we see another Saladin box working at a distillery in Scotland. Bruichladdich have advanced plans for reintroducing on-site malting, and when they do – it will be a Saladin box!

There are no visible remains of the original Benrinnes distillery dating back to 1826. The current distillery is in fact a creation from the 1950s. The equipment consists of an 8.5 ton semi-lauter mash tun, eight washbacks made of Oregon pine with a fermentation time ranging from 65 to 100 hours. There are also two wash stills and four spirit stills. From 1966 until 2009, these were run three and three with a partial triple distillation. This system has now been abandoned and one wash still now serves two spirit stills. In the last couple of years, Benrinnes has been alternating between a seven-day production week and a five-day with either 21 or 15 mashes per week.

The Benrinnes style of single malt often goes against the traditional opinion on how a Speyside whisky is supposed to taste. It can often be quite heavy and meaty. Most of the production goes into blended whiskies – J&B, Johnnie Walker and Crawford's 3 Star – and there is currently only one official single malt, the **Flora & Fauna 15 year old**. In 2010 a **Manager's Choice** from 1996 was released and in autumn 2014 it was time for a **21 year old Special Release**.

History:

1826 Lyne of Ruthrie distillery is built at Whitehouse Farm by Peter McKenzie.

1829 A flood destroys the distillery and a new distillery is constructed by John Innes a few kilometres from the first one.

1834 John Innes files for bankruptcy and William Smith & Co takes over.

1864 William Smith & Co goes bankrupt and David Edward becomes the new owner.

1896 Benrinnes is ravaged by fire which prompts major refurbishment. Alexander Edward takes over.

1922 John Dewar & Sons takes over ownership.

1925 John Dewar & Sons becomes part of Distillers Company Limited (DCL).

1956 The distillery is completely rebuilt.

1964 Floor maltings is replaced by a Saladin box.

1966 The number of stills doubles to six.

1984 The Saladin box is taken out of service and the malt is purchased centrally.

1991 The first official bottling from Benrinnes is a 15 year old in the Flora & Fauna series.

1996 United Distillers releases a 21 year old cask strength in their Rare Malts series.

2009 A 23 year old is launched as a part of this year´s Special Releases.

2010 A Manager´s Choice 1996 is released.

2014 A limited 21 year old is released.

Tasting notes Benrinnes 15 years old:

GS – A brief flash of caramel shortcake on the initial nose, soon becoming more peppery and leathery, with some sherry. Ultimately savoury and burnt rubber notes. Big-bodied, viscous, with gravy, dark chocolate and more pepper. A medium-length finish features mild smoke and lively spices.

15 years old

Benromach

[ben•ro•mack]

Owner:
Gordon & MacPhail

Region/district:
Speyside

Founded: 1898 **Status:** Active (vc) **Capacity:** 700 000 litres

Address: Invererne Road, Forres, Morayshire IV36 3EB

Website: benromach.com **Tel:** 01309 675968

With single malt Scotch being hotter than ever, it has become increasingly difficult for independent bottlers to acquire casks of maturing whisky from the producers. The solution for the bigger independents is to build a distillery of their own.

At least eight of them have done just that but the first to do so was without doubt Gordon & MacPhail. In 1993 the family-owned company bought the closed Benromach distillery and re-opened it five years later. Actually this wasn't the first attempt by the company to buy a distillery. Already in 1950, the head of the family at the time, John Urquhart, placed a bid on Strathisla when it was up for sale. He was willing to pay £70,000 but the distillery went to Seagrams who offered £71,000!

The distillery is equipped with a 1.5 ton semi-lauter mash tun with a copper dome and 13 washbacks made of larch with a fermentation time of 67-115 hours. There is also one pair of stills with the condensers outside. The barley is predominantly peated to a phenol specification of 12ppm. The cut points for the middle cut are 72%-60% but they are lower when producing heavily peated spirit. The 2021 plan entails 14 mashes per week for 44 weeks and 400,000 litres of pure alcohol including 11,000 litres of peated spirit. There are seven dunnage and racked warehouses on site (two new since 2020) with space for 35,000 casks.

The core range consists of **10, 15** and **21 year old** (new since October 2020 and matured in a combination of ex-sherry and ex-bourbon) as well as **Cask Strength Vintage 2009**. In August 2021 the first of annual releases of a **40 year old** appeared. Recent limited releases include a **1978 single cask**, a **2009 Triple Distilled** and a **20th Anniversary** bottling. There are also special editions in the Contrasts range; **Organic 2012** and **Peat Smoke 2010**. A special version of the latter is **Peat Smoke Sherry Cask Matured 2012** which was released in summer 2021. Fairly recent wood finishes include **Chateau Cissac 2010** and **Sassicaia 2011** and in October 2019, a **50 year old**, distilled in 1969 was released. However, since 2018, Benromach is not just about whisky. That year their Red Door Gin was released.

History:

1898 Benromach Distillery Company starts the distillery.

1911 Harvey McNair & Co buys the distillery.

1919 John Joseph Calder buys Benromach and sells it to Benromach Distillery Ltd.

1931 The distillery is mothballed.

1937 The distillery reopens.

1938 Joseph Hobbs buys Benromach and sells it on to National Distillers of America (NDA).

1953 NDA sells Benromach to Distillers Company Ltd.

1968 Floor maltings is abolished.

1983 Benromach is mothballed.

1993 Gordon & McPhail buys Benromach.

1998 The distillery is once again in operation.

2004 The first bottle distilled by the new owner is 'Benromach Traditional'.

2005 A Port Wood finish, a Vintage 1968 and Classic 55 years ar released.

2006 Benromach Organic is released.

2007 Peat Smoke, the first heavily peated whisky from the distillery, is released.

2008 Benromach Origins Golden Promise is released.

2009 Benromach 10 years old is released.

2011 New edition of Peatsmoke, a 2001 Hermitage finish and a 30 year old are released.

2014 Three new bottlings are launched; a 5 year old, 100 Proof and Traveller´s Edition.

2015 A 15 year old and two wood finishes (Hermitage and Sassicaia) are released.

2016 A 35 year old and 1974 single cask are released.

2017 A 1976 single cask and a 2009 Triple Distilled are released.

2018 A 20th Anniversary bottling and a Sassicaia 2010 are released.

2019 Peat Smoke Sherry Cask Matured and a 50 year old are released.

2020 A new core range is released.

2021 A 40 year old is released together with Peat Smoke Sherry Cask Matured 2012.

Tasting notes Benromach 10 year old:

GS – A nose that is initially quite smoky, with wet grass, butter, ginger and brittle toffee. Mouth-coating, spicy, malty and nutty on the palate, with developing citrus fruits, raisins and soft wood smoke. The finish is warming, with lingering barbecue notes.

10 years old

Bladnoch

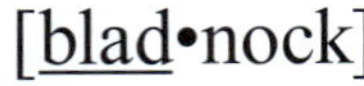

[blad•nock]

Owner: David Prior

Region/district: Lowlands

Founded: 1817

Status: Active (vc)

Capacity: 1 500 000 litres

Address: Bladnoch, Wigtown, Wigtonshire DG8 9AB

Website: bladnoch.com

Tel: 01988 402605

In 1993, it seemed as if Bladnoch distillery had reached the end of the road. Small and archaic and under the wings of the giant United Distillers who wanted large distilleries to produce malts for blends, the distillery had little hope of surviving.

Enter Raymond Armstrong, an Irish entrepreneur who wanted to buy it and make it into holiday homes. UD agreed under the condition that no whisky would be produced and no stock was included in the deal. Soon, the local community persuaded Armstrong to resurrect the distillery and a deal was struck with Diageo (to which UD now belonged) that permitted distillation of whisky. The deal even entailed that if Armstrong could supply Diageo with mature stocks of any malt whisky, they would be willing to swap it for casks of Bladnoch single malt distilled between 1989 and 1993. Fast forward, a family feud prevented Raymond Armstrong from continuing with Bladnoch and the distillery company was liquidated in 2014. A year later it was taken over by the current owner and the oldest surviving Lowland distillery continued to operate.

Bladnoch is equipped with a five ton stainless steel semi-lauter mash tun and six Douglas fir washbacks. Fermentations used to be a combination of short (76 hours) and long (100 hours) ones, but due to increased production it is now at 60 hours. There is also two pairs of stills. The plan for 2021 is to do 16 mashes per week which will amount to 1,5 million litres of pure alcohol. A small part of heavily peated production (60-80ppm) started already in 2017 and will continue in 2021.

The core range today consists of **11** and **19 year old**. There are two expressions without age statement; **Samsara** matured in ex-bourbon and casks that had contained Californian red wine and **Vinaya** matured in a combination of first fill bourbon and sherry casks. In autumn 2020, the first expression in a distillery exclusive series named **Waterfall** was launched. Over 5 years a new bottling with a new maturation story will be released annually.

History:

1817 Founded by Thomas and John McClelland.

1878 John McClelland's son Charlie reconstructs and refurbishes the distillery.

1905 Production stops.

1911 Dunville & Co. buys T. & A. McClelland Ltd. Production is intermittent until 1936.

1937 Dunville & Co. is liquidated and Bladnoch is wound up. Ross & Coulter from Glasgow buys the distillery after the war. The equipment is dismantled and shipped to Sweden.

1956 A. B. Grant (Bladnoch Distillery Ltd.) takes over and restarts production with four new stills.

1964 McGown and Cameron becomes new owners.

1973 Inver House Distillers buys Bladnoch.

1983 Arthur Bell and Sons take over.

1985 Guiness Group buys Arthur Bell & Sons which, from 1989, are included in United Distillers.

1988 A visitor centre is built.

1993 United Distillers mothballs Bladnoch in June.

1994 Raymond Armstrong buys Bladnoch in October.

2000 Production commences in December.

2003 The first bottles from Armstrong are launched, a 15 year old cask strength from UD casks.

2008 First release of whisky produced after the takeover in 2000 - three 6 year olds.

2009 An 8 year old of own production and a 19 year old are released.

2014 The distillery is liquidated.

2015 The distillery is bought by David Prior.

2016 Samsara, Adela and Talia are released.

2017 Production starts again and a Vintage 1988 is released.

2018 A 10 year old is released.

2019 A visitor centre is opened.

2020 An 11 year old and the Waterfall collection is launched.

10 years old

Tasting notes Bladnoch 10 year old:

IR – Fresh and grassy on the nose with sweet notes of honey and lilac, citrus, vanilla and a hint of cardamom. Rich and herbal on the palate with eucalyptus, ginger, pineapple, liquorice and milk chocolate coming through. Lovely mouthfeel.

Blair Athol

[blair <u>ath</u>•ull]

Owner: **Region/district:**
Diageo   Southern Highlands

Founded: **Status:**   **Capacity:**
1798   Active (vc)   2 800 000 litres

Address: Perth Road, Pitlochry, Perthshire PH16 5LY

Website: **Tel:**
malts.com   01796 482003

Blair Athol single malt has always been an important part of Bell's blended Scotch and while the Bell family bought the distillery in 1933 it was not a family member who would finally bring the brand the fame and status it enjoys today.

That credit goes to Raymond Miquel who made it the best selling whisky in England. Miquel joined the company in 1956 and became managing director in 1968. He soon discovered that the company had a very traditional way of doing things or, as he himself would put it: "I thought I'd gone back to the Middle Ages." His way of improving things led to a sales increase in the home market from £20m in 1970 to £159m ten years later. The success attracted the interest from the Guinness Group and its manager, Ernest Saunders. A hostile take-over bid (and – later to be found – a fraudelent one) was launched and Bell's was absorbed into the giant brewing company. A disappointed Miquel soon went into other business opportunities and towards the end of his life he was living at the legendary Gleneagles Hotel which he himself bought in 1984 on behalf of Arthur Bell & Sons. In January 2021 Raymond Miquel died at the age of 89.

Blair Athol is by far the most visited of all the Diageo distilleries and number four in Scotland. Around 80,000 people travel here every year. The distillery equipment consists of an 8.2 ton semi-lauter mash tun, six washbacks made of stainless steel and two pairs of stills. The part of the spirit which goes into Bell's is matured mainly in bourbon casks, while the rest is matured in sherry casks. The last couple of years, the distillery has been working a five-day week with 12 mashes per week and around two million litres of alcohol. This also means a scheme of short (46 hours) and long (104 hours) fermentations. A very cloudy wort gives Blair Athol new make a nutty and malty character.

The only official bottling is the **12 year old Flora & Fauna**. In autumn 2017, however, a **23 year old**, matured in ex-bodega European oak butts was released as part of the Special Releases.

History:

1798 John Stewart and Robert Robertson found Aldour Distillery, the predecessor to Blair Athol. The name is taken from the adjacent river Allt Dour.

1825 The distillery is expanded by John Robertson and takes the name Blair Athol Distillery.

1826 The Duke of Atholl leases the distillery to Alexander Connacher & Co.

1860 Elizabeth Connacher runs the distillery.

1882 Peter Mackenzie & Company Distillers Ltd of Edinburgh (future founder of Dufftown Distillery) buys Blair Athol and expands it.

1932 The distillery is mothballed.

1933 Arthur Bell & Sons takes over by acquiring Peter Mackenzie & Company.

1949 Production restarts.

1973 Stills are expanded from two to four.

1985 Guinness Group buys Arthur Bell & Sons.

1987 A visitor centre is built.

2003 A 27 year old cask strength from 1975 is launched in Diageo's Rare Malts series.

2010 A distillery exclusive with no age statement and a single cask from 1995 are released.

2016 A distillery exclusive without age statement is released.

2017 A 23 year old is released as part of the Special Releases.

12 years old

Tasting notes Blair Athol 12 years old:

GS – The nose is mellow and sherried, with brittle toffee. Sweet and fragrant. Relatively rich on the palate, with malt, raisins, sultanas and sherry. The finish is lengthy, elegant and slowly drying.

Bowmore

[bow•moor]

Owner: Beam Suntory

Region/district: Islay

Founded: 1779

Status: Active (vc)

Capacity: 2 150 000 litres

Address: School Street, Bowmore, Islay, Argyll PA43 7GS

Website: bowmore.com

Tel: 01496 810441

History:

1779 Bowmore Distillery is founded by David Simpson and becomes the oldest Islay distillery.

1837 The distillery is sold to James and William Mutter of Glasgow.

1892 After additional construction, the distillery is sold to Bowmore Distillery Company Ltd, a consortium of English businessmen.

1925 J. B. Sheriff and Company takes over.

1929 Distillers Company Limited (DCL) takes over.

1950 William Grigor & Son takes over.

1963 Stanley P. Morrison buys the distillery and forms Morrison Bowmore Distillers Ltd.

1989 Japanese Suntory buys a 35% stake in Morrison Bowmore.

1993 The legendary Black Bowmore is launched.

1994 Suntory now controls all of Morrison Bowmore.

1996 A Bowmore 1957 (38 years) is bottled at 40.1% but is not released until 2000.

1999 Bowmore Darkest with three years finish on Oloroso barrels is launched.

2000 Bowmore Dusk with two years finish in Bordeaux barrels is launched.

2001 Bowmore Dawn with two years finish on Port pipes is launched.

2002 A 37 year old Bowmore from 1964 and matured in fino casks is launched in a limited edition of 300 bottles (recommended price £1,500).

2003 Another two expressions complete the wood trilogy which started with 1964 Fino - 1964 Bourbon and 1964 Oloroso.

2005 Bowmore 1989 Bourbon (16 years) and 1971 (34 years) are launched.

2006 Bowmore 1990 Oloroso (16 years) and 1968 (37 years) are launched.

With the exception of Caol Ila most distilleries on Islay are either small or medium-sized in terms of capacity. Another observation is that the majority of them are now producing at full capacity, an obvious effect of the huge demand for peated whisky around the world.

For many years, Bowmore was working a five-day week with both short and long fermentations and producing around 65% of their capacity. In 2018 the decision was taken to increase production and in 2019 they moved to a six-day week. Since 2020 the capacity is utilized to the full, seven days per week. This is also in line with the rest of the Scottish distilleries in the Beam Suntory group.

Bowmore is equipped with an eight ton stainless steel semi-lauter mash tun with a copper lid which was previously in use at Jura distillery. There are also two magnificent and unusual hot water tanks made of copper to feed the mash tun. The six washbacks are made of Oregon pine and all named after previous owners of the distillery, Working a 7-day week with 16 mashes per week, the fermentation time is now 62 hours. One washback will feed one of the two wash stills and is then in its turn split between the two spirit stills. In 2021, the plan is to do 16 mashes per week which amounts to 2,15 million litres of alcohol. Bowmore is one of three on the island having their own floor maltings. Thirty percent of the malt requirement is produced in-house and the green malt is dried for 18 hours using peat and then for 42 hours with dry air. The remaining part is bought from Simpson's. Both parts have a phenol specification of 25-30 ppm and are always mixed on a ratio of 2.5 tons in house malt and 5.5 tons of malt from Simpsons.

The domestic core range includes **12, 15, 18** and **25 years.** There is also an annual but limited release of a **30 year old.** The entry level expression, No. 1 without an age statement, has now been discontinued. Recent limited bottlings (both released in spring 2021) are the first two parts in the new Timeless collection. The first was a **27 year old** matured for 15 years in a combination of ex-sherry and ex-bourbon casks and then transferred to oloroso butts for a 15 year second maturation. This was followed by a **31 year old,** matured for 29 years in ex-bourbon and then finished for two years in Spanish oak Matusalem sherry butts for two years. Other limited releases include a range highlighting the influence from the famous warehouse Vault No. 1. This was first introduced in 2016 and the final installment was named **Peat Smoke.** Another range, focusing on how wine casks interact with Bowmore single malt, was introduced in 2017 with a **27 year old** port finish being the last. The Feis Ile bottling for 2021 was an **18 year old** matured in first fill oloroso casks. The duty free range consists of **10 year old** (Dark and Intense), **15 year old** (Golden and Elegant) and **18 year old** (Deep and Complex). Limited releases for duty free include **21** and **22 year old** as well as single casks from **1995** and **1997.**

History continued:

2007 An 18 year old is introduced. 1991 (16yo) Port and Black Bowmore are released.

2008 White Bowmore and a 1992 Vintage with Bourdeaux finish are launched.

2009 Gold Bowmore, Maltmen´s Selection, Laimrig and Bowmore Tempest are released.

2010 A 40 year old and Vintage 1981 are released.

2011 Vintage 1982 and new batches of Tempest and Laimrig are released.

2012 100 Degrees Proof, Springtide and Vintage 1983 are released for duty free.

2013 The Devil´s Casks, a 23 year old Port Cask Matured and Vintage 1984 are released.

2014 Black Rock, Gold Reef and White Sands are released for duty free.

2015 New editions of Devil´s Cask, Tempest and the 50 year old are released as well as Mizunara Cask Finish.

2016 A 9 year old, a 10 year old travel retail exclusive and Bowmore Vault Edit1on are released as well as the final batch of Black Bowmore.

2017 No. 1 is released together with three new expressions for travel retail.

2018 Vintner´s Trilogy is launched.

2019 Vault Edit1on Peat Smoke, a 21 year old for duty free and the 36 year old Dragon Edition are released.

2020 Black Bowmore DBS is launched.

2021 Timeless 27 and 31 years old are released.

Tasting notes Bowmore 12 year old:

GS – An enticing nose of lemon and gentle brine leads into a smoky, citric palate, with notes of cocoa and boiled sweets appearing in the lengthy, complex finish.

Vintner´s Trilogy
27 year old Port Cask

Timeless
31 years old

18 years old
Travel Retail

12 years old

15 years old

25 years old

Braeval

[bre•<u>vaal</u>]

Owner: **Region/district:**
Chivas Brothers (Pernod Ricard) Speyside

Founded: **Status:**   **Capacity:**
1973   Active   4 200 000 litres

Address: Chapeltown of Glenlivet, Ballindalloch,
Banffshire AB37 9JS

Website: **Tel:**
-                                  01542 783042

Braes of Glenlivet, the area south of Glenlivet and east of the B9008, has been described as exposed, wild, pastoral, rugged and even forlorn. Different people see different things but one thing is for sure – it is remote.

Because it was so difficult to reach and to travel around, it served as the perfect spot for two very different activities. One was illicit distilling and whisky smuggling. To this very day you can walk in the foot steps of the smugglers on paths and trails that are clearly marked and named after smugglers or gaugers (excise men). The second activity, favored by the secluded location was the performance of a religion banned during the 18th century by the authorities – catholicism. Many believers took refuge in isolated parts of the Highlands and close to where the distillery lies today, Scalan, a college where young men could train to be priests, was secretly built. It was closed in 1799 when a new law granted the Catholics their rights again. Right next to Braeval Distillery lies a catholic church built in 1826 – Our Lady of Perpetual Succour. The church can seat as many as 350 people and the interior is very beautiful.

The equipment at Braeval consists of a 9 ton stainless steel, full lauter mash tun, 13 stainless steel washbacks with a fermentation time of 70 hours and six stills. Two of them are wash stills with aftercoolers and four are spirit stills, and with the possibility of producing 26 mashes per week, the distillery can now make 4.2 million litres per year.

The first official bottling appeared in 2017: a 16 year old single cask available only at Chivas' visitor centres. Then, in July 2019, a new range called The Secret Speyside Collection was launched – a total of 15 bottlings from four different distilleries where Braeval was one. Initially they were reserved for travel retail but were later rolled out to domestic markets as well. The three from Braeval are **25, 27** and **30 year old**, all matured in ex-bourbon barrels and hogsheads. Finally there is an **18 year old** available in the Distillery Reserve Collection available at the visitor centres.

25 years old

History:

1973 The distillery is founded by Chivas Brothers (Seagram´s) and production starts in October.

1975 Three stills are increased to five.

1978 Five stills are further expanded to six.

1994 The distillery changes name to Braeval.

2001 Pernod Ricard takes over Chivas Brothers.

2002 Braeval is mothballed in October.

2008 The distillery starts producing again in July.

2017 The first official bottling, a 16 year old single cask, is released.

2019 Three new official bottlings in a new range, The Secret Speyside Collection, are released.

Tasting notes Braeval 16 year old:

GS – Marzipan, milk chocolate-coated Turkish Delight and orange peel on the nose. The palate is sweet and fruity, with stewed apples, sugared almonds, nutmeg and ginger. Medium to long in the finish, consistently sugary and spicy.

Trailblazers of Malt Whisky

Yu-Ting Lee
Kavalan, Taiwan

All of the world´s ten largest malt whisky distilleries must have been built by one of the three giant spirits conglomerates and surely it must be located in Scotland? Anything else would seem crazy. And yet, there is one of the Top 10 that can be found in Taiwan and it opened up as late as in 2006. The story of Kavalan doesn´t follow the usual narrative of a "new world" distillery where a passionate whisky enthusiast is desperately searching for financial means for building a distillery. And yet, Kavalan was founded out of love for whisky but with an entirely different starting-point. This is the story.

In 1956, Tien-Tsai Lee at the age of 18, started the Chu Chen company producing insecticides and cleaning products. The company expanded to include a number of other household products. Tien-Tsai´s family also lived in the building with the factory being on the ground floor and their home on the first floor. In 1979 Tien-Tsai founded the King Car Group and this is when he joined the beverage business. A plant was set up in Zhongli in Taoyuan manufacturing root beer, the canned Mr. Brown coffee, energy drinks and more. Within the next couple of decades, the group grew into a virtual conglomerate including frozen noodles, fast food, mineral water, health food, shrimps and an orchid cultivation center.

But during all these years of building an enterprise, Tien-Tsai nurtured a dream. Being an avid whisky lover he wanted to build a distillery to produce Taiwan´s first single malt. The first attempt in the alcohol business (producing beer) in 1995 was given a cold shoulder by the authorities. The government, with its Taiwan Tobacco and Liquor Corporation, was not prepared to abandon their state monopoly for alcohol production in the country. At this time one of Tien-Tsai´s sons, Yu-Ting had been employed in the company. He had studied business management in Japan and at the age of 27 he joined his father. With Yu-Ting also being a whisky aficionado, the two now worked tirelessly together to break up the monopoly and the turning point came in 2002 when Taiwan joined the World Trade Organization. Having climbed the ladder to CEO, it now became Yu-Ting´s task to commence the building of the first malt whisky distillery in Taiwan.

His first step was to find someone who could design not only the distillery but also draw up the plans for the distillation, maturation and future launch of the whisky. He decided to contact Dr. Jim Swan in Scotland and he could not have chosen wiser. Dr Swan, with a PhD in chemistry, had been working with whisky analysis for three decades, first at Pentlands Scotch Whisky Research and later at Tatlock & Thomson. When he received Yu-Ting Lee´s phone call in early 2000, Dr. Swan had just decided to set up his own business as a whisky consultant and he agreed to take on the assignement of designing the distillery. Around the same time, the company hired Ian Chang as a reserach fellow. Guided by Yu-Ting Lee´s passion and ambitious plans, the Scottish whisky sorcerer and his young Taiwanese apprentice, was the perfect couple to make the dream of the Lee family come true. The distillery was completed in record time in December 2005 and in March 2006, the first drops of spirit trickled from the stills. Located in the Yilan province in the north-east of Taiwan just an hour drive from Taipei, the distillery was named Kavalan after the old name of Yilan county.

A couple of things were clear to Yu-Ting Lee from the very start; due to the hot and humid climate in Taiwan, the Kavalan whisky would mature much quicker than its counterparts in Scotland. This of course was a major advantage making it possible to release the whisky at a young age. Secondly, and most important to Yu-Ting, the ambition was to make a world class whisky and not just a decent copy of a Scotch malt.Two years later, in 2008, the distillery reached two milestones – the first whisky was released and a visitor centre which would challenge all the others in the whisky world was inaugurated. When I was at Kavalan the first time, in 2010, my jaw dropped at the sight of the huge centre which one year later (and a second time in 2021) was awarded the Icons of Whisky "Visitor Attraction of the Year". Eventually, around one million visitors would come here every year.

Following the release of Kavalan Classic in 2008, new bottlings were launched rapidly and a new range of single casks, matured or finished in a variety of casks, under the name Solist turned out to become the icebreaker internationally. But it wasn´t just the range that was expanded. Being the entrepreneur that he is, Yu-Ting knew he had to plan for future increases in sales and decided to expand the distillery. In autumn 2016 more stills had been installed bringing the total capacity to nine million litres of alcohol which made Kavalan one the ten largest malt whisky distilleries in the world!

The company has continued harvesting awards for its whiskies at competitions around the world but undoubtedly one of the highest accolades for their work in bringing the first Taiwanese whisky to the world came in 2018. Both Yu-Ting and his father Tien-Tsai were inducted into the World Whiskies Awards Hall of Fame at the Waldorf Hotel in London. This is an honour bestowed on very few people and the Lees were the first father and son inductees.

Kavalan is now exported to more than 60 countries and they have also been succesful in conquering what many consider to be the most important market of all – the USA. The introduction to the US consumers was definitely not a quiet one. I still remember going to New York in autumn 2017 and standing on Times Square. I looked up at the huge billboard screens and I saw the name Kavalan in huge letters flashing towards me. In Yu-Ting´s own words that was Kavalan´s way of saying "We´re here and we´re in business".

In recent years the Lees have started the production of Buckskin beer, they have launched a Kavalan gin as well as a whole new range of ready-to-drink spirits. Designated Kavalan whisky bars have opened up in Taiwan where consumers can try the whisky at cask strength. All this has happened in the scope of 15 years and if you listen to Yu-Ting, this is only the beginning.

Challenging the conservative whisky industry which has been dominated by a handful of countries for centuries must be daunting. To do it in the conspicuous way that father and son Lee have done it with Kavalan, takes passion, perseverance and, let´s be honest, money. But most of all – it takes guts. I´ll let Yu-Ting Lee have the final word. "When you see a challenge, that is an opportunity."

Bruichladdich

[brook•lad•dee]

Owner: Rémy Cointreau   **Region/district:** Islay

Founded: 1881   **Status:** Active (vc)   **Capacity:** 2 000 000 litres

Address: Bruichladdich, Islay, Argyll PA49 7UN

Website: bruichladdich.com   **Tel:** 01496 850221

Distilleries around the world are currently working on different solutions how to minimize their environmental impact. Bruichladdich is at the forefront when it comes to renewable energy sources and during spring 2021 a new technology was tested.

The project, named HyLaddie, includes a DCC chamber which, by using only oxygen and hydrogen which is combusted in a vacuum, will meet the distillery's heating requirements. The process creates water which can be recycled and, more importantly, eliminates any emission of CO_2.

The distillery is equipped with a 7 ton cast iron, open mash tun with rakes, six washbacks made of Oregon pine with a fermentation time between 60 and 105 hours and two pairs of stills. All whisky produced is based on Scottish barley. Around half comes from Islay and 5% is organically grown. During 2021, the plan is to mash 9-10 times per week and make 1,1 million litres of alcohol. The breakdown of the three whisky varieties will be 50% Bruichladdich, 40% Port Charlotte and 10% Octomore. It also includes filling around 20 barrels of rye whisky.

The malting floors at Bruichladdich were closed in 1961 but it has been decided to start up own maltings again within the next two to four years. Instead of traditional floor malting, Saladin boxes will be installed. The main reason for this is to maintain the consistency of the spirit since Baird's, their current malt supplier, are using that same technique. The malting will be located in one of the current warehouses.

Bruichladdich has three product lines; unpeated Bruichladdich, heavily peated (40ppm) Port Charlotte and ultra-heavily peated (in the excess of 100ppm) Octomore. The only core expressions, in the sense that they are widely available, are **The Classic Laddie** and **Port Charlotte 10 year old**. The following appear every year with new batches/vintages; for Bruichladdich there are **Islay Barley 2012, Bere Barley 2011** and **The Organic 2010** and for Port Charlotte, **Islay Barley 2013** and the new **PAC:01**. The latter is an 8 year old matured in ex-bourbon casks with 25% of the volume being finished for one year in French wine casks.

Since last year, the duty free range has diminished and is now made up of **The Laddie Eight** and **Bruichladdich 1990**. There is also the mysterious 26 year old **Black Art 8**. In autumn 2021, another batch of the heavily peated Octomore, all of them 5 years old, was released; **12.1** matured in first fill bourbon casks was bottled at 59,9%, **12.2** bottled at 57,3% had received a finish in sauternes casks and **12.3** was the result of a maturation in both ex-bourbon and PX sherry casks and bottled at 62,1%. There were two special bottling for Feis Ile 2021; one of them was **Laddie Origins** with a recipe that included the very first spirit after the resurrection of the distillery as well some of the first triple distilled spirit. Whisky was drawn from nine different cask types and from 12 vintages. The second festival bottling was a **17 year old** matured in 2nd fill sherry.

History:

1881 Barnett Harvey builds the distillery with money left by his brother William III to his three sons William IV, Robert and John Gourlay.

1886 Bruichladdich Distillery Company Ltd is founded and reconstruction commences.

1929 Temporary closure.

1936 The distillery reopens.

1938 Joseph Hobbs, Hatim Attari and Alexander Tolmie purchase the distillery through the company Train & McIntyre.

1952 The distillery is sold to Ross & Coulter.

1960 A. B. Grant buys Ross & Coulter.

1961 Own maltings ceases.

1968 Invergordon Distillers take over.

1975 The number of stills increases to four.

1983 Temporary closure.

1993 Whyte & Mackay buys Invergordon Distillers.

1995 The distillery is mothballed in January.

1998 In production again for a few months.

2000 Murray McDavid buys the distillery from JBB Greater Europe for £6.5 million.

2001 The first distillations of Port Charlotte and Bruichladdich starts in July.

2002 Octomore, the world's most heavily peated whisky (80ppm) is distilled.

2004 Second edition of the 20 year old (nick-named Flirtation) and 3D, also called The Peat Proposal, are launched.

2005 Several new expressions are launched - the second edition of 3D, Infinity, Rocks, Legacy Series IV, The Yellow Submarine and The Twenty 'Islands'.

2006 The first official bottling of Port Charlotte; PC5.

2007 New releases include Redder Still, Legacy 6, PC6 and an 18 year old.

History continued:

2008 New expressions include the first Octomore, Bruichladdich 2001, PC7 and Golder Still.

2009 New releases include Classic, Organic, Black Art, Infinity 3, PC8, Octomore 2 and X4+3 - the first quadruple distilled single malt.

2010 PC Multi Vintage, Organic MV, Octomore/3_152, Bruichladdich 40 year old are released.

2011 The first 10 year old from own production is released as well as PC9 and Octomore 4_167.

2012 Ten year old versions of Port Charlotte and Octomore are released as well as Laddie 16 and 22, Bere Barley 2006, Black Art 3 and DNA4. Rémy Cointreau buys the distillery.

2013 Scottish Barley, Islay Barley Rockside Farm, Bere Barley 2nd edition, Black Art 4, Port Charlotte Scottish Barley, Octomore 06.1 and 06.2 are released.

2014 PC11 and Octomore Scottish Barley are released.

2015 PC12, Octomore 7.1 and High Noon 134 are released.

2016 The Laddie Eight, Octomore 7.4 and Port Charlotte 2007 CC:01 are released.

2017 Black Art 5 and 25 year old sherry cask are launched. The limited Rare Cask series is launched.

2018 The Port Charlotte range is revamped and a 10 year old and Islay Barley 2011 are released.

2019 Bere Barley 10, Organic 10, Black Art 7 and Octomore 10.1, 10.2, 10.3 and 10.4 are released.

2020 Port Charlotte OLC:01, Port Charlotte 16 year old and four new Octomore are released.

2021 Port Charlotte PAC:01 and Islay Barley 2013 are launched together with Bruichladdich Islay Barley 2012, Bere Barley 2011 and The Organic 2010. Three new Octomore are also released.

Tasting notes The Classic Laddie:

IR – Fresh on the nose with notes of pears, green apples, vanilla, citrus and paint. The palate starts with a sweet maltiness and lively pepper followed by malted barley, vanilla and pears.

Tasting notes Port Charlotte 10 year old:

IR – Smoked herring and clams on the nose together with notes of tobacco, mint, dried grass and a hint of orange. Great mouth feel with a soothing smokiness, apple pie, digestive, liquorice, nutmeg, roasted coco flakes and some honey sweetness.

Black Art 7   Bere Barley 2011   Islay Barley 2012

The Classic Laddie Scottish Barley

Port Charlotte PAC:01 2011

Port Charlotte 10 year old

Bunnahabhain

[buh•nah•hav•enn]

Owner:
Distell International Ltd.

Region/district:
Islay

Founded: 1881

Status: Active (vc)

Capacity: 2 700 000 litres

Address: Port Askaig, Islay, Argyll PA46 7RP

Website:
bunnahabhain.com

Tel:
01496 840646

Bunnahabhain is situated at the north part of the Sound of Islay, which parts Islay from Jura. The view from the pier is classical, with the three highest mountains on neighbouring Jura, The Paps, clearly visible. Dolphins and Killer Whales can be spotted with some luck in the waters.

It is the northernmost of the nine distilleries on Islay and definitely the most inaccessible. It has long deserved a Visitor's Centre and in summer 2021, delayed by the covid pandemic, it was ready to receive it's first guests. A consdierable improvement to the small shop that was found on site previously.

The distillery is equipped with a 12.5 ton traditional stainless steel mash tun with a copper lid, six washbacks made of Oregon pine and two pairs of stills. Two of the washbacks were replaced in July 2021 while another two, dating back to 1963/64, are due for replacement soon. The fermentation time varies between 55 and 110 hours. The production plan for 2021 is 2,5 million litres, split between 35% peated and 65% unpeated. The peating level has increased during the last years and the barley now has a phenol specification of 35-45ppm.

The core range consists of **12, 18, 25** and a **40 year old**. The peated side of Bunnahabhain is represented by **Toiteach a Dha** without age statement and matured in both bourbon and sherry casks and **Stiùireadair**, matured in first and re-fill sherry casks. Recent limited releases include the first in the new Elements series – a **39 year old**, launched in June 2019. July 2020 saw the release of three bottlings ; a **2008 manzanilla matured**, a **1997 Moine PX finish** and a **2005 burgundy finish** (distillery exclusive) and in May 2021, two releases for Feis Ile 2021 appeared – a **2013 Moine Bordeaux finish** and a **2001 Marsala finish**. Finally, there are three travel retail exclusives – **Cruach-Mhòna** which comprises of young, heavily peated Bunnahabhain, **Eirigh Na Greine**, a vatting of whisky from bourbon, sherry and red wine casks and the sherry-matured **An Cladach**.

History:

1881 William Robertson founds the distillery together with the brothers William and James Greenless.

1883 Production starts in January.

1887 Islay Distillers Company Ltd merges with William Grant & Co. in order to form Highland Distilleries Company Limited.

1963 The two stills are augmented by two more.

1982 The distillery closes.

1984 The distillery reopens. A 21 year old is released to commemorate the 100th anniversary.

1999 Edrington takes over Highland Distillers and mothballs Bunnahabhain but allows for a few weeks of production a year.

2001 A 35 year old from 1965 is released during Islay Whisky Festival.

2002 Auld Acquaintance 1968 is launched at the Islay Jazz Festival.

2003 Edrington sells Bunnahabhain and Black Bottle to Burn Stewart Distilleries for £10 million. A 40 year old from 1963 is launched.

2004 The first limited edition of the peated version is a 6 year old called Moine.

2005 Three limited editions are released - 34 years old,18 years old and 25 years old.

2006 14 year old Pedro Ximenez and 35 years old are launched.

2008 Darach Ur is released for the travel retail market and Toiteach (a peated 10 year old) is launched on a few selected markets.

2009 Moine Cask Strength is released.

2010 The peated Cruach-Mhòna and a limited 30 year old are released.

2013 A 40 year old is released.

2014 Eirigh Na Greine and Ceobanach are released.

2017 Moine Oloroso, Stiùireadair and An Cladach are released.

2018 Toiteach a Dha and a 20 year old Palo Cortado are released.

2019 A 2007 brandy finish and a 39 year old are released.

2020 A 2008 manzanilla, a 1997 PX finish and a 2005 burgundy finish are released.

Tasting notes Bunnahabhain 12 years old:

GS – The nose is fresh, with light peat and discreet smoke. More overt peat on the nutty and fruity palate, but still restrained for an Islay. The finish is full-bodied and lingering, with a hint of vanilla and some smoke.

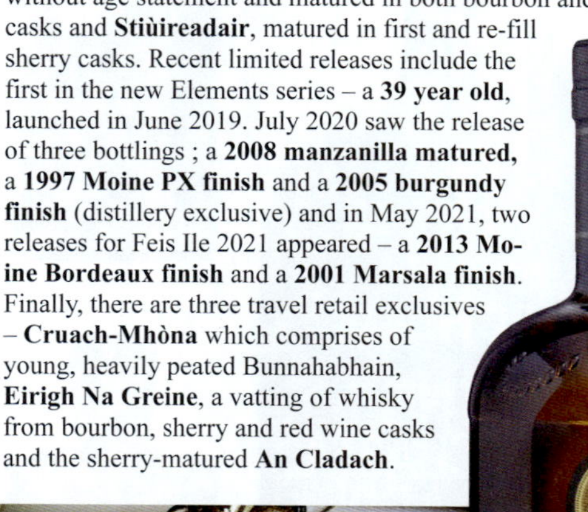

12 years old

Caol Ila

[cull eel•a]

Owner: Diageo   **Region/district:** Islay

Founded: 1846   **Status:** Active (vc)   **Capacity:** 6 500 000 litres

Address: Port Askaig, Islay, Argyll PA46 7RL

Website: malts.com   **Tel:** 01496 302760

A distillery situated on Islay, the world's whisky island number one and home to peated malts, would seem to have a safe route to the market and to fame. But it's not as simple as that.

With nine distilleries on Islay, competition is fierce and a handful of them have been present in whisky shops and bars for many decades now with plenty of marketing effort to bolster their success. Caol Ila is different. It wasn't until 2002 that Diageo began to treat the malt as a stand alone brand and while they have created a comprehensive range they haven't put that much money into advertising it. The sales curve for the past ten years is evidence of this: The Kildalton three have increased substantially; Laphroaig (+60%), Lagavulin (+77%) and Ardbeg (+157%). For Caol Ila, on the other hand, volumes are up by just 4% in the same time.

This isn't something that worries the owners though. The malt from the island's largest distillery is far too important for their blends, Johnnie Walker in particular. The connection with the world's most sold Scotch will be even more emphasized in 2022 when the new visitor experience will be ready as the final part of a huge investment which also includes new visitor centres at Clynelish, Glenkinchie and Cardhu as well as a Johnnie Walker Experience in Edinburgh.

Caol Ila is equipped with a 12.5 ton full lauter mash tun, eight wooden washbacks and two made of stainless steel and three pairs of stills. In recent years, the distillery has either been working a seven-day week with 26 mashes or a five-day week with 16 mashes. On a five-day week production, there is a mix of short (55 hours) and long (120 hours) fermentations. Caol Ila is known for its peated whisky but unpeated new-make is also produced.

The core range consists of **Moch** without age statement, **12, 18** and **25 year old, Distiller's Edition** with a moscatel finish and **Cask Strength**. The release for Feis Ile 2021 was a **12 year old**, bottled at 56,6%, that had been matured in refill American oak and finished in moscatel casks. In July 2020, a **35 year old**, matured in a refill sherry butt and bottled at 50,8% was part of the new Prima & Ultima range.

History:

1846 Hector Henderson founds Caol Ila.

1852 Henderson, Lamont & Co. is subjected to financial difficulties and Henderson is forced to sell Caol Ila to Norman Buchanan.

1863 Norman Buchanan sells to the blending company Bulloch, Lade & Co. from Glasgow.

1879 The distillery is rebuilt and expanded.

1920 Bulloch, Lade & Co. is liquidated and the distillery is taken over by Caol Ila Distillery.

1927 DCL becomes sole owners.

1972 All the buildings, except for the warehouses, are demolished and rebuilt.

1974 The renovation, which totals £1 million, is complete and six new stills are installed.

1999 Experiments with unpeated malt.

2002 The first official bottlings since Flora & Fauna/Rare Malt appear; 12 years, 18 years and Cask Strength (c. 10 years).

2003 A 25 year old cask strength is released.

2006 Unpeated 8 year old and 1993 Moscatel finish are released.

2007 Second edition of unpeated 8 year old.

2009 The fourth edition of the unpeated version (10 year old) is released.

2010 A 25 year old, a 1999 Feis Isle bottling and a 1997 Manager´s Choice are released.

2011 An unpeated 12 year old and the unaged Moch are released.

2012 An unpeated 14 year old is released.

2013 Unpeated Stitchell Reserve is released.

2014 A 15 year old unpeated and a 30 year old are released.

2016 A 15 year old unpeated is released.

2017 An 18 year old unpeated is released.

2018 Two bottlings in the Special Releases - a 15 year old and a 35 year old.

2020 A 35 year old is released as part of the new Prima & Ultima range.

Tasting notes Caol Ila 12 year old:

GS – Iodine, fresh fish and smoked bacon feature on the nose, along with more delicate, floral notes. Smoke, malt, lemon and peat on the slightly oily palate. Peppery peat in the drying finish.

12 years old

Cardhu

[car•doo]

Owner:	**Region/district:**
Diageo	Speyside
Founded: **Status:**	**Capacity:**
1824 Active (vc)	3 400 000 litres

Address: Knockando, Aberlour, Moray AB38 7RY

Website:	**Tel:**
malts.com	01479 874635

Three years ago, a £185m investment by Diageo was announced which included a huge Johnnie Walker Experience in Edinburgh as well as completely new visitor centres at four of their distilleries.

The "four corner distilleries" have in common that they are all pivotal to the profile of the Johnnie Walker blend. Situated in four corners of Scotland, Glenkinchie was first to open up their new facilities in 2020 and was followed by Clynelish in April 2021. In June 2021 it was time for Cardhu to welcome visitors to a completely new venue with several tours to choose from. These include a warehouse experience and a Tasting Kitchen where visitors can enjoy whisky and highballs.

Cardhu was the first distillery to be bought by John Walker & Sons (in 1893) and has always been important for the world's number one Scotch whisky. Yet at the same time, Cardhu single malt is very much a brand of its own. In 2019 it was Diaego's number two single malt after The Singleton (which actually is made up of three distilleries) and sold 3,5 million bottles. This means that the brand is also number eight of the top selling single malts in the world.

The distillery is equipped with an eight ton stainless steel full lauter mash tun with a copper top, ten washbacks (eight of wood and two of stainless steel in a separate room), all with a fermentation time of 75 hours, and three pairs of stills. Four of the wooden washbacks are new and made of Oregon pine, having replaced four old ones made of larch. For several years now, the distillery has been producing on a seven-day week with 21 mashes per week and a total of 3.4 million litres of alcohol.

The core range from the distillery is **12, 15** and **18 year old** and two expressions without age statement – **Amber Rock** and **Gold Reserve**. There is also a **Special Cask Reserve** matured in rejuvenated bourbon casks. In April 2021 a limited **16 year old** Four Corners of Scotland bottling, available only at the distillery, was launched. Recent limited releases include a **14 year old** Rare by Nature in autumn 2021 which had been finished in red wine casks.

History:

1824 John Cumming applies for and obtains a licence for Cardhu Distillery.

1846 John Cumming dies and his wife Helen and son Lewis takes over.

1872 Lewis dies and his wife Elizabeth takes over.

1884 A new distillery is built to replace the old.

1893 John Walker & Sons purchases Cardhu for £20,500.

1908 The name reverts to Cardow.

1960 Reconstruction and expansion of stills from four to six.

1981 The name changes to Cardhu.

1998 A visitor centre is constructed.

2002 Diageo changes Cardhu single malt to a vatted malt with contributions from other distilleries in it.

2003 The whisky industry protests sharply against Diageo's plans.

2004 Diageo withdraws Cardhu Pure Malt.

2005 The 12 year old Cardhu Single Malt is relaunched and a 22 year old is released.

2009 Cardhu 1997, a single cask in the new Manager´s Choice range is released.

2011 A 15 year old and an 18 year old are released.

2013 A 21 year old is released.

2014 Amber Rock and Gold Reserve are launched.

2016 A distillery exclusive is released.

2019 A 14 year old appears in the Special Releases and Cardhu is also part of the Game of Thrones series.

2020 An 11 year old Rare by Nature bottling is released.

2021 A 14 year old Rare by Nature and a 16 year old Four Corners of Scotland bottling are released.

14 years old
Rare by Nature

Tasting notes Cardhu 12 years old:

GS – The nose is relatively light and floral, quite sweet, with pears, nuts and a whiff of distant peat. Medium-bodied, malty and sweet in the mouth. Medium-length in the finish, with sweet smoke, malt and a hint of peat.

Websites to watch

There are a lot of great blogs and websites
to be found on the internet and, to be honest, some not so great.
These are the ones I follow frequently and while they are all well worth
visiting, the ones marked with * are my personal favourites.

allthingswhisky.com *

bestshotwhiskyreviews.com *

blog.thewhiskyexchange.com *

bozzy.org

canadianwhisky.org *

edinburghwhiskyblog.com *

greatdrams.com *

insidethecask.com *

jason-scotchreviews.blogspot.com

maltandoak.com

maltermagasin.se *

maltfascination.com

maltimpostor.com

malt-review.com *

masterofmalt.com/blog *

meleklerinpayi.com

ozwhiskyreview.com.au *

scotchmaltwhisky.co.uk *

scotchnoob.com

scotchwhisky.com *

scotch-whisky.org.uk

speller.nl

spiritedmatters.com

spiritsjournal.klwines.com

spiritsnews.se

taswhiskytrail.com

thedramble.com

thewhiskeyjug.com

thewhiskeywash.com *

thewhiskylady.net

thewhiskyphiles.com

thewhiskyviking.blogspot.com

thewhiskywire.com *

timeforwhisky.com

tjederswhisky.se *

tomswhiskyreviews.com

topwhiskies.com

whiskeyapostle.com

whisky.buzz

whiskyandwisdom.com

whiskyboys.com

whiskycast.com *

whiskycritic.com

whisky-distilleries.net *

whiskyfacile.com

whiskyfanblog.de

whiskyforeveryone.blogspot.com *

whiskyfun.com *

whiskyintelligence.com *

whiskyisrael.co.il *

whiskymonster.com

whiskymylife.wordpress.com

whisky-news.com *

whiskynotes.be *

whiskeyreviewer.com

whiskyreviews.net

whiskysaga.com *

whiskysponge.com *

whiskywaffle.com

wordsofwhisky.com

Clynelish

[cline•leash]

Owner:
Diageo

Region/district:
Northern Highlands

Founded: 1967   **Status:** Active (vc)   **Capacity:** 4 800 000 litres

Address: Brora, Sutherland KW9 6LR

Website: malts.com   **Tel:** 01408 623003 (vc)

Named the "Highland Home of Johnnie Walker" by the owners, Clynelish opened up its new visitor experience in April 2021. It is part of a £185m investment also including a Johnnie Walker Experience in Princess street in Edinburgh.

On top of that, another two distilleries with strong links to the Johnnie Walker blend have had their visitor centres completely rebuilt (Glenkinchie and Cardhu) and a third, Caol Ila, will open in 2022. Visitors to Clynelish will have access to an interactive story room, secret rooms and hidden keys, a large shop and a terrace bar overlooking the Brora hills.

What makes the Clynelish site even more exciting this year is that the closed Brora distillery re-opened and started distillation at the same time. The current Clynelish distillery was built in 1967, next to Brora, which was founded in 1819, and the two distilleries first went under the names Clynelish A and B but this was later changed to Clynelish for the new distillery and Brora for the old. The reason for the new distillery getting the "old" name was that the old distillery had always been known to the locals as the Brora distillery. Finally, Brora shut the doors in 1983 and remained closed for 38 years.

Following a year-long upgrade which was completed in 2017, Clynelish is equipped with a 12.5 ton full lauter mash tun, eight wooden washbacks and two made of stainless steel. The still room, with its three pairs of stills, has stunning views towards the village of Brora and the North Sea. Clynelish is usually operational seven-days a week, producing around 4.8 million litres of alcohol.

Official bottlings include a **14 year old** and a **Distiller's Edition**, with an Oloroso Seco finish. Recent limited bottlings include a **26 year old** matured in refill American oak which was part of the new Prima & Ultima range launched in July 2020. In April 2021 a **16 year old** distillery exclusive (Four Corners of Scotland Clynelish) matured in ex-bourbon hogsheads was launched.

History:

1819 The 1st Duke of Sutherland founds a distillery called Clynelish Distillery.

1827 The first licensed distiller, James Harper, files for bankruptcy and John Matheson takes over.

1846 George Lawson & Sons become new licensees.

1896 James Ainslie & Heilbron takes over.

1912 James Ainslie & Co. narrowly escapes bankruptcy and Distillers Company Limited (DCL) takes over together with James Risk.

1916 John Walker & Sons buys a stake of James Risk's stocks.

1931 The distillery is mothballed.

1939 Production restarts.

1960 The distillery becomes electrified.

1967 A new distillery, also named Clynelish, is built adjacent to the first one.

1968 'Old' Clynelish is mothballed in August.

1969 'Old' Clynelish is reopened as Brora and starts using a very peaty malt.

1983 Brora is closed in March.

2002 A 14 year old is released.

2006 A Distiller's Edition 1991 finished in Oloroso casks is released.

2009 A 12 year old is released for Friends of the Classic Malts.

2010 A 1997 Manager's Choice single cask is released.

2014 Clynelish Select Reserve is released.

2015 Second version of Clynelish Select Reserve is released.

2017 The distillery produces again after a year long closure for refurbishing.

2019 Clynelish House Tyrell is released as part of the Game of Thrones series.

2020 A 26 year old Prima & Ultima is released.

2021 A 16 year old Four Corners of Scotland is launched.

16 years old
Four Corners of Scotland

Tasting notes Clynelish 14 year old:

GS – A nose that is fragrant, spicy and complex, with candle wax, malt and a whiff of smoke. Notably smooth in the mouth, with honey and contrasting citric notes, plus spicy peat, before a brine and tropical fruit finish.

Cragganmore

[crag•an•moor]

Owner: Diageo
Region/district: Speyside

Founded: 1869
Status: Active (vc)
Capacity: 2 200 000 litres

Address: Ballindalloch, Moray AB37 9AB

Website: malts.com
Tel: 01479 874700

Despite the fact that Cragganmore is one of the original six Classic Malts, it keeps a rather low profile in the Diageo portfolio. Around 200,000 bottles were sold last year with more than 90% going to the export market.

Some of the owner's big sellers have had geographical strong holds for many years – Knockando and Cardhu in southern Europe and Oban in America. Others, like Lagavulin, Talisker and the three Singletons, have in the last decades consequently been globally promoted resulting in millions of bottles sold. However, Cragganmore's absence in the very top os sales lists is compensated by its importance in a blended whisky. The heavy, complex style makes wonders in any blend much in the same way as stablemates such as Benrinnes, Mortlach, Dailuaine and Glen Elgin. All five produce a sulphury, sturdy newmake and all five use worm tubs for condensing the spirits. Cragganmore sits quite close to the Speyside artery A95 but while Ballindalloch to the east and Tormore to the west are visible from the road, Cragganmore is a distillery you have to seek out and it's worth while doing so. The visitor centre may be small but the distillery and the equipment is quite unique.

Cragganmore is equipped with a 6.8 ton stainless steel full lauter mash tun with a copper canopy and six washbacks made of Oregon pine. Since they are working a five-day week there will be six short (60 hours) and six long (90 hours) fermentations. There are two wash stills and two spirit stills, all attached to worm tubs for cooling the spirit vapours. In 2021, the production will amount to around 1.65 million litres of alcohol.

The single malt plays an important part in the Old Parr blend which was first introduced in 1909 and is very popular in Japan and Latin America. The official core range of Cragganmore is made up of a **12 year old** and a **Distiller's Edition** with a finish in port pipes. In July 2020, a **48 year old**, matured in first fill sherry (the last remaining cask from when Cragganmore used coal fired stills) was part of the new Prima & Ultima range and in the Rare by Nature series in autumn 2020 a **20 year old** appeared.

History:

1869 John Smith, who already runs Glenfarclas distillery, founds Cragganmore.

1886 John Smith dies and his brother George takes over operations.

1893 John's son Gordon, at 21, is old enough to assume responsibility for operations.

1901 The distillery is refurbished and modernized with help of the famous architect Charles Doig.

1912 Gordon Smith dies and his widow Mary Jane supervises operations.

1917 The distillery closes.

1918 The distillery reopens and Mary Jane installs electric lighting.

1923 The distillery is sold to the newly formed Cragganmore-Glenlivet Distillery Co. where Mackie & Co. and Sir George Macpherson-Grant of Ballindalloch Estate share ownership.

1927 White Horse Distillers is bought by DCL which thus obtains 50% of Cragganmore.

1964 The number of stills is increased from two to four.

1965 DCL buys the remainder of Cragganmore.

1988 Cragganmore 12 years becomes one of six selected for United Distillers´ Classic Malts.

1998 Cragganmore Distillers Edition Double Matured (port) is launched for the first time.

2002 A visitor centre opens in May.

2006 A 17 year old from 1988 is released.

2010 Manager´s Choice single cask 1997 and a limited 21 year old are released.

2014 A 25 year old is released.

2016 A Special Releases vatting without age statement and a distillery exclusive are released.

2019 A 12 year bottled at cask strength appears in the Special Releases series.

2020 A 48 year old and a 20 year old are released.

12 years old

Tasting notes Cragganmore 12 years old:

GS – A nose of sherry, brittle toffee, nuts, mild wood smoke, angelica and mixed peel. Elegant on the malty palate, with herbal and fruit notes, notably orange. Medium in length, with a drying, slightly smoky finish.

Craigellachie

[craig•ell•ack•ee]

Owner:
John Dewar & Sons (Bacardi)

Region/district:
Speyside

Founded: 1891 **Status:** Active **Capacity:** 4 100 000 litres

Address: Aberlour, Banffshire AB38 9ST

Website: craigellachie.com **Tel:** 01340 872971

Craigellachie was founded by Alexander "Sandy" Edward – one of the most dynamic entrepreneurs in Scotland during the late 19th century. Today his name has faded behind better known names of the industry such as Walker, Dewar and Bell.

At the age of 26 and together with the legendary Peter Mackie he founded Craigellachie distillery. The small town of Craigellachie was close to his heart and he believed he could contribute greatly in order to make the town prosper. At this point in time, it was popular for the English upper class to visit Scotland and hunting, amongst other pastimes, was a main attraction and Craigellachie sat conveniently beside the Strathspey railway line. In 1896 he built what would eventually become the whisky world's most legendary hotel, The Craigellachie Hotel, and he managed to do this whilst also building Aultmore and taking over Benrinnes. Two years earlier he founded Dallas Dhu and over time he gained ownership of Oban and Yoker distilleries. When he died in 1946 at the age of 81 at his Sanquhar Estate in Forres, the obituary in the Elgin Courant and Courier referred to him as "one of the oldest and best-known distillers in Scotland".

Craigellachie distillery is equipped with a 10 ton Steinecker full lauter mash tun, eight 47,000 litre washbacks made of larch with a fermentation time of 56-60 hours and two pairs of stills. Of the five malt distilleries owned by Dewar's, Craigellachie is the only one using worm tubs to condense the spirit vapours. The old cast iron tubs were exchanged for stainless steel in 2014 and the existing copper worms were moved to the new tubs. The production plan for 2021 is 21 mashes per week and 3.9 million litres of alcohol.

The core range, introduced in 2014, consists of **13, 17** and **23 year old**. A **33 year old**, originally released for duty free, has now been added to the domestic core range. Occasionally some very limited bottlings for the travel retail market are released in **The Exceptional Cask** series.

History:

1890 The distillery is built by Craigellachie–Glenlivet Distillery Company which has Alexander Edward and Peter Mackie as part-owners.

1891 Production starts.

1916 Mackie & Company Distillers Ltd takes over.

1924 Peter Mackie dies and Mackie & Company changes name to White Horse Distillers.

1927 White Horse Distillers are bought by Distillers Company Limited (DCL).

1930 Administration is transferred to Scottish Malt Distillers (SMD), a subsidiary of DCL.

1964 Refurbishing takes place and two new stills are bought, increasing the number to four.

1998 United Distillers & Vintners (UDV) sells Craigellachie together with Aberfeldy, Brackla and Aultmore and the blending company John Dewar & Sons to Bacardi Martini.

2004 The first bottlings from the new owners are a new 14 year old which replaces UDV's Flora & Fauna and a 21 year old cask strength from 1982 produced for Craigellachie Hotel.

2014 Three new bottlings for domestic markets (13, 17 and 23 years) and one for duty free (19 years) are released.

2015 A 31 year old is released.

2016 A 33 year old and a 1994 Madeira single cask are released.

2018 A 24 year old and and a 17 year old palo cortado finish are released for duty free and the oldest official Craigellachie so far, 51 years old, is launched.

2019 A 19 and a 23 year old are released.

2020 A 39 year old is launched.

2021 A 33 year old is added to the core range.

13 years old

Tasting notes Craigellachie 13 years old:

GS – Savoury on the early nose, with spent matches, green apples and mixed nuts. Malt join the nuts and apples on the palate, with sawdust and very faint smoke. Drying, with cranberries, spice and more subtle smoke.

Dailuaine

[dall•yoo•an]

Owner: Diageo   **Region/district:** Speyside

Founded: 1852   **Status:** Active   **Capacity:** 5 200 000 litres

Address: Carron, Banffshire AB38 7RE

Website: malts.com   **Tel:** 01340 872500

Dailuaine is probably not the first single malt that comes to mind if you would make a list of what you've enjoyed recently. Being one of Diageo's 28 malt distilleries, its main task is to produce malt for blends.

However in the late 1980s, well before single malt had become what it is today, United Distillers decided to release whiskies from most of their distilleries in the Rare Malts range. This was followed up in the early 1990s by the Flora & Fauna range nicknamed as such by the one and only Michael Jackson because of the labels. The whisky from all of the company's distilleries at the time was bottled as a single malt and Dailuaine was blessed with a badger on the label. Whisky enthusiasts soon fell in love with the malt which represented an archaic style of flavourful and full-bodied whisky much akin to the likes of Benrinnes and Mortlach.

Dailuaine has cemented its place in whisky history thanks to a new innovation that was tested here for the first time in 1889. At that time the architect, Charles Cree Doig, constructed the first pagoda roof (as it was named later) to make it easier to ventilate the smoke coming from the kiln. Unfortunately, the roof collapsed in 1917 but the same design can still be seen today at many of the distilleries around Scotland although the vast majority of them these days are just ornamental.

Today, the distillery is equipped with a stainless steel, 11.25 ton full lauter mash tun, eight washbacks made of Douglas fir plus two stainless steel ones placed outside and three pairs of stills. All the condensers are made of copper as usual but, until a few years ago, some were made of stainless steel to help achieve a sulphury style of new make. In 2015, the fermentation time was changed to produce a more waxy character to the spirit. The plan for 2021 is to do three short (80 hours) and nine long fermentations (107 hours) per week amounting to 2.6 million litres of pure alcohol.

The only core bottling is the **16 year old Flora & Fauna**. In 2015, a **34 year old** from 1980 was launched as part of the Special Releases.

History:

1852 The distillery is founded by William Mackenzie.

1865 William Mackenzie dies and his widow leases the distillery to James Fleming, a banker from Aberlour.

1879 William Mackenzie's son forms Mackenzie and Company with Fleming.

1891 Dailuaine-Glenlivet Distillery Ltd is founded.

1898 Dailuaine-Glenlivet Distillery Ltd merges with Talisker Distillery Ltd and forms Dailuaine-Talisker Distilleries Ltd.

1915 Thomas Mackenzie dies without heirs.

1916 Dailuaine-Talisker Company Ltd is bought by the previous customers John Dewar & Sons, John Walker & Sons and James Buchanan & Co.

1917 A fire rages and the pagoda roof collapses.

1920 The distillery reopens.

1925 Distillers Company Limited (DCL) takes over.

1960 Refurbishing. The stills increase from four to six and a Saladin box replaces the floor maltings.

1965 Indirect still heating through steam is installed.

1983 On site maltings is closed down and malt is purchased centrally.

1991 The first official bottling, a 16 year old, is launched in the Flora & Fauna series.

1996 A 22 year old cask strength from 1973 is released as a Rare Malt.

1997 A cask strength version of the 16 year old is launched.

2000 A 17 year old Manager's Dram matured in sherry casks is launched.

2010 A single cask from 1997 is released.

2012 The production capacity is increased by 25%.

2015 A 34 year old is launched as part of the Special Releases.

16 years old

Tasting notes Dailuaine 16 years old:

GS – Barley, sherry and nuts on the substantial nose, developing into maple syrup. Medium-bodied, rich and malty in the mouth, with more sherry and nuts, plus ripe oranges, fruitcake, spice and a little smoke. The finish is lengthy and slightly oily, with almonds, cedar and slightly smoky oak.

Dalmore

[dal•moor]

Owner:
Whyte & Mackay Ltd
(Emperador Inc)

Region/district:
Northern Highlands

Founded: 1839

Status: Active (vc)

Capacity: 4 300 000 litres

Address: Alness, Ross-shire IV17 0UT

Website: thedalmore.com

Tel: 01349 882362

Anyone remotely interested in whisky knows of Richard Paterson. He is the Master Blender for Whyte & Mackay and this colourful and knowledgeable gentleman joined the company in September 1970.

Those who have met him, and they are many, can testify to the passion Richard has for Scotch whisky. He has now decided to step back from the involvement in the wider Whyte & Mackay portfolio to focus solely on The Dalmore brand. The rest of the whiskies however, including malts such as Jura, Fettercairn and Tamnavulin, are in safe hands. Already in 2016 Richard chose his successor, Greg Glass, who is now responsible for the entire range bar Dalmore. An often used term for the blender who is supposed to take over from the master is apprentice. In Greg's case though that epithet doesn't cut it. During his eleven years with Compass Box he showed over and over again what an accomplished, talented and innovative blender he is.

Dalmore distillery is equipped with a 10.4 ton stainless steel, semi-lauter mash tun, eight washbacks made of Oregon pine with a fermentation time of 50 hours and four pairs of stills. The spirit stills are equipped with water jackets, which allow cold water to circulate between the reflux bowl and the neck of the stills, thus increasing the reflux. The owners expect to mash 23 times per week during 2021, producing 4.3 million litres of alcohol which is more or less less the capacity for the distillery.

The core range consists of **12, 15, 18 and 25 year old, 1263 King Alexander III, Cigar Malt Reserve** and **Port Wood Reserve**. A recent addition, in autumn 2020, is the **12 year Sherry Cask Select**. This has been matured for 10 years in ex-bourbon with another two years in a selection of ex-oloroso and ex-PX casks. In 2019, the entire travel retail range was replaced by three new bottlings, **The Trio, The Quartet** and **The Quintet**, finished in three, four and five casks respectively. Recent limited bottlings include **30, 35, 40, 45** and **51 year old**, a range called **Vintage Port Collection** with three different expressions and a **60 year old**. In August 2021 **The Dalmore Decades** was launched with three collections comprising whiskies going back to 1951..

History:

1839 Alexander Matheson founds the distillery.

1867 Three Mackenzie brothers run the distillery.

1891 Sir Kenneth Matheson sells the distillery for £14,500 to the Mackenzie brothers.

1917 The Royal Navy moves in to start manufacturing American mines.

1922 The distillery is in production again.

1956 Floor malting replaced by Saladin box.

1960 Mackenzie Brothers (Dalmore) Ltd merges with Whyte & Mackay.

1966 Number of stills is increased to eight.

1982 The Saladin box is abandoned.

1990 American Brands buys Whyte & Mackay.

1996 Whyte & Mackay changes name to JBB (Greater Europe).

2001 Through management buy-out, JBB (Greater Europe) is bought from Fortune Brands and changes name to Kyndal Spirits.

2002 Kyndal Spirits changes name to Whyte & Mackay.

2007 United Spirits buys Whyte & Mackay. A 15 year old, and a 40 year old are released.

2008 1263 King Alexander III is released.

2009 New releases include an 18 year old, a 58 year old and a Vintage 1951.

2010 The Dalmore Mackenzie 1992 is released.

2011 More expressions in the River Collection and 1995 Castle Leod are released.

2012 The visitor centre is upgraded and Constellaton Collection is launched.

2013 Valour is released for duty free.

2014 Emperador Inc buys Whyte & Mackay.

2016 Three new travel retail bottlings are released as well as a 35 year old and Quintessence.

2017 Vintage Port Collection is launched.

2018 The Port Wood Reserve is released.

2019 A new travel retail range is launched.

2020 A 51 year old is released.

2021 A 30 year old and The Dalmore Decades are released.

Tasting notes Dalmore 12 years old:

GS – The nose offers sweet malt, orange mar-malade, sherry and a hint of leather. Full-bodied, with a dry sherry taste though sweeter sherry develops in the mouth along with spice and citrus notes. Lengthy finish with more spices, ginger, Seville oranges and vanilla.

12 years old

Dalwhinnie

[dal•whin•nay]

Owner:	**Region/district:**
Diageo	Speyside
Founded: **Status:**	**Capacity:**
1897 Active (vc)	2 200 000 litres

Address: Dalwhinnie, Inverness-shire PH19 1AB

Website:	**Tel:**
malts.com	01540 672219 (vc)

Dalwhinnie is easily spotted from the A9 when the road reaches its highest point (462 metres), Drumochter Summit, in the Cairngorms. The two pagoda roofs stand out but another feature will also attract you attention – the worm tubs.

The two huge, wooden vats are placed on a white footing in the court yard. Only 15% of the distilleries in Scotland use this technique for cooling the spirit vapours and Dalwhinnie is one of them. Worm tubs were first introduced in Scotland in the mid 1500s. Before that, the distillers relied on inefficient air cooling and, later, leading the tube from the still straight through a tub of water. When the worm, a copper spiral emerged in water through which the vapours were lead, was introduced it resulted in a much more efficient cooling and a higher yield. In the second half on the 19th century, distilleries began to use shell and tube condensers which are the most common ones used today. Condensing the spirit with worm tubs, like at Dalwhinnie, Mortlach and Benrinnes, gives more sulphur because of the lesser copper contact in the worms. Longer maturation is therefore required to finally complete the elimination of sulphur.

Dalwhinnie is equipped with a 7.3 ton full lauter mash tun and six wooden washbacks with the fermentation split into four short sessions of 60 hours and six long, fermenting over the weekend, of 110 hours. There is one pair of stills, replaced in 2018, attached to worm tubs which were replaced with new ones in 2015. The production plan for 2021 is a five-day production week which means 10 mashes per week resulting in 1.4 million litres of alcohol in the year.

The core range is made up of a **15 year old, Distiller's Edition** with a finish in oloroso casks and **Dalwhinnie Winter's Gold**. In 2018, **Lizzie's Dram**, a distillery exclusive was launched. In spring 2019, Dalwhinnie was also part of the series named after the popular TV series Game of Thrones with **Winter's Frost**. Finally, in autumn 2020, a **30 year old** bottled at 51,9% was launched in the Rare by Nature range

History:

1897 John Grant, George Sellar and Alexander Mackenzie commence building the facilities. The first name is Strathspey.

1898 The owner encounters financial troubles and John Somerville & Co and A P Blyth & Sons take over and change the name to Dalwhinnie.

1905 Cook & Bernheimer in New York, buys Dalwhinnie for £1,250 at an auction.

1919 Macdonald Greenlees & Willliams Ltd headed by Sir James Calder buys Dalwhinnie.

1926 Macdonald Greenlees & Williams Ltd is bought by Distillers Company Ltd (DCL) which licences Dalwhinnie to James Buchanan & Co.

1930 Operations are transferred to Scottish Malt Distilleries (SMD).

1934 The distillery is closed after a fire in February.

1938 The distillery opens again.

1968 The maltings is decommissioned.

1987 Dalwhinnie 15 years becomes one of the selected six in United Distillers´ Classic Malts.

1991 A visitor centre is constructed.

1992 The distillery closes and goes through a major refurbishment costing £3.2 million.

1995 The distillery opens in March.

2002 A 36 year old is released.

2006 A 20 year old is released.

2012 A 25 year old is released.

2014 A triple matured bottling without age statement is released for The Friends of the Classic Malts.

2015 Dalwhinnie Winter´s Gold and a 25 year old are released.

2016 A distillery exclusive without age statement is released.

2018 Lizzie´s Dram, a distillery exclusive bottling, is released.

2019 Dalwhinnie Winter´s Frost, part of the Game of Thrones series, is released as well as a 30 year old in the annual Special Releases.

2020 A 30 year old is released as part of the Rare by Nature series.

15 years old

Tasting notes Dalwhinnie 15 years old:

GS – The nose is fresh, with pine needles, heather and vanilla. Sweet and balanced on the fruity palate, with honey, malt and a very subtle note of peat. The medium length finish dries elegantly.

Deanston

[deen•stun]

Owner: Distell International Ltd.

Region/district: Southern Highlands

Founded: 1965

Status: Active (vc)

Capacity: 3 000 000 litres

Address: Deanston, Perthshire FK16 6AG

Website: deanstonmalt.com

Tel: 01786 843010

During its 180 years as a cotton mill, Deanston (or Adelphi as it was called in the start) was powered by water wheels using the water from the river Teith. At one time there were eight wheels supplying the plant with electricity.

One of them, Hercules, was the largest in Europe measuring more than 11 metres in diameter. Footage of the colossal wheel in action is included as part of the distillery tour. In 1949 the last water wheel was replaced by modern hydro turbines and in 2020 the turbine was replaced by a more efficient one. The turbine not only powers the distillery but the surplus power produced is sold to the national grid.

Deanston is equipped with a 10.5 ton traditional open top, stainless steel mash tun with rakes and eight stainless steel washbacks. Four of the washbacks have stainless steel lids while the other four have wooden lids. The fermentation time is 85 hours. There are also two pairs of stills with ascending lyne arms. In 2020 the distillery worked 5 days per week and that lasted until March 2021 when a 7-day week was resumed. This will mean a total of 2,3 million litres of pure alcohol. Having started in 2000, organic spirit is produced every year. Due to the demand for "traditional" Deanston single malt, the volume of organic spirit has been reduced to around 10,000 litres per year.

The core range is a **12** and an **18 year old**, the **Virgin Oak** matured in ex-bourbon and with a finish in virgin oak casks and the **15 year old Organic**. New additions in 2021 were **Kentucky Cask**, an entry level expression without age statement and **Dragon's Milk** which had been finished in stout casks from New Holland Brewing Company. Recent limited bottlings, released in July 2020, include a **1991 Muscat finish**, a **2002 Organic Pedro Ximenez** and a **2002 Pinot Noir finish**. The only available duty-free exclusive is a **10 year old Bordeaux red wine cask finish**. Finally, there are two recent distillery exclusives – a **2002 Port finish** and a **2007 Calvados finish**.

History:

1965 A weavery from 1785 is transformed into Deanston Distillery by James Findlay & Co. and Brodie Hepburn Ltd.

1966 Production commences in October.

1971 The first single malt is named Old Bannockburn.

1972 Invergordon Distillers takes over.

1974 The first single malt bearing the name Deanston is produced.

1982 The distillery closes.

1990 Burn Stewart Distillers from Glasgow buys the distillery for £2.1 million.

1991 The distillery resumes production.

1999 C L Financial buys an 18% stake of Burn Stewart.

2002 C L Financial acquires the remaining stake.

2006 Deanston 30 years old is released.

2009 A new version of the 12 year old is released.

2010 Virgin Oak is released.

2012 A visitor centre is opened.

2013 Burn Stewart Distillers is bought by South African Distell Group for £160m

2014 An 18 year old cognac finish is released.

2015 An 18 year old is released.

2016 Organic Deanston is released.

2017 A 40 year old and Vintage 2008 are released.

2018 A 10 year old Bordeaux finish is released for duty free.

2019 1997 Palo Cortado finish, 2006 Cream Sherry finish and a 2012 Beer finish are launched.

2020 A 1991 Muscat finish, a 2002 Organix PX and a 2002 Pinot Noir finish are released.

2021 Kentucky Cask and Dragon´s Milk are released.

12 years old

Tasting notes Deanston 12 years old:

GS – A fresh, fruity nose with malt and honey. The palate displays cloves, ginger, honey and malt, while the finish is long, quite dry and pleasantly herbal.

Dufftown

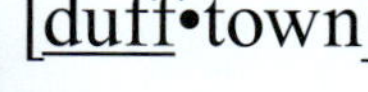

[duff•town]

Owner:
Diageo

Region/district:
Speyside

Founded: 1896

Status: Active

Capacity: 6 000 000 litres

Address: Dufftown, Keith, Banffshire AB55 4BR

Website:
malts.com
thesingleton.com

Tel:
01340 822100

The Malt Whisky Yearbook prides itself on being objective and unbiased. That is why these following lines may seem a bit unusual: the 8 year old Dufftown-Glenlivet was the first single malt I bought with my own money.

I picked it up in London in the summer of 1980 and shared it with a friend on the sleeper to Inverness. The following week, renting a car and driving along the Whisky Trail sent me on a life-long journey of love for Scotch malt whisky. Forty years on, I find myself tasting a whisky from Dufftown distillery that was distilled in 1966 and bottled in 2020. Aged for 54 years and finished in a PX-cask, this is not only the oldest ever bottling from Dufftown – it is also the oldest official bottling of a Diageo single malt!

Of the 28 malt distilleries owned by Diageo, Dufftown is the fifth largest in terms of capacity. In fact, before Roseisle opened in 2009, it was the biggest together with Caol Ila. The distillery is equipped with a 13 ton full lauter mash tun, 12 stainless steel washbacks and three pairs of stills. Furthermore, all stills have sub coolers. The style of Dufftown single malt is green and grassy which is achieved by a clear wort and long fermentation (75 hours minimum). In a seven-day week, no less than 165 still runs are completed (110 in the wash stills and 55 in the spirits stills) which clearly shows what a busy distillery it is. Dufftown has been working 24/7 since 2007 and during 2021 the plan is to produce 6 million litres of alcohol.

The core range consists of **The Singleton of Dufftown 12, 15** and **18 year old**. A new expression was added to the line-up two years ago – **Malt Master's Selection**. Without age statement, the whisky has been matured in a combination of bourbon and sherry casks. A range for duty-free consists of **Trinité, Liberté** and **Artisan**. In autumn 2019 a **53 year old** was released in the series Paragon of Time Collection, in July 2020 a **30 year old** was part of the new Prima & Ultima range and in the autumn, a **17 year old** was part of the Rare by Nature series. Finally, in June 2021 – the **54 old** Singleton of Dufftown was released.

History:

1895 Peter Mackenzie, Richard Stackpole, John Symon and Charles MacPherson build the distillery Dufftown-Glenlivet in an old mill.

1896 Production starts in November.

1897 The distillery is owned by P. Mackenzie & Co., who also owns Blair Athol in Pitlochry.

1933 P. Mackenzie & Co. is bought by Arthur Bell & Sons for £56,000.

1968 The floor maltings is discontinued and malt is bought from outside suppliers. The number of stills is increased from two to four.

1974 The number of stills is increased from four to six.

1979 The stills are increased by a further two to eight.

1985 Guinness buys Arthur Bell & Sons.

1997 Guinness and Grand Metropolitan merge to form Diageo.

2006 The Singleton of Dufftown 12 year old is launched as a special duty free bottling.

2008 The Singleton of Dufftown is made available also in the UK.

2010 A Manager's Choice 1997 is released.

2013 A 28 year old cask strength and two expressions for duty free - Unité and Trinité - are released.

2014 Tailfire, Sunray and Spey Cascade are released.

2016 Two limited releases are made - a 21 year old and a 25 year old.

2018 Malt Master's Selection is released.

2020 A 30 year old Prima & Ultima and a 17 year old Rare by Nature are released.

2021 A 54 year old is released.

Tasting notes Dufftown 12 years old:

GS – The nose is sweet, almost violet-like, with underlying malt. Big and bold on the palate, this is an upfront yet very drinkable whisky. The finish is medium to long, warming, spicy, with slowly fading notes of sherry and fudge.

Singleton of Dufftown 12 year

Edradour

[ed•ra•<u>dow</u>•er]

Owner:
Signatory Vintage
Scotch Whisky Co. Ltd

Region/district:
Southern Highland

Founded: **Status:** **Capacity:**
1825 Active (vc) 260 000 litres

Address: Pitlochry, Perthshire PH16 5JP

Website: **Tel:**
edradour.com 01796 472095

The owner of Edradour is the "independent bottler" Signatory Vintage but the irony is that in spite of what the label implies, nowadays these companies enjoy much less independency than they used to do.

The definition of an independent bottler is that they don't have a distillery of their own but instead buy casks from other producers and bottle them under their own label. Due to a growing consumer interest in single malt, whisky producers have become more reluctant over the years to sell casks to others. Signatory anticipated this early on and in 2002 they bought Edradour to level out the risks. The distillery however was very small and in 2018 a second distillery was commissioned which doubled the capacity. At that time Signatory Vintage represented 60% of the company's turnover but the gap is closing and the owners are working to make Edradour single malt the main source of revenue in the future.

Since 2018, the combined equipment for the two distilleries consists of two open, traditional cast iron mash tuns with a mash size of 1.1 tons, two Morton refrigerators to cool the wort and eight washbacks made of Oregon pine, with enough room left to install more in the future. The two stills in each distillery are attached to worm tubs on the outside and new warehouses have also been erected next to the new still house. Lately, Edradour has been doing 5 mashes per week at each distillery with three short at 48 hours and two long at 96 hours. This will equate to 200,000 litres of alcohol. Due to rapidly increasing demand for the unpeated Edradour, the amount of peated production has diminished in the last couple of years with only around 10 to 15,000 litres being distilled per year.

The core range consists of a **10 year old** and the **12 year old Caledonia Selection**. Both are vattings of 1ˢᵗ and 2ⁿᵈ fill Oloroso casks. In the range are also recurrent versions of **Cask Strength Sherry** and **Cask Strength Bourbon**, often between 10 and 13 years old. There is also the peated **Ballechin 10 year old**. The Ibisco Decanter range are all fully matured in different casks. Some of the latest include a **13 year old Bourbon** from 2007 and a **12 year old Sherry** distilled in 2009. Recent wood finishes include **21 year old Bordeaux** and **21 year old Barolo**.

History:

1825 Probably the year when a distillery called Glenforres is founded by farmers in Perthshire.

1837 The first year Edradour is mentioned.

1841 The farmers form a proprietary company, John MacGlashan & Co.

1886 John McIntosh & Co. acquires Edradour.

1933 William Whiteley & Co. buys the distillery.

1982 Campbell Distilleries (Pernod Ricard) buys Edradour and builds a visitor centre.

1986 The first single malt is released.

2002 Edradour is bought by Andrew Symington from Signatory for £5.4 million. The product range is expanded with a 10 year old and a 13 year old cask strength.

2003 A 30 year old and a 10 year old are released.

2004 A number of wood finishes are launched as cask strength.

2006 The first bottling of peated Ballechin is released.

2007 A Madeira matured Ballechin is released.

2008 A Ballechin matured in Port pipes and a 10 year old Edradour with a Sauternes finish are released.

2009 Fourth edition of Ballechin (Oloroso) is released.

2010 Ballechin #5 Marsala is released.

2011 Ballechin #6 Bourbon and a 26 year old PX sherry finish are relased.

2012 A 1993 Oloroso and a 1993 Sauternes finish as well as the 7ᵗʰ edition of Ballechin (Bordeaux) are released.

2013 Ballechin Sauternes is released.

2014 The first release of a 10 year old Ballechin.

2015 Fairy Flag is released.

2017 New releases include an 8 year old vatting of Edradour and Ballechin.

2018 The new distillery is commissioned.

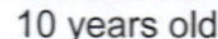

10 years old

Tasting notes Edradour 10 years old:

GS – Cider apples, malt, almonds, vanilla and honey ar present on the nose, along with a hint of smoke and sherry. The palate is rich, creamy and malty, with a persistent nuttiness and quite a pronounced kick of slightly leathery sherry. Spices and sherry dominate the medium to long finish.

Fettercairn

[fett•er•cairn]

Owner: Whyte & Mackay (Emperador)

Region/district: Eastern Highlands

Founded: 1824

Status: Active (vc)

Capacity: 2 200 000 litres

Address: Fettercairn, Laurencekirk, Kincardineshire AB30 1YB

Website: fettercairnwhisky.com

Tel: 01561 340205

In 1952 Alistair Menzies, the distillery manager at the time, decided to change the character of the Fettercairn new make to make it lighter and more fruity. His way of doing it turned out to be quite unique.

He added a cooling ring to the spirit still which sprayed the head of the still with water which was then collected at the base for circulation towards the top again. This effectively increased the reflux during distillation. The effect however would years later be mitigated by another installation of equipment – stainless steel condensers. These made the spirit robust with a burnt note. The steel condensers have not been used since 1995 while the the cooling ring is still very much in place.

The current manager of the distillery is Stewart Walker who was born and bred in Fettercairn. He started as a warehouseman in 1990, became brewer in 2003 and manager in 2015. In the 2021 Icons of Whisky Scotland he won the Distillery Manager of the Year award.

Fettercairn distillery is equipped with a traditional, five ton cast iron mash tun and eleven washbacks with a fermentation time of 60 hours. There are also two pairs of stills. During 2020 they managed to make 1,5 million litres of pure alcohol and the production goal for 2021 is 24 mashes per week and a total of 2,1 million litres.

The core range consists of **12, 16, 22** and **28 year old**. The 16 year old, made from chocolate malt and finished for two years in both sherry and port casks, was first released in summer 2020 and a new batch with a different recipe appeared in November 2021. The 22 year old, matured in first fill ex-bourbon, was also a new addition in 2020. Older versions in the range include **40, 46** and **50 year old**. In March 2021 the first in a new series named **Warehouse 2** was released. **Batch No. 1**, matured in a combination of bourbon, sherry and port casks, was followed in August by **Batch No. 2**. For the duty free market there is a **12 year old PX sherry finish** as well as a one litre version of the **16 year old** and a **23 year old**.

History:

1824 Sir Alexander Ramsay founds the distillery.

1830 Sir John Gladstone buys the distillery.

1887 A fire erupts and the distillery closes for repair.

1890 Thomas Gladstone dies and his son John Robert takes over. The distillery reopens.

1912 John Gladstone buys out the other investors.

1926 The distillery is mothballed.

1939 The distillery is bought by Associated Scottish Distillers Ltd. Production restarts.

1960 The maltings discontinues.

1966 The stills are increased from two to four.

1971 The distillery is bought by Tomintoul-Glenlivet Distillery Co. Ltd.

1973 Tomintoul-Glenlivet Distillery Co. Ltd is bought by Whyte & Mackay Distillers Ltd.

1974 The mega group of companies Lonrho buys Whyte & Mackay.

1988 Lonrho sells to Brent Walker Group plc.

1989 A visitor centre opens.

1990 American Brands Inc. buys Whyte & Mackay for £160 million.

1996 Whyte & Mackay and Jim Beam Brands merge to become JBB Worldwide.

2001 Kyndal Spirits buys Whyte & Mackay from JBB Worldwide.

2002 The whisky changes name to Fettercairn 1824.

2003 Kyndal Spirits changes name to Whyte & Mackay.

2007 United Spirits buys Whyte & Mackay. A 23 year old single cask is released.

2009 24, 30 and 40 year olds are released.

2010 Fettercairn Fior is launched.

2012 Fettercairn Fasque is released.

2015 Emperador Inc buys Whyte & Mackay.

2018 A new range is launched; 12, 28, 40 and 50 year old.

2019 A 12 year old PX finish is released for duty free.

2020 A 16 year old and a 22 year old are added to the core range.

2021 Two first batches of Warehouse 2 are released.

Tasting notes Fettercairn 12 years old:

IR – A delicious combination of pineapple, banana and mango together with coffee beans, cured ham and dried flowers. Still fruity on the palate but also becomes more spicy and malty and with a bit of mint at the end.

12 years old

Glenallachie

[glen•<u>alla</u>•key]

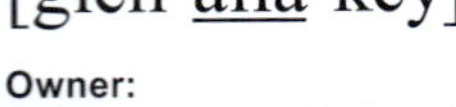

Owner:	**Region/district:**
The Glenallachie Distillers Co.	Speyside
Founded: **Status:**	**Capacity:**
1967 Active (vc)	4 000 000 litres

Address: Aberlour, Banffshire AB38 9LR

Website: **Tel:**
www.theglenallachie.com   01236 422120

When Billy Walker took over BenRiach in 2004 and later GlenDronach and Glenglassaugh, he spent the first time nosing through the inventory to get to know the character and get a sense of what he would be able to achieve in the future.

The procedure was repeated after he had bought GlenAllachie. With almost 50,000 casks in the warehouses when he took over, it was an extensive task to fulfill. The robust Glenallachie spirit is ideal for long maturations but can also cope with finishes in a wide range of casks without being overpowered.

The distillery is equipped with a 9.4 ton semi-lauter mash tun, six washbacks made of mild steel, but lined with stainless steel, plus another two washbacks made from stainless steel which were brought in from Caperdonich when that was demolished. The latter two have now been converted to low wines and feints vessels for peated and unpeated spirit to facilitate the switch between the two styles. There are also two pairs of unusually wide stills with horizontal condensers. Distilling 700,000 litres in a distillery built to make 4 million litres allows for very long fermentations – in GlenAllachie's case up to 160 hours. 100,000 litres of heavily peated spirit with an 80ppm phenol specification is also made.

The Glenallachie core range consists of a **10 year old cask strength** (currently batch 5), **12, 15** and **18 year old.** Added to the range in autumn 2020 was a **21 year old cask strength** matured in PX casks and in May 2021, a **30 year old cask strength** from PX, oloroso and chinquapin virgin oak appeared. Recent limited expressions include three 12 year olds making up the **Virgin Oak Finish** series (French, Spanish and Chinquapin) released in October 2020 and they were followed up by a **Wine Cask Finish** series in April 2021 including Grattamaco, Sauternes and Rioja. Various single cask bottlings have also been released for selected markets. Finally there are two peated, blended malts (12 and 21 year old) called MacNair's Lum Reek. The name MacNair is also used for a new range of rum, launched in July 2021 – 7 year old, 7 year old peated and 15 year old.

History:

1967 The distillery is founded by Mackinlay, McPherson & Co., a subsidiary of Scottish & Newcastle Breweries Ltd. William Delmé Evans is architect.

1985 Scottish & Newcastle Breweries Ltd sells Charles Mackinlay Ltd to Invergordon Distillers which acquires both Glenallachie and Isle of Jura.

1987 The distillery is decommissioned.

1989 Campbell Distillers (Pernod Ricard) buys the distillery, increases the number of stills from two to four and takes up production again.

2005 The first official bottling for many years is a Cask Strength Edition from 1989.

2017 Glenallachie Distillery Edition is released and the distillery is sold to The Glenallachie Consortium.

2018 A series of single casks is released followed by a core range consisting of 12, 18 and 25 year old.

2019 A range of wood finishes is launched as well as a 15 year old core bottling. A visitor centre is opened.

2020 A 21 year old cask strength and three new wood finishes are launched; rye, port and moscatel.

2021 A 30 year old cask strength and the Wine Cask Finish series are launched.

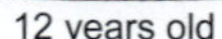

12 years old

Tasting notes Glenallachie 12 years old:

IR – Baked apples with almonds and custard, lemon zest and pine needles on the nose. Rich and lively on the palate, sweet spices, ginger, bananas, liquorice, raisins and hints of pepper.

Glenburgie

[glen•<u>bur</u>•gee]

Owner:	**Region/district:**
Chivas Brothers	Speyside
(Pernod Ricard)	
Founded: **Status:**	**Capacity:**
1810 Active	4 250 000 litres

Address: Glenburgie, Forres, Morayshire IV36 2QY

Website: **Tel:**
- 01343 850258

For a long time there have been semi-official bottlings of Glenburgie single malt from Gordon & MacPhail (mainly a 10 year old) and other independent bottlers have also released their fair share. The owners themselves have been more reluctant.

There have been a few cask strength versions but only available at Chivas Brothers' visitor centres. Fans of Glenburgie single malt, which are quite a few, were therefore delighted when a 15 year old was released in 2017 in a new range called Ballantine's Single Malt Scotch. Two other distilleries, Miltonduff and Glentauchers, were also represented and the idea was to highlight the three signature malts that set the flavour profile of the world's second best selling blend. The distance behind the number one, Johnnie Walker, is considerable but during the difficult year 2020 when most brands struggled, Ballantines did comparatively well. The decline stayed at 9% and 84 million bottles while Johnnie Walker lost 23% of its volumes having sold 169 million.

For slightly more than two decades, 1958-1981, two Lomond stills were operative at Glenburgie. Instead of the traditional swan neck, they had columns with a number of adjustable plates inside. The whisky from these stills is known as Glencraig.

Glenburgie is equipped with a 7.5 ton full lauter mash tun, 12 stainless steel washbacks and three pairs of stills. In older days, the fermentation time used to be around 70 hours, but has now been reduced to 52. The majority of the production is filled into bourbon casks and a part thereof is matured in four dunnage, two racked and two palletized warehouses.

There are two official bottlings of Glenburgie – **15** and **18 year old** both aged in ex-bourbon casks and bottled at 40%. A **17 year old cask strength** in the range The Distillery Reserve Collection is also available at Chivas' visitor centres.

History:

1810 William Paul founds Kilnflat Distillery. Official production starts in 1829.

1870 Kilnflat distillery closes.

1878 The distillery reopens under the name Glenburgie-Glenlivet, Charles Hay is licensee.

1884 Alexander Fraser & Co. takes over.

1925 Alexander Fraser & Co. files for bankruptcy and the receiver Donald Mustad assumes control of operations.

1927 James & George Stodart Ltd (owned by James Barclay and R A McKinlay since 1922) buys the distillery which by this time is inactive.

1930 Hiram Walker buys 60% of James & George Stodart Ltd.

1936 Hiram Walker buys Glenburgie Distillery in October. Production restarts.

1958 Lomond stills are installed producing a single malt, Glencraig. Floor malting ceases.

1981 The Lomond stills are replaced by conventional stills.

1987 Allied Lyons buys Hiram Walker.

2002 A 15 year old is released.

2004 A £4.3 million refurbishment and reconstruction takes place.

2005 Chivas Brothers (Pernod Ricard) becomes the new owner through the acquisition of Allied Domecq.

2006 The number of stills are increased from four to six in May.

2017 A 15 year old is released.

2019 An 18 year old is released.

15 years old

Tasting notes Glenburgie 15 years old:

IR – Very fruity on the nose with notes of pears, apple pie, honey, marzipan and roasted nuts. The palate reveals tropical fruits, white chocolate, marmalade, vanilla and caramel.

Glencadam

[glen•ka•dam]

Owner:
Angus Dundee Distillers

Region/district:
Eastern Highlands

Founded: **Status:**
1825   Active

Capacity:
1 300 000 litres

Address: Brechin, Angus DD9 7PA

Website:
glencadamwhisky.com

Tel:
01356 622217

An astonishing addition to Glencadam distillery was installed in May 2021. Right in the heart of the distillery there is now a water wheel running and its purpose is not just to charm the visitors but to supply the distillery with electricity.

When Glencadam was built in 1825 it was equipped with a water wheel and it operated for nearly a century. As Angus Dundee took over the ownership in 2003, a key thing was to reinstate the wheel. A local engineer was commissioned to construct the wheel from stainless steel and wood and, measuring 4,3 metres in diameter and with 32 wooden buckets, it was built in four quarters to be able to fit it into the narrow spot where the original had been operating. The wheel takes its water from Barrie's Burn and it will become the centrepiece of the new visitor centre that is about to be built. The current office building will be extended with a shop and visitor centre on the ground floor and a café and outdoor terrace on the first floor.

Glencadam, together with Tomintoul, is owned by Angus Dundee Distillers which is controlled by the Hillman family. The founder, Terry Hillman is now in his late eighties and his two children Tania and Aaron are responsible for the daily business.

The equipment consists of a traditional, 4.9 ton cast iron mash tun, six stainless steel washbacks with a fermentation time of 52 hours and one pair of stills. On site, two dunnage warehouses from 1825, three from the 1950s and one modern racked can be found. The distillery is currently working a 7-day week, which enables 16 mashes per week and 1.3 million litres of alcohol. The owners also produce a large number of blends. These are blended in 16 huge steel tanks next to the distillery. From here the spirit is sent to the bottling plant in Coatbridge east of Glasgow.

The core range consists of **Origin 1825, Reserva Andalucia, 10, 13, 15, 21** and **25 year old**. Two wood finishes (17 year old port finish and a 19 year old oloroso finish) were discontinued in 2021. Rare single cask bottlings are also regularly released, usually aged between 25 and 35 years old.

History:

1825   George Cooper founds the distillery.

1827   David Scott takes over.

1837   The distillery is sold by David Scott.

1852   Alexander Miln Thompson becomes the owner.

1857   Glencadam Distillery Company is formed.

1891   Gilmour, Thompson & Co Ltd takes over.

1954   Hiram Walker takes over.

1959   Refurbishing of the distillery.

1987   Allied Lyons buys Hiram Walker Gooderham & Worts.

1994   Allied Lyons changes name to Allied Domecq.

2000   The distillery is mothballed.

2003   Allied Domecq sells the distillery to Angus Dundee Distillers.

2005   The new owner releases a 15 year old.

2008   A re-designed 15 year old and a new 10 year old are introduced.

2009   A 25 and a 30 year old are released in limited numbers.

2010   A 12 year old port finish, a 14 year old sherry finish, a 21 year old and a 32 year old are released.

2012   A 30 year old is released.

2015   A 25 year old is launched.

2016   Origin 1825, 17 year old port finish, 19 year old oloroso finish, an 18 year old and a 25 year old are released.

2017   A 13 year old is released.

2019   The 15 year old is back in the range and batch two of the 25 year old is released.

2020   Reserva Andalucia is released.

10 years old

Tasting notes Glencadam 10 years old:

GS – A light and delicate, floral nose, with tinned pears and fondant cream. Medium-bodied, smooth, with citrus fruits and gently-spiced oak on the palate. The finish is quite long and fruity, with a hint of barley.

GlenDronach

[glen•<u>dro</u>•nack]

Owner: **Region/district:**
Benriach Distillery Co   Highlands
(Brown Forman)

Founded: **Status:**   **Capacity:**
1826   Active (vc)   2 000 000 litres

Address: Forgue, Aberdeenshire AB54 6DB

Website: **Tel:**
glendronachdistillery.com   01466 730202

Things are starting to heat up at GlenDronach. For many years now, the distillery has been working a 5-day week producing around 1,3 million litres of alcohol. Since last year, production has increased to 27 mashes per week and two million litres.

It looks like the owners are forecasting an increase in future demands and when you look at the sales figures it becomes quite obvious. Ten years ago Glendronach was selling 200,000 bottles – the same as its stablemate Benriach. Since then sales of Glendronach has increased by 420% to 1 million bottles while Benriach "only" managed to double the figures during the same period, reaching 400,000 bottles. Without giving any details, the owners have indicated some big changes at GlenDronach distillery within the next five years.

The distillery equipment consists of a 3.7 ton cast iron mash tun with rakes, nine washbacks made of larch with a fermentation time of 50 to 65 hours and two pairs of stills. The visitor centre was completely renovated in early 2020 and includes a new tasting room, whisky bar, lounge area and a shop. There is also a display with old and rare bottles including the distillery's oldest bottle of GlenDronach from 1913.

The core range is **The Hielan 8 years, Original 12 years, Revival 15 years, Allardice 18 years, Parliament 21 years** and **Traditionally Peated**. Recent limited releases include **Cask Strength Batch 9** (released in spring 2021), the 10th edition of the **27 year old Grandeur, Port Wood, Peated Port Wood, Master Vintage 1993** (a combination of oloroso and PX casks) and **Kingsmans Edition Vintage 1991**. In December 2020, batch 18 of the **Cask Bottlings** was launched including no less than **18 single casks** aged between 11 and 30 years. The first GlenDronach for duty free appeared in autumn 2018 when **10 year old Forgue** was launched followed in May 2019 by the **16 year old Boynsmill** using port pipes to supplement the sherried profile.

History:

1826 The distillery is founded by a consortium with James Allardes as one of the owners.

1837 Parts of the distillery is destroyed in a fire.

1852 Walter Scott (from Teaninich) takes over.

1887 Walter Scott dies and Glendronach is taken over by a consortium from Leith.

1920 Charles Grant buys Glendronach for £9,000.

1960 William Teacher & Sons buys the distillery.

1966 The number of stills is increased to four.

1976 Allied Breweries takes over William Teacher & Sons.

1996 The distillery is mothballed.

2002 Production is resumed on 14th May.

2005 The distillery closes to rebuild from coal to indirect firing by steam. Reopens in September. Chivas Brothers (Pernod Ricard) becomes new owner through the acquisition of Allied Domecq.

2008 Pernod Ricard sells the distillery to the owners of BenRiach distillery.

2009 Relaunch of the whole range including 12, 15 and 18 year old.

2010 A 31 year old, a 1996 single cask and a total of 11 vintages and four wood finishes are released. A visitor centre is opened.

2011 The 21 year old Parliament and 11 vintages are released.

2012 A number of vintages are released.

2013 Recherché 44 years and a number of new vintages are released.

2014 Nine different single casks are released.

2015 The Hielan, 8 years old, is released.

2016 Brown Forman buys the distillery. Peated GlenDronach and Octaves Classic are released.

2017 A range of new single casks is released.

2018 Two bottlings for duty free are released - 10 year old Forgue and 16 year old Boynsmill.

2019 Port Wood, Traditionally Peated and batch 18 of the Cask Bottlings are released.

2021 Cask Strength batch 9 is released.

12 years old Original

Tasting notes GlenDronach 12 years old:

GS – A sweet nose of Christmas cake fresh from the oven. Smooth on the palate, with sherry, soft oak, fruit, almonds and spices. The finish is comparatively dry and nutty, ending with bitter chocolate.

Glendullan

[glen•<u>dull</u>•an]

Owner:	**Region/district:**
Diageo	Speyside
Founded: **Status:**	**Capacity:**
1897 Active	5 000 000 litres

Address: Dufftown, Keith, Banffshire AB55 4DJ

Website:	**Tel:**
thesingleton.com	01340 822100

Built by a whisky blender in 1896, Glendullan distillery continued to be a part of the anonymous blending business for more than a century. Then, in 2007, the whisky became a brand of its own – The Singleton of Glendullan.

But let's go back to the beginning. The founder, a blender from Aberdeen by the name of William Williams, was well acquainted with the owners of Glenfiddich, the Grant family, and when Glenfiddich started producing in 1888, an agreement was made where Williams bought the entire volume produced at the distillery. This contract was dissolved in 1890, when the two parties had differing opinions about the terms and conditions. Two years later, when the Grants founded Balvenie, Williams approached them again, looking for a new agreement but was rejected. Finally he had no alternative other than to build his own distillery, Glendullan, on a site by the river Fiddich just one kilometre south of Glenfiddich. The working distillery we see today is of a much later date, built in 1972 and the two plants operated simultaneously until 1985 when the old distillery was closed. The old buildings are now used by Diageo's distillery engineering team.

The distillery is equipped with a 12 ton full lauter stainless steel mash tun, 8 washbacks made of larch and two made of stainless steel with a fermentation time of 75 hours as well as three pairs of stills. In 2021 the distillery will be doing 21 mashes per week, producing 5 million litres of alcohol. Of the three Singletons (Glen Ord and Dufftown being the other two) Glendullan, producing a green/grassy newmake, is definitely the lightest.

The core range consists of **12, 15** and **18 year old**. The Singleton Reserve Collection with **Classic** (American oak), **Double Matured** (American and European oak and then married together) and **Master's Art** (Muscat finish) is exclusive to duty free. The most recent limited expressions include a **19 year old**, part of the Rare by Nature series and with a finish in cognac casks and a **28 year old** Prima & Ultima with a 14 year second maturation in madeira casks. Both appeared in autumn 2021.

History:

1896 William Williams & Sons, a blending company with Three Stars and Strahdon among its brands, founds the distillery.

1902 Glendullan is delivered to the Royal Court and becomes the favourite whisky of Edward VII.

1919 Macdonald Greenlees buys a share of the company and Macdonald Greenlees & Williams Distillers is formed.

1926 Distillers Company Limited (DCL) buys Glendullan.

1930 Glendullan is transferred to Scottish Malt Distillers (SMD).

1962 Major refurbishing and reconstruction.

1972 A brand new distillery is constructed next to the old one and both operate simultaneously during a few years.

1985 The oldest of the two distilleries is mothballed.

1995 The first launch of Glendullan in the Rare Malts series is a 22 year old from 1972.

2005 A 26 year old from 1978 is launched in the Rare Malts series.

2007 Singleton of Glendullan is launched in the USA.

2013 Singleton of Glendullan Liberty and Trinity are released for duty free.

2014 A 38 year old is released.

2015 Classic, Double Matured and Master´s Art are released.

2018 The Forgotten Drops 40 years old is released.

2019 House of Tully, part of the Game of Thrones series, as well as a 41 year old are released.

2021 A 19 year old with a cognac finish and a 28 year old with a second maturation in madeira casks are released.

12 years old

Tasting notes Singleton of Glendullan 12 years:

GS – The nose is spicy, with brittle toffee, vanilla, new leather and hazelnuts. Spicy and sweet on the smooth palate, with citrus fruits, more vanilla and fresh oak. Drying and pleasingly peppery in the finish.

Glen Elgin

[glen el•gin]

Owner:
Diageo

Region/district:
Speyside

Founded: **Status:** **Capacity:**
1898 Active 2 700 000 litres

Address: Longmorn, Morayshire IV30 8SL

Website: **Tel:**
malts.com 01343 862100

The vast majority of Scottish blended brands took a severe beating in terms of sales during the pandemic year of 2020. Many of them lost more than 10 percent of their volumes in just twelve months. But there were a few exceptions to be found.

At least since the 1920s, Glen Elgin has been one of the most important malts in the White Horse blend and this world famous Scotch managed to grow the volumes during 2020 by no less than 20% to 25 million bottles sold. You may wonder why this particular brand fared so well in a turbulent year. One of the reasons could be the momentum for the brand. In five years sales have increased by more than 60% and it's easier to struggle through hard times in a tailwind. A second reason is that lower priced spirits are preferred by customers when the future is uncertain. Finally, White Horse isn't as exposed as Johnnie Walker Black and Chivas Regal to the travel retail market which more or less vanished during 2020. The re-born White Horse blend has made an impressive journey during the past five years where it has overtaken seven of its worst competitors and is now in the 11th place on the top list.

Glen Elgin distillery, hidden away in the tiny hamlet of Fogwatt on the A941 between Elgin and Rothes, is equipped with an 8.4 ton Steinecker full lauter mash tun, nine washbacks made of larch and six small stills. The stills are connected to six wooden worm tubs in which the spirit vapours are condensed. Although worm tubs might indicate a heavy and perhaps sulphury newmake, the long fermentation (between 80 and 120 hours) and the slow distillation produce a fruity spirit with depth, perfect for a blended whisky. The distillery alternates between 12 and 16 mashes in a five-day week which interprets to 1.8 million litres of alcohol.

The only official bottling is a **12 year old**, but a limited **18 year old**, matured in ex-bodega European oak butts was one of the Special Releases in 2017.

History:

1898 The former manager of Glenfarclas, William Simpson and banker James Carle found Glen Elgin.

1900 Production starts in May but the distillery closes just five months later.

1901 The distillery is auctioned for £4,000 to the Glen Elgin-Glenlivet Distillery Co. and is mothballed.

1906 The wine producer J. J. Blanche & Co. buys the distillery for £7,000 and production resumes.

1929 J. J. Blanche dies and the distillery is put up for sale again.

1930 Scottish Malt Distillers (SMD) buys it and the license goes to White Horse Distillers.

1964 Expansion from two to six stills plus other refurbishing takes place.

1992 The distillery closes for refurbishing and installation of new stills.

1995 Production resumes in September.

2001 A 12 year old is launched in the Flora & Fauna series.

2002 The Flora & Fauna series malt is replaced by Hidden Malt 12 years.

2003 A 32 year old cask strength from 1971 is released.

2008 A 16 year old is launched as a Special Release.

2009 Glen Elgin 1998, a single cask in the new Manager´s Choice range is released.

2017 An 18 year old is launched as part of the Special Releases.

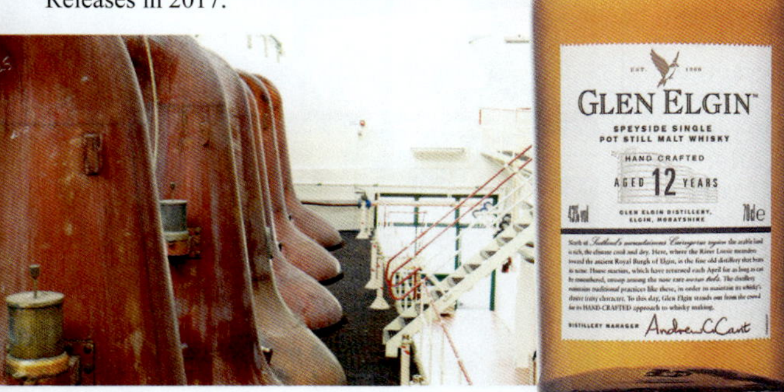

12 years old

Tasting notes Glen Elgin 12 years old:

GS – A nose of rich, fruity sherry, figs and fragrant spice. Full-bodied, soft, malty and honeyed in the mouth. The finish is lengthy, slightly perfumed, with spicy oak.

Glenfarclas

[glen•<u>fark</u>•lass]

Owner:
J. & G. Grant

Region/district:
Speyside

Founded: 1836

Status:
Active (vc)

Capacity:
3 500 000 litres

Address: Ballindalloch, Banffshire AB37 9BD

Website:
glenfarclas.com

Tel:
01807 500257

This year, Glenfarclas celebrates its 185th anniversary and the Grants have been a part of that journey since 1865. The perks of being family-owned is that you can walk your own way, caring about the consumers but not having to worry about share holders.

Glenfarclas single malt is old style in the best sense of the word. In his excellent book "The World Atlas of Whisky", Dave Broom describes it as "having a feeling of permanence". Apparently the customers like this because on the sales list of single malts, Glenfarclas is in spot 13, just after Lagavulin and ahead of brands such as Highland Park and Bowmore. Around 2,5 million bottles were sold last year.

A hugely important part of the Glenfarclas character is the use of ex-sherry casks. However, for a new make spirit to cope with a long maturation in the dominant and demanding sherry casks it takes a certain style. If it is too delicate and light it will not manage the wood. Glenfarclas newmake is heavy, pungent and fruity. They start collecting the middle cut at 72% abv but while the vast majority of Scottish distilleries stop well over 60%, Glanfarclas carry on down to 58% in order to catch some heavier spirits which will then be transformed during maturation to earthy and leathery notes that add depth and complexity.

The distillery is equipped with a 16.5 ton semi-lauter mash tun, the largest in Scotland, and twelve stainless steel washbacks with a minimum fermentation time of 60 hours but with a current average of 102 hours. There are three pairs of directly fired stills and the wash stills are equipped with rummagers. In the pandemic 2020, they produced 1,8 million litres of pure alcohol but the goal for 2021 is to make 2,5 million litres. On site are 38 dunnage warehouses with another four being added in 2021.

The Glenfarclas core range consists of **8, 10, 12, 15, 21** and **25 year old**, as well as the lightly sherried **Heritage** which comes without an age statement and the **105 Cask Strength**. The latter was the first commercially available cask strength single malt in the industry. There is also a **17 year old** destined for the USA, Japan and Sweden. The **30** and **40 year olds** are limited but new editions occur regularly. An 18 year old exclusive to travel retail was launched in 2014 but has now been discontinued. The owners quite often produce spectacular limited releases and the rarity of the expressions clearly show the impressive selection that they have available in their warehouses. In autumn 2020 a **60 year old** was released which, together with a 60 year old in 2014, was the oldest official bottling from the company. Two Pagoda bottlings (**62** and **63 years old**) released in 2020 were made available through a private company in Asia. To celebrate the **185th anniversary**, a special edition was launched in May 2021 and in the autumn that same year, a **35 year old** and a **50 year old** were released. The owners also continue to release bottlings in their **Family Casks** series with vintages ranging from **1954** to **2005**.

History:

1836 Robert Hay founds the distillery on the original site since 1797.

1865 Robert Hay passes away and John Grant and his son George buy the distillery. They lease it to John Smith at The Glenlivet Distillery.

1870 John Smith resigns in order to start Cragganmore and J. & G. Grant Ltd takes over.

1889 John Grant dies and George Grant takes over.

1890 George Grant dies and his widow Elsie takes over the license while sons John and George control operations.

1895 John and George Grant take over and form The Glenfarclas-Glenlivet Distillery Co. Ltd with the infamous Pattison, Elder & Co.

1898 Pattison becomes bankrupt. Glenfarclas encounters financial problems after a major overhaul of the distillery but survives by mortgaging and selling stored whisky to R. I. Cameron, a whisky broker from Elgin.

1914 John Grant leaves due to ill health and George continues alone.

1948 The Grant family celebrates the distillery's 100th anniversary, a century of active licensing. It is 9 years late, as the actual anniversary coincided with WW2.

1949 George Grant senior dies and sons George Scott and John Peter inherit the distillery.

1960 Stills are increased from two to four.

1968 Glenfarclas is first to launch a cask-strength single malt. It is later named Glenfarclas 105.

1972 Floor maltings is abandoned and malt is purchased centrally.

1973 A visitor centre is opened.

1976 Enlargement from four stills to six.

2002 George S Grant dies and is succeeded as company chairman by his son John L S Grant.

History continued:

2003 Two new gift tins are released (10 years old and 105 cask strength).

2005 A 50 year old is released to commemorate the bi-centenary of John Grant´s birth.

2007 Family Casks, a series of single cask bottlings from 43 consecutive years, is released.

2008 New releases in the Family Cask range. Glenfarclas 105 40 years old is released.

2009 A third release in the Family Casks series.

2010 A 40 year old and new vintages from Family Casks are released.

2011 Chairman´s Reserve and 175th Anniversary are released.

2012 A 58 year old and a 43 year old are released.

2013 An 18 year old for duty free is released as well as a 25 year old quarter cask.

2014 A 60 year old and a 1966 single fino sherry cask are released.

2015 A 1956 Sherry Cask and Family Reserve are released.

2016 40 year old, 50 year old, 1981 Port and 1986 cask strength are released.

2018 A 22 year old version of the 105 Cask Strength is released.

2019 Glenfarclas Trilogy is released.

2020 Pagoda Ruby Reserve 62 and 63 years old are released.

2021 A 185th anniversary bottling is launched together with a 35 year old and a 50 year old.

Tasting notes Glenfarclas 10 year old:

GS – Full and richly sherried on the nose, with nuts, fruit cake and a hint of citrus fruit. The palate is big, with ripe fruit, brittle toffee, some peat and oak. Medium length and gingery in the finish.

105 Cask Strength

60 years old

12 years old

18 years old

Family Cask 1959

185th Anniversary

40 years old

Glenfiddich

[glen•fidd•ick]

Owner: William Grant & Sons

Region/district: Speyside

Founded: 1886

Status: Active (vc)

Capacity: 21 000 000 litres

Address: Dufftown, Keith, Banffshire AB55 4DH

Website: glenfiddich.com

Tel: 01340 820373 (vc)

Glenfiddich is often described as the first global single malt. The launch of their Straight Malt in 1963 was a major milestone in the history of Scotch and paved the way for other brands and the entire category of single malts.

The man behind it was Sandy Grant Gordon whose great grandfather William Grant had built Glenfiddich in the late 1800s. Together with his older brother Charles he took over the leadership of the company in 1953 when their father prematurely passed away. Both were only in their mid twenties but proved to be more than able to run the company. While Charles focused on getting the Girvan grain distillery built, Sandy put a lot of effort into launching the single malt, which was used for their famous blend, as a brand of its own and his methods were quite progressive. Global marketing campaigns, also on television, gave Glenfiddich a headstart and since then the brand has kept its pole position as the world's most sold single malt. Sandy retired from the business in 1996 and then spent a lot of time pursuing one of his great interests – birdwatching. He died in December 2020 at the age of 89.

In December 2015, William Grant were granted planning approval for an expansion of the distillery which at the time was already the biggest in the industry. The first indications from the company said the new distillery would be up and running by the end of 2018. This was later changed to mid 2019 and then again to mid 2020. Finally, in December 2020, spirit was distilled in the new facility. Today, Glenfiddich is equipped with four, stainless steel full lauter mash tuns – all with a ten ton mash. There are 48 washbacks made of Douglas fir with a minimum fermentation time of 68 hours (but typically 72 hours). The total number of stills is 43 (16 wash stills and 27 spirit stills) and 15 of them in the old still house number two are directly fired using gas. The plan for 2021 is to do 105 mashes per week and 21 million litres of pure alcohol which is at the capacity level of the distillery.

The Glenfiddich core range consists of **12, 15, 18, 21, 30, 40** and **50 years old**. A new addition to the core range appeared in September 2019 with **Grand Cru 23 year old**, finished in champagne casks and this was followed in 2020 by the **Grande Couronne 26 years old** with a cognac finish. A **14 year old Bourbon Barrel Reserve** is available only in the USA , Canada, France and Israel and for China and Taiwan there is the **Gran Cortes 22 years old**.

Recent limited releases include **Glenfiddich The Original** and the **38 year old Glenfiddich Ultimate**. In the Experimental Series, **IPA Experiment** and **Project XX** are ongoing items. A third bottling, the **21 year old Winter Storm**, was released in 2018 followed by **Fire & Cane**. In spring 2020, two **1975 Vintages 44 years old** from the Rare Collection were released in the US. Included in the duty free range is the Cask Collection with **Select Cask, Reserve Cask, Vintage Cask** and **Finest Solera**. Another duty free exclusive is **Rare Oak 25 years**. Finally, a **15 year old Distillery Edition** is available in duty-free and at the distillery.

History:

1886 The distillery is founded by William Grant.

1887 The first distilling takes place on Christmas Day.

1892 William Grant builds Balvenie.

1898 The blending company Pattisons, largest customer of Glenfiddich, files for bankruptcy and Grant decides to blend their own whisky. Standfast becomes one of their major brands.

1903 William Grant & Sons is formed.

1957 The famous, three-cornered bottle is introduced.

1958 The floor maltings is closed.

1963 Glennfiddich becomes the first whisky to be marketed as single malt in the UK and the rest of the world.

1964 A version of Standfast's three-cornered bottle is launched for Glenfiddich in green glass.

1969 Glenfiddich becomes the first distillery in Scotland to open a visitor centre.

1974 16 new stills are installed.

2001 1965 Vintage Reserve is launched in a limited edition of 480 bottles. Glenfiddich 1937 is bottled (61 bottles).

2002 Glenfiddich Gran Reserva 21 years old, Caoran Reserve 12 years and Glenfiddich Rare Collection 1937 (61 bottles) are launched.

2003 1973 Vintage Reserve (440 bottles) is launched.

2004 1991 Vintage Reserve (13 years) and 1972 Vintage Reserve (519 bottles) are launched.

2005 Circa £1.7 million is invested in a new visitor centre.

2006 1973 Vintage Reserve, 33 years (861 bottles) and 12 year old Toasted Oak are released.

Sandy Grant Gordon (right)

History continued:

2007 1976 Vintage Reserve, 31 years is released.

2008 1977 Vintage Reserve is released.

2009 A 50 year old and 1975 Vintage Reserve are released.

2010 Rich Oak, 1978 Vintage Reserve, the 6th edition of 40 year old and Snow Phoenix are released.

2011 1974 Vintage Reserve and a 19 year old Madeira finish are released.

2012 Cask of Dreams and Millenium Vintage are released.

2013 A 19 year old red wine finish and 1987 Anniversary Vintage are released. Cask Collection with three different expressions is released for duty free.

2014 The 26 year old Glenfiddich Excellence, Rare Oak 25 years and Glenfiddich The Original are released.

2015 A 14 year old for the US market is released.

2016 Finest Solera is released for travel retail. Two expressions in the Experimental Series are launched; Project XX and IPA Experiment.

2017 Winter Storm is released.

2018 Fire & Cane is released.

2019 Grand Cru 23 year old and Rare Collection Cask No. 20050 are released.

2020 Gran Cortes 22 year old, Grande Couronne 26 year old and two 1975 Vintages are released.

Tasting notes Glenfiddich 12 year old:

GS – Delicate, floral and slightly fruity on the nose. Well mannered in the mouth, malty, elegant and soft. Rich, fruit flavours dominate the palate, with a developing nuttiness and an elusive whiff of peat smoke in the fragrant finish.

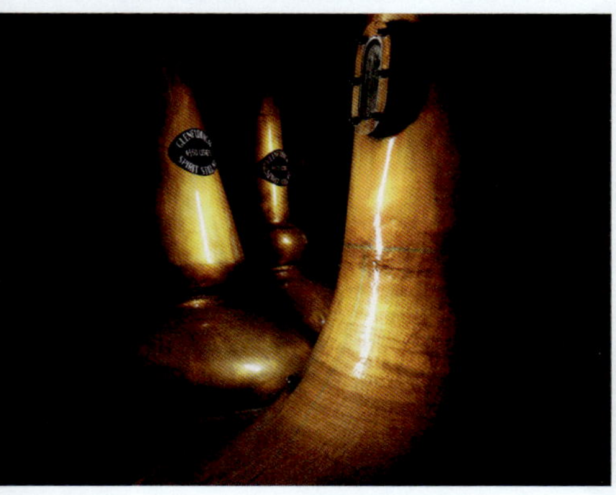

Project XX

Grand Cru

IPA Experiment

Reserve Cask

Grande Couronne
26 years

Our Original
Twelve

Our Solera
Fifteen

Our Small Batch
Eighteen

Glen Garioch

[glen gee•ree]

Owner:
Beam Suntory

Region/district:
Eastern Highlands

Founded:
1797

Status:
Active (vc)

Capacity:
1 370 000 litres

Address: Oldmeldrum, Inverurie, Aberdeenshire
AB51 0ES

Website:
glengarioch.com

Tel:
01651 873450

In last year's book I could report on an unusual change at the distillery where the wash still was to change from indirect heating to being directly gas-fired. This has now been completed, adding a new pot but keeping the same design as the old still.

Lots of other work has been going on since last year at a total cost of £6 million; one more washback, new effluent tanks, a new hot water system and a new CIP system. As if that wasn't enough, the owners decided to re-install floor malting at the distillery – a practice abandoned in 1995. Very few distilleries in Scotland are still using it. The work commenced in April 2021 and the plan is to have it finalized end of the year. If running at full capacity, the in-house maltings will cover 35% of their needs. This makes Glen Garioch the third in the Beam Suntory group of Scottish distilleries to practice floor malting with Bowmore and Laphroaig being the other two.

The distillery is equipped with a four ton full lauter mash tun, nine stainless steel washbacks (one new installed in 2020) with an average fermentation time of 72 hours, one wash still and one spirit still. A redundant third still was removed in 2020 and the copper was recycled at Forsyth's in Rothes. Glen Garioch was shut down for five months in 2020 and produced 450,000 litres of pure alcohol. In 2021 they were back in full production with 18 mashes per week and a total of 1,3 million litres.

The core range is the **1797 Founder's Reserve** (without age statement) and a **12 year old**, both of them bottled at 48%. A limited **15 year old** matured in oloroso casks was launched, mainly for the duty free market, in 2018. Since 2013 there is also the limited **Virgin Oak**, fully matured in virgin American white oak. Other recent limited expressions released a few years ago were four bottlings (15, 16, 17 and 18 years old) in a series called **The Rennaisance**.

History:

1797 John Manson founds the distillery.

1798 Thomas Simpson becomes licensee.

1825 Ingram, Lamb & Co. bcome new owners.

1837 The distillery is bought by John Manson & Co.

1884 The distillery is sold to J. G. Thomson & Co.

1908 William Sanderson buys the distillery.

1933 Sanderson & Son merges with the gin maker Booth's Distilleries Ltd.

1937 Booth´s Distilleries Ltd is acquired by Distillers Company Limited (DCL).

1968 Glen Garioch is decommissioned.

1970 It is sold to Stanley P. Morrison Ltd.

1973 Production starts again.

1978 Stills are increased from two to three.

1994 Suntory controls all of Morrison Bowmore Distillers Ltd.

1995 The distillery is mothballed in October.

1997 The distillery reopens in August and from now on, it is using unpeated malt.

2004 Glen Garioch 46 year old is released.

2005 15 year old Bordeaux Cask Finish is launched. A visitor centre opens in October.

2006 An 8 year old is released.

2009 Complete revamp of the range - 1979 Founders Reserve (unaged), 12 year old, Vintage 1978 and 1990 are released.

2010 1991 vintage is released.

2011 Vintage 1986 and 1994 are released.

2012 Vintage 1995 and 1997 are released.

2013 Virgin Oak, Vintage 1999 and 11 single casks are released.

2014 Glen Garioch Renaissance Collection 15 years is released.

2018 The fourth and final installment of the Rennaisance Collection is released.

2021 Floor malting is re-installed.

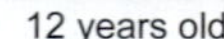

12 years old

Tasting notes Glen Garioch 12 years old:

GS – Luscious and sweet on the nose, peaches and pineapple, vanilla, malt and a hint of sherry. Full-bodied and nicely textured, with more fresh fruit on the palate, along with spice, brittle toffee and finally dry oak notes.

Trailblazers of Malt Whisky

Gilles Leizour
Armorik, France

The people that invented cognac, calvados and armagnac are also the world biggest consumers of Scotch whisky. In fact, the French enjoy more of the latter in a year than the three indigenous spirits together. With such love for the amber liquid, it is surprising that it would last until 1998 before the first 100% French malt whisky was launched.

But let's go back to the year 1900 when it all began. The Warenghem family, with Léon at the helm, opened up a distillery in Lannion on the pink granite coast in Brittany - the northwesterly tip of France. The focus was on plant liqueurs and their big seller Elixir d´Armorique, a blend of 35 plants. The brand was exported to markets all over the world and in 1919 when Léon´s son Henri took over the business, he expanded the product range to also include liqueurs made from mint, black currant, kirsch etc.

Henri steered the family company through the second world war with continued success, but in the early 1960s, he needed to think about the succession in the company. His son, Paul-Henri, had been in the army fighting in the French-Algerian war in the late 50s and early 60s. and took his place in the family company. His father then felt that both Paul-Henri and the business would benefit from someone outside the family joining in.

Enter Yves Leizour. He was a businessman and a graduate from HEC, the famous university in Paris and the plan was that Paul-Henri would take care of sales while Yves would be in charge of the rest. He also got a share of the company and years later, the company was owned (and still is) by the Leizour family.

In 1974, the distillery was moved from the town centre to the outskirts of Lannion but this was also a time when the company started to struggle in a highly competitive market. Yves Leizour was succeeded by his son Gilles in the early 80s. At the age of thirty, Gilles was running a pharmacy together with his wife in Lannion. The revival of the Warenghem company became his first task and his ideas centered around the distillery's location - in Brittany, one of the Celtic nations. In his mind, regional products was the way forward. The first new addition to the range was mead but soon Gilles´ mind began to focus on whisky.

Every year since 1790, the French have celebrated the storming of the Bastille and the birth of the republic on the 14th July. Part of this " Fête nationale" is a military parade in Paris and a gathering at the presidential palace. In 1983 media reported that a French whisky was being served at the palace. In reality, it was whisky imported from Scotland that had been partly matured and blended in France.

This gave Gilles the proper motivation. A French whisky should be 100% produced in France and in 1987 he released WB Breton whisky, a blended whisky made in France. The reactions from the market were probably not what Gilles had been hoping for. The minds and palates of conservative consumers and critics in France were adjusted to Scotch and how could a French whisky compete with that? The fact that WB Breton was sold in super markets didn't help things either.

But Gilles wasn't deterred. The next step was to build a designated whisky distillery. Nowadays, a presumptive distiller from the "new world of whisky" will hire a knowledgeable consultant to build the distillery. Gilles on the other hand preferred to learn everything by himself. He did go to Scottish distilleries but more as a tourist and although the stills were designed with the help of a Scottish engineer, they were built in Cognac and from the producers in the same region, he acquired a lot of his knowledge. In 1993, the first drops of single malt whisky trickled from the new stills and five years later, Armorik, the first French single malt, was officially launched.

The release of Armorik though did not immediately change the view of French whisky. Whisky shops and distributors were still hesitant about the new kid on the block. It actually took 15 years before the first official recognition appeared. In 2013, Armorik Double Maturation was voted Best European Whisky at the World Whiskies Awards and the year after it received double gold at the San Francisco World Spirits Competition. Before that, in 2009, Gilles actually did seek advice from someone outside of France. Jim Swan, legendary whisky consultant, was brought in to give his opinions on everything from yeast, distillation and maturation to give Armorik that extra push.

At the same time, Gilles´ daughter and son in law, David Roussier, joined the company. David had a business background specialising in finance and no knowledge about whisky making. His grandfather was a wine maker in Loire and David soon found that the creation of whisky and wine involved the same passion not least in how the local climate influences the end product. The range of whiskies grew rapidly including several different types of maturations, peated whisky and, released in 2018 to celebrate the 30th anniversary of the first Armorik, a 10 year old. Today 75% of the sales consists of whisky with other spirits making up the rest. Of the whisky part, 65% is made up of Armorik single malt.

Gilles retired in 2016 and David and his wife are now the sole owners of the company. In recent years Armorik have also been the forerunners in the creation of the geographical indication of Breton Whisky, regulating how the whisky should be mashed, fermented, distilled and aged in Brittany.

Today, France is one of the really interesting countries in the new world of whisky making. From the one distillery in 1993, Armorik, no less than 80 whisky distilleries have opened up in the country and while most of the whisky is still sold in the home market there is no doubt that French single malt will be heard of internationally in the next years.

The story of Warenghem and Armorik is a fascinating tale of a family company struggling through booms and busts, bringing in new ideas, new people and coming out on the other side stronger than before. But it is also an account of one person, Gilles Leizour, who never got the proper credit for being the forerunner of a wave of whisky producers in a country that loves whisky. And truth be told, he never sought it - he just wanted to make something new to be proud of. Happily retired, Gilles now sees the prospering company in the safe hands of his daughter and son-in-law but every now and then he turns up at the distillery, eager to taste some of the upcoming new expressions of whisky from his beloved Brittany.

Glenglassaugh

[glen•gla•ssa]

Owner:
Glenglassaugh Distillery Co
(BenRiach Distillery Co.)

Region/district:
Highlands

Founded: **Status:** **Capacity:**
1875   Active (vc)   1 100 000 litres

Address: Portsoy, Banffshire AB45 2SQ

Website:
glenglassaugh.com

Tel:
01261 842367

Glenglassaugh is a good example of how painstakingly difficult it can be to establish a new brand in the crowded Scotch single malt market. Although resurrected as a distillery more than ten years ago, it still only sells around 100,000 bottles per year.

There are many reasons for the slow pace. When Scaent Group opened up the distillery after 22 years of silence, they had to start from scratch. A stock of very old whisky of high quality was included but volumes were small and once bottled the whisky obviously did not come cheap. The new owners gave up after four years, just having launched the first single malt from the new production. Billy Walker took over but was also preoccupied with his two other brands – BenRiach and GlenDronach. Just three years later he sold all three distilleries to Brown Forman, the current owner. The combination of several owners in a short period of time, the complete lack of brand history and offering either young whisky or very old and expensive whisky has not been to Glenglassaugh's advantage. Hopefully the endurance and the financial muscles of a huge conglomerate such as Brown Forman will levitate Glenglassaugh in the near future.

The equipment of the distillery consists of a 5.2 ton Porteus cast iron mash tun with rakes, four wooden washbacks and two stainless steel ones, with a fermentation time between 54 and 80 hours and one pair of stills. The production is around 800,000 litres of pure alcohol, and usually 5% is is peated (30ppm).

The core range is **Revival, Evolution** and the peated **Torfa** without age statement. Limited releases include **30, 40** and a recently launched **50 year old**, as well as single casks in the **Rare Cask Series**. There is also the second release of **Octaves Classic** and **Octaves Peated,**. A series of wood finishes include **Port, PX Sherry, Peated Port** and **Peated Virgin Oak**. In October 2020 the oldest expressions so far from the new production were released in a range called **Coastal Casks**. All ten single casks were destined for selected markets around the world.

History:

1873 The distillery is founded by James Moir.

1887 Alexander Morrison embarks on renovation work.

1892 Morrison sells the distillery to Robertson & Baxter. They in turn sell it on to Highland Distilleries Company for £15,000.

1908 The distillery closes.

1931 The distillery reopens.

1936 The distillery closes.

1957 Reconstruction takes place.

1960 The distillery reopens.

1986 Glenglassaugh is mothballed.

2005 A 22 year old is released.

2006 Three limited editions are released - 19 years old, 38 years old and 44 years old.

2008 The distillery is bought by the Scaent Group for £5m. Three bottlings are released - 21, 30 and 40 year old.

2009 New make spirit and 6 months old are released.

2010 A 26 year old replaces the 21 year old.

2011 A 35 year old and the first bottling from the new owners production, a 3 year old, are released.

2012 A visitor centre is inaugurated and Glenglassaugh Revival is released.

2013 BenRiach Distillery Co buys the distillery and Glenglassaugh Evolution and a 30 year old are released.

2014 The peated Torfa is released as well as eight different single casks and Massandra Connection (35 and 41 years old).

2015 The second batch of single casks is released.

2016 Brown Forman buys the distillery. Octaves Classic and Octaves Peated are released.

2017 Three wood finishes are released.

2018 Batch three in the Rare Cask series and the second release of Octaves are released

2020 Ten single casks in the series Coastal Casks are launched.

Evolution

Tasting notes Glenglassaugh Evolution:

GS – Peaches and gingerbread on the nose, with brittle toffee, icing sugar, and vanilla. Luscious soft fruits dipped in caramel figure on the palate, with coconut and background stem ginger. The finish is medium in length, with spicy toffee.

Glengoyne

[glen•goyn]

Owner:
Ian Macleod Distillers

Region/district:
Southern Highlands

Founded: 1833

Status: Active (vc)

Capacity: 1 100 000 litres

Address: Dumgoyne by Killearn, Glasgow G63 9LB

Website: glengoyne.com

Tel: 01360 550254 (vc)

The use of ex-sherry casks for maturation is a key component in creating not only the Glengoyne flavour profile but also to give the owner's other distillery, Tamdhu, its character.

Even if some of Glengoyne's newmake is filled into ex-bourbon casks, the owners rely heavily on sherry wood. Air-dried European oak from Galicia as well as American oak is used for the butts that are then filled with sherry in Jerez to season the casks. The entire process from cutting down a tree to the stage when the cask is filled at Glengoyne can take up to six years. The distillery, with a magnificent location in the scenic region of the Trossarchs, is situated at the base of Dumgoyne Hill and right on the border between the Lowlands and the Highlands. Every year, around 85,000 visitors come to the distillery to enjoy a wide range of tours and tastings

Glengoyne is equipped with a 3.84 ton semi lauter mash tun. There are also six Oregon pine washbacks, as well as the rather unusual combination of one wash still and two spirit stills. Both short (56 hours) and long (110 hours) fermentations are practiced. The production plan for 2021 is to do 16 mashes per week and 966,000 litres of alcohol.

The core range consists of **10, 12, 18** and **21 and 25 year old.** There is also batch eight of the **Cask Strength**. Older expressions are part of a range called Fine & Rare and include **25** and **30 year olds** and, since November 2020, a **50 year old** – the oldest ever expression released from the distillery. Other recent limited releases include a new series called **Glengoyne Legacy** where **Chapter Two** was launched in autumn 2020 and is a whisky predominantly matured in ex-bourbon casks but also contains a proportion of refill sherry casks. Other limited releases are batch 7 of the popular **The Teapot Dram** and the **17 year old Duncan's Dram**. The line-up for duty free consists of four expressions; **Cuartillo** (American oak oloroso), **Balbaina** (European oak oloroso), **28 year old** (a combination of American and European oak oloroso) and **Glengoyne PX** (American and European oak with a finish in PX casks).

History:

1833 The distillery is licensed under the name Burnfoot Distilleries by the Edmonstone family.

1876 Lang Brothers buys the distillery and changes the name to Glenguin.

1905 The name changes to Glengoyne.

1965 Robertson & Baxter takes over Lang Brothers and the distillery is refurbished. The stills are increased from two to three.

2001 Glengoyne Scottish Oak Finish (16 years old) is launched.

2003 Ian MacLeod Distillers Ltd buys the distillery plus the brand Langs from the Edrington Group for £7.2 million.

2005 A 19 year old, a 32 year old and a 37 year old cask strength are launched.

2006 Nine "choices" from Stillmen, Mashmen and Manager are released.

2007 A new version of the 21 year old, two Warehousemen´s Choice, Vintage 1972 and two single casks are released.

2008 A 16 year old Shiraz cask finish, three single casks and Heritage Gold are released.

2009 A 40 year old, two single casks and a new 12 year old are launched.

2010 Two single casks, 1987 and 1997, released.

2011 A 24 year old single cask is released.

2012 A 15 and an 18 year old are released as well as a Cask Strength with no age statement.

2013 A limited 35 year old is launched.

2014 A 25 year old is released.

2018 A new range for duty free is released – Cuartillo, Balbaine, a 28 year old and Glengoyne PX.

2019 Glengoyne Legacy is launched.

2020 A 50 year old and Glengoyne Legacy Chapter Two are released.

12 years old

Tasting notes Glengoyne 12 years old:

GS – Slightly earthy on the nose, with nutty malt, ripe apples, and a hint of honey. The palate is full and fruity, with milk chocolate, ginger and vanilla. The finish is medium in length, with milky coffee and soft spices.

Glen Grant

[glen grant]

Owner: Campari Group

Region/district: Speyside

Founded: 1840

Status: Active (vc)

Capacity: 6 200 000 litres

Address: Elgin Road, Rothes, Banffshire AB38 7BS

Website: glengrant.com

Tel: 01340 832118

Part of the success of single malt Scotch around the world can be attributed to the symbiosis between whisky producers and independent bottlers. There are few better examples of that than the relation between Glen Grant and Gordon & MacPhail.

The first steps into fame for Glen Grant came in the early 1960s when the Italian hotel owner and whisky lover Armando Giovinetti came to the distillery to negotiate the purchase of a substantial number of cases of the single malt. He focused on the 5 year old and soon the Italians had fallen in love with the young whisky and sales rocketed. Around the same time George Urquhart, part of the family who owned the independent bottler Gordon & MacPhail, took an interest in the Italian whisky market. A range of single malts named Connoiseur's Choice, including Glen Grant which was a favourite of Georges, was introduced. Instead of very young expressions, Gordon & MacPhail focused on older bottlings. The range was (and still is) a success and old Glen Grant single malts in particular have continued to grace the market. Two of the most recent examples are a 72 year old bottled in 2020 and the 67 year old Mr George Legacy (in honour of George Urquhart) which appeared in 2021.

Glen Grant distillery is equipped with a 12.3 ton semi-lauter mash tun, ten Oregon pine washbacks with a minimum fermentation time of 48 hours and four pairs of stills. The wash stills are peculiar in that they have vertical sides at the base of the neck and all eight stills are fitted with purifiers. An extremely efficient £5m bottling hall was inaugurated in 2013. It has a capacity of 12,000 bottles an hour and Glen Grant is alone among the large distillers in bottling the entire production on site. In 2015 a second line for the premium range was installed. The production plan for 2021 is to do 22 mashes per week for 30 weeks which will amount to 3.1 million litres of pure alcohol.

The core range consists of **Major's Reserve** with no age statement, a **5 year old** sold in Italy, **Arboralis**, matured in a combination of ex-bourbon and ex-sherry, a **10 year old,** a **12 year old** matured in both bourbon and sherry casks and an **18 year old** bourbon matured. There are two expressions for the duty free market – one **without age statement** and a **12 year old.** A **15 year old,** matured in first fill bourbon is available for the American market as well as for duty free. The current distillery exclusive bottling is a **12 year old Apleton rum finish**. In 2021, the legendary Dennis Malcolm, former distillery manager of Glen Grant and today the Master Distiller, celebrates his 60th anniversary in the Scotch whisky industry. He was born on the site of Glen Grant, where his father worked, in 1946 and at the age of 15 he started as an apprentice cooper at the distillery. His career includes being responsible for the production of all the Chivas distilleries. The company will launch a **Dennis Malcolm anniversary bottling** of Glen Grant on the 5th of October this year but at the time of writing no details about the whisky were available.

History:

1840 The brothers James and John Grant, managers of Dandelaith Distillery, found the distillery.

1861 The distillery becomes the first to install electric lighting.

1864 John Grant dies.

1872 James Grant passes away and the distillery is inherited by his son, James junior (Major James Grant).

1897 James Grant decides to build another distillery across the road; it is named Glen Grant No. 2.

1902 Glen Grant No. 2 is mothballed.

1931 Major Grant dies and is succeeded by his grandson Major Douglas Mackessack.

1953 J. & J. Grant merges with George & J. G. Smith who runs Glenlivet distillery, forming The Glenlivet & Glen Grant Distillers Ltd.

1961 Armando Giovinetti and Douglas Mackessak found a friendship that leads to Glen Grant becoming the most sold malt whisky in Italy.

1965 Glen Grant No. 2 is back in production, but renamed Caperdonich.

1972 The Glenlivet & Glen Grant Distillers merges with Hill Thompson & Co. and Longmorn-Glenlivet Ltd to form The Glenlivet Distillers.

1973 Stills are increased from four to six.

1977 The Chivas & Glenlivet Group (Seagrams) buys Glen Grant Distillery. Stills are increased from six to ten.

2001 Pernod Ricard and Diageo buy Seagrams Spirits & Wine, with Pernod acquiring Chivas Group.

History continued:

2006 Campari buys Glen Grant for €115m.

2007 The entire range is re-packaged and re-launched and a 15 year old single cask is released. Reconstruction of the visitor centre.

2008 Two limited cask strengths - a 16 year old and a 27 year old - are released.

2009 Cellar Reserve 1992 is released.

2010 A 170th Anniversary bottling is released.

2011 A 25 year old is released.

2012 A 19 year old Distillery Edition is released.

2013 Five Decades is released and a bottling hall is built.

2014 A 50 year old and the Rothes Edition 10 years old is released.

2015 Glen Grant Fiodh is launched.

2016 A 12 year old and an 18 year old are launched and a 12 year old non chill-filtered is released for travel retail.

2018 A 15 year old is released for the duty free market.

2020 Arboralis with no age statement is released.

2021 A Dennis Malcolm Anniversary bottling is released.

Tasting notes Glen Grant 12 year old:

GS – A blast of fresh fruit – oranges, pears and lemons – on the initial nose, before vanilla and fudge notes develop. The fruit carries over on to the palate, with honey, caramel and sweet spices. Medium in length, with cinnamon and soft oak in the finish.

12 years old

Arboralis

18 years old

10 years old

The Major´s Reserve

Glengyle

[glen•gajl]

Owner: **Region/district:**
Mitchell´s Glengyle Ltd   Campbeltown

Founded: **Status:**   **Capacity:**
2004   Active   750 000 litres

Address: Glengyle Road, Campbeltown,
Argyll PA28 6LR

Website: **Tel:**
kilkerran.com   01586 551710

The most prosperous time for Campbeltown was in the Victorian days when shipbuilding, fishing and coal mining made most of the inhabitants quite wealthy.

This was also the time when at least 25 whisky distilleries were operating in this little town with, today, only 5,000 people. The downturn came during the first world war and by 1934, when Rieclachan closed, only two distilleries remained – Glen Scotia and Springbank. Seventy years later the number grew to three when Glengyle (also closed in 1925) was re-opened by the owners of Springbank.

The distillery is equipped with a 4.5 ton semi-lauter mash tun, two washbacks made of boat skin larch and two made of Douglas fir. The fermentation varies between 72 and 110 hours. There is also one set of stills. Malt is obtained from the neighbouring Springbank and operations are managed by the same staff. The capacity is 750,000 litres, but considerably smaller amounts have been produced over the years. However, production has increased in later years and the plan for 2021 is to mash five times per week between September and December. This will amount to around 100,000 litres with 85% made up of "regular" Kilkerran and the rest of heavily peated spirit. Over the years, the owners have been conducting some interesting experimental production at Glengyle including quadruple distillation.

After many years of "work in progress" bottlings, the first core **12 year old** was launched in 2016. It was a vatting of bourbon- (70%) and sherry-matured (30%) whisky. In spring 2017, an **8 year old cask strength** was added to the range with a new batch, fully matured in oloroso casks, released in February 2021. The first batch of **Kilkerran Heavily Peated** was released in spring 2019 with batch 4 appearing in May 2021. The word "heavily" is no exaggeration – the phenol specification of the barley is around 80ppm! The main event in terms of new releases however, came in autumn 2020 when a **16 year old**, the oldest Kilkerran so far, was launched with a second batch being released in September 2021.

History:

1872 The original Glengyle Distillery is built by William Mitchell.

1919 The distillery is bought by West Highland Malt Distilleries Ltd.

1925 The distillery is closed.

1929 The warehouses (but no stock) are purchased by the Craig Brothers and rebuilt into a petrol station and garage.

1941 The distillery is acquired by the Bloch Brothers.

1957 Campbell Henderson applies for planning permission with the intention of reopening the distillery.

2000 Hedley Wright, owner of Springbank Distillery and related to founder William Mitchell, acquires the distillery.

2004 The first distillation after reconstruction takes place in March.

2007 The first limited release - a 3 year old.

2009 Kilkerran "Work in progress" is released.

2010 "Work in progress 2" is released.

2011 "Work in progress 3" is released.

2012 "Work in progress 4" is released.

2013 "Work in progress 5" is released and this time in two versions - bourbon and sherry.

2014 "Work in progress 6" is released in two versions - bourbon and sherry.

2015 "Work in progress 7" is released in two versions - bourbon and sherry.

2016 Kilkerran 12 years old is released.

2017 Kilkerran 8 year old cask strength is released.

2019 Kilkerran Heavily Peated is released.

2020 A 16 year old is released.

2021 Batch four of Heavily Peated and batch two of the 16 year old are released.

12 years old

Tasting notes Kilkerran 12 year old:

GS – Initially, quite reticent on the nose, then peaty fruit notes develop. Oily and full on the palate, with peaches and more overt smoke, plus an earthy quality. Castor oil and liquorice sticks. Slick in the medium-length finish, with slightly drying oak and enduring liquorice.

Trailblazers of Malt Whisky

Magnus Dandanell
Mackmyra, Sweden

The story of eight friends from university, rejoining years after graduation in a small winter resort in the far north with plenty of whisky on the table sounds like the perfect plot for a Hollywood movie. But instead of an evening of reminiscing and sorting out emotions, the guys are looking forward. They are all in the midst of their careers but the sense of wanting something more is in the air of the room and questions about "the meaning of life" arise. This is when the idea of building a malt whisky distillery comes up - the first in Sweden in modern times. In a country known for vodka and aquavit!

That was how Mackmyra started and the story is well-known to Mackmyra fans and has been told by the company many times. The driving force behind this crazy idea and later the company CEO for 21 years was Magnus Dandanell. Born and raised a stones throw from the distillery, he later on graduated as a Master of Science in Chemical Engineering. Not a bad choice for anyone wanting to make it big in whisky production but that wasn't the thought at the time. After graduation he did his spell at a couple of pharmaceutical companies until that famous evening in Sälen where everything took a new turn. Within the group, Dandanell was the natural choice for the leader for two reasons. While in uni he often assumed the role as Project Manager and, not least important, he had the knowledge in chemistry.

Most of the friends kept their dayjobs in the beginning of the adventure while perusing the possibilities of producing a Swedish malt whisky full time. From the start, there was no doubt that they were aiming for a Swedish malt whisky – not a good copy of a Scotch. As Dandanell put it after a research trip to Scotland in 1998; "why would we try to build the 104th Scottish distillery in Sweden, always being looked at as the second best, when we could start the first Swedish distillery and add something to the industry". He notes that this is how many successful Swedish companies were born. You study processes around the world, build up knowledge and then take it back to Sweden using local raw material and do it your own way.

Instead of forging ahead with a full scale distillery, the team decided to spend three years working on their skills and recipes in a small pilot plant. You could say the plan was conservative but brave with no distillation of gin, vodka or other spirits that quickly could create a cash flow. Single malt whisky was the thing! In 2002, they were ready to start their first production distillery with the ambition to produce whisky for sales to the consumers. A rather unconventional plan at the time was to fill small casks (30 litres) and offer them directly to consumers to be bottled 3-5 years later. This of course was a vital part of the financing of the company but also established the brand and (due to the small casks and quick maturation) made it possible for the consumers to try a mature Mackmyra from early on.

For Magnus it was actually much more than that. In an interview from that time he says that it is better to have fans than customers. When I ask him today what he meant he says that what they were doing at the time was building a community where people could be a part of the journey. The company was in a constant dialogue with their customers by emails and blogs and they were also invited to numerous events. Mackmyra was building up the anticipation and the loyalty and hoping that some of these people would become advocates of the brand. It should be noted that this was before social media were the name of the game and most of the other whisky companies´ similar attempts came much later.

Already in 2006/2007, the first whiskies from Mackmyra were released. From the company´s side, the six Preludium bottlings were meant to be an opportunity for the consumer to join the ride to see how Mackmyra single malt would evolve from early days on. The whiskies were of course young (which was the whole idea) and perhaps due to the high anticipation from Swedish whisky enthusiasts and partly due to how the company marketed the whiskies, the idea back fired. The six whiskies were not meant to be a statement of how Mackmyra whiskies would taste in the future but rather an invitation to the consumer to be a part of the adventure from the very beginning. In Magnus Dandanells own words more like how Ardbeg re-launched their 10 year old from Very Young to Almost There. Nevertheless, this first release of young whiskies would haunt them for years, at least in the small circles of whisky enthusiasts. The general whisky drinker on the other hand seemed unaffected.

The company embarked on a giant endeavor when their current gravity distillery was built in 2012. This meant a huge financial commitment and at the same time the company was trying to create a foothold on the notoriously difficult American market. Soon enough they had to scale down their export ambitions and in 2014 they had settled for Germany. Magnus admits that, at the time, they underestimated the problems launching a Swedish whisky to the export market. Years later they are present in the UK as well as in several EU countries and also Taiwan. A lot of this success is due to having their own organisation present in these markets. According to Magnus, the future success of Mackmyra lies in the export market.

When talking to Magnus it becomes obvious that the early years of their corporate adventure were formed by comparing themselves to Scottish distilleries, yet aiming for a Swedish whisky. It wasn't until 2013 when he visited Australia and met with Bill Lark and Patrick Maguire that he realized that antipod distilleries had faced the same challenges just a few years before Mackmyra, trying to convince the consumers that malt whisky could be made outside of Scotland.

Early 2020, Magnus left his job as CEO of Mackmyra after 21 years. At that time, sales to the three biggest export markets alone exceeded sales in the home market. He took on a new role in the company, working with business development focusing on consumer patterns and web-based sales. He recognized the importance of digital D2C communication and sales (Direct to Consumer) in which cosmetics and apparels have already made the transformation and which is surprisingly similar to the analogue method Mackmyra used in the early days. Still a minority share holder but no longer working in the company, Magnus is now writing a book on the forging of Mackmyra which will no doubt serve as a blueprint of how to start a whisky distillery in a non-traditional market.

Glen Keith

[glen <u>keeth</u>]

Owner:
Chivas Brothers
(Pernod Ricard)

Region/district:
Speyside

Founded: 1957

Status: Active

Capacity: 6 000 000 litres

Address: Station Road, Keith, Banffshire AB55 3BU

Website:
-

Tel:
01542 783042

History:

1957 The Distillery is founded by Chivas Brothers (Seagrams).

1958 Production starts.

1970 The first gas-fuelled still in Scotland is installed, the number of stills increases from three to five.

1976 Own maltings (Saladin box) ceases.

1983 A sixth still is installed.

1994 The first official bottling, a 10 year old, is released as part of Seagram's Heritage Selection.

1999 The distillery is mothballed.

2001 Pernod Ricard takes over Chivas Brothers from Seagrams.

2012 The reconstruction and refurbishing of the distillery begins.

2013 Production starts again.

2017 A Distillery Edition is launched.

2019 Three bottlings in The Secret Speyside Collection are launched.

Every time I came to Keith during the first years of the new millenium, I was confused by the fact that Glen Keith was not producing. Obviously being a new and large distillery and owned by one of the big companies – it didn't make sense to me.

To understand the reason we need to look at some figures. In 1998 stocks of whisky were at its highest since 1980. At the same time consumption as percentage of whisky distilled were at its lowest since 1979 – only 79,6%. In other words, there were signs that too much whisky was produced. With the decline of whisky sales in the late 1970s and the mass closure of distilleries in 1983/84 in fresh memory, the reasons for producing conservatively were obvious.. Glen Keith was mothballed in 1999 and a year earlier, Imperial. In 2002, both Allt-a-Bhainne and Braeval stopped production – all four distilleries owned by Chivas Brothers. But it only took a few years before the predictions changed. While Imperial remained closed, Allt-a-Bhainne and Braeval reopened in 2005 and 2008 and Glen Keith in 2013.

From the very start, the malt from Glen Keith was intended to be a part of one of the new blended Scotch of the time – 100 Pipers. At the same time the distillery served as a testing plant where trials with triple distillation and peated production were carried out

Glen Keith is equipped with a Briggs 8 ton full lauter mash tun and six stainless steel washbacks. In the old building there are nine washbacks made of Oregon pine and six, old but refurbished stills. The distillery has the capacity to make 6 million litres with the possibility of producing 40 mashes per week.

The only official core bottling from the distillery is the **Distillery Edition**. In July 2019, Chivas launched The Secret Speyside Collection with 15 bottlings from four distilleries (Glen Keith, Longmorn, Braeval and Caperdonich). The three Glen Keith expressions were **21, 25** and **28 years old**. Finally, there is a **22 year old cask strength** bottling, distilled in 1998, in the Distillery Reserve Collection, available at all Chivas visitor centres.

Distillery Edition

Tasting notes Glen Keith Distillery Edition:

IR – Sweet and fruity on the nose with notes of toffee and apples. Smooth on the palate, vanilla, tropical fruits, marzipan, sponge cake, honey, pears and a hint of dry oak in the finish.

Glenkinchie

[glen•kin•chee]

Owner: **Region/district:**
Diageo   Lowlands

Founded: **Status:**   **Capacity:**
1837   Active (vc)   2 500 000 litres

Address: Pencaitland, Tranent,
East Lothian EH34 5ET

Website: **Tel:**
malts.com   01875 342004

In 2018 Diageo announced that they would be building a Johnnie Walker experience in Edinburgh as well as new visitor centres at distilleries located in four corners of Scotland. Glenkinchie was the first to open as part of this £185m investment.

In October 2020 the gates of a completely new visitor centre swinged open to visitors. Four different tours are on offer and the red brick warehouse has become an important part of the experience. Leading up to the distillery, a large landscaped garden with an orchard and specially selected plants native to East Lothian has been constructed. Every year the distillery is visited by 50,000 people and you can go their using a shuttle bus straight from Edinburgh city centre to the distillery doors.

At the beginning of the new millenium, there were only two malt distilleries left in the Lowlands – Auchentoshan and Glenkinchie. When the latter was founded in 1825, there were 115! Things have changed though and today there are 18 distilleries operating. There are two reasons for Glenkinchie having survived as a distillery when so many others were decommissioned. One was the formation of Scottish Malt Distillers with four other distilleries which took it through the hard years after the First World War. The other is the proximity to Edinburgh which makes it easy to visit and also may have contributed to Glenkinchie being selected as one of six Classic Malts in 1988.

The distillery is equipped with a full lauter mash tun (nine tons) and six wooden washbacks with a fermentation of up to 100 hours. There are two stills where the wash still has the biggest charge in Scotland – 21,000 litres (the actual capacity is 32,000 litres). In recent years the distillery has been working a five-day week with 10 mashes, producing just under 2 million litres of alcohol.

The core range consists of a **12 year old** and a **Distiller's Edition** with a finish in amontillado sherry casks. A limited **16 year old** bottled at 50,6% and aivailable only at the distillery was released in October 2020.

History:

1825 A distillery known as Milton is founded by John and George Rate.

1837 The Rate brothers are registered as licensees of a distillery named Glenkinchie.

1853 John Rate sells the distillery to a farmer by the name of Christie who converts it to a sawmill.

1881 The buildings are bought by a consortium from Edinburgh.

1890 Glenkinchie Distillery Company is founded. Reconstruction and refurbishment is on-going for the next few years.

1914 Glenkinchie forms Scottish Malt Distillers (SMD) with four other Lowland distilleries.

1939-
1945 Glenkinchie is one of few distilleries allowed to maintain production during the war.

1968 Floor maltings is decommissioned.

1969 The maltings is converted into a museum.

1988 Glenkinchie 10 years becomes one of selected six in the Classic Malt series.

1998 A Distiller's Edition with Amontillado finish is launched.

2007 A 12 year old and a 20 year old cask strength are released.

2010 A cask strength exclusive for the visitor centre, a 1992 single cask and a 20 year old are released.

2016 A 24 year old and a distillery exclusive without age statement are released.

2019 A limited version is released in connection with The Royal Edinburgh Military Tattoo.

2020 A new visitor experience is opened and a 16 year old distillery exclusive is released.

Tasting notes Glenkinchie 12 years old:

GS – The nose is fresh and floral, with spices and citrus fruits, plus a hint of marshmallow. Notably elegant. Water releases cut grass and lemon notes. Medium-bodied, smooth, sweet and fruity, with malt, butter and cheesecake. The finish is comparatively long and drying, initially rather herbal.

12 years old

Glenlivet

[glen•liv•it]

Owner: **Region/district:**
Chivas Brothers   Speyside
(Pernod Ricard)

Founded: **Status:**   **Capacity:**
1824   Active (vc)   21 000 000 litres

Address: Ballindalloch, Banffshire AB37 9DB

Website: **Tel:**
theglenlivet.com   01340 821720 (vc)

In 2020, Glenlivet did what every distillery tried to do – keep the production going as smoothly as possible. Lots of new regulations had to be taken into consideration but most distilleries managed to keep the stills running. The visitor side of the business though, took a huge blow.

Some distilleries accepted visitors for a few months before being forced to close again. Others didn't open up at all and Glenlivet belonged to them. Instead they used the closure to completely refurbish the visitor centre. The last time that happened was 23 years ago. In July 2021, the owners opened up the gates to a one thousand square metres completely transformed experience. Apart from telling the brand story new features have been included such as an indoor field of local barley, an archive wall with the distillery's rarest bottlings and a sampling room with the opportunity to try not only their single malt but also the talked about cocktail capsules.

Glenlivet has been the second best selling single malt after Glenfiddich for many years now but the 2020 sales figures for the two brands are so close that we have decided to call it a draw this year. While Glenfiddich lost 21% of their volumes, Glenlivet fared better with a decrease of only 4%. This means bot brands sold around 14,5 million bottles.

With a second distillery commissioned in 2018, Glenlivet is now equipped with two Briggs full lauter mash tuns, each with a 13.5 ton charge. Sixteen wooden washbacks were augmented by another 16 of stainless steel. Fourteen pairs of stills are divided with four pairs in the oldest still room, three in the room that was built in 2010 and another seven in the third and latest still room.

The core range is made up of **Founder's Reserve, Captain's Reserve** with a finish in cognac casks, **Caribbean Reserve** finished in rum casks, **12 year old, 15 year old French Oak Reserve, 18 year old, 21 year old Archive** and **Glenlivet XXV**. As an exclusive to the American market, a **14 year old** cognac finish was released in 2019. A special range of non-chill filtered whiskies called Nàdurra include: **Oloroso Cask Strength, First Fill Selection Cask Strength** and **Peated Whisky Cask Finish**. All three are available at cask strength but the first two are also bottled at 48% for duty free. The smoky notes in the latter come from a finish in casks that had previously held peated Scotch whisky. The travel retail range includes **Triple Cask Distiller's Reserve, Triple Cask White Oak Reserve** and **Triple Cask Rare Cask**. There is also a recent **35 year old** exclusive to Dubai

Recent limited expressions include the **12 year old Illicit Still** which was released in November 2020. This was the first in a new series called Original Stories. The Glenlivet Cellar Collection includes **30, 33, 38** and **40 year olds**, available on-line or at the distillery. Finally, there are ten cask strength bottlings – from **8** to **25 years old** – in the Distillery Reserve Collection.

History:

1817 George Smith inherits the farm distillery Upper Drummin from his father Andrew Smith who has been distilling on the site since 1774.

1840 George Smith buys Delnabo farm near Tomintoul and leases Cairngorm Distillery.

1845 George Smith leases three other farms, one of which is situated on the river Livet and is called Minmore.

1846 William Smith develops tuberculosis and his brother John Gordon moves back home to assist his father.

1858 George Smith buys Minmore farm and obtains permission to build a distillery.

1859 Upper Drummin and Cairngorm close and all equipment is brought to Minmore which is renamed The Glenlivet Distillery.

1871 George Smith dies and his son John Gordon takes over.

1880 John Gordon Smith applies for and is granted sole rights to the name The Glenlivet.

1890 A fire breaks out and some of the buildings are replaced.

1896 Another two stills are installed.

1901 John Gordon Smith dies.

1904 John Gordon's nephew George Smith Grant takes over.

1921 Captain Bill Smith Grant, son of George Smith Grant, takes over.

1953 George & J. G. Smith Ltd merges with J. & J. Grant of Glen Grant Distillery and forms the company Glenlivet & Glen Grant Distillers.

1966 Floor maltings closes.

1970 Glenlivet & Glen Grant Distillers Ltd merges with Longmorn-Glenlivet Distilleries Ltd and Hill Thomson & Co. Ltd to form The Glenlivet Distillers Ltd.

1978 Seagrams buys The Glenlivet Distillers Ltd. A visitor centre opens.

History continued:

2000 French Oak 12 years and American Oak 12 years are launched

2001 Pernod Ricard and Diageo buy Seagram Spirits & Wine. Pernod Ricard thereby gains control of the Chivas group.

2004 This year sees a lavish relaunch of Glenlivet. French Oak 15 years replaces the previous 12 year old.

2005 Two new duty-free versions are introduced – The Glenlivet 12 year old First Fill and Nadurra. The 1972 Cellar Collection (2,015 bottles) is launched.

2006 Nadurra 16 year old cask strength and 1969 Cellar Collection are released.

2007 Glenlivet XXV is released.

2009 Four more stills are installed and Nadurra Triumph 1991 is released.

2010 Another two stills are commissioned and Glenlivet Founder´s Reserve is released.

2011 Glenlivet Master Distiller´s Reserve is released for the duty free market.

2012 1980 Cellar Collection is released.

2013 The 18 year old Batch Reserve and Glenlivet Alpha are released.

2014 Nadurra Oloroso, Nadurra First Fill Selection, The Glenlivet Guardian´s Chapter and a 50 year old are released.

2015 Founder´s Reserve is released as well as Solera Vatted and Small Batch.

2016 The Glenlivet Cipher and the second edition of the 50 year old are launched.

2018 Captain´s Reserve and Code are released. A new distillery is commissioned.

2019 Enigma and a 14 year old cognac finish are released.

2020 Spectra, Carribean Reserve and Illicit Still are released.

Tasting notes Glenlivet 12 year old:

GS – A lovely, honeyed, floral, fragrant nose. Medium-bodied, smooth and malty on the palate, with vanilla sweetness. Not as sweet, however, as the nose might suggest. The finish is pleasantly lengthy and sophisticated.

Tasting notes Glenlivet Founder´s Reserve:

GS – The nose is fresh and floral, with ripe pears, pineapple, tangerines, honey and vanilla. Medium-bodied, with ginger nuts, soft toffee and tropical fruit on the smooth palate. Soft spices and lingering fruitiness in the finish.

Distiller´s Reserve

Illicit Still
12 years old

Carribean Reserve

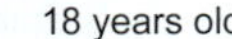

18 years old   40 years old

Founder´s Reserve

Nàdurra
Oloroso

12 years old

Glenlossie

[glen•<u>loss</u>•ee]

Owner: Diageo   **Region/district:** Speyside

Founded: 1876   **Status:** Active   **Capacity:** 3 700 000 litres

Address: Birnie, Elgin, Morayshire IV30 8SS

Website: malts.com   **Tel:** 01343 862000

Glenlossie is located just south of Elgin in an area that is like a veritable bee's nest of distilleries. No less than eight distilleries are situated within a radius of a mere 4 kilometres.

To the west lies Miltonduff, to the north Glen Moray and Linkwood, to the south BenRiach, Longmorn and Glen Elgin and on the same site as Glenlossie, there is Mannochmore, built as late as in 1971. Glenlossie was founded almost 100 years before that and the malt whisky has, over the years, earned a reputation amongst blenders to be one of the best there is to work with when creating a blended Scotch. Glenlossie has always been an integral part of Haig's and Dimple, both brands emanating from the Haig family which could probably be called Scotland's oldest whisky dynasty. Already in 1667, Robert Haig was rebuked for distilling on the Sabbath! The golden years of Haig whisky were from 1930-1970 when it was the brand leader in the UK. It was actually the first Scotch to sell one million cases (12 million bottles) in a year in the UK alone! The slogan that was used is still a classic, "Don't be vague - ask for Haig". Ever since the 1970's sales have decreased but, despite that, around 4 million bottles are still being sold every year. In recent years the Haig brand has been extended with two all-grain versions – Haig Club and Haig Club Clubman. The two whiskies are aimed at the on-trade market for use in cocktails and drinks and in 2020 two pre-mixed versions appeared – one with ginger ale and another with cola.

Glenlossie was closed for 18 months from January 2018 for a major upgrade which, amongst many other things, included the installation of another two external washbacks. Today's equipment consists of an eight ton stainless steel full lauter mash tun, eight washbacks made of larch and two made of stainless steel with a fermentation time of 65 and 106 hours. There are three pairs of stills with the spirit stills equipped with purifiers. During the last couple of years, the distillery has been making 12 mashes per week producing 2 million litres of alcohol.

The only official bottling of Glenlossie single malt available today is a **10 year old Flora & Fauna**.

History:

1876 John Duff, former manager at Glendronach Distillery, founds the distillery. Alexander Grigor Allan (to become part-owner of Talisker Distillery), the whisky trader George Thomson and Charles Shirres (both will co-found Longmorn Distillery some 20 years later with John Duff) and H. Mackay are also involved in the company.

1895 The company Glenlossie-Glenlivet Distillery Co. is formed. Alexander Grigor Allan passes away.

1896 John Duff becomes more involved in Longmorn and Mackay takes over management of Glenlossie.

1919 Distillers Company Limited (DCL) takes over the company.

1929 A fire breaks out and causes considerable damage.

1930 DCL transfers operations to Scottish Malt Distillers (SMD).

1962 Stills are increased from four to six.

1971 Another distillery, Mannochmore, is constructed by SMD on the premises. A dark grains plant is installed.

1990 A 10 year old is launched in the Flora & Fauna series.

2010 A Manager´s Choice single cask from 1999 is released.

10 years old

Tasting notes Glenlossie 10 years old:

GS – Cereal, silage and vanilla notes on the relatively light nose, with a voluptuous, sweet palate, offering plums, ginger and barley sugar, plus a hint of oak. The finish is medium in length, with grist and slightly peppery oak.

Trailblazers of Malt Whisky

Bill Lark
Lark Distillery, Australia

The epithet "Godfather of Australian Whisky" is not a marketing cliché invented for a brand. It is commonly used by whisky enthusiasts and fellow whisky producers to describe Bill Lark's importance to the modern Australian whisky industry. An industry that has grown from the one distillery Bill Lark opened in 1992 to 75 working malt distilleries today! As Lark has personally been involved in several of these operations, either as a consultant or co-founder, one realises that he has earned his reputation justly.

In the 1980s, Bill was working as a land surveyor in Tasmania. One day he was fly fishing with his father-in-law Max at Lake Sorell and while they were preparing their catch for dinner with their respective wives, Max presented him with a bottle of Scotch single malt. Enjoying their drams they started discussing why no one produced whisky in Tasmania with its abundance of barley and excellent water. After all, there was a time in the early 1800s when there were at least 16 legal whisky distilleries on the island and probably many more illegal ones. All of these disappeared in 1838 when the wife of the governor at the time, John Franklin, allegedly said to her husband that "I would prefer barley be fed to pigs than it be used to turn men into swine." Obviously taken by her words, the governor banned the making of whisky and all the distilleries were shut down.

Bill Lark decided it was time to put Tasmania on the whisky map again and he managed to buy a small copper pot still at an auction. That was when he faced the next problem. The existing law from 1901 had been prepared to regulate the making of spirits on an industrial scale and there was no way Bill's plans for a small craft distillery would fit in. He shared his grief with the local MP in Hobart, Duncan Kerr and Kerr, being a whisky fan himself, began pulling some strings with the federal government in Canberra. A change in law came through and in 1992 Lark got his license for a small whisky distillery. Two weeks after the license was granted, he received a surprising phone call from Scotland. John Grant from Glenfarclas Distillery had heard from his distributor in Hobart that Lark had managed to get the first license to make whisky in modern days in Tasmania and he wanted to hear if he could offer any advice. A solid recognition from the homeland of malt whisky!

Working together with his wife Lyn they soon developed a Bush Liqueur using native pepper berries and six years later, in 1998, the couple released their first malt whisky and, as it were, the first legal whisky produced in Tasmania since 1839! While being a passionate entrepreneur, Bill still had the good sense of keeping his day time job as a land surveyor until 1998 when he let his business partner take over the running of their company in order to pursue his passion for whisky.

Following Bill's overturning of the archaic law and the set up of Lark Distillery the word spread quickly around the island and in 1994 Tasmania Distillery (or Sullivan's Cove Distillery as it is known today) was established. In 1999 Bill Lark took over as distillery manager while still running his own distillery but soon enough handed over the responsibility to a friend of his, Patrick Maguire. In a way this highlights the influence Bill Lark has had on, not only Tasmanian but also Australian, whisky production ever since. He has been involved in numerous projects both as a consultant and sometimes as co-owner. And not only in Australia. When the people behind Kingsbarns Distillery in Fife, Scotland were working on their initial plans, Bill was called in to advise them.

With his wife Lyn by his side, Lark Distillery was always a family business and in 2007 their daughter Kristy became general manager. Lark single malt became known also outside Australia and when asked what cemented the success of the whisky Bill is very clear on one thing – using small casks. Barrels from Seppetsfield that had been used to mature Para Port were cut down to quarter casks (around 100 litres) then shaved and recharred. The remaining influence from the wine and the small size with a faster maturation created a whisky which showed high quality in a much shorter time.

Lark Distillery was growing, as was the Australian whisky scene, and in 2010 when Bill went to Scotland with a friend to ride around on motorbikes and visiting distilleries, the future looked brighter than ever. One night in Glasgow though, Bill suffered a stroke. The idea to cut down on the amount of work had been there before but that incident triggered him to sell the distillery. Another reason was that the company had reached a point where a lot of investment was needed to grow the business. The sale went through in 2013 but ever since Bill has, not surprisingly, occupied an ambassadorial role in the company. In 2016, his daughter Kristy moved on to build a distillery of her own – Killara distillery which recently moved from Hobart to Richmond.

The major share holder of Lark Distillery since 2018 is Australian Whisky Holdings (AWH) and two years ago they decided to upgrade the distillery capacity through a substantial investment. And not only that. The name Lark is so important that the holding company (which has interest in other distilleries as well) was renamed in 2020 to Lark Distilling Co. Next up in the strategy is to turn Lark whisky from a local brand to a global hero. Before that will happen, Bill Lark has already become a global hero. His knowledge and passion has inspired many distillers both in Australia and abroad and in March 2015 his deeds were recognised in an astonishing way. He became a member of the Whisky Hall of Fame as the seventh person outside of Scotland or Ireland to be inducted and the first distiller in the southern hemisphere to be recognised. A special celebratory bottling was released that year and in 2021 it was followed by two rare 19 year old expressions named Legacy with his signature on the label. Not bad for a guy who sold his distillery eight years ago and the name of the expression could not have been more appropriate. Bill Lark's legacy as a reviver of Australian whisky is unquestionable.

After his startup in 1992 he was followed by just a handful of other distilleries during the next decade. It was as if the rest wanted to see how Bill was doing before they took a leap of faith and joined in the game. Today 75 malt whisky distilleries are operating in Australia, 31 of them in Tasmania alone. I think Bill Lark must be both proud of and astonished by the way his first small pot still gave birth to an entire industry.

Glenmorangie

[glen•<u>mor</u>•run•jee]

Owner: **Region/district:**
The Glenmorangie Co   Northern Highlands
(Moët Hennessy)

Founded: **Status:**   **Capacity:**
1843   Active (vc)   6 500 000 litres

Address: Tain, Ross-shire IV19 1PZ

Website: **Tel:**
glenmorangie.com   01862 892477 (vc)

For as long as most of us can remember, Bill Lumsden has personified Glenmorangie – first as distillery manager and later as master blender and head of whisky creation. Seven years ago, it seemed like the first steps on finding his successor were taken.

Brendan McCarron was hired to work alongside Lumsden and eventually take over the role as master blender. Over the years Brendan has been responsible for amazing bottlings of both Glenmorangie and Ardbeg and his most recent job title was head of maturing whisky. Before joining Glenmorangie, he worked for many years with several Diageo distilleries and apparently he missed the production side of whiskymaking: in March 2021, surprising news about Brendan leaving the company to take up the role as master distiller at Distell appeared. Glenmorangie has not yet made it public who will be Bill Lumsden's new "apprentice".

Glenmorangie is currently equipped with a full lauter mash tun with a charge of 10,3 tons, 12 stainless steel washbacks with a fermentation time of 52 hours and six pairs of stills. The production plan for 2021 is to make around 6,2 million litres of pure alcohol. On site are also 18 warehouses (4 dunnage, 6 racked and 8 palletised). An innovation plant, nicknamed the Lighthouse project and including mashing and fermentation equipment as well as two stills, is due to be completed later in 2021. With a capacity of one million litres, the new distillery will facilitate various experiments without interfering with the on-going production.

The core range consists of **Original** (10 year old) and **18 year old**. The 25 year old has now been discontinued. There are three wood finishes: **Quinta Ruban**, which used to be a 12 year old but is now a 14 year old that has been finished in a combination of 225 litre ruby barriques and 670 litre ruby pipes. **Lasanta** is 12 year old with a finish in a combination of oloroso casks (75%) and PX sherry casks (25%). Finally, there is **Nectar D'Or** with no age statement that has been finished in Sauternes casks. Added to the core range is **Signet**, an unusual piece of work with 20% of the whisky made using chocolate malt. A new addition to the core range appeared in May 2021 when **X by Glenmorangie** was released. Matured in ex-bourbon, finished in charred virgin oak and bottled at 40%, the new expression has been designed for mixing with for example tonic, soda, cola or ginger ale.

Recent limited releases include the **Glenmorangie Grand Vintage Malt 1997**. Launched in June 2021 it had matured for almost a decade when part of it was transferred to casks that had held Ch. Montrose Bordeaux wine. At the same time a **13 year old cognac cask finish** was released and later in autumn **Tale of Winter**, finished in marsala casks, appeared. There is also **The Cadboll Estate 2020**, exclusive to North America. For travel retail there are 12 year old **The Accord**, 14 year old **The Elementa**, 16 year old **The Tribute** and a **19 year old**. Finally, **Signet Ristretto** made with 100% chocolate malt was released as an exclusive to South Korea's Incheon Airport in August 2021.

History:

1843 William Mathesen applies for a license for a farm distillery called Morangie, which is rebuilt by them. Production took place here in 1738, and possibly since 1703.

1849 Production starts in November.

1887 The distillery is rebuilt and Glenmorangie Distillery Company Ltd is formed.

1918 40% of the distillery is sold to Macdonald & Muir Ltd and 60 % to the whisky dealer Durham. Macdonald & Muir takes over Durham's share by the late thirties.

1931 The distillery closes.

1936 Production restarts in November.

1980 Number of stills increases from two to four and own maltings ceases.

1990 The number of stills is doubled to eight.

1994 A visitor centre opens. Glenmorangie Port Wood Finish is released.

1995 Glenmorangie´s Tain l´Hermitage is launched.

1996 Two different wood finishes are launched, Madeira and Sherry. Glenmorangie plc is formed.

2001 Cask strength port wood finish, Cote de Beaune Wood Finish and Three Cask (ex-Bourbon, charred oak and ex-Rioja) are launched.

2002 A 20 year old Sauternes finish is launched.

2003 Burgundy Wood Finish and cask strength Madeira-matured are released.

2004 Glenmorangie buys the Scotch Malt Whisky Society. The Macdonald family decides to sell Glenmorangie plc (including the distilleries Glenmorangie, Glen Moray and Ardbeg) to Moët Hennessy at £300 million. A new version of Glenmorangie Tain l´Hermitage (28 years) is released as well as Glenmorangie Artisan Cask.

History continued:

2005 A 30 year old is launched.

2007 The entire range gets a complete makeover with
15 and 30 year olds being discontinued
and the rest given new names as well as new
packaging.

2008 An expansion of production capacity is started.
Astar and Signet are launched.

2009 The expansion is finished and Sonnalta PX is
released for duty free.

2010 Glenmorangie Finealta is released.

2011 28 year old Glenmorangie Pride is released.

2012 Glenmorangie Artein is released.

2013 Glenmorangie Ealanta is released.

2014 Companta, Taghta and Dornoch are released.

2015 Túsail and Duthac are released.

2016 Milsean, Tayne and Tarlogan are released.

2017 Bacalta, Astar and Pride 1974 are released.

2018 Spios, Cadboll and Grand Vintage Malt 1989
and 1993 are released.

2019 Allta, Cask 1784 and Grand Vintage Malt 1991
are launched.

2020 A new range of travel retail exclusives is
released as well as the 26 year Truffle Oak,
Grand Vintage Malt 1996 and A Tale of Cake.

2021 X by Glenmorangie, Grand Vintage Malt 1997,
a 13 year old cognac finish, Signet Ristretto and
Tale of Winter are launched.

Tasting notes Glenmorangie Original 10 year old:

GS – The nose offers fresh fruits, butterscotch and
toffee. Silky smooth in the mouth, mild spice, vanilla,
and well-defined toffee. The fruity finish has a final
flourish of ginger.

The Tribute   A Tale of Winter   Quinta Ruban

Original 10 years old   13 years old
Cognac Cask Finish   X by Glenmorangie

Glen Moray

[glen **mur**•ree]

Owner:
La Martiniquaise (COFEPP)

Region/district:
Speyside

Founded:
1897

Status:
Active (vc)

Capacity:
5 700 000 litres

Address: Bruceland Road, Elgin,
Morayshire IV30 1YE

Website:
glenmoray.com

Tel:
01343 542577

When long-time distillery manager and master blender Graham Coull left Glen Moray in late 2019 he was, at least on the blending side, succeeded by Kirstie McCallum who had spent several years with Burn Stewart.

McCallum's spell at La Martiniquaise and Glen Moray however would not last very long. In January 2021 it was announced that she was leaving to join Halewood Artisanal Spirits to work with their Scotch whisky Crabbie, the Irish The Pogues and the Welsh Aber Falls. The new head of whisky creation and stock at Glen Moray is Stephen Woodcock. He has spent the last few years overseeing the production at Distell's three Scottish distilleries – Bunnahabhain, Tobermory and Deanston (the same distilleries that McCallum used to work with) and before that he was the manager of several Diageo distilleries. Woodcock will not only be responsible for Glen Moray single malt but also three major blends owned by La Martiniquaie – Label 5, Sir Edward's and Cutty Sark

Glen Moray is equipped with a 10.1 ton full lauter mash tun. There are 14 stainless steel washbacks placed outside with a fermentation time of 60 hours. In summer 2021, another two were installed in order to increase the fermentation time. Finally there are nine stills (3 wash and 6 spirit). The current capacity is 5.7 million litres of alcohol. In 2021, the owners plan to mash 27 times per week and produce 5 million litres of alcohol. Usually, a small batch of peated newmake (48ppm in the barley) is made every year.

The core range consists of **Classic, Classic Port Finish, Classic Chardonnay Finish, Classic Sherry Finish, Classic Cabernet Sauvignon Finish** and **Classic Peated** as well as **10 year old Fired Oak, 12, 15** and **18 year old**. Limited releases include a **21 year old portwood finish**, a **30 year old sherry finish** (in autumn 2021) and a **14 year old Sauternes matured**, part of the Warehouse 1 Collection. Three finishes, reserved for the UK market and released in 2021, were **2005 Tokaji, 2008 Manzanilla** and **1998 Barolo**.

History:

1897 Elgin West Brewery, dated 1830, is reconstructed as Glen Moray Distillery.

1910 The distillery closes.

1920 Financial troubles force the distillery to be put up for sale. Buyer is Macdonald & Muir.

1923 Production restarts.

1958 A reconstruction takes place and the floor maltings are replaced by a Saladin box.

1978 Own maltings are terminated.

1979 Number of stills is increased to four.

1996 Macdonald & Muir Ltd changes name to Glenmorangie plc.

1999 Three wood finishes are introduced - Chardonnay (no age) and Chenin Blanc (12 and 16 years respectively).

2004 Louis Vuitton Moët Hennessy buys Glenmorangie plc and a 1986 cask strength, a 20 and a 30 year old are released.

2006 Two vintages, 1963 and 1964, and a new Manager's Choice are released.

2007 New edition of Mountain Oak is released.

2008 The distillery is sold to La Martiniquaise.

2009 A 14 year old Port finish and an 8 year old matured in red wines casks are released.

2011 Two cask finishes and a 10 year old Chardonnay maturation are released.

2012 A 2003 Chenin Blanc is released.

2013 A 25 year old port finish is released.

2014 Glen Moray Classic Port Finish is released.

2015 Glen Moray Classic Peated is released.

2016 Classic Chardonnay Finish and Classic Sherry Finish are released as well as a 15 and an 18 year old.

2017 Glen Moray Mastery is launched.

2018 10 year old Fired Oak is released.

2019 Glen Moray Rhum Agricole is released.

2020 A 13 year old Madeira Cask is released.

2021 A 30 year old sherry finish and a 14 year old matured in Sauternes casks are launched.

12 years old

Tasting notes Glen Moray 12 years old:

GS – Mellow on the nose, with vanilla, pear drops and some oak. Smooth in the mouth, with spicy malt, vanilla and summer fruits. The finish is relatively short, with spicy fruit.

Glen Ord

[glen <u>ord</u>]

Owner: Diageo

Region/district: Northern Highlands

Founded: 1838   **Status:** Active (vc)   **Capacity:** 11 000 000 litres

Address: Muir of Ord, Ross-shire IV6 7UJ

Website: malts.com   **Tel:** 01463 872004 (vc)

Glen Ord is one of only two distilleries malting all the barley themselves – the other is Springbank. But the similarities stop there. While Springbank is practicing floor malting and small volumes, the malting at Glen Ord are of an industrial scale.

Glen Ord's floor malting stopped in 1961 when a Saladin box was installed. This was later replaced by a huge drum malting which was built in 1968. The barley is soaked for two days in 18 steeping vessels and then germinated for four days in the 18 drums. There are four kilns to dry the malt – two that are always used for unpeated production and two where they exchange between using peat and hot air. The total capacity is 45,000 tons per year which, when converted to litres of pure alcohol, is close to 20 million – double the distillation capacity of Glen Ord. But the maltings also produce malt mainly for Talisker and for a few other Diageo distilleries.

The distillery is situated 15 miles west of Inverness in the fertile Black Isle and with one of the best visitor centres in the industry, it is well worth a visit. Since 2011, Glen Ord distillery has been expanded rapidly in several stages and with its latest expansion in 2015, the distillery now has a capacity of 11 million litres. This makes it the second largest in the Diageo group and number six in Scotland. The complete set of equipment comprises of two stainless steel mashtuns, each with a 12.5 ton mash. There are 22 wooden washbacks with a fermentation time of 75 hours and no less than 14 stills.

The core range is the **Singleton of Glen Ord 12, 15** and **18 year old**. A sub-range, The Singleton Reserve Collection, is exclusive to duty free and consists of **Signature, Trinité, Liberté** and **Artisan**. The Forgotten Drops Series is made up of old and limited releases. The most recent, and final release, was a **43 year old** in July 2019, matured in two types of sherry casks and then finished both in ex-muscat casks and small firkin casks. An **18 year old** also appeared in the 2019 Special Releases. Finally, there is a bottling available exclusively at the distillery.

History:

1838   Thomas Mackenzie founds the distillery.

1855   Alexander MacLennan and Thomas McGregor buy the distillery.

1870   Alexander MacLennan dies and the distillery is taken over by his widow who marries the banker Alexander Mackenzie.

1877   Alexander Mackenzie leases the distillery.

1878   Alexander Mackenzie builds a new still house and barely manages to start production before a fire destroys it.

1896   Alexander Mackenzie dies and the distillery is sold to James Watson & Co. for £15,800.

1923   John Jabez Watson, James Watson's son, dies and the distillery is sold to John Dewar & Sons. The name changes from Glen Oran to Glen Ord.

1961   A Saladin box is installed.

1966   The two stills are increased to six.

1968   Drum maltings is built.

1983   Malting in the Saladin box ceases.

1988   A visitor centre is opened.

2002   A 12 year old is launched.

2003   A 28 year old cask strength is released.

2004   A 25 year old is launched.

2005   A 30 year old is launched as a Special Release from Diageo.

2006   A 12 year old Singleton of Glen Ord is launched.

2010   A Singleton of Glen Ord 15 year old is released in Taiwan.

2011   Two more washbacks are installed, increasing the capacity by 25%.

2012   Singleton of Glen Ord cask strength is released.

2013   Singleton of Glen Ord Signature, Trinité, Liberté and Artisan are launched.

2015   The Master´s Casks 40 years old is released.

2017   A 41 year old reserved for Asia is released.

2018   A 14 year old triple-matured is launched as part of the Special Releases.

2019   A 43 year old is released as well as an 18 year old in the Special Releases.

Tasting notes Glen Ord 12 years old:

GS – Honeyed malt and milk chocolate on the nose, with a hint of orange. These characteristics carry over onto the sweet, easy-drinking palate, along with a biscuity note. Subtly drying, with a medium-length, spicy finish.

12 years old

Glenrothes

[glen•roth•iss]

Owner: The Edrington Group

Region/district: Speyside

Founded: 1878 **Status:** Active **Capacity:** 5 600 000 litres

Address: Rothes, Morayshire AB38 7AA

Website: theglenrothes.com **Tel:** 01340 872300

Glenrothes is often referred to as the single malt that was always released as a vintage. While it's true that Glenrothes pioneered this, at least for whisky, unusual scheme it was actually a quite recent strategy which has now been abandoned.

Let's go back a century in time. In 1923 the legendary Berry Brothers & Rudd in London launched a new Scotch called Cutty Sark and as the backbone of the blend they used Glenrothes single malt which they bought from the distillery owners at the time – Highland Distillers. Fast forward to 1982 when BBR decided to launch a single malt for their customers. Having had a 60 year long relationship with Highland Distillers for their blend, they decided that Glenrothes could be a good choice. In 1987 a 12 year old was launched but sales were slow. With one foot firmly placed in the world of wine and vintages, BBR took the bold step to re-brand Glenrothes as a vintage and in 1993, the vintage 1979 was released. While this approach put Glenrothes single malt on the map, it was only 12 years later (in 2005) that Select Reserve, without vintage and age statement, was launched. Finally in 2018, and now with Edrington as the brand owner, the vintage concept was abandoned and a range with age on the label was introduced.

The distillery is equipped with a 5.5 ton stainless steel full lauter mash tun. Twelve washbacks made of Oregon pine are in one room, whilst an adjacent tun room houses eight stainless steel washbacks – all of them with a 58 hour fermentation time. There are also five pairs of stills. For 2021, they are aiming for 44 mashes per week, producing just over 4 million litres of alcohol.

The core range, named Soleo Collection, consists of **10 year old, 12 year old, Whisky Maker's Cut, 18 year old** and **25 year old**. The Aqua Collection intended for sale on-line has now been discontinued. Exclusive to travel retail are **Robur Reserve, Manse Reserve, Elder's Reserve, Minister's Reserve** and the **25 year old Ancestor's Reserve**. Recent limited releases include a **13 year old Halloween Edition** from October 2019. Exceptionally old expressions, **40** and **50 years old**, have also recently been released.

History:

1878 James Stuart & Co. begins planning the new distillery with Robert Dick, William Grant and John Cruickshank as partners.

1879 Production starts in December.

1884 The distillery changes name to Glenrothes-Glenlivet.

1887 William Grant & Co. joins forces with Islay Distillery Co. and forms Highland Distillers Company.

1897 A fire ravages the distillery.

1903 An explosion causes substantial damage.

1963 Expansion from four to six stills.

1980 Expansion from six to eight stills.

1989 Expansion from eight to ten stills.

1999 Edrington and William Grant & Sons buy Highland Distillers.

2002 Four single casks from 1966/1967 are launched.

2005 A 30 year old is launched together with Select Reserve and Vintage 1985.

2008 1978 Vintage and Robur Reserve are launched.

2009 The Glenrothes John Ramsay, Alba Reserve and Three Decades are released.

2010 Berry Brothers takes over the brand.

2011 Editor´s Casks are released.

2013 2001 Vintage and the Manse Brae range are released.

2014 Sherry Cask Reserve and 1969 Extraordinary Cask are released.

2015 Glenrothes Vintage Single Malt is released.

2016 Peated Cask Reserve and Ancestor´s Reserve are released.

2017 The brand returns to Edrington and The Glenrothes Wine Merchant´s Collection is introduced.

2018 The entire range is revamped and four new bottlings with age statements are introduced.

2019 A 40 year old and a 50 year old are released.

2020 A 13 year old Halloween Edition is released.

Tasting notes Glenrothes Soleo 12 year old:

IR – Fresh and fruity on the nose with notes of strawberries/raspberries and a hint of cinnamon. The taste if fruity and spicy with notes of pear, cinnamon, nutmeg, lemon zest and, in the finish, brown sugar and a little ginger.

12 years old

Trailblazers of Malt Whisky

Steve McCarthy
McCarthy´s Oregon Single Malt
USA

As a young man, Steve McCarthy didn't harbour secret dreams of producing spirits. In fact, it wasn´t until the early 1980s, when Steve was 40, that the idea of building a distillery entered his mind. In the first four decades of his life though, both dedication and passion were evident – qualities that would later make him the first to produce an American single malt whisky.

He was born in Seattle in 1943 and later moved with his family to Myrtle Creek in Oregon. As a teenager, Steve loved hiking and he could spend hours climbing Mount Hood. But he longed for a bigger adventure and together with two college friends he went to Nepal in autumn 1963 to do some serious climbing. It ended with a tragedy when one of Steve´s friends died on the mountain. Four years later he wrote an article for Sports Illustrated (Ordeal Above Tesi Lapcha) about the life-changing episode. Back in the USA, Steve started studying at Columbia Law School and graduated in 1969. He practised law for two years but was simultaneously looking for ways where his skills could make a more direct impact on peoples´ lives and on the community. In the early 1970s, the famous political activist Ralph Nader gave a speech at Oregon State University. He encouraged the students to engage in consumer rights and environmental issues, urging them to power up to change the world. The Oregon Student Public Interest Research Group (OSPIRG) was founded and Steve became the first director of the organisation. One of the issues he and the organisation addressed was, due to the increasing car traffic, the alarming air pollution in Portland (and most other cities in America). Through OSPIRG he worked hard to improve public transport and was eventually handpicked by the governor to manage the local transit company – Tri-Met – where he stayed on for four years.

In 1977, Steve joined his father´s succesful gun accessory company and eventually took over the leadership. Part of the job included visiting customers in Europe and, especially, in France. This was by no means his first travels across the Atlantic. He made his first trip in 1961, for university studies, which brought him to Grenoble, a centre for skiing and climbing. His local friends often brought a bottle of home-made eau de vie when they socialized and Steve was intrigued by the taste and, not least, the process of turning fruits into liquor. During the next couple of decades he would come back to France many times and became more and more familiar with spirits distilled from fruits. His interest actually didn´t come out of the blue. His family had vast orchards of pears and apples back in Oregon. Sometimes the harvest would give a surplus of fruit for which they weren´t paid that much. So, Steve came up with the idea of starting a distillery to make the beautiful eau de vie he had enjoyed on his travels.

With no knowledge about distillation, Steve turned to Jörg Rupf for advice. Hailing from Germany, Rupf had started the St George distillery in San Francisco in 1982. Today he is often referred to as the father of the modern American artisan distillation movement. Steve told Rupf about his plans and made it clear from the start that since they would eventually become competitors, Steve would pay him $75,000 to share his knowledge. Rupf agreed and Steve ordered his first Holstein still. It arrived broken and it wasn´t until summer 1985 when a new still arrived that the production started. He named the distillery Clear Creek Distillery after the name of the family orchards and eventually bought a second still. He also sold the gun company with a profit that could have lasted him for the rest of his life doing nothing. That gave him the opportunity and the financial freedom to experiment at Clear Creek, creating a product that he himself liked, without having to think about building a brand that would sell to the masses within the next couple of years. This new adventure did cost a lot of money though and eventually he had to start thinking of how to sell his product. He had significant help with that from the rave reviews of his pear eau de vie.

In the early 1990s, Steve and his wife went on a fishing trip to Ireland. The Emerald Isle lived up to its reputation and it was raining most of the time. The couple were staying in a friend´s house where there was a huge collection of Scottish single malts. With plenty of time indoors, Steve and his friend went through the whiskies and Steve was particularly intrigued by the peated stuff from Islay, not least Lagavulin 16 year old. Back in Oregon he decided to make a try at producing whisky from malted barley – something that no one had done before in the States. With his other produce, the local touch was important where the pears and other fruits were being sourced "next door". If he wanted to make a peated single malt, he realised that he would have to buy the peated malted barley from Scotland as it couldn´t be found in USA. So in order to add a sense of "terroir" to the future whisky he knew that he would have to come up with an additional feature. He found it in the barrels that matured the spirit. The local *Quercus garryana* oak would become one of the cornerstones in building the flavour of McCarthy´s single malt. He filled the new make into sherry casks and then finished it off in garry oak. In fact, today the distillery is using only garry oak but with a mix of new wood and 1st, 2nd and 3rd fill casks.

His heavily peated, 3 year old McCarthy´s Oregon Single Malt, released in 1999 was the first American single malt and the reviews could not have been more overwhelming. In fact Steve constantly struggled to leave some stock to mature for more than three years but failed. The demand was huge and every batch that was released sold out instantly. Joe O´Sullivan, the current Master Distiller for McCarthy´s, was working with Steve from early on and he recalls one time when customers at the back end of the line at the distillery had to be turned down because the new batch had sold out in twenty minutes. That was when Joe went up to the office, picked up the few bottles that Steve had reserved for himself and sold them to the eager fans.

In 2014 Steve sold Clear Creek Distillery to Hood River Distillers who eventually, in 2017, moved the distillery to Hood River. Steve stayed on for a short while as a consultant and then left the business. At the age of 78, his legacy lives on, not least on every label of McCarthy´s Oregon Single Malt. Undoubtedly Steve McCarthy, through the benefit of the family businesses, was handed the means to do something extraordinary but it takes a true entrepreneur equipped with passion, courage and curiosity to actually seize that opportunity.

Glen Scotia

[glen <u>sko</u>•sha]

Owner: **Region/district:**
Loch Lomond Group   Campbeltown
(Hillhouse Capital Management)

Founded: **Status:**   **Capacity:**
1832   Active (vc)   800 000 litres

Address: High Street, Campbeltown, Argyll PA28 6DS

Website: **Tel:**
glenscotia.com   01586 552288

The transformation of Glen Scotia from a malt known only to a few whisky enthusiasts to a brand well respected in a wider market is impressive.

A couple of attempts by the previous owner to establish Glen Scotia as a brand failed miserably and it wasn't until Exponent Equity (later bought by Hillhouse) took over in 2014 that things started to happen. A much needed re-design of both bottles and labels was made and, more importantly, an entire new range of bottlings was launched. The brain behind the new expression is Michael Henry who joined the company as a warehouseman in 2007 and later advanced to master blender. Around the same time Iain McAllister became the distillery manager and he has worked tirelessly to transform the worn-out distillery to a beautiful and efficient site which includes a visitor centre.

Glen Scotia is equipped with a traditional 2.8 ton cast iron mash tun, nine washbacks made of stainless steel with an average fermentation time of 128 hours and one pair of stills. The shortest fermentation time is 70 hours and the longest up to 140 hours. The cut points for the middle cut are 73%-63% and slightly lower for the peated version. During the extreme year of 2020, the distillery managed to produce only 220,000 litres of alcohol but for 2021 it's back to 10 mashes per week and 500,000 litres. The latest peated share of the production was eight weeks of medium (23.5ppm) and heavily peated (54.5ppm).

The core range consists of **Double Cask, 15, 18** and **25 year old** and the gently peated **Victoriana** which has been bottled at cask strength. There is also **Glen Scotia Harbour**, a 100% first fill bourbon, which is an exclusive to Waitrose and Tesco Scotland as well as a new **10 year old** exclusive to Germany and Japan. The 10 year old peated sold only in USA and Germany has been discontinued. The duty free range (due for an update in 2022) consists of **Glen Scotia Campbeltown 1832** finished in PX sherry casks, a **16 year old** and a **vintage 1991**. Limited expressions include a **30 year old** released in 2020, a **10 year old Bordeaux red wine cask finish** for the Campbeltown Malts Festival and, due for release at the end of 2021, a **46 year old**.

History:

1832 The families of Stewart and Galbraith start Scotia Distillery.

1895 The distillery is sold to Duncan McCallum.

1919 Sold to West Highland Malt Distillers.

1924 West Highland Malt Distillers goes bankrupt and Duncan MacCallum buys back the distillery.

1930 The distillery closes and Duncan MacCallum commits suicide

1933 Bloch Brothers Ltd take over and production restarts.

1954 Hiram Walker takes over.

1955 A. Gillies & Co. becomes new owner.

1970 A. Gillies & Co. becomes part of Amalgamated Distilled Products.

1979 Reconstruction takes place.

1984 The distillery closes.

1986 Amalgamated Distilled Products is taken over by Gibson International.

1989 Production starts again.

1994 Glen Catrine Bonded Warehouse Ltd takes over and the distillery is mothballed.

1999 The distillery re-starts under Loch Lomond Distillery supervision using staff from Springbank.

2000 Loch Lomond Distillers runs operations with its own staff from May onwards.

2005 A 12 year old is released.

2006 A peated version is released.

2012 A new range (10, 12, 16, 18 and 21 year old) is launched.

2014 A 10 year old and one without age statement are released - both heavily peated.

2015 A new range is released; Double Cask, 15 year old and Victoriana.

2017 A 25 year old and an 18 year old as well as two bottlings for duty-free are released.

2019 The distillery is sold to Hillhouse Capital Management. A 2003 Vintage and a 45 year old are released.

2021 A 46 year old is released.

Tasting notes Glen Scotia Double Cask:

GS – The nose is sweet, with bramble and redcurrant aromas, plus caramel and vanilla. Smooth mouth-feel, with ginger, sherry and more vanilla. The finish is quite long, with spicy sherry and a final hint of brine.

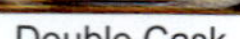

Double Cask

Glen Spey

[glen spey]

Owner: Diageo

Region/district: Speyside

Founded: 1878

Status: Active

Capacity: 1 500 000 litres

Address: Rothes, Morayshire AB38 7AU

Website: malts.com

Tel: 01340 831215

The third smallest of the Diageo group of distilleries and virtually unknown to most whisky drinkers, Glen Spey is a distillery rarely heard of. You pass it in a blink of an eye even though it is located on the main street of Rothes.

The village of Rothes on the other hand is famous as an epicentre of everything that relates to whisky production. Another three, large distilleries can be found here (Glen Grant, Glenrothes and Speyburn) and the town is also home to the famous Forsyths Coppersmiths, making pot stills and other equipment for distilleries all over the world. A few hundred metres from Forsyths lies a dark grains plant where pot ale is turned into animal food and since 2013 there is also a bio plant where draff from the whisky production is burned together with wood chips to create electricity. Both plants are co-owned by the local distilleries through CoRD (Combination of Rothes Distilleries). And as if that wasn't enough, the family owned Simpsons Malt with two plants in England, have plans to open a state of the art maltings on a 40-acre site near Rothes.

Glen Spey distillery is equipped with a 4.4 ton semi-lauter mash tun, eight stainless steel washbacks with both short (46 hours) and long (100 hours) fermentations and two pairs of stills. The two spirit stills are equipped with purifiers which add reflux and also help eliminate the heavier esters. Due to a cloudy wort, the Glen Spey new make is nutty and slightly oily. Even though a new control room was installed in 2017, Glen Spey is still run largely as a manual distillery. The distillery is usually producing on a 5-day week with 18 mashes per week (ten short and eight long) and 1.5 million litres of pure alcohol in the year.

Virtually all of the produce goes into blends and especially J&B, the sixth biggest brand in the world. The only official single malt is the **12 year old Flora & Fauna** bottling. In 2010, two limited releases were made – a **1996 single cask** from new American oak and a **21 year old** with maturation in ex-sherry American oak.

History:

1878 James Stuart & Co. founds the distillery which becomes known by the name Mill of Rothes.

1886 James Stuart buys Macallan.

1887 W. & A. Gilbey buys the distillery for £11,000 thus becoming the first English company to buy a Scottish malt distillery.

1920 A fire breaks out and the main part of the distillery is re-built.

1962 W. & A. Gilbey combines forces with United Wine Traders and forms International Distillers & Vintners (IDV).

1970 The stills are increased from two to four.

1972 IDV is bought by Watney Mann which is then acquired by Grand Metropolitan.

1997 Guiness and Grand Metropolitan merge to form Diageo.

2001 A 12 year old is launched in the Flora & Fauna series.

2010 A 21 year old is released as part of the Special Releases and a 1996 Manager's Choice single cask is launched.

12 years old

Tasting notes Glen Spey 12 years old:

GS – Tropical fruits and malt on the comparatively delicate nose. Medium-bodied with fresh fruits and vanilla toffee on the palate, becoming steadily nuttier and drier in a gently oaky, mildly smoky finish.

Glentauchers

[glen•tock•ers]

Owner: **Region/district:**
Chivas Brothers   Speyside
(Pernod Ricard)

Founded: **Status:**   **Capacity:**
1897   Active   4 200 000 litres

Address: Mulben, Keith, Banffshire AB55 6YL

Website: **Tel:**
-                 01542 860272

For an enthusiast, the majority of Scottish distilleries are more or less familiar, at least when it comes to the whisky itself. If official releases are scarce, independent bottlers make up for the loss. But whisky lovers also want to visit the distilleries they adore.

Even though many distilleries nowadays have visitor centres, quite a few are considered as production units by their owners and do not allow people entering the site. This approach should of course always be respected but there is nothing preventing you from stopping by on your journey to take pictures. Distillery spotting if you like! Glentauchers is one of these hidden gems and since it's located right on the busy A95 between Keith and Craigellachie, I have two suggestions for photo opportunities without entering the distillery or obstructing the traffic. Coming from Keith, you take a left opposite the distillery on to a small dirt track, park and climb the small hill. Or you take right just after the distillery and take pictures from the railway side of the distillery.

The distillery is equipped with a 12.2 ton stainless steel full lauter mash tun. There are six washbacks made of Oregon pine and three pairs of stills. The distillery is now doing 18 mashes per week and a total of 4 million litres per year. In February 2020, Pernod Ricard announced that they had plans to turn Glentauchers into their first carbon-neutral distillery by using biofuel within two years. The plan is part of a grander scheme where the emission of greenhouse gases for all of their plants will be reduced by a further 20%.

Over the years Glentauchers' role has been to produce malt whisky for blends: Buchanan's Black & White, Teachers and Ballantines. Official bottlings have been scarce but in 2017 a **15 year old** was launched as a part of the Ballantine's Single Malt Series which was recently accompanied by a **23 year old**. There are also three cask strength bottlings in the Distillery Reserve Collection, available at all Chivas' visitor centres – two **13** and one **21 year old**.

History:

1897 James Buchanan and W. P. Lowrie, a whisky merchant from Glasgow, found the distillery.

1898 Production starts.

1906 James Buchanan & Co. takes over the whole distillery and acquires an 80% share in W. P. Lowrie & Co.

1915 James Buchanan & Co. merges with Dewars.

1923 Mashing house and maltings are rebuilt.

1925 Buchanan-Dewars joins Distillers Company Limited (DCL).

1930 Glentauchers is transferred to Scottish Malt Distillers (SMD).

1965 The number of stills is increased from two to six.

1969 Floor maltings is decommissioned.

1985 DCL mothballs the distillery.

1989 United Distillers (formerly DCL) sells the distillery to Caledonian Malt Whisky Distillers, a subsidiary of Allied Distillers.

1992 Production recommences in August.

2000 A 15 year old Glentauchers is released.

2005 Chivas Brothers (Pernod Ricard) become the new owner through the acquisition of Allied Domecq.

2017 A 15 year old is released in the Ballantine´s Single Malt Series.

2021 A 23 year old is launched.

15 years old

Tasting notes Glentauchers 15 years old:

IR – Delicious on the nose, both floral and fruity, vanilla, pastry, heather and honey. Still fruity on the palate with additional notes of roasted nuts, toffee and milk chocolate..

Glenturret

[glen•turr•et]

Owner: **Region/district:**
Lalique Group/Hansjörg Wyss   Southern Highlands

Founded: **Status:**   **Capacity:**
1775   Active (vc)   340 000 litres

Address: The Hosh, Crieff, Perthshire PH7 4HA

Website: **Tel:**
theglenturret.com   01764 656565

The debate over which the oldest working distillery in Scotland is, resurrects every now and then. Among the contenders for the title have been distilleries such as Bowmore, Glen Garioch and Glenturret.

For quite some time consensus has been that Glenturret deserves the title and it has often been said it was established around the year 1775 as Hosh distillery. Recent findings however indicate the distillery could have been founded even earlier than that. A rental document of Sir Patrick of Ochtertye, 4th Baronet Murray, who died in 1764, refers to Thurot Distillery. The Murray family owned extensive lands and property and part of it was rented out to tennants, in this case to one who started a distillery. In 1990, Glenturret was bought by Highland Distillers (Edrington) who twelve years later turned it into the spiritual home of the blend Famous Grouse. In 2018 it was sold to Lalique, a Swiss company specializing in luxury products such as crystal glassware, jewelry and furniture. The visitor centre has been considerably revamped and it is no longer connected to Famous Grouse.

The distillery is equipped with a 1.05 ton stainless steel, open mash tun, eight Douglas fir washbacks with a fermentation time of up to 120 hours and one pair of stills. The production target for 2021 is 8-10 mashes per week 250,000 litres. A small part of the production is usually made up of the heavily peated (80ppm) Ruadh Maor. The owners plan to increase production, without adding any new equipment, to 500,000 litres within the next couple of years.

A completely new range was introduced in September 2020 and the core range now consists of seven expressions, all with different abv; **Triple Wood** (43%), **10 year old Peat Smoked** (50%), **12 year old** (46%), **15 year old** (55%), **25 year old** (44,5%) and **30 year old** (45,7%). A range of very limited bottlings, **The Trinity**, was also introduced with a **33 year old** as the first expression. Finally in collaboration with the car company Jaguar, a **Glenturret Jaguar E-Type** at least 30 years old has also been released.

History:

1775 Whisky smugglers establish a small illicit farm distillery named Hosh Distillery.

1818 John Drummond is licensee until 1837.

1826 A distillery in the vicinity is named Glenturret, but is decommissioned before 1852.

1852 John McCallum is licensee until 1874.

1875 Hosh Distillery takes over the name Glenturret Distillery and is managed by Thomas Stewart.

1903 Mitchell Bros Ltd takes over.

1921 Production ceases and the buildings are used for whisky storage only.

1929 Mitchell Bros Ltd is liquidated, the distillery dismantled and the facilities are used as storage for agricultural needs.

1957 James Fairlie buys the distillery and re-equips it.

1959 Production restarts.

1981 Remy-Cointreau buys the distillery and invests in a visitor centre.

1990 Highland Distillers takes over.

1999 Edrington and William Grant & Sons buy Highland Distillers for £601 million. The purchasing company, 1887 Company, is a joint venture between Edrington (70%) and William Grant (30%).

2002 The Famous Grouse Experience, a visitor centre costing £2.5 million, is inaugurated.

2003 A 10 year old Glenturret replaces the 12 year old as the distillery´s standard release.

2007 Three new single casks are released.

2013 An 18 year old bottled at cask strength is released as a distillery exclusive.

2014 A 1986 single cask is released.

2015 Sherry, Triple Wood and Peated are released.

2016 Fly´s 16 Masters is released.

2017 Cameron´s Cut, Jamieson´s Jigger Edition and Peated Drummond Edition are launched.

2019 Lalique Group and Hansjörg Wyss buy the distillery.

2020 A completely new core range is launched.

2021 Glenturret Jaguar E-Type is released.

Tasting notes Glenturret 12 years old:

GS – Initial hints of Christmas cake and old leather, warm spices, dried fruits and old oak. Sweet and rich on the palate with tangy orange notes, cinnamon, dates, walnuts, caramel and lingering ginger.

12 years old

Highland Park

[hi•land <u>park</u>]

Owner:
The Edrington Group

Region/district:
Highlands (Orkney)

Founded: 1798
Status: Active (vc)
Capacity: 2 500 000 litres

Address: Holm Road, Kirkwall, Orkney KW15 1SU

Website:
highlandparkwhisky.com

Tel:
01856 874619

In March 2021, Highland Park released the third version of their 50 year old single malt and the story behind it serves as an interesting description of the genesis of a very old whisky.

In 1968 numerous casks of Highland Park newmake were filled to eventually become part of the standard 12 year old a little more than a decade later. When remaining casks were examined in the early 1990s, it became obvious that some of these refill casks had produced a whisky that was too pale for a Highland Park. They were put aside to eventually be used as a vintage in the future. In 2008, nine of these casks were assessed again and since the whisky was still light in colour the spirit was re-racked into first fill sherry casks made of European oak. Twelve years later the whisky had adopted both a darker colour, tannins and flavour of dried fruits, the quality was exceptional and master blender Gordon Motion used it as the foundation of the 50 year old.

The distillery is equipped with a 12 ton semi-lauter mash tun, twelve Oregon pine washbacks with a fermentation time between 50 and 80 hours, and two pairs of stills. In the last couple of years there has been 22 mashes per week which means a total of 2.5 million litres of alcohol. Highland Park is malting 30% of its malt themselves and there are five malting floors with a capacity of almost 36 tons of barley. The phenol content is 30-40 ppm in its own malt and the malt which has been bought from Simpson's is unpeated. The distillery has an excellent visitor centre attracting 15,000 people every year and recently the owners opened a shop right in the centre of Kirkwall. Apart from selling Highland Park whisky, the shop houses a gallery and an education area.

The core range of Highland Park consists of **10 year old Viking Scars, 12 year old Viking Honour,** the new **15 year old Viking Heart** which was launched in September 2021, **18 year old Viking Pride** as well as **21, 25, 30** and **40 year olds**. In autumn 2020 a **Cask Strength** was added to the range and included are also **Dragon Legend** and **Viking Tribe**. The duty free range, called the Warrior Series, has been around for several years and the more expensive ones, **Sigurd, Ragnvald** and **Thorfinn**, are still available, although in limited numbers. The rest were replaced in 2018 by **Spirit of the Bear** (matured mainly in American oak ex-sherry), **Loyalty of the Wolf** (14 years old, matured in a combination of American oak ex-sherry and ex-bourbon), **Wings of the Eagle** (16 years old, predominantly from European oak ex-sherry) and a duty free version of the **18 year old Viking Pride**.

Recent limited expressions include a new edition of the **50 year old** released in March 2021. There is also the **16 year old Twisted Tattoo** which was partly matured in ex-Rioja casks, the third instalment in the Viking Legend series, **Valfather**, and **Triskelion**. The latter, released in late 2019, was created by the distillery's current master whisky maker Gordon Motion together with his predecessors John Ramsay and Max McFarlane. Every year a number of single casks are also released.

History:

1798 David Robertson founds the distillery. The local smuggler and businessman Magnus Eunson previously operated an illicit whisky production on the site.

1816 John Robertson, an Excise Officer who arrested Magnus Eunson, takes over production.

1826 Highland Park obtains a license and the distillery is taken over by Robert Borwick.

1840 Robert´s son George Borwick takes over but the distillery deteriorates.

1869 The younger brother James Borwick inherits Highland Park and attempts to sell it as he does not consider the distillation of spirits as compatible with his priesthood.

1895 James Grant (of Glenlivet Distillery) buys Highland Park.

1898 The distillery is expanded from two to four stills.

1937 Highland Distilleries buys Highland Park.

1979 Highland Distilleries invests considerably in marketing Highland Park as single malt which increases sales markedly.

1986 A visitor centre, considered one of Scotland's finest, is opened.

1997 Two new Highland Park are launched, an 18 year old and a 25 year old.

1999 Highland Distillers are acquired by Edrington Group and William Grant & Sons.

2000 Visit Scotland awards Highland Park "Five Star Visitor Attraction".

2005 Highland Park 30 years old is released. A 16 year old for the Duty Free market and Ambassador´s Cask 1984 are released.

2006 The second edition of Ambassador´s Cask, a 10 year old from 1996, is released.

History continued:

2007 The Rebus 20, a 21 year old duty free exclusive, a 38 year old and a 39 year old are released.

2008 A 40 year old and the third and fourth editions of Ambassador´s Cask are released.

2009 Two vintages and Earl Magnus 15 year are released.

2010 A 50 year old, Saint Magnus 12 year old, Orcadian Vintage 1970 and four duty free vintages are released.

2011 Vintage 1978, Leif Eriksson and 18 year old Earl Haakon are released.

2012 Thor and a 21 year old are released.

2013 Loki and a new range for duty free, The Warriors, are released.

2014 Freya and Dark Origins are released.

2015 Odin is released.

2016 Hobbister, Ice Edition, Ingvar and King Christian I are released.

2017 Valkyrie, Dragon Legend, Voyage of the Raven, Shiel, Full Volume, The Dark and The Light are released.

2018 New duty free bottlings include Spirit of the Bear, Loyalty of the Wolf and Wings of the Eagle. The limited Valknut is also released.

2019 Twisted Tattoo, Valfather, Triskelion and a 21 year old are released.

2020 A cask strength is added to the core range.

2021 A 15 year old and a 50 year old are released.

Tasting notes Highland Park 12 year old:

GS – The nose is fragrant and floral, with hints of heather and some spice. Smooth and honeyed on the palate, with citric fruits, malt and distinctive tones of wood smoke in the warm, lengthy, slightly peaty finish.

21 years old   Twisted Tattoo   Triskelion

12 years old

Cask Strength

Loyalty of the Wolf

Inchgower

[inch•gow•er]

Owner: **Region/district:**
Diageo   Speyside

Founded: **Status:**   **Capacity:**
1871   Active   3 200 000 litres

Address: Buckie, Banffshire AB56 5AB

Website: **Tel:**
malts.com   01542 836700

That the owners of Inchgower, Alexander Wilson & Co, went bankrupt in 1936 might not have been so strange, as the previous years were amongst the toughest ever for the Scottish whisky industry.

The Wall Street crash in 1929 had led to a deep recession and in 1933 only two pot distilleries (Glenlivet and Glen Grant) and 13 grain distilleries were working in Scotland. The total production of malt whisky during that year was only 285,000 gallons, the lowest since 1824. But when Franklin D. Roosevelt became president of the USA in the same year, he pledged to abolish prohibition and, slowly but surely, the market for Scotch improved. Arthur Bell & Co had in the meanwhile kept ahead of the game and already acquired Blair Athol, as well as Dufftown in 1933. When they bought Inchgower in 1938 the amount of malt whisky produced was over 10 million gallons. For almost 50 years Inchgower was run by Bells until the Guinness group acquired Bells for £356m. The distillery is owned by Diageo today and it continues to produce mainly for the blended industry.

For at least 80 years Ingower single malt has been one of the most important malts in Bell's blended Scotch. The famous brand is the second best selling blend in the UK and in the difficult year of 2020 it managed much better than most brands with an impressive increase of 13% to 25 million bottles.

The distillery is equipped with an 8.4 ton stainless steel semilauter mash tun where the cloudy wort adds to the spirit character. Six washbacks made from Oregon pine with an average fermentation time of 48-53 hours are complemented by two pairs of stills. The production plan for 2021 is a seven-day operation with 19 mashes per week and 3,2 million litres. It also entails fermentations of 50-52 hours as opposed to a combination of short (42 hours) and long (90 hours) when operating a five-day week.

Besides the official **Flora & Fauna 14 year old**, there have also been a few limited bottlings of Inchgower single malt. The most recent was a **27 year old** in autumn 2018 which was part of the yearly Special Releases.

History:

1871   Alexander Wilson & Co. founds the distillery. Equipment from the disused Tochineal Distillery, also owned by Alexander Wilson, is installed.

1936   Alexander Wilson & Co. becomes bankrupt and Buckie Town Council buys the distillery and the family's home for £1,600.

1938   The distillery is sold on to Arthur Bell & Sons for £3,000.

1966   Capacity doubles to four stills.

1985   Guinness acquires Arthur Bell & Sons.

1987   United Distillers is formed by a merger between Arthur Bell & Sons and DCL.

1997   Inchgower 1974 (22 years) is released as a Rare Malt.

2004   Inchgower 1976 (27 years) is released as a Rare Malt.

2010   A single cask from 1993 is released.

2018   A 27 year old is launched as part of the Special Releases.

Tasting notes Inchgower 14 years old:

GS – Ripe pears and a hint of brine on the light nose. Grassy and gingery in the mouth, with some acidity. The finish is spicy, dry and relatively short.

14 years old

Jura

[joo•rah]

Owner: **Region/district:**
Whyte & Mackay   Highlands (Jura)
(Emperador Inc)

Founded: **Status:**   **Capacity:**
1810   Active (vc)   2 400 000 litres

Address: Craighouse, Isle of Jura PA60 7XT

Website: **Tel:**
jurawhisky.com   01496 820240

There may be many expressions from the distillery that have been partly matured in various sherry and wine casks but starting in 1995 all of the new make spirit from Jura is initially filled into first fill bourbon casks.

The stock from pre 1995 however, had been filled into wood of a lesser quality and this initiated a gigantic re-racking programme which lasted from 1998 until 2016. No less than 30,000 casks were emptied and the maturing whisky was filled into casks of a better quality.

Jura distillery has a 5 ton semi-lauter mash tun, six stainless steel washbacks with a fermentation time of 54 hours and two pairs of stills . In summer 2021 four complete new stills were installed during the silent season. Starting with clear worts and due to the tall stills with large pots, narrow waists and slightly ascending lye pipes the Jura new make is light and fruity. The production plan for 2021 is 28 mashes per week and close to 2,4 million litres of alcohol and as usual this will include a couple of weeks of peated production (45ppm).

The core range consists of **Journey, 10 year old, 12 year old, Seven Wood, 18 year old** and the **21 year old Tide**. All the expressions have an amount of peated Jura in the recipe. There is also **French Oak** and a new series called **Cask Editions** which is part of the signature range but sold seasonally. The latest include **Red Wine Cask, Winter Edition** and **Rum Cask**. For duty-free there are **The Sound, The Road, The Loch** and the **19 year old The Paps** – all of them finished in PX casks. There is also the **21 year old Jura Time**, finished in ex-peated malt casks and, exclusive to travel retail in Asia, the **12 year old The Bay**. Recent limited releases include the **13 year old Two-One-Two** which was finished in casks made of Chinkapin oak, a **28 year old, Very Rare Vintage 1975** and four other vintages; **1988, 1989, 1990** and **1993**. The last two were released in September 2021. Finally, the Feis Ile 2021 bottling was an **18 year old** fully matured in a refill sherry butt.

History:

1810 Archibald Campbell founds a distillery named Small Isles Distillery.

1853 Richard Campbell leases the distillery to Norman Buchanan from Glasgow.

1867 Buchanan files for bankruptcy and J. & K. Orr takes over the distillery.

1876 Licence transferred to James Ferguson & Sons.

1901 Ferguson dismantles the distillery.

1960 Charles Mackinlay & Co. extends the distillery. Newly formed Scottish & Newcastle Breweries acquires Charles Mackinlay & Co.

1963 The first distilling takes place.

1985 Invergordon Distilleries acquires Charles Mackinlay & Co. from Scottish & Newcastle.

1993 Whyte & Mackay (Fortune Brands) buys Invergordon Distillers.

1996 Whyte & Mackay changes name to JBB (Greater Europe).

2001 The management buys out the company and changes the name to Kyndal.

2002 Isle of Jura Superstition is launched.

2003 Kyndal reverts back to its old name, Whyte & Mackay. Isle of Jura 1984 is launched.

2006 The 40 year old Jura is released.

2007 United Spirits buys Whyte & Mackay.

2008 A series of four different vintages, called Elements, is released.

2009 Prophecy and Paps of Jura are released.

2012 The 12 year old Jura Elixir is released.

2013 Camas an Staca, 1977 Juar and Turas-Mara are released.

2014 Whyte & Mackay is sold to Emperador Inc.

2016 The 22 year old "One For The Road" is released.

2017 The limited One and All is released.

2018 A new core range is released; 10, 12 and 18 year old as well as Journey and Seven Wood.

2019 A new range for duty-free is released.

2020 Red Wine Cask and Winter Edition are released.

2021 Cask Editions and two vintages (1990 and 1993) are launched.

Tasting notes Jura 10 years old:

GS – Resin, oil and pine notes on the delicate nose. Light-bodied in the mouth, with malt and drying saltiness. The finish is malty, nutty, with more salt, plus just a wisp of smoke.

12 years old

Kilchoman

[kil•ho•man]

Owner:
Kilchoman Distillery Co.

Region/district:
Islay

Founded: **Status:**
2005   Active (vc)

Capacity:
650 000 litres

Address: Rockside farm, Bruichladdich,
Islay PA49 7UT

Website:
kilchomandistillery.com

Tel:
01496 850011

Kilchoman sells around 300,000 bottles per year but the owner, Anthony Wills, is definitely aiming for substantially larger volumes in the future. His investments in the distillery the past couple of years are evidence of a strong belief in the future.

In spring 2019 a second distillery was opened next to the existing one and a new malting floor and kiln was also part of that year's expansion. In 2020 a fully automated bottle filler was installed as well as a second semi-automatic line for single casks and small batches. Then, in summer 2021, two more washbacks were added which brings the capacity for the distillery to 650,000 litres of alcohol per year. Over the years more warehouses have been built and in 2015 Wills bought Rockside farm, whose lands surround the distillery. Every year they harvest 200 tons of barley that is used for Kilchoman 100% Islay

The distillery is equipped with two 1.2 ton stainless steel semi-lauter mash tuns, 14 stainless steel, 6,000 litre washbacks with an average fermentation time of 90 hours and two pairs of stills. Last year 365,000 litres of alcohol were distilled and in 2021 the plan is to increase that to 500,000 litres. Around 30% of their malt requirement is malted in-house, typically with a phenol content of 20ppm. The rest (50ppm) is bought from Port Ellen.

The core range consists of **Machir Bay** and **Sanaig**. Limited, but regular releases are **Loch Gorm** matured in oloroso casks and **100% Islay** made from 100% barley grown and malted on the island. Other recent limited releases include **Am Burach** ("the mess" in Gaelic), which was the result of a serendipitous mix of Machir Bay and port matured Kilchoman during vatting, a **fino sherry cask-matured** and **Machir Bay Cask Strength**. Limited bottlings in May 2021 were a **bourbon/sherry maturation** for Feis Ile that had been made from barley harvested and malted at Kilchoman and a **PX sherry cask matured**. These were then followed in September by a **Madeira cask matured**. For the UK duty free market there is **Coull Point** and for global duty free, **Saligo Bay** is available.

History:

2002 Plans are formed for a new distillery at Rockside Farm on western Islay.

2005 Production starts in June.

2006 A fire breaks out in the kiln causing a few weeks' production stop but malting has to cease for the rest of the year.

2007 The distillery is expanded with two new washbacks.

2009 The first single malt, a 3 year old, is released on 9th September followed by a second release.

2010 Three new releases and an introduction to the US market. John Maclellan from Bunnahabhain joins the team as General Manager.

2011 Kilchoman 100% Islay is released as well as a 4 year old and a 5 year old.

2012 Machir Bay, the first core expression, is released together with Kilchoman Sherry Cask Release and the second edition of 100% Islay.

2013 Loch Gorm and Vintage 2007 are released.

2014 A 3 year old port cask matured and the first duty free exclusive, Coull Point, are released.

2015 A Madeira cask maturation is released and the distillery celebrates its 10th anniversary.

2016 Sanaig and a Sauternes cask maturation are released.

2017 A Portugese red wine maturation and Vintage 2009 are released.

2018 Original Cask Strength and 2009 Vintage are released.

2019 Capacity is doubled with two more stills. A limited STR Cask Matured is released.

2020 Am Burach and a fino sherry cask are released.

2021 Two bottlings matured in PX sherry cask and madeira cask respectively are launched.

Machir Bay

Tasting notes Kilchoman Machir Bay:

GS – A nose of sweet peat and vanilla, undercut by brine, kelp and black pepper. Filled ashtrays in time. A smooth mouth-feel, with lots of nicely-balanced citrus fruit, peat smoke and Germolene on the palate. The finish is relatively long and sweet, with building spice, chili and a final nuttiness.

Kininvie

[kin•in•vee]

Owner: William Grant & Sons

Region/district: Speyside

Founded: 1990

Status: Active

Capacity: 4 800 000 litres

Address: Dufftown, Keith, Banffshire AB55 4DH

Website: kininvie.com

Tel: 01340 820373

Kininvie is what the owners, William Grant & Sons, like to call "our free-thinking distillery". Some whisky enthusiasts refer to their malt as "a whisky made by geeks for geeks". But the birth of the distillery was far less adventurous.

In the late 1980s sales of the Grant's blended Scotch were booming and more stock of malt whisky was needed. At the same time Glenfiddich single malt, as a brand of its own, was on the rise. More malt capacity became essential and so Kininvie was built on the grounds of Balvenie (also owned by the Grant family). For twenty years Kininvie produced malt for blends. When the company's fourth distillery, Ailsa Bay, was built in 2007 there was an opportunity to do something more with Kininvie. That was when new grain varieties and triple distillation was introduced as part of the production.

Kininvie distillery consists of one still house with three wash stills and six spirit stills. There is a 9.6 ton stainless steel full lauter mash tun which is placed next to Balvenie's in the Balvenie distillery. Ten Douglas fir washbacks with a minimum fermentation time of 70 hours (typically 75 hours) can be found in two separate rooms. In 2021 the distillery will be doing 20 mashes per week but due to an extended silent period the total volume will be one million litres less than usual which means 3 million litres compared to just under 4 million liters. Innovative distillation has been a part of Kininvie for quite some time now and while production of rye whisky is still ongoing, triple distillation hasn't been on the menu for several years.

The first official bottling appeared in 2013 and later both a 17 year old and a 23 year old were released. In 2019, three experimental whiskies were launched under the name Kininvie Works. The **KVSM001** is a 5 year old triple distilled single malt while the **KVSG002** is a whisky made of 11% malted rye and 89% malted barley and matured in virgin American oak for three years. Finally, there is **KVSB003** which is a blend of double distilled malt and the aforementioned rye/barley whisky.

History:

1990 Kininvie distillery is inaugurated and the first distillation takes place on 25th June.

1994 Another three stills are installed.

2006 The first expression of a Kininvie single malt is released as a 15 year old under the name Hazelwood.

2008 In February a 17 year old Hazelwood Reserve is launched at Heathrow´s Terminal 5.

2013 A 23 year old Kininvie is launched in Taiwan.

2014 A 17 year old and batch 2 of the 23 year old are released.

2015 Batch 3 of the 23 year old is released and later in the year, the batches are replaced by a 23 year old signature bottling. Three 25 year old single casks are launched.

2019 Three expressions in the Kininvie Works series are released.

Tasting notes Kininvie 17 years old:

GS – The nose offers tropical fruits, coconut and vanilla custard, with a hint of milk chocolate. Pineapple and mango on the palate, accompanied by linseed oil, ginger, and developing nuttiness. The finish dries slowly, with more linseed, plenty of spice, and soft oak.

Kininvie KVSB003

Knockando

[nock•<u>an</u>•doo]

Owner: Diageo.

Region/district: Speyside

Founded: 1898

Status: Active

Capacity: 1 400 000 litres

Address: Knockando, Morayshire AB38 7RT

Website: malts.com

Tel: 01340 882000

Knockando distillery was closed in December 2017 subject to a major refurbishment. Usually that would mean no production for two years but it took until summer 2021 before the stills were fired up again.

Allegedly, the distillery will, at least to start with, work for six months per year and the staff will alternate between Knockando and another Diageo distillery. Eleven of the 28 Diageo malt distilleries produce whisky more or less for blends only, yet at the same time they are represented in the official Flora & Fauna range of single malts. That range celebrates its 30th anniversary this year and also made Diageo the first major Scotch whisky producer to make sure that single malts from all of their distilleries were available as official bottlings. Knockando on the other hand, albeit important to the J&B blend, has been a brand of its own for many decades now, popular not least in Spain and France. The latest sales figures were 500,000 bottles and hopefully the re-start of the distillery is a sign from the owners that they intend to continue with the brand. Knockando is beautifully situated on the Spey river at the end of the road with Tamdhu and Cardhu as its nearest distillery neighbours.

The distillery is equipped with a small (4.4 ton), semi-lauter mash tun, eight Douglas fir washbacks and two pairs of stills. Knockando has always worked a five-day week with 16 mashes per week, 8 short fermentations (50 hours) and 8 long (100 hours). The nutty character of the newmake, a result of the cloudy worts coming from the mash tun, has given it its fame. However, in order to balance the taste, the distillers also wish to create the typical Speyside floral notes by using boiling balls on the spirit stills to increase reflux.

Even though Knockando is a vital part of the J&B blend, it is also Diageo's 8th most sold single malt. The core range consists of **12 year old, 15 year old Richly Matured, 18 year old Slow Matured** and the **21 year old Master Reserve**. In 2011 a **25 year old** matured in first fill European oak was released as part of the Special Releases.

History:

1898 John Thompson founds the distillery. The architect is Charles Doig.

1899 Production starts in May.

1900 The distillery closes in March and J. Thompson & Co. takes over administration.

1903 W. & A. Gilbey purchases the distillery for £3,500 and production restarts in October.

1962 W. & A. Gilbey merges with United Wine Traders (including Justerini & Brooks) and forms International Distillers & Vintners (IDV).

1968 Floor maltings is decommissioned.

1969 The number of stills is increased to four.

1972 IDV is acquired by Watney Mann who, in its turn, is taken over by Grand Metropolitan.

1978 Justerini & Brooks launches a 12 year old Knockando.

1997 Grand Metropolitan and Guinness merge and form Diageo; simultaneously IDV and United Distillers merge to United Distillers & Vintners.

2010 A Manager´s Choice 1996 is released.

2011 A 25 year old is released.

2017 The distillery closes for refurbishing.

2021 Production starts again.

12 years old

Tasting notes Knockando 12 years old:

GS – Delicate and fragrant on the nose, with hints of malt, worn leather, and hay. Quite full in the mouth, smooth and honeyed, with gingery malt and a suggestion of white rum. Medium length in the finish, with cereal and more ginger.

Knockdhu

[nock•<u>doo</u>]

Owner:
Inver House Distillers
(Thai Beverages plc)

Region/district:
Highland

Founded: 1893 **Status:** Active (vc) **Capacity:** 2 000 000 litres

Address: Knock, By Huntly, Aberdeenshire AB54 7LJ

Website: ancnoc.com **Tel:** 01466 771223

With more than 50 years in the whisky business, the owners of Knockdhu, Inver House, is one of the dominant players in the industry today. But the company has had its fair share of ups and downs.

Founded in 1964 by an American, Harry Publicker, and based in Scotland, the company employed over 1,000 people in Airdrie, North Lanarkshire in its heyday. However, a serious decline for Scotch whisky in the late 70s and early 80s, combined with the death of Harry Publicker, had put an end to the glory days for the company. Intervention by way of a management buyout in 1988, Inver House managed to overcome the hard times and that same year, it bought its first distillery of five – Knockdhu. For many years, the distillery produced malt for the company's blends but in 2003, a genuine investment was made in anCnoc single malt and, since then, the brand has gained more and more devoted followers. In 2019, 163,000 bottles were sold. A substantial part of anCnoc single malt still goes into the well-respected blend Hankey Bannister which sold close to 4 million bottles worldwide in 2019. It also lends its flavour profile to Barrogill blended malt which is endorsed by Prince Charles for his Mey Selections range.

Knockdhu distillery is equipped with a 5 ton stainless steel lauter mash tun, eight washbacks made of Oregon pine (two of them used as intermediate vats), with fermentation time now increased to 65 hours and one pair of stills with worm tubs. Oddly enough there is also a shell and tube condenser fitted on the wash still just before the worm tub. In 2021 the distillery is working seven days per week which means 20 mashes and a total of 1.8 million litres of pure alcohol. At least 200,000 litres will be heavily peated (45ppm).

The core range consists of **12, 18** and **24 years old**. In addition to that there is the smoky **Peatheart** made from 40ppm barley. Recent limited bottlings, launched in 2019, were a **16 year old cask strength** matured in ex-bourbon barrels, **Peat**, a smoky expression (40ppm) with an extra maturation in Spanish oak sherry butts, **Vintage 2002** and **Sherry Cask Finish** (exclusive to Sweden). For the duty-free market there are **Black Hill Reserve** and the peated (20ppm) **Rùdhan**.

History:

1893 Distillers Company Limited (DCL) starts construction of the distillery.

1894 Production starts in October.

1930 Scottish Malt Distillers (SMD) takes over production.

1983 The distillery closes in March.

1988 Inver House buys the distillery from United Distillers.

1989 Production restarts on 6th February.

1990 First official bottling of Knockdhu.

1993 First official bottling of anCnoc.

2001 Pacific Spirits purchases Inver House Distillers at a price of $85 million.

2003 Reintroduction of anCnoc 12 years.

2004 A 14 year old from 1990 is launched.

2005 A 30 year old from 1975 and a 14 year old from 1991 are launched.

2006 International Beverage Holdings acquires Pacific Spirits UK.

2007 anCnoc 1993 is released.

2008 anCnoc 16 year old is released.

2011 A Vintage 1996 is released.

2012 A 35 year old is launched.

2013 A 22 year old and Vintage 1999 are released.

2014 A peated range with Rutter, Flaughter, Tushkar and Cutter is introduced.

2015 A 24 year old, Vintage 1975 and Peatlands are released as well as Black Hill Reserve and Barrow for duty free.

2016 Vintage 2001, Blas and Rùdhan are released.

2017 Vintage 2002 and Peatheart are released.

2019 A 16 year old cask strength is released.

Tasting notes anCnoc 12 years old:

GS – A pretty, sweet, floral nose, with barley notes. Medium bodied, with a whiff of delicate smoke, spices and boiled sweets on the palate. Drier in the mouth than the nose suggests. The finish is quite short and drying.

12 years old

Lagavulin

[lah•gah•voo•lin]

Owner:
Diageo

Region/district:
Islay

Founded: 1816

Status: Active (vc)

Capacity: 2 600 000 litres

Address: Port Ellen, Islay, Argyll PA42 7DZ

Website:
malts.com

Tel:
01496 302749 (vc)

With 2,5 million bottles sold last year, Lagavulin single malt obviously doesn't lack followers. One of the more enthusiastic fans is American actor Nick Offerman known not least from the sitcom "Parks & Recreation".

In 2014 he was engaged in a couple of commercials for Lagavulin and five years later he could put his name on his own Lagavulin bottling – the 11 year old Offerman Edition. In May 2021 it was time again for an 11 year old Offerman edition but this time it had been finished for four months in Guinness beer casks from the Open Gate Brewery in Maryland.

Even though Laphroaig had been exported to foreign markets, not least USA, in the 1920s and 30s, it could be said that it was Lagavulin that started the peated whisky trend during the last two decades of the old millenium. In the late 1990s it was by far the most sold Islay malt. In the following years, mostly due to small production years before and thereby lack of stock, Lagavulin was surpassed by both Laphroaig and Bowmore. In recent years it has climbed to second place on the sales list with 2,5 million bottles sold last year.

Lagavulin distillery was, for a period of time, owned by Peter Mackie, creator of the famous White Horse blend. He also acted as sales agent for Laphroaig but lost the agency in 1907. Disappointed and infuriated by this, he then decided to build a distillery on the site of Lagavulin that would produce a whisky identical to Laphroaig. The Malt Mill distillery started production in 1908, but, unfortunately, the whisky had little resemblance with Laphroaig single malt, and was only used for various blends until 1962 when it finally closed. A bottle of Malt Mill new make from the last distillation is now on display at the distillery.

The distillery is equipped with a 4.4 ton stainless steel full lauter mash tun and ten washbacks made of larch with a 55 hour fermentation cycle. There are two pairs of stills where the spirit stills are actually larger than the wash stills. The newmake is, almost without exception, filled into ex-bourbon hogsheads. There are only 5,000 casks maturing at the distillery and all of the new production is now shipped to the mainland for maturation. The production plan for 2021 is a 7-day week with 29 mashes per week and close to 2.6 million litres of alcohol.

The core range of Lagavulin consists of an **8 year old**, a **12 year old cask strength** which actually forms part of the yearly Rare by Nature series, a **16 year old** and the **Distiller's Edition**, a Pedro Ximenez sherry finish. Recent limited bottlings include the aforementioned **Offerman Edition** and, part of the Special Releases, a **26 year old** that had been matured in a combination of first fill PX and oloroso casks. The special bottling for Feis Ile 2021 was quite unusual for a Lagavulin. It was a **13 year old** which had been finished in high char ex-port casks. Another rare release in September 2021 was a **28 year old** matured in freshly charred American oak which was part of the Prima & Ultima range.

History:

1816 John Johnston founds the distillery.

1825 John Johnston takes over the adjacent distillery Ardmore.

1836 John Johnston dies and the two distilleries are merged and operated under the name Lagavulin. Alexander Graham, a wine and spirits dealer from Glasgow, buys the distillery.

1861 James Logan Mackie becomes a partner.

1867 The distillery is acquired by James Logan Mackie & Co. and refurbishment starts.

1878 Peter Mackie is employed.

1889 James Logan Mackie passes away and nephew Peter Mackie inherits the distillery.

1890 J. L. Mackie & Co. changes name to Mackie & Co. Peter Mackie launches White Horse onto the export market with Lagavulin included in the blend.

1908 Peter Mackie uses the old distillery buildings to build a new distillery, Malt Mill, on the site.

1924 Peter Mackie passes away and Mackie & Co. changes name to White Horse Distillers.

1927 White Horse Distillers becomes part of Distillers Company Limited (DCL).

1930 The distillery is administered under Scottish Malt Distillers (SMD).

1952 An explosive fire breaks out and causes considerable damage.

1962 Malt Mills distillery closes and today it houses Lagavulin's visitor centre.

1974 Floor maltings are decommisioned and malt is bought from Port Ellen instead.

1988 Lagavulin 16 years becomes one of six Classic Malts.

1998 A Pedro Ximenez sherry finish is launched as a Distillers Edition.

History continued:

2002 Two cask strengths (12 years and 25 years) are launched.

2006 A 30 year old is released.

2010 A new edition of the 12 year old and a Manager´s Choice single cask are released.

2011 The 10th edition of the 12 year old cask strength is released.

2012 The 11th edition of the 12 year old cask strength and a 21 year old are released.

2013 A 37 year old and the 12th edition of the 12 year old cask strength are released.

2014 A triple matured for Friends of the Classic Malts and the 13th edition of the 12 year old cask strength are released.

2015 The 14th edition of the 12 year old cask strength is released.

2016 An 8 year old and a 25 year old are launched.

2017 A new edition of the 12 year old cask strength is released.

2018 An 18 year old is released for Feis Ile.

2019 A 19 year old is released for Feis Ile, a 9 year old House Lannister in the Game of Thrones series and a 10 year old for duty free.

2020 The 11 year old Offerman Edition, the 1991 Prima & Ultima and a 20 year old for Feis Ile are released.

2021 A second Offerman Edition, a 13 year old for Feis Ile, a 28 year old Prima & Ultima and a 26 year old are launched.

Tasting notes Lagavulin 16 year old:

GS – Peat, iodine, sherry and vanilla merge on the rich nose. The peat and iodine continue on to the expansive, spicy, sherried palate, with brine, prunes and raisins. Peat embers feature in the lengthy, spicy finish.

Offerman Edition
11 years old

13 years old
Feis Ile 2021

Prima & Ultima
28 years old

16 years old

8 years old

26 years old
Rare by Nature

Laphroaig

[lah•froyg]

Owner:
Beam Suntory

Region/district:
Islay

Founded: **Status:**
1815   Active (vc)

Capacity:
3 300 000 litres

Address: Port Ellen, Islay, Argyll PA42 7DU

Website:
laphroaig.com

Tel:
01496 302418

With close to four million bottles sold last year Laphroaig is the most popular peated single malt in the world. It is number one on Islay and on the global sales list the brand occupies spot number 7. But regardless of how big a brand is, success does not come without effort – not even for Laphroaig.

In the last four years sales volumes have increased by 7% compared to the previous four-year period when the increase was 35%. And if you look at some of the competitors, Balvenie in place six increased their volumes during the last four years by 36% and Cardhu in place eight by 32%. The owners are not idle however and in late 2020 a commercial ad for TV and social media was launched. Playing on the smoky character which often is described as "love it or hate it" (people are rarely indifferent), the ad was named "You'll always remember your first Laphroaig."

The distillery is equipped with a 5.5 ton stainless steel full lauter mash tun and six stainless steel washbacks with a minimum fermentation time of 53 hours. The distillery uses an unusual combination of three wash stills, three smaller spirit stills and a fourth spirit still, double the size. Three of the spirit stills were exchanged for new ones in 2020. All stills are fitted with ascending lyne arms and foreshots are unusually long – 45 minutes. The middle cut starts at 72% and goes down to 60%. It is one of very few distilleries with its own maltings which, using two malting floors, produces 15% of its requirements. The malt is dried for 12-15 hours using peat and then for another 10 hours on hot air. The in-house malt has a phenol specification of 50-60ppm, while the remaining malt from Port Ellen or the mainland comes in at a minimum of 45ppm. Loading and unloading the kilns has been a pretty laboursome work until recently when the owners had a company converting snow shovels into battery operated malting equipment. The distillery has been running at full capacity for several years now but a nine week closure in 2020 due to the pandemic halted that. In 2021 they are back on track producing 3,3 million litres of pure alcohol. which means 34 mashes per week and 3.3 million litres. Around 70% of the production is destined to be bottled as single malt and the rest is used for blends.

The core range consists of **Select** without age statement, **10 year old, 10 year old cask strength, Quarter Cask, Triple Wood, Lore,** a **16 year old** and a **25 year old.** A new addition to the core range was made in April 2021 – a **10 year old Sherry Oak Finish** with 12 to 18 months in oloroso casks. The travel retail range consists of **Four Oak,** the **1815 Edition** and **PX Cask.** Also a part of the duty free range is the **Bessie Williamson Story 25 years old.** Recent limited releases include **Ian Hunter Story, Book Three: Source Protector.** This 33 year old is the third of five in a series of bottlings celebrating the legendary Ian Hunter, the last of the Johnston family to own Laphroaig. Other expressions are **Port Wood** (previously known as Brodir) and **Cairdeas Triple Wood.** The 2021 Feis Ile bottling was **Cairdeas PX Cask** bottled at 58,9%.

History:

1815   Brothers Alexander and Donald Johnston found Laphroaig.

1836   Donald buys out Alexander and takes over.

1837   James and Andrew Gairdner found Ardenistiel a stone's throw from Laphroaig.

1847   Donald Johnston is killed in an accident in the distillery. The Manager of neigh-bouring Lagavulin, Walter Graham, takes over.

1857   Operation is back in the hands of the Johnston family when Donald's son Dougald takes over.

1877   Dougald, being without heirs, passes away and his sister Isabella, married to their cousin Alexander takes over.

1907   Alexander Johnston dies and the distillery is inherited by his two sisters Catherine Johnston and Mrs. William Hunter (Isabella Johnston).

1908   Ian Hunter arrives in Islay to assist his mother and aunt with the distillery.

1924   The two stills are increased to four.

1927   Catherine Johnston dies and Ian Hunter takes over.

1928   Isabella Johnston dies and Ian Hunter becomes sole owner.

1950   Ian Hunter forms D. Johnston & Company

1954   Ian Hunter passes away and management of the distillery is taken over by Elisabeth "Bessie" Williamson.

1967   Seager Evans & Company buys the distillery through Long John Distillery, having already acquired part of Laphroaig in 1962. The number of stills is increased from four to five.

1972   Bessie Williamson retires. Another two stills are installed bringing the total to seven.

1975   Whitbread & Co. buys Seager Evans (now renamed Long John International) from Schenley International.

History continued:

1989 The spirits division of Whitbread is sold to Allied Distillers.

1994 The Friends of Laphroaig is founded.

1995 A 10 year old cask strength is launched.

2001 A 40 year old is released.

2004 Quarter Cask is launched.

2005 Fortune Brands becomes new owner.

2007 A vintage 1980 and a 25 year old are released.

2008 Cairdeas, Cairdeas 30 year old and Triple Wood are released.

2009 An 18 year old is released.

2010 A 20 year old for French Duty Free and Cairdeas Master Edition are launched.

2011 Laphroaig PX and Cairdeas - The Ileach Edition are released.

2012 Brodir and Cairdeas Origin are launched.

2013 QA Cask, An Cuan Mor, 25 year old cask strength and Cairdeas Port Wood Edition are released.

2014 Laphroaig Select and a new version of Cairdeas are released.

2015 A 21 year old, a 32 year old sherry cask and a new Cairdeas are released and the 15 year old is re-launched.

2016 Lore, Cairdeas 2016 and a 30 year old are released.

2017 Four Oak, The 1815 Edition and a 27 year old are released.

2018 A 28 year old and Cairdeas Fino are released.

2019 A 30 year old is the first release in a new series named The Ian Hunter Story.

2020 The Ian Hunter Story chapter 2, Cairdeas Port & Wine Casks and a 16 year old are released.

2021 A 10 year old sherry oak finish and The Ian Hunter Story chapter 3 are released.

Tasting notes Laphroaig Select:

GS – The nose offers chocolate and malt notes set against peat, citrus fruit and iodine. Citrus fruit is most apparent on the relatively light palate, along with ginger, cinnamon and dried fruits. The peat is muted. The finish offers bright spices, new oak and medicinal notes.

Tasting notes Laphroaig 10 year old:

GS – Old-fashioned sticking plaster, peat smoke and seaweed leap off the nose, followed by something a little sweeter and fruitier. Massive on the palate, with fish oil, salt and plankton, though the finish is quite tight and increasingly drying.

Select   Quarter Cask   16 years old

10 year old sherry finish    The 1815 Edition

10 years old

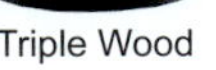

Triple Wood

Cairdeas PX Cask

Linkwood

[link•wood]

Owner:
Diageo

Region/district:
Speyside

Founded: **Status:** **Capacity:**
1821 Active 5 600 000 litres

Address: Elgin, Morayshire IV30 8RD

Website: **Tel:**
malts.com 01343 862000

When Alfred Barnard made his famous tour of 150 distilleries in Scotland, Ireland and England in 1886 he didn't seem overly impressed with Linkwood. In his book about the journey, he only devoted one page to the distillery.

Two decades later, the interest in the distillery and its whisky had changed. Largely responsible for that was the major stakeholder of the distillery at the time, Innes Cameron. Born in 1860, he began as a grocer's apprentice in Elgin but soon moved on to become a spirit merchant. Except for Linkwood, Cameron was also involved in Teaninich and Tamdhu. Buying large stocks of whisky from Glenfarclas, he helped the Grant family reclaiming the 50% of the distillery that was in the hands of the Pattison brothers when the whisky market imploded in 1898. Cameron realized the qualities that Linkwood single malt had as a blending component and today, blenders can only agree with him. The whisky makes an important contribution, not only to Diageo blends such as Johnnie Walker and White Horse, but also to whiskies from many other companies

The old part of the distillery worked in tandem with the new site (built in 1971) but stopped producing in 1996. In connection with an upgrade in 2013, the old buildings from the 1800s facing Linkwood Road were demolished and an extension of the current still house, which houses two of the stills and the tunroom, was conducted. The only original buildings from 1872 left standing are No. 6 warehouse and the redundant, old kiln with the pagoda roof. The set up of equipment is one 12.5 ton full lauter mash tun, 11 wooden washbacks and three pairs of stills. The fermentation time during a five-day week production varies between 65 and 105 hours. Production during the last couple of years has varied between 3.6 and 5.6 million litres of alcohol, depending on having a five or seven-day production week.

The only official core bottling is a **12 year old Flora & Fauna**. In 2021, a **39 year old** matured in American oak that had been seasoned with both PX and oloroso sherry was launched as part of the Prima & Ultima range.

History:

1821 Peter Brown founds the distillery.

1868 Peter Brown passes away and his son William inherits the distillery.

1872 William demolishes the distillery and builds a new one.

1897 Linkwood Glenlivet Distillery Company Ltd takes over operations.

1902 Innes Cameron, a whisky trader from Elgin, joins the Board and eventually becomes the major shareholder and Director.

1932 Innes Cameron dies and Scottish Malt Distillers takes over in 1933.

1962 Major refurbishment takes place.

1971 The two stills are increased by four. Technically, the four new stills belong to a new distillery referred to as Linkwood B.

1985 Linkwood A (the two original stills) closes.

1990 Linkwood A is in production again for a few months each year until 1996.

2002 A 26 year old from 1975 is launched as a Rare Malt.

2005 A 30 year old from 1974 is launched as a Rare Malt.

2008 Three different wood finishes (all 26 year old) are released.

2009 A Manager´s Choice 1996 is released.

2013 Expansion of the distillery including two more stills.

2016 A 37 year old is released.

2021 A 39 year old in the Prima & Ultima range is released.

39 years old
Prima & Ultima

Tasting notes Linkwood 12 years old:

GS – Floral, grassy and fragrant on the nutty nose, while the slightly oily palate becomes increasingly sweet, ending up at marzipan and almonds. The relatively lengthy finish is quite dry and citric.

Loch Lomond

[lock low•mund]

Owner:
Loch Lomond Group
(Hillhouse Capital Management)

Region/district:
Western Highlands

Founded: 1965
Status: Active
Capacity: 5 000 000 litres

Address: Lomond Estate, Alexandria G83 0TL

Website: lochlomondwhiskies.com
Tel: 01389 752781

It may sound harsh but for many years Loch Lomond single malt was something that a whisky enthusiast wouldn't come near let alone buy. It was considered a cheap malt of low quality. Today the attitude is one of admiration and curiosity.

The distillate was well made but in the past always intended for blends and occasionally sold far too young as a single malt. New owners and a talented master blender, Michael Henry, have created a brand that has increased its sales volumes by 200% in the past decade and now sells almost 1 million bottles per year.

Loch Lomond has an extremely unusual equipment setup. Founded in 1966, one pair of straight neck pot stills were instal- led. Yet another pair were installed in 1990 and four years later a grain distillery with two continuous stills was opened. One pair of traditional swan neck pot stills were installed in 1998 and in 2007 a single grain coffey still was added. Complemented with a third pair of straight neck stills the distillery now has 11 stills of four different kinds! Of the 5 million litres on the malt side, 70% is distilled in the Coffey still with Loch Lomond Single Grain (ac- tually a single malt but not accepted as such by the SWA) being the big seller. The Loch Lomond is distilled in the traditional pot stills but mixed before bottling with whisky from the straight neck stills. The rest of the equipment consists of a 9.5 ton full lauter mash tun, 21 stainless steel washbacks (with a fermentation time of 92 to 160 hours) for the malt side of the production and another 18 for the grain side. The plan for 2021 is to make 2,8 million litres of malt spirit and 2 million litres of grain

The core range consists of **Loch Lomond Classic, Original, 10, 12, 14, 18, 21** and **30 year old**. Further- more there is **Loch Lomond Inchmurrin 12 year old** and **Loch Lomond Inchmoan 12 year old**. The duty-free range is made up of **Original, Madeira Wood Finish, 12 year old, 14 year old Peated** and **18 year old**. Recent limited releases include a **45 year old oloroso finish,** the first in a new series named Remarkable Stills and the **12 year old Open Special Edition**. Finally, there are two core grain expressions, the **Single Grain** and the **Single Grain Peated**.

History:

1965 The distillery is built by Littlemill Distillery Company Ltd owned by Duncan Thomas and American Barton Brands.

1966 Production commences.

1971 Duncan Thomas is bought out.

1984 The distillery closes.

1985 Glen Catrine Bonded Warehouse Ltd buys Loch Lomond Distillery.

1987 The distillery resumes production.

1993 Grain spirits are also distilled.

1997 A fire destroys 300,000 litres of maturing whisky.

1999 Two more stills are installed.

2005 Inchmoan and Craiglodge as well as Inchmurrin 12 years are launched.

2006 Inchmurrin 4 years, Croftengea 1996 (9 years), Glen Douglas 2001 (4 years) and Inchfad 2002 (5 years) are launched.

2010 A peated Loch Lomond with no age statement is released as well as a Vintage 1966.

2012 New range for Inchmurrin released – 12, 15, 18 and 21 years.

2014 The distillery is sold to Exponent Private Equity. Organic versions of 12 year old single malt and single blend are released.

2015 Loch Lomond Original Single Malt is released together with a single grain and two blends, Reserve and Signature.

2016 A 12 year old and an 18 year old are launched.

2017 This year´s releases include Inchmoan 12 year old and Inchmurrin 12 and 18 year old.

2018 A 50 year old Loch Lomond is released.

2019 The distillery is sold to Hillhouse Capital Management and a 50 year old is released.

2020 The core range is revamped and expanded.

2021 The 45 year old oloroso finish Remarkable Stills is released.

Tasting notes Loch Lomond 12 years old:

IR – Starts out malty on the nose followed by pears, apple pie with custard and digestive. Herbal at first on the palate with cinnamon and thyme, roasted root vegetables and nuts, caramel, vanilla and a hint of peat.

Loch Lomond 12 year old

Lochranza

[lock•<u>ran</u>•sa]

Owner:	**Region/district:**
Isle of Arran Distillers	Highlands (Arran)

Founded:	**Status:**	**Capacity:**
1993	Active (vc)	1 200 000 litres

Address: Lochranza, Isle of Arran KA27 8HJ

Website:	**Tel:**
arranwhisky.com	01770 830264

When the distillery in Lochranza started distilling in 1995, the founder, Harold "Hal" Currie was 71 years old. Born in Liverpool, his working life had been a long and successful career with Chivas Brothers.

After retiring from Chivas he nurtured a dream of building a distillery of his own. Together with his two sons, he travelled the Lake District to find the perfect spot with perfect water. His good friend, and architect, David Hutchison suggested he should focus on Arran instead. An island with thousands of visitors every year would be ideal for a distillery. Hal followed his advice but his plans were not met with enthusiasm by all of the islanders. The impact on the environment was one issue and in the early 1990s few could predict the popularity that single malt would achieve a few years further on. Hal worked on tirelessly and proved his opponents wrong. Hal was one of the last great whisky gentlemen and died in 2016, aged 91.

Lochranza is equipped with a 2.5 ton semi-lauter mash tun, six Oregon pine washbacks with an average fermentation time of 60 hours and four stills. The production plan for 2021 entails 13 mashes per week and 600,000 litres of pure alcohol, all unpeated. The distillery is by far the most visited distillery in Scotland with well over 100,000 people coming here annually.

The core range consists of **10, 18, 21** and **25 year old, Quarter Cask The Bothy** and **Sherry Cask The Bodega** as well as **Barrel Reserve** and **Robert Burns**. The peated side of Arran is represented by the re-branded **Machrie Moor** without age statement and bottled both at 46% and at cask strength as well as a new **10 year old** version. Limited expressions include **Machrie Moor Fingal's Cut** with two varieties; quarter cask finish and sherry finish. Recent limited expressions of the unpeated Lochranza include three wood finishes – **Amarone, Port** and **Sauternes** – as well as **Kildonan & Pladda** and **Drumadoon Point**, the third and fourth installments in the Explorer's Series. Finally two 15 year olds in the Rare Batch range were released in autumn 2021 – **French Oak Argonne** and **French Oak Bordeaux**.

History:

1993 Harold Currie founds the distillery.

1995 Production starts in full on 17th August.

1998 The first release is a 3 year old.

1999 The Arran 4 years old is released.

2002 Single Cask 1995 is launched.

2003 Single Cask 1997, non-chill filtered and Calvados finish is launched.

2004 Cognac finish, Marsala finish, Port finish and Arran First Distillation 1995 are launched.

2005 Arran 1996 and two finishes, Ch. Margaux and Grand Cru Champagne, are launched.

2006 After an unofficial launch in 2005, Arran 10 years old is released as well as a couple of new wood finishes.

2007 Four new wood finishes and Gordon's Dram are released.

2008 The first 12 year old is released as well as four new wood finishes.

2009 Peated single casks, two wood finishes and 1996 Vintage are released.

2010 A 14 year old, Rowan Tree, three cask finishes and Machrie Moor (peated) are released.

2011 The Westie, Sleeping Warrior and a 12 year old cask strength are released.

2012 The Eagle and The Devil's Punch Bowl are released.

2013 A 16 year old and a new edition of Machrie Moor and released.

2014 A 17 year old and Machrie Moor cask strength are released.

2015 A 18 year old and The Illicit Stills are released.

2017 The Exciseman is released.

2018 A 21 year old and Brodick Bay are released.

2019 The core range is revamped and the limited Lochranza Castle is released.

2020 A 25 year old and the 21 year old Kildonan & Pladda are released.

2021 Drumadoon Point and two 15 year olds are released.

Tasting notes Arran 14 year old:

GS – Very fragrant and perfumed on the nose, with peaches, brandy and ginger snaps. Smooth and creamy on the palate, with spicy summer fruits, apricots and nuts. The lingering finish is nutty and slowly drying.

10 years old

Longmorn

[long•morn]

Owner:
Chivas Brothers
(Pernod Ricard)

Region/district:
Speyside

Founded: 1894
Status: Active
Capacity: 4 500 000 litres

Address: Longmorn, Morayshire IV30 8SJ

Website:
-

Tel:
01343 554139

In the fifth edition of his Malt Whisky Companion, Michel Jackson says the following about Longmorn; "It is to be hoped that the new owners make this distillery's whisky more readily available".

By "new owners" he was refering to Chivas Brothers who took over in 2001. He then continues; "Longmorn is one of the finest Speyside malts, cherished by connoisseurs but not widely known". He eloquently describes the status Longmorn single malt has had amongst whisky enthusiasts for many years. Especially the expressions distilled in the 1960s and 70s are highly regarded. Another bottling that is held in high esteem is the official 15 year old which was first released in 1994 and eventually replaced by a 16 year old thirteen years later. Even though another couple of bottlings were later added to the core range and the brand was completely revamped, Longmorn is still difficult to come by. In 2019 only 22,000 bottles were sold globally. The owners are probably not that concerned. While they obviously thought it was worth a try to make Longmorn more known, the malt from the distillery is extremely important to some of their high end blends such as Chivas Regal 18 year old and Royal Salute.

Longmorn distillery is equipped with an 8.5 ton Briggs full lauter mash tun and ten stainless steel washbacks. The eight, onion-shaped stills with declining lyne arms are big and fitted with sub-coolers and the wash stills have external heat exchangers. In the last few years, production has been running for five days per week with 18 mashes which means roughly 3 million litres of alcohol.

The core range consists of **The Distiller's Choice**, a **16 year old** and a **23 year old**. In 2019, another three bottlings appeared in the new Chivas series named The Secret Speyside Collection. Two of them, **18 and 23 year old**, had been matured in American oak barrels and hogsheads and the third, a **25 year old**, had been filled into a combination of ex-bourbon and ex-sherry. Finally, there are four cask strength bottlings in the Distillery Reserve Collection, available at all Chivas' visitor centres – from **15 to 24 years old**.

History:

1893 John Duff & Company, which founded Glenlossie already in 1876, starts construction. John Duff, George Thomson and Charles Shirres are involved in the company. The total cost amounts to £20,000.

1894 First production in December.

1897 John Duff buys out the other partners.

1898 John Duff builds another distillery next to Longmorn which is called Benriach (at times aka Longmorn no. 2). Duff declares bankruptcy and the shares are sold by the bank to James R. Grant.

1970 The distillery company is merged with The Glenlivet & Glen Grant Distilleries and Hill Thomson & Co. Ltd. Own floor maltings ceases.

1972 The number of stills is increased from four to six. Spirit stills are converted to steam firing.

1974 Another two stills are added.

1978 Seagrams takes over through The Chivas & Glenlivet Group.

1994 Wash stills are converted to steam firing.

2001 Pernod Ricard buys Seagram Spirits & Wine together with Diageo and Pernod Ricard takes over the Chivas group.

2004 A 17 year old cask strength is released.

2007 A 16 year old is released replacing the 15 year old.

2012 Production capacity is expanded.

2015 The Distiller's Choice is released.

2016 A 16 year old and a 23 year old are released.

2019 Three expressions in the new The Secret Speyside Collection are released.

Distiller´s Choice

Tasting notes Longmorn Distiller´s Choice:

GS – Barley sugar, ginger, toffee and malt on the sweet nose. The palate reveals caramel and milk chocolate, with peppery Jaffa orange. Toffee, barley and a hint of spicy oak in the medium-length finish.

Macallan

[mack•al•un]

Owner: Edrington Group

Region/district: Speyside

Founded: 1824

Status: Active (vc)

Capacity: 15 000 000 litres

Address: Easter Elchies, Craigellachie, Morayshire AB38 9RX

Website: themacallan.com

Tel: 01340 871471

Few brands have an extensive single malt range like Macallan. It spans from an affordable and widely available core range to limited releases that make you marvel and reach (or not) for your wallet. The latter category often steals the headlines.

The latest ultra premium expressions from the distillery was The Red Collection launched in November 2020 which comprised of six bottlings – the youngest a 40 year old and the oldest a 78 year old. The latter was the oldest bottling released of the brand. In fact, it was the oldest single malt from any distillery ever released for a few months until Gordon & MacPhail presented an 80 year old Glenlivet in June 2021. The first set of six bottles of the Red Collection, sold at Sotheby's in October 2020 to raise funds for charity, went for £756,400! Master whisky maker Kirsteen Campbell has an overall responsibility for the collection but the three oldest expressions (71, 74 and 78 year old), which by the way will change over time, will be selected by one of the other Macallan whisky makers – in this case Sarah Burgess.

The distillery is equipped with a full lauter mash tun with a 17 ton mash and 21 washbacks made of stainless steel with a fermentation time of 60 hours. There are 12 wash stills and 24 spirit stills. The capacity is 15 million litres of pure alcohol per year and during 2021, they plan to mash 35-40 times per week resulting in 11-11.5 million litres of alcohol. There are 16 dunnage and 35 racked warehouses on site. The old distillery has been closed since December 2018 and has no plans to reopen. The equipment is still in place though: two mash tuns, 22 stainless steel washbacks and six made of wood, seven wash stills and 14 spirit stills. The capacity when working was 11 million litres.

The core range of Macallan consists of three styles. **Sherry Oak** (100% sherry maturation) is represented by **12, 18, 25** and **30 years old**. **Triple Cask**, a combination of whisky matured in bourbon and sherry casks, is represented by a **12 year old**. **Double Cask**, finally, is currently made up of **Gold** without age statement, **12, 15** and **18 year old**. In this case, Double Cask means a mix of sherry casks from both American and European Oak. Finally, **Macallan Estate** made from barley grown on the Macallan estate, is also a core expression.

The Macallan Quest Collection is reserved for duty-free including **Quest, Lumina, Terra** and **Enigma** as well as **Oscuro, Rare Cask Black** and **Concept No.3**. Apart from the already mentioned **The Red Collection**, there is a range of prestige bottlings called The Macallan Masters Decanter Series which include; **Reflexion, No 6, M Rare Cask** and **M Black**. Recent limited releases include **Edition No. 5, Classic Cut** and **Genesis**. In December 2020 **Distil Your World: The London Edition** was launched in collaboration with the restaurant El Cellar de Can Roca. In August 2021 **Tales of The Macallan Volume I** was released at a price of £60,000. Finally, there is the **Fine and Rare Collection** with single casks from 1926 to 1993.

History:

1824 The distillery is licensed to Alexander Reid under the name Elchies Distillery.

1847 Alexander Reid passes away and James Shearer Priest and James Davidson take over.

1868 James Stuart takes over the licence. He founds Glen Spey distillery a decade later.

1886 James Stuart buys the distillery.

1892 Stuart sells the distillery to Roderick Kemp from Elgin. Kemp expands the distillery and names it Macallan-Glenlivet.

1909 Roderick Kemp passes away and the Roderick Kemp Trust is established to secure the family's future ownership.

1965 The number of stills is increased from six to twelve.

1966 The trust is reformed as a private limited company.

1968 The company is introduced on the London Stock Exchange.

1974 The number of stills is increased to 18.

1975 Another three stills are added, now making the total 21.

1984 The first official 18 year old single malt is launched.

1986 Japanese Suntory buys 25% of Macallan-Glenlivet plc stocks.

1996 Highland Distilleries buys the remaining stocks. 1874 Replica is launched.

1999 Edrington and William Grant & Sons buys Highland Distilleries for £601 million through The 1887 Company with 70% held by Edrington and 30% by William Grant & Sons. Suntory still holds 25% in Macallan.

2000 The first single cask from Macallan (1981) is named Exceptional 1.

2001 A new visitor centre is opened.

History continued:

2002 Elegancia replaces 12 year old in the duty-free range. 1841 Replica, Exceptional II and Exceptional III are also launched.

2003 1876 Replica and Exceptional IV, single cask from 1990 are released.

2004 Exceptional V, single cask from 1989 is released as well as Exceptional VI, single cask from 1990. The Fine Oak series is launched.

2005 New expressions are Macallan Woodland Estate, Winter Edition and the 50 year old.

2007 1851 Inspiration and Whisky Maker´s Selection are released as a part of the Travel Retail range.

2008 Estate Oak and 55 year old Lalique are released.

2009 The mothballed No. 2 stillhouse is re-opened. The Macallan 1824 Collection and a 57 year old Lalique bottling is released.

2010 Oscuro is released for Duty Free.

2011 Macallan MMXI is released for duty free.

2012 Macallan Gold, the first in the new 1824 series, is launched.

2013 Amber, Sienna and Ruby are released.

2014 1824 Masters Series (with Rare Cask, Reflexion and No. 6) is released.

2015 Rare Cask Black is released.

2016 Edition No. 1 and 12 year old Double Cask are released.

2017 Folio 2 is released. The new distillery is commissioned.

2018 The Quest Collection is released for duty free and Macallan M Black and Genesis are launched. Concept No. 1 and a 72 and a 52 year old are released.

2019 Macallan Estate, Edition No. 5 and Concept No. 2 are released.

2020 Double Cask 15 and 18 year old are released as well as the Red Collection.

2021 The third and final bottling in the Concept range is launched as well as Tales of The Macallan Volume I.

Tasting notes Macallan 12 year old Sherry oak:

GS – The nose is luscious, with buttery sherry and Christmas cake characteristics. Rich and firm on the palate, with sherry, elegant oak and Jaffa oranges. The finish is long and malty, with slightly smoky spice.

Tasting notes Macallan 12 year old Triple Cask:

GS – The nose is perfumed and quite complex, with marzipan and malty toffee. Expansive on the palate, with oranges, marmalade, milk chocolate and oak. Meidum in length, balanced and comparatively sweet.

Gold   Sherry Oak 12 years   Triple Cask 12 years

Enigma   78 years old   Concept No. 3

Double Cask 12 years   Macallan Estate   Rare Cask Black   Rare Cask Batch 3

Macduff

[mack•<u>duff</u>]

Owner:
John Dewar & Sons Ltd (Bacardi)

Region/district:
Highlands

Founded: 1960

Status: Active

Capacity: 3 400 000 litres

Address: Banff, Aberdeenshire AB45 3JT

Website:
lastgreatmalts.com

Tel:
01261 812612

History:

1960 The distillery is founded by Marty Dyke, George Crawford, James Stirrat and Brodie Hepburn (who is also involved in Tullibardine and Deanston). Macduff Distillers Ltd is the name of the company.

1964 The number of stills is increased from two to three.

1967 Stills now total four.

1968 The first bottling from the distillery is launched - the 5 year old Macduff Pure Highland Malt Scotch Whisky.

1972 William Lawson Distillers, part of General Beverage Corporation which is owned by Martini & Rossi, buys the distillery from Glendeveron Distilleries.

1990 A fifth still is installed.

1993 Bacardi buys Martini Rossi (including William Lawson) and eventually transfered Macduff to the subsidiary John Dewar & Sons.

2013 The Royal Burgh Collection (16, 20 and 30 years old) is launched for duty free.

2015 A new range is launched - 10, 12 and 18 years old.

Conceived as a fairly anonymous brand by many whisky drinkers today, Glen Deveron, as it was called then, sold more than the likes of Talisker and Highland Park in the early days of the new millenium.

Part of the success could be attributed to the brand's popularity in France and Italy. In 2010 it was still the biggest single malt brand in the Dewar's portfolio but since then Aberfeldy has taken over. The numbers are still good with more than 600,000 bottles last year but pale in comparison with Aberfeldy's 1,5 million!

Undisputed though is the malt's importance as a key component of Lawson's blended Scotch. Currently occupying place nine on the Top 10 of blends in terms of volume (selling close to 30 million bottles per year), the brand was registered in 1889 by an Irish blending company called E. & J. Burke. The whisky is named after William Lawson who became export manager of the company one year before the blend was launched. Sales increased steadily, but it wasn't until Martini & Rossi took over in 1963 that volumes began to skyrocket.

Macduff is equipped with a 6.75 ton stainless steel semi-lauter mash tun and nine washbacks (29,800 litres each) made of stainless steel with a fermentation time of 55 hours. There is also a rather unusual set-up of five stills – two wash stills and three spirit stills. In order to fit the stills into the still room, the lyne arms on four of the stills are bent in a peculiar way and on one of the wash stills it is U-shaped. In 2021, the plan is to mash 26 times per week for 48 weeks, producing 3.3 million litres of alcohol.

Since 2015, the core range from the distillery is known under the name The Deveron and consists of a **10 year old** (with a new design of the bottle and label), a **12 year old** and an **18 year old**. For duty free there is a range, first launched in 2013, named Glen Deveron encompassing a **16**, a **20** and a new **28 year old**. The 30 year old that used to be has now been discontinued.

10 years old

Tasting notes The Deveron 12 years old:

GS – Soft, sweet and fruity on the nose, with vanilla, ginger, and apple blossom. Medium-bodied, gently spicy, with butterscotch and Brazil nuts. Caramel contrasts with quite dry spicy oak in the finish.

Mannochmore

[man•och•moor]

Owner: **Region/district:**
Diageo   Speyside

Founded: **Status:**   **Capacity:**
1971   Active   6 000 000 litres

Address: Elgin, Morayshire IV30 8SS

Website: **Tel:**
malts.com   01343 862000

In 2013, a new mash tun and more stills were installed at Mannochmore. This increased the production capacity from 3,5 million litres of alcohol per year to 6 million. But Mannochmore was not the only one of Diageo's distilleries expanding at the time.

From 2008 to 2014 Diageo grew their malt capacity by 76% starting with the building of Roseisle but also including major expansions of other distilleries such as Caol Ila, Glen Ord, Talisker, Glen Elgin, Glendullan, Linkwood and, as mentioned, Mannochmore. Other producers did the same. New markets, not least in Asia, showed rapidly growing sales figures and it was critical that you had sufficient stock for the future. The total Scotch malt capacity increased by 90 million litres and Diageo's share of the growth was 52 million. If we look at the following six years (2015 -2021), Diageo has increased malt capacity by less than one percent so obviously they feel that they are sufficiently geared for an increase in demand.

On the same site as Mannochmore lies Glenlossie which was built almost 100 years earlier. There is also a dark grains plant which converts pot ale into cattle feed, as well as a biomass burner which generates draff into steam that powers the entire site.

Since 2013 Mannochmore is equipped with an 11.1 ton Briggs full lauter mash tun, eight wooden washbacks and another eight external made of stainless steel with a fermentation time of up to 100 hours and four pairs of stills. The plan for 2021 is to mash 26 times per week and produce 5 million litres of alcohol.

Mannochmore is the signature malt for Haig, a brand first introduced in the late 1880s and which today sells almost 5 million bottles per year. The Haig family belonged to the elite of Scottish whisky aristocracy and had been involved in distilling since the middle of the 17th century.

The only current official bottling is a **12 year old Flora & Fauna**. In autumn 2016, a **25 year old** distilled in 1990 and bottled at 53.4%, was launched as part of the Special Releases.

History:

1971 Distillers Company Limited (DCL) founds the distillery on the site of their sister distillery Glenlossie. It is managed by John Haig & Co. Ltd.

1985 The distillery is mothballed.

1989 In production again.

1992 A Flora & Fauna series 12 years old becomes the first official bottling.

2009 An 18 year old is released.

2010 A Manager's Choice 1998 is released.

2013 The number of stills is increased to eight.

2016 A 25 year old cask strength is released.

12 years old

Tasting notes Mannochmore 12 years old:

GS – Perfumed and fresh on the light, citric nose, with a sweet, floral, fragrant palate, featuring vanilla, ginger and even a hint of mint. Medium length in the finish, with a note of lingering almonds.

Miltonduff

[mill•ton•<u>duff</u>]

Owner: **Region/district:**
Chivas Brothers   Speyside
(Pernod Ricard)

Founded: **Status:**   **Capacity:**
1824   Active   5 800 000 litres

Address: Miltonduff, Elgin, Morayshire IV30 8TQ

Website: **Tel:**
-                         01343 547433

Miltonduff distillery is situated 7 kilometres south-west of Elgin, in peaceful rural surroundings called Pluscarden. Once called the Garden of Scotland, this is excellent land for growing barley.

That was one of the reasons for an abbey to be founded here by Alexander II in 1230. The influence of the abbey grew and a big part of the surroundings soon belonged to the monks of Pluscarden, including the site where Miltonduff now lies. The clear water from the Black Burn and the surplus of good barley created good conditions for building a brew house and producing beer and, who knows, perhaps even whisky. In any case, there is a legend which tells the story of a ceremony in the 15th century where the abbot, kneeling on a stone, blessed the water "and any product distilled therefrom". What is believed to be the stone, can now be seen imbedded in the water wheel pit at Miltonduff distillery.

Miltonduff is – since at least 1936 when Hiram Walker, the owner of the Ballantines brand at the time, bought the distillery – one of the signature malts for Ballantines blend. Official bottlings of the single malt were rare until 2017 when Miltonduff, together with Glenburgie and Glentauchers, were released in a new range called Ballantine's Single Malt Series. The launch took place in Taiwan, one of the most vibrant malt whisky scenes in the world and the Swedes were the next to enjoy it. Later the range has spread to other markets as well.

The distillery is equipped with an eight ton full lauter mash tun with a copper dome, 16 stainless steel washbacks with a fermentation time of 56 hours and six, large stills. In 1964, two Lomond stills were installed at Miltonduff. They were equipped with columns with adjustable plates with the intention of distilling different styles of whisky from the same still. They were dismantled in 1981 but the special whisky produced, Mosstowie, can still, with a bit of luck, be found.

The official bottling is a **15 year old** and it was accompanied in 2020 by a **19 year old,** exclusive to Asia. There is also a **12 year old cask strength** in the Distillery Reserve Collection, available at all Chivas' visitor centres.

History:

1824   Andrew Peary and Robert Bain obtain a licence for Miltonduff Distillery. It has previously operated as an illicit farm distillery called Milton Distillery but changes name when the Duff family buys the site it is operating on.

1866   William Stuart buys the distillery.

1895   Thomas Yool & Co. becomes new part-owner.

1936   Thomas Yool & Co. sells the distillery to Hiram Walker Gooderham & Worts. The latter transfers administration to the newly acquired subsidiary George Ballantine & Son.

1964   A pair of Lomond stills is installed to produce the rare Mosstowie.

1974   Major reconstruction of the distillery.

1981   The Lomond stills are decommissioned and replaced by two ordinary pot stills, the number of stills now totalling six.

1986   Allied Lyons buys 51% of Hiram Walker.

1987   Allied Lyons acquires the rest of Hiram Walker.

1991   Allied Distillers follow United Distillers´ example of Classic Malts and introduce Caledonian Malts in which Tormore, Glendro-nach and Laphroaig are included in addition to Miltonduff. Tormore is later replaced by Scapa.

2005   Chivas Brothers (Pernod Ricard) becomes the new owner through the acquisition of Allied Domecq.

2017   A 15 year old is released.

2020   A 19 year old exclusive to Asia is released.

15 years old

Tasting notes Miltonduff 15 years old:

IR – Fresh citrus and honey on the nose together with heather, ginger and peaches. More spicy on the palate with cinnamon and clove, vanilla, honey, red berries and liquorice.

Mortlach

[mort•lack]

Owner: Diageo

Region/district: Speyside

Founded: 1823

Status: Active

Capacity: 3 800 000 litres

Address: Dufftown, Keith, Banffshire AB55 4AQ

Website: mortlach.com, malts.com

Tel: 01340 822100

Dufftown is often referred to as the whisky capital of the world with no less than six distilleries in a small town with just 1500 inhabitants. Some of the distilleries are global stars in terms of sales figures but to a whisky geek, Mortlach is the chosen one.

This has nothing to do with the likes of Glenfiddich, Balvenie or the two Singletons being inferior. Instead it's the enthusiasts love for rarity and oddity in terms of character and production. Mortlach was the first distillery to start producing in Dufftown. The first 30 years were colourful with changes in ownership, closures and the distillery periodically being used as a church or brewery. In 1867 en engineer named Georg Cowie became the sole owner. His technical background was well suited to expand the distillery and make it more efficient. His son Alexander introduced the unique 2,81 distillation scheme which remains to this very day. The love from the aficionados originated from the 16 year old Flora & Fauna bottling which was first released in 1988.

Mortlach is equipped with a 12 ton full lauter mash tun and six washbacks made of Douglas fir, currently with six short fermentations (55 hours) and six long (110 hours). There are three wash stills and three spirit stills – all of them attached to worm tubs for cooling the spirit vapours. The production plan for 2021 is a five-day week with 12 mashes per week with a target of making 2.6 million litres.

The core range consists of **12 year old Wee Witchie, 16 year old Distiller's Dram, 20 year old Cowie's Blue Seal** and, for duty-free, the **14 year old Alexander's Way.** In 2019, the first in Mortlach's Singing Stills series appeared when a **47 year old** was released. In autumn 2021 Mortlach appeared in the Rare by Nature series with a **13 year old** which had been partly matured in virgin oak and at the same time a **25 year old** Prima & Ultima matured in a first fill PX/Oloroso butt was released.

History:

1823 The distillery is founded by James Findlater.

1824 Donald Macintosh and Alexander Gordon become part-owners.

1831 The distillery is sold to John Robertson for £270.

1832 A. & T. Gregory buys Mortlach.

1837 James and John Grant of Aberlour become part-owners. No production takes place.

1842 The distillery is now owned by John Alexander Gordon and the Grant brothers.

1851 Mortlach is producing again after having been used as a church and a brewery for some years.

1853 George Cowie joins and becomes part-owner.

1867 John Alexander Gordon dies and Cowie becomes sole owner.

1896 Alexander Cowie joins the company.

1897 The number of stills is increased from three to six.

1923 Alexander Cowie sells the distillery to John Walker & Sons.

1925 John Walker becomes part of Distillers Company Limited (DCL).

1964 Major refurbishment.

1968 Floor maltings ceases.

1996 Mortlach 1972 is released as a Rare Malt.

1998 Mortlach 1978 is released as a Rare Malt.

2004 Mortlach 1971, a 32 year old cask strength is released.

2014 Four new bottlings are released - Rare Old, Special Strength, 18 year old and 25 year old.

2018 A new range is presented; 12 year old Wee Witchie, 16 year old Distiller´s Dram and 20 year old Cowie´s Blue Seal.

2019 The oldest official Mortlach bottling ever, 47 years, is released and a 26 year old appears in the Special Releases.

2020 A 25 year old Prima & Ultima is released followed by a 21 year old Rare by Nature.

2021 A 13 year old, partly matured in virgin oak, is released as well as a 25 year old Prima & Ultima.

Tasting notes Mortlach 12 years old:

IR – Fresh and intense on the nose with notes of sherry, apple cider, dark plums, tobacco and toffee. The palate is robust with orange marmalade, dark chocolate, espresso and chili pepper.

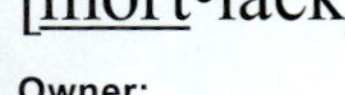

12 years old

Oban

[oa•bun]

Owner: Diageo

Region/district: Western Highlands

Founded: 1794

Status: Active (vc)

Capacity: 870 000 litres

Address: Stafford Street, Oban, Argyll PA34 5NH

Website: malts.com

Tel: 01631 572004 (vc)

Historically, most Scottish distilleries were placed where there was a reliable access to clean water. Consequently, most are thus found otuside of the major cities. A handful of urban distilleries, among them Oban, make up an exception.

But while many of these distilleries were established in an already existing town, In Oban's case it's the opposite. The distillery was born before the town. When Oban was built in 1793 the location was inhabited by a few fishermen. Oban's existence can be seen as the catalyst for establishing the town. The energetic brothers John and Hugh Stevenson took the initiative and over the years they built a business empire which also included a quarry, tannery, shipyard, brewery and a construction company. Nowadays the distillery is squeezed in between other buildings on Stafford Street, and a giant cliff towers over it on the back side. This makes it more or less impossible to expand, even if the owners probably would be interested, In terms of production capacity, Oban may be the second smallest distillery within the Diageo group but as a brand it's the fifth best seller of all the Diageo malts and in the last decade sales figures have more than doubled, to 1.7 million bottles in 2019. The only other Diageo malts that have achieved similar growths are The Singleton and Talisker.

The equipment consists of a 7 ton traditional stainless steel mash tun with rakes. The four wooden washbacks are made from Oregon pine and there is one pair of stills attached to a rectangular, stainless steel, double worm tub. The fruity character of Oban single malt is partly due to long fermentations, hence they can only manage six mashes per week with five long (110 hours) and one short (65 hours). The production plan for 2021 is to produce around 840,000 litres.

The core range consists of **Little Bay,** a **14 year old,** an **18 year old** and a **Distiller's Edition** with a montilla fino sherry finish. Recent limited editions include the **Night's Watch – Oban Bay Reserve, Old Teddy** and a **12 year old,** released in autumn 2021 in the Rare by Nature series.

History:

1793 John and Hugh Stevenson found the distillery.

1820 Hugh Stevenson dies.

1821 Hugh Stevenson's son Thomas takes over.

1829 Bad investments force Thomas Stevenson into bankruptcy. His eldest son John takes over.

1830 John buys the distillery from his father's creditors for £1,500.

1866 Peter Cumstie buys the distillery.

1883 Cumstie sells Oban to James Walter Higgins who refurbishes and modernizes it.

1898 The Oban & Aultmore-Glenlivet Co. takes over with Alexander Edwards at the helm.

1923 The Oban Distillery Co. owned by Buchanan-Dewar takes over.

1925 Buchanan-Dewar becomes part of Distillers Company Limited (DCL).

1931 Production ceases.

1937 In production again.

1968 Floor maltings ceases and the distillery closes for reconstruction.

1972 Reopening of the distillery.

1979 Oban 12 years is on sale.

1988 United Distillers launches Classic Malts and Oban 14 year old is included.

1998 A Distillers' Edition is launched.

2002 The oldest Oban (32 years) so far is launched.

2004 A 1984 cask strength is released.

2009 Oban 2000, a single cask, is released.

2010 A no age distillery exclusive is released.

2013 A limited 21 year old is released.

2015 Oban Little Bay is released.

2016 A distillery exclusive without age statement is released.

2018 A 21 year old is launched as a part of the Special Releases.

2019 Night´s Watch - Oban Bay Reserve and Oban Old Teddy are released.

2021 A 12 year old Rare by Nature is released.

12 years old
Rare by Nature

Tasting notes Oban 14 years old:

GS – Lightly smoky on the honeyed, floral nose. Toffee, cereal and a hint of peat. The palate offers initial cooked fruits, becoming spicier. Complex, bittersweet, oak and more gentle smoke. The finish is quite lengthy, with spicy oak, toffee and new leather.

Pulteney

[poolt•ni]

Owner:
Inver House Distillers
(Thai Beverages plc)

Region/district:
Northern Highlands

Founded: 1826   **Status:** Active (vc)   **Capacity:** 1 800 000 litres

Address: Huddart St, Wick, Caithness KW1 5BA

Website: oldpulteney.com   **Tel:** 01955 602371

Pulteney distillery is named after Sir William Pulteney who, at the beginning of the 1800s, decided to build an entirely new town with a fishing harbour situated next to Wick in the very north of Scotland.

Pulteney, as governor of the British Fisheries Society, gave the famous engineer, Thomas Telford, the assignment to build the city named Pulteneytown, to the south side of the river Wick. One of the reasons was to supply work to the many farmers who were evicted from their homes during the Highland Clearances. Over time, the town reputedly became the biggest herring port in Europe and, during its heydays, 800 boats could set sail from the harbour during a single day.

The distillery is equipped with a stainless steel semi-lauter mash tun with a copper canopy. There are seven washbacks made of stainless steel with a fermentation time between 50 and 110 hours. The wash still is equipped with a huge boil ball and a very thick lye pipe. Both stills use stainless steel worm tubs for condensing the spirit. In 2021 the distillery is working a 5-day week producing around 1.3 million litres of alcohol.

The core range is made up of **12 years old**, matured in ex-bourbon casks and bottled at 40%, the smoky **Huddart** without age statement and **15, 18** and **25 years old**, all three matured in a combination of ex-bourbon and ex-sherry casks. For the travel retail market there is a **10 year old** matured in ex-bourbon barrels, a **16 year old** with a finish ex-oloroso casks and a **Vintage 2006** which had spent time in first fill ex-bourbon barrels.

A number of limited single casks have also occurred with a **34 year old** sherry finish for the Chinese market in May 2020 as one of the most recent. In 2013, the **Flotilla** series was introduced as an exclusive to France but lately they have become available in other markets as well. These are small batch expressions with new vintages every year. The latest, a **10 year old** from 2010, was released in 2020.

History:

1826   James Henderson founds the distillery.

1920   The distillery is bought by James Watson.

1923   Buchanan-Dewar takes over.

1930   Production ceases.

1951   In production again after being acquired by the solicitor Robert Cumming.

1955   Cumming sells to James & George Stodart, a subsidiary to Hiram Walker & Sons.

1958   The distillery is rebuilt.

1959   The floor maltings close.

1961   Allied Breweries buys James & George Stodart Ltd.

1981   Allied Breweries changes name to Allied Lyons.

1995   Allied Domecq sells Pulteney to Inver House Distillers.

1997   Old Pulteney 12 years is launched.

2001   Pacific Spirits (Great Oriole Group) buys Inver House at a price of $85 million.

2004   A 17 year old is launched.

2005   A 21 year old is launched.

2006   International Beverage Holdings acquires Pacific Spirits UK.

2010   WK499 Isabella Fortuna is released.

2012   A 40 year old and WK217 Spectrum are released.

2013   Old Pulteney Navigator, The Lighthouse range (3 expressions) and Vintage 1990 are released.

2014   A 35 year old is released.

2015   Dunnet Head and Vintage 1989 are released.

2017   Three vintages (1983, 1990 and 2006) are released together with a 25 year old.

2018   A completely new core range is launched; 12 years old, Huddart, 15 years old and 18 years old.

2020   A limited 34 year old is released.

Tasting notes Old Pulteney 12 years old:

GS – The nose presents pleasingly fresh malt and floral notes, with a touch of pine. The palate is comparatively sweet, with malt, spices, fresh fruit and a suggestion of salt. The finish is medium in length, drying and decidedly nutty.

12 years old

Royal Brackla

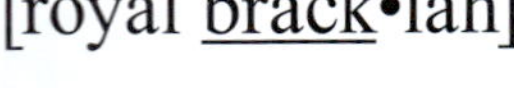

[royal brack•lah]

Owner:
John Dewar & Sons
(Bacardi)

Region/district:
Highlands

Founded: **Status:**   **Capacity:**
1812   Active   4 240 000 litres

Address: Cawdor, Nairn, Nairnshire IV12 5QY

Website: **Tel:**
lastgreatmalts.com   01667 402002

Royal Brackla is connected to an important character of the Scotch whisky industry – Andrew Usher, who is credited for creating one of the first commercial blends of Scotch whiskies.

He set up his own business in 1813 and later became responsible for selling the entire output from Glenlivet distillery. He then became an agent for Royal Brackla where he launched his first blended whisky (a vatting of malt whiskies) called Old Vatted Glenlivet. After his death in 1853 his son, Andrew II, continued the experiments but now used grain whisky and malt whisky as the components, something that had become legal to do under bond (i. e. without payment of duty until you bottled it) through the Spirits Act of 1860. Andrew II later became one of the directors of Royal Brackla and whisky from the distillery thus became part of some of the first blended Scotch that was sold.

Royal Brackla is equipped with a 12.9 ton (a slight increase from the previous 12.3 tons) full lauter mash tun. There are six wooden washbacks and another two made of stainless steel – all with a fermentation time of 70 hours. Finally, there are also two pairs of stills. In 2021, the production plan is 17 mashes per week, translating into 4,24 million litres of alcohol which equates to the full capacity of the distillery. With a mash tun producing a clear wort, long fermentations, long foreshots (30 minutes), a slow distillation and lots of reflux from the stills due to ascending lyne arms – the house style of Brackla is elegant and fruity. The Dewar's master blender since 2006, Stephanie Macleod, soon discovered that Brackla new make is perfect for being finished in ex-sherry casks, which is evident from the line of expressions.

The core range used to consist of a **12, 16** and **21 year old**. In 2021 the 16 and 21 year old were discontinued and the **18 year old palo cortado finish** and the **20 year old** finished in a combination of PX, oloroso and palo cortado that previously were travel retail exclusives became part of the core range. Henceforth the travel retail range will consist of limited and exclusive expressions in **The Exceptional Casks** series.

History:

1812 The distillery is founded by Captain William Fraser.

1833 Brackla becomes the first of three distilleries allowed to use 'Royal' in the name.

1852 Robert Fraser & Co. takes over the distillery.

1897 The distillery is rebuilt and Royal Brackla Distillery Company Limited is founded.

1919 John Mitchell and James Leict from Aberdeen purchase Royal Brackla.

1926 John Bisset & Company Ltd takes over.

1943 Scottish Malt Distillers (SMD) buys John Bisset & Company Ltd and thereby acquires Royal Brackla.

1964 The distillery closes for a big refurbishment
-1966 and the number of stills is increased to four. The maltings closes.

1970 Two stills are increased to four.

1985 The distillery is mothballed.

1991 Production resumes.

1993 A 10 year old Royal Brackla is launched in United Distillers´ Flora & Fauna series.

1997 UDV spends more than £2 million on improvements and refurbishing.

1998 Bacardi–Martini buys Dewar´s from Diageo.

2004 A new 10 year old is launched.

2014 A 35 year old is released for Changi airport in Singapore.

2015 A new range is released; 12, 16 and 21 year old.

2019 A new range for travel retail, including 12, 18 and 20 year olds, is launched.

2021 The 18 year old palo cortado finish and the 20 year old sherry finish (three different types of sherry) become part of the core range.

12 years old

Tasting notes Royal Brackla 12 years old:

GS – Warm spices, malt and peaches in cream on the nose. The palate is robust, with spice and mildly smoky soft fruit. Quite lengthy in the finsh, with citrus fruit, mild spice and cocoa powder.

Royal Lochnagar

[royal loch•nah•gar]

Owner: Diageo

Region/district: Eastern Highlands

Founded: 1845

Status: Active (vc)

Capacity: 500 000 litres

Address: Crathie, Ballater, Aberdeenshire AB35 5TB

Website: malts.com

Tel: 01339 742700

The distillery lies beautifully in the lush greenery of the Royal Deeside – a wonderful area which stretches from the village of Banchory in the east to Braemar in the west.

This is a spectacular part of Scotland and my favourite route to the distillery is coming from the north on the old military road (A939), turning right at Gairnshiel Lodge onto the B976, enjoying the scenery as I continue south, driving a few hundred metres on the A93, then back on the B976 which crosses the river Dee right where the Balmoral car park is and then leading you to the distillery.

Royal Lochnagar is one of very few whisky brands holding a royal warrant. The background is the unlikely story of the owner at the time, John Begg, inviting his "neighbours", Queen Victoria and Prince Albert, in 1848 to come and visit the distillery. Prince Albert had recently acquired Balmoral Castle, just a kilometre away, and the royals apparently took a liking to the whisky and awarded Begg a royal warrant. Currently there are seven brands or companies in the Scotch whisky business that have earned the same recognition; Royal Lochnagar, Laphroaig, Dewar's, Johnnie Walker, Matthew Glog & Sons (Famous Grouse), Berry Brothers and Justerini & Brooks. After the Duke of Edinburgh died there are now only two members of the royal family who can issue a royal warrant – The Queen and Prince Charles.

The distillery is equipped with a 5.4 ton open, traditional stainless steel mash tun. There are two wooden washbacks with short fermentations of 70 hours and long ones of 110 hours. The two stills are quite small and the spirit vapours are condensed in cast iron worm tubs. Four mashes per week during 2021 will result in 450,000 litres of pure alcohol.

The official core range of single malts consists of the **12 year old** and **Selected Reserve**. The latter is a vatting of casks, usually around 18-20 years of age. Recent limited releases include an unusual appearance in the Rare by Nature range for 2021 by way of a **16 year old**, matured in refill casks and bottled at 57,5%.

History:

1823 James Robertson founds a distillery in Glen Feardan on the north bank of River Dee.

1826 The distillery is burnt down by competitors but Robertson decides to establish a new distillery near the mountain Lochnagar.

1841 This distillery is also burnt down.

1845 A new distillery is built by John Begg, this time on the south bank of River Dee. It is named New Lochnagar.

1848 Lochnagar obtains a Royal Warrant.

1882 John Begg passes away and his son Henry Farquharson Begg inherits the distillery.

1896 Henry Farquharson Begg dies.

1906 The children of Henry Begg rebuild the distillery.

1916 The distillery is sold to John Dewar & Sons.

1925 John Dewar & Sons becomes part of Distillers Company Limited (DCL).

1963 A major reconstruction takes place.

2004 A 30 year old cask strength from 1974 is launched in the Rare Malts series (6,000 bottles).

2008 A Distiller´s Edition with a Moscatel finish is released.

2010 A Manager´s Choice 1994 is released.

2013 A triple matured expression for Friends of the Classic Malts is released.

2016 A distillery exclusive without age statement is released.

2019 House Baratheon is released as part of the Game of Thrones series.

2021 A 16 year old Rare by Nature is released.

16 years old
Rare by Nature

Tasting notes Royal Lochnagar 12 years old:

GS – Light toffee on the nose, along with some green notes of freshly-sawn timber. The palate offers a pleasing and quite complex blend of caramel, dry sherry and spice, followed by a hint of liquorice before the slightly scented finish develops.

Scapa

[ska•pa]

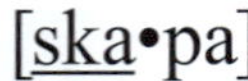

Owner:	**Region/district:**
Chivas Brothers	Highlands (Orkney)
(Pernod Ricard)	
Founded: **Status:**	**Capacity:**
1885 Active	1 300 000 litres

Address: Scapa, St Ola, Kirkwall, Orkney KW15 1SE

Website: **Tel:**
scapawhisky.com 01856 876585

If you go to Orkney you are bound to end up on Mainland, the largest of 70 islands. You will reach it either by boat from Scrabster to Stromness or by flying in from Aberdeen to Kirkwall.

Regardless of how you travel, you will have two whisky distilleries to visit once you're there. The obvious Highland Park, located on the outskirts of Kirkwall overlooking the town and Scapa, a mere 15 minute walk to the south-west, down by Scapa Flow. It wasn't until six years ago that Scapa opened to visitors and last year some 8,000 people found their way to the distillery. One could hope for a wider range of bottlings being released by the owners but the problem with Scapa is that the stock of matured whisky is rather intermittent. with the distillery being more or less closed from 1994 until 2006.

The equipment consists of a 2.9 ton semi-lauter mash tun with a copper dome, twelve washbacks and two stills. Until recently, there were eight washbacks with four of them made from Corten steel. With the Corten replaced by stainless steel and another four added, there are now twelve made of stainless steel. At the same time, the boiler was also replaced. Due to increased production, fermentation time was down to 52 hours from the previous 160 but with the additional washbacks, it is now possible to increase fermentation time again. The wash still, sourced from Glenburgie distillery in 1959, is only one of two surviving Lomond stills in the industry but on the Scapa still, the adjustable plates were removed in 1979.

The core range consists of **Skiren** with no age statement and matured in first fill bourbon as well as **Glansa**, matured in American oak and then finished in casks that previously held peated whisky. A range of rare bottlings named Scapa Single Cask Vintage Edition was launched in 2020 including three vintages – **1977, 1979** and **1990**. Currently there are also no less than nine different cask strength bottlings in the Distillery Reserve Collection, available at all Chivas' visitor centres from **10** to **26 years old** – three from sherry butts and the rest matured in first or second fill ex-bourbon barrels.

History:

1885 Macfarlane & Townsend founds the distillery with John Townsend at the helm.

1919 Scapa Distillery Company Ltd takes over.

1934 Scapa Distillery Company goes into voluntary liquidation and production ceases.

1936 Production resumes.

1936 Bloch Brothers Ltd (John and Sir Maurice) takes over.

1954 Hiram Walker & Sons takes over.

1959 A Lomond still is installed.

1978 The distillery is modernized.

1994 The distillery is mothballed.

1997 Production takes place a few months each year using staff from Highland Park.

2004 Extensive refurbishing takes place at a cost of £2.1 million. Scapa 14 years is launched.

2005 Production ceases in April and phase two of the refurbishment programme starts. Chivas Brothers becomes the new owner.

2006 Scapa 1992 (14 years) is launched.

2008 Scapa 16 years is launched.

2015 The distillery opens for visitors and Scapa Skiren is launched.

2016 The peated Glansa is released.

2020 Three vintages are released - 1977, 1979 and 1990.

Scapa Skiren

Tasting notes Scapa Skiren:

GS – Lime is apparent on the early nose, followed by musty peaches, almonds, cinnamon, and salt. More peaches on the palate, with tinned pear and honey. Tingling spices in the drying finish, which soon becomes slightly astringent.

Speyburn

[spey•burn]

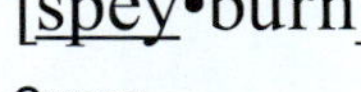

Owner:	**Region/district:**
Inver House Distillers (Thai Beverages plc)	Speyside

Founded:	**Status:**	**Capacity:**
1897	Active	4 500 000 litres

Address: Rothes, Aberlour, Morayshire AB38 7AG

Website:	**Tel:**
speyburn.com	01340 831213

Driving south on the A941 from Elgin, the road makes a left bend just before entering the town of Rothes and that is where you usually would get your best images of Speyburn distillery down in the glen.

Not anymore though. The trees have grown much taller and you can barely spot the distillery, let alone take any pictures. While the distillery may be hidden, the single malt Speyburn is not. The brand sells around 500,000 bottles per year and it has a special fan base in America. The strong position in the USA can probably be attributed to the fact that Inver House has had American owners for the first 24 years. Publicker Industries founded the company in 1964 and then sold it to Standard Brands in 1979. A management buyout in 1988, however, ended the American ownership. The relationships that were established during these years led to an agreement in 1993 with Barton Brands to distribute Speyburn single malt on the American market. The agreement with Barton expired in 2009 and since 2015, the US importer for all the Inver House brands has been 375 Park Avenue Spirits.

An impressive expansion of the distillery was completed in 2015 and it is now equipped with a 6.25 ton stainless steel mash tun. There are four wooden washbacks and 15 made of stainless steel. Finally, there is one large wash still with a shell and tube condenser and two spirit stills that are connected to a worm tub. The distillery has recently changed from a five-day week production to seven days which means the fermentation will be 72 hours. The goal is to produce 4,2 million litres of alcohol during 2021.

The core range consists of a **10 year old**, a **15 year old**, an **18 year old** and **Bradan Orach** without age statement. Limited bottlings include **Companion Cask**, a series of single casks matured in first fill ex Buffalo Trace bourbon casks and, limited to USA, **Arranta Casks**. Three bottlings are available in travel retail; a **10 year old** (ex-bourbon and ex-sherry), the **Hopkins Reserve** that has been matured in casks that previously held a peated whisky and a **16 year** old aged in ex-bourbon barrels.

History:

1897 Brothers John and Edward Hopkins and their cousin Edward Broughton found the distillery through John Hopkins & Co. They already own Tobermory. The architect is Charles Doig. Building the distillery costs £17,000 and the distillery is transferred to Speyburn-Glenlivet Distillery Company.

1916 Distillers Company Limited (DCL) acquires John Hopkins & Co. and the distillery.

1930 Production stops.

1934 Productions restarts.

1962 Speyburn is transferred to Scottish Malt Distillers (SMD).

1968 Drum maltings closes.

1991 Inver House Distillers buys Speyburn.

1992 A 10 year old is launched as a replacement for the 12 year old in the Flora & Fauna series.

2001 Pacific Spirits (Great Oriole Group) buys Inver House for $85 million.

2005 A 25 year old Solera is released.

2006 Inver House changes owner when International Beverage Holdings acquires Pacific Spirits UK.

2009 The un-aged Bradan Orach is introduced for the American market.

2012 Clan Speyburn is formed.

2014 The distillery is expanded.

2015 Arranta Casks is released.

2017 A 15 year old and Companion Casks are launched.

2018 Two expressions for duty free are released - a 10 year old and Hopkins Reserve. A core 18 year old is launched.

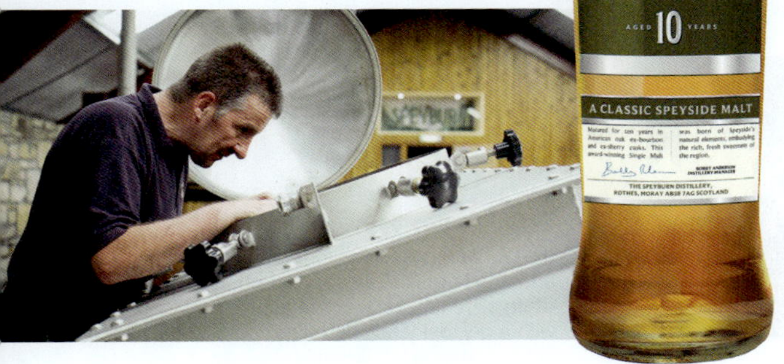

10 years old

Tasting notes Speyburn 10 years old:

GS – Soft and elegant on the spicy, nutty nose. Smooth in the mouth, with vanilla, spice and more nuts. The finish is medium, spicy and drying.

Speyside

[spey•side]

Owner: **Region/district:**
Speyside Distillers Co.   Speyside

Founded: **Status:**   **Capacity:**
1990   Active   600 000 litres

Address: Glen Tromie, Kingussie, Inverness-shire PH21 1NS

Website: **Tel:**
speysidedistillery.co.uk   01540 661060

For years there have been rumours about Speyside Distillers looking to build yet another distillery. There has been no confirmation from the company although a location has been discussed – Rothiemurchus, some 15 km north of the current distillery.

In January 2021, things took another direction when it was announced that the blender and bulk whisky supplier Glasgow Whisky had bought the Tromie Mills Distillery Ltd, the company that owns the land and the buildings that comprise Speyside Distillery. Since 2012, when Harvey's of Edinburgh took over the Spey brand and the running of Speyside distillery, they have been leasing the site and the building. The lease expires in 2025 and this is why they are looking to move to another location while the new owners have the intention of building a complete new distillery. It remains to be seen if Glasgow Whisky will keep the beautiful stone buildings that were erected between 1962 and 1987.

Speyside distillery is equipped with a 4.2 ton semi-lauter mash tun, four stainless steel washbacks with a 70-120 hour fermentation time and one pair of stills. For the last couple of years they have been working a six-day week with a total production of 600,000 litres of alcohol. There have been hints from the owners that the production is due to increase and the hiring of another two distillery operators in spring 2021 could mean the change is imminent. In nearby Aviemore, a visitor experience opened up a few years ago. Named The Snug, the centre is selling the distillery's range and also arranges tastings.

The core range of Spey single malt is made up of **Tenné** (with a 6 months port finish), **Trutina** which is a 100% bourbon maturation, **Fumare**, similar to Trutina but distilled from peated barley, **Chairman's Choice** and **Royal Choice**. The latter two are multi-vintage marriages from both American and European oak. Also part of the core range is **Beinn Dubh** which replaced the black whisky Cu Dubh. Recent limited releases include the third batch of **cask strength** versions of Trutina and Fumare, a **12 year old peated** and a **12 year old tawny port finish**.

History:

1956 George Christie buys a piece of land at Drumguish near Kingussie.

1957 George Christie starts a grain distillery near Alloa.

1962 George Christie (founder of Speyside Distillery Group in the fifties) commissions the drystone dyker Alex Fairlie to build a distillery in Drumguish.

1986 Scowis assumes ownership.

1987 The distillery is completed.

1990 The distillery is on stream in December.

1993 The first single malt, Drumguish, is launched.

1999 Speyside 8 years is launched.

2000 Speyside Distilleries is sold to a group of private investors including Ricky Christie, Ian Jerman and Sir James Ackroyd.

2001 Speyside 10 years is launched.

2012 Speyside Distillers is sold to Harvey's of Edinburgh.

2014 A new range, Spey from Speyside Distillery, is launched (NAS, 12 and 18 year old).

2015 The range is revamped again. New expressions include Tenné, 12 years old and 18 years old.

2016 "Byron's Choice - The Marriage" and Spey Cask 27 are released.

2017 Trutina and Fumare are released.

2019 Cask strength versions of Tenné, Trutina and Fumare are released.

2020 A 10 year old bourbon/port, a peated 12 year old and a 12 year old port cask are released.

Trutina

Tasting notes Spey Trutina:

IR – A floral nose, with lemon, granola, shortbread and dried grass. A sweet start on the palate, honey, white chocolate, sweet red apples and then ends with a dry, oaky note.

Trailblazers of Malt Whisky

Andrew Nelstrop
The English Whisky Company
England

To say that the Nelstrops know a thing or two about farming is definitely an understatement. In 1335, when Edward III was king of England and the country was on the verge of engaging in The Hundred Year's War with France, William Nelstroppe was recorded as farming in Yorkshire. Through the centuries, the family continued working the land while also branching out into businesses that were related to farming, like for instance starting a mill in Cheshire which still, over 200 years later, is run by the family. Closely connected with farming is of course also whisky production but it would take well over 600 years before the first Nelstrop opened a distillery.

James Nelstrop was born in 1945 in Lincolnshire into a – yes, you guessed it – farming family. Being the younger son, James didn't have a farm to tend so he began working as a farm manager for an estate in Lincolnshire and then became a tenant farmer near Stamford. But equipped with an adventurous mind he wanted to see more of the world. He emigrated to Australia with his family and with a talent for business, his career led him to different parts of the world where he was involved in innovative agricultural projects. Having enjoyed a successful professional life and nearing his sixties he realised that early retirement was not what he was aiming for. He wanted to do something he'd never done before but still with a farming connection.

He had always had a keen interest in whisky and thought it was a shame that all this barley grown in England had to go all the way to Scotland to be turned into liquid gold. Consequently, James gathered his family including his son Andrew and proposed producing an incredible English whisky – the first to be distilled in more than a century. Previously the family had bought land at Roudham in Norfolk and with an abundance of water underground and the best barley in the UK growing in the fields nearby this would be the perfect place for a distillery.

James saw this more or less as a suitable hobby and he and Andrew decided early on that they should aim for a micro distillery, producing just a few casks every year but of the highest quality. That was when Her Majesty's Customs & Excise came into the picture. The law did not permit the small stills that the Nelstrops had in mind – at least 1,800 litres were required – so they installed a 1,800 litre spirit still and a 2,800 litre wash still. Finally, on 12th December 2006 the first spirit at St. George's distillery was produced. At the same time as he was helping his father, Andrew was managing director of a building company and he wisely chose to keep that job during the first few years before wholeheartedly joining the distillery full-time.

Father and son Nelstrop obviously realised that the first spirit run was a historical moment but were hardly able to anticipate the huge impact this would have on the future of English whisky as a category. But more on that later. With no experience in whisky-making the Nelstrops had the good sense of hiring someone who knew the drill. At that time Iain Henderson, the legendary whisky maker at Laphroaig, had been retired but James managed to persuade him to come to Norfolk and make sure the family was on the right track. The first whisky was launched in December 2019 and in the following years many more bottlings saw the light of day. To be honest, it was not an easy task getting to grips with the range. The whisky was released in Chapters (up to 17 of them) and some consumers, being used to a clear and obvious core range, were confused. In hindsight, Andrew Nelstrop has said that he's not convinced that their route to the market was the best and that it possibly delayed the brand awareness they were aiming for. In 2013 however, a more comprehensible range was introduced and since 2016 there are two core bottlings, The Original and The Smokey. On top of that a variety of exciting limited releases appear every year.

A few years after the distillery had started, James Nelstrop handed over the responsibility as managing director to Andrew and instead took on the role as the chairman of the company. While James had the privilege of being the first to distill a whisky in England in more than a century, he never really saw the huge impact St. George's Distillery had on the growing English whisky scene. He passed away in 2014 at the age of 69 and by that time only four more malt whisky distilleries had been founded in England – today there are over twenty and more are being built as I write this

Andrew Nelstrop, together with head distiller David Fitt, has continued what he and his father started and on top of that he has expanded the business into many more markets and also introduced new and innovative spirits. In 2017 a subrange by the name of The Norfolk was introduced. Under this brand David Fitt and his team can excel in innovative types of whiskies and other spirits, not least by using different types of grains. Andrew is convinced that not having a background in whisky production has been beneficial to the company. By not feeling restrained by a history of what works and what doesn't he and his team have had the freedom of trying new things. At the same time, the methods they use show in the end that they largely follow the rules that apply to a Scottish whisky maker. For instance they have the freedom to use other types of wood than oak for maturation but have decided not to do so.

Part of the success for The English Whisky Company is the visitor experience that was opened in summer of 2007. Already in the first year they received 25,000 visitors. The centre was recently expanded and nowadays more than 50,000 people find their way here.

Selling an English single malt whisky in a world that is completely dominated by Scotch hasn't been easy. It often boils down to finding the right importer that is willing to put a little more effort into explaining not just the brand but also the category. Other distillers that have experienced something similar are the producers of the Welsh Penderyn single malt. What is clear though is that The English Whisky Company has paved the way for all other English whisky producers in the same way as the other "trailblazers" in this edition of the Malt Whisky Yearbook have done in their respective countries. It takes guts, passion and perseverance to be the first because mistakes will happen and for other distillers that follow it must be a blessing to be able to learn from others and not having to make them yourself.

Springbank

[spring•bank]

Owner:
Springbank Distillers
(J & A Mitchell)

Region/district:
Campbeltown

Founded: 1828

Status: Active (vc)

Capacity: 750 000 litres

Address: Well Close, Campbeltown, Argyll PA28 6ET

Website: springbankwhisky.com

Tel: 01586 551710

Many whisky drinkers believe that Springbank has always been the one distillery which walks its own path, always relying on sales of their single malts for their success.

But this was not always the case. In the 1960s and 1970s, part of the whisky produced was sold to blenders and that is also why Springbank, like many others, were hit by the crash in the 1980s. They were forced to close the distillery from 1979 to 1987 and when they reopened, Hedley Wright, the owner and the great-great-grandson of one of the founders, made a decision. Never again should they sell their whisky to third parties but instead build their success on single malts. Springbank has also been famous for being the only Scottish distillery malting all their barley themselves, although from 1960 to 1992 the maltings were closed. Today, however, Springbank is widely considered as a producer of high quality malts with a style of its own.

The distillery is equipped with a 3.5 ton open cast iron mash tun, six washbacks made of Scandinavian larch with a fermentation time of up to 110 hours, one wash still and two spirit stills. The wash still is unique in Scotland, as it is fired by both an open oil-fire and internal steam coils. Ordinary condensers are used to cool the spirit vapours, except in the first of the two spirit stills, where a worm tub is used. Springbank is also the only distillery in Scotland that malts its entire need of barley using own floor maltings. Currently there are ten warehouses on site (dunnage and racked).

Springbank produces three distinctive single malts with different phenol contents in the malted barley. Springbank is distilled two and a half times (12-15ppm), Longrow is distilled twice (50-55 ppm) and the unpeated Hazelburn is distilled three times. When Springbank is produced, the malted barley is dried using 6 hours of peat smoke and 30 hours of hot air, while Longrow requires 48 hours of peat smoke. Production during 2020 proved to be difficult due to the pandemic and only 120,000 litres were distilled. In 2021 however, they are back on 5 mashes per week which means 220,000 litres of Springbank and 30,000 litres each of Longrow and Hazelburn.

The core range is **Springbank 10, 15** and **18 year old**, as well as **12 year old cask strength** (latest batch in autumn 2021). There are also limited but yearly releases of a **21 year old** and a **25 year old**. Other recent limited releases include **Springbank Local Barley 10 years old** (the latest in March 2021) and a **17 year old madeira cask matured**. Longrow is represented by **Longrow without age statement** and the **18 year old**. A limited yet annual release is **Longrow Red** with a **10 year old malbec finish** released in February 2021 being the latest. A limited and old Longrow (**21 years**) was released in November 2020. For Hazelburn, the core expression is a **10 year old** complemented by limited annual releases. In October 2020 it was a **Hazelburn 14 year old** matured in oloroso casks. The oldest official Hazelburn, a **21 year old**, is scheduled for a release in late 2021 or early 2022.

History:

1828 The Reid family, in-laws of the Mitchells (see below), founds the distillery.

1837 The Reid family encounters financial difficulties and John and William Mitchell buy the distillery.

1897 J. & A. Mitchell Co Ltd is founded.

1926 The depression forces the distillery to close.

1933 The distillery is back in production.

1960 Own maltings ceases.

1979 The distillery closes.

1985 A 10 year old Longrow is launched.

1987 Limited production restarts.

1989 Production restarts.

1992 Springbank takes up its maltings again.

1997 First distillation of Hazelburn.

1998 Springbank 12 years is launched.

1999 Dha Mhile (7 years), the world's first organic single malt, is launched.

2000 A 10 year old is launched.

2001 Springbank 1965 'Local barley' is launched.

2002 Number one in the series Wood Expressions is a 12 year old with five years in rum casks.

2004 Springbank 10 years 100 proof is launched as well as Longrow 14 years old, Springbank 32 years old and Springbank 14 years Port Wood.

2005 Springbank 21 years, the first version of Hazelburn (8 years) and Longrow Tokaji Wood Expression are launched.

2006 Longrow 10 years 100 proof, Springbank 25 years, Springbank 9 years Marsala finish, Springbank 11 years Madeira finish and a new Hazelburn 8 year old are released.

2007 Springbank Vintage 1997 and a 16 year old rum wood are released.

2008 The distillery closes temporarily. Three new releases of Longrow - CV, 18 year old and 7 year old Gaja Barolo.

History continued:

2009 Springbank Madeira 11 year old, Springbank 18 year old, Springbank Vintage 2001 and Hazelburn 12 year old are released.

2010 Springbank 12 year old cask strength and a 12 year old claret expression together with new editions of the CV and 18 year old are released.

2011 Longrow 18 year old and Hazelburn 8 year old Sauternes wood expression are released.

2012 Springbank Rundlets & Kilderkins, Springbank 21 year old and Longrow Red are released.

2013 Longrow Rundlets & Kilderkins, a new edition of Longrow Red and Springbank 9 year old Gaja Barolo finish are released.

2014 Hazelburn Rundlets & Kilderkins, Hazelburn 10 year old and Springbank 25 years old are launched.

2015 New releases include Springbank Green 12 years old and a new edition of the Longrow Red.

2016 Springbank Local Barley and a 9 year old Hazelburn barolo finish are released.

2017 Springbank 14 year old bourbon cask and Hazelburn 13 year old sherrywood are released.

2018 Local Barley 10 year old, 14 year old Longrow Sherry Wood and a new Longrow Red are released.

2019 Springbank 25, Hazelburn 14 and a 21 year old Longrow are released.

2020 Springbank Local Barley 10 years old, a 17 year old madeira finish and Longrow Red Cabernet Sauvignon are released.

2021 Longrow Red 10 year old malbec and a 21 year old Hazelburn are released.

Tasting notes Springbank 10 years old:

GS – Fresh and briny on the nose, with citrus fruit, oak and barley, plus a note of damp earth. Sweet on the palate, with developing brine, nuttiness and vanilla toffee. Coconut oil and drying peat in the finish.

Tasting notes Longrow NAS:

GS – Initially slightly gummy on the nose, but then brine and fat peat notes develop. Vanilla and malt also emerge. The smoky palate offers lively brine and is quite dry and spicy, with some vanilla and lots of ginger. The finish is peaty with persistent, oaky ginger.

Tasting notes Hazelburn 10 years old:

GS – Pear drops, soft toffee and malt on the mildly floral nose. Oiliness develops in time, along with a green, herbal note and ultimately brine. Full-bodied and supple on the smoky palate, with barley and ripe, peppery orchard fruits. Developing cocoa and ginger in the lengthy finish.

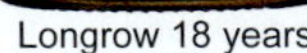

Longrow 18 years   Springbank 18 years   Hazelburn 10 years

Longrow NAS   Longrow Red

Springbank 10 years   Springbank 17 years Madeira   Springbank Local Barley

Strathisla

[strath•<u>eye</u>•la]

Owner:
Chivas Bros (Pernod Ricard)

Region/district:
Speyside

Founded: | **Status:** | **Capacity:**
1786 | Active (vc) | 2 450 000 litres

Address: Seafield Avenue, Keith,
Banffshire AB55 5BS

Website: | **Tel:**
chivas.com | 01542 783044

The location and the old-fashioned beauty makes Strathisla one of the loveliest distilleries in Scotland but to be perfectly blunt – as a single malt brand, Strathisla is virtually non-existent.

In 2019 the official 12 year old sold 25,000 bottles which is less than one percent of total Aberlour sales. Even the newly launched, and to most consumers completely unknown, Allt-a-Bhainne sells twice as much. These figures are by no means a failure on behalf of the Pernod Ricard sales department nor is it a sign of poor quality. Strathisla's owners have focused on producing the single malt as the backbone of Chivas Regal for at least seven decades, as well as making the distillery the spiritual home of the blend.

Chivas Regal was in 2019 the third best selling Scotch blend in the world but 2020, the year of the pandemic, was brutal on the brand. No less than 27% of the volume disappeared and both Grant's and William Lawson managed to overtake it on the top list. The brand's problem was the exposure to the travel retail segment – a sales channel which more or less disappeared. The on-trade business (bars and restaurants) is also important to Chivas Regal and with restrictions and closures all over the world, the brand suffered even more. However, signs of improved sales figures became obvious already in late 2020, not least in the important Chinese market.

Strathisla is equipped with a 5.12 ton traditional mash tun with a raised copper canopy, seven washbacks made of Oregon pine and three of larch – all with a 54 hour fermentation cycle. There are two pairs of stills. The wash stills are of lantern type with descending lyne arms and the spirit stills have boiling balls with the lyne arms slightly ascending.

The only core expression is the **12 year old** but currently there are also no less than six cask strength bottlings in the Distillery Reserve Collection, available at all Chivas' visitor centres. Three of them, **13, 16** and **25 year old** were matured in sherry butts while the other three, **17, 27** and **29 year old**, came from either bourbon hogsheads of barrels.

History:

1786 Alexander Milne and George Taylor found the distillery under the name Milltown, but soon change it to Milton.

1823 MacDonald Ingram & Co. purchases the distillery.

1830 William Longmore acquires the distillery.

1870 The distillery name changes to Strathisla.

1880 William Longmore retires and hands operations to his son-in-law John Geddes-Brown. William Longmore & Co. is formed.

1890 The distillery changes name to Milton.

1942 Jay Pomeroy acquires a majority of the shares in William Longmore & Co. Pomeroy is jailed as a result of dubious business transactions and the distillery goes bankrupt in 1949.

1950 Chivas Brothers buys the run-down distillery at a compulsory auction for £71,000 and starts restoration.

1951 The name reverts to Strathisla.

1965 The number of stills is increased from two to four.

1970 A heavily peated whisky, Craigduff, is produced but production stops later.

2001 The Chivas Group is acquired by Pernod Ricard.

2019 Chivas Distillery Collection Strathisla 12 year old is released.

12 years old

Tasting notes Strathisla 12 years old:

GS – Rich on the nose, with sherry, stewed fruits, spices and lots of malt. Full-bodied and almost syrupy on the palate. Toffee, honey, nuts, a whiff of peat and a suggestion of oak. The finish is medium in length, slightly smoky and with a final flash of ginger.

Strathmill

[strath•mill]

Owner: Diageo

Region/district: Speyside

Founded: 1891

Status: Active

Capacity: 2 600 000 litres

Address: Keith, Banffshire AB55 5DQ

Website: malts.com

Tel: 01542 883000

When a whisky tourist comes to Keith these days, perhaps by way of the heritage Keith and Dufftown railway, it is definitely not to see Strathmill. The goal is the neighbouring Strathisla.

Neatly tucked away right by the River Isla, Strathmill's apearance is of a classic, late 19th century distillery. At the dead end of the road, you can climb the tiny slope to take some decent photos but don't expect to walk around the distillery as it doesn't accept visitors. This is a true working distillery with a main purpose of producing malt whisky to be used in blends, in particular J&B.

It was bought by the famous gin producer W. & A. Gilbey in 1895 who changed the name of the distillery from Glenisla to Strathmill. The company already owned Glen Spey and were later (in 1904) to buy Knockando as well. They used Strathmill for blends while marketing the single malt for export markets at the same time. In the Australian newspaper of December 1905, The Manawatu Times, one could read the following. "Of eight of the most popular whiskies submitted for analysis, the Western Australian Government analyst in his annual report to Parliament, pronounces Strathmill to be the most genuine matured malt whisky."

The equipment consists of a 9.1 ton stainless steel semi-lauter mash tun and six stainless steel washbacks. There are two pairs of stills and Strathmill is one of few distilleries still using purifiers on the spirit stills. This device is mounted between the lyne arm and the condenser and acts as a mini-condenser, allowing the lighter alcohols to travel towards the condenser and forcing the heavier alcohols to go back into the still for another distillation. The result is a lighter spirit. Lately, the distillery has been working a five-day week producing around two million litres of pure alcohol in the year. Although not confirmed by the owners, it seems that, for at least this year, Strathmill will be producing less while sharing workforce with another Diageo distillery – the newly re-opened Knockando.

The only official bottling is the **12 year old Flora & Fauna**, but a limited **25 year old** was launched in 2014 as part of the Special Releases.

History:

1891 The distillery is founded in an old mill from 1823 and is named Glenisla-Glenlivet Distillery.

1892 The inauguration takes place in June.

1895 The gin company W. & A. Gilbey buys the distillery for £9,500 and names it Strathmill.

1962 W. & A. Gilbey merges with United Wine Traders (including Justerini & Brooks) and forms International Distillers & Vintners (IDV).

1968 The number of stills is increased from two to four and purifiers are added.

1972 IDV is bought by Watney Mann which later the same year is acquired by Grand Metropolitan.

1993 Strathmill becomes available as a single malt for the first time since 1909 as a result of a bottling (1980) from Oddbins.

1997 Guinness and Grand Metropolitan merge and form Diageo.

2001 The first official bottling is a 12 year old in the Flora & Fauna series.

2010 A Manager´s Choice single cask from 1996 is released.

2014 A 25 year old is released.

12 years old

Tasting notes Strathmill 12 years old:

GS – Quite reticent on the nose, with nuts, grass and a hint of ginger. Spicy vanilla and nuts dominate the palate. The finish is drying, with peppery oak.

Talisker

[tal•iss•kur]

Owner:	**Region/district:**
Diageo	Highlands (Skye)

Founded:	**Status:**	**Capacity:**
1830	Active (vc)	3 300 000 litres

Address: Carbost, Isle of Skye,
Inverness-shire IV47 8SR

Website:	**Tel:**
malts.com	01478 614308 (vc)

The location of Talisker in the Hebrides and the history of the MacAskill brothers rowing from Eigg to Skye in 1830 to found the distillery, inspired the current owners, Diageo, to launch the Talisker Whisky Atlantic Challenge in 2015.

This is a competition where rowers, on their own or in a team, cross the Atlantic ocean from La Gomera in the Canary Islands to Antigua in the West Indies. Around 30 solo rowers or teams participate every year and in the fifth race which started in December 2019, one of the teams was Broar which was made up of three brothers (Ewan, James and Lachlan), sons of the renowned whisky authority Charles MacLean. In early 2020 the adventurist James Aiken single-handedly sailed the same route in 24 days. On his boat, The Oaken Yarn, he brought staves that were later used to build 10 casks in which the exclusive Talisker 43 year old Xpedition Oak was later finished.

Talisker is equipped with a stainless steel lauter mash tun with a capacity of 8 tonnes and eight washbacks made of Oregon pine. Before mashing, the malted barley is mixed to a ratio of 25% unpeated and 75% peated which has a phenol specification of 20-25ppm. There are five stills – two wash stills and three spirit stills. The wash stills are equipped with a special type of "purifiers" or, more specifically, return pipes, which use the colder outside air, and there is also a u-bend in the lyne arms. The return pipes and the peculiar bend of the lyne arms allow for more copper contact and increases the reflux during distillation. All of the stills are connected to wormtubs. The fermentation time is quite long (60-65 hours) and the middle cut from the spirit still is collected between 76% and 65% which, together with the phenol specification, gives a medium peated spirit. The number 1 wash still and number 3 spirit still were replaced in February 2020 due to age as were the wooden worm tubs on spirit stills 2 and 3. The production plan for 2021 is 20 mashes per week which accounts for 3.3 million litres of alcohol.

Talisker's core range consists of **Skye** and **Storm**, both without age statement, **10, 18, 25** and **30 year old, Distiller's Edition** with an Amoroso sherry finish and **Port Ruighe**, finished in ruby port casks. There is also **Dark Storm**, the peatiest Talisker so far, which is exclusive to duty free together with **Neist Point**. Included in recent limited bottlings (launched in spring 2021) is the oldest Talisker ever released by the owners - the above mentioned **43 year old**, A new range of limited bottlings was introduced in summer 2018 – the Bodega Series which explores the impact of different sherry cask finishes. The second installment, released in July 2019, was a **41 year old** finished in Manzanilla casks. Launched around the same time was **Talisker Select Reserve House Greyjoy** as part of the Game of Thrones series. Finally, in autumn 2021, an **8 year old** bottled from the smokiest stock in the warehouses was part of the yearly Rare by Nature series and at the same time a **41 year old Prima & Ultima** was released.

History:

1830 Hugh and Kenneth MacAskill found the distillery.

1848 The brothers transfer the lease to North of Scotland Bank and Jack Westland from the bank runs the operations.

1854 Kenneth MacAskill dies.

1857 North of Scotland Bank sells the distillery to Donald MacLennan for £500.

1863 MacLennan experiences difficulties in making operations viable and puts the distillery up for sale.

1865 MacLennan, still working at the distillery, nominates John Anderson as agent in Glasgow.

1867 Anderson & Co. from Glasgow takes over.

1879 John Anderson is imprisoned after having sold non-existing casks of whisky.

1880 New owners are now Alexander Grigor Allan and Roderick Kemp.

1892 Kemp sells his share and buys Macallan Distillery instead.

1894 The Talisker Distillery Ltd is founded.

1895 Allan dies and Thomas Mackenzie, who has been his partner, takes over.

1898 Talisker Distillery merges with Dailuaine-Glenlivet Distillers and Imperial Distillers to form Dailuaine-Talisker Distillers Company.

1916 Thomas Mackenzie dies and the distillery is taken over by a consortium consisting of, among others, John Walker, John Dewar, W. P. Lowrie and Distillers Company Limited (DCL).

1928 The distillery abandons triple distillation.

1960 On 22nd November the distillery catches fire and substantial damage occurs.

1962 The distillery reopens after the fire.

1972 Own malting ceases.

1988 Classic Malts are introduced, Talisker 10 years included. A visitor centre is opened.

History continued:

1998 A new stainless steel/copper mash tun and five new worm tubs are installed. Talisker is launched as a Distillers Edition with an amoroso sherry finish.

2004 Two new bottlings appear, an 18 year old and a 25 year old.

2005 To celebrate the 175th birthday of the distillery, Talisker 175th Anniversary is released.

2006 A 30 year old and the fourth edition of the 25 year old are released.

2007 The second edition of the 30 year old and the fifth edition of the 25 year old are released.

2008 Talisker 57° North, sixth edition of the 25 year old and third edition of the 30 year old are launched.

2009 New editions of the 25 and 30 year old are released.

2010 A 1994 Manager´s Choice single cask and a new edition of the 30 year old are released.

2011 Three limited releases - 25, 30 and 34 year old.

2012 A limited 35 year old is released.

2013 Four new expressions are released – Storm, Dark Storm, Port Ruighe and a 27 year old.

2014 A bottling for the Friends of the Classic Malts is released.

2015 Skye and Neist Point are released.

2016 A distillery exclusive without age statement is released.

2018 A 40 year old, the first in the new Bodega Series, and an 8 year old Special Release are launched.

2019 A 41 year old Bodega Series and House Greyjoy in the Game of Thrones series are released.

2020 A 31 year old Prima & Ultima and an 8 year old rum finish Rare by Nature are released.

2021 A 41 year old Prima & Ultima and an 8 year old Rare by Nature are released

Tasting notes Talisker 10 years old:

GS – Quite dense and smoky on the nose, with smoked fish, bladderwrack, sweet fruit and peat. Full-bodied and peaty in the mouthy; complex, with ginger, ozone, dark chocolate, black pepper and a kick of chilli in the long, smoky tail.

Tasting notes Talisker Storm:

GS – The nose offers brine, burning wood embers, vanilla, and honey. The palate is sweet and spicy, with cranberries and blackcurrants, while peat-smoke and black pepper are ever-present. The finish is spicy, with walnuts, and fruity peat.

Port Ruighe

Storm

Skye

Prima & Ultima 1988

43 years old

10 years old

8 year old
Rare by Nature

Distiller´s Edition

Tamdhu

[tam•doo]

Owner:
Ian Macleod Distillers

Region/district:
Speyside

Founded: **Status:**
1897   Active

Capacity:
4 000 000 litres

Address: Knockando, Aberlour,
Morayshire AB38 7RP

Website:
tamdhu.com

Tel:
01340 872200

The owners of Tamdhu, Ian Mecleod Distillers, are not only the owners of three distilleries associated with single malt. They also have a vast number of blended Scotch brands in their range and they produce blends for other companies as well.

In fact, in terms of volume more than 90% of the company´s sales are blends with 10 million bottles sold in 2019. If one adds another 5 million bottles of other spirits on top of that, it becomes obvious that warehousing is high on the agenda. The storage capacity at the headquarter in Broxburn is not enough so in the past five years they have added another 18 warehouses at Tamdhu to the ten that were already there.

The flavour profile of Tamdhu rests firmly on the use of ex-sherry casks for maturation and, to be specific, we are talking about first and second fill oloroso cask made from both European and American Oak. This is the same type of maturation that lends its character to the sister malt Glengoyne.

Tamdhu is equipped with an 11.8 ton semilauter mash tun, nine Oregon pine washbacks with a fermentation time of 59 hours and three pairs of stills. An on-site cooperage for repairing and testing casks became operational in 2019. The production plan for 2021 is 16 mashes per week which translates to 3.1 million litres for the entire year.

The core range consists of a **10 year old** exclusive to the UK market, a **12 year old**, the non-chill filtered **Batch Strength** (with the sixth edition launched in August 2021) and the limited **15 year old**. A very limited bottling (100 decanters and now sold out) was a rare **50 year old** released in 2017 to celebrate the 120th anniversary of the distillery. More recently, we have seen the release of **Tamdhu Cigar Malt** and – available only in the distillery webshop – part four of **Dalbeallie Dram**, the **16 year old Iain Whitecross Single Cask** and **Tamdhu Club Single Cask**. Finally, there are two expressions reserved for the travel retail market; **Ámbar 14 year old** and the **Gran Reserva First Edition**.

History:

1896 The distillery is founded by Tamdhu Distillery Company, a consortium of whisky blenders with William Grant as the main promoter. Charles Doig is the architect.

1897 The first casks are filled in July.

1898 Highland Distillers Company, which has several of the 1896 consortium members in managerial positions, buys Tamdhu Distillery Company.

1911 The distillery closes.

1913 The distillery reopens.

1928 The distillery is mothballed.

1948 The distillery is in full production again in July.

1950 The floor maltings is replaced by Saladin boxes when the distillery is rebuilt.

1972 The number of stills is increased from two to four.

1975 Two stills augment the previous four.

1976 Tamdhu 8 years is launched as single malt.

2005 An 18 year old and a 25 year old are released.

2009 The distillery is mothballed.

2011 The Edrington Group sells the distillery to Ian Macleod Distillers.

2012 Production is resumed.

2013 The first official release from the new owners – a 10 year old.

2015 Tamdhu Batch Strength is released.

2017 A 50 year old is released.

2018 A 12 year old, a 15 year old and the Dalbeallie Dram are released.

2019 Two expressions for duty-free - Ámbar and Gran Reserva First Edition.

2020 Iain Whitecross Single Cask and Cigar Malt are launched

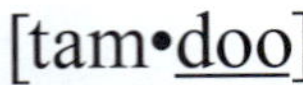

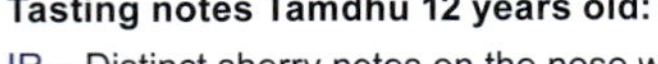

12 years old

Tasting notes Tamdhu 12 years old:

IR – Distinct sherry notes on the nose with raisins and prunes as well as menthol and green leaves. The taste is wellbalanced with dried fruit, crème brûlée, roasted nuts, bananas and cinnamon.

Tamnavulin

[tam•na•voo•lin]

Owner:
Whyte & Mackay (Emperador)

Region/district:
Speyside

Founded: 1966

Status: Active

Capacity: 4 200 000 litres

Address: Tomnavoulin, Ballindalloch,
Banffshire AB3 9JA

Website:
tamnavulinwhisky.com

Tel:
01807 590285

The presence of official bottlings of Tamnavulin single malt in whisky shops is quite recent. In fact, it wasn't until two years ago that there was an entire core range available.

With the exception of a few limited vintages, the whiskies are without age statement which is not surprising. The distillery was more or less closed from 1996 to 2007 so obviously there are still some gaps in the stock to fill. In some markets it hasn't taken long for whisky consumers to start appreciating Tamnavulin. In Sweden for example, the brand in 2020 went from 36th place on the single malt sales list to the top spot. An old carding mill next to the distillery was used as a visitor centre until the late 1990s and the owners are now contemplating starting up something similar again. It is highly unlikely though that the old mill will be used this time as this is now home to 700 pipistrelle bats!

Tamnavulin distillery is equipped with a full lauter mash tun with an 11 ton charge, nine washbacks made of stainless steel with a fermentation time of 54-60 hours and three pairs of stills. The wash stills, with horizontal lyne arms, are all equipped with sub-coolers while the spirit stills with their descending lyne arms have purifiers. The foreshots are running for 25 minutes and the heart is collected from 75% down to 60% resulting in a slightly grassy new make. On the environmental side, the distillery is since September 2018 running on LPG (liquefied petroleum gas) rather than heavy fuel oil and a new bioplant has been installed to take care of the residues from the distillation. In spite of the pandemic, the owners managed to produce 3,3 million litres of pure alcohol during 2020 and in 2021, the plan is to do 21-22 mashes per week and 4,2 million litres.

The core expression is **Double Cask** with a sherry finish. In 2019 a **Sherry Cask Edition** with a finish in three types of oloroso casks was launched together with a **Tempranillo finish** for duty free. Recent limited bottlings include four **vintages** (from 1970 to 2000) for Taiwan and, released in 2020, three wine cask finishes for select markets - **Cabernet Sauvignon**, **Grenache** and **Pinot Noir**.

History:

1966 Tamnavulin-Glenlivet Distillery Company, a subsidiary of Invergordon Distillers Ltd, founds Tamnavulin.

1993 Whyte & Mackay buys Invergordon Distillers.

1995 The distillery closes in May.

1996 Whyte & Mackay changes name to JBB (Greater Europe).

2000 Distillation takes place for six weeks.

2001 Company management buy out operations for £208 million and rename the company Kyndal.

2003 Kyndal changes name to Whyte & Mackay.

2007 United Spirits buys Whyte & Mackay. Tamnavulin is opened again in July after having been mothballed for 12 years.

2014 Whyte & Mackay is sold to Emperador Inc.

2016 Tamnavulin Double Cask is released.

2019 Sherry Cask Edition and Tempranillo Finish are released.

2020 Three wine cask finishes are released; cabernet sauvignon, grenache and pinot noir.

Tasting notes Tamnavulin Double Cask:

GS – The nose offers malt, soft toffee, almonds and tangerines. Finally, background earthiness. Smooth on the palate, with ginger nut biscuits, vanilla and orchard fruits, plus walnuts. The finish is medium in length, with lingering fruity spice.

Double Cask

Teaninich

[tee•ni•nick]

Owner:
Diageo

Region/district:
Northern Highlands

Founded: **Status:**
1817   Active

Capacity:
10 200 000 litres

Address: Alness, Ross-shire IV17 0XB

Website:
malts.com

Tel:
01349 885001

In 2016, Diageo released their first expressions in a new range named Johnnie Walker Blenders' Batch. This is an innovative range of whiskies where master blender Jim Beveridge and his team display the versatility of the worlds number one Scotch.

The initiative involves experiments within raw materials, distillation and maturation and the series was created first and foremost with bartenders in mind. In a highly competitive spirits business, staying relevant in the on-trade business has become increasingly important for Scotch whisky brands. One part of the innovation formula is having distilleries that are adaptable and ready to handle different types of grain and this is where Teaninich excels. The distillery is equipped with a hammer mill and a mash filter instead of a traditional mill and a mash tun. This facilitates handling for example grains such as rye and different types of malted barley. While still an important supplier of "classic" single malt for a variety of blends, Teaninich has also become a distillery where the owner can conduct all kinds of trials for future releases.

The grain is ground into a fine flour without husks in a hammer mill. This is the basis for a higher spirit yield but also entails that one can use grain varieties that wouldn't mill as well in a traditional mill with rollers. The grist is mixed with water in a conversion vessel. Once the conversion from starch to sugar is done, the mash passes through a mash filter which consists of a number of mesh bags. The filter compresses the bags and the wort is collected for the next step – fermentation

Apart from the mash filter. the equipment consists of 18 wooden washbacks and two made of stainless steel – all with a fermentation time of 75 hours and six pairs of stills. Due to a major expansion in 2015 the capacity was doubled and Teaninich is now the third largest malt distillery in the Diageo group. In the past few years the distillery has alternated between 16 and 28 mashes per week.

The only official core bottling is a **10 year old** in the Flora & Fauna series but a limited **17 year old** matured in refill American oak was launched in autumn 2017 as part of the Special Releases.

History:

1817   Captain Hugh Monro, owner of the estate Teaninich, founds the distillery.

1831   Captain Munro sells the estate to his younger brother John.

1850   John Munro, who spends most of his time in India, leases Teaninich to the infamous Robert Pattison from Leith.

1869   John McGilchrist Ross takes over the licence.

1895   Munro & Cameron takes over the licence.

1898   Munro & Cameron buys the distillery.

1904   Robert Innes Cameron becomes sole owner of Teaninich.

1932   Robert Innes Cameron dies.

1933   The estate of Robert Innes Cameron sells the distillery to Distillers Company Limited.

1970   A new distillation unit with six stills is commissioned and becomes known as the A side.

1975   A dark grains plant is built.

1984   The B side of the distillery is mothballed.

1985   The A side is also mothballed.

1991   The A side is in production again.

1992   United Distillers launches a 10 year old Teaninich in the Flora & Fauna series.

1999   The B side is decommissioned.

2000   A mash filter is installed.

2009   Teaninich 1996, a single cask in the new Manager´s Choice range is released.

2015   The distillery is expanded with six new stills and the capacity is doubled.

2017   A 17 year old is launched as part of the Special Releases.

Tasting notes Teaninich 10 years old:

GS – The nose is initially fresh and grassy, quite light, with vanilla and hints of tinned pineapple. Mediumbodied, smooth, slightly oily, with cereal and spice in the mouth. Nutty and slowly drying in the finish, with pepper and a suggestion of cocoa powder notes.

10 years old

Tobermory

[tow•bur•<u>mo</u>•ray]

Owner:	**Region/district:**
Distell International Ltd.	Highland (Mull)
Founded: **Status:**	**Capacity:**
1798 Active (vc)	1 000 000 litres

Address: Tobermory, Isle of Mull, Argyllsh. PA75 6NR

Website: **Tel:**
tobermorydistillery.com 01688 302647

The distillery was known as Tobermory from 1798 until its closure in 1930. In 1972, when the distillery was re-opened, the new owners decided to name the distillery Ledaig Distillery.

Seven years later it was time for yet another change of owner-ship when Stewart Jowett took over. During the sporadic production years of his ownership, he continued to use the name Ledaig. However, to confuse matters even further, he also launched both a blended whisky and a vatted malt under the name Tobermory. Nine years after Burn Stewart's take-over in 1993, a decision was taken to use Tobermory as the brand for unpeated malts while Ledaig was reserved for all peated expressions with a phenol content of 30-40 ppm. Production from 1972 to 1993 was intermittent and of a hugely varying quality. The first task for Master Blender, Ian MacMillan was therefore to separate casks worthy of being bottled as single malts, while the rest was being used for blends.

The equipment consists of a 45 year old traditional five ton cast iron mash tun which is probably due to be replaced like for like in the coming years. There are four, new washbacks made of Oregon pine with a fermentation time of 48 to 100 hours and two pairs of stills. Two of the stills were replaced in 2014 and the other two in summer 2019. The production plan for 2021 is to do 9 mashes per week (800,000 litres of alcohol) with a 50/50 split between the peated Ledaig and the unpeated Tobermory. There is also a recently installed 2,000 litre gin still producing Tobermory Hebridean Gin.

The core range consists of the **12 year old Tobermory** and the **10** and **18 year old Ledaig**. Two additions were made in September 2020 – the **23 year old Tobermory oloroso finish** and the NAS **Ledaig Sinclair rioja finish**. More expressions can be expected in the Sinclair series. Recent limited expressions include a **Tobermory 2004 oloroso cask matured** and a **Ledaig 1999 PX cask matured**. Available only at the distillery are **Tobermory 2003 madeira cask finish** and **Ledaig 2008 amarone cask finish**.

History:

1798 John Sinclair founds the distillery.

1837 The distillery closes.

1878 The distillery reopens.

1890 John Hopkins & Company buys the distillery.

1916 Distillers Company Limited (DCL) takes over John Hopkins & Company.

1930 The distillery closes.

1972 A shipping company in Liverpool and the sherrymaker Domecq buy the buildings and embark on refurbishment. When work is completed it is named Ledaig Distillery Ltd.

1975 Ledaig Distillery Ltd files for bankruptcy and the distillery closes again.

1979 The estate agent Kirkleavington Property buys the distillery, forms a new company, Tobermory Distillers Ltd and starts production.

1982 No production. Some of the buildings are converted into flats and some are rented to a dairy company for cheese storage.

1989 Production resumes.

1993 Burn Stewart Distillers buys Tobermory.

2002 CL Financial buys Burn Stewart Distillers.

2005 A 32 year old from 1972 is launched.

2007 A Ledaig 10 year old is released.

2008 A Tobermory 15 year old is released.

2013 Burn Stewart Distillers is sold to Distell Group Ltd. A 40 year old Ledaig is released.

2015 Ledaig 18 years and 42 years are released together with Tobermory 42 years.

2018 Two 19 year old Ledaig are released.

2019 A 12 year old Tobermory is released, replacing the 10 year old.

2020 Two additions to the core range; 23 year old Tobermory oloroso finish and Ledaig Sinclair rioja finish.

Tasting notes Tobermory 12 years old:

IR – Butterscotch and heather honey on the nose with peaches and a hint of orange peel. Mouthcoating, rich and malty with notes of fudge, Danish pastry, citrus, pineapple and a hint of pepper. The finish is slightly salty.

Tasting notes Ledaig 10 years old:

GS – The nose is profoundly peaty, sweet and full, with notes of butter and smoked fish. Bold, yet sweet on the palate, with iodine, soft peat and heather. Developing spices. The finish is medium to long, with pepper, ginger, liquorice and peat.

12 years old

Tomatin

[to•mat•in]

Owner: **Region/district:**
Tomatin Distillery Co   Highland
(Takara Shuzo Co., Kokubu & Co., Marubeni Corp.)

Founded: **Status:**   **Capacity:**
1897   Active (vc)   5 000 000 litres

Address: Tomatin, Inverness-shire IV13 7YT

Website: **Tel:**
tomatin.com   01463 248144 (vc)

It wasn't until 2004 that a widely available 12 year old Tomatin single malt was released. Since then the range has grown and sales figures have rocketed. Today the brand sells more than 750,000 bottles every year.

Tomatin is a perfect example of a distillery that decade after decade tirelessly produced malts for blends but where the owners, noticing the increased interest in malt whisky in the new millenium, changed direction and created a single malt brand instead. Others are Ardmore, Tullibardine and Tamnavulin.

The distillery is equipped with a nine ton stainless steel, full lauter mash tun, 12 stainless steel washbacks and six pairs of stills (with only four of the spirit stills being used). Usually they have a combination of short and long fermentations but this year they are focusing on fermentations that are 140 hours or longer. There are also eleven racked warehouses and two dunnage on site with a capacity to store 200,000 casks. The goal is to produce 1.55 million litres in 2021, including 80,000 litres of peated production at 40ppm.

The core range consists of **Legacy, 12, 18, 30** and **36 year old.** Included are also **Cask Strength, 14 year old port finish** and a **2006 Fino sherry cask** exclusive to the UK. Recent limited releases include the highly exclusive **Decades II** which is a vatting of casks from five decades starting from the 1970s and the **Frech Collection**, released in April 2021. This series is aimed at highlighting the impact on flavour imparted by the finish in three different types of French wine casks - **Monbazillac, Sauternes** and **Rivesaltes.** The series will be completed later in 2021 with a **Cognac** finish. The distillery's duty free range consists of **8, 12, 15, 21** and **40 year old** while the smoky side of Tomatin is represented by the stand-alone brand **Cù Bòcan** with **Signature, Creation #1** and **Creation #2.** For the last two, the maturation story is innovative to say the least involving both virgin oak as well as casks that have previously held imperial stout, moscatel and shochu. **Creation #3** and **#4** are due for release in late autumn 2021.

History:

1897 The distillery is founded by Tomatin Spey Distillery Company.

1906 Production ceases.

1909 Production resumes through Tomatin Distillers.

1956 Stills are increased from two to four.

1958 Another two stills are added.

1961 The six stills are increased to ten.

1974 The stills now total 23 and the maltings closes.

1985 The distillery company goes into liquidation.

1986 Takara Shuzo Co. and Okara & Co., buy Tomatin through Tomatin Distillery Co.

1998 Okara & Co is liquidated and Marubeni buys out part of their shareholding.

2004 Tomatin 12 years is launched.

2005 A 25 year old and a 1973 Vintage are released.

2006 An 18 year old and a 1962 Vintage are launched.

2008 A 30 and a 40 year old as well as several vintages from 1975 and 1995 are released.

2009 A 15 year old, a 21 year old and four single casks (1973, 1982, 1997 and 1999) are released.

2010 The first peated release - a 4 year old exclusive for Japan.

2011 A 30 year old and Tomatin Decades are released.

2013 Cù Bòcan, the first peated Tomatin, is released.

2014 14 year old port finish, 36 year old, Vintage 1988, Tomatin Cuatro, Cù Bòcan Sherry Cask and Cù Bòcan 1989 are released.

2015 Cask Strength and Cù Bòcan Virgin Oak are released.

2016 A 44 year old Tomatin and two Cù Bòcan vintages (1988 and 2005) are released.

2017 New releases include Wood, Fire and Earth as well as a 2006 Cù Bòcan.

2018 A 30 year old and a 50 year old are released.

2019 The entire range of Cù Bòcan is relaunched with three new expressions.

2020 A Vintage 1975 is released.

2021 The French Collection and Cù Bócan Creation #3 and #4 are released.

Tasting notes Tomatin 12 years old:

GS – Barley, spice, buttery oak and a floral note on the nose. Sweet and medium-bodied, with toffee apples, spice and herbs in the mouth. Medium-length in the finish, with sweet fruitiness.

12 years old

Tomintoul

[tom•in•<u>towel</u>]

Owner:
Angus Dundee Distillers

Region/district:
Speyside

Founded: 1965
Status: Active
Capacity: 3 300 000 litres

Address: Ballindalloch, Banffshire AB37 9AQ

Website:
tomintouldistillery.co.uk

Tel:
01807 590274

Tomintoul distillery became operational in 1965 and while the first 35 years were eventful, there was little focus on the distillery's single malts.

No less than six different owners came and went, one of them being Lonhro which was led by the controversial Tiny Rowlands. He was the son of a German adventurer and during WWII, he got involved in the Hitler Youth. After the war he was interned on the Isle of Man and then immigrated to South Rhodesia where he began to create a fortune for himself. With considerably more focus, the owners since 2000, Angus Dundee, has taken on the task of managing the distillery. Admittedly, they use the bulk part of the whisky for their many blends and for own-label whiskies, but they have also put in a lot of work in establishing Tomintoul as a single malt of note.

Tomintoul is equipped with a 12 ton semi lauter mash tun, six stainless steel washbacks with a fermentation time of 54-60 hours and two pairs of stills. There are currently 15 mashes per week, which means that capacity is used to its maximum, and the 13 warehouses have a storage capacity of 120,000 casks. The malt used for mashing is unpeated, but every year since 2001, small batches of heavily peated (55ppm) spirit has been produced. On the site there is also a blending centre with 14 large blending vats.

The core range consists of **Tlàth** without age statement, **10, 14, 16, 18, 21** and **25 year old**. Since January 2021, the new **Cigar Malt** is also included in the range. There are also two finishes; a **12 year old oloroso sherry cask** and a **15 year old port finish**. The peaty side of Tomintoul is represented by **Peaty Tang**, either without age statement or as a newly released **15 year old**. As a stand-alone range, there is also the heavily peated **Old Ballantruan** without age statement as well as a **10** and **15 year old**. Recent limited releases include **Seiridh**, launched in March 2020 and without age statement. Finally there are two single cask **Robert Fleming 30th Anniversary** – one **30 year old PX sherry butt** bottled at 51,1% and a **25 year old sherry cask** bottled at 57,4%.

History:

1965 The distillery is founded by Tomintoul Distillery Ltd, which is owned by Hay & MacLeod & Co. and W. & S. Strong & Co.

1973 Scottish & Universal Investment Trust, owned by the Fraser family, buys both the distillery and Whyte & Mackay.

1974 The two stills are increased to four and Tomintoul 12 years is launched.

1978 Lonhro buys Scottish & Universal Investment Trust.

1989 Lonhro sells Whyte & Mackay to Brent Walker.

1990 American Brands buys Whyte & Mackay.

1996 Whyte & Mackay changes name to JBB (Greater Europe).

2000 Angus Dundee plc buys Tomintoul.

2002 Tomintoul 10 year is launched.

2003 Tomintoul 16 years is launched.

2004 Tomintoul 27 years is launched.

2005 The peated Old Ballantruan is launched.

2008 1976 Vintage and Peaty Tang are released.

2009 A 14 year old and a 33 year old are released.

2010 A 12 year old Port wood finish is released.

2011 A 21 year old, a 10 year old Ballantruan and Vintage 1966 are released.

2012 Old Ballantruan 10 years old is released.

2013 A 31 year old single cask is released.

2015 Five Decades and a 40 year old are released.

2016 A 40 year old and Tlàth without age statement are launched.

2017 15 year old Peaty Tang and 15 year old Old Ballantruan are launched.

2018 Tomintoul 1965 The Ultimate Cask is released.

2020 Seiridh and a number of bottlings celebrating Robert Fleming's 30th anniversary are released.

10 years old

Tasting notes Tomintoul 10 years old:

GS – A light, fresh and fruity nose, with ripe peaches and pineapple cheesecake, delicate spice and background malt. Medium-bodied, fruity and fudgy on the palate. The finish offers wine gums, mild, gently spiced oak, malt and a suggestion of smoke.

Tormore

[tor•more]

Owner:
Chivas Bros (Pernod Ricard)

Region/district:
Speyside

Founded: 1958

Status: Active

Capacity: 4 800 000 litres

Address: Tormore, Advie, Grantown-on-Spey, Morayshire PH26 3LR

Website:
tormoredistillery.com

Tel:
01807 510244

Among the previous owners of Tormore Distillery there have been a couple of controversial characters that stick out. Less so for their knowledge of the production of whisky but more for their unorthodox and sometimes dubious ways of conducting business.

First was Lewis Rosenstiel, owner of the company that founded Tormore – Schenley Industries. He made it big during prohibition as a dealer in spirits and wines and was indicted but never convicted for bootlegging. It wasn't until after his death in 1976, that the truth about Rosenstiel's connections with Mafia members such as Frank Costello and Meyer Lansky really became known. Schenley Industries (including Tormore) was sold to Rapid American in 1968. The owner of that company, Meshulam Riklis, became known as the "inventor" of junk bond transactions and leveraged buyouts. When his company went bankrupt it had debts up to $3 billion. He was also suspected of manipulating the share price of Guinness which helped to beat off competitors when Guinness took over DCL in 1986.

From the outside, Tormore is without competition the most unusual looking distillery in Scotland, at least until the new Macallan was opened. It is impossible to miss as it lies on the right hand side when driving the A95 from Grantown-on-Spey to Craigellachie. Before a 2014 re-launch, there had been two attempts to establish Tormore single malt as a brand. In 1991 it became part of Caledonian Malts, a range introduced by Allied Distillers. The second time was in 2004 when a 12 year old was launched under the name "The Pearl of Speyside".

The distillery is equipped with a stainless steel full lauter mash tun, 11 stainless steel washbacks and four pairs of stills. Tormore's fruity and light character is achieved by a clear wort, slow distillation and by using purifiers on all the stills.

The only official bottlings are a **14 year old** bottled at 43% and a **16 year old**, non chill-filtered, bottled at 48%. There are also two cask strength bottlings (**12** and **20 years old**) in the Distillery Reserve Collection, available at all Chivas' visitor centres.

History:

1958 Schenley International, owners of Long John, founds the distillery.

1960 The distillery is ready for production.

1972 The number of stills is increased from four to eight.

1975 Schenley sells Long John and its distilleries (including Tormore) to Whitbread.

1989 Allied Lyons (to become Allied Domecq) buys the spirits division of Whitbread.

1991 Allied Distillers introduce Caledonian Malts where Miltonduff, Glendronach and Laphroaig are represented besides Tormore. Tormore is later replaced by Scapa.

2004 Tormore 12 year old is launched as an official bottling.

2005 Chivas Brothers (Pernod Ricard) becomes new owners through the acquisition of Allied Domecq.

2012 Production capacity is increased by 20%.

2014 The 12 year old is replaced by two new expressions - 14 and 16 year old.

14 years old

Tasting notes Tormore 14 years old:

GS – Vanilla, butterscotch, summer berries and light spice on the nose. Milk chocolate and tropical fruit on the smooth palate, with soft toffee. Lengthy in the finish, with a sprinkling of black pepper.

Tullibardine

[tully•<u>bar</u>•din]

Owner:
Terroir Distillers
(Picard Vins & Spiritueux)

Region/district:
Highlands

Founded: **Status:** **Capacity:**
1949 Active (vc) 3 000 000 litres

Address: Blackford, Perthshire PH4 1QG

Website: **Tel:**
tullibardine.com 01764 682252

In the last couple of years, the Tullibardine single malt has received a lot more attention, not least thanks to a wide and comprehensive range introduced by the current owners.

At the same time, the distillery is the spiritual home to the famous brand Highland Queen where Tullibardine malt plays a significant part. The brand was first launched in 1893 by Roderick Macdonald, who 15 years later, took over Glenmorangie distillery. The brand had its heyday in the 1970s when it was sold all over the world. In 2008 it was taken over by the Picard family. The range now consists of four blends and six single malts, the oldest being a 40 year old.

The equipment consists of a 6.2 ton stainless steel semi-lauter mash tun, nine stainless steel washbacks with a fermentation of 55-60 hours, two 21,000 litre wash stills and two 16,000 litre spirit stills. During 2021, they will be working 27 mashes per week which will result in 3 million litres of alcohol.

Some of the most popular botttlings from Tullibardine are the ones in the Marquess Collection first introduced in 2016. It is named after the 2nd Marquess of Tullibardine, William Murray. He was a devoted Jacobite and was one of the Seven Men of Moidart who accompanied Prince Charles (the young pretender) from France to Scotland in 1745 in an attempt to reclaim the Scottish throne. He was also the one who unfurled the Royal Standard at the landing at Glenfinnan. Following the defeat at Culloden, William Murray was taken prisoner and brought to the Tower of London where he died in 1746.

The core range consists of **Sovereign** without age statement, **225 Sauternes finish, 228 Burgundy finish, 500 Sherry finish**, and 15, 20 and **25 year old**. The 15 year old, added to the range in spring 2020, was the oldest whisky yet released to have been made from spirit distilled after the re-opening in 2003. Custodian's Collection was introduced in 2015 and the latest in that range was **Vintage 1964**. Six expressions have so far been released in the Marquess Collection with **The Murray Double Wood Finish** as the latest (February 2021).

History:

1949 The architect William Delmé-Evans founds the distillery.

1953 The distillery is sold to Brodie Hepburn.

1971 Invergordon Distillers buys Brodie Hepburn Ltd.

1973 The number of stills increases to four.

1993 Whyte & Mackay buys Invergordon Distillers.

1994 Tullibardine is mothballed.

1996 Whyte & Mackay changes name to JBB (Greater Europe).

2001 JBB (Greater Europe) is bought out from Fortune Brands by management and changes name to Kyndal (Whyte & Mackay from 2003).

2003 A consortium buys Tullibardine for £1.1 million. The distillery is in production again.

2005 Three wood finishes from 1993, Port, Moscatel and Marsala, are launched together with a 1986 John Black selection.

2006 Vintage 1966, Sherry Wood 1993 and a new John Black selection are launched.

2007 Five different wood finishes and a couple of single cask vintages are released.

2008 A Vintage 1968 40 year old is released.

2009 Aged Oak is released.

2011 Three vintages and a wood finish are released. Picard buys the distillery.

2013 A completely new range is launched – Sovereign, 225 Sauternes, 228 Burgundy, 500 Sherry, 20 year old and 25 year old.

2015 A 60 year old Custodian Collection is released.

2016 A Vintage 1970 and The Murray from 2004 are released.

2017 Vintage 1962 and The Murray Chateauneuf-du-Pape are released.

2018 The Murray Marsala Finish is released.

2019 A Vintage 1964 is released.

2020 A 15 year old is released.

2021 The Murray Double Wood Finish is released

Tasting notes Tullibardine Sovereign:

GS – Floral on the nose, with new-mown hay, vanilla and fudge. Fruity on the palate, with milk chocolate, brazil nuts, marzipan, malt, and a hint of cinnamon. Cocoa, vanilla, a squeeze of lemon and more spice in the finish.

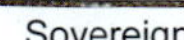
Sovereign

After refurbishing, the pagoda roof at Brora is put back in place

New
distilleries

Since last year´s book, we have four distilleries
that have started production – three of them brand new
and the fourth, Brora, being revived after a 38 year long dormancy.
But there is more to come. At least twenty distilleries are in
various stages of planning or construction.
Read more about them in the chapter
The Year That Was, pages 272-274.

Aberargie

[aber•<u>ar</u>•jee]

Owner: **Region/district:**
Morrison Scotch Whisky   Lowlands
Distillers Ltd.

Founded: **Status:**   **Capacity:**
2017   Active   750 000 litres

Address: Aberargie, Perthshire PH2 9LX

Website: **Tel:**
morrisondistillers.com   01738 787044

The distillery was built on the same grounds in Fife as Morrison & Mackay, independent bottler and producer of Scottish liqueurs, and a company which can trace it´s roots back to 1982.

Founded as John Murray & Co., the company was taken over in 2005 by Kenny Mackay and Brian Morrison, once the chairman of Morrison Bowmore, and his son Jamie. The production of liqueurs, continued while bottling of Scotch single malts (The Carn Mor) was added to the business. Later on, they also took over the Old Perth brand from Whyte & Mackay and relaunched it as a blended malt. The company name was changed to Morrison & Mackay in 2014. In 2019, when Brian and Jamie Morrison became the sole owners, the name was changed to Morrison Scotch Whisky Distillers Ltd.

The company has a blending and bottling facility in Fife and just a stone´s throw from that, construction on a whisky distillery started in summer 2016 and the first spirit was distilled in November 2017.

The distillery is equipped with a 2 ton semilauter mash tun, six stainless steel washbacks with a fermentation time of 72 hours, one 15,000 litre wash still and one 10,000 litre spirit still. The stills, both with steeply descending lyne arms, were made by Forsyths and are heated with panels instead of coils or pans. With a maturation in a mixture of first fill sherry butts, first fill bourbon barrels and second fill sherry/bourbon casks, the owners are aiming for a fruity character which will be enhanced by occasional peated spirit runs. Different barley varieties are being used, including Golden Promise, and they are all grown in 300 acres of field owned by the Morrison family and that surround the distillery.

Abhainn Dearg

[aveen <u>jar</u>•rek]

Owner: **Region/district:**
Mark Tayburn   Highlands (Isle of Lewis)

Founded: **Status:**   **Capacity:**
2008   Active (vc)   c 20 000 litres

Address: Carnish, Isle of Lewis,
Na h-Eileanan an Iar HS2 9EX

Website: **Tel:**
abhainndeargdistillery.co.uk   01851 672429

In September 2008, spirit flowed from a newly constructed distillery in Uig on the island of Lewis in the Outer Hebrides.

This was the first distillery on the island since 1840 when Stornoway distillery was closed. The conditions for new distilleries being built at that time were not improved when James Matheson, a Scottish tradesman, bought the entire island in 1844. Even though he had made his fortune in the opium trade, he was an abstainer and a prohibitionist and did not look kindly on the production or use of alcohol.

The Gaelic name of the new distillery is Abhainn Dearg which means Red River, and the founder and owner is Mark "Marko" Tayburn who was born and raised on the island. There are two 500 kg mash tuns made of stainless steel and two 7,500 litre washbacks made of Douglas fir with a fermentation time of 4 days. The wash still has a capacity of 2,112 litres and the spirit still 2,057 litres. Both have very long necks and steeply descending lye pipes leading out into two wooden worm tubs. Both bourbon and sherry casks are used for maturation. The plan is to use 100% barley grown on Lewis and in 2013 the first 6 tonnes of Golden Promise (15% of the total requirement) were harvested. Over the years, production has been limited to around 10,000 litres of pure alcohol yearly even though the distillery has the capacity to do more.

The first release from the distillery was The Spirit of Lewis in 2010 and the first single malt was a limited release of a 3 year old in October 2011, followed up by a cask strength version (58%) in 2012. The distillery´s first 10 year old appeared in late 2018 when 10,000 bottles were released, bottled at 46%. At the same time 100 bottles of a limited 10 year old single cask, also bottled at 46% were launched. Since then a number of single casks with different maturations (including madeira and sauternes) have been released for various markets.

Ailsa Bay

[ail•sah bey]

Owner:	**Region/district:**
William Grant & Sons	Lowlands
Founded: **Status:**	**Capacity:**
2007 Active	12 000 000 litres

Address: Girvan, Ayrshire KA26 9PT

Website:	**Tel:**
ailsabay.com	01465 713091

Commissioned in September 2007, it only took nine months to build this distillery on the same site as Girvan Distillery near Ayr on Scotland´s west coast.

Initially, it was equipped with a 12,1 tonne full lauter mash tun, 12 washbacks made of stainless steel and eight stills. In 2013 however, it was time for a major expansion when yet another mash tun, 12 more washbacks and eight more stills were commissioned, doubling the capacity to 12 million litres of alcohol.

Each washback will hold 50,000 litres and fermentation time is 60 hours for the heavier styles and 72 hours for the lighter ”Balveniestyle”. The stills are made according to the same standards as Balvenie's and one of the wash stills and one of the spirit stills have stainless steel condensers instead of copper. That way, they have the possibility of

making batches of a more sulphury spirit if desired. To increase efficiency and to get more alcohol, high gravity distillation is used. Maturation for the part that is bottled as single malt starts in small (25-100 litres) ex-bourbon barrels from Tuthilltown distillery and after 6-9 months the spirit is tranferred to regular sized barrels as well as into new oak. The plan for 2020 is to do around 50 mashes per week, producing 10 million litres of alcohol.

Five different types of spirit are produced. The most common is a light and rather sweet spirit. Then there is a heavy, sulphury style and three peated with the peatiest having a malt specification of 50ppm. The production is destined to become a part of Grant´s blended Scotch but in 2016, a peated single malt Ailsa Bay was released. In September 2018 Ailsa Bay Sweet Smoke was launched. Definitely sweeter and slighly smokier, it replaced the inaugural bottling. The ppm on the label (22) is the actual phenol content of the liquid itself and not the barley.

Annandale

[ann•an•dail]

Owner:	**Region/district:**
Annandale Distillery Co.	Lowlands
Founded: **Status:**	**Capacity:**
2014 Active (vc)	500 000 litres

Address: Northfield, Annan, Dumfriesshire DG12 5LL

Website:	**Tel:**
annandaledistillery.com	01461 207817

In 2010 Professor David Thomson and his wife, Teresa Church, obtained consent from the local council for the building of the new Annandale Distillery in Dumfries and Galloway in the south-west of Scotland.

The old one had been producing since 1836 and was owned by Johnnie Walker from 1895 until it closed down in 1918. From 1924 to 2007, the site was owned by the Robinson family, who were famous for their Provost brand of porridge oats. David Thomson began the restoration of the site in June 2011 with the two, old sandstone warehouses being restored to function as two-level dunnage warehouses. The distillery was in a poor condition and the mash house and the tun room was largely reconstructed while the other buildings were refurbished substantially. The old maltings have been turned into an excellent visitor centre.

The distillery is equipped with a 2.5 ton semi-lauter mash tun with a copper dome. There are three wooden washbacks (a fermentation time of 72-96 hours), one wash still (12,000 litres) and two spirit stills (4,000 litres).

The first cask was filled in November 2014 and both unpeated and peated (45ppm) whisky is distilled. In June 2018, the first two single malts were released, both matured in ex-Buffalo Trace barrels. The Man O´Words is unpeated while the Man O´Swords is heavily peated. All expressions are bottled at cask strength, un chill-filtered and without colouring. The Founder´s Selection range are all single casks with the two latest being bottled in July 2021. There are also two other ranges, Vintage and Rare Vintage, that are vattings of several casks. During the first years it was mainly bourbon and sherry casks that were filled but an interesting variety of casks have followed; tequila, rye, rum, wheated bourbon and, not least, wine casks that have been shaved, toasted and re-charred (STR).

Arbikie

[ar•<u>bi</u>•ki]

Owner: **Region/district:**
The Stirling family   Eastern Highlands

Founded: **Status:**   **Capacity:**
2015   Active   200 000 litres

Address: Inverkeilor, Arbroath, Angus DD11 4UZ

Website: **Tel:**
arbikie.com   01241 830770

The Stirling family has been farming since the 17th century and the 2000-acre Arbikie Highland Estate in Angus has now been in their possession for four generations.

The three brothers (John, Iain and David) started their careers within other fields but have now returned to the family lands to open up a single-estate distillery. The definition of a single-estate distillery is that, not only does the whole chain of production take place on site, but all the ingredients are also grown on the farm.

The first vodka from potatoes was distilled in October 2014 which was followed by gin in May 2015. Trials with malt whisky, started in March 2015, went over to full production in October 2015. Responsible for the production side at the distillery is master distiller Kirsty Black. The barley is grown in fields of their own and then sent to Boorts malt in Montrose. The distillery is equipped with a stainless steel, semi-lauter mash tun with a 0.75 ton charge and four washbacks (two 4,400 litre and two 9,000 litre) with a fermentation time of 96-120 hours. There is also one 4,000 litre wash still and one 2,400 litre spirit still. For the final stage of vodka and gin production, there is a 40 plate rectification column. The Stirlings don´t intend to launch their first single malt whisky until 2029/2030.

In 2015 Arbikie started trials with rye whisky made from 52% unmalted rye, 33% unmalted wheat and 15% malted barley grown on their own farm. Matured for three years in American oak and finished in ex-PX casks, it was released in December 2018 as the first rye whisky made in Scotland for more than 100 years. The latest release, in early 2021, was the 1794 Highland Rye Scotch matured in virgin oak. The same year, Arbikie was awarded craft producer of the year in Whisky Icons of Scotland.

Ardnahoe

[ard•na•<u>hoe</u>]

Owner: **Region/district:**
Hunter Laing & Company   Islay

Founded: **Status:**   **Capacity:**
2017   Active (vc)   1 000 000 litres

Address: Isle of Islay, Port Askaig PA46 7RU

Website: **Tel:**
ardnahoedistillery.com   01496 840711

Ardnahoe, the newest distillery on Islay, came on stream in November 2018. The location, between Caol Ila and Bunnahabhain and overlooking Jura, is absolutely stunning!

The distillery, owned by independent bottler Hunter Laing, is equipped with a 2.75 ton (an increase from the previous 2.5 ton) semi lauter mash tun with a copper lid. The lauter gear is used as little as possible to get a clear wort. There are four washbacks made from Oregon pine with a fermentation time between 60 and 70 hours, one wash still (12,500 litres) and one spirit still (7,500 litres) with a slow distillation, both with the longest lyne arms in Scotland (7,5 metres). The distillery is equipped with wooden worm tubs (the only ones on Islay) with a 77 metre copper tube in each. Another unusual piece of equipment is the 4-roller Boby mill from the 1920s which was brought in from Fettercairn. The distillery produces a variety of single malts from unpeated to peated on several levels (from 5ppm up to 40ppm) with the malt being bought from Port Ellen maltings. The production plan for 2021 is to do 14 mashes per week which amounts to 650,000 litres. Eighty percent of the newmake goes into first fill bourbon and the rest is matured in sherry casks. There is currently one warehouse on site but more will be built – a mix of dunnage and racked.

Ardnahoe is the first new distillery on the island since Kilchoman was opened in 2005 and the 9th on Islay. The distillery visitor centre is surprisingly huge (given the size of the distillery) with a large shop and a café/whisky bar with an excellent view towards the paps of Jura and with Mull in the distance. In the first year (2019), the distillery received 25,000 visitors and was also presented with a Five Star award from Visit Scotland.

Ardnamurchan

[ard•ne•mur•ken]

Owner:
Adelphi Distillery Ltd

Region/district:
Western Highlands

Founded: **Status:** **Capacity:**
2014 Active (vc) 500 000 litres

Address: Glenbeg, Ardnamurchan, Argyll PH36 4JG

Website:
adelphidistillery.com

Tel:
01972 500 285

It takes a good 90 minutes to go from Fort William to the distillery on the Ardnamurchan peninsula north of Mull by car but it's well worth the journey.

Winding single track roads beg for careful driving but the stunning scenery it also a good reason for driving slowly. The distillery is owned by independent bottler Adelphi Distillery. In 2007, they realised that the supply of good whisky could become scarce in years to come for those companies not having a distillery of their own. They decided to build one and part of the reason for choosing this remote site was that the land was owned by one of the directors of Adelphi Distillery, Donald Houston.

Ardnamurchan distillery came on stream on 11th July 2014 and is equipped with a two tonne semi lauter mash tun made of stainless steel with a copper canopy, four wooden washbacks and three made of stainless steel. The initial wooden washbacks were made from oak, having been used as cognac vats in France but two of them were exchanged in 2018 for Oregon pine. The fermentation time is 72-96 hours. There is one wash still (10,000 litres) and one spirit still (6,000 litres) and quite recently, sub-coolers made from stainless steel were also fitted. Two different styles of whisky are produced; peated and unpeated and for the peated spirit, the barley has a phenol specification of 30-35ppm. The goal for 2021 is to do 12 mashs per week and 400,000 litres of alcohol. There are also plans to malt some of their barley themselves and a malting floor is already in place but hasn't been used so far.

Since 2016 they have released young spirit and the final bottling had been matured in a combination of hogsheads, butts and octaves – all seasoned with oloroso and PX sherry. Finally, in October 2020, the owners released their inaugural single malt – the AD/09.20:01. The latest bottling is AD/04.21:03 and recently there have also been several limited single cask releases.

Ardross

[ard•ross]

Owner:
Greenwood Distillers

Region/district:
N Highland

Founded: **Status:** **Capacity:**
2019 Active 1 000 000 litres

Address: Ardross Mains, Ardross, Alness

Website:
theardross.com

Tel:
-

An old, derelict 19th century farm site north of Inverness, has recently been transformed into one of Scotland's newest distilleries.

The nearest distillery neighbors are Teaninich and Dalmore, some 5 km to the southeast. A planning application was approved in 2017 and behind the project lies Greenwood Distillers Ltd. and that company, in turn, is an affiliate of Vevil International, owner of Ned Hotel and the Wolseley restaurant in London. The CEO of Greenwood Distillers is Barthelemy Brosseau and one of the directors is Andrew Rankin who was Operations Director and Chief Blender at Morrison Bowmore for almost 25 years. As Distillery Manager, the company hired Sandy Jamieson with a long career in the Scotch whisky business, most recently as manager of Speyside Distillery near Kingussie. The company also has a connection in Mexico with a mezcal producer, in France with a producer of armagnac, in Japan with a cooperage making mizunara casks and in Kentucky where Copper Pheasant distillery is about to be built.

The distillery was commissioned in August 2019 and is equipped with a 3 ton semi-lauter mash tun, six wooden washbacks (20,000 litres each and with a fermentation time of 120 hours), one 15,000 litre wash still and one 12,000 litre spirit still. The capacity is an impressive one million litres of pure alcohol and the new make is sent in tankers to the company´s bond in Cumbernauld. The signature style will be unpeated but peated newmake was produced for four weeks in the beginning of 2021.

The first release from the distillery was Theodore gin which appeared in August 2019. It features 16 botanicals inspired by those that the Picts may have encountered on their travels to Scotland. The gin will not just be a way of creating cash flow until the future whisky has been released, as a designated gin distillery has been built on the site.

Ballindalloch

[bal•lin•da•lock]

Owner: The Macpherson-Grant family

Region/district: Speyside

Founded: 2014

Status: Active (vc)

Capacity: 100 000 litres

Address: Ballindalloch, Banffshire AB37 9AA

Website: ballindallochdistillery.com

Tel: 01807 500 331

In the heart of Speyside, the owners of Ballindalloch Castle, the Macpherson-Grant family, decided in 2012 to turn the Lagmore farm steading from 1820 into a whisky distillery.

Previous generations of the family had been involved in distilling from the 1860s and from 1923 to 1965, they owned part of Cragganmore distillery, not far away from the castle. The old farm building was meticulously renovated with attention given to every little detail and the result is an amazingly beautiful distillery which can be seen from the A95 between Aberlour and Grantown-on-Spey.

Ballindalloch distillery takes its water from the nearby Garline Springs and all the barley is grown on the Estate. All of the distillery equipment are gathered on the second floor which makes it easy for visitors to get a good view of the production. The equipment consists of an extraordinary 1 ton semi lauter, copper clad mash tun with a copper dome. There are four washbacks made of Oregon pine with four long fermentations (140 hours) and one short (92 hours). Finally there is a 5,000 litre lantern-shaped wash still and a 3,600 litre spirit still with a reflux ball. Both stills are connected to two wooden worm tubs for cooling the spirit vapours. The worms are run sligthly hotter than conventional worms in an attempt to increase the conversion between the spirit vapour and the copper. The water from the tubs is also passed over a cooling tower and returned to the tub. These features will make for a very light, delicate and fruity spirit. The distillery is working 5 days a week, making 100,000 litres of alcohol. More than 4,000 casks have now been filled since the start in 2014. The first single malt release is expected in 2022.

The distillery is open for visitors by appointment and there is also the opportunity to take part in The Art of Whisky Making, which means spending a day with the crew and learning about whisky from mashing to warehousing.

Bonnington

[bon•ing•tun]

Owner: John Crabbie & Co. (Halewood)

Region/district: Lowlands

Founded: 2020

Status: Active

Capacity: 500 000 litres

Address: 21 Graham Street, Edinburgh EH6 5QN

Website: crabbiewhisky.com

Tel: 0151 480 8800

The second malt whisky distillery to open up in Edinburgh in recent times could have been the first if archeologists hadn't made some amazing discoveries during construction.

Bonnington is owned by John Crabbie & Co, a subsidiary of Halewood Wines & Spirits, founded in 1978, which is a company that has interests in wines and spirits all over the world. John Crabbie was a co-founder of North British grain distillery in 1885 and a notable whisky blender in his time. When excavations for the distillery began, just a few hundred metres from the original site where John Crabbie matured and blended his whisky, archeologists found the remnants of a whisky distillery from the 1700s but also evidence of Bonnington House, a mansion dating back to the 11th century. The findings meant the time frame for the new distillery was delayed by a year. Construction of the distillery started in January 2019 and was finished in December that year. But, already in 2018 a small pilot distillery was opened in Granton not far away from the current distillery. Producing just one cask a week, here the owners could trial different malts, yeasts, fermentation lengths, cut points and distillation methods before starting at Bonnington.

The first distillation took place in March 2020 and the distillery is equipped with a two ton semi lauter mash tun, six stainless steel washbacks with a fermentation time of 48-70 hours, a 10,500 litre wash still and an 8,000 litre spirit still. The owners managed to find their own production water on site through a borehole to an ancient aquifer. While 90% of the whisky will be unpeated the remaining 10% will be made using peated malt (50ppm). The newmake is filled into a variety of casks (bourbon, sherry, virgin oak, port, marsala and sweet wine). A visitor centre is planned to be opened in 2021.

The Borders

[<u>boar</u>•ders]

Owner:
The Three Stills Co. Ltd.

Region/district:
Lowlands

Founded:
2017

Status:
Active (vc)

Capacity:
1 600 000 litres

Address: Commercial Road, Hawick TD9 7AQ

Website:
thebordersdistillery.com

Tel:
01450 374330

On the 6th of March 2018, the first whisky distillery in the Borders in 180 years started production and the distillery opened to the public a few weeks later.

Behind the Borders Distillery in Hawick is a company called The Three Stills Company which was founded in 2013. The owners include four men who had all previously worked for William Grant & Sons – George Tait, Tony Roberts, John Fordyce and Tim Carton. In 2016, the company started to renovate the beautiful buildings dating from the late 1880s and which used to be an electric company and turned it into a distillery. The river Teviot is running just behind the distillery and like the textile companies that Hawick is renowned for were using the water for dyeing and power, the distillery now uses it for cooling the spirit vapours.

The distillery is equipped with a 5 ton mash tun, eight stainless steel washbacks with a fermentation time of 80 hours, two wash stills (12,500 litres) and two spirit stills (7,500 litres) with all equipment provided by Forsyths. The whisky produced is un-peated and floral. Other spirits are also produced, for instance vodka and gin, where the barley spirit from the pot stills is redistilled in a Carterhead still. The vodka is unique in the way that it is not filtered as a liquid but instead is steamed through charcoal inside the still in order to preserve the character of the barley in the taste. The owners also have plans to install an anaerobic bio plant on the site. The company has already released a blended Scotch from sourced whisky called Clan Fraser and a blended malt named Lower East Side. The first bottling of spirit actually made at the distillery appeared in July 2018 when William Kerr´s Borders Gin was launched and this was later followed by Puffing Billy Steam Vodka.

Brew Dog

[<u>bru</u>•dog]

Owner:
Brewdog plc.

Region/district:
Highlands

Founded:
2016

Status:
Active

Capacity:
450 000 litres

Address: Balmacassie Commercial Park, Ellon, Aberdeenshire AB41 8BX

Website:
brewdog.com

Tel:
01358 724924

In spring 2019, the distillery changed the name from Lone Wolf to Brew Dog in order to tap into the name and fame of the well-known brewery

Founded in 2007 Brew Dog grew to become the biggest independent brewery in the UK and in 2014 a decision was taken to open up also a distillery. It is situated next to the brewery in Ellon outside of Aberdeen and as director distilling operations, Steven Kersley who had a background at several Diageo distilleries, was called in. In autumn 2018, David Gates who previously ran Diageo Futures and worked as brand director for Johnnie Walker, joined the company as managing director.

The adjacent brew house provides the wash for the distillery which has the following equipment; one 3,000 litre pot still with an 8 plate rectification column which will be used for stripping the wash for vodka, whisky and rum, another 3,000 litre still with a 60-plate column is used for the final distillation of vodka and whisky, a 600 litre pot still is dedicated to gin and brandy production, while a 50 litre pot still is used for research and experimentation.

The initial production was gin and vodka and the first bottles were launched in spring 2017. Whisky and rum production has also commenced and while the botanical rum Five Hundred Cuts was recently launched, no whisky has yet been released. In 2017, Lone Wolf became one of the first Scottish distilleries in modern times to distill a rye whisky. In spring 2019, the company entered into a collaboration with three other whisky makers (Millstone, Compass Box and Duncan Taylor) who all designed one whisky each to be paired with Brew Dog beers. An unusual and exciting release turned up in 2020 with a shochu named Inugami which means "spirit of the dog".

Brora

[bro•rah]

Owner:	**Region/district:**
Diageo	Northern Highlands
Founded: **Status:**	**Capacity:**
2021 (1819) Active (vc)	800 000 litres
Address: Clynelish Rd, Brora, Sutherland KW9 6LR	
Website:	**Tel:**
malts.com	-

Brora distillery was closed in 1983 and as the years passed, the prospects of a resurrection more or less vanished. Not even the biggest enthusiasts believed it would produce again.

That's why it came as a huge surprise in October 2017 when Diageo announced that not only Brora but also Port Ellen were to be restored and rebuilt as a part of a £35m investment. Brora was founded as Clynelish in 1819 by the 1st Duke of Sutherland and operated under that name until 1969 when it was changed to Brora. At that time a modern distillery had also been built on the same site and was named Clynelish. Both distilleries worked in tandem for 16 years with Brora focusing on peated spirit. The final distillation at the old distillery was in 1983.

Starting 2019 the old distillery has been restored to its former glory. The original stills (wash still 14,400 litres and spirit still 13,200) were sent to Abercrombie in Alloa for refurbishing while a new traditional 6 ton mash tun with rake and plough and new washbacks made of Oregon pine were manufactured in accordance with the old drawings and specifications that could be found in the Diageo archive. A modern feature to the distillery is a bio-mass boiler powered by wood chips. The first cask was filled in May 2021 and the new distillery manager for Brora is Stewart Bowman, born and bred in Brora and son of the distillery's last exciseman.

Since 1995, old stock of Brora single malt has been released on a yearly basis and it quickly got the attention from whisky enthusiasts with prices going through the roof. Recent limited bottlings include a 39 year old from 1982 released in spring 2021 and which is only available at the distillery. On top of that, a set of three 50cl bottles named Brora Triptych was released made up of three vintages; 1972 (48 years), 1977 (43 years) and 1982 (38 years).

Burn O´Bennie

[burn•o•benni]

Owner:	**Region/district:**
Ardent Spirits	Eastern Highlands
Founded: **Status:**	**Capacity:**
2020 Active	180 000 litres
Address: Burn Ó Bennie Road, Banchory, Aberdeenshire AB31 5NN	
Website:	**Tel:**
burnobennie.com	01330 202172

In 2017, Mike Bain opened up a small experimental craft distillery in Banchory and named it Deeside Distillery after the surrounding area. It only worked for 18 months though before it closed.

It was a part of Deeside Brewery in Lochton of Leys, also owned by Bain, but it was more or less intended from the beginning that this would serve as a pilot distillery where the team could put some of their ideas into practice. Only 100 casks were filled at Deeside of which 88 were sold to help finance the new distillery. The remaining 12 will be matured for at least ten years before being bottled.

Mike Bain founded an information technology company in the late 1990s which he eventually sold in 2015. Already three years before that he had started the Deeside Brewery in Banchory. In 2019 he teamed up with Liam Pennycook and moved the operation to larger premises in a business park in near-by Hill of Banchory. Liam Pennycook's background is in distilling, lately with the Strathearn distillery.

The new distillery, which started production in 2020, is equipped with a 1,6 ton mash tun, five stainless steel wash-backs with a fermentation time of 168 hours, one 5,000 litre wash still and one 3,600 litre spirit still. Foreshots are one hour and a slow distillation is practiced. Mash tun, washbacks, coolers etc were made by Gravity Systems while the stills were ordered from Germany. So far the distillery has only produced unpeated single malt as well as small batches of rye. One feature which stands out is the owners' interest in various speciality malts that are typically used in the brewing business but not so much by distilleries. These include for instance crystal and chocolate malt. For maturation, ex-bourbon and ex-oloroso casks are used.

The Clydeside

[k<u>laj</u>dsajd]

Owner: **Region/district:**
Morrison Glasgow Distillers   Lowlands

Founded: **Status:**   **Capacity:**
2017   Active (vc)   500 000 litres

Address: 100 Stobcross Road, Glasgow G3 8QQ

Website: **Tel:**
theclydeside.com   0141 2121401

If Tim Morrison, the owner of independent bottler AD Rattray. ever wanted to found a distillery he couldn´t have picked a better spot.

The queens Docks in Glasgow oozes of whisky history with ships coming in with barley and coal and going out with barrels of whisky, To add to the picture, Tim´s great grandfather designed the pumphouse which was used to power the hydraulic gates allowing ships in and out of the Queens Dock and which is now the site of Clydeside distillery. Tim Morrison represents the fourth generation of one of Scotland´s best known whisky families. Today, Tim´s son Andrew is the managing director of Clydeside Distillery.

The distillery is beautifully situated on the river Clyde with well-known attractions such as the Riverside Museum, Glasgow Science Centre and the SEC Centre as its closest neighbours. The equipment consists of a 1.5 ton semi lauter mash tun made of stainless steel, 8 stainless steel washbacks with a fermentation time of 72 hours, a 7,500 litre wash still and a 5,000 litre spirit still. The foreshots are 15 minutes with a slow distillation and the cutpoints for the spirit run are 76-71%. In spite of the covid pandemic, the distillery managed to fulfill their goal of producing 440,000 litres during 2020 and the aim for 2021 is to distill 465,000 litres of alcohol on 17 mashes per week. The inaugural release of a Clydeside single malt is planned for late 2021.

An excellent visitor centre has been constructed within the old Pump House building from 1877 while an adjacent, modern building houses the distillery. Apart from a variety of tours, the distillery shop also offers a wide range of whiskies including new make spirit from the distillery itself. Around 70,000 visitors came here in 2019.

Daftmill

[daf•mil]

Owner: **Region/district:**
Francis Cuthbert   Lowlands

Founded: **Status:**   **Capacity:**
2005   Active   c 65 000 litres

Address: By Cupar, Fife KY15 5RF

Website: **Tel:**
daftmill.com   01337 830303

The distillery may be one of the smallest in Scotland but few single malt releases have been more eagerly awaited by the whisky enthusiasts than the inaugural release from Daftmill.

Ever since December 2008, when the spirit legally became whisky, questions to the owners Francis and Ian Cuthbert about when the first whisky would be launched have always been answered by ”when it´s ready”. In 2017, they signed a distribution agreement with Berry Brothers and in May 2018, a ballot was opened for buying one of the first 629 bottles of a 12 year old matured in ex-bourbon casks. The first release was followed by a Summer Relase in June where seven casks rendered 1665 bottles. More bottlings have followed, including eight single casks in autumn 2020 exclusive to certain markets or retailers.

Daftmill´s first distillation was on 16th December 2005 and it is run as a typical farmhouse distillery. The barley is grown on the farm and they also supply other distilleries. The malting is done without peat at Crisp´s in Alloa. The equipment consists of a one tonne semi-lauter mash tun with a copper dome, two stainless steel washbacks with a fermentation between 72 and 100 hours and one pair of stills with slightly ascending lyne arms. The equipment is designed to give a lot of copper contact, a lot of reflux. The wash still has a capacity of 3,000 litres and the spirit still 2,000 litres and around 100 casks are filled very year.

The Cuthbert´s aim is to do a light, Lowland style whisky. In order to achieve this they have very short foreshots (five minutes) and the spirit run starts at 78% to capture all of the fruity esters and already comes off at 73%. Taking care of the farm during spring and autumn obviously prohibits Francis from producing whisky full time. Whisky production is therefore reserved for two months in the summertime and two in the winter.

Dalmunach

[dal•<u>moo</u>•nack]

Owner: Chivas Brothers

Region/district: Speyside

Founded: 2015

Status: Active

Capacity: 10 000 000 litres

Address: Carron, Banffshire AB38 7QP

Website: -

Tel: -

One of the newest distilleries in Scotland, and one of the most beautiful, has been built on the site of the former Imperial distillery.

Imperial distillery was founded in 1897, the year of Queen Victoria´s Diamond Jubilee and on the top of the roof there was even a large cast iron crown to mark the occasion. The founder was Thomas Mackenzie who at the time already owned Dailuaine and Talisker. The timing was not the best though. One year after the opening, the Pattison crash brought the whisky industry to its knees and the distillery was forced to close. Eventually it came into the hands of DCL who owned it from 1916 until 2005, when Chivas Brothers took over. It was out of production for 60% of the time until 1998 when it was mothballed. The owners probably never planned to use it for distillation again as it was put up for sale in 2005 to become available as residential flats. Soon after, it was withdrawn from the market and, in 2012, a decision was taken to tear down the old distillery and build a new. Demolition of the old distillery began in 2013 and by the end of that year, nothing was left, except for the old warehouses.

Construction on the new Dalmunach distillery started in 2013 and it was commissioned in October 2014. The exceptional and stunning distillery is equipped with an efficient (4 hour mash) 13 ton Briggs full lauter mash tun and 16 stainless steel washbacks charged with 56,000 litres and with a fermentation time of 56-62 hours. There are four pairs of stills of a considerable size – wash stills 28,000 litres and spirits stills 18,000. They are all positioned in a circle with a hexagonal spirit safe in the middle. The distillery, which cost £25m to build, is the company´s most ennergy efficient distillery and uses 38% less energy and 15% less water than the industry average. In autumn 2019, the first official release of Dalmunach single malt appeared – a 4 year old bottled at cask strength (59%).

Dornoch

[<u>dor</u>•nock]

Owner: Thompson Bros Distillers

Region/district: Northern Highlands

Founded: 2016

Status: Active

Capacity: 30 000 litres

Address: Castle Street, Dornoch, Sutherland, IV25 3 SD

Website: thompsonbrosdistillers.com

Tel: 01862 810 216

Getting to grips with the style of a completely new single malt by glancing through the list of old whiskies available in a hotel bar in northern Scotland may seem ludicrous.

Yet at the Dornoch Castle Hotel the clues are there – black on white. Whiskies made in the 60s and 70s with methods and ingredients rarely seen today fill the shelves. The hotel is owned by the Thompson family and the second generation, Phil and Simon, are passionate about old-style whisky. So passionate that they decided in 2016 to open a distillery in an old fire station at the back of the hotel. The idea was to try and recreate whisky as it was made decades ago, not worrying about yield. All the barley is floor malted, often using old heritage varieties and different strains of brewer´s yeast. They are also working as independent bottlers having released more than 100 expressions.

The distillery building is only 47 square metres and the brothers have struggled to fit all the equipment into the limited space. In May 2021 however a new racked warehouse eased the burden. Currently, the distillery is equipped with a 300 kg stainless steel, semi-lauter mash tun, six washbacks made of oak with a minimum fermentation time of seven days, a 1,000 litre wash still and a 600 litre spirit still. The stills are directly fired using gas but they are also equipped with steam coils as an alternative heating method. There is also a 2,000 litre still with a column for the production of gin and other spirits. The distillery has a yearly capacity of 30,000 litres of pure alcohol of which 15,000 litres are dedicated to whisky. Their first release was gin in spring 2017 while the first whisky-to-be was filled in July 2017. The first single malt release appeared in November 2020 when a first fill oloroso sherry butt made from organic Plumage Archer barley rendered 893 bottles.

Eden Mill

[eden mill]

Owner: Anthony Kelly et al
Region/district: Lowlands

Founded: 2014
Status: Active (vc)
Capacity: 100 000 litres

Address: St Andrews, Fife, KY16 0UU

Website: edenmill.com
Tel: 01334 834038

In 2012, Paul Miller, the former Molson Coors Sales Director and Tony Kelly, the current CEO of the company, opened up the successful Eden Brewery in Guardbridge, west of St Andrews.

The site was an old paper mill and only 50 metres away, there was a distillery called Seggie which was operative between 1810 and 1860 and owned by the Haig family. As an extension of the brewery, the owners decided to build a distillery called Eden Mill Distillery. The distillery, with a capacity of 100,000 litres per year, mainly produces malt whisky, but gin is also on the map. The distillery is equipped with two wash stills and one spirit still of the alembic type. Made by Hoga in Portugal, all three stills are of the same size – 1,000 litres.

Whisky production started in 2014 and the first release of a single malt appeared in 2018, matured in a combination of French virgin oak, American virgin oak, and Pedro Ximenez casks. Meanwhile a series of different 20cl bottlings called the Hip Flask Series has been launched. All of them have been made from different mashbills and matured in different types of casks. The latest two releases in January 2021, boath peated, were #16 (matured in ex-Islay casks) and #17 (aged in bourbon refill casks).

In 2018, the owners announced that they had plans to move the entire operation to a new distillery. As a part of an £8m investment programme, £3.1m has been set aside for an expansion of the production. The new distillery will increase the whisky capacity to 200,000 lpa per year and it will be powered by St Andrews University´s biomass power plant thus making it one of the first carbon-neutral distilleries in Scotland. The covid pandemic has delayed the opening but the current plan is to commission the distillery during 2021.

Falkirk

[fall•kirk]

Owner: Stewart family
Region/district: Lowlands

Founded: 2020
Status: Active (vc)
Capacity: 1 200 000 litres

Address: Grandsable Rd, Polmont, Falkirk FK2 0WA

Website: falkirkdistillery.com
Tel: 01324 281086

The road from idea to distillery is not always as straightforward as planned. Falkirk is a good example of navigating a long and winding road.

As early as in 2008 the plans for a distillery were on the table. There was even talk about buying the equipment from the closed Rosebank distillery and acquiring the rights to the Rosebank brand name. Planning approval was granted in spring 2010 but Historic Scotland raised objections that the distillery would be built too close to the remnants of the Antonine Wall from the Roman period. That prompted a lot of compulsory surveys, including archaeological digs, before the green light was given. Then in 2010, most of the Rosebank equipment was stolen but the founders, George Stewart and his daughter Fiona, didn't lose hope though. They adjusted their plans and carried on and in July 2020 the distillery became fully operational and in September the first drops of spirit were distilled. In the words of George Stewart himself; "The whole process has been one of passion and patience."

The distillery is equipped with a 4,6 ton ex-Caperdonich traditional mash tun with rakes and made of copper, six 20,000 litre stainless steel washbacks with a fermentation time of 100 plus hours, one 10,000 litre wash still and a 7,100 litre spirit still – both from Caperdonich. The plan is to produce a light, traditional Lowland malt which will mature mainly in ex-oloroso and first fill bourbon casks. It will probably be until 2025 before the first core expression is released but there are plans for "work-in-progress" bottlings as well. As distillery manager, the family hired an industry veteran, Graham Brown, formerly of Distell where he has worked at both Tobermory and Deanston. A visitor centre is also in place and benefitting from Falkirk's three existing visitor attractions (Callendar House, The Falkirk Wheel and The Kelpies) the owners hope to attract over 80,000 visitors every year.

Glasgow

[glas•go]

Owner: **Region/district:**
Liam Hughes, Ian McDougall   Lowlands

Founded: **Status:**   **Capacity:**
2015   Active   365 000 litres

Address: Deanside Rd, Hillington, Glasgow G52 4XB

Website: **Tel:**
glasgowdistillery.com   0141 4047191

When Glasgow Distillery was opened in Hillington Business Park, it became the first new whisky distillery in Glasgow in modern times.

There were stills within the Strathclyde grain distillery producing the malt whisky Kinclaith from 1958-1975 but Liam Hughes, Mike Hayward and Ian McDougall built the first proper malt distillery in Glasgow in more than a hundred years. The distillery started production in February 2015 and the first distillation of whisky was unpeated. Since then peated spirit (50ppm) has become part of the production and since January 2017, triple distillation is also practised one month per year. The distillery is equipped with a one ton mash tun, 8 stainless steel washbacks with a minimum fermentation of 72 hours, two 2,500 litre wash still, two 1,400 litre spirit still and one 450 litre gin still – all from Firma Carl in Germany. Two of the stills were installed as late as in November 2019.

The first product to be bottled was the Makar gin which now exists in several versions. In the beginning, the owners also bottled old, sourced single malts under the name Prometheus. The fourth and final release in January 2020 was a 30 year old. The first single malt from their own production appeared in June 2018. Aged in ex-bourbon barrels and finished in virgin oak, the whisky was called 1770 Glasgow Single Malt, named after Glasgow's first distillery which was founded at Dundashill in 1770. Since then a signature range of three whiskies has evolved; The Original (fresh and fruity), Peated (rich and smoky) and, first released in May 2020, Triple Distilled (smooth and complex). They are released in batches with the type of wood changing slightly for every batch. In June 2020 the owners launched Malt Riot Blended Malt with their own malt as the main part and in April 2021, the first distillery exclusive, The Cooper's Cask Release, sold out in a couple of hours.

GlenWyvis

[glen•wivis]

Owner   **Region/district:**
GlenWyvis Distillery Ltd.   Highlands

Founded: **Status:**   **Capacity:**
2017   Active (vc)   140 000 litres

Address: Upper Docharty, Dingwall IV15 9UF

Website: **Tel:**
glenwyvis.com   01349 862005

In 2015, the local farmer John McKenzie, came up with the idea to establish a distillery that was owned by the local people – the first ever 100% community-owned distillery.

A planning application was submitted to the local council in March 2016 and by summer more than £2.5 million had been raised via a community share offer with more than 3,000 people investing. Construction started in January 2017 and later that year, the owners managed to hire one of the most experienced distillers in Scotland as the manager, Duncan Tait, who was succeeded by Matthew Farmer in August 2020. The first distillation was on the 30th of January 2018 and the production goal for 2021 is to average 6 mashes per week and produce 55,000 litres of pure alcohol. The distillery is equipped with a 0.5 ton semi lauter mash tun, six washbacks (4,400 litres each) made of stainless steel with a fermentation time of 96-144 hours, one 2,500 litre wash still and one 1,700 litre spirit still. In October 2019 there was a fire in the distillery's woodchip store and even though the fire was contained to a small area, it took until March 2020 before they were producing again. They have one dunnage warehouse on site and are currently working on the restoration of an old farm steading into a second one.

The style of the newmake is a combination o fruity and green/grassy and the unpeated spirit, which is mainly filled into American oak, was released for sale in November 2019. The first, limited whisky release for shareholders will appear around Christmas 2021. A dedicated 400 litre gin still was installed in spring 2018 and the distillery has three types of gin for sale; Good Will Gin, Quercus Alba (matured in bourbon casks) and a third expression matured in first fill oloroso casks.

Harris

[har•ris]

Owner: Isle of Harris Distillers Ltd.
Region/district: Highlands (Isle of Harris)

Founded: 2015
Status: Active (vc)
Capacity: 399 000 litres

Address: Tarbert, Isle of Harris, Na h-Eileanan an Iar HS3 3DJ

Website: harrisdistillery.com
Tel: 01859 502212

More than ten years ago, Anderson Bakewell had conjured up an idea to build a distillery on the Isle of Harris.

Joining Bakewell, who had been connected to the island for more than 40 years, was Simon Erlanger, a former marketing director for Glenmorangie and now the MD of the new distillery. Construction started in 2014 and the distillery came into production in September 2015. The total cost for the whole project was £11.4m. The distillery, located in Tarbert, was the second distillery after Abhainn Dearg on Lewis to be founded in the Outer Hebrides.

The first spirit to be distilled in September 2015 was gin and this was followed by whisky in December. The gin has already been released and apart from traditional botanicals, local ingredients are also used such as sugar kelp.

The equipment consists of a 1.2 tonne semi lauter mash tun made of stainless steel but clad with American oak and 8 washbacks made of Oregon pine with a fermentation time of 72-96 hours. There are also one 7,000 litre wash still and a 5,000 litre spirit still - both with descending lyne arms and made in Italy. From 2016 to 2019, the production increased from 5 to 9 mashes per week and a total of 180,000 litres and that is the target also for 2021. A second warehouse was built in 2021. The style of the whisky, which will be called Hearach (the Gaelic word for a person living on Harris), is medium peated with a phenol specification in the barley of 12-14ppm although they have also distilled a few batches of heavily peated malt (30ppm) made with local peat.

In a normal year the distillery receives no less than 100,000 visitors. During 2020 however, due to the pandemic, they only managed to have the shop often for a few months but still attracted 20,000 visitors.

Holyrood

[holly•rude]

Owner: The Holyrood Distillery Ltd.
Region/district: Lowlands

Founded: 2019
Status: Active (vc)
Capacity: 250 000 litres

Address: 19 St Leonard´s Lane, Edinburgh EH8 9SH

Website: holyrooddistillery.co.uk
Tel: 0131 2858977

The first whisky distillery in almost 100 years to open up in Edinburgh, Holyrood has become known as one of the most versatile distilleries in Scotland.

The use of a variety of different types of yeast (including yeast from Champagne, Bordeaux and Burgundy) has been implemented in partnership with Berry Brothers. Different mash bills based on traditionally malted barley but also including varieties such as crystal and chocolate malt further increases the number of styles of newmake. Recently they have also started experimenting with different filling strengths.

Co-founders of Holyrood are whisky veteran David Robertson (ex Macallan master distiller) and the Canadian couple Kelly and Rob Carpenter together with 60 other investors. The distillery manager Jack Mayo left in summer 2020 and was succeeded by Marc Watson with a background at Eden Mill and, most recently, Bonnington distillery. In January 2021, Nick Ravenhall who in the past has worked with Morrison Bowmore and Atom Brands, became managing director.

The distillery is equipped with a one ton semi-lauter mash tun and six 5,000 litre washbacks made of stainless steel with a fermentation time of 48-168 hours depending on the style they're making. There are one 5,000 litre wash still and one 3,750 litre spirit still – both very tall and fitted with descending lyne arms and boil balls. Attached to the spirit still is a water-cooled purifier. Foreshots vary from 6 to 30 minutes depending on the spirit style.

The distillery is located in a listed building from 1835 and in July 2019 the distillery opened to the public. Apart from whisky, the distillery also produces other sprits including gin.

InchDairnie

[inch•dairnie]

Owner:	**Region/district:**
John Fergus & Co. Ltd	Lowlands
Founded: **Status:**	**Capacity:**
2015 Active	2 000 000 litres

Address: Whitecraigs Rd, Glenrothes, Fife KY6 2RX

Website:	**Tel:**
inchdairniedistillery.com	01595 510010

For InchDairnie´s distillery manager Ian Palmer there are three key words that govern operation – flavour, innovation and experimentation.

Opened in May 2016, a few miles west of Glenrothes in Fife, the distillery has a capacity of two million litres per year with a possibility of expanding to four million. It is owned by John Fergus & Co. which was founded by Ian Palmer, who has more than 40 years of experience in the Scotch whisky industry. Palmer's unorthodox ideas start already with the equipment. The distillery has a hammer mill and a Meura mash filter, instead of a traditional mash tun. There are four washbacks with a fermentation time of 72 hours and one pair of traditional pot stills with double condensers and after-coolers to increase the copper to spirit ratio. The two stills are complemented by a Lomond still with six plates to provide the opportunity for triple and experimental distillation. A unique yeast recipe is used and high gravity fermentation will create a fruitier character of the newmake. Furthermore, Palmer is working with both the standard spring barley as well as winter barley to give the possibility for a broader palette of flavours.

Five different types of whisky are produced; first of all Inchdairnie Single Malt which going forward will form the core range together with RyeLaw, first distilled in December 2017 from malted rye and malted barley, and KinGlassie which is a peated expression, distilled once a year for only two weeks in December. The first to be released of these three will be RyeLaw. Furthermore there is Strathenry which constitutes 80% of the distillery´s production and will be used for blended whisky. The final expression is The Prinlaws Collection which will be a range of spirits from different yeasts, cereals and oaks. The first attempt in this series was made in June 2019 when a whisky from oats was distilled. This was in fact the first time in over a century that whisky made from oat was produced in Scotland.

Isle of Raasay

[ajl ov r**a**ssay]

Owner:	**Region/district:**
R&B Distillers	Highlands (Raasay)
Founded: **Status:**	**Capacity:**
2017 Active (vc)	200 000 litres

Address: Borodale House, Raasay, By Kyle IV40 8PB

Website:	**Tel:**
rbdistillers.com	01478 470177

The owners, R&B Distillers, were working on establishing a distillery in The Borders when a new plan surfaced – to build a distillery on the small island of Raasay, east of Skye.

Alasdair Day, with an ancestral interest in Scotch whisky, teamed up with entrepreneur Bill Dobbie and bought Borodale House. With more buildings added for the whisky production, the old Victorian house is now the hotel part of the distillery. With a stunning view towards the Cuillin Mountains on the Isle of Skye, this is an excellent way of spending a night on Raasay.

The distillery is equipped with a 1,1 ton mash tun and six stainless steel (5,000 litre) washbacks with cooling jackets currently with four short fermentations (67 hours) and six long (118 hours) adding up to 211,000 litres of alcohol in 2021. The 5,000 litre wash still has a cooling jacket around the lyne arm and there's also a 3,600 litre spirit still with a copper column attached should they want to use it for special runs. The production is a 50/50 combination of peated (50 ppm) and unpeated spirit. Some of the barley is grown on Raasay, including rare varieties such as Brage, Iskria and Salome, and it is then sent off to the mainland to be floor malted. All Raasay single malt is distilled, matured and bottled on the island.

A wide variety of casks are used for maturation. The inaugural and limited lightly peated release in November 2020 was matured for two years in first fill bourbon and another year in Bordeaux red wine casks. The first core expression appeared in June 2021 and had been matured in a combination of virgin chinkapin oak, Bordeaux red wine barriques and first fill rye casks from Woodford. It was followed by a second batch in September and in October by a limited, peated expression matured in rye casks and finished in ex oloroso.

Kingsbarns

[kings•barns]

Owner: Wemyss family

Region/district: Lowlands

Founded: 2014

Status: Active (vc)

Capacity: 600 000 litres

Address: East Newhall Farm, Kingsbarns, St Andrews KY16 8QE

Website: kingsbarnsdistillery.com

Tel: 01333 451300

The plans for this distillery near St Andrews in Fife, were drafted in 2008 and came to fruition in 2014 when the distillery was opened.

The idea was to restore a derelict farm-steading from the late 18th century and turn it into a modern distillery. Planning permission was received in March 2011 and in 2012 the Wemyss family invested £3m into the project and becoma the new owners. The company is behind the independent bottling company, Wemyss Malts, and also owns other companies in the field of wine and gin.

The distillery is equipped with a 1.5 ton stainless steel mash tun, four 7,500 litre stainless steel washbacks with a fermentation time of 72-120 hours, one 7,500 litre wash still and one 4,500 litre spirit still. A slow distillation and an early cut are important to achieve the fruity character. Mainly first fill bourbon barrels are used for maturation together with STR casks (wine barriques that have been shaved, toasted and re-charred). The first casks were filled in March 2015 and the current yearly production is 200,000 litres of alcohol.

The first release of Kingsbarns single malt was in 2018 when a limited number of bottles were made available to the members of the Founder's Club. Their first generally available malt, Dream to Dram, was a vatting of ex-bourbon casks and STR red wine barriques and was released in 2019. In summer 2020 a cask strength version named Family Reserve was released and this was followed in November by the 6 year old Founder's Reserve 2020, the 6 year old Distillery Reserve 2020 and a 5 year old matured in oloroso butts made of American oak. The latter is now the core expression under the name Balcomie. In spring 2021 the limited Bell Rock was launched. This was the first time where the owners had vatted whisky from ex-bourbon and ex-oloroso casks.

Lagg

[laag]

Owner: Isle of Arran Distillers Ltd.

Region/district: Lowlands (s. Arran)

Founded: 2019

Status: Active (vc)

Capacity: 750 000 litres

Address: Kilmory, Isle of Arran KA27 8PG

Website: laggwhisky.com

Tel: 01770 870565

The success for Arran distillery, which was opened in 1993, encouraged the owners to open yet another distillery on the island. Work on Lagg distillery began in February 2017 and the first distillation took place in March 2019.

With Arran distillery (now renamed Lochranza) located in the village with the same name on the northern tip of the island, Lagg is situated in the south. Since the old diversion line between the Highlands and the Lowlands cuts through isle of Arran, the two distilleries belong to two different whisky regions with Lagg being a Lowland distillery.

Lochranza is by far the most visited distillery in Scotland with more than 100,000 visitors last year and the owners anticipate that the combined distilleries will see more than 200,000 visitors in a couple of years. For those wanting to do more than just visiting the distillery, there is the possibility of buying entire casks for future bottling.

The distillery is equipped with a four ton semilauter mash tun, four Oregon pine washbacks holding 24,000 litres and with a fermentation time of 72 hours, one wash still (10,000 litres) and one spirit still (7,000 litres). However, there is space for an additional four washbacks and one more pair of stills in the future. All of Arran Distillers' peated production has now moved from Lochranza to Lagg who uses barley with a phenol specification of 50ppm. The peat used to dry the barley is sourced from different places in Scotland and also from abroad Also, Lagg will act as an experimental plant with trials of different yeast strains and types of barley and they have plans to produce their own cider and apple brandy in the future. The target for 2021 is to do 5-7 mashes per week which means 400,000 litres of pure alcohol. In spring 2020, newmake from both Lochranza and Lagg were vatted together to eventullay become an Arran blended malt.

Lindores Abbey

[linn•doors aebi]

Owner: The Lindores Distilling Co.

Region/district: Lowlands

Founded: 2017

Status: Active (vc)

Capacity: 225 000 litres

Address: Lindores Abbey House, Abbey Road, Newburgh, Fife KY14 6HH

Website: lindoresabbeydistillery.com

Tel: 01337 842547

The famous, first written record of whisky was a letter to Friar John Cor, a monk at the Abbey of Lindores, dated 1494 where, by order of King James IV, he was instructed to make "aqua vitae, VIII bolls of malt".

The archeologial and historical evidence for Lindores being the birthplace of Scotch whisky are by no way inconclusive but further excavations of the site may reveal some evidence. Be that as it may, the current owners of the abbey in ruins are Drew and Helen McKenzie Smith and in December 2017 they commissioned a distillery next to the old monastery. The location is stunning and with all the production equipment on one level you have a spectacular view of the surroundings. Behind the washbacks you catch a glimpse of Dundee and from the stills you look down on the abbey ruins with the river Tayne in the background.

Lindores Abbey is one of few producers of a single estate whisky in Scotland. Starting in 2020, all the barley used has been grown in surrounding fields which were under the original ownership of the abbey back in the 15th century. The equipment consists of a 2 ton semi lauter mash tun with a copper lid, four Douglas fir washbacks with two short (68 hours) and three long (114 hours) fermentations, one 10,000 litre wash still and two 3,500 litre spirit stills. The foreshots are 15-20 minutes and the spirit cut starts at 75% and goes down to 67%. The production goal for 2021 is 188,000 litres of pure alcohol. In spring 2021, the first 1494 bottles of their inaugural release, available only to members of The 1494 Preservation Society, appeared and this was followed in July by the first widely available expression - the Lindores MCDXCIV bottled at 46%.

An excellent visitor centre with a wide range of activities, including whisky and champagne afternoon teas and an apothecary experience is also a part of the distillery.

Lochlea

[lock•lee]

Owner: Lochlea Distilling Co.

Region/district: Lowlands

Founded: 2018

Status: Active

Capacity: 200 000 litres

Address: Lochlea Farm, South Ayrshire KA1 5NN

Website: lochleadistillery.com

Tel: 07585 661 605

The foundation of Lochlea definitely goes against the birth pattern of most other new distilleries. Usually press releases are sent out years before the shovel is in the ground but Lochlea decided to fly under the radar.

The owner, Neil McGeoch, received planning permission in autumn 2015 and while that is public information few, if any, details about the ongoing work in the years to come reached the public eye. The first distillation was in April 2018 but at that time the distillery had no website and no presence in social media. The strategy was clear - when we have something to show for (i.e. a bottled whisky) we'll come forward. Neil McGeoch's grandfather built a business of clothing retail stores in the 1950s which today is known as M&Co. Neil took his place in the family business while at the same time working as a beef farmer at the Lochlea

farm. In 2014, he sold his herd of Simmental and pursued his career as a whisky distiller.

Loch Lea is situated on a farm from the 1700s in Ayrshire just south of Kilmarnock. What makes it so special is that Robert Burns, the famous bard, actually lived and worked here during his formative years (1777-1784) and it was at that time he wrote some of his most famous poems and also founded the Bachelor's Club.

The distillery is equipped with one mash tun, six washbacks with a long fermentation and two, tall stills. All the barley used for the whisky is grown on the farm. The style of the spirit will be more full-bodied than a traditional Lowland and peated production is also in the pipeline. For maturation the owners use 14 different cask types although predominantly first fill bourbon and oloroso. The inaugural, limited whisky appeared in autumn 2021 with the first signature style Lochlea planned for an early 2022 release.

Nc'nean

[nook•<u>knee</u>•anne]

Owner:		Region/district:
Nc'nean Distillery Ltd.		Western Highlands

Founded:	Status:	Capacity:
2017	Active (vc)	100 000 litres

Address: Drimnin, By Lochaline PA80 5XZ

Website:	Tel:
ncnean.com	01967 421698

Sustainability has been at the heart of the founder Annabel Thomas and her team from the moment the first plans for Nc'nean distillery were drawn up.

That is also why 2021 will be remembered as perhaps the most important year in the distillery's history. In 2021 Nc'nean became a certified net zero emissions whisky distillery - the first in the UK to achieve this and 20 years ahead of the Scotch industry target. The distillery is powered with 100% renewable energy from a biomass boiler fired by woodchips from a forest two miles from the distillery and all the trees are replanted. The distillery is also certified organic using only organic Scottish barley and the whisky is finally bottled in 100% recycled glass bottles.

The distillery is equipped with a one ton semi lauter mash tun and four stainless steel washbacks with a fermentation time between 65 and 115 hours. Furthermore there is a 5,000 litre wash still and a 3,500 litre spirit still, both with slightly descending lyne arms and sub coolers although the latter are currently not being used. The plan for 2021 is to do five mashes per week and 94,000 litres of pure alcohol. The owner is working on two basic recipes of fruity whisky – "new style" to be enjoyed young and "old style", with lower cut points and destined for a longer maturation.

A botanical spirit including wild herbs and flowers foraged from the surroundings of the distillery, was launched in autumn 2018. The first single malt, Ainnir, matured in red wine casks and American bourbon barrels, was released in September 2020 and this was followed by a speecial edition in autumn 2021.

The distillery is beautifully situated on the Drimnin estate on the Morvern peninsula with an astounding view towards Mull and Tobermory. Open to visitors, Nc'nean was recently named one of the top 10 Scottish distilleries to visit by The Guardian.

Roseisle

[rose•<u>eyel</u>]

Owner:		Region/district:
Diageo		Speyside

Founded:	Status:	Capacity:
2009	Active	12 500 000 litres

Address: Roseisle, Morayshire IV30 5YP

Website:	Tel:
-	01343 832100

Roseisle distillery is located on the same site as the already existing Roseisle maltings just west of Elgin. The distillery has won several awards for its ambition towards sustainable production.

The distillery is equipped with two stainless steel, full lauter mash tuns with a 12.5 tonne charge each. There are 14 huge (112,000 litres) stainless steel washbacks and 14 stills with the wash stills being heated by external heat exchangers while the spirit stills are heated using steam coils. The spirit vapours are cooled through copper condensers but on three spirit stills and three wash stills there are also stainless steel condensers attached, that you can switch to for a more sulphury spirit. The fermentation time for a Speyside style of whisky is 90-100 hours and for a heavier style it is 50-60 hours. The plan for 2020 is to do 23 mashes per week and a total of 12 million litres of alcohol.

The total cost for the distillery was £40m and how to use the hot water in an efficient way was very much a focal point from the beginning. For example, Roseisle is connected by means of two long pipes with Burghead maltings, 3 km north of the distillery. Hot water is pumped from Roseisle and then used in the seven kilns at Burghead and cold water is then pumped back to Roseisle. The pot ale from the distillation will be piped into anaerobic fermenters to be transformed into biogas and the dried solids will act as a biomass fuel source. The biomass burner on the site, producing steam for the distillery, covers 72% of the total requirement. Furthermore, green technology has reduced the emission of carbon dioxide to only 15% of an ordinary, same-sized distillery.

Destined to be used for blends, Roseisle single malt was in autumn 2017 for the first time used in a different role. It was part of the blended malt Collectivum XXVIII where Diageo had used whiskies from all 28 malt distilleries.

Strathearn

[strath•<u>earn</u>]

Owner:	**Region/district:**
Douglas Laing	Southern Highlands
Founded: **Status:**	**Capacity:**
2013 Active	c 30 000 litres

Address: Bachilton Farm Steading, Methven PH1 3QX

Website:	**Tel:**
strathearndistillery.com	01738 840 100

When Tony Reeman-Clark founded Strathearn back in 2013, it was probably fair to label it as Scotland´s first micro distillery.

They were one of the pioneers of Scottish craft distilling and they were keen to challenge the rules stipulated by the Scotch Whisky Association. One example was their experimentation with different types on non-oak wood for maturation. Chestnut, mullberry and cherry wood was used.and in order to apply with the SWA rules it was sold as Uisge Beatha, the ancient name for Scotch, rather than whisky.

In autumn 2019 a surprising announcement was made by independent bottler Douglas Laing that they had bought Strathearn. It was surprising because at the same time Douglas Laing was working on establishing their own Clutha distillery on the banks of Clyde in Glasgow. The new owners stated that the style of Strathearn will stay the same with the exception of the unusual types of casks used for maturation or as they themselves put it "a slight revamp to the cask policy."

All the equipment is fitted into one room and consists of a stainless steel mash tun, two stainless steel washbacks, one 1,000 litre wash still and a 500 litre spirit still. Both stills are of the Alembic type with vertical tube copper condensers. The new owners have plans to install both a new still and a new mashtun raising the capacity to just under 150,000 litres. Both peated and un-peated whisky is produced.

The first single malt Scotch from the distillery was released in December 2016. The first from the new owners however, appeared in December 2019. Distilled in 2013 and 2014 the whisky had matured in a combination of virgin European oak and first fill oloroso and bottled at 46,6% without chill filtration. A second batch is in the pipeline and several gins have also been released over the years with Scottish Gin and Heather Rose being the big sellers.

Torabhaig

[tor•a•<u>vaig</u>]

Owner:	**Region/district:**
Mossburn Distillers	Highlands (Skye)
Founded: **Status:**	**Capacity:**
2016 Active (vc)	500 000 litres

Address: Teangue, Sleat, Isle of Skye IV44 8RE

Website:	**Tel:**
torabhaig.com	01471 833447

The company behind the second distillery on Skye (with Talisker being the first) is Mossburn Distillers but Torabhaig is definitely not their only engagement in the whisky business.

Also known as an independent bottler, the company recently opened the small Reivers distillery in the Scottish Borders with plans to build a much larger one in a few years. On top of that they are co-founders of the Kaikyo distillery in Japan.

The entire set of production equipment is situated on one level with a 1.5 ton stainless steel semi lauter mash tun with a copper top. There are eight washbacks made of Douglas fir (10,000 litres) with a fermentation time between 80 and 120 hours, one 8,000 litre wash still and one 5,000 litre spirit still. The production plan for 2021 is 400,000 litres of pure alcohol. The owners produce a heavily peated whisky with a phenol specification of up to 75ppm in the malted barley. The first single malt from the distillery, 2017. The Legacy Series, was supposed to be released in autumn 2020 but due to the pandemic the 32,000 bottles were delayed to February 2021. Made from heavily peated barley (55-60ppm) it had matured in first fill bourbon barrels. It was followed in July 2021 by Allt Gleann with a third, sherry-matured expression already in the pipeline.

In order to open up for innovation and experiments, an interesting program has been implemented at the distillery called The Journeyman Projects. Different distillers on site are given the chance to create their own designed spirit for a month each. That means laborating with different yeasts and malts but also experimenting with fermentation times, distillation itself and maturation. Last year´s recipes included the distillery´s highest peated malt at 137ppm and a batch of imperial malt which had been fermented with a Norwegian brewer´s yeast - Voss Kveik

Wolfburn

[wolf•burn]

Owner:
Aurora Brewing Ltd.

Region/district:
Northern Highlands

Founded:
2013

Status:
Active (vc)

Capacity:
135 000 litres

Address: Henderson Park, Thurso,
Caithness KW14 7XW

Website:
wolfburn.com

Tel:
01847 891051

The most northerly distillery on the Scottish mainland, Wolfburn, is situated in an industrial area on the outskirts of Thurso.

The owners have chosen a site that is situated 350 metres from the ruins of the old Wolfburn Distillery. Construction work commenced in August 2012 and the first newmake came off the stills at the end of January 2013. The distillery is equipped with a 1.1 ton semi-lauter stainless steel mash tun with a copper canopy, four stainless steel washbacks with a fermentation time of 70-92 hours, holding 5,500 litres each, one wash still (5,500 litres) and one spirit still (3,600 litres).

The main part (80%) of the malt is unpeated but since 2014, a lightly peated (10 ppm) spirit has also been produced. The inaugural bottling from the distillery appeared in early 2016 and had a smoky profile due to the fact that it had partly been matured in quarter casks from Islay. This limited release was followed by a more widely available bourbon matured whisky which in September 2016 was re-named Northland. At the same time a second bottling appeared, Aurora, which had been partly matured in oloroso sherry casks. The core range was expanded in 2017 with Morven, the distillery´s first peated whisky and currently their biggest seller, and September 2018 saw the fourth expression being released – Langskip, matured in ex-bourbon barrels and bottled at 58%. A range of limited bottlings started in 2017 with the lightly peated Batch 128 and the most recent, in February 2020, was Batch 155 with a maturation for almost five years in first fill bourbon and another six months in port hogsheads. Another limited range is Kylver where batch 7 (Gebo) was released in October 2020 followed by the oloroso matured batch 8 (Wunjo) in April 2021. Limited releases in 2021 include a Father´s Day special matured in ex-bourbon quarter casks and Manager´s Cask from an oloroso sherry butt. Visitors also have the opportunity of filling their own bottle at the distillery – currently a PX hogshead distilled in 2013.

Lochlea, Lindores Abbey and Isle of Raasay released their inaugural bottlings in 2021

Active distilleries per owner

Diageo
Auchroisk
Benrinnes
Blair Athol
Brora
Caol Ila
Cardhu
Clynelish
Cragganmore
Dailuaine
Dalwhinnie
Dufftown
Glendullan
Glen Elgin
Glenkinchie
Glenlossie
Glen Ord
Glen Spey
Inchgower
Knockando
Lagavulin
Linkwood
Mannochmore
Mortlach
Oban
Roseisle
Royal Lochnagar
Strathmill
Talisker
Teaninich

Pernod Ricard
Aberlour
Allt-a-Bhainne
Braeval
Dalmunach
Glenburgie
Glen Keith
Glenlivet
Glentauchers
Longmorn
Miltonduff
Scapa
Strathisla
Tormore

Edrington Group
Glenrothes
Highland Park
Macallan

Inver House (Thai Beverage)
Balblair
Balmenach
Knockdhu
Pulteney
Speyburn

John Dewar & Sons (Bacardi)
Aberfeldy
Aultmore
Craigellachie
Macduff
Royal Brackla

William Grant & Sons
Ailsa Bay
Balvenie
Glenfiddich
Kininvie

Whyte & Mackay (Emperador)
Dalmore
Fettercairn
Jura
Tamnavulin

Beam Suntory
Ardmore
Auchentoshan
Bowmore
Glen Garioch
Laphroaig

Distell International
Bunnahabhain
Deanston
Tobermory

Benriach Dist. Co. (Brown Forman)
Benriach
Glendronach
Glenglassaugh

Loch Lomond Group
Glen Scotia
Loch Lomond

J & A Mitchell
Glengyle
Springbank

Glenmorangie Co. (LVMH)
Ardbeg
Glenmorangie

Angus Dundee Distillers
Glencadam
Tomintoul

Ian Macleod Distillers
Glengoyne
Tamdhu

Campari Group
Glen Grant

Isle of Arran Distillers
Lagg
Lochranza

Signatory
Edradour

Tomatin Distillery Co.
Tomatin

J & G Grant
Glenfarclas

Rémy Cointreau
Bruichladdich

David Prior
Bladnoch

Gordon & MacPhail
Benromach

La Martiniquaise
Glen Moray

Ben Nevis Distillery Ltd (Nikka)
Ben Nevis

Picard Vins & Spiritueux
Tullibardine

Harvey´s of Edinburgh
Speyside

Kilchoman Distillery Co.
Kilchoman

Cuthbert family
Daftmill

Mark Tayburn
Abhainn Dearg

Aurora Brewing Ltd
Wolfburn

Douglas Laing
Strathearn

Annandale Distillery Co.
Annandale

Adelphi Distillery Co.
Ardnamurchan

Wemyss
Kingsbarns

Mcpherson-Grant family
Ballindalloch

Paul Miller
Eden Mill

Isle of Harris Distillers
Harris

The Glasgow Distillery Company
Glasgow Distillery

John Fegus & Co. Ltd
Inchdairnie

Stirling family
Arbikie

Brewdog plc
Brew Dog Distillery

Thompson family
Dornoch

Mossburn Distillers
Torabhaig

R & B Distillers
Isle of Raasay

The Lindores Distilling Company
Lindores Abbey

Morrison Glasgow Distillers
Clydeside

Nc´nean Distillery Ltd.
Nc´nean

The Three Stills Co.
The Borders

The Glenallachie Distillers Co.
Glenallachie

Morrison Scotch Whisky Distillers
Aberargie

GlenWyvis Distillery Ltd.
GlenWyvis

Hunter Laing
Ardnahoe

The Holyrood Distillery Ltd.
Holyrood

Greenwood Distillers
Ardross

Lalique Group/Hansjörg Wyss
Glenturret

John Crabbie & Co.
Bonnington

Lochlea Distilling Co.
Lochlea

Stewart family
Falkirk

Ardent Spirits
Burn O´Bennie

Closed
distilleries

The distilleries on the following pages
have all been closed and some of them even demolished.
One is tempted to say that none of them will ever produce again
but two - Port Ellen and Rosebank - are actually being re-opened in 2022.
As for the rest, the best chances of finding new
bottlings from old stock are probably Caperdonich,
Convalmore, Dallas Dhu, Imperial, Ladyburn, Littlemill
and Pittyvaich. Old bottlings from the others show
up at whisky auctions from time to time
but few, if any, casks remain.

Opposite page; Coleburn Distillery - closed in 1985

Port Ellen

[port <u>ell</u>•en]

Owner: | **Region/district:**
Diageo | Islay

Founded: | **Status:** | **Capacity:**
1825 | Dismantled | -

Address: Port Ellen, Isle of Islay, Argyll PA42 7AJ

The announcement that Port Ellen and Brora distilleries would be reopened, came at the same time in autumn 2017 but while renovation on Brora started in early 2019, the owners did not receive an approval from the council for Port Ellen until December 2019.

Both distilleries stopped producing in 1983 but the main difference between the two is that no equipment remains at Port Ellen and very few of the buildings can be used. A new distillery will be built in the courtyard between the maltings and the old warehouses. The old drawings of the equipment still exist and one pair of stills with shell and tube condensers will be fabricated. There will also be a second, smaller pair with the intention of creating experimental whiskies. The distillery, with an 800,000 litre capacity should be up and running sometime in 2022 and will have a brand home as Diageo calls its visitor centres.

The founder of the distillery, Alexander Mackay, went bankrupt a few months after the distillery had opened and it was a relative of his, John Ramsay, who would run the distillery instead until the late 1800s and he did so with great success. There was no intention of ever bottling the spirit as a single malt – all the production went to blends. In 1930 the distillery was mothballed and didn't reopen until 1967. The final era would last but 16 years and in 1983 the distillery was closed for good (or so it would seem). At its height, Port Ellen was equipped with four stills, producing 1.7 million litres of alcohol.

Port Ellen single malt has been released twice in the Rare Malts range (1998 and 2000). It wasn't until 2001, when the first Port Ellen Special Release turned up that things started to change and the malt became a cult whisky. There is still some stock of old Port Ellen left but going forward, this will not be launched in the Special Releases as it used to be. However, a new range from Diageo, Untold Stories, appeared in spring 2019 with a **39 year old** as the inaugural release. This was followed up by a **40 year old** in 2020 together with another **40 year old** in the Prima & Ultima range. Both were distilled in 1979.

History:

1825 Alexander Kerr Mackay assisted by Walter Campbell founds the distillery. Mackay runs into financial troubles after a few months and his three relatives John Morrison, Patrick Thomson and George Maclennan take over.

1833 John Ramsay, a cousin to John Morrison, comes from Glasgow to take over.

1836 Ramsay is granted a lease on the distillery from the Laird of Islay.

1892 Ramsay dies and the distillery is inherited by his widow, Lucy.

1906 Lucy Ramsay dies and her son Captain Iain Ramsay takes over.

1920 Iain Ramsay sells to Buchanan-Dewar who transfers the administration to the company Port Ellen Distillery Co. Ltd.

1925 Buchanan-Dewar joins Distillers Company Limited (DCL).

1930 The distillery is mothballed.

1967 In production again after reconstruction and doubling of the number of stills from two to four.

1973 A large drum maltings is installed.

1980 Queen Elisabeth visits the distillery and a commemorative special bottling is made.

1983 The distillery is mothballed.

1987 The distillery closes permanently but the maltings continue to deliver malt to all Islay distilleries.

2001 Port Ellen cask strength first edition is released.

2014 The 14th release of Port Ellen - a 35 year old from 1978.

2015 The 15th release of Port Ellen - a 32 year old from 1983.

2016 The 16th release of Port Ellen - a 37 year old from 1978.

2017 The 17th release of Port Ellen - a 37 year old from 1979. Diageo announces that the distillery will re-open in 2020.

2019 A 39 year old is released as the first in a new range – Untold Stories.

2020 Two 40 year olds in the Untold Stories and Prima & Ultima range respectively are released.

40 years old

Rosebank

[rows•bank]

Owner:
Ian Macleod Distillers

Region/district:
Lowlands

Founded: **Status:**
1840 Closed

Capacity:
6-800,000 litres

Address: Falkirk FK1 4DS

Website:
rosebank.com

Tel:
-

Lovers of the elegant, triple distilled Lowland single malt from Rosebank have had their hopes for a long time that someone would come along och take pity on the closed distillery.

There were several interested parties over the years and there were even rumours that none less than Diageo would re-open it, but no change of state took place. Eventually, in autumn 2017, Ian Macleod (owners of Glengoyne and Tamdhu) bought the property from Scottish Canals, to whom Diageo had sold to in 2002, and acquired the trademark and stock from Diageo. In early 2019, they received planning permission from Falkirk council. Construction work started in December 2019 but stopped in March 2020 due to the covid pandemic. It was resumed 1st February 2021 and the plan now is to commission the distillery in autumn 2022. The new distillery, with the iconic chimney being kept, will be equipped with three stills (for triple distillation) and wormtubs with a capacity to produce 1 million litres of pure alcohol per year. The cost for the project is estimated to be £12m.

Established in 1798, Rosebank single malt enjoyed a good reputation during most of its lifespan even though the distillery also produced its fair share of grain whisky which was common especially in the Lowlands at the time. Most of the production went into blends but in 1982, Rosebank 8 year old single malt became a part of the owners Ascot Malt Cellar range together with Lagavulin, Talisker and Linkwood. Six years later, The Classic Malts saw the light of day and when the owners were to decide which malt to represent the Lowlands, their choice was Glenkinchie.

The latest bottling of Rosebank from the previous owners was a 21 year old in the Special Releases autumn 2014. In February 2020, Ian Macleod released **two single casks**, both bottled at cask strength and distilled in 1993, the same year that the distillery closed. These were followed in October 2020 by a **30 year old** and a **Vintage 1990** for travel retail.

History:

1840 James Rankine founds the distillery.

1845 The distillery is expanded.

1864 Rankine buys Camelon Distillery on the west bank of the Forth-Clyde canal.

1894 Rosebank Distillery Company is formed.

1914 Rosebank, togehter with Clydesdale, Glenkinchie, St. Magdalene and Grange form Scottish malt Distillers (SMD).

1919 SMD becomes a part of Distillers company Limited (DCL).

1982 DCL launches the series The Ascot Malt Cellar with Rosebank, Linkwood, Talisker, Lagavulin and two blendeed malts.

1993 The distillery closes in June.

2002 The buildings are bought by British Waterways.

2008 The stills and other equipment are stolen.

2014 A 21 year old is launched as part of the Special Releases.

2017 The site is bought from Scottish Canals by Ian Macleod Distillers and at the same time they acquire the trademark and stocks from Diageo.

2020 Two single casks distilled in 1993 are released together with a 30 year old and a Vintage 1990.

1993 single cask

Banff

Owner:	Region:	Founded:	Status:
Diageo	Speyside	1824	Demolished

The distillery has a tragic history of numerous fires, explosions and bombings. The most spectacular incident was when a lone Junkers Ju-88 bombed one of the warehouses in 1941. The distillery was closed in 1983 and the buildings were destroyed in a fire in 1991.

Ben Wyvis

Owner:	Region:	Founded:	Status:
Whyte & Mackay	N Highlands	1965	Dismantled

Built on the same site as Invergordon grain distillery, the distillery was equipped with one mash tun, six washbacks and one pair of stills. The stills are in use today at Glengyle distillery. Production stopped in 1976 and in 1977 the distillery was closed and dismantled.

Caperdonich

Owner:	Region:	Founded:	Status:
Chivas Bros.	Speyside	1897	Demolished

Founded by the owners of Glen Grant. Five years after the opening, the distillery was shut down but was re-opened again in 1965 under the name Caperdonich. In 2002 it was mothballed yet again. Sold in 2010 to Forsyth´s in Rothes and the buildings were demolished.

Coleburn

Owner:	Region:	Founded:	Status:
Diageo	Speyside	1897	Dismantled

Coleburn was used as an experimental workshop where new production techniques were tested. In 1985 the distillery was mothballed and never opened again. Since 2014, the warehouses are used by Aceo Ltd, who owns the independent bottler Murray McDavid.

Convalmore

Owner:	Region:	Founded:	Status:
Diageo	Speyside	1894	Dismantled

This distillery is still intact and can be seen in Dufftown next to Balvenie distillery. The buildings are used by William Grant´s for storage while Diageo still holds the rights to the brand. In the early 20th century, distilling of malt whisky in continuous stills took place. Closed in 1985.

Dallas Dhu

Owner:	Region:	Founded:	Status:
Diageo	Speyside	1898	Closed

The distillery is still intact, equipment and all, but hasn´t produced since 1983. Today it is run by Historic Scotland as a museum which is open all year round. In 2013 a feasibility study was commissioned to look at the possibilities of re-starting production again.

Glen Albyn

Owner:	Region:	Founded:	Status:
Diageo	N Highlands	1844	Demolished

One of three Inverness distilleries surviving into the 1980s. In 1866 the buildings were transformed into a flour mill. but then converted back to a distillery in 1884 and continued producing whisky until 1983 when it was closed. Three years later the distillery was demolished.

Glenesk

Owner:	Region:	Founded:	Status:
Diageo	E Highlands	1897	Demolished

Operated under many names; Highland Esk, North Esk, Montrose and Hillside. In 1968 a large drum maltings was built adjacent to the distillery and the Glenesk maltings still operate today under the ownership of Boortmalt. The distillery building was demolished in 1996.

Glen Flagler

Owner:	Region:	Founded:	Status:
InverHouse	Lowlands	1965	Demolished

Glen Flagler was one of two malt distilleries (Killyloch being the other) that were built on the site of Garnheath grain distillery. Killyloch was closed in the early 1970s, while Glen Flagler continued to produce until 1985. A year later, Garnheath was closed only to be demolished in 1988.

Glenlochy

Owner:	Region:	Founded:	Status:
Diageo	W Highlands	1898	Demolished

Glenlochy was one of three distilleries in Fort William at the beginning of the 1900s. For a period of time, the distillery was owned by Joseph Hobbs who, after having sold the distillery to DCL, bought the second distillery in town, Ben Nevis. Glenlochy was closd in 1983.

Glen Mhor

Owner:	Region:	Founded:	Status:
Diageo	N Highlands	1892	Demolished

Glen Mhor was one of the last three Inverness distilleries and probably the one with the best reputation when it comes to the whisky that it produced. Glen Mhor was closed in 1983 and three years later the buildings were demolished. Today there is a supermarket on the site.

Glenugie

Owner:	Region:	Founded:	Status:
Chivas Bros	E Highlands	1831	Demolished

Glenugie produced whisky for six years before it was converted into a brewery. In 1875 whisky distillation started again, but production was very intermittent until 1937 when Seager Evans took over. Following several ownership changes, the distillery closed in 1983.

Glenury Royal

Owner:	Region:	Founded:	Status:
Diageo	E Highlands	1825	Demolished

The founder of Glenury was the eccentric Captain Robert Barclay Allardyce, the first to walk 1000 miles in 1000 hours in 1809. The distillery closed in 1983 and part of the building was demolished a decade later with the rest converted into flats.

Imperial

Owner:	Region:	Founded:	Status:
Chivas Bros	Speyside	1897	Demolished

In over a century, Imperial distillery was out of production for 60% of the time, but when it produced it had a capacity of 1,6 million. In 2012, the owners announced that a new distillery would be built. The old distillery was demolished and in 2015 Dalmunach distillery was commissioned.

Inverleven

Owner:	Region:	Founded:	Status:
Chivas Bros	Lowlands	1938	Demolished

Inverleven was built on the same site as Dumbarton grain distillery, equipped with one pair of traditional pot stills. In 1956 a Lomond still was added. Inverleven was mothballed in 1991 and finally closed. The Lomond still is now working again since 2010 at Bruichladdich.

Killyloch

Owner:	Region:	Founded:	Status:
InverHouse	Lowlands	1965	Demolished

Publicker Industries converted a paper mill in Airdrie into a grain distillery (Garnheath) and two malt distilleries (Glen Flagler and Killyloch). Killyloch (originally named Lilly-loch after the water source) was closed in the early 1970s, while Glen Flagler continued to produce until 1985.

Kinclaith

Owner:	Region:	Founded:	Status:
Chivas Bros	Lowlands	1957	Demolished

The last malt distillery to be built in Glasgow and constructed on the grounds of Strathclyde grain distillery by Seager Evans. In 1975 it was dismantled to make room for an extension of the grain distillery. It was later demolished in 1982.

Ladyburn

Owner:	Region:	Founded:	Status:
W Grant & Sons	Lowlands	1966	Dismantled

In 1963 William Grant & Sons built their huge grain distillery in Girvan in Ayrshire. Three years later they also decided to build a malt distillery on the site which was given the name Ladyburn. The distillery was closed in 1975 and finally dismantled during the 1980s.

Littlemill

Owner:	Region:	Founded:	Status:
Loch Lomond Co.	Lowlands	1772	Demolished

Scotland´s oldest working distillery until production stopped in 1992. Triple distillation was practised until 1930. In 1996 the distillery was dismantled and part of the buildings demolished and in 2004 much of the remaining buildings were destroyed in a fire.

Lochside

Owner:	Region:	Founded:	Status:
Chivas Bros	E Highlands	1957	Demolished

Most of the output from the distillery was made for blended whisky. One of the owners combined grain and malt whisky production. In 1992 the distillery was mothballed and five years later all the equipment and stock were removed. The distillery buildings were demolished in 2005.

Millburn

Owner:	Region:	Founded:	Status:
Diageo	N Highlands	1807	Dismantled

The oldest of those Inverness distilleries that made it into modern times. With one pair of stills, the capacity was 300,000 litres. In 1985 it was closed and three years later all the equipment was removed. The buildings are now a hotel and restaurant owned by Premier Inn.

North Port

Owner:	Region:	Founded:	Status:
Diageo	E Highlands	1820	Demolished

The names North Port and Brechin are used interchangeably on the labels of this single malt. The distillery had one pair of stills and produced 500,000 litres per year. Closed in 1983, it was dismantled piece by piece and was finally demolished in 1994 to make room for a supermarket.

Pittyvaich

Owner:	Region:	Founded:	Status:
Diageo	Speyside	1974	Demolished

Built by Arthur Bell & Sons on the same ground as Dufftown distillery. For a few years in the 1990s, Pittyvaich was also a back up plant for gin distillation (Gordon´s gin). The distillery was mothballed in 1993 and has now been demolished.

St Magdalene

Owner:	Region:	Founded:	Status:
Diageo	Lowlands	1795	Dismantled

The distillery came into ownership of DCL in 1912 and was at the time a large distillery with 14 washbacks, five stills and with the possibility of producing more than one million litres of alcohol. Ten years after the closure in 1983, the distillery was re-built into flats.

Distilleries
around the globe

Including the subsections:
Europe
North America | Australia & New Zealand
Asia | Africa | South America

Adding new countries to this ever-growing family of malt whisky producing nations is always a pleasure. This year we can for the first time present a Chinese distillery and what a debut. Located in Qionglai, the Laizhou distillery has the capacity to produce five million litres of malt whisky and 20 million litres of grain every year! A little smaller but still of an impressive size, the Three Societies Distillery is the first malt whisky distillery in South Korea, at least in modern times. And while these two distilleries may be thousands of miles from Scotland, the epicentre of malt whisky making, the copper stills they are using were manufactured in Prestonpans near Edinburgh and in Rothes in Speyside.

Meanwhile, the hardships of the pandemic during 2020 don´t seem to have offset too many plans of opening up new distilleries around the world and two countries that definitely stand out are Australia and USA. I doubt whether Bill Lark, who founded his distillery in Tasmania in 1992, or Steve McCarthy, who released the first American single malt back in Oregon in 1999, had any idea of what kind of movement they started in their respective countries. You can by the way read more about them on pages 117 and 123. This plethora of distilleries popping up around the world also brings new blood to the entire malt whisky scene which in turn makes the spirit we love relevant and appealing to new consumers.

Opposite page: The world's first cast copper pot stills also known as Zemon stills at Saburomaru Distillery, Japan

Europe

Austria

casks. There are also several limited releases including heavily peated as well as a 10 year old released in June 2020.

Destillerie Haider

Roggenreith, founded in 1995

waldviertlerwhisky.at

The owners released the first Austrian whisky in 1998. In 2005, they opened up a Whisky Experience World with tours and tastings. The distillery is equipped with two 450 litre Christian Carl copper stills. The main part of the production is made from either 100% malted rye or a combination of rye and malted barley while the rest is from malted barley. Five expressions make up the core range and apart from them there are peated versions as well and limited releases are launched regularly. In autumn 2020 the company´s first blended malt was released.

Broger Privatbrennerei

Klaus, founded in 1976 (whisky since 2008)

broger.info

The production of whisky is supplementing the distillation and production of eau de vie from apples and pears. The distillery is equipped with a 150 litre Christian Carl still. The current range of whiskies consists of Triple Cask, Medium Smoked, Burn Out and the limited Distiller´s Edition. A new range of four whiskies is Hoamat with the grain coming from neighbouring farms.

Other distilleries in Austria

Dachstein Destillerie

Radstadt, founded in 2007

mandlberggut.com

Apart from production of various spirits from berries, malt whisky is also produced. Their only release so far is the five year old Rock-Whisky which is distilled 2,5 times.

Ebner, Brennerei

Absam, founded in 1930 (whisky since 2005)

brennereiebner.at

Whisky is produced in this combination of a guesthouse, brewery and distillery. Besides a single malt from barley, they have also released whiskies made from maize, dinkel and wheat.

Farthofer, Destillerie

Öhling, founded in 1867 (whisky since 2014)

destillerie-farthofer.at

A classic Austrian distillery that has been producing schnapps and various liqueurs for more than a century. Whisky production started in recent years and apart from the blend AWA, the owners have released both single rye and single malt whiskies. The production is organic and they also have their own maltings.

Franz Kostenzer, Edelbrennerei

Maurach/Achensee, founded in 1998, whisky since 2006

schnaps-achensee.at

A huge range of different spirits as well as whisky is produced. Several expressions under the name Whisky Alpin have been released including an 8 year old single malt with a sherry cask finish, an 8 year old single malt rye and, the oldest whisky so far from the owners, an 11 year old single malt doublewood.

Hermann Pfanner, Destillerie

Lauterach, founded in 1854 (whisky since 2005)

pfanner-weine.com

Two core whisky expressions are produced, Pfanner Single Malt Classic and Single Malt Red Wood with a maturation in red wine

Keckeis Destillerie

Rankweil, founded in 2003 (whisky since 2008)

destillerie-keckeis.at

The core expression is Keckeis Single Malt but in early 2021 the limited Stillman´s Finest was launched. Part of the barley has been smoked with beech and maturation takes place in small ex-sherry casks.

Kuenz Naturbrennerei

Dölsach, founded in1643 (whisky since 2014)

kuenz-schnaps.at

With an impressive legacy from the 17th century and owned by the same family for 12 generations, the distillery recently added whisky to their range. The first expression, named Rauchkofel, was released in late 2017 and one of the latest bottlings had been matured in virgin Styrian oak and finished in a sherry cask.

Old Raven

Neustift, founded in 2004

oldraven.at

More than 250,000 litres of beer are produced yearly and the wash from the brewery is used for distillation of whisky. The triple distilled Old Raven comes in three expressions – Old Raven, Old Raven Smoky and the limited edition Old Raven Black Edition.

Pfau Brennerei

Klagenfurt, founded in 1987

pfau.at

Focused on production of "Edelbrände" from fruits and berries, the owners also make whisky. The core expression is a 7 year old single malt but recently a limited 15 year old has also been released.

Puchas, Destillerie (former Lagler, Spezialitätenbrennerei)

Kukmirn, founded in 2009

destillerie-puchas.at

One of few distilleries that are using vacuum distillation. Two single malts are available under the name Kukmirn.

Reisetbauer & Son

Kirchberg-Thening, founded in 1994 (whisky since 1995)

reisetbauer.at

Specialising in brandies and fruit schnapps, a range of malt whiskies is also produced. The current range of whiskies have all been matured in casks that have previously contained Chardonnay and Trockenbeerenauslese and include a 7, a 12 and a 15 year old.

Rogner, Destillerie

Rappottenstein, founded in 1997

destillerie-rogner.at

Producer of a variety of spirits including whisky. The range consists of Rogner Waldviertel Whisky 3/3 (malted and unmalted). Rye Whisky No. 13 and a single malt, Whisky No. 2. A peated 12 year old named Old Power was released in June 2019.

Weutz, Destillerie

St. Nikolai im Sausal, founded in 2002

weutz.at

The distillery added whisky to the range in 2004. Some of the whiskies are produced in the traditional Scottish style while others are more unorthodox, for example based on elderflower.

Wieser Destillerie

Wösendorf in der Wachau, founded in 1996

wieserwachau.com

Traditionally producing schnaps and liqueur, they have also launched the quadruple distilled Uuahouua whisky; American oak, French oak, Pinot Noir and Smoke on the Water.

Belgium

The Owl Distillery

Grâce Hollogne, founded in1997

belgianwhisky.com

The first commercial bottling of Belgium's first single malt, 'The Belgian Owl', appeared in November 2008 and the core expression today is the 3 year old Belgian Owl bottled at 46% or at cask strength. Limited releases include whiskies aged up to 12 years. The distillery is equipped with a 2.1 ton mash tun, four washbacks and two stills that had previously been used at Caperdonich distillery. All the barley used for production comes from farms close to the distillery.

De Molenberg Distillery

Blaasveld, founded in 1471 (whisky since 2003)

stokerijdemolenberg.be

In 2010, the brewer Charles Leclef started a distillery at the family estate Molenberg. The wash still has a capacity of 3,000 litres and the spirit still 2,000 litres. The first bottles under the name Gouden Carolus Single Malt, appeared on the market in 2008 and this 3 year old (including a special sherry oak version) is still the core expression. A limited range called Pure Taste include three different bottlings; Bourbon, Anker and Oloroso and the 7th anniversary edition with a finish in white port casks appeared in autumn 2020.

Other distilleries in Belgium

Braeckman Distillery

Oudenaarde, founded in 1918 (whisky since 2007)

braeckman.eu

A family owned genever distillery with whisky also on the map. Their first release in 2017 was a 9 year old single grain and in 2019, they launched their first 10 year old single malt. They are also distilling the San Graal 5 and 7 year old single malt for the De Graal brewery.

Filliers

Bachte-Maria-Leerne, founded in 1880 (malt whisky since 2008)

filliers.be

For many years, only gin and genever was produced but in 2007 a blended whisky was launched and today there is a range of Goldlys, a single grain whisky, aged up to 14 years. In 2018 two pot stills from Forsyths were installed and malt whisky is now also produced.

Pirlot, Brouwerij

Zandhoven, founded in 1998 (whisky since 2011)

brouwerijpirlot.be

Originally a brewery, their distillery is equipped with a German continuous still and the spirit is matured for 18 months in ex-bourbon casks and then another 18 months in quarter casks from Laphroaig. The first batch of Kempisch Vuur single malt was released in 2016 and several releases have followed.

Radermacher, Distillerie

Raeren, founded in 1836

distillerie.biz

In a wide range of products from this classic distillery, there is also whisky to be found. The brand name is Lambertus and the range consists of both single grain and single malt, aged up to 10 years.

Sas Distillery

Stekene, founded in 2014

sasdistilleries.com

Founded by Benedikt Sas who is a professor in organic chemistry. In a personally designed 200 litre column still, Sas is producing gin, rum, absinthe and whisky according to old recipes. In 2019 the Ignis Templi single malt bottled at 44% was released.

Wilderen, Brouwerij & Distilleederij

Wilderen-St. Truiden, founded in 2011

brouwerijwilderen.be

A combination of a beer brewery with a history going back to 1642 and a distillery founded in 2011. The current core bottling of a single malt is Wild Weasel bottled at either 46% or 60% and a limited sherry cask finish was released in autumn 2019.

.

Stills from the closed Caperdonich now working at the Owl Distillery in Belgium

Czech Republic

Svachovka Distillery

České Budějovice, founded in 2016

svachovkadomu.cz

Owned by Vaclav Cvach, this is a combination of a brewery, distillery, hotel, restaurant and spa. Equipped with stainless steel washbacks and copper stills the distillery produces fruit brandy as well as 5-10,000 litres of Svach´s Old Well single malt whisky yearly. The first 3 year old single malt was launched in autumn 2019 and a wide variety of expressions have been released since.

Gold Cock Distillery

Vizovice, founded in 1877

rjelinek.cz

The whisky is produced in three versions – a 3 year old blended whisky, a 12 year old single malt and different versions of Small Batch single malt including a 20 year old. Production was stopped for a while but after the brand and distillery were acquired by R. Jelinek a.s. the whisky began life anew.

Denmark

Stauning Whisky

Stauning, founded in 2006

stauningwhisky.dk

The first Danish purpose-built malt whisky distillery entered a more adolescent phase in 2009, after having experimented with two small pilot stills bought from Spain. More stills were installed in 2012. The preconditions, however, were completely changed in 2015 when it was announced that Diageo´s incubator fund project, Distil Ventures, would spend £10m to increase the capacity of Stauning. In 2018, it became evident what the investment had meant to the company. A new distillery with no less than 24 copper stills, all directly fired, was opened. The floor malting were increased to 1,000 m² on four floors and the total production capacity is now 900,000 litres of pure alcohol. The core range was redesigned in late 2020 and now consists of Rye, Kaos Triple Malt (both rye and barley) and Smoke Single Malt. A recent limited expression was the Stauning El Clásico – a rye which has been finished in vermouth casks.

Braunstein

Köge, founded in 2005 (whisky since 2007)

braunstein.dk

Denmark's first micro-distillery, built in an already existing brewery in Køge, just south of Copenhagen. The wash comes from the own brewery and a Holstein type of still, with four plates in the rectification column, is used for distillation. A substantial part of the required barley is ecologically grown in Denmark. The first release from the distillery and the first release of a malt whisky produced in Denmark was in 2010. The most recent releases include Library Collection 21:1, an unpeated whisky matured in PX sherry casks and Edition No: 12, peated and oloroso matured. There is also Danica which is reserved for the duty-free market.

Other distilleries in Denmark

Als, Destilleriet

Sydals, founded in 2018

destillerietals.dk

Built as a combined gin- and whisky distillerie with aid from Henric Molin of Spirit of Hven fame, the whisky is distilled in a 350 litre column still. The first single malt is due in 2021.

Copenhagen Distillery

Copenhagen, founded in 2014

copenhagendistillery.com

The first distillery was situated in a listed building close to the Copenhagen Airport but a few years ago it was moved closer to the city. A bus garage has been turned into a combination of a distillery and a creative hot spot including a bar and plenty of space for concerts and other gatherings. A wide range of gin, vodka and liqueurs have been produced as an initial "bread and butter" but this is first and foremost a whisky distillery with some unusual features. The grain is milled using a Skiold plate mill and then mashed in a 0.6 ton mash tun. Following a 7-10 day fermentation

The Stauning Distillery which houses no less than 24 copper pot stills

on the grain, the liquid is distilled one time in a 1,050 litre copper hybrid still by Müller which has a 2-plate column attached as well as dephlegmator to increase the options while distilling. The spirit is mainly matured in toasted 100-litre casks made of Hungarian oak but more unusual casks are used as well. There are three different ranges; Refine which is a more traditional whisky, Raw where the all the flavours are "dialled up" and the experimental Rare bottlings where sometimes alternative grains are used. The First Edition was released in February 2020 and followed later in the year by Raw Edition and Rare Edition batch 1.Rare Edition batch 2 (aged in the distillery's own gin casks) appeared in summer 2021.

Enghaven, Braenderiet

Mellerup, founded in 2014

enghaven-whisky.dk

Producing also rum and gin, the first whisky release, in autumn 2017, was a rye matured in both bourbon casks and port casks and in October 2018, the first single malt from a rum cask was released. The latest was the wine-finished Single Malt No. 3 in late 2020.

Falster Destilleri & Bryghus

Væggerløse, founded in 2019

falsterdestilleri.dk

A combined brewery and distillery producing several different types of spirits in two Portuguese pot stills, including malt whisky. The first whisky will not be released until early 2023.

Fary Lochan Destilleri

Give, founded in 2009

farylochan.dk

The main part of the malted barley is imported from the UK but they also malt some themselves. The first whisky was released in 2013 and a number of bottlings have been released since then. One of the latest was an 8 year old single bourbon cask in March 2021. The distillery has also been represented in the Scotch Malt Whisky Society range as well as in Nordic Casks from Berry Brothers.

Limfjorden, Braenderiet

Roslev, founded in 2013

braenderiet.dk

The distillery moved to a new location in 2018 and a brewery was added. Apart from peated and unpeated single malt and rye, the distillery also produces gin and rum. The first single malt was released in 2016 and was later followed by Lindorm whisky with the third edition (a 6 year old, peated PX sherry cask) released in March 2020. Three months later a 6 year old grain whisky appeared.

Mosgaard Whisky

Oure, founded in 2015

mosgaardwhisky.dk

Three alambic stills (two wash stills and one spirit still), were designed by the owners and made in Portugal. There is also a 150 kilo mash tun and four stainless steel washbacks with a 7 day fermentation. The whisky is produced from organically grown barley and the maturation takes place primarily in small 50 litre casks. The first single malts, matured in oloroso casks and PX sherry appeared in spring 2019. Since then there have been a number of releases including Peated No. 6 (a combination of French and American oak). In autumn 2020 a new range called Experiment Series was introduced where the first expression was a vatting of whiskies from bourbon, virgin French oak, PX and oloroso.

Nordisk Brænderi/Thy Whisky

Fjerritslev, founded in 2009 (whisky since 2011)

nordiskbraenderi.dk, thy-whisky.dk

The ecological barley used for the production is grown in fields surrounding the distillery. In the first 8-9 years around ten whiskies have been released under the name Thy Whisky, the first in 2014. One of the latest, in March 2021, is No. 14 Bøg, a beech-smoked single malt from an oloroso cask.

Nyborg Destilleri

Nyborg, founded in 1997 (whisky since 2009)

fioniawhisky.com

Opened as an extension to an existing brewery, the distillery moved in 2017 to new premises. The distillery is equipped with two copper pot stills with attached columns. The first release of Isle of Fionia single malt was in 2012. The new range of whiskies is called Ardor with Peated, Black and Danish Oak as some of the latest releases. Another range of special and limited releases is called Adventurous Spirit which includes a 10 year old and Darling (a combination os STR casks and oloroso).

Radius Distillery

Præstø, founded in 2019

radiusdistillery.com

A farmhouse distillery focused on gin and apple brandy but also producing malt whisky from their own barley. Unusually, the whisky is distilled on the grain with an anticipated release in 2024.

Sall Whisky Distillery

Sall, founded in 2018

sallwhisky.com

Gin but above all, malt whisky made from ecologically grown barley from the land of one of the owners is produced. New make was launched in late 2019 and the first whisky is expected in 2022.

Søgaards Bryghus

Aalborg, founded in 2010 (whisky since 2018)

soegaardsbryghus.dk

Originally a brewery, the owners embarked on an exciting distillery adventure in 2018. Four farmers on four different islands in northern Jutland were sent Odyssey sowing barley in spring 2018. The barley was harvested and malted in autumn that same year and used at the brewery/distillery in Aalborg to distill new make in spring 2019. This was filled into Jack Daniels casks and then sent back to each of the islands for maturation. The whisky will be released in spring 2022 under the name Vindblæst (Windswept) . A true terroir experiment if ever there was one!

Trolden Distillery

Kolding, founded in 2011

trolden.com

The distillery is a part of a brewery and the wash from the brewery is fermented for 4-5 days before distillation. The first single malt release was Nimbus in 2014 and in May 2020, the distillery moved to new premises. The seventh release, in December 2020, was a vatting of bourbon and sherry casks.

Ærø Whisky

Ærøskøbing, founded in 2013

ærøwhisky.dk

Situated on the small island of Ærø the distillation started in stills from Portugal. In 2016, new and larger stills were installed and the production increased. The first bottling was a bourbonmatured single cask released in 2017 while the current range consists of one whisky matured in American oak and several special maturations (Danish oak, oloroso and French red wine casks).

England

St. George´s Distillery

Roudham, Norfolk, founded in 2006

englishwhisky.co.uk

St. George´s Distillery near Thetford in Norfolk was started by father and son, James and Andrew Nelstrop, and came on stream in December 2006. This made it the first English malt whisky distillery for over a hundred years. In December 2009, it was time for the release of the first legal whisky called Chapter 5 (the first four chapters had been young malt spirit). This was then followed by several more chapters (up to 17) but the sometimes uncomprehensible range was then exhanged for a range with two core expressions; The English Original and The English Smokey. There are also regular, limited releases in the Small Batch series including Virgin Oak, Smokey Virgin and Rum Cask. The latest small batch were Gently Smoked Sherry Cask and Triple Distilled Unpeated. In June 2020 The English 11 years old (the first with an age statement) was released and in early 2021 Triple Distilled Peated single cask appeared. In 2017 an innovative sub range was introduced – The Norfolk – with whiskies made from different grains. Currently there are two expressions, Farmers and Parched.

The distillery is equipped with a stainless steel semi-lauter mash tun with a copper top and three stainless steel washbacks with a fermentation time of 85 hours. There is one pair of stills, a 2,800 litre wash still and a 1,800 litre spirit still. All the whiskies from the distillery are un chill-filtered and without colouring. The distillery also has an excellent, newly expanded visitor centre, including a shop with more than 300 different whiskies.

Cotswolds Distillery

Stourton, founded in 2014

cotswoldsdistillery.com

The distillery is the brainchild of Dan Szor who recently made his debut as an author as well with Spirit Guide: In Search of an Authentic Life. Production of both whisky and gin started in September 2014. There are four stills; one wash still (2,400 litres), one spirit still (1,600 litres) and two Holstein stills for production of gin and other spirits. The rest of the equipment includes a 0.5 ton mash tun and eight stainless steel wash backs with a fermentation time of four days. All the barley is grown locally and is floor malted at Warminster Maltings. The first product for sale was their gin in 2014 while the first single malt, the 3 year old Odyssey, was launched in 2017. In early 2018, the distillery started experimenting with rye whisky and in August that same year the owners made their first trials producing rum. Today, the core whisky expression is the Cotswolds Single Malt which has been matured in a combination of ex-bourbon and STR casks. Widely available, bottled at cask strength and produced in yearly batches are Sherry Cask, Founder´s Choice and Peated Cask. In 2020 the first release in the limited Hearts & Craft series appeared with the second, a full time maturation in Pineau Des Charentes casks, being launched in April 2021. The visitor centre, which was recently rebuilt, welcomes 30,000 people every year.

Lakes Distillery

Bassenthwaite Lake, founded in 2014

lakesdistillery.com

Headed by Paul Currie, who was the co-founder of Isle of Arran distillery, a consortium of private investors founded the distillery. The distillery is equipped with two stills for the whisky production, each with both copper and stainless steel condensers, and a third still for the distillation of gin. A £4.25m investment from Comhar Capital made it possible to install another eight washbacks in November 2020 thereby trebling the production capacity to more than 1 million bottles per year. The inaugural bottling, The Lakes Malt Genesis, was released on 29th June 2018. A widely available core expression has yet to emerge. Instead the single malts are divided into three series. In September 2019, the first installment in a four-year collection of single malts called The Quatrefoil Collection was released with numbers three and four following in 2020 and 2021. In September 2019, the distillery launched its first limited edition in the sherry-led Whiskymaker´s Reserve series with the fourth expression being released in April 2021. Finally, there is the Whiskymaker´s Editions where the distillery´s whisky maker Dhavall Gandhi can play around with one-off releases that differ from the house style.

The two stills at St George´s Distillery in Norfolk

Spirit of Yorkshire Distillery

Hunmanby, founded in 2016

spiritofyorkshire.com

The distillery, founded by Tom Mellor and David Thompson, is actually situated in two separate locations with a one ton mash tun and two 10,000 litre washbacks standing at Tom´s farm which also houses World Top Brewery while the 5,000 litre wash still and a 3,500 litre spirit still are 2,5 miles down the road in Hunmanby. A four plate column is designed to run in tandem with the spirit still and part of the production is distilled using the column to achieve a lighter character of the new make. All the barley comes from the farm and the distillery produces 80,000 litres of pure alcohol a year and that also includes small volumes made from rye. There are plans to increase capacity and the distillery also has a visitor centre with daily tours. Their core bottling, first released in 2019, is the bourbonmatured Filey Bay Flagship. Recent limited expressions include batch 2 of their moscatel finish, an IPA finish and a sherry cask reserve batch 2 – all of them released in autumn 2021. Their first rye whisky will not be released until at least 2024.

Bimber Distillery

London, founded in 2015

bimberdistillery.co.uk

The distillery buys its floor malted barley from Warminster Maltings and the spirit is distilled in a 1,000 litre wash still and a 600 litre spirit still – both alembic made in Portugal and direct fired. The owners use open top wooden washbacks with a seven day fermentation and more were installed in 2019. They have also done trials with peated poduction using barley that they floor malted themselves. Distillation began in May 2016 and the first release from the distillery was a vodka. In September 2019, it was time for the distillery´s inaugural single malt bottling – aptly named The First. Among the latest are an oloroso cask and the first port matured from the distillery, both in March 2021. In July 2021 a range of 14 single malts destined for different international markets was launched and later that year another seven bottlings were added to the Country Collection.

Other distilleries in England

Adnams Copper House Distillery

Southwold, founded in 2010

adnams.co.uk

Adnams Brewery in Suffolk added distillation of spirits to their production in December 2010 and, apart from whisky – gin, vodka and absinthe are produced. The first whisky was released in 2013 and the range now consists of Single Malt, Rye Malt (75% rye and 25% barley) and Triple Malt (wheat, barley and oats).

Chase Distillery

Rosemaund Farm, Hereford, founded in 2008

chasedistillery.co.uk

The main product from the distillery is Chase Vodka made from potatoes and gin has also become part of their range. By the end of 2011, the first whisky was distilled but so far it hasn´t been released. The distillery is equipped with a copper still with a five plate column and an attached rectification column with another 42 plates. In October 2020, Diageo bought the distillery.

Circumstance Distillery

Bristol, founded in 2018

circumstancedistillery.com

The owners idea is to make whisky and rum in a flexible distillery equipped with a pot still with attached columns. The very first bottling in March 2019 was Circumstantial Barley 1:1:1:1:6, a spirit from 100% malted barley that had matured for two months using charred oak spindles and then another four months in ex-bourbon

casks. The five digit number in this and following releases is a code identifying batch, fermentation (including mash bill), distillation, maturation and age in months.

Cooper King Distillery

Sutton-on-the-Forest, founded in 2018

cooperkingdistillery.co.uk

Inspired by a trip to Australia, Abbie Neilson and Chris Jaume decided to equip their distillery with a Tasmanian copper pot still. The barley if floor malted at Warminster Maltings, the mash is stirred by hand and fermentation times are 6-7 days. The owners released their first gin in 2018, whisky production started in June 2019 and the first malt whisky is expected in 2024. The distillery practises a combination of vacuum distillation and traditional distillation.

Copper Rivet Distillery

Chatham, founded in 2016

copperrivetdistillery.com

Situated in an old pump house in the Chatham Docks, the distillery is equipped with a copper pot still with a column attached as well as a special gin still. Dockyard Gin and Vela Vodka were released early on and in April 2017, Son of a Gun, an 8 week old grain spirit (rye, wheat and barley) was released. The first Masthouse single malt was released in June 2020 with a second batch in early 2021.

Dartmoor Distillery

Bovey Tracey, founded in 2016

dartmoorwhiskydistillery.co.uk

Greg Millar and Simon Crow acquired a 50 year old alembic still in Cognac. The brought it to England, refurbished it and attached a copper ”wash warmer” to pre warm the wash and increase the copper contact. the first single malt was launched in February 2020 and the current core range of three includes ex-bourbon, ex-oloroso and ex-Bordeaux wine casks.

Durham Whisky

Durham, founded in 2014 (whisky since 2018)

durhamwhisky.co.uk

The distillery started producing gin and vodka and in 2018 whisky was added to the range. In 2021, the distillery (as well as bar and visitor centre) moved to larger premises. Using local malt, the distillery is equipped with a 1,200 litre wash still and a 1,000 litre spirit still. So far, no single malt has been released.

Forest Distillery, The

Macclesfield, founded in 2014

theforestdistillery.com

Established in a 17th century stone barn in the Peak District National Park, the 500 litre pot still was later moved to the legendary Cat & Fiddle Inn and thus becoming Britain´s highest altitude whisky distillery. Gin has been released as well as sourced whisky with their first own single malt expected in 2022.

Henstone Distillery

Oswestry, Shropshire, founded in 2017

henstonedistillery.com

Commissioned in December 2017, the distillery first released gin, vodka, apple brandy and (in early 2020) a corn ”whisky”. The first malt whisky, distilled in a Kothe copper hybrid still, was released in January 2021 with more bottlings following during the year.

Isle of Wight Distillery

Newport, founded in 2015

isleofwightdistillery.com

The distillery is currently focused on vodka and their Mermaid

Gin. For the whisky, the fermented wash is bought from a local brewery and distilled in hybrid copper stills. The first whisky was distilled in December 2015 but has not yet been released.

London Distillery Company, The

London, founded in 2012

londondistillery.com

The first release was Dodd´s Gin in 2013 and in December the same year, production of whisky started. A rye whisky was launched in 2018 and a single malt made from barley, Cask 109, was released in early 2019.. Facing administration, the distillery was bought in early 2020 by honey-infused spirits brand The British Honey Company. They now have plans to move the distillery to Tusmore Estate in Oxfordshire.

Ludlow Distillery

Craven Arms, founded in 2014

ludlowdistillery.co.uk

Equipped with a 200 litre still, this tiny distillery just south of Shrewsbury released its first single malt, Young Prince, in November 2018. They also produce wine, brandy and eau de vie

Wharf Distillery

Towcester, founded in 2015

wharfdistillery.co.uk

Probably the smallest whisky distillery in England also producing gin and rum. The first malt whisky release appeared in January 2019 and their fifth barrel was filled in December 2020.

White Peak Distillery

Ambergate, Derbyshire, founded in 2017

whitepeakdistillery.co.uk

The distillery made the first distillation in April 2018. Gin, rum, and a 30 months old malt spirit have been released but the first bottlings of the lightly peated malt are not expected until 2021.

Whittaker´s Distillery

Harrogate, founded in 2015 (whisky since 2019)

whittakersgin.com

The owners have already had success with Whittaker Gin but whisky was in their thoughts from the beginning. In summer 2019, two new, larger stills were installed and whisky production started in the autumn. The release of their single malt is planned for 2025.

Faroe Islands 

Einar´s Distillery

Klaksvik, founded in 2016

einarsdistillery.com

Following a change in local laws, the first legal distillery in the Faroe Islands was built adjacent to the Föroya Bjór brewery founded in 1888. Today the company is run by the third and fourth generations of the family - Einar Waag and his daughter Annika. The wash obviously comes from the brewery´s 2 ton mash tun and is then fermented in three stainless steel washbacks and distilled in a pot still from Arnold Holstein. The owners also have plans for a second still. The distillery has a capacity of 50,000 litres and the first product was an aquavit and in October 2016, the first whisky was distilled. The first single malt, matured in a combination of ex-bourbon and ex-oloroso, was released in November 2020 followed by another three in February, May and July 2021.

Finland 

Teerenpeli

Lahti, founded in 2002

teerenpeli.com

The original distillery, located in a restaurant in Lahti, is equipped with one wash still (1,500 litres) and one spirit still (900 litres). A completely new distillery, with one 3,000 litre wash still and two

Einar Waag, founder of the first distillery in the Faroe Islands, with his grand daughter Elisa by his side

900 litre spirit stills, was opened in 2015 in the same house as the brewery and today the old distillery serves as a "laboratory" for new spirits. The core range consists of a 10 year old matured in bourbon casks, Kaski which is a 100% sherry maturation, Portti which is finished for 1.5 years in port casks, the peated Savu and the 7 year old Kulo, matured in a combination of PX and oloroso sherry casks. Recent limited bottlings include Lemmon Lintu, the first in a series of three called Rum Cask trilogy, a cask strength version of Savu and a 10 year old Port single cask.

Other distilleries in Finland

Helsinki Distilling Company

Helsinki, founded in 2014

hdco.fi

  Equipped with one mash tun, three washbacks and two stills. A gin was released in 2014 and on the whisky side, the focus is on malted rye but also single malt made from barley and whisky made from corn. The latest single malt from barley was a 4 year old PX finish in 2020. In spring 2021 they distilled their first organic whisky.

Ägräs Distillery

Fiskars, founded in 2017

agradistillery.com

  Located in the south of Finland in a small factory village dating back to the 17th scentury. Today it is renowned for its artisan community with a variety of activities within art, craft and design, Ägräs Distillery produces various spirit such as aqvavit, gin and also malt whisky. No whisky has yet been released

France

Distillerie Warenghem

Lannion, Bretagne, founded in1900 (whisky since 1994)

distillerie-warenghem.com

  Leon Warenghem founded the distillery and in 1967, his grandson Paul-Henri Warenghem, together with his associate, Yves Leizour, took over the reins. They moved the distillery to its current location on the outskirts of Lannion in Brittany. Gilles Leizour, Yves' son, took over at the end of the 1970's and it was he who added whisky to the Warenghem range. WB, a blend from malted barley and wheat, saw the light in 1987 and Armorik – the first ever French single malt – was released in 1998. The distillery is equipped with a 6,000 litre semi-lauter mashtun, six stainless steel washbacks and two, traditional copper pot stills (a 6,000 litre wash still and a 3,500 litre spirit still). Around 180,000 litres of pure alcohol (including 20% grain whisky) are produced yearly. The single malt core range consists of Armorik Édition Originale and Armorik Sherry Finish. Both are around 4 years old, matured in ex-bourbon casks and with a finish in sherry butts. Armorik Classic, a mix of 4 to 8 year old whiskies and the 7 year old Armorik Double Maturation which has spent time in both new oak and sherry wood are earmarked for export as well as the Armorik Sherry Cask and a 10 year old. Warenghem has also distilled rye whisky with the 10 year old Roof Rye being released in September 2021. In 2018 the first peated expression, Triagoz, was released and in July 2021 the Armorik 16 year old became the oldest French whisky ever sold.

Distillerie Rozelieures

Rozelieures, Grand Est, founded in 1860 (whisky since 2003)

whiskyrozelieures.com

  Hubert Grallet and his son-in-law, Christophe Dupic started with whisky production in 2003 and launched the Glen Rozelieures brand in 2007. With a production of 200,000 litres, Rozelieures is one of the largest distilleries in France. Five versions are currently available: Original Collection aged in ex-fino casks, the lightly peated Rare Collection matured in ex-sauternes, Fumé Collection (20ppm) matured in ex-fino, Tourbé Collection and the un-peated Subtil Collection. In 2018 they opened a malting plant with a capacity of 2,000 tons and in September 2021, they released a batch of whiskies made from their own barley and malted on site.

Distillerie des Menhirs

Plomelin, Bretagne, founded in 1986 (whisky since 1998)

distillerie.bzh

  Originally a portable column still distillery, Guy Le Lay and his wife Anne-Marie settled down in 1986 and the first lambig with the

In 2019 a new visitor centre was built at Warenghem Distillery in Brittany

name Distillerie des Menhirs was released in 1989. Shortly after, Guy Le Lay came up with the idea of producing a 100% buckwheat whisky. Eddu Silver was launched in 2002, followed by Eddu Gold, Eddu Silver Brocéliande and Eddu Diamant. Ed Gwenn, aged for 4 years in ex-cognac barrels, was released in 2016 and in 2019, Les Menhirs released a vintage 2004 which was the first whisky distilled from malted buckwheat. In 2021 the distillery launched a a new Eddu Collection and a 15 year old Vintage 2005.

Domaine des Hautes-Glaces

Saint Jean d´Hérans, Auvergne-Rhône Alpes, founded in 2009 (whisky since 2014)

hautesglaces.com

At an altitude of 900 metres in the the French Alps, Jérémy Bricka and Frédéric Revol decided to produce whisky from barley to bottle. Apart from growing their own barley, all the parts of whisky production take place at the distillery – malting, brewing, distillation, maturation and bottling. They are producing the first French single estate whisky and organically too. Principium, the first whisky made at the distillery has been available since 2014. Domaine des Hautes Glaces was bought by Rémy Cointreau in 2015 and a second distillery started operating in June 2020. The core range includes two whiskies, Les Moissons Malt and Les Moissons Rye. Single cask bottlings such as Ceros or Secale (rye), Flavis, Tekton, Ampelos or Obscuros (barley) are released from time to time.

Miclo

Lapoutroie, Grand Est, founded in 1970 (whisky since 2012)

distillerie-miclo.com

Founded by Gilbert Miclo the distillery started by specialising in fruit spirits. It is equipped with four Holstein waterbath pot stills and since 2012, wort from a local brewery is fermented and distilled into malt whisky. In September 2021 the range was revamped and now consists of Welche Classique ex-Sauternes, Welche Fumé, Welche Tourbé and Welche Classique ex-Bourgogne.

Bercloux

Bercloux, Nouvelle Aquitaine, founded in 2000 (whisky since 2014)

distillerie-bercloux.fr

Philippe Laclie opened his brewery in 2000 and in 2014 he took the next step and bought an 800 litre Stupfler pot still. The first two bottlings of Bercloux Single Malt Whisky were released in 2018. In November 2019, the distillery was bought by the company Les Bienheureux. Their intention was to secure stock and production for their own brand – Bellevoye triple malt whisky which was launched at the end of 2015. In 2021, Bercloux launched a new brand, Lefort.

Domaine Mavela

Corsica, founded in 1991 (whisky since 2001)

domaine-mavela.com

The creators of the P&M brand are the Pietra family, responsible for Pietra beer since 1996, and Venturini family who set up the Mavela distillery in 1991. Distilled in a Holstein still and aged in ex-Corsican muscat casks, the P&M single malt was sold for the first time in 2004. End of 2017, the distillery released its first 12 year old and in 2018 the owners unveiled a completely new range of three expresions: P&M Signature, P&M Red Oak (aged in ex-red-wine casks) and P&M Tourbé (peated). Recently both a 13 and a 14 year old have been released and the owners are now expanding with a brewery of their own, a second still and a new warehouse.

Glann ar Mor

Pleubian, Bretagne, founded in 1999

glannarmor.com

The founder, Jean Donnay, started his first trials in 1999 while regular production commenced in 2005. Two small stills are

directly fired and worm tubs are used for condensing the spirit. The fermentation in wooden washbacks is long and the distillation is very slow. There are two versions of the whisky – the unpeated Glann ar Mor and the peated Kornog. Core expressions are usually bottled at 46% but every year a number of limited releases are made including single casks and cask strength bottlings. Early 2019, Glann Ar Mor released its oldest bottling, a Kornog 12 year old, the first ever French triple distilled single malt called Teir Gwech and Ar Seizh Greun, distilled from a mash of seven malted cereals: barley, wheat, rye, oat, millet, spelt and triticale. In 2020 Jean Donnay sold the distillery to Maison Villevert.

Hepp, Distillerie

Uberach, Grand Est, founded in 1972 (whisky since 2005)

distillerie-hepp.com

A family-owned distillery with two main expressions without age statement; Tharcis Hepp (matured in bourbon and sherry) and Johnny Hepp (bourbon and white wine). In 2018 three new bottlings were released; Ouisky, Tharcis Hepp Tourbé and French Flanker. Hepp is also behind the brand Roborel de Climens, launched in 2019 by Aymeric Roborel. The idea is to present whiskies finished in single grape wine cask. Merlot, Sauvignon, Semillon, Rolle, Grenache and Ugni Blanc have already been released.

Castan, Distillerie

Villeneuve Sur Vère, Occitanie, founded in 1946 (whisky since 2010)

distillerie-castan.com

In 2010 Sébastien Castan moved the portable still that had been in the family for generations into a proper distillery and the same year he distilled his first whisky. In 2016, a brewery was built to supply the beer. The range consists of five bottlings: Villanova Berbie (ex-white wine casks), Gost (new cask), Terrocita (peated), Roja (ex-red wine casks) and Segala (rye). In June 2019 the construction of a new distillery started which has now been completed.

Distillerie Naguelann

Languenan, Bretagne, founded in 2014

naguelann.bzh

Lenaïck Lemaitre launched Naguelann Company as an independent bottler, sourcing malt spirits and whiskies from other producers before ageing them in different casks. The range includes Mesk, Gran'pa, Ed Unan and Ruz!. While working as a bottler, Lenaïck started to build his own distillery fitted with two small stills. Dieil Tantad released in 2020 is his first bottling from own production.

Rouget de Lisle

Bletterans, Bourgogne-Franche Comté, founded in 1994 (whisky since 2006),

brasserie-rouget-lisle.com

Rouget de Lisle is a brewery created by Bruno Mangin and his wife. In 2006, they commissioned the Brûlerie du Revermont to distil whisky for them. The first Rouget De Lisle single malt whisky was released in 2009 and in 2012, Bruno Mangin bought his own still. Current bottlings are from the numerous casks he filled during his association with the Tissot family. End of 2018, Bruno Mangin renamed the brand BM Signature. The core range consists of two NAS aged in ex-vin de paille and ex-Macvin casks. Apart from that there are a lof of vintages ranging from 2008 to 2015.

Other distilleries in France

Bertrand, Distillerie

Uberach, Grand Est, founded in 1874 (whisky since 2002)

distillerie-bertrand.com

The manager Jean Metzger, gets the malt from a local brewer and distils it in Holstein type stills. The core bottling is a single malt aged in new barrels and barrels which have previously contained the fortified wine Banyuls. Being a wine connoisseur, Metzger started to experiment with ageing and finishing whisky in casks having held different French wines including casks from the famous Domaine de la Romanée Conti.

BOWS

Montauban, Occitanie, founded in 2017

bowsdistillerie.com

Bows, which stands for Brave Occitan Wild Spirits, is a project started by Benoit Garcia, a former engineer. He designed and built the distillery himself including a 900 litre still fitted with a rectifying column. The first malt spirit, Bestiut, was released in 2017 while the first whiskies, Benleioc Original and Benleioc Tourbe Intense both made from a stout beer, appeared in spring 2021.

Breuil, Château du

Le Breuil en Auge, Normandie, founded in 1952 (whisky since 2015)

chateau-breuil.biz

Le Chateau du Breuil is one of the most beautiful estates in Normandy. The reputation of its Calvados is well established and it is one of the two French leaders in the cider brandy category. Fitted with two Charentais stills the distillery recently started producing also malt whisky. The first expressions, including a smoky version after maturation in Laphroaig casks, appeared in March 2021 under the name Le Breuil (the wood, in old French).

Brûlerie du Revermont

Nevy sur Seille, Bourgogne-Franche Comté, founded in 1991 (whisky since 2003)

marielouisetissot-levin.com

For years, the Tissot family were travelling distillers offering their services to local wine producers. Relying upon a unique distillation set-up, a Blavier still with three pots, they have been producing single malt whisky since 2003. Pascal and Joseph Tissot launched their own whisky brand Prohibition in 2011, aged in "feuillettes" which is 114 litre half-casks.

Brunet, Distillerie

Cognac, Nouvelle Aquitaine, founded in 1920 (whisky since 2006)

drinkbrenne.com

In 2006, Stéphane Brunet made the bold move to start whisky production in the Poitou-Charentes region - famous for its cognac production. His whisky, Tradition Malt, was released in 2009 and was launched in the USA by whisky enthusiast Allison Parc under the brand Brenne. In September 2015 a 10 year old version was released in small quantities in the USA. Since 2015 Brenne Cuvée Spéciale is also available in France.

Bughes, Distillerie des

Solignac, Auvergne, founded in 2017

homedistillers.fr

The founder, Béranger Mayoux, started with three stills, directly heated using gas and with a capacity of 300 litres. Now, twelve stills are in operation! The profile of La Distillerie des Bughes is that of an American moonshiner or Scottish illegal still. Hence the brand name, Home Distillers. Their first whisky was aged in sherry casks.

Castor, Distillerie du

Troisfontaines, Grand Est, founded in 1985 (whisky since 2011)

distillerie-du-castor.com

Equipped with two small stills the distillery produces whisky as well as fruit and pomace brandies. The distillate is aged in ex-white wine (sauvignon blanc) casks and then finished in ex-sherry casks. The whisky is sold under the name St Patrick.

Charlier & Fils

Warcq, Grand Est, founded in 2015

facebook.com/laquinarde

It was Yann Charlier's ambition already from start to create his own whisky from indigeneous yeast and practising long fermentations (7 to 8 days). The first Charlier whisky was released in May 2020. The production will increase in the coming years as Yann Charlier recently bought another still from Gilbert Holl.

Claeyssens de Wambrechies, Distillerie

Wambrechies, Hauts de France, founded in 1817 (whisky since 2000)

wambrechies.com

One of the oldest distilleries in France famous for its genever. The first whisky, a 3 year old, was released in 2003 followed by an 8 year old in 2009. In 2019, the distillery was bought by Saint-Germain brewery/distillery. It is currently mothballed but a new Holstein still is expected to make its appearance soon. The range consists of Wambrechies 5 year old, Sherry and the peated Tourbé.

Didier Barbe Entreprise

Lusigny Sur Barse, Grand Est, founded in 2012

didierbarbeentreprise.com

Using and old still Didier Barbe started producing brandies and gin. In 2017 the first whisky was produced from the wash from local breweries. The first whisky, aged in ratafia barrels, Barbe & Fils, was launched in May 2020.

Dreumont

Neuville-en-Avesnois, Hauts de France, founded in 2005 (whisky since 2011)

ladreum.com

In 2011 Jérôme Dreumont built his own 300 litre still and has since then been filling only one cask per year. His first whisky, distilled from a mix of peated and non-peated barley, was launched in 2015 and has since then been followed by more releases.

Ergaster, Distillerie

Passel, Hauts de Frances, founded in 2015

distillerie-ergaster.com

Fitted with a Stupfler pot still, peated and unpeated spirit is slowly aging in ex-Cognac, ex-Pineau des Charentes, ex-Vin Jaune and ex-Banyuls casks. The first whisky, the organic Ergaster Nature was launched in 2018 and was followed by Ergaster Tourbé in 2019.

Fabrique à Alcools, La

Pecqueuse, Ile de France, founded in 2016

lafabriqueaalcools.com

After studies at Heriot Watt University in Edinburgh, Eric Esnault founded Parisis Brewery in 2003. In 2017, together with Christophe Astorri, he bought two Holstein stills and started to distill whisky. In June 2021 a single cask named Le Premier de la Fabrique was launched followed by Alliage, Chevreuse and Fromenteau.

Hagmeyer

Balbronn, Alsace, founded in 2016

distillerie-hagmeyer.com

Originally fruit producers for several generations, Willy and his brother André started whisky production after sourcing beer from Perle brewery. The first edition of WAH was launched in October 2019, after 42 months in Alsatian wine barrels.

Hautefeuille Esquisse, Distillerie

Beaucourt En Santerre, Hauts de France, founded in 2015

distilleriedhautefeuille.com

Founded by the farmer Étienne d'Hautefeuille and drink specialist and retailer Gaël Mordac. Fitted with an 800 litre Stupfler still, a new warehouse and a filling/bottling room was built in 2020. The first whisky, Loup Hardi distilled at another distillery, was launched in December 2018. The first release from their own production appeared in May 2020.

Laurens, Domaine

Clairvaux d'Aveyron, Occitanie, founded in 1983 (whisky since 2014)

domaine-laurens.com

The wine estate Domaine Laurens was founded in 1983 and in 2014, whisky production started with the help of a neighbouring brewery. The first versions. Red Léon, aged in white dry aveyron wine ex-casks, and Blue Léon, red ratafia ex-casks, were launched in 2017.

Lehmann, Distillerie

Obernai, Grand Est, founded in 1850 (whisky since 2001)

distillerielehmann.com

Yves Lehmann inherited the old family distillery in 1982 and in 1993 he decided to move all the equipment to a new distillery. The first regular bottling, aged for seven years in Bordeaux casks, was launched in 2008. The range now includes Elsass Origine (4-6 years) and Elsass Gold (6-8 years), both matured in ex-white wine casks, and Elsass Premium (8 years) matured in ex-Sauternes casks. Florent Lehmann joined his father in 2020 and soon after launched a new range, Birdy, with three bottlings celebrating the legendary French art de vivre: Coup de Foudre, C'est la vie and Rendez-vous.

Leisen

Malling, Grand Est, founded in 1898 (whisky since 2012)

distillerie-leisen-petite-hettange.fr

Since 1898, the Leisen family has distilled fruit spirits but also spirits made from rye and barley. The distillery is equipped with two Carl stills (250 and 350 litres respectively). In 2018, Jean-Marie Leisen released his first bottles under the JML brand.

Merlet & Fils

Saint-Sauvant, Nouvelle Aquitaine, founded in 1850 (whisky since 2015)

distillerie-merlet.com

Internationally renowned for their liqueurs, aperitifs and cognacs, the Merlet family started to produce whisky in 2015. The distillery is equipped with five Charentais stills and in December 2020 the first whisky was released under the name Coperies

Meyer, Distillerie

Hohwarth, Grand Est, founded in 1958 (whisky since 2004)

distilleriemeyer.fr

The first bottlings from the distillery were launched by Jean-Claude Meyer in 2007 one year before he passed away and his two sons took over the operation. There are two malt whiskies for sale, Meyer's Pur Malt and Meyer Pur Malt Le Fumé.

Michard, Brasserie

Limoges, Nouvelle Aquitaine, founded in 1987 (whisky since 2008)

bieres-michard.com

Started as a craft brewery, Jean Michard began to also produce whisky in 2008 and the first bottling was released in 2011. It was followed by a second batch in 2013. Jean Michard has now retired and the still does not work very often but a brand new bottle and packaging design has been launched, announcing a new start.

Moon Harbour

Bordeaux, Nouvelle Aquitaine, founded in 2017

moonharbour.fr

With the help of the well-known whisky consultant John McDougall, Jean-Philippe Ballanger and Yves Médina founded the distillery in the heart of Bordeaux. A nearby former submarine base was also acquired and will eventually serve as a warehouse. The distillery is equipped with two 1,000 litre Stupfler stills. The first

Twelve Distillery in Laguiole

whiskies, matured in ex-bourbon casks and with a Bordaeux wine finish, were released in September 2020 under the name Dock.

Moutard

Buxeuil, Grand Est, founded in 1892 (whisky since 2017)

famillemoutard.com

Recently, the winemaker François Moutard and his sons, Alexandre and Benoit, started buying wash from local breweries in order to make whisky. Their distillery is fitted with five pot stills and production started in April 2017. Matured in Champagne ratafia barrels, the first whisky was released in May 2020.

Nalin, Distillerie

La Chana, Auvergne-Rhône Alpes, founded in 1919 (whisky since 2015)

distillerie-nalin.fr

A family distillery for three generations, the Nalin family distilled mainly pear eaux-de-vie for other companies. In 2015, they started whisky production and the first bottling has been sold under the name of NP since November 2018.

Ninkasi

Tarare, Auvergne-Rhône Alpes, founded in 2015

ninkasi.fr

The whisky is distilled in a 2,500-litre Prulho Chalvignac still and aged in different types of wine barrels. A second still was installed in 2019. The limited Track01 was released in 2018 followed by Track 2, 3 and 4 and the first core expression, Ninkasi Chardonnay, appeared in May 2021.

Northmaen, Distillerie de

La Chapelle Saint-Ouen, Normandie, founded in 1997 (whisky since 2002)

northmaen.com

Originally a craft brewery but later equipped with a portable still. the 3 year old Thor Boyo was released in 2003. the 8 year old Slepinir in 2013, the 5 year old peated Fafnir in 2015 and the 6 year old Kenning in 2018. The still is not portable anymore but now works in a real distillery.

Ouche Nanon

Ourouer Les Bourdelins, Centre-Val de Loire, founded in 2015 (whisky since 2018)

ouche-nanon.fr

Originally a brewery, Thomas Mousseau acquired an old 500 litre Guillaume still heated with wood. The first whisky, La Petite Bertha aged in ex-Sauternes casks, was released in November 2018 and was followed in 2019 by the peated Frog´s Peat.

Paris, Distillerie de

Paris, Île de France, founded in 2016

distilleriedeparis.com

Sébastien and Nicolas Julhès installed a small 400 litre Holstein still in 2016 and obtained license No. 1, the first one granted to Paris for over a century. The first Parisian whisky was launched in September 2019 and was followed in 2021 by the first whiskies in France made from corn and rice.

Piautre, La

Ménitré Sur Loire, Pays de Loire, founded in 2004 (whisky since 2014)

lapiautre.fr

Ten years after Yann Leroux and Vincent Lelièvre had founded a brewery, they decided to start malting their own barley and to start experiments with distillation. La Piautre is now equipped with two Charentais direct-fire heated stills. The company released their first Loire Valley whiskies in January 2018: Malt, Tourbé and Seigle.

Quintessence, La

Herrberg, Grand Est, founded in 2008 (whisky since 2013)

distillerie-quintessence.com

Nicolas Schott produces fruit spirits (raspberry, pear, plum, quetsche or quince) and also liqueurs (spices or asperule). End of 2016, he surprised everyone with the release of his first single malt whisky, Schott's, bottled at 42%.

Roche Aux Fées, La

Sainte-Colombe, Bretagne, founded in 1996 (whisky since 2010)

distillerie-larocheauxfees.com

Gonny Keizer installed a micro-brewery in 1996 and became the first female master-brewer in France. In 2010, Gonny and her husband Henry bought a 400 litre portable automatic batch still. The still is wood-heated and equipped with a worm-tub condenser. The first Roc'Elf bottling, distilled from three malted cereals (barley, wheat, oat), was released in 2016 followed by a second in 2017. In 2020, the brewery moved to a new and larger site.

Saint-Palais

Saint-Palais de Negrignac, Nouvelle Aquitaine, founded in 2016

alfredgiraud.com

In 1896, Louis Gautriaud built a distillery, Chevanceaux, which was taken over by his son and grandson. In 1963, a new distillery was built with ten stills to be enlarged in 1990 when the number was doubled. In 1995, Philippe Giraud joined the company to form the Alfred Giraud French Malt Whisky in association with Julien Nau who in 2016 built a brewery dedicated to whisky production. Three versions of a blended malt have been released, Harmonie, Héritage and Voyage and in September 2021 the distillery´s first own single malt, Pointe Blanche, was launched.

T. O. S. Distillery

Aix-Noulette, Hauts de France, founded in 2017

tosdistillery.fr

Since 2003 Saint-Germain brewery has been one of the greatest successes in the revival of French beer production and in 2017 the owners also plunged into whisky production. Distilled in a 1,200 litre Holstein still the first whisky, Artesia single malt, was released in December 2020 followed by Artesia Rye in June 2021.

Twelve, Distillerie

Laguiole, Occitanie, founded in 2017

whiskytwelve.fr

Founded by twelve friends who acquired the former presbytery of Laguiole to set up a whisky distillery. The distillery became operational in 2017. The brewing unit is housed in a very small room in the presbytery while the still is installed in an adjacent building. The first malt whisky, Basalte, was released in November 2020 and was followed by several single casks.

Vercors, Distillerie

Saint-Jean En Vercors, Auvergne-Rhône Alpes, founded in 2015 (whisky since 2019)

distillerie-vercors.com

The distillery is an atypical installation equipped with a Charentais copper still and a steel boiler which works under vacuum for the first run. First distillation is carried out at low temperature (around 50°C). Sequoia Première Impression and Sequoïa Tourbé, two malt spirits, were launched in 2018 and in April 2020 the first "proper" whisky was launched followed by a peated version in 2021.

Germany

Whisky-Destillerie Blaue Maus

Eggolsheim-Neuses, 1980

fleischmann-whisky.de

The oldest malt whisky distillery in Germany distilling their first whisky in 1983. It took, however, 15 years before the first whisky, Glen Mouse 1986, appeared. A completely new distillery became operational in 2013. All whisky from Blaue Maus are single cask and there are around ten single malts in the range. Some of them are released at cask strength while others are reduced to 40%.

Slyrs Destillerie

Schliersee, founded in 1928 (whisky since 1999)

slyrs.de

The malt, smoked with beech, comes from locally grown grain and the spirit is distilled in 1,500 litre stills. The non chill-filtered whisky is called Slyrs after the original name of the surrounding area, Schliers. The core expressions are a 3 year old bottled at 43%, the 51 which has matured in casks that previously held sherry, port or sauternes and a 12 year old. Limited editions include various finishes including an 12 year old Islay cask as well as Mountain Edition, with a new batch released yearly around 1st of May, where the whiskies have been matured at a high altitude.

Hercynian Distilling Co (formerly known as Hammerschmiede)

Zorge, founded in 1984 (whisky since 2002)

hercynian-distilling.de

The distillery´s main products used to be spirits from fruit, berries and herbs but whisky distilling was embarked on in 2002. The first bottles were released in 2006. The core range used to be called Glen Els but the name was changed to Elsburn in September 2019. One subrange is called Alrik represented by experimental and smoky whiskies while the Willowburn range consists of whiskies finished in different types of casks and Emperor´s Way is all about peated whisky. Several new releases appear every year in small batches and often sell out quickly.

Bayerwald-Bärwurzerei und Spezialitäten-Brennerei Liebl

Kötzting, founded in 1970 (whisky since 2006)

coillmor.com

In 2009 the first bottles bearing the name Coillmór were released. There is a wide range aged between 4 and 12 years currently available. Recent limited editions include the 8 year old Bavaria & Toscana with a finish in Caberlot casks (a cross breed of cabernet franc and merlot) as well as the peated Albanach.

St Kilian Distillers

Rüdenau, founded in 2015

stkiliandistillers.com

St Kilian is one of few German distilleries designated to make only whisky. The distillery has a capacity of producing 200,000 litres of alcohol. The first single malt, Signature Edition One released in 2019, was a 3 year old matured in bourbon casks and the most recent, Edition Six, has been matured in a combination of casks – bourbon, rye and Spätburgunder. The first core bottling is expected in 2022/2023.

Finch Whiskydestillerie

Heroldstatt, founded in 2001

finch-whisky.de

One of Germany´s biggest distilleries with a yearly production of 250,000 litres. The range of whiskies is large and they are made from a variety of different grains. The age is between 5 and 8 years and included is a 5 year old single malt matured in e-sherry casks.

Eifel Whisky

Koblenz, founded in 2009

eifelwhisky.de

This is not a distillery per se. Instead the owner of the company, Stephan Mohr, decides on the mash bills and the malted barley and

Hercynian Distillery formerly known as Hammerschmiede

other grains are then sent to Feinbrennerei Sasse to be processed and distilled to Mohr´s specification. The newmake is then sent back to Eifel Whisky´s warehouses in Koblenz for maturation and blending. There are currently three ranges; Signatur, around 4 years old and including malt, rye and malt/rye, Reserve, 6-8 years old represented by both malt and rye and 746.9 Series, 10-12 years old with one peated malt and two rye whiskies.

Other distilleries in Germany

Altstadthof, Hausbrauerei

Nürnberg, founded in 1984

hausbrauerei-altstadthof.de

The current range of Ayrer´s organic single malts consists of Red, PX, Bourbon and Ayla (peated). Limited expressions include the 5 year old Mastercut bottled at 75,2% and the 5 year old Alligator.

Am Hartmannsberg, Schaubrennerei

Freital, founded in 2011

hartmannsberger.de

Working on a range of various spirits, the owner also produces small volumes of whisky. The first whisky was released in 2015 and the latest was a 7 year old single malt, matured in ex-sherry casks.

Avadis Distillery

Wincheringen, founded in 1824 (whisky since 2006)

avadisdistillery.de

Matured in French oak casks that have previously matured white Mosel wine. Threeland Whisky is between 3 and 6 years old and the range also consists of finishes in oloroso and port casks.

Bellerhof Brennerei

Owen, founded in 1925 (whisky since 1990)

dannes.de

The production of whisky made from barley, wheat and rye started in 1990 and today there is a range of various whiskies under the name Danne´s.

Birgitta Rust Piekfeine Brände

Bremen, founded in 2011

br-piekfeinebraende.de

A producer of gin and other spirits but also single malt whisky. One of the latest releases is the Van Loon 5 year old single malt with a port finish.

Birkenhof-Brennerei

Nistertal, founded in 1848 (whisky since 2002)

birkenhof-brennerei.de

The first release from the distillery in 2008 was the 5 year old rye Fading Hill followed by a single malt. One of the most recent bottlings was Peated Edition No. 4.

Bosch Edelbrand

Lenningen, founded in 1948 (whisky since 1997)

bosch-edelbrand.de

A family company run by the third generation, the distillery produces gin, edelbrände and single malt whisky. The range consists of whiskies (both grain and malt) up to ten years of age.

Brauhaus am Lohberg

Wismar, whisky since 2010

brauhaus-wismar.de, hinricusnoyte.de

The first release of Baltach single malt was in 2013. It was a 3 year old sherry finish. One of the latest editions of Baltach, finished in PX sherry casks was released in November 2019.

Burger Hofbrennerei

Burg, founded in 2007 (whisky since 2012)

sagengeister.de

Apart from distillates from fruits and berries, the distillery also produces whisky made from malted barley. The first release of Der Kolonist single malt was in spring 2015.

Dolleruper Destille

Dollerup, founded in 1990 (whisky since 2014)

dolleruper-destille.de

A huge variety of spirits from fruits, berries and nuts are produced but also single malt whisky. A variety of different bottlings, including peated, have been released.

Drexler, Destillerie

Arrach, whisky since 2007

drexlers-baerwurz.de

Malt whisky has been produced since 2009. The first release of Bayerwoid Single Malt was in 2011 and the latest was a 5 year old single cask (58,7%) from American oak in late 2020.

Druffel, Brennerei

Oelde-Stromberg, founded in 1792 (whisky since 2010)

brennerei-druffel.de

A variety of spirits are produced including malt whisky. One of the latest releases of Prum single malt (autumn 2020) was a 5 year old matured in a combination of PX, bourbon and plum wood.

Dürr Edelbranntweine

Neubulach, founded in 2002

blackforest-whiskey.com

The first release from the distillery, the 4 year old Doinich Daal, reached the market in 2012. The latest release, Erbenwald, appeared in December 2020.

Edelbrände Senft

Salem-Rickenbach, founded in 1988 (whisky since 2009)

senft-destillerie.de

The first Senft Bodensee Whisky was released in 2012 and then followed by a cask strength version. The latest release, Torf, was a 6 year old that had spent the final year maturing in a peat bog!

Faber, Brennerei

Ferschweiler, founded in 1949

faber-eifelbrand.de

A producer of eau-de vie from fruits and berries, whisky has also been included in the production. The only whisky so far is a single malt that has matured for 6 years in American white oak.

Feller, Brennerei

Dietenheim-Regglisweiler, founded in 1820 (whisky since 2008)

brennerei-feller.de

In 2012 the 3 year old single malt Valerie matured in bourbon casks, was released. It has since been followed by whiskies aged from 3 to 6 years including the smoky Torf.

Fitzke, Kleinbrennerei

Herbolzheim-Broggingen, founded in 1874 (whisky since 2004)

kleinbrennerei-fitzke.de

The first release of Derrina single malt was in 2007 and new batches have been launched ever since. The different varieties are made from malted grains (barley, rye, wheat, oats) or unmalted (barley, oats, buckwheat, rice, triticale, sorghum or maize).

Glina Whiskydestillerie

Werder a.d. Havel, founded in 2004

glina-whisky.de

The first Glina Single Malt was released in 2008. Most of the whiskies are between 3 and 5 years old. The oldest whisky so far is 10 year old single malt matured in a combination of wine casks including Port, Bordeaux and Knupperkirschwein (cherry).

Grumsiner Distillery

Angermünde, founded in 2015

grumsiner.de

The first whiskies were released in 2019 and the current range consists of a 6 year old single malt matured in acacia wood, finished in sherry casks. Single rye and single grain are also available.

Gutsbrennerei Joh. B. Geuting

Bocholt Spork, founded in 1837 (whisky since 2010)

muensterland-whisky.de

The first releases, two single malts and two single grain, appeared in 2013. More releases of the J.B.G. Münsterländer Single Malt have followed, the latest a 6 year old matured in ex-bourbon casks.

Heinrich, Brennerei

Kriftel, founded in 1983 (whisky since 2009)

brennerei-henrich.de, www.gilors.de

The first release was the 3 year old single malt Gilors in 2012. Several more expressions aged up to seven years have followed with a port finish as one of the latest in February 2021.

Höhler, Brennerei

Aarbergen, founded in 1895 (whisky since 2001)

brennerei-hoehler.de

The first whisky was released in 2004 as a 3 year old. A couple of the more recent releases of their Whesskey include versions made from rye, oat, triticale and pilsner.

Kammer-Kirsch, Destillerie

Karlsruhe, founded in1961 (whisky since 2006)

kammer-kirsch.de

Working with a brewery the distillery is making their own Black Forest Rothaus whisky as well the new single malt Bird of Prey, finished in madeira casks, for the spirits company Bauernkirsch.

Kinzigbrennerei

Biberach, founded in 1937 (whisky since 2004)

biberacher-whisky.de

The first single malt release was the 4 year old Biberacher in 2010. Later releases include Schwarzwälder Rye, Kinzigtäler and Geroldsecker. The oldest whisky so far is the 15 year old Annorum XV bottled at both 40% and cask strength (54%).

Kymsee Whisky

Grabenstätt, founded in 1994 (whisky since 2012)

kymsee-whisky.de

In 2015 the first triple-distilled Kymsee single malt was released.

Later editions include Triple Oak and two finishes - quarter cask and sherry cask.

Landgasthof Gemmer

Rettert, founded in 1908 (whisky since 2008)

landgasthof-gemmer.de

The only single malt released is the 3 year old Georg IV which has matured for two years in toasted Spessart oak casks and finished for one year in casks that have contained Banyuls wine.

Lübbehusen Malt Distillery

Emstek, founded in 2014

theluebbehusen.com

With one of the largest pot stills in the country, the distillery currently has three single malts in the range; Unpeated small batch 4 years old, Peated small batch 5 years old and a Vintage 2014.

Marder Edelbrände

Albbruck-Unteralpfen, founded in 1953 (whisky since 2009)

marder-edelbraende.de

The first release in 2013 was the 3 year old Marder Single Malt. The latest limited edition was a 5 year old single amarone cask.

Märkische Spezialitäten Brennerei

Hagen, whisky since 2010

msb-hagen.de

The spirit is distilled four times, matured for 12 months and then brought to a cave, with low temperature for further maturation. The first whisky was released in 2013 and is now called DeCavo.

Mösslein, Destillerie

Zeilitzheim, founded in 1984 (whisky since 1996)

weingeister.de

Originally a winery, the first whisky was released in 2003 and the core range consists of a single malt and a grain whisky, both 5 years old. In 2017, the first 12 year old, Ernest 25, was released.

Nordik Edelbrennerei

Jork, founded in 2012

nordik-edelbrennerei.de

A variety of spirits including whisky are produced. Their latest single malts, released in 2020, include two 5 year olds, both matured in red wine casks.

Nordpfälzer Edelobst & Whiskydestille Höning

Winnweiler, founded in 2008

nordpfalz-brennerei.de

The first release was in 2011, a 3 year old single malt by the name Taranis with a full maturation in a Sauternes cask. Every year in September, a new version is released.

Number Nine Spirituosen-Manufaktur

Leinefelde-Worbis, founded in 1999 (whisky since 2013)

number-nine.eu

The production was expanded in 2013 to include rum, gin and whisky. The first single malt under the label The Nine Springs was launched in 2016. Some of the latest (in 2020/2021) are a 7 year old rioja maturation and a 5 year old amontillado finish.

Old Sandhill Whisky

Bad Belzig, founded in 2012

sandhill-whisky.com

The first whisky was released as a 3 year old single malt in 2015.

The current range of five expressions (all seven years old) are Oloroso, Bordeaux, German oak, American oak and a port finish..

Preussische Whiskydestillerie

Mark Landin, founded in 2009

preussischerwhisky.de

The spirit is distilled five to six times in a 550 litre copper still with a rectification column. Since 2013 only organic barley is used. The first whisky was launched as a 3 year old in 2012. Since 2015, all the whiskies have been at least 5 years old.

Ralf Hauer, Destillerie

Bad Dürkheim, founded in 1989 (whisky since 2012)

sailltmor.de

The first release appeared in 2015 with the 3 year old Saillt Mor single malt. The current range of five whiskies are all 5 years old; PX Sherry, Peated Oloroso, Port Cask, Palatinate Oak and Pfälzer Eiche.

Rieger & Hofmeister

Fellbach, founded in 1994 (whisky since 2006)

rieger-hofmeister.de

First release was in 2009 and there are now five expressions – a single malt matured in pinot noir casks, a malt & grain from chardonnay casks, a malted rye, a single grain and a smoky, 8 year old triple wood.

Sauerländer Edelbrennerei

Kallenhardt, founded in 2000 (whisky since 2004)

sauerlaender-edelbrennerei.de

The first release of the 3 year old Thousand Mountains McRaven appeared in 2007. One of the latest bottlings (December 2020) was Double Raven #3, cask strength and matured in bourbon and sherry.

Scheibel Mühle

Kappelrodeck, founded in 2015

scheibel-muehle.de

Originally distillers of Kirschwasser the owners are now also producing whisky. The Emill range of single malts consists of Feinwerk, Stockwerk and, bottled at 58,7%, Kraftwerk.

Schlitzer Destillerie

Schlitz, founded in 2006

schlitzer-destillerie.de

Apart from a range of different spirits, whisky is also produced. There are currently three Schlitzer single malt - 3 year old Classic, 3 year old Peaty and 8 year old Pedro Ximénez as well as grain whisky and one made from wheat.

Schloss Neuenburg, Edelbrennerei

Freyburg, founded in 2012

schlossbrennerei.eu

The first whisky appeared in August 2016 while the most recent releases of Schlosswhisky include the 4 year old, peated No. 6 matured in red wine and port casks and the 3 year old, unpeated No. 7 matured in new French oak.

Schwarzwaldbrennerei Walter Seeger

Calw-Holzbronn, founded in 1952 (whisky since 1990)

krabba-nescht.de

The first single malt was launched in 2009. Currently there are two expressions in the range; the 4 year old Black-Wood single malt matured in amontillado casks and an 8 year old wheat whisky.

Seitz, Gasthof

Gräfenberg, founded in 2007 (whisky since 2013)

gasthof-seitz.de, elch-whisky.de

A combination of a brewery and a distillery. A 3 year old peated malt whisky with the name Elch has been matured in three types of wood – ex-bourbon, ex-sherry and acacia.

Simon´s Feinbrennerei

Alzenau-Michelbach, founded in 1879 (whisky since 1998)

simon-brennt.de

In 2013 a new Holstein still was installed increasing production. A single pot still whisky has since been released as well as rye whisky and whisky made from rice and emmer.

Singold Whisky

Wehringen, founded in 2017

singold-whisky.de

Although founded in 2017, the brand was produced at another distillery already in 2012. The core range consists of Singold Malt Whisky including a cask strength version and Singold Sherry Cask.

Steinhauser Destillerie

Kressbronn, founded in 1828 (whisky since 2008)

weinkellerei-steinhauser.de

The main products are spirits derived from fruits, but whisky also has its niche. The first release was the single malt Brigantia which appeared in 2011 and an 8 year old has followed since.

Steinwälder Hausbrennerei

Erbendorf, founded in 1818 (whisky since 1920)

brennerei-schraml.de

A kind of whisky was made here already in the early 1900s but was sold as "Kornbrand". When the current owner took over, the spirit was relaunched as a 10 year old single grain by the name Stonewood 1818. Other releases include two 3 year old single malts.

Stickum Brennerei (Uerige)

Düsseldorf, founded in 2007

stickum.de

With the wash coming from their own brewery the owners produce a single malt by the name of BAAS. Currently 3 and 5 year olds are for sale.

Stork Club Whiskey-Destillerie

Schlepzig, founded in 2004

stork-club-whisky.com

The distillery had a history of producing a wide range of spirits but new owners decided to focus mainly on rye whisky. The range is called Stork Club and also includes a single malt made from barley.

Tecker Whisky-Destillerie

Owen, founded in 1979 (whisky since 1989)

tecker.eu

Apart from a variety of other spirits, whisky is also produced. The core expression is the 10 year old Tecker Single Malt matured for five years in ex-bourbon barrels, followed by five years in oloroso casks. There is also a 5 year old single grain (wheat and barley).

Thomas Sippel, Destillerie

Weisenheim am Berg, founded in 1992 (whisky since 2011)

destillerie-sippel.de

Wines as well as distillates of all kinds are on the menu with whisky being introduced in 2011. The first release of the Palatinatus Single Malt came in 2014 and there are several expressions available, including a 6 year old peated version.

Volker Theurer, Brennerei

Tübingen, founded in 1991

schwaebischer-whisky.de

The first whisky was released in 2003 as a 7 year old. Since then they have released the 8 year old Sankt Johann and the 10 year old Tammer (both single malts) as well as the blend Original Ammertal.

Wild Brennerei

Gengenbach, founded in 1855 (whisky since 2002)

wild-brennerei.de

Three 5 year old whiskies have been released so far – Wild Whisky Single Malt matured for 3 years in American white oak and another 2 in either sherry or port casks, Blackforest Wild Whisky Sherry Cask and Blackforest Wild Whisky Peated.

Zeitzer Whisky Manufaktur

Zeitz, founded in 2014

whisky-zeitz.de

The distillery is equipped with a Lomond still as well as a still built in Germany in 1935. A wide variety of newmake and 3 year old single malt from different casks has been released.

Ziegler, Brennerei

Freudenberg, founded in 1865

brennerei-ziegler.de

Maturation takes place not only in oak casks, but also made from chestnut! The current core bottling is a 5 year old called Aureum 1865 and there is also a cask strength version. Limited releases, also peated, occur regularly and the oldest so far is an 8 year old.

Hungary

Gemenc Distillery

Pörböly, founded in 2014

gemencdistillery.hu

Unlike so man other distilleries in Hungary producing pálinka, Gemenc is completely focused on whisky. The owner´s, Lajos Szöke, interest lies mainly in various grain whiskies which are distilled in a 4 plate copper still. Maturation takes place in 55-110 litre casks made from Hungarian oak or acacia and three different levels of charring are used. The current distillery is quite small but the long term plan is to build a larger facility. Since 2017, Szöke has also filled circa 30 casks with both peated and unpeated single malt made from barley. One single malt, made from chocolate malt, has so far been bottled but can only be obtained at the distillery.

Iceland

Eimverk Distillery

Reykjavik, founded in 2012

flokiwhisky.is

The country´s first whisky distillery where only organic barley grown in Iceland is used for the production and everything is malted on site. Both peat and sometimes sheep dung is used to dry the malted barley. The distillery has a capacity of 100,000 litres where 50% is reserved for gin and aquavite and the rest for whisky. The first, limited release of a 3 year old whisky was in late 2017 and

more bottlings have followed since then. Two of the latest limited releases are Double Wood Reserve with a finish in stout casks and Birch Finish where toasted staves made of birch were put into the barrels for a few weeks.

Republic of Ireland 

Midleton Distillery

Midleton, Co. Cork, founded in 1975

irishdistillers.ie

Midleton is by far the biggest distillery in Ireland and the home of Jameson´s Irish Whiskey. The production at Midleton comprises of two sections – grain whiskey and single pot still whiskey. The grain whiskey is needed for the blends, where Jameson´s is the biggest seller. Single pot still whiskey, on the other hand, is unique to Ireland. This part of the production is also used for the blends but is being bottled more and more on its own.

Instead of mash tuns, Midleton is equipped with mash filters and following two major upgrades of the distillery (in 2013 and 2017) the distillery is now equipped with 48 washbacks, 6 column stills and 10 pot stills. A new maturation facility with 40 warehouses has also been built in Dungourney, not far from Midleton. In autumn 2015, a new micro distillery adjacent to the existing distillery, was opened. With a production capacity of 400 casks per year, it will be used for experiments and innovation. However, in spring 2019, a commercial release of Method and Madness Gin made at the micro distillery appeared.

Of all the brands produced at Midleton, Jameson´s blended Irish whiskey is by far the biggest. In 2020 the brand sold 92 million bottles! Apart from the core expression with no age statement, there are Crested (which used to be called Cresten Ten), Black Barrel and an 18 year old. Since 2015, a number of special series have been launched; Deconstructed with three bottlings – Bold, Lively and Round, The Whiskey Maker´s Series with The Cooper´s Croze and The Blender´s Dog and Jameson Caskmates with three whiskies finished in various beer barrels. Other blended whiskey brands include Powers and the exclusive, yearly releases of Midleton Very Rare. The latter is also the name of a newly released series of exceptionally old whiskies – Midleton Very Rare Silent Distillery. They have all been distilled at the old Midleton Distillery which closed in 1975. The second installment in April 2021 was a 46 year old single pot still and the remaining four releases will appear with one new bottling every year.

In recent years, Midleton has invested increasingly in their second category of whiskies, single pot still, and that range now includes Redbreast 10 (launched in March 2021), 12, 12 cask strength, 15, 21, Lustau Edition and, launched in March 2020, a 27 year old as core bottlings. Limited releases include the Redbreast Dream Cask 32 years old and the 20 year old Redbreast Dream Cask Pedro Ximénez Edition. Furthermore, there is Green Spot without age statement, the 12 year old Leoville Barton bordeaux finish and the Chateau Montelena finish, Yellow Spot 12 years old, Red Spot 15 year old and, launched in 2020, Blue Spot - a 7 year old matured in a combination of bourbon, sherry and madeira. Powers (John´s Lane, Signature and Three Swallow) and Barry Crocket Legacy are other eaxmples of their single pot still whiskies. The third release of an Irish whiskey finished in virgin Irish oak, the Dair Ghaelach Knockrath Forest, appeared in early 2020. More innovation was displayed in 2017 when a range of experimental whiskeys was introduced under the name Method and Madness. Recent releases include finishes in acacia wood, wild cherry wood and, launched in March 2021, a mulberry cask finish - all three are single pot stills.

Tullamore Dew Distillery

Clonminch, Co. Offaly, founded in 2014

tullamoredew.com

Until 1954, Tullamore D.E.W. was distilled at Daly´s Distillery in Tullamore. When it closed, production was temporarily moved to Power's Distillery in Dublin, and was later moved to Midleton Distillery and Bushmill's Distillery. William Grant & Sons acquired Tullamore D.E.W. in 2010 and in May 2013, they started to build a new distillery at Clonminch, situated on the outskirts of Tullamore. The four stills produce both malt whiskey and single pot still whiskey and the capacity is 3.6 million litres of pure alcohol. In autumn 2017, a bottling hall and a grain distillery with a capacity of doing 8 million litres of grain spirit was opened on the same site. All whiskies at Tullamore are triple distilled. Tullamore D.E.W. is the second biggest selling Irish whiskey in the world after Jameson with more than 14 million bottles sold in 2020. The core range consists of Original (without age statement), 12 year old Special Reserve and 14 and 18 year old Single Malts. Limited releases include Phoenix and Old Bonded Warehouse. As an exclusive to duty free, the Tullamore D.E.W Cider Cask Finish was launched in 2015 and this was followed in 2017 by a Carribean Rum Cask Finish.

Cooley Distillery

Cooley, Co. Louth, founded in 1987

thetyrconnellwhiskey.com, connemarawhiskey.com

In 1987, the entrepreneur John Teeling bought the disused Ceimici Teo distillery and renamed it Cooley distillery. Two years later he installed two pot stills and in 1992 he released the first single malt from the distillery, called Locke's Single Malt. A number of brands were launched over the years. In 2011 Beam Inc. acquired the distillery and in 2014, Suntory took over Beam with the new company being renamed Beam Suntory. Cooley distillery is equipped with one mash tun, four malt and six grain washbacks all made of stainless steel, two copper pot stills and two column stills. There is a production capacity of 650,000 litres of malt spirit and 2,6 million litres of grain spirit. The range of whiskies is made up of several brands. Connemara single malts, which are all more or less peated, consist of a no age, a 12 year old and a cask strength. Another brand is Tyrconnell with a core expression bottled without age statement. Other Tyrconnell varieties include three 10 year old wood finishes and Tyrconnell 16 year old with a finish in both oloroso and moscatel casks. Finally, there is the lightly peated Locke's 8 year old

Teeling Distillery

Dublin, founded in 2015

teelingwhiskey.com

After the Teeling family had sold Cooley and Kilbeggan distilleries to Beam in 2011, the family started a new company, Teeling Whiskey. John Teeling's two sons, Jack and Stephen, then opened a new distillery in Newmarket, Dublin in June 2015. This was the first new distillery in Dublin in 125 years. In summer 2017, Bacardi acquired a minority stake in Teeling Whiskey for an undisclosed sum. This is the first time Bacardi gets involved with Irish whiskey. The distillery also has an impressive visitor centre.

Teeling is equipped with two wooden washbacks, four made of stainless steel and three stills made in Italy; wash still (15,000 litres), intermediate still (10,000 litres) and spirit still (9,000 litres) and the capacity is 500,000 litres of alcohol. Both pot still and malt whisky is produced. The core range from the distillery consists of the blend Small Batch, the biggest seller, which has been finished in rum casks, Single Grain which has been fully matured in Californian red wine barrels, Single Malt - a vatting of five different whiskies that have been finished in five different types of wine casks and Single Pot Still (50% malted and 50% unmalted barley), the first of the whiskies being entirely distilled at the current distillery. The others had been distilled at Cooley. In October 2020 an extension to the range appeared when Blackpitts Peated Single Malt, triple distilled and matured in ex-bourbon and ex-Sauternes, was released. Recent limited bottlings include the Renaissance series which appeared first in 2020 with the third installment launched in spring 2021. All three are 18 years old and have received a finish in madeira casks, Australian shiraz casks and muscat casks respectively. Finally, the third installment in the Wonders of Wood series appeared in August 2021. This time it was a triple distilled single pot still that had been fully matured in brandy PX chestnut casks.

Roayl Oak Distillery (fomerly known as Walsh Whiskey Distillery)

Carlow, Co. Carlow, founded in 2016

royaloakdistillery.com, thebusker.com

With succesful brands such as The Irishman and Writer's Tears (both produced at Midleton), Bernard Walsh opened his own

Tullamore Dew Distillery

distillery at Royal Oak, Carlow. With a back-up from the major Italian drinks company, Illva Saronno, construction began in late 2014 and the distillery was commissioned in 2016. The capacity is 2.5 million litres of alcohol and all types of whiskey is produced including grain- malt- and pot still whiskey. The equipment consists of a 3 ton semi-lauter mash tun, six washbacks, a 15,000 litre wash still, a 7,500 litre intermediate still and a 10,000 litre spirit still. There is also a column still for grain whiskey production. In January 2019, it was announced that Illva Saronno would take full control of the distillery while Bernard Walsh would continue with the brands Writer's Tears and The Irishman, trading under the name Walsh Whiskey and in the future relying on whiskey from Irish Distillers (Midleton) for his needs. The new owners introduced their own brand, Busker, in November 2020 and the range now consists of Single Grain, Single Malt, Single Pot Still and Triple Cask.

Great Northern Distillery

Dundalk, Co. Louth, founded in 2015

gndireland.com

In 2013, the Irish Whiskey Company (IWC), with the Teeling family as the majority owners, took over the Great Northern Brewery in Dundalk and turned it into a distillery. When it became operational in August 2015, it was the second biggest distillery in Ireland, with the capacity to produce 3.6 million litres of pot still whiskey and 8 million litres of grain spirit. The distillery is equipped with three columns for the grain spirit production and three pot stills for producing malt and single pot still whiskey. In summer 2019, another two washbacks were added to increase production with an additional three being installed in late 2020 and early 2021. The main part of the business is supplying whiskey to private label brands but since 2017, the owners have their own brand of Irish single malt called Burke's Irish Whiskey, which had been distilled during the family's Cooley days.

Waterford Distillery

Waterford, Co. Waterford, founded in 2015

waterforddistillery.ie

Founded by the former co-owner of Bruichladdich distillery, Mark Reynier. In 2014 he bought Waterford Brewery and in December 2015, the first spirit was distilled. The distillery is equipped with two pot stills (which replaced the old Inverleven stills in August 2021) and one column still and, even though grain spirit will be produced, malt whiskey is the number one priority. The distillery also has a mash filter instead of a mash tun. There is a focus on local barley sourced from 72 farms on 19 different soil types. The distillery has a capacity of 1 million litres but the owners have plans to go up to 3 million litres in the future. After having distilled Ireland's first organic whiskey in 2016, Reynier decided to also produce the first biodynamic whiskey in 2018. In April 2020, Pilgrimage, the first general whiskey release from the distillery appeared. In June, Bannow Island and Ballykilcavan, the distillery's first two single farm whiskies were released and were followed by many more. Organic Gaia 1.1, the first certified organic single malt produced in Ireland, was launched in November 2020.

Roe & Co. Distillery

Dublin, founded in 2019

roeandcowhiskey.com

The opening of Roe & Co Distillery marked Diageo's return to the Irish whiskey scene which they left in 2014 when they sold Bushmills. A blend named Roe & Co made from sourced whiskies was launched already in 2017 and at the same time plans to build a distillery in Dublin were revealed. The distillery is situated in The Liberties district in the former Guinness Power Station. Three stills made by Abercrombie in Alloa and wooden washbacks make up part of the equipment and the production capacity of double- and tripledistilled whiskey is 500,000 litres. In November 2020 a 13 year old cask strength single malt, obviously sourced from another distillery, was released.

West Cork Distillers

Skibbereen, Co. Cork, founded in 2004

westcorkdistillers.com

The distillery, equipped with eight pot stills, two column stills and with a yearly capacity of no less than 4,5 million litres of pure alcohol, produces both malt whiskey and grain whiskey and some of the malting is done on site. The whiskey range is quite substantial including also peated whiskey and a range of wood finished expressions. In February 2021 the limited blend Stout Cask Finish was released. In autumn 2019 the founders bought out the majority stake in the business held by Halewood Group and in 2020 the company moved to a new and expanded distillery in Marsh Road in Skibbereen.

Other distilleries in Ireland

Achill Island Distillery

Achill Island, Co. Mayo, founded in 2019

irishamericanwhiskeys.com

Situated on the most westerly tip of Europe, this is Irelands first island-based whiskey distillery, owned by the IrishAmerican Trading Company, a family owned company with offices both in Dublin and Boston. The distillery is equipped with two copper pot stills from Forsyths in Speyside and started distilling in summer 2019. The current products for sale are both sourced whiskies – a blend and a 10 year old single malt.

Ballykeefe Distillery

Ballykeefe, Co. Kilkenny, founded in 2017

ballykeefedistillery.ie

A classic farm distillery growing their own barley and the first to operate in Kilkenny for over 200 years. The distillery is equipped with three copper pot stills and the first triple distillation was in spring 2018. Gin, vodka and poitin were released early on while the first Ballykeefe single pot still appeared in March 2021.

Blacks Brewery & Distillery

Kinsale, Co. Cork, founded in 2013 (whiskey since 2020)

blacksbrewery.com

Starting off as a brewery, the owners later went on with distillation of gin and rum. In 2020, they purchased two copper pot stills (2,800 and 1,600 litres respectively) from Frilli in Italy and the first whiskey distillation was made later that year. Both single malt whiskey and single pot still are produced.

Blackwater Distillery

Ballyduff, Co. Kerry, founded in 2014

blackwaterdistillery.ie

Originally located in Cappoquin, Co. Waterford, the distillery moved in 2018 to Ballyduff. At that time the company was already famous for their gin. In their new distillery, equipped with three stills from Frilli in Italy, whiskey is now also produced. Director and co-founder Peter Mulryan is passionate about single pot still. The current legislation says it must be produced from malted and unmalted barley and that only 5% of other grains can be a part of the mash bill. According to legislators this is the traditional way. Going through hundreds of recipes from the 19th and 20th century Irish distilleries, Mulryan has shown that a substantially higher percentage of other grains were involved. Apart from making some single malt, Mulryan has spent 2019 making single pot still from a huge variety of these ancient recipes. The first release from their own production is expected in 2022.

Boann Distillery

Drogheda, Co. Meath, founded in 2016

boanndistillery.ie

Assisted by the well-known whisky consultant, John McDougall, Pat Cooney built the distillery which is equipped with three Italian-made copper pot stills and a gin still. The first single pot still whiskey distillation was in December 2019 but in common with most Irish distillery start-ups, they have already launched a range of sourced whiskey called The Whistler. The owners also started trials in late 2020 with different mash bills in order to revive the old Irish way of using a range of different grains.

Burren Distillery

Ballyvaughan, Co. Clare, founded in 2019

burrendistillers.com

The owners are using locally grown barley which is floor malted at the distillery, distillation takes place in traditional copper pot stills and for some of the maturation, casks made of Irish oak are used. Both single pot still and single malt whiskey is produced.

Clonakilty Distillery

Clonakilty, Co. Cork, founded in 2016

clonakiltydistillery.ie

For nine successive generations, the Scully family have farmed the coastal lands near the resort town Clonakilty in West Cork. Production started in early 2019 with Paul Corbett (former Teeling Whiskey Company) as the head distiller. The main product will be a triple distilled pot still whiskey and the first release is planned for late 2021 with sourced whiskey already in the range.

Connacht Whiskey Company

Ballina, Co. Mayo, founded in 2016

connachtwhiskey.com

Equipped with three pot stills made in Canada the distillery has the capacity to produce 300,000 litres of pure alcohol per year. The first distillation of whiskey (double-distilled) was made in April 2016 and in 2017, triple distillation started as well. Apart from malt whiskey and single pot still, the owners also produce vodka, gin and poitin. In June 2021 a limited release from the first cask filled in 2016 as well as a general release of Single Malt Batch 1 occured. Sourced whiskies are also sold.

Crolly Distillery

Crolly, Co. Donegal, founded in 2020

thecrollydistillery.com

The former Crolly Doll factory from 1902 has been converted into a distillery with two beautiful cognac stills and the ability to produce 50,000 litres of pure alcohol yearly. The first distillation was in November 2020.

Dingle Whiskey Distillery, The

Milltown, Dingle, Co. Kerry, founded in 2012

dingledistillery.ie

Equipped with three pot stills and a combined gin/vodka still, the first production of gin and vodka was in October 2012 with whiskey production commencing in December. The first general release of a single malt whiskey appeared in autumn 2016. The most recent bottlings are Batch No. 5 of the single malt and Batch No. 4 of the single pot still. Both expressions are also available at cask stregth.

Dublin Liberties Distillery, The

Dublin founded in 2018

thedld.com

After eight years of preparations, the distillery finally started the production in early 2019, It is owned by Quintessential Brands (75%) and East European drinks company Stock Spirits (25%). The master distiller is Darryl McNally who spent 17 years working for Bushmills. The three coper pot stills produce both double and triple distilled whiskey as well as peated expressions and the total capacity is 700,000 litres of pure alcohol per year. The whiskeys currently available (from 5 to 16 years) have all been produced at either Bushmills or Cooleys.

Glendalough Distillery

Newtown Mount Kennedy, Co. Wicklow, founded in 2012

glendaloughdistillery.com

For the first three years, the company acted as an independent bottler. In 2015 stills were installed and gin production began. Apart from gin, the company regularly releases sourced whiskies. In 2016, the Canadian drinks distribution group Mark Anthony Brands invested €5.5m taking over 40% of the distillery and in December 2019 they took over the remaining 60%.

Glendree Distillery

Glendree, Co. Clare, founded in 2019

glendreedistillery.ie

Originally a brewery, it was later on expanded with a distillery. Using the wash from the brewery and equipped with a 1,500 litre hybrid copper still with three columns, the distillery produces vodka, gin and whiskey. Apart from a lightly peated single malt, they will also make whiskies from rye and wheat. A very unusual feature is that they will be using 100% rainwater for the production.

Kilbeggan Distillery

Kilbeggan, Co. Westmeath, founded in 1757

kilbegganwhiskey.com

Brought back to life in 2007, Kilbeggan is the oldest producing whiskey distillery in the world, equipped with a wooden mash tun, four Oregon pine washbacks and two stills. The first single malt from the new production came in 2010 and limited batches have been released since. The core blended expression of Kilbeggan is a no age statement bottling but limited releases of aged bottlings have occurred. There is also a Kilbeggan Single Pot Still, a Kilbeggan Single Grain produced at Cooley distillery and, released in spring 2021, the peated Kilbeggan Black.

Lough Gill Distillery

Hazelwood House, Co. Sligo, founded in 2019

loughgilldistillery.com, athru.com

A group of investors led by David Raethorne came up with the idea in 2014 to build a distillery adjacent to the 18th century Hazelwood House. Planning permission was secured in 2017 and in late 2019 the distillery was commissioned. Equipped with three pot stills from Frilli in Italy, the distillery is unusually large with a capacity of 1 million litres (300,000 litres in 2020). Several releases of sourced whiskey can be found under the brand name Athrú.

Lough Mask Distillery

Tourmakeady, Co. Mayo, founded in 2017

loughmaskdistillery.com

Equipped with two alambic stills, the distillery started production in early 2018. Due to the covid pandemic, plans to make whiskey were postponed but once the production begins, The Loch Measc malt will be double distilled and both peated and unpeated spirit will be produced. Gin and vodka are already for sale.

Pearse Lyons Distillery

Dublin, founded in 2017

pearselyonsdistillery.com

Dr Pearse Lyons, who passed away in 2018, was a native of

Ireland and used to work for Irish Distillers in the 1970s. In 1980 he changed direction and founded a company specializing in animal nutrition and feed supplements. In 2008, he opened a whiskey distillery in Lexington, Kentucky. Four years later he started a distillery in Carlow, Ireland. After a few years, the stills were moved to Dublin where Dr Lyons restored the old St James´ church and converted it to a distillery. The distillery is equipped with a traditional wash still with a descending lyne arm while the spirit still has four rectification plates to further refine the spirit. The first distillation was in September 2017 but the owners already have a range of aged malt whiskies made from whisky produced at Carlow and other distilleries. In July 2019 they also started distilling pot still whiskey and in 2020 they began using oats in some of their mashbills.

Powerscourt Distillery

Enniskerry, Co. Wicklow, founded in 2017

powerscourtdistillery.com

The distillery is situated at the Powerscourt Estate, owned by the Slazenger family, south of Dublin. Three pot stills were ordered from Forsyths in Scotland, distillation started in autumn 2018 and a visitor centre was opened in summer 2019. Noel Sweeney from Cooley Distillery is in charge of the distillery which has a capacity of producing 1 million bottles per year. A range of sourced whiskies have already been released under the name Fercullen.

Shed Distillery, The

Drumshanbo, Co. Leitrim, founded in 2014

thesheddistillery.com

Founded by entrepreneur and drinks veteran P J Rigney, the distillery is equipped with five pot stills, three column stills and six washbacks. The focus for the owners is triple distilled single pot still whiskey but Drumshanbo gin has been on the market for years. The first whiskey distillation was in late 2014 and in December 2019 the 5 year old Drumshanbo Single Pot Still was released.

Slane Distillery

Slane, Co. Meath, founded in 2017

slaneirishwhiskey.com

The Conyngham family established a whiskey brand a few years ago which became popular not least in the USA. The whiskey was produced at Cooleys but the family decided to start a distillery of their own. After an unsuccesful partnership with Camus Wine & Spirits, Brown-Forman stepped in and took over the entire project in 2015. Equipped with three copper pot stills, six column stills and washbacks made of wood, the distillery started production in summer 2018. Three types of whiskey are produced; single malt, single pot still and grain whiskey.

Tipperary Boutique Distillery

Clonmel, Co. Tipperary, founded in 2020

tipperarydistillery.ie

Jennifer Nickerson and her husband Liam Ahearn chose the Ahearn family farm, Ballindoney, between Clonmel and Tipperary as the spot for Tipperary Boutique Distillery. They also took in Jennifer's father in the business. Stuart Nickerson is well-known to lovers of Scotch after having held the position as Distillery Manager at Glenmorangie. Sourced whiskey was released from early on and in November 2020, the first whiskey made from their own barley and distilled at another Irish distillery was released. Simultaneously, the owners made their first distillation at their own distillery which is equipped with four stills from Hoga in Portugal.

Jennifer Nickerson - co-founder of the Tipperary Boutique Distillery which began production in late 2020

Italy

Puni Destillerie

Glurns, South Tyrol, founded in 2012

puni.com

There are two things that distinguish this distillery from most others. One is the design of the distillery – a 13-metre tall cube made of red brick. The other is the raw material where they use a combination of three malted cereals in the recipe – barley, rye and wheat. In 2016, however, they also started distilling 100% malted barley. The distillery is equipped with five washbacks with a fermentation time of 96 hours. There is also one pair of stills. The first single malt was released in 2015 and the current core range consists of Alba (marsala casks with a finish in Islay casks), Sole (two years in ex-bourbon and two years in PX casks), Gold (5 years in ex-bourbon) and Vina (5 years in marsala casks). Recent limited releases include the first two expressions in the Puni Arte range. Edition 2 (released in July 2021) is interesting as it is a vatting of the distillery´s three malt recipe and their first single malt.

Psenner Destillerie

Tramin, founded in 1947 (whisky since 2013)

psenner.com

A producer of fruit spirits and grappa, tried their hands at whisky for the first time 7 years ago. Their inaugural release of the 3 year old single malt eRètico appeared in October 2016 and had been matured in a combination of ex-grappa and ex-oloroso casks.

The Netherlands

Zuidam Distillers

Baarle Nassau, founded in 1974 (whisky since 1996)

zuidam.eu

Zuidam Distillers was started in 1974 as a traditional, family distillery producing liqueurs, genever, gin and vodka and is today managed by Patrick van Zuidam. The first release of the Millstone single malt was bottled in 2007 as a 5 year old. The current range is a 5 year old which comes in both peated and unpeated versions, American oak 10 years, French oak 10 years, Sherry oak 12 years and PX Cask 1999. Apart from single malts there is also a Millstone 100% Rye which is bottled at 50%. Limited expressions include the 8 year old Double Sherry Cask (oloroso and PX), American Oak Peated Moscatel, the 4 year old 92 Rye, the 7 year old Peated PX and, not least, a 23 year old oloroso single cask released in November 2019. This was by far their oldest expression. Two more stills from Forsyths were commissioned in 2020 and the distillery has also started to grow their own barley and rye at a nearby farm.

Other distilleries in The Netherlands

Den Hool Distillery

Holsloot, founded in 2015

denhoolwhisky.nl

Originally a farm, the owners started brewing beer in the late 1990s. In 2009 some of the wash was sent to Zuidam Distillers for distillation into whisky. The first release appeared as a 6 year old Veenhaar single malt in 2016 and the latest was an 10 year old in September 2020. Since 2015, distillation is carried out on the farm and they are also taking care of their own malting.

Eaglesburn Distillery

Ede, founded in 2015

eaglesburndistillery.com

The owner, Bart Joosten, is a firm believer in long fermentation and the wort is fermented for at least 10-12 days. The first release of a 3 year old malt whisky (ex-bourbon) was in October 2018 while the latest appeared in April 2021 – a 3 year old matured in virgin oak which was followed in October by a 4 year old rum finish.

Hemel Brewery and Distillery, De

Nijmegen, founded in 1983

brouwerijdehemel.nl

Situated in a 12th century monastery, a brewery has now been complemented by a distillery. The two releases of Anima whisky are technically "Bierbrands", i. e. distilled from a hopped beer.

Horstman Distillery

Losser, founded in 2000

distilleerderijhorstman.nl

Producers of genever and whisky, the distillery released their first bottling in 2016 (a 5 year old matured in port casks). The current range includes both grain and single malt, matured in various casks.

Ijsvogel Distillery, De

Arcen, founded in 2012

ijsvogel.com

A huge variety of different spirits are distilled including malt whisky. The first whisky was bottled in 2015 and the latest, released in March 2021, was a 42 months old matured in a combination of ex-bourbon, ex-Laphroaig and PX casks.

Kalkwijck Distillers

Vroomshoop, founded in 2009

kalkwijckdistillers.nl

The distillery is equipped with a 300 litre pot still with a column attached. The main part of the production is jenever, korenwijn and liqueurs but also whisky. In spring 2015, the first Eastmoor single malt was released as a 3 year old made from barley grown on the estate. One of the latest releases was the 5 year old 10th anniversary bottling released in 2019.

Lepelaar Distillery

Texel, founded in 2009 (whisky since 2014)

landgoeddebontebelevenis.nl

Joscha and Inge Schoots started a brewery and shop in 2009 and continued five years later by adding distilling equipment. The business is a part of a larger crafts centre. Single malt (both peated and unpeated) as well as grain whisky and genever is produced. A first, limited release of Texelse Whisky was made for the crowd funders in 2018 and was later followed by a general release.

Stokerij Sculte

Ootmarsum, founded in 2004 (whisky since 2011)

stokerijsculte.nl

The distillery is equipped with a 500 litre stainless steel mashtun, 4 stainless steel washbacks and two stills. The first Sculte Twentse Whisky was released in 2014 and this was followed by a 4 year old in 2016. The third release was heavily peated (30ppm) and this has recently been followed by a sixth and seventh batch.

Us Heit Distillery

Bolsward, founded in 2002

usheit.com

Frysk Hynder was the first Dutch whisky and made its debut in 2005 at 3 years of age. The barley is grown in surrounding Friesland and malted at the distillery. The whisky (3 to 5 years old) is matured in a variety of casks. A cask strength version has also been released.

Northern Ireland 

Bushmill´s Distillery

Bushmills, Co. Antrim, founded in 1784

bushmills.com

Being the second biggest of the Irish distilleries after Midleton, Bushmills became a part of Irish Distillers Group in 1972. Irish Distillers were later (1988) purchased by Pernod Ricard who, in turn, sold Bushmill´s to Diageo in 2005. Diageo invested heavily into the distillery bringing the capacity to 4,5 million litres per year with ten stills. In 2014, Diageo took the market by surprise when they announced that they were selling the distillery. The buyer was the tequila maker Casa Cuervo, producer of José Cuervo. The new owners applied for a planning permission to expand the capacity and also to build another 29 warehouses over the next two decades on adjacent farmland. The local council gave the green light in April 2019 and with the second distillery equipped with one mash tun, eight washbacks and another ten stills, Bushmills will double their capacity to 9 million litres. It is expected that the new distillery will be ready by late 2021 or early 2022.

At Bushmill´s, single malt whiskey is produced. For their range of blended whiskies, the grain part is brought in from Midleton Distillery. Black Bush and Bushmill´s Original are the two main blended whiskeys but in 2017 a third expression was added – Bushmills Red Bush. The core range of single malts consists of a 10 year old, a 16 year old Triple Wood with a finish in Port pipes and a 21 year old finished in Madeira casks for two years. In 2016, Bushmill´s launched their first whiskey exclusive for duty free, The Steamship Collection, with special cask matured whiskies and in 2018, Bushmills became one of the first distilleries in the world to release a whiskey matured in acacia wood. In October 2020 a 28 year old single malt became the first in a new range – The Rare Casks. December 2020 saw the launch of the limited The Causeway Collection where a total of ten single malts, aged up to 30 years and that had been finished in different casks were bottled at cask strength. In April 2021, finally, two Bushmills Original Cask Finish were released. The two single malts, bottled at 40% had been finished in American oak and rum respectively. Bushmills is the third most sold Irish whiskey after Jameson and Tullamore D.E.W.

Other distilleries in Northern Ireland

Copeland Distillery

Donaghadee, Co. Down, founded in 2016

copelanddistillery.com

In early 2019, the founder Gareth Irvine moved his distillery in Saintfield 20 kilometres south of Belfast to Donaghadee by the coast. Already established as a gin producer, the owners filled their first cask of malt whiskey in November 2019. The distillery is equipped with a still from Arnold Holstein.

Echlinville Distillery

Kircubbin, Co. Down, founded in 2013

echlinville.com

Founded by Shane Braniff and located near Kircubbin on the Ards Peninsula, the distillery started production in August 2013. The distillery, having its own floor maltings, was further expanded with more equipment in 2015 and in 2016, a visitor centre opened. Currently the distillery is undergoing a huge £9m expansion to increase the capacity and grow the brand. Apart from single pot still and single malt whiskey, vodka and gin is also produced. Using sourced whiskey Braniff has revived the old Dunville´s brand of blended whiskey and included also single malt.

Hinch Distillery

Ballynahinch, Co. Down, founded in 2020

hinchdistillery.com

The owner of Chateau de La Ligne in Bordeaux, Terry Cross, is the founder of this distillery within the grounds of Killaney Lodge just south of Belfast. A wide range of sourced whiskies were launched early on. The covid pandemic delayed the opening of the distillery but in November 2020, the first distillation was made. The distillery, practising triple distillation, is equipped with three pot stills (10,000 l, 5,500 l and 2,500 l).

Fiona and David Boyd-Armstrong - owners of Rademon Estate Distillery

Killowen Distillery

Newry, Co. Down, founded in 2017

killowendistillery.com

Founded by Brendan Carty, the distillery started producing gin in 2017. Whiskey was always on the charts however and in early 2019 the first batch of pot still whiskey was distilled. Carty's approach is a bit different compared to many other Irish distillers as the spirit is double distilled and peated and the mash bill contains not only malted and unmalted barley but also other grains (like oats). Furthermore, fermentation takes place in open top wash backs for a week and sometimes longer, the two Portuguese stills are direct heated and worm tub condensers are being used. In 2019 the first in a range of sourced whiskeys called Bonded Experimental was launched and in February 2021, they released a series of poitín called The Cuige.

Rademon Estate Distillery

Downpatrick, Co. Down, founded in 2012

shortcrosswhiskey.com

Since its inception, their main product for Rademon has been Shortcross gin which quickly became a success story. In summer 2015 the production was expanded into whiskey, both single malt and single pot still. Through a £2.5m investment, the capacity of the distillery was further increased in 2018 with a new gin still as well as a new still for the whiskey production. The owners had plans to release their first Shortcross whiskey in 2020 but it will now most likely happen during 2021.

Norway 

Det Norske Brenneri

Grimstad, founded in 1952 (whisky since 2009)

detnorskebrenneri.no

Founded in 1952 the company mainly produced wine from apples and other fruits. Whisky production started in 2009 and two Holstein stills are used for the distillation. In 2012, Audny, the first single malt produced in Norway was launched. Recent bottlings include Eiktyrne Quadruple Batch 2. It is double distilled while Quadruple refers to the four different types of casks used for maturation; virgin American oak, bloodtub oloroso, brandy and PX.

Other distilleries in Norway

Arcus

Gjelleråsen, founded in 1996 (whisky since 2009)

arcus.no

Arcus is the biggest supplier and producer of wine and spirits in Norway with subsidaries in Denmark, Finland and Sweden. The first whisky produced by the distillery was launched in 2013. Under the name Gjoleid, two whiskies made from malted barley and malted wheat were released. More and older expressions have followed and in late 2020 the 10 year old Mesterbrevet, made from 65% malted barley and 35% malted wheat was released.

Aurora Spirit

Tromsö, founded in 2016

bivrost.com

At 69.39ºN, Aurora is the northernmost distillery in the world. The mash is bought from a brewery, fermented at the distillery and distilled in the 1,200 litre Kothe pot still with an attached column. Apart from single malt whisky, the owners also produce gin, vodka and aquavit. All their products are sold under the name Bivrost and until the first core bottling is released (around 2025) a number of limited expressions will occur. The first three, starting in May 2020, were Niflheim, Nidavellir and Muspelheim.

Berentsen Distillery

Egersund, founded in 1895 (whisky since 2018)

berentsens.no

A producer of mineral water for more than 100 years, the company started brewing beer 15 years ago and just recently expanded into distillation of spirits (vodka, aquavit and whisky). By way of a £5m investment, with stills from Arnold Holstein in Germany and with the aid of Frank McHardy as a consultant, the owners hope to become one of the biggest whisky producers in Norway. No whisky released yet.

Feddie Distillery

Island of Fedje, founded in 2019

feddiedistillery.no

On Fedje, the most westerly, populated island in Norway, an already existing brewery was complemented by a distillery in 2019 and production of organic whisky started in November that year. By October 2021 500 casks had been filled and a gin has already been released. Founded by Anne Koppang, the distillery is owned by more than 100 investors, all women. The bigger goal for the company is to contribute to the island by way of investments and inspiration and thus ensuring a thriving and growing community.

Klostergården Distillery

Tautra, founded in 2017

klostergardentautra.no

Equipped with two copper stills from Hoga in Portugal (1,000 and 600 litres repectively), this distillery is situated on the island of Tautra in the Trondheim fiord. There is also a brewery, hotel, restaurant and shop. No official bottling has yet been released.

Myken Distillery

Myken, founded in 2014

mykendestilleri.no

This distillery lies in Myken, a group of islands in the Atlantic ocean, 32 kilometres from mainland Norway. The equipment consists of copper stills produced by Hoga and in 2020 production was increased. Both peated and unpeated whisky is produced. The first launch of their single Malt was in September 2018. Recent expressions in spring 2021 include Extra Virgin Swede matured in virgin Swedish oak and ex-bourbon and United Americans, matured in a combination of virgin American oak and bourbon barrels.

Oss Craft Distillery

Flesland, founded in 2016

osscraft.no

Specialising in gin and other spirits made from herbs and botanicals, the distillery has already launched a range of spirits under the name Bareksten. In 2017, production of malt whisky began as well and in 2019 the distillery was expanded.

Slovakia 

Nestville Distillery

Hniezdne, founded in 2008

nestville.sk

The distillery is owned by BGV which was founded in 2001 and focuses mainly on production of ethanol and grain alcohol for industrial use. Whisky production started in 2008 and in 2012 the first Nestville whisky, a blend, was released as a three year old. Currently there are six different blends, all based on 90% grain made with a mash bill of malted barley, triticale and corn and 10% malt whisky. The first single malt was released in 2018 followed by a 6 year old in 2019.

Spain

Distilerio Molino del Arco
Segovia, founded in 1959

dyc.es

Equipped with six copper pot stills, the distillery has the capacity for producing eight million litres of grain whisky and two million litres of malt whisky per year. The big seller when it comes to whiskies is a blend simply called DYC which is around 4 years old. It is supplemented by an 8 year old blend and, since 2007, also by DYC Pure Malt, a blend of malt from the distillery and from Scottish distilleries. A new range called Colección Maestros Destiladores was launched in 2018 with a 12 year old blend as the first release. This was followed by a 15 year old single malt in 2019 to commemorate the distillery's 60th anniversary.

Other distilleries in Spain

Destilerias Liber
Padul, Granada, founded in 2001

destileriasliber.com

Apart from whisky, the distillery produces rum, marc, gin and vodka. For the whisky production, the spirit is double distilled after a fermentation of 48-72 hours. Maturation takes place in PX sherry casks that have been previously used in a solera system for 20-30 years as opposed to casks made of new oak and then seasoned with sherry for a few years. Until recently, the only available whisky on the market has been a 5 year old single malt called Embrujo de Granada. Starting 2020, a number of single casks aged 12-16 years have been released in small numbers.

Sweden

High Coast Distillery (former BOX Distillery)
Bjärtrå, founded in 2010

highcoastwhisky.se

Set in buildings from the 19th century, the distillery started production in November 2010. Eventually sales of their whisky exceeded the owners´ expectations and in 2018 the distillery was expanded. The equipment now consists of a semilauter mash tun with a capacity of 1,5 tonnes, ten stainless steel washbacks, two wash stills (3,800 litres) and two spirit stills (2,500 litres). The expansion has increased capacity from 100,000 litres to 300,000. In 2014 an excellent visitor centre was opened which today attracts more than 10,000 visitors yearly. The distillery makes two types of whisky – fruity/unpeated and peated. With a slow distillation, the flavour of the spirit is also impacted by the effective condensation using 2-6ºC water from a nearby river. A fermentation time of 72-96 hours also affects the character.

The first whisky, The Pioneer, was released in 2014 and in 2017 the first core expression, Dàlvve, was launched. This was replaced in 2019 by a new core range; the bourbon matured, heavily peated Timmer, the medium peated Hav with some of the whisky matured in new oak from Sweden and Hungary, the unpeated Älv matured in first fill bourbon and unpeated Berg matured in PX sherry casks. This was followed in 2020 with the limited Cinco, matured in a combination of five different types of sherry casks. At the same time the peated Marieberg, the first in a range to honour closed saw mills working in the vicinity of the distillery, was released. It was later followed by Sandö and Svanö and in February 2021 the 8 year old, peated Alba with a maturation in new American oak was launched. The High Coast head distiller Roger Melander was awarded Distillery Manager of the Year – Rest of the World in the 2021 Icons of Whisky.

Mackmyra Svensk Whisky
Valbo, founded in 1999

mackmyra.se

Mackmyra´s first distillery was built in 1999 and, ten years later, the company revealed plans to build a brand new facility in Gävle, a few miles from the present distillery. In 2012, the distillery was ready and the first distillation took place in spring of that year. The construction of the new distillery is quite extraordinary and with its 37 metre structure, it is perhaps one of the tallest distilleries in the world. Since April 2013, all the distillation takes place at this new gravitation distillery. In 2017 however, the old distillery was re-opened as the Lab Distillery where the company aim to develop innovative spirits. Two different gins have already been released.

Mackmyra whisky is based on two basic recipes, one which produces a fruity and elegant whisky, while the other is smokier. The first release was in 2006 and the distillery now has four core expressions; Svensk Ek, Brukswhisky, the peated Svensk Rök and MACK by Mackmyra. Since summer 2021 there is also an older,

High Coast Distillery

limited version of Brukswhisky named DLX. A range of limited editions called Moment was introduced in 2010 and consists of exceptional casks selected by the Master Blender, Angela D`Orazio. The latest edition is Körsbärsrök where part of the whisky had been matured in casks that had previously held cherry wine. Seasonal expressions are also released regularly with Björksav in March 2021 as one of the latest. Part of the maturation was enhanced by casks that had been seasoned with birch sap. In autumn 2019, the distillery launched the first whisky in the world where AI (artificial intelligence) had been involved in the creation process.

Spirit of Hven

Hven, founded in 2007

hven.com

The distillery is situated on the island of Hven right between Sweden and Denmark and the first distillation took place in May 2008. Henric Molin, founder and owner, is a trained chemist and very concerned about what type of yeast and grain he uses not to mention the right oak for his casks. The distillery is equipped with a 0,5 ton mash tun, six washbacks made of stainless steel, one wash still, one spirit still and a designated gin still. Apart from that, a unique wooden Coffey still has been installed to be used mainly for distillation of rye and corn. Part of the barley is malted on site using Swedish peat, sometimes mixed with seaweed and sea-grass, for drying. Apart from whisky, other products include rum made from sugar beet, vodka, gin and aquavit.

Their first whisky was the lightly peated Urania, released in 2012. The second launch was the start of a new series of eight limited bottlings called The Seven Stars released over seven years. The first and so far only core expression, Tycho´s Star, was released in 2015. New and innovative bottlings include Sweden´s first rye whisky, Hvenus Rye, and Mercurious, the first whisky in Sweden made predominantly (88%) from corn which had been grown on the distillery grounds. One of the latest single malt bottlings (September 2021) was Stjerneborg.

Smögen Whisky

Hunnebostrand, founded in 2010

smogenwhisky.se

Pär Caldenby – lawyer, whisky enthusiast and the author of Enjoying Malt Whisky – is the founder of this distillery on the west coast of Sweden. Equipped with three washbacks (1,600 litres each), a wash still (900 litres) and a spirit still (600 litres), the capacity is 35,000 litres of alcohol a year. An interesting addition to the equipment setup was made in summer 2018 when Pär installed worm tubs to cool the spirits. Heavily peated malt is imported from Scotland and the aim is to produce an Islay-type of whisky. The first release from the distillery was the 3 year old Primör in 2014. This has over the years been followed by many limited releases, mostly single casks. In 2020 there was the release of a 6 year old ”100 proof” from sherry seasoned quarter casks and an 8 year old bourbon and sherry maturation. These were followed in September 2021 by an 8 year old sherry puncheon.

Agitator Whiskymakare

Arboga, founded in 2017

agitatorwhisky.se

The owners of this new distillery have chosen some rather unusual techniques in the production. Water is added during the milling in order to make the mashing more efficient. The same fermented wash is split in half and distributed to the two pairs of stills in order to achieve different characters. The stills, by the way, operate under vacuum which is extremely rare in pot still whisky making. The distillery is experimenting with different kinds of grain apart from barley - oat, wheat and rye. Finally, the maturation sometimes takes place in casks where extra staves have been inserted, some of them made from chestnut. The distillery has a capacity of 500,000 litres of pure alcohol and the first distillation was made in February 2018. The first two bottlings (in November 2021) were made from

the unpeated recipe and one of them had been finished in chestnut casks. These were followed in spring 2022 by a whisky that had been matured both in ex-Islay casks as well as chestnut casks. At the same time the Blind Seal Straight Rye Whiskey and a blended whisky were released.

Other distilleries in Sweden

Gammelstilla Whisky

Torsåker, founded in 2005

gammelstilla.se

Built by the owners, the wash still has a capacity of 600 litres and the spirit still 300 litres and the annual capacity is 20,000 litres per year. The first, limited release for shareholders was in May 2017 with a general release in January 2018 of the 4 year old Jern. The two most recent releases were Hyttan in autumn 2020 and ”2021”, a combination of ex-bourbon and virgin Swedish oak, in April 2021.

Gotland Whisky

Romakloster, founded in 2011

gotlandwhisky.se

The distillery is equipped with a 1,600 litre wash still and a 900 litre spirit still. Local barley is ecologically grown and part of it is malted on site. Unpeated and peated whisky is produced and the capacity is 60,000 litres per year. The first release of Isle of Lime was in 2017. Recent bottlings in summer 2021 were Sangelstain which had matured in a combination of ex-bourbon, virgin American oak, ex-sherry and Hungarian oak and the 6 year old Tjaukle.

Nordmarkens Destilleri

Årjäng, founded in 2014 (whisky since 2018)

nordmarkensdestilleri.se

In 2015 the owners produced newmake spirit at another Swedish distillery and following maturation at Nordmarken, Traukiol was released in March 2021. The first whisky distillation on their own premises was in summer 2018 and both peated and unpeated spirit is produced.

Norrtelje Brenneri

Norrtälje, founded in 2002 (whisky since 2009)

norrteljebrenneri.se

The production consists mainly of spirits from fruits and berries. Since 2009, a single malt whisky from ecologically grown barley is also produced. The first bottling was released in summer 2015 and several limited editions have followed.

Tevsjö Destilleri

Järvsö, founded in 2012 (whisky since 2017)

tevsjodestilleri.se

The owners are primarily focused on distillation of aquavit and other white spirits but whisky production is also included. In December 2019 the first malt whisky and ”bourbon” were released.

Uppsala Destilleri

Uppsala, founded in 2015

uppsaladestilleri.se

One of the smallest distilleries in the country. Production started with a 100 litre alambic still from Portugal but yet another still has been installed. Apart from whisky, gin and rum are also produced.

Switzerland 

Käsers Schloss (a.k.a Whisky Castle)

Elfingen, Aargau, founded in 2001

kaesers-schloss.ch

The first whisky from this distillery, founded by Ruedi Käser, reached the market in 2004. It was a single malt under the name Castle Hill. Since then the range of malt whiskies (now with the name Whisky Castle) has been expanded and today includes Doublewood (3 years old matured both in casks made of chestnut and oak), Smoke Barley (at least 3 years old matured in new oak), the portmatured Family Reserve and the 8 year old Edition Käser, the distillery´s premium expression.

Brauerei Locher

Appenzell, founded in 1886 (whisky since 1999)

saentismalt.com

Brauerei Locher is unique in using old beer casks for the maturation, sometimes with a finish in other types of casks. The core range consists of three expressions; Himmelberg, Dreifaltigkeit which is slightly peated having matured in toasted casks and Sigel which has matured in very small casks. There is also a range of limited bottlings with the Edition Genesis being one of the latest.

Langatun Distillery

Langenthal, Bern, founded in 2007

langatun.ch

The distillery was built under the same roof as a brewery. A variety of casks are used for maturation and the core single malts include Old Deer, Old Bear and the smoky Old Crow. Other bottlings are Old Eagle rye, Old Mustang "bourbon" and the organic Old Woodpecker. Limited releases occur with various finishes (rioja, marsala, port and PX finish) and the second edition of their oldest expression, a 10 year old, appeared in 2020.

Other distilleries in Switzerland

Etter Distillerie

Zug, founded in 1870 (whisky since 2007)

etter-distillerie.ch

The main produce from this distillery is eau de vie from various fruits and berries but whisky production commenced in 2007. The first release of Johnett Single Malt was made in 2010 and the current 8 year old has a peated touch from ex-Laphroaig casks.

Hollen, Whisky Brennerei

Lauwil, Baselland, founded in 1999

single-malt.ch

The first Swiss whisky! In the beginning most bottlings were 4-5 years old but in 2009 the first 10 year old was released and there has also been a 12 year old from the distillery.

Humbel Brennerei

Stetten, Aargau, founded in 2004

humbel.ch

With a history going back to 1918, the distillery uses a wash from the brewery Unser Bier in Basel to produce their ValeReuss Whisky.

Lüthy, Bauernhofbrennerei

Muhen, Aargau, founded in 1997 (whisky since 2005)

brennerei-luethy.ch

The distillery is equipped with its own malting floor and the first single malt was Insel-Whisky, matured in Chardonnay casks and released in 2008. Several releases have since followed. Starting in 2010, the yearly bottling was given the name Herr Lüthy and the 13th release from these had been matured in a combination of oloroso casks and first fill bourbon barrels. Whisky from rye, corn, rice and dinkel are also produced.

Macardo Distillery

Strohwilen, Thurgau, founded in 2007

macardo.ch

Built on a former cheese factory, the distillery moved to new premises in 2020. The core single malt, without age statement, is bottled at 42%. Recent limited releases include the smoky Chapter 1 bottled at 53,7% and the Opening Edition 1904 bottled at either 42% or 53,7%.

Rugen Distillery

Interlaken, Bern, founded in 2010

rugenbraeu.ch

A brewery founded in 1892 was later expanded with a distillery. The whisky brand name is Swiss Mountain and the core range consists of Classic and Double Barrel. Limited releases include Rock Label with a finish in Swiss oak and the sought after Ice Label where the latest edition (11 years old) received a second maturation of 7 years in the ice of Jungfraujoch at an altitude of 3,454 m. Another limited expression is the 9 year old Master Distiller Edition III, matured in a cognac cask and finished in a red wine cask.

Sempione Distillery

Brig-Glis, Valais, founded in 1976 (whisky since 2011)

sempione-distillery.ch

A family-owned distillery of fruits and berries but now focusing on whisky. Current single malts made from barley are Wallisky and Swiss Stone Eagle while Sempione and 1815 – 3 Sterne also include dinkel and rye.

Stadelmann, Brennerei

Altbüron, Luzern, founded in 1932 (whisky since 2003)

schnapsbrennen.ch

The distillery is equipped with three Holstein-type stills and the first generally available bottling (a 3 year old) appeared in 2010. Small volumes of Luzerner Hinterländer Single Malt are released yearly. The first whisky from smoked barley was distilled in 2012.

Z´Graggen Distillerie

Lauerz, Schwyz, founded in 1948

zgraggen.ch

Focusing on spirits distilled from fruits and berries, the owners also produce gin, vodka and whisky. The distillery is quite large, with a combined production of 400,000 litres per year. There are three single malts in the range – 3, 8 and the 10 year old Bergsturz.

Zürcher, Spezialitätenbrennerei

Port, Bern, founded in 1954 (whisky from 2000)

lakeland-whisky.ch

The main focus of the distillery is specialising in various distillates of fruit, absinth and liqueur but a Lakeland single malt is also in the range. The current core expression is a vatting of 4 and 7 year old whiskies, matured in oloroso casks while a recent limited edition had matured for 9 years in a port cask.

Wales

Penderyn Distillery

Penderyn, founded in 2000

penderyn.wales

When Penderyn began producing in 2000, it was the first Welsh distillery in more than a hundred years. A new type of still, developed by David Faraday for Penderyn, differs from the Scottish and Irish procedures in that the whole process from wash to new make takes place in one single still producing a spirit at 92% abv. In 2013, a second still (almost a replica of the first still) was commissioned and in 2014, two traditional pot stills, as well as their own mashing equipment was installed. In May 2021, the owners opened yet another distillery in Llandudno in north Wales. This is also equipped with the trademark Faraday still but production at the new distillery will be focused on production of peated single malt. The distillery has a visitor centre which the owners hope will attract 60,000 people yearly. A third distillery in Swansea, due to open in 2022/2023, is also in the plans.

The first single malt was launched in 2004. The core range today is divided into two groups. Dragon consists of the Madeira finished Legend, Myth which is fully bourbon matured and Celt with a peated finish. The other range is Gold with Madeira, Peated, Portwood, Sherrywood and, most recently, Rich Oak which has matured in bourbon casks and then finished in rejuvenated ex-wine casks. The smoky notes from the distillery´s peated expressions comes from maturation in ex-Islay casks. An exclusive to travel retail is Penderyn Faraday. Over the years, the company has released many single casks and limited releases and two of the latest, released in June 2020, are a Moscatel wine finish and a Tawny Port pipe full maturation. Both are bottled at cask strength.

Other distilleries in Wales

Aber Falls Distillery

Abergwyngregyn, founded in 2017

aberfallsdistillery.com

In common with so many other distilleries, Aber Falls started producing and selling gin. Malt whisky, however, is also produced and in spring 2019, they distilled rye for the first time. Their inaugural, limited single malt was released in May 2021. It had been matured in a combination of American virgin oak, ex-sherry and orange wine casks. More bottles were released in autumn.

Dà Mhìle Distillery

Llandyssul, founded in 2013

damhile.co.uk

Focusing on gin and grain whisky, malt whisky is also produced in a wood fired still. Aged, organic single malts, distilled by Springbank back in the 1990s, have been offered for a while and in December 2019, their first organic single malt from own production was released - The Tarian Edition from a single first fill oloroso cask. It was followed in January 2021 by Glynhynod.

The unique Faraday stills at Penderyn

North America

USA

Westland Distillery

Seattle, Washington, founded in 2011

westlanddistillery.com

Until 2012, Westland was a medium sized craft distillery where they brought in the wash from a nearby brewery and had the capacity of doing 60,000 litres of whiskey per year. During the summer of 2013 the owners moved to another location equipped with a 6,000 litre brewhouse, five 10,000 litre fermenters and two Vendome stills. The capacity is now 260,000 litres per year. In 2017, global spirits giant Remy Cointreau bought Westland Distillery. Sine the start the distillery has been focusing on local barley varieties and also local peat.

The first core expression, Westland American Single Malt Whiskey, was released in 2013. Until recently, the core range consisted of American Oak and Peated Malt, both matured in a combination of new American oak and first fill bourbon casks and Sherry Wood which had matured in new American oak as well as in casks that previously held Oloroso and PX sherry. All three varieties had been mashed with a 5-malt grain bill. In June, this range was replaced by Westland American Single Malt Whiskey based on a 6-malt grain bill and matured for a minimum of 40 months in a combination of five different types of casks. A limited range called Outpost was introduced in order to highlight the owners´ interest in exploring new frontiers of whiskey making. The two first expressions are Garryana where the native garry oak has been used for the maturation and Colere which has been made using the local six-row winter barley Alba. Still maturing in the warehouses, with an expected release in 2023, is Solum which is based on local peat.

In summer 2019 three expressions made from different barley types (Maris Otter, Golden Promise and Pilsen malt) were released in order to highlight the flavours that the grains impart. Celebrious was finished in a tequila barrel while Cask 3204 was heavily peated and matured in an oloroso cask. In January 2020, the 6th edition of the limited Peat Week was released and in February, Coldfoot, a collaboration between Westland and maker of outerwear and workwear Filson was released.

Balcones Distillery

Waco, Texas, founded in 2008

balconesdistilling.com

Originally founded by Chip Tate who left the company in 2014, All of Balcones´ whisky is mashed, fermented and distilled on site and they were the first to use Hopi blue corn for distillation. The core range currently consists of five expressions; Texas Single Malt, two corn whiskies made from blue corn, Baby Blue and True Blue 100 Proof, Texas 100 Rye and Pot Still Bourbon.

Limited but yearly expressions include Rumble, Mirador, Fr. Oak and Single Malt Rum Cask. In summer 2021 a new range called Pilgrimage (which will be permanent in the lineup going forward) was introduced. The first expression had been made from Golden Promise barley and finished in sauternes casks. Limited releases in 2021 include two single malts named Dusk and Dawn - both finished in Texas madeira casks. All whiskies from the distillery are un chill-filtered and without colouring. In early 2014, another four, small stills were installed. The big step though, was a completely new distillery which was built 5 blocks from the old site. Distillation started in February 2016 and the official opening was in April. The new distillery is equipped with two pairs of stills and five fermenters and they now distill approximately 350,000 litres per year.

Stranahans Whiskey Distillery

Denver, Colorado, founded in 2003

stranahans.com

Founded by Jess Graber and George Stranahan, the distillery was bought by New York based Proximo Spirits in 2010. Rob Dietrich took over as head distiller in 2011 but left the company in 2019. His succesor Owen Martin began revamping part of the range. The Classic expression was in spring 2021 replaced by Original made up of older whiskies. Before that, in 2020, the four year old Blue Peak, matured using a solera system, was launched together with the oldest expression so far from the distillery - the 10 year old Mountain Angel fully matured in new American oak. In spring 2021 a new, limited range called Experimental Series, only available at the distillery, was launched. From the old range there is still

Matt Hoffman of Westland Distillery selecting staves of Garryana oak for limited releases

Diamond Peak, a vatting of casks that are around 4 years old, a Single Barrel and Sherry cask. Every year in December there is also the release of the limited Snowflake edition which usually sells out in hours.

Hood River Distillers

Hood River, Oregon, 1934

hrdspirits.com

Since the foundation, the company acts as importer, distiller, producer and bottler of all kinds of spirits. Some of the products are distilled in-house while others are sourced. The role in the single malt segment came through buying Clear Creek Distillery in 2014. Founded by Steve McCarthy Clear Creek Distillery was the first to produce single malt whiskey in the USA. The only single malt whiskey produced by the company is the peated McCarthy´s Oregon Single Malt. In December 2017, Clear Creek closed their distillery in Portland and moved to Hood River.

Tuthilltown Spirits

Gardiner, New York, founded in 2003

tuthilltown.com

The distillery, 80 miles north of New York City, was founded in 2003 by Ralph Erenzo and Brian Lee. In 2010, William Grant & Sons aquired the Hudson Whiskey brand while the founders still owned the distillery. In spring 2017, William Grant followed up the deal by buying the entire company. Launched in 2006, the brand has undergone a complete revamp in late 2020 and it looks as though their single malt has been discontinued, at least for the time being. In an attempt to highlight the fact that the four whiskies in the new core range are made in New York, they are now called Bright Lights Big Bourbon (a straight bourbon), Do The Rye Thing (a straight rye), Short Stack (rye finished in maple syrup casks) and Back Room Deal (a rye finished in barrels that had previously contained peated Scotch).

Copper Fox Distillery

Sperryville, Virginia, founded in 2000

copperfoxdistillery.com

Founded in 2000 by Rick Wasmund, the distillery moved to another site in 2006 and in November 2016, he opened up a second distillery in Williamsburg. He is currently planning for a third distillery. Wasmund does his own floor malting of barley and it is dried using smoke from selected fruitwood (apple and cherry). After mashing, fermentation and distillation, the spirit is filled into oak barrels, together with hand chipped and toasted chips of apple wood and oak wood. In 2019 the entire range was rebranded and the core expressions are the signature Original Single Malt, the Original Rye, the Peachwood Single Malt, the Sassy Single Malt Rye (smoked with sassafras wood) and, introduced in spring 2020, the four year old Dawson´s Reserve Bourbon. In the limited Sperryville Collection you will find both malted barley and malted rye finished in either brandy barrels or port wood style barrels as well as a cognac finished rye.

St. George Distillery

Alameda, California, founded in 1982

stgeorgespirits.com

The distillery is situated in a hangar at Alameda Point, the old naval air station at San Fransisco Bay. It was founded by Jörg Rupf, who came to California in 1979 and who was to become one of the forerunners when it came to craft distilling in America. In 1996, Lance Winters joined him and today he is Distiller, as well as co-owner. In 2005, the two were joined by Dave Smith who now has the sole responsibility for the whisky production. The main produce is based on eau-de-vie and a vodka named Hangar One. Whiskey production was picked up in 1996 and the first single malt appeared on the market in 1999. St. George Single Malt, based on a highly complex mashbill, used to be sold as a three year old

but, nowadays, comes to the market as a blend of whiskeys aged from 5 to 21 years! The latest release is Lot 21 in autumn 2021. Introduced a few years ago, and having become a favourite amongst bartenders, there is the single malt Baller which has been matured in a combination of ex-bourbon barrels and French oak wine casks. After a filtration through maple charcoal, the whiskey is finished in casks that have held umeshu - a Japanese plum liqueur.

Westward Whiskey (House Spirits Distillery)

Portland, Oregon, founded in 2004

westwardwhiskey.com

In 2015, Christian Krogstad and Matt Mount moved their distillery a few blocks to bigger premises. That was also the year when fermentation of the wash was brought in-house, having relied on local breweries before.In the early days, the main products for House Spirits used to be Aviation Gin and Krogstad Aquavit but with their new equipment they drastically increased whiskey capacity from 150 barrels per year to 4,000 barrels. In September 2018, Diageo´s ”spirits accelerator” Distill Ventures acquired a minority stake in the brand which helped expand the capacity even further. The first three whiskies were released in 2009 and in 2012 it was time for the first, widely available single malt under the name of Westward American Single Malt. In autumn 2020 the brand was revamped and the core range now consists of American Single Malt, American Single Malt Stout Cask and American Single Malt Pinot Noir Cask.

Corsair Distillery

Bowling Green, Kentucky and Nashville, Tennessee, founded in 2008

corsairdistillery.com

The two founders of Corsair, Darek Bell and Andrew Webber, first opened up a distillery in Bowling Green, Kentucky and two years later, another one in Nashville, Tennessee (followed by a second one in Nashville a few years later). In March 2018 a third site in Nashville was acquired for $6,8m and in January 2020, the distillery was expanded with a new and larger mash tun. Corsair Distillery has always had a wide range of whiskies often made from experimental grains. This changed in 2020 when the owners settled for both a new design of the bottles and a more comprehensice range. This now consists of Triple Smoke, a single malt smoked using cherry wood, beech wood and peat, Dark Rye made from malted rye and chocolate rye and two gins - barreled and unbarreled.

Kings County Distillery

Brooklyn, New York, founded in 2010

kingscountydistillery.com

Founded by Colin Spoelman and David Haskell, this is the oldest distillery in Brooklyn. The wash is fermented in open-top, wooden fermenters and they practise double distillation in copper pot stills. A third pot still from Vendome was also recently installed. The first single malt (60% unpeated and 40% peated) was launched in 2016. It has then been released in batches aged between 1.5 and 4 years. In later years, focus has been more on other styles of whiskey and the current range is made up of several bourbons; straight, peated, bottled-in-bond, barrel strength and wine finish. On the rye side there is Empire rye and a bottled-in-bond version.

Virginia Distillery

Lovingston, Virginia, 2008 (production started 2015)

vadistillery.com

The whole idea for this distillery was conceived in 2007. The copper pot stills arrived from Turkey in 2008 but following several changes in ownership and struggling with the financing, the first distillation didn´t take place until November 2015. The distillery has the capacity of making 1.1 million litres of alcohol and is equipped with a 3.75 ton mash tun, 8 washbacks, a 10,000 litre wash still and a 7,000 litre spirit still. Their first single malt from own production was a very limited release of Prelude: Courage & Conviction in autumn 2019 followed by a general launch in April 2020. This is now the flagship expression made up of 50% matured in bourbon casks and 25% each matured in ex-sherry and ex.wine (cuvée) casks respectively. In March 2021, another three versions representing each of the individual maturation styles were launched.

Long Island Spirits

Baiting Hollow, New York, founded in 2007

lispirits.com

Long Island Spirits, founded by Rich Stabile, is the first distillery on the island since the 1800s. The starting point for The Pine Barrens Whisky, the first single malt from the distillery, is a finished ale with hops and all. The beer is distilled twice in a potstill and matures for one year in a 10 gallon, new, American, white oak barrel. The whisky was first released in 2012 and was followed in 2018 by a bottle-in-bond version (at least four years old) and later by an expression that is cherrywood smoked. The whiskey range also includes Rough Rider bourbon and rye. Apart from that a huge variety of spirits are distilled and they have also recently introduced canned cocktails

Great Wagon Road Distilling Co.

Charlotte, North Carolina, founded in 2014

gwrdistilling.com

The distillery, founded by Ollie Mulligan, started with a 15 litre still but moved to a new location in 2020 and is now equipped with a 3,000 litres Kothe still and in April 2021 a second still was installed. The mash comes from a neighbouring brewery and the fermentation is made in-house. The first batch of the Rua Single Malt was launched at Christmas 2015 and several batches have since followed, including vodka and Drumlish poteen. New releases in 2018 included a straight Rua single malt, two finishes - port and sherry - and a rye whiskey. They were followed in 2019 by their first cask strength release (at 63%) and a Rua matured for nine months in virgin oak and another 20 months in a sherry cask.

Hamilton Distillers

Tucson, Arizona, founded in 2011

whiskeydelbac.com

Stephen Paul came up with the idea of drying barley over mesquite, instead of peat. He started his distillery using a 40 gallon still but since 2014, a 500 gallon still is in place. In 2015, new malting equipment was installed which made it possible to malt the barley in 5,000 lbs batches, instead of the previous 70 lbs! The first bottlings of Del Bac single malt appeared in 2013 and they now have three expressions – aged Mesquite smoked (Dorado), aged unsmoked (Classic), unaged Mesquite smoked (Old Pueblo) and aged unsmoked, bottled at cask strength (Distiller's Cut).

Deerhammer Distilling Company

Buena Vista, Colorado, founded in 2010

deerhammer.com

The location of the distillery at an altitude of 2,500 metres with drastic temperature fluctuations and virtually no humidity, have a huge impact on the maturation of the spirit. Owners Lenny and Amy Eckstein released their first single malt, aged for only 9 months, in 2012. More and older batches (2 to 3 years) of their Deerhammer Single Malt have followed including several different finishes. In autumn 2019, the first edition of a new series, Progeny, was released. The second release, in December 2020, was the 5 year old single malt Cask Savant made from a hopped beer from the local brewery Crooked Stave,

Hillrock Estate Distillery

Ancram, New York, founded in 2011

hillrockdistillery.com

What makes this distillery unusual, at least in the USA, is that

they are not just malting their own barley – they are floor malting it. When Jeff Baker founded the distillery he equipped it with a 250 gallon Vendome pot still and five fermentation tanks. In spring 2019, the distillery was substantially expanded with a new pot still, a lauter mash tun and more fermentation tanks. This tripled the capacity to 20,000 cases of whiskey per year. The first release from the distillery was in 2012, the Solera Aged Bourbon. Today, the range has been expanded with a Single Malt and a Double Cask Rye. Over the years, limited bottlings have appeared such as the peated Single Malt and a Napa cabernet cask finished bourbon.

Santa Fe Spirits

Santa Fe, New Mexico, founded in 2010

santafespirits.com

Colin Keegan uses copper stills from Christian Carl in Germany for his distillation and the whiskey gets a hint of smokiness from mesquite. The first product, Silver Coyote released in 2011, was an unaged malt whiskey. The first release of an aged single malt whiskey, Colkegan, was in 2013. Since then, the range has been expanded to include also a version finished in apple brandy casks, a four year old (released in 2021) finished for one year in PX sherry casks and a third bottled at cask strength.

Copperworks Distilling Company

Seattle, Washington, founded in 2013

copperworksdistilling.com

Jason Parker and Micah Nutt obtain their wash from a local brewery and then ferment it on site. The distillery is equipped with two, large copper pot stills for the whiskey production, one smaller pot still for the gin and one column still. The first distillation was in 2014 and the first batch of the single malt was released in 2016. Among the latest releases are batch 33 in November 2020, a whisky that had partly been matured in fino sherry casks, a month later batch 34 which was the distillery's first peated single malt and batch 35 in March 2021, made from the local Baronesse barley.

Rogue Ales & Spirits

Newport, Oregon, founded in 2009

rogue.com

The company consists of one brewery, two combined brewery/pubs and two distillery pubs scattered over Oregon, Washington and California. The main business is producing Rogue Ales but apart from whiskey, rum and gin are also distilled. The first malt whiskey, Dead Guy Whiskey, was launched in 2009 and is still in the core range. Later additions are Oregon Single Malt and Oregon Straight Rye Malt - matured for five and three years respectively. There is also Rolling Thunder Stouted Whiskey and a special range of limited whiskies that have matured in unusual casks, the Single Barrel Project.

FEW Spirits

Evanston, Illinois, founded in 2010

fewspirits.com

Former attorney (and founder of a rock and roll band) Paul Hletko started this distillery in Evanston, a suburb in Chicago in 2010. It is equipped with three stills; a Vendome column still and two Kothe hybrid stills. The first single malt (preceeded by both bourbon and rye) was released in 2015. The current core range consists of American Straight Whiskey (a blend of bourbon, rye and malt), Single Malt smoked with cherry wood, Straight Bourbon and Straight Rye. Recent experimental bottlings include Cold Cut Bourbon made with cold brew coffee and Immortal Rye where oolong tea has enhanced the flavours.

Sons of Liberty Spirits Co.

South Kingstown, Rhode Island, founded in 2010

solspirits.com

The distillery is equipped with a stainless steel mash tun, stainless steel, open top fermenters and a combined pot and column still from Vendome and is first and foremost a whiskey distillery. In 2011 the double distilled Uprising American Whiskey was launched, made from a stout beer and it was followed in 2014 by Battle Cry made from a Belgian style ale. Both Uprising and Battle Cry have also been released as PX and oloroso finishes respectively. Recent limited releases include Oktoberfest Single Malt in 2019 and Wheated Single Malt (70% malted barley and 30% malted wheat) in 2020.

High West Distillery

Park City, Utah, founded in 2007

highwest.com

The founder, David Perkins, made a name for himself mainly as a blender of sourced rye whiskies. None of these were distilled at High West distillery. In 2015, they opened another distillery at Blue Sky Ranch in Wanship, Utah and in 2016 Constellation Brands (makers of Corona beer and Svedka vodka) bought High West Distillery for a sum of $160 million. Even though they consider themselves blenders first and foremost, the 2018 versions of Rendezvous Rye and Double Rye, were the first expressions which included whiskey from their own production. In December 2019, the first single malt made entirely by themselves and named High Country, was released. In January 2021, yet another edition of the legendary Bourye (a blend of bourbon and rye) was launched and there is also a limited range of bourbon and rye finished in unusual casks named Barrel Select.

Golden Moon Distillery

Golden, Colorado, founded in 2008

goldenmoondistillery.com

Distillery veteran Stephen Gould has built a distillery equipped with six custom designed pot stills as well as four antique stills. Working also as an independent bottler the products from the company are a combination of sourced whiskey (mainly bourbon) and whiskies produced in-house. At least 15 different kinds of spirits are distilled and three single malts whiskies have so far been released, the latest being Principium and Triple.

Bently Heritage Distillery

Minden, Nevada, founded in 2016

bentlyheritage.com

A true estate distillery, growing their own grains and floor malting it themselves, Bently Heritage is located in an old mill from the early 1900s. The equipment consists of a Briggs mash tun, oak fermenters, one pair of copper pot stills made by Forsyths and hybrid stills with columns for the distillation of vodka, gin and all whiskies except single malt.The first distillation was in 2018 and the owners have so far released gin and vodka but have also laid down a substantial amount of casks for future whiskey releases.

Other distilleries in USA

2nd Street Distilling Co

Walla Walla, Washington, founded in 2011

2ndstreetdistillingco.com

Formerly known as River Sands Distillery, the company has been around since 1968 but the distillery only started in 2011. Different types of gin and vodka are produced, as well as a single malt – R J Callaghan. In 2016 a 100% malted rye, Reser´s Rye, was also released.

3 Howls Distillery

Seattle, Washington, founded in 2013

3howls.com

Malted barley is imported from Scotland including a small amount of pated malt. For the distillation they use a 300 gallon hybrid still with a stainless steel belly and a copper column. Their first whiskies were released in 2013, a single malt and a hopped rye, and these were followed in 2014 by a rye whiskey and a bourbon.

10th Street Distillery

San José, California, founded in 2017

10thstreetdistillery.com

Inspired by a two-week apprentice program on Islay, Scotland, Virag Saksena and Vishal Gauri went on to build their own distillery in California. So far they have released Peated Single Malt, STR Single Malt and a limited pinot noir cask finish.

Alley 6 Craft Distillery

Healdsburg, California, founded in 2014

alley6.com

A small craft distillery in Sonoma county with rye whiskey as the main product. The first bottles were released in summer 2015 followed by a single malt in May 2016. The owners are experimenting with a range of different barley varieties.

Amalga Distillery

Juneau, Alaska, founded in 2017

amalgadistillery.com

The distillery uses a 250 gallon pot still from Vendome and they are also floor malting their own barley, some of it grown in Alaska. The first core single malt was released in August 2020, later followed by the sherry-finished Winter Solstice Solera.

Andalusia Whiskey

Blanco, Texas, founded in 2016

andalusiawhiskey.com

Focusing entirely on whiskey production, the spirit is double-distilled in a 250 gallon pot still and the first single malts were released in late 2016; Stryker, where mesquite and oak have been used to dry the barley and the lightly peated Revenant Oak. This was followed up end of 2017 by Andalusia Triple-Distilled. There is also a special range with cask-finished whiskies with PX sherry being the latest.

Arizona Distilling Company

Tempe Arizona, founded in 2012

azdistilling.com

The first release from the distillery was a bourbon sourced from Indiana. The ensuing releases, which started with Desert Durum made from wheat, have all been produced in their distillery. Humphrey's – a single malt – was first released in late 2014. The distillery is one of few using open top fermenters.

ASW Distillery

Atlanta, Georgia, founded in 2016

aswdistillery.com

The distillery is equipped with two traditional Scottish copper pot stills but with the American twist of fermenting and distilling on the grain. Among the latest releases are Duality, made from 50% malted barley and 50% malted rye, the heavily peated Tire Fire, the triple distilled Druid Hill and Burns Night Single Malt.

Atelier Vie Distillery

New Orleans, Louisiana, founded in 2012

ateliervie.com

The first product, released in 2013, was Riz - a whiskey made from Louisiana rice, Owner Jedd Haas then went on to distil also malt whiskey from barley. Louisiana Single Malt was first released in 2019 and the third version (2 years old) appeared in late 2020.

Axe and the Oak Distillery

Colorado Springs, Colorado, founded in 2013

axeandtheoak.com

A combination of a distillery, bar and restaurant, Axe and the Oak have so far released both a bourbon and a rye whiskey but there is also single malt maturing.

Bendt Distilling Co. (former Witherspoon Distillery)

Lewisville, Texas, founded in 2011

bendtdistillingco.com

The main products from this distillery used to be bourbon and rum but they have also made small runs of Witherspoon Single Malt. The distillery recently changed names to Bendt Distilling Co and the current big seller is Bendt No. 5, a blended whiskey.

Bent Brewstillery

Roseville, Minnesota, founded in 2014

bentbrewstillery.com

This combined brewery and distillery produces, apart from a range of beers, also gin and whiskey. A rye whiskey named Dark Fatha has been released and also Double IPA-Skey, made from one of their hopped beers.

Big Bottom Distilling

Hillsboro, Oregon, founded in 2015

bigbottomdistilling.com

The company started out as a blender and bottler of sourced whiskey, not least bourbon finished in different wine casks. A distillery was built in 2015 and in June 2018, their first own 2 year old single malt was released.

Black Heron Spirits

West Richland, Washington, founded in 2011

blackheronspirits.com

The owner started out as a winemaker, then decided to sell the company and open a distillery instead. A wide variety of spirits are produced, including bourbon, a corn whiskey and a limited peated single malt which was first released in January 2017.

Blaum Bros. Distilling

Galena, Illinois, founded in 2012

blaumbros.com

The distillery equipment consists of a 2,000 litre mash tun, five 2,000 litre wash backs and a 2,000 litre Kothe hybrid still. Apart from gin and vodka, the first two releases were the sourced Knotter Bourbon and Knotter Rye. The first whiskey from their own production was a rye in 2015 followed by a straight bourbon in 2018. It will be a few years before the first single malt is released.

Bogue Sound Distillery

Bogue, North Carolina, founded in 2018

boguesounddistillery.com

The distillery is equipped with a 500-gallon still and the first spirits released included gin, vodka and rye. A single malt, to be released under the John A.P. Conoley brand, is currently maturing.

Boston Harbor Distillery

Boston, Massachusetts, founded in 2015

bostonharbordistillery.com

The distillery concentrates mainly on whiskey but is also making a variety of spirits based on different Samuel Adams´ beers. The whiskies, currently several versions of rye single malt, are released under the Putnam New England label. Apart from the distillery with its 150-gallon Vendome copper pot still, the facility consists of a shop, tasting room and an event space.

Breckenridge Distillery

Breckenridge, Colorado, founded in 2008

breckenridgedistillery.com

Situated at a an altitude of 2,900 metres and claiming to be the world´s highest distillery, Breckenridge was founded by Bryan Nolt following a number of isnpirational tours to Scotland. The first spirits, vodka and bourbon, appeared in 2011. Bourbon, not least many cask finished versions, is still the main product but Dark Arts, a 10 year old single malt, is also on offer.

Brickway Distillery recently quadrupled the capacity

Breuckelen Distilling

Brooklyn, New York, founded in 2010

brkdistilling.com

Founded by Brad Estabrooke who left the world of finance for a distilling career, the company focused first on gin and whiskies made from rye, corn and wheat. When locally malted barley became available the range was expanded and the first single malt, the 6 year old Brownstone Malt Whiskey, was released in 2020.

Brickway Brewery & Distillery (former Borgata)

Omaha, Nebraska, founded in 2013

drinkbrickway.com

All the wash for the distillation comes from their own brewery and distillation takes place in a 550 gallon Canadian wash still, and a 400 gallon spirit still. The owners are focused on single malt whiskey but they also produce smaller amounts of bourbon and rye as well as gin and rum. Their first whisky was released in 2014 and there is now an aged version under the name Brickway Single Malt A recent expansion of the distillery made it possible to quadruple the whisky production.

Bull Run Distillery

Portland, Oregon, founded in 2011

bullrundistillery.com

The distillery is equipped with two pot stills (800 gallons each) and the main focus is on 100% Oregon single malt whiskey. First release was the sourced bourbon Temperance Trader. The first release of a single malt under the name Bull Run was a 4 year old in 2016 (now 5 years old) and there is also a version finished in Oregon pinot noir casks.

Caiseal Beer & Spirits Company

Hampton, Virginia, founded in 2017

caiseal.com

A combined brewery and distillery where the brewery produces the mash for various distilled products. The first spirits were released in May 2018 and included vodka, gin and bourbon and was followed in June 2019 by a 14 months old single malt.

Cannon Beach Distillery

Cannon Beach, Oregon, founded in 2012

cannonbeachdistillery.com

The owner's philosophy is never to make the same whiskey twice. All the whiskies are made in small batches and one of the latest was Mike Drop Oregon Malt Whiskey made from three different kinds of malt and matured for two years in Garryana oak.

Cedar Ridge Distillery

Swisher, Iowa, founded in 2003

cedarridgewhiskey.com

Malt whiskey production started in 2005 and in 2013 the first single malt was launched with more releases being made since then, including the current solera aged The Quintessential. Other spirits in the range include both bourbon, malted rye and malted wheat.

Charbay Winery & Distillery

St. Helena, California, founded in 1983

charbay.com

With a wide range of products such as wine, vodka, grappa, pastis, rum and port, the owners decided in 1999 to also enter in to whiskey making. They were pioneers distilling whiskey from hopped beer and over the years several releases have been made including Double-Barrel Release, Doubled & Twisted, Pilsner Whiskey and Charbay R5. In spring 2017, the company was split in two with Marko and his wife Jenni focusing on the spirit side while Marko's father Miles continues with the wine production.

Chattanooga Whiskey

Chattanooga, Tennessee, founded in 2015

chattanoogawhiskey.com

Production started in what the owners call their Experimental Distillery and in 2017, the much larger Riverfront Distillery came on stream. This is where their signature high malt bourbon is now produced. A couple of whiskies made entirely from 100% malted barley have been released - the 2 year old Batch #8 in May 2018 and the almost 3 year old Barrel #50 in March 2019.

Coppersea Distilling

New Paltz, New York, founded in 2011

coppersea.com

A "farm-to-glass" distillery with the barley malted on site, open-top wooden washbacks and direct-fired alembic stills. Another thing that make Coppersea stand out is that they don't dry the malted barley but instead produce a mash from green, unkilned barley. The one year old Big Angus is made from 100% green barley and in the range there is also Excelsior Straight Bourbon and Rye, Bonticou Crag Straight Rye Malt and the blend, Springtown Straight Whisky.

Cotherman Distilling

Dunedin, Florida, founded in 2015

cothermandistilling.com

All the whiskies are made from 100% malted barley. The mash is brought in from local breweries, fermented at the distillery and then distilled in a pot still and a 3-plate bubble-cap still. First launched in July 2016, several batches have followed since. Apart from whiskey – gin and vodka are also produced.

Current Spirits

Elmsford, New York, founded in 2019

currentspirits.com

Scott Vaccaro, owner of Captain Lawrence Brewing, recently opened up a distillery next door focused on gin, vodka, rye and many versions of bourbon. In March 2020 the first cask strength version of their single malt was released but most of the stock is maturing for future releases.

Cut Spike Distillery (formerly Solas Distillery)

La Vista, Nebraska, founded in 2009

cutspike.com

In 2010 single malt whiskey was distilled and the first bottles were launched in August 2013. New batches of the 2 year old whiskey have then appeared regularly and various special editions include single malt aged in cabernet barrels as well as finished in maple syrup barrels, oatmeal stout barrels and PX sherry casks. Peated production commenced in January 2020.

Cutwater Spirits (former spirit division of Ballast Point)

San Diego, California, founded in 2016

cutwaterspirits.com

In 2015, Ballast Point Brewing was bought by Constellation Brands four years later it was sold on to Kings & Convicts. The distilling side of Ballast Point, which started in 2008, was never a part of the deal and during 2016, a handful of executives and co-founders started a new company and distillery called Cutwater Spirits. That company in turn was sold to brewing giant Anheuser-Busch InBev in February 2019. The whiskyside of the business consists of Devil's Share Whiskey which comes in two versions - single malt and bourbon.

Dallas Distilleries Inc.

Garland, Texas, founded in 2008

dallasdistilleries.com

The distillery is primarily focused on whiskey. The first products in their Herman Marshall range were launched in 2013. It was a bourbon and a rye and they were later followed by a single malt. Two recent additions to the malt range are the 7 months old Temptress and the 22 months old Divine.

Dampfwerk Distillery, The

St. Louis Park, Minnesota, founded in 2016

thedampfwerk.com

A family company founded by Ralf Loeffelholz. Inspired by German drinking culture, they offer fruit brandies and herbal liqueurs as well as gin and single malt whiskey. The first single malt, made from pale ale and chocolate malt and finished in red wine barrels, was launched as a four year old in 2020.

Dark Island Spirits

Alexandria Bay, New York, founded in 2015

darkislandspirits.com

By way of a device inside the casks, the owners are maturing their spirits with the help of soundwaves created by different genres of music. Musically Matured is trademarked and so far apple brandy, vodka, gin, bourbon, corn whiskey and small volumes of Eleanor Glen Single Malt Whisky have been launched.

Deaf Shepherd Distilling Co.

San Diego, California, founded in 2019

deafshepherddistilling.com

Owned by Josh Christy, a former Navy EOD Operator, the distillery is making bourbon, rye whiskey, rum, gin and a single malt which is due for release in 2021.

Dirty Water Distillery

Plymouth, Massachusetts, founded in 2013

dirtywaterdistillery.com

Starting with vodka, gin and rum, the distillery expanded into malt whiskey in 2015. The first release, Bachelor Single Malt, came in 2016 and was followed by Boat For Sale Malt Whiskey which had been made using a beer from Independent Fermentations.

Distillery 291

Colorado Springs, Colorado, founded in 2011

distillery291.com

Founded by photographer Michael Myers, the distillery now has a core range that consists of several ryes, bourbons and American whiskies. In a limited, experimental range there are also two single malts made from 100% barley. In February 2021, the distillery moved to a new facility and doubled their capacity.

Dogfish Head Distillery

Milton, Delawere, founded in 1995

dogfish.com

Opened up as a brewery, the company later expanded into being a distillery as well. Two copper stills and a copper column are used to make rum, gin and vodka. On the whiskey side there is also single malt from malted barley. One of the latest releases was the 3 year old Let´s Get Lost made from four kinds of malted barley.

Door County Distillery

Sturgeon Bay, Wisconsin, founded in 2011

doorcountydistillery.com

A winery founded in 1974 was complemented by a distillery in 2011. Gin, vodka and brandy are the main products but they also make single malt whiskey. The first Door County Single Malt was released in 2013 and there are also bourbon and rye in the range.

Dorwood Distillery

Buellton, California, founded in 2014

dorwood-distillery.com

The distillery (which recently changed its name from Brothers Spirits) started producing malt whisky in 2016. The barley is dried using mesquite smoke and the triple distillation takes place in two reflux stills. The unaged White Hawk Malt Whiskey has been released and several barrels have been laid down for maturation.

DownSlope Distilling

Centennial, Colorado, founded in 2008

downslopedistilling.com

Made from 65% malted barley and 35% rye, Double-Diamond Whiskey was released in 2010 and it is still the core expression. It was followed by a number of varieties of bourbon, rye and a 4 year old single malt matured in a combination of six different casks.

Dry Fly Distilling

Spokane, Washington, founded in 2007

dryflydistilling.com

Several types of whisky have been released – bourbon, wheat and triticale - but also the single pot still O´Danaghers made from malted and unmalted barley. A new 4,500 litre Carl still was installed in 2020 and the distillery moved to a new location.

Eastern Kille Distillery (former Gray Skies Distillery)

Grand Rapids, Michigan, founded in 2014

easternkille.com

The equipment is made up of a 1,800 litre mash kettle, four fermenters and a 2,500 litre pot still with an attached column. Bourbon and rye are produced and the first bottle of Michigan Single Malt appeared in 2016 while the latest batch (almost three years old) appeared in 2020. In 2019, following a trademark dispute with Campari, the distillery changed the name to Eastern Kille.

Edgefield Distillery

Troutdale, Oregon, founded in1998

mcmenamins.com

The distillery is a part of the McMenamin chain of more than 60 pubs and hotels in Oregon and Washington. More than 20 of the pubs have adjoining microbreweries and the chain's first distillery opened in 1998 in Troutdale with the first whiskey, Hogshead Whiskey, being bottled in 2002. Limited releases occur every year on St Patrick´s Day under the name The Devil´s Bit with the 2020 edition beeing a 7 year old rye aged in heavily charred American oak. A second distillery was opened in 2011 at the company´s Cornelius Pass Roadhouse location in Hillsboro.

Eleven Wells Distillery

St. Paul, Minnesota, founded in 2013

11wells.com

The distillery is equipped with a 650 gallon mash tun, stainless steel open-top fermentation tanks and two stills. Whiskey is the main product and the first two releases, aged bourbon and rye, were released in 2014 followed by a wheat whiskey in 2015 and finally a subtly smoky single malt made from malted barley.

Elgin Distillery (Arizona Craft Beverage)

Elgin, Arizona, founded in 2015

azwhiskies.com

What started out as a wi nery founded in 1982 by Bill Letarte, was later expanded to also a brewery and a distillery by Bill´s daughter Kathy and her husband Gary Ellam. Gin, rum, bourbon, rye and a 5 year old malt whiskey from 100% barley are produced. Everything is done in-house, even the malting.

Fainting Goat Spirits

Greensboro, North Carolina, founded in 2015

faintinggoatspirits.com

First spirits on the shelves for this distillery, as for many others, were gin and vodka. In December 2017, Fisher´s single malt whiskey was launched as a 2 year old with another batch being released in July 2019. Fisher´s Straight Rye has also been released.

Glacier Distilling

Coram, Montana, founded in 2010

glacierdistilling.com

The distillery produces a wide range of all kinds of spirits. On the malt whiskey side there is Bearproof flavoured with huckleberry juice, Wheatfish which is a malted wheat whiskey and Two Med made from an ale from Great Northern Brewing Company.

Good Shepherd Distillery

Mamaroneck, New York, founded in 2016

goodshepherddistillery.com

Founded by Vincent and Carly Miata, the distillery launched vodka and brandy before adding malt whiskey to the range. The Sound Shore single malt made from malted barley grown in New York was first launched in early 2019 as a one year old.

Grand Teton Distillery

Driggs, Idaho, founded in 2012

tetondistillery.com

The first and foremost product from the distillery is vodka made from potatoes. Actor Channing Tatum has invested in the company and the Born and Bred Vodka. Various whiskies are also produced, including a 4 year old single malt matured in ex-bourbon barrels and finished in Jackson Hole Winery red wine barrels.

Great Lakes Distillery

Milwaukee, Wisconsin, founded in 2004

greatlakesdistillery.com

Included in the extensice range of various spirits are bourbon, rye and malt whiskey. The Kinnickinnic blend has been around for a few years and in 2019 the limited 10 year old Menomonee single malt was launched.

Hewn Spirits

Pipersville, Pennsylvania, founded in 2013

hewnspirits.com

Apart from rum, gin and vodka the distillerty produces bourbon, rye and the Reclamation American Single Malt Whiskey. After maturing the malt whiskey in barrels for 1-4 months, it receives a second maturation in stainless steel vats where charred staves of chestnut and hickory wood add to the profile.

High Peaks Distilling

Lake George, New York, founded in 2016

highpeakdistilling.com

John Carr left his job at Adirondack Brewery in 2016 to start High Peak Distilling but he is still very much involved with his old employer. High Peaks obtains all of their fermented wash from the brewery which is then distilled and matured on site. The first release in spring 2018 was the peated Cloudsplitter Single Malt which was followed by Night Spirit Bourbon and Sugar Moon in spring 2019.

Highside Distilling

Bainbridge Island, Washington, founded in 2018

highsidedistilling.com

The first spirit, a gin, was released in November 2018. Since then Amaro has also been launched while production of single malt whiskey started in January 2019 with an anticipated release in 2021 and with a peated version in the pipeline for 2023.

Hogback Distillery

Boulder, Colorado, founded in 2017

hogbackdistillery.com

The distillery founder and owner is the Scotsman Graeme Wallace who moved to Colorado. The focus is to do a Scottish style single malt made from malt from Gleneagles Maltings, some of it peated. The first single malt (peated) was released in September 2020 and there is also bourbon and rye in the range.

Idlewild Spirits

Winter Park, Colorado, founded in 2015

idlewildspirits.com

Production of the first batch of malt whiskey was in June 2016. For maturation they have moved from 5 gallon barrels, via 10 and 30 gallons to the full-size 50 gallon barrels that they use today. Fermentation and distillation being on the grain add to the over-all character. Their Colorado Single Malt was released in 2018.

Immortal Spirits

Medford, Oregon, founded in 2008

immortalspirits.com

A wide range of spirits are produced including gin, rum, vodka and limoncello. The only whiskey made from barley (unmalted) is the 5 year old Single Grain. The Single Barrel range of selected casks has sometimes been represented by a single malt but lately it was a 4 year old made from barley and corn.

Ironton Distillery

Denver, Colorado, founded in 2018

irontondistillery.com

Located in the River North area of Denver, the distillery produces vodka, gin, genever and rum. The first whiskies (bourbon, rye and malt) were all released in autumn 2019. The malt whiskey is made from malted barley smoked with beech.

Jersey Spirits Distilling Co

Fairfield, New Jersey, founded in 2015

jerseyspirits.com

Apart from gin and vodka, the owners have two bourbon varieties for sale - Crossroads and Patriot´s Trail. The first distillation of a single malt was in summer 2018 and in April 2020, Apple Wood Smoked and Cherry Wood Smoked single malts were released. In 2020, the owners opened a second distillery in Brooklyn.

John Emerald Distilling Company

Opelika, Alabama, founded in 2014

johnemeralddistilling.com

With the wash being fermented on the grain, the main product is John´s Alabama Single Malt which gets its character from barley smoked with a blend of southern pecan and peach wood. The first release was made in 2015 and is currently aged for three years.

Journeyman Distillery

Three Oaks, Michigan, founded in 2010

journeymandistillery.com

The first release from the distillery (Ravenswood Rye) was

sourced from Koval Distillery in Ravenswood. The range of whiskies distilled at their own premises now include bourbon, rye, wheat and single malt. The first release of Three Oaks Single Malt Whiskey was in 2013 and it has been aged in a combination of casks that have previously contained bourbon, rye and rum.

Laws Whiskey House

Denver, Colorado, founded in 2011

lawswhiskeyhouse.com

Alan and Marianne Laws released their first 3 year old in 2014 and all of their following releases have been at least 2 years old. The flagship in the range is Four Grain Straight Bourbon but they also have rye, corn, wheat and a 4 year old single malt called Henry Road on the menu. Beginning of 2020, the distillery was closed for a month for a substantial upgrade of equipment.

Liberty Call Spirits

Spring Valley, California, founded in 2014

libertycall.com

This distillery outside San Diego, uses a range of barley varieties including caramel malts and the rare Maris Otter. Apart from bourbon, gin and rum there is also a single malt named Old Ironsides. In spring 2020, they opened up a second restaurant/distillery in Barrio Logan, south central San Diego and the capacity of the distillery has recently been expanded.

Liquid Brands Distillery

Spokane, Washington, founded in 2018

warriorliquor.com

Rich and Mary Clemson produce gin, vodka, bourbon, rye whiskey and a single malt made from malted barley.

Liquid Riot Bottling Co.

Portland, Maine, founded in 2013

liquidriot.com

At the waterfront in the Old Port, Liquid Riot, Maine's first brewery/distillery/resto-bar, produces an extensive range of beers and spirits which include bourbon, rye, oat, rum, vodka, agave spirit and the almost three years old Old Port Single Malt.

Loch & Union Distilling

American Canyon, California, founded in 2017

lochandunion.com

A fairly large distillery with an impressive set of two copper pot stills for whiskey distillation and a third still designated for gin making – all fabricated by Carl in Germany. The first gin was released in 2018 and they have single malt made from barley and malted rye maturing in the warehouse..

Los Angeles Distillery

Culver City, California, founded in 2018

ladistillery.com

While gin and rum may be a part of the product range, the distillery is very much focusing on whiskey. Different versions of bourbon and rye are produced as well as three varieties of malt whiskey from barley; Virgin Oak, Triple Cask and Light Smoked. For maturation, the owners use American and Hungarian oak.

Lyon Distilling Co.

Saint Michaels, Maryland, founded in 2013

lyondistilling.com

Focusing mainly on rum but also whiskey, the distillery is equipped with a 2,000 litre mash tun, stainless steel fermenters and five small pot stills. The first, unaged, malt whiskey was released in late 2015 and the first aged release came one year later.

Mad River Distillers

Warren, Vermont, founded in 2011

madriverdistillers.com

The distillery was built on a 150 year old farm in the Green Mountains. Focus is on rum, brandy and whiskey. The only single malt so far is Hopscotch which was first released in late 2016 with batch six launched in October 2020.

Maine Craft Distilling

Portland, Maine, founded in 2013

mainecraftdistilling.com

The distillery offers vodka, gin, rum, Chesuncook, which is a botanical spirit using barley and carrot distillates, as well as the Fifty Stone single malt in limited batches. The barley is floor malted on site and both peat moss and seaweed is used to dry the barley.

Maplewood Brewery and Distillery

Chicago, Illinois, founded in 2014

maplewoodbrew.com

This combination of brewery and distillery has released three malts; Fat Pug made from pale malt, dark crystal, dark munich, chocolate malt and roasted malt, Oaty Otter with Maris Otter barley and oats and recently, Fest, which was released in September 2020.

Montgomery Distillery

Missoula, Montana, founded in 2012

montgomerydistillery.com

The owners use a hammer mill and the wash is then fermented on the grain. The first whiskey was a rye in 2015, followed up by the 3 year old Montgomery Single Malt in 2016 and a 4 year old a year later. The latest release, in November 2020, was a 5 year old matured in ex-oloroso casks and new American oak.

Motor City Gas

Royal Oak, Michigan, founded in 2014

motorcitygas.com

The owners have an experimental approach to whiskey making and use unusual and old grains, different yeast strains and unusual woods. The expressions so far have been both unpeated and heavily peated. A series of Irish style whiskies has recently been introduced with the 4 year old Scrapper as one of the first releases.

Nashoba Valley Winery

Bolton, Massachusetts, founded in 1978 (whiskey since 2003)

nashobawinery.com

Mainly about wines, the business was expanded with a brewery and a distillery as well. In 2009, Stimulus, the first single malt was released. The second release of a 5 year old came in 2010 and a one-off 11 year old was launched in 2016

New Holland Brewing Co.

Holland, Michigan, founded in 1996 (whiskey since 2005)

newhollandbrew.com

The first cases of New Holland Artisan Spirits were released in 2008 and among them were Zeppelin Bend, a 3 year old straight malt whiskey which is now their flagship brand. Included in the range is also the 4 year old Zeppelin Bend Reserve which has been finished in sherry casks.

New Liberty Distillery

Philadelphia, Pennsylvania, founded in 2014

newlibertydistillery.com

The distillery is working with whiskey on two tracks - the New

Liberty which is produced at the distillery (including a Smoked Malt and Dutch Malt Whiskey) and Kinsey which is sourced from other distilleries. On the malt whiskey side, the distillery has a collaboration with Deer Creek Malthouse supplying them with floor malted barley.

Noco Distillery

Fort Collins, Colorado, founded in 2016

nocodistillery.com

Using four small hand-crafted copper pot stills, a fermentation of up to three weeks, slow distillation and up to nine different types of woods for maturation, the distillery produces gin, rum, vodka, bourbon, rye whiskey as well as single malt. The latter was first released in March 2019.

Oak & Grist Distilling Co.

Black Mountain, North Carolina, founded in 2015

oakandgrist.com

Inspired by Scotch, the owners are focusing on whiskey made from locally grown and malted barley. So far, apart from a genever style gin, the distillery has released a blended, malted whiskey and in June 2020, their first 3 year old single malt whiskey was released. Two of the founders are father and son Ed and Russell Dodson. Ed, with a 40 year plus track record in the Scotch whisky industry, was the distillery manager of Glen Moray until 2005.

Old Home Distillers

Lebanon, New York, founded in 2014

oldhomedistillers.com

The distillery produces bourbon, corn whiskey and single malt whiskey. The mash is fermented on the grain for 4-5 days, distillation takes place in a 100 gallon hybrid column still and the spirit is matured in charred, new American oak for at least seven months.

Old Line Spirits

Baltimore, Maryland, founded in 2014

oldlinespirits.com

The owners bought the equipment from Golden Distillery when that was about to close down and brought it to Baltimore. Distilling started in 2016 and a peated version from their own production was launched in 2017, a sherry cask finish appeared in autumn 2018, a cask strength a year later, Golden Edition (an 8 year old from the first distillery) was released in late 2019 and a port cask finish appeared in early 2021.

Old Route Two Spirits

Barre, Vermont, founded in 2017

oldroutetwo.com

Starting with gin and rum, the distillery started making single malt whiskey in November 2018. This, however is not due for release until 2021/2022.

Old Trestle Distillery

Truckee, California, founded in 2012

oldtrestle.com

Using their own underground aquifer as the water source, the distillery is focused on whiskey production but the first spirit releases were vodka and gin. In summer 2020, their 3 year old Sierra Bourbon was launched while the first American single malt is expected during 2021.

Orange County Distillery

Goshen, New York, founded in 2013

orangecountydistillery.com

The distillery malts their own barley and even use their own peat when needed. Since 2014, they have launched a wide range of whiskies, including corn, bourbon, rye and peated single malt. The first aged single malt was launched in 2015 and the latest, in December 2019, was made using Black Dirt Malt from a local malting company and was matured for two years in virgin oak.

Orcas Island Distillery

Orcas, Washington, founded in 2014

orcasislanddistillery.com

Apple brandy is the main produce but in 2019 the distillery also won the Best American Single Malt Whiskey award from

Old Line Spirits distillery in Baltimore

the American Distilling Institute for his West Island Single Malt Whiskey which was first released in 2018.

Painted Stave Distilling

Smyrna, Delaware, founded in 2013

paintedstave.com

Most of the production is centered on bourbon and rye but there is also Ye Old Barley made from 100% malted barley, Diamond State Pot Still Whiskey made from malted barley and rye and Festskey, made from beer from a local brewery.

Peach Street Distillers

Palisade, Colorado, founded in 2005

peachstreetdistillers.com

An extensive range of various spirits is complemented by a bourbon (first released in 2008) and (soon to be released) a smoky rye and a peated single malt whiskey made from barley.

Pine Bluffs Distilling

Pine Bluffs, Wyoming, founded in 2018

pinebluffsdistilling.com

Malting the barley themselves, the distillery has been relying on vodka, bourbon, malted rye and corn whiskey for their first releases. In December 2019, Burly Malt Whiskey and Munich Style Whiskey, both made from 100% malted barley, were released.

Pioneer Whisky (formerly known as III Spirits)

Talent, Oregon, founded in 2014

pioneerwhisky.com

Focusing mainly on single malts, there are currently two single malts in the range; Oregon Highlander made from a grain bill of brewer's malt, Munich malt and crystal malt and Islay Style Peated Whisky produced from 100% heavily peated malt from Scotland.

PostModern Distilling

Knowville, Tennessee, founded in 2017

postmodernspirits.com

While focusing on gin, vodka and liqueur, the owners released their first single barrel single malt whiskey in 2018 with while one of the latest (October 2020) was Brewer's Stave in collaboration with the nearby Crafty Bastard Brewery.

Prichard´s Distillery

Kelso and Nashville, Tennessee, founded in 1999

prichardsdistillery.com

The main track of the production is rum. The first single malt was launched in 2010 and later releases usually have been vattings from barrels of different age (some up to 10 years old).

Quincy Street Distillery

Riverside, Illinois, founded in 2011

quincystreetdistillery.com

The distillery produces an impressive range of spirits including gin, vodka, absinth, bourbon, corn whiskey and rye. The only single malt released so far is the 2 year old Golden Prairie which was launched in December 2015 for the first time only to return in 2020.

Ranger Creek Brewing & Distilling

San Antonio, Texas, founded in 2010

drinkrangercreek.com

Focusing on beer brewing and whiskey production, the first whiskey release was Ranger Creek .36 Texas Bourbon in 2011. Their first single malt, Rimfire, was launched in 2013. In June 2019, Heavy Smoke Rimfire made from mesquite hand-smoked barley, was released followed by a 5 year old cask strength in 2020.

Rennaisance Artisan Distillers

Akron, Ohio, founded in 2013

renartisan.com

Apart from whiskey, the distillery produces gin, brandy, grappa and limoncello. The first whiskey release, The King´s Cut single malt, was made from a grain bill including toasted and caramel malts and new batches appear every 6 months. In March 2021 Kilted Peat Malt Whiskey was released.

Rock Town Distillery

Little Rock, Arkansas, founded in 2010

rocktowndistillery.com

A true grain-to-glass distillery where the grains are grown within 125 miles of the property. The backbone of the production is made up of several bourbons, rye, wheat whiskey and vodka but there is also a 4 year old single malt matured in toasted French oak.

Sand Creek Distillery

Hugo, Colorado, founded in 2013

sandcreekdistillery.com

Founded by Lucas Hohl, this micro distillery is entirely focused on American malt whiskey. The first Sand Creek single malt was released in 2017 and it was followed by American Redux in 2020.

San Diego Distillery

Spring Valley, California, founded in 2015

sddistillery.com

A distillery focused almost entirely on whiskey. In March 2016 the first six whiskies were released; a bourbon, a rye and an Islay peated single malt. Since then several single malts have been released including a cask strength, a peated, a French oak finish and one that had been matured in a barrel that had held brew coffee.

SanTan Spirits

Chandler and Phoenix, Arizona, founded in 2007 (2015)

santanbrewing.com

With two locations in Arizona, this brewery/restaurant added distilling to its concept in 2015. So far vodka, gin and whiskey has been released. Sacred Stave Single Malt occurs in two versions both finished in red wine barrels with one being bottled at cask strength.

Sauvage Distillery (former KyMar Farm Winery & Distillery)

Charlotteville, New York, founded in 2011

drinksauvage.com

Before Sauvage Beverages bought the distillery in May 2020, the former owners had, apart from wine, liqeurs and apple brandy, managed to release a single malt whiskey as well. It remains to be seen if whiskey from malted barley will remain in the product line.

Seattle Distilling

Vashon, Washington, founded in 2013

seattledistilling.com

The distillery produces gin, vodka, coffee liqueur and malt whiskey. The latter, named Idle Hour, is made from both malted and unmalted barley with an addition of honey and matured in barrels that used to hold local cabernet sauvignon wine.

Seven Caves Spirits

San Diego, California, founded in 2016

the7caves.com

Apart from gin and rum, Geoff Longenecker also makes whiskey from malted barley. The first single malt was released in 2019.

Seven Stills Distillery

San Francisco, California, founded in 2013

sevenstillsofsf.com

On the whiskey side, this combined distillery/brewery/taproom/ restaurant is completely focused on distilling single malt whiskey from craft beer - either from their own beer or from other breweries (collaboration whiskeys). Starting in 2016 in Bayview with beer brewing added in 2017, they moved in autumn 2019 to a much larger facility in Mission Bay.

Shadow Ridge Spirits

Oceanside, California, founded in 2017

srdistilled.com

While rum and (recently) gin may be a part of the range, the distillery is focused on whiskey. Bourbon, rye and American single malt have all been released, the latter made from a combination of different malts and smoked using peat and cherry wood.

Sinister Distlling

Albany, Oregon, founded in 2015

sinisterdeluxe.com

Part of a brewstillery with DeLuxe Brewing as the other half. A variety of spirits are produced in a pot still from Portugal including the 4 year old single barrel Howard Jacob single malt.

Snitching Lady Distillery

Fairplay, Colorado, founded in 2018

snitchingladydistillery.com

The distillery, which moved to new premises in August 2019, has so far released peach brandy, bourbon, rye and blue corn spirit. Single malt made from barley was distilled for the first time in March 2019 but hasn´t been released yet.

South Mountain Distilling

Connelly Springs, North Carolina, founded in 2015

southmountaindistillery.com

Focus is very much on moonshine but there are also matured whiskies in the range including Dignified Single Malt and a corn whiskey named Sinister.

Spirit Hound Distillers

Lyons, Colorado, founded in 2012

spirithounds.com

The distillery´s signature spirits are gin and malt whiskey. The barley for the whiskey is grown, malted and peat-smoked in Alamosa by Colorado Malting. The first bottles hit the shelves in summer 2015 and by summer 2021 close to two-hundred single barrels had been released as well as a cask strength version.

Spirit Lab Distilling

Charlottesville, Virginia, founded in 2016

spiritlabdistilling.com

Founded by the Norway immigrant Ivar Aass, the distillery is making gin, brandy and American malt whiskley. Using a solera system, around ten batches of the cask strength Aass single malt made from Virginia grown barley have been released so far.

Spirits of St Louis Distillery (formerly known as Square One)

St. Louis, Missouri, founded in 2006

spiritsofstlouisdistillery.com

A combined brewery and restaurant. Apart from rum, gin, vodka and absinthe, the owners also produce J.J. Neukomm Whiskey, a malt whiskey made from 25% cherry wood smoked malt.

Stark Spirits

Pasadena, California, founded in 2013

starkspirits.com

The first single malt whiskey was distilled in July 2015 and the first official distillery release of single malt (both peated and un-peated) came in February 2017. They have two stills with one reserved for all the peated production.

Storm King Distilling Co.

Montrose, Colorado, founded in 2017

stormkingdistilling.com

Inspired by a passion for whiskey, the owners released a wheat whiskey and a rye in 2020 while bourbon and single malt is still maturing. Currently for sale are also gin, vodka, rum and different spirits made from agave.

Stoutridge Distillery

Marlboro, New York, founded in 2017

stoutridge.com

A winery was founded in 2006 and was expanded with a distillery in 2017. The range consists of vodka, gin, brandy and whiskey. Their Southern Ulster Single Malt is made from in-house malted barley and matured in ex-Laphroaig casks.

Sugar House Distillery

Salt Lake City, Utah, founded in 2014

sugarhousedistillery.net

The first release from the distillery in 2014 was a vodka, followed later that year by a single malt whisky. More releases of the single malt have followed (as well as bourbon, rye and rum) and a limited single malt finished in Malbec casks was launched in February 2021.

Sweetgrass Distillery

Portland, Maine, founded in 2007

sweetgrasswinery.com

Focusing from the start on wine and the distillation of gin, brandy, rum and liqueur, the distillery went on to producing malt whiskey. Their Sunk Haze malt whiskey is currently released at the age of seven years old.

Talnua Distillery

Denver, Colorado, founded in 2017

talnua.com

With a career in the oil- and gas business, Patrick and Meagan Miller started the distillery with the aim to produce single pot still whiskey in the traditional Irish style. That means, in their case, using a mashbill of 50% unmalted and 50% malted barley as well as practising triple distillation. Their initial pot still was recently replaced by three new ones and the range is made up of Quarter Cask Whiskey (single pot still) and Heritage Selection Whiskey (a blend of pot still and grain whiskey). Limited releases include Olde Saint´s Keep, aged in virgin oak and finished in port casks.

Telluride Distilling

Telluride, Colorado, founded in 2014

telluridedistilling.com

Vodka and malt whiskey is produced in a distillery equipped with open top fermenters and a column still. Maturation is in new charred oak for two years followed by 6 months in port barrels. The first single malt was released in 2016.

Thumb Butte Distillery

Prescott, Arizona, founded in 2013

thumbbuttedistillery.com

A variety of gin, dark rum and vodka, as well as whiskey are produced by the owners. Crown King Single Malt as well as rye and bourbon has been released. The latest version of the single malt has been made from barley smoked by using Arizona pecan wood.

Timber Creek Distillery

Crestview, Florida, founded in 2014

timbercreekdistillery.com

Fermentation and distillation is off the grain and they use a traditional worm tub to cool the spirits. Releases include a rye, a wheated bourbon, a four grain whiskey and Florida Single Malt.

Town Branch Distillery

Lexington, Kentucky, founded in 1999

lexingtonbrewingco.com

In 1980 Dr Pearse Lyons founded Alltech Inc, a biotechnology company specializing in animal nutrition and feed supplements. Alltech purchased Lexington Brewing Company in 1999 and in 2008, two traditional copper pot stills were installed. The first single malt whiskey was released in 2010 under the name Pearse Lyons Reserve and has since been replaced by the 7 year old Town Branch Malt. There is also a limited 11 year old, matured in oloroso casks. In June 2018, Alltech opened yet another distillery in Pikeville - Dueling Barrels Brewery and Distillery.

Triple Eight Distillery

Nantucket, Massachusetts, founded in 2000

ciscobrewers.com

Apart from whiskey, Triple Eight also produces vodka, rum and gin. The first 888 bottles of single malt whiskey were released on 8th August 2008 as an 8 year old. More releases of Notch (as in "not Scotch") have followed and currently there is a 12 year old and a 15 year old.

Two James Spirits

Detroit, Michigan, founded in 2013

twojames.com

Equipped with a 500 gallon pot still with a rectification column attached, the distillery has released vodka, gin, bourbon (even a peated version) and rye while a single malt is still maturing in the warehouse. Aged in ex-sherry casks the whiskey has been made from peated Scottish barley.

Up North Distillery

Post Falls, Idaho, founded in 2015

upnorthdistillery.com

Randy and Hilary Mann had their eyes set on malt whiskey when they started production but the first releases were honey spirits and apple brandy. The first release of North Idaho Single Malt Whiskey was in autumn 2020.

Van Brunt Stillhouse

Brooklyn, New York, founded in 2012

vanbruntstillhouse.com

Part of the Brooklyn Spirits Trail in New York, the distillery made their first release of Van Brunts American Whiskey in 2012. This has been followed by bourbon, rye and corn whiskey. The Van Brunt Single Malt is bottled biannually, produced from a mash bill of eight different malts and fermented on the grain.

Vapor Distillery (formerly known as Roundhouse Spirits)

Boulder, Colorado, founded in 2007

vapordistillery.com

Since 2014 and using a 3,800 litre copper pot still, Ted Palmer and Alastair Brogan focus on American malt whiskey. Currently the distillery has four single malt whiskies in the range – an American Oak Boulder American Single Malt Whiskey, a peated version of the same, one that has been finished in port casks and one bottled in bond.

Venus Spirits

Santa Cruz, California, founded in 2014

venusspirits.com

Production is focused on whiskey, but gin and spirits from blue agave have also been released. The first single malt was Wayward Whiskey, matured in port and sherry casks and released in 2015. This was followed up by a rye and later a bourbon.

Vikre Distillery

Duluth, Minnesota, founded in 2012

vikredistillery.com

Together with whisky - gin, vodka and aquavit are produced at

The owners of Talnua Distillery specialise in production of traditional Irish-style whiskey

the distillery. Whiskies include Iron Range American Single Malt, Northern Courage Smokey Rye, Sugarbush Whiskey and Honor Brand Hay & Sunshine.

Warfield Distillery

Ketchum, Idaho, founded in 2015

drinkwarfield.com

Warfield Organic American Whiskey was launched in December 2019 with a second release in November 2020 and is distilled from organic pale and crystal malts. Gin, vodka, brandy and beer is also produced. In summer 2020 the distillery was expanded with two copper pot stills (3,800 litres each) made by Forsyths in Scotland.

Woodstone Creek Distillery

Cincinnati, Ohio, founded in 1999

woodstonecreek.com

Opened as a farm winery in 1999, a distillery was added to the business in 2003. The first bourbon, was released in 2008 followed by a 10 year old single malt. Whiskey production is very small and just a handfull of releases have appeared since.

Wood´s High Mountain Distillery

Salida, Colorado, founded in 2011

woodsdistillery.com

The first expression (and current big seller), Tenderfoot Whiskey, is a triple malt and so is the release that followed, Sawatch, a 4 year old made from malted barley (a mix of chocolate malt and cherrywood smoked malt), malted rye and malted wheat. The latest version (with a second release in 2021) is the limited 5 year old Dawn Patrol made from 45% cherry-wood smoked barley.

Wright & Brown Distilling Co.

Oakland, California, founded in 2015

wbdistilling.com

The distillery is focused on barrel aged spirits. The first release, a rye whiskey (70/30 rye/barley), appeared in autumn of 2016 and was followed by a bourbon in autumn 2017. In February 2020 it was time for the first single malt, a bottled in bond expression aged for 4,5 years and batch 2 was launched in February 2021.

Canada 

Shelter Point Distillery

Vancouver Island, British Columbia, founded in 2009

shelterpointdistillery.com

Founded by dairy farmer Patrick Evans who in 2005 switched to growing crops and four years later added a distillery. The equipment consists of a one ton mash tun, five stainless steel washbacks and one pair of stills. Distillation started in 2011 and the barley used is grown on the farm. Apart from whisky, gin and vodka is also produced. In 2016, the first 5 year old single malt was released and this is still the core expression. Limited releases in 2021 include Forbidden batch 2 which is a 6 year old made from malted wheat, the sixth version of Double Barreled this time finished in French oak wine barrels, the first edition of Smoke & Oak where spirit made from 100% unmalted barley had been finished in barrels that had been smoked with applewood and peat and, finally, a 10 year old version of their cask strength.

Still Waters Distillery

Concord, Ontario, founded in 2009

stillwatersdistillery.com

The distillery is equipped with a 3,000 litre mash tun, two 3,000 litre washbacks and a Christian Carl 450 litre pot still. The still also has rectification columns. The focus is on whisky but they also produce vodka, brandy and gin. Their first single malt, named Stalk & Barrel Single Malt, was released in 2013 and it was followed in 2014 by the first rye whisky. The range now consists of Blue Blend, Red Blend, Rye and Single Malt. In June 2020 the Three Barrel Whisky, a blend of rye, single malt and corn whisky, was released.

Victoria Caledonian Distillery

Victoria, British Columbia, founded in 2016

victoriacaledonian.com

Founded by the Scotsman Graeme Macaloney the distillery is equipped with a one ton semilauter mash tun, 7 stainless steel washbacks, a 5,500 litre wash still and a 3,600 litre spirit still. Some of the barley is malted on site and there is also a craft beer brewery. In late 2017 the owners released the Mac Na Braiche, a 12 months malt spirit. The first 3 year old single malt was released in 2020. Recently, Macaloney and his distillery has become involved in a legal debate about the use of words like ”island” and ”Macaloney” on the product´s labels and the Scotch Whisky Association has filed a lawsuit against the company.

Glenora Distillery

Glenville, Nova Scotia, founded in 1990

glenoradistillery.com

Situated in Nova Scotia, Glenora was the first malt whisky distillery in Canada. The first launch of in-house produce came in 2000, an 8 year old named Glen Breton Rare and a 10 year old is now the core expression. Other expressions have occured - 14, 19, 21 and 25 year olds. Glen Breton Ice, aged in an ice wine barrel, was launched in 2006 and the latest edition was a 19 year old. A recent limited release is the Glen Breton Alexander Keith´s 18 year old which was distilled from an IPA made at a local brewery.

Other distilleries in Canada

Arbutus Distillery

Nanaimo, British Columbia, founded in 2014

arbutusdistillery.com

The distillery is focusing on vodka, gin and other spirits but single malt whisky is also on the agenda. The first 3 year old appeared in December 2018 and the most recent is Double Barrel launched in November 2019.

Bridgeland Distillery

Calgary, Alberta, founded in 2018

bridgelanddistillery.com

Equipped with an unusual copper pot still where the lyne arm is extended with a large copper spiral leading to a condenser. A single malt spirit was released in August 2019 and Taber Corn Berbon (a Canadian take on bourbon) appeared in spring 2021.

Central City Brewers & Distillers

Surrey, British Columbia, founded in 2013

centralcitybrewing.com

One of Canada´s largest craft breweries added a distillery in 2013. The whisky is sold under the Lohin McKinnon Single Malt brand including special bottlings such as peated, chocolate malt and one finished in Niagara wine barrels.

De Vine Wine & Spirits

Victoria, British Columbia, founded in 2007

devinevineyards.ca

Starting as winemakers, the owners added a distillery in 2014. The first whisky was the 3 year old single malt Glen Saanich which was first released in 2017. Made from floor malted barley it was later followed up by Ancient Grains which had been made from a combination of barley, spelt, emmer, einkorn and kamut.

Dubh Glas Distillery, The

Oliver, British Columbia, founded in 2015

thedubhglasdistillery.com

The whisky is double distilled in an Arnold Holstein still and gin is also produced. Initial products were Noteworthy Gin and Virgin Spirits Barley (a newmake). The first release of a single malt was the peated Against All Odds in June 2019. During the pandemic Grant Stevely has been extremely prolific with a number of whisky releases; a series of four called Pandemic (Quarantine, Isolation, Social Distance and Lockdown), single barrels like Smoke on the Water, Fire in the Sky and Hardly Typical and finally, A Beautiful Man - matured in ex Glenglassaugh octaves.

Eau Claire Distillery

Turner Valley, Alberta, founded in 2014

eauclairedistillery.ca

The distillery's first limited single malt whisky appeared in December 2017 with Batch 4 (a combination of ex-bourbon and new European oak) released in November 2020. The range also includes Ploughman's Rye and the blend Rupert's Whisky.

Ironworks Distillery

Lunenburg, Nova Scotia, founded in 2010

ironworksdistillery.com

Focusing on rum, brandy and vodka, Lynne MacKay and Pierre Guevremont started to produce also whisky. Heart Iron single malt was released in 2020 followed by a second edition in March 2021.

Last Mountain Distillery

Lumsden, Saskatchewan, founded in 2010

lastmountaindistillery.com

Equipped with two copper stills with columns from Carl in Germany, the distillery produces vodka, gin, rum, limoncello and whisky including rye, wheat and single malt from barley. The latest single malt bottling was 4 years old.

Liberty Distillery, The

Vancouver, British Columbia, founded in 2010

thelibertydistillery.com

Equipped with two copper stills with columns from Carl in Germany, the distillery produces gin, vodka and a wide range of whiskies made from organic grain. Sold under the brand name Trust Whiskey, there are two single malts matured in madeira and burgundy casks respectively as well as rye, corn and grain whiskies.

Lucky Bastard Distillers

Saskatoon, Saskatchewan, founded in 2012

lbdistillers.ca

Founded by Michael Goldney, Cary Bowman and Lacey Crocker, in 2012. The first releases were vodka, gin and a variety of liqueurs. In summer 2016 the first single malt appeared and this is now released in small batches.

Maison Sivo

Hinchinbrooke, Quebec, founded in 2014

maisonsivo.ca

Inspired by production of fruit brandies in Hungary where he grew up, Janos Sivo produces different kinds of spirit including whisky. Le Single Malt finished in Sauternes casks and Le Rye were both released in 2018. There is also the limited Le Sélection Single Malt.

Odd Society Spirits

Vancouver, British Columbia, founded in 2013

oddsocietyspirits.com

The first two whiskies appeared in late 2018; the Commodore single malt and the Prospector rye. This was followed in late 2019 by Maple - a single malt that had been smoked with maple wood and matured in casks that had previously contained maple syrup.In March 2020 the single malt Blender's Release was launched.

Okanagan Spirits

Vernon and Kelowna, British Columbia, founded in 2004

okanaganspirits.com

The first Okanagan distillery was started in 1970 but closed in 1995. In 2004 Okanagan Spirits was established and a distillery was opened in Vernon. A variety of spirits including gin, vodka and whisky are being produced. In 2013 the Laird of Fintry single malt was released with different expressions. The calvados matured Packinghouse Amber was added to the range in April 2021.

Pemberton Distillery

Pemberton, British Columbia, founded in 2009

pembertondistillery.ca

Vodka made from potatoes was the distillery's first product. In 2010, the owner started their first trials distilling a single malt whisky using organic malted barley. The first release was in 2013 when a 3 year old unpeated version was launched. Since 2015, the owners have a regular expression called Pemberton Valley Organic Single Malt Whisky with a 10 year old being the latest release.

Phillips Fermentorium

Victoria, British Columbia, founded in 2014

fermentorium.ca

Started as a brewery, distillation of spirits was added 13 years later. The first release was gin and this was followed in late 2019 by the 5 year old single malt Small Talk Whiskey which had been matured in a combination of ex-pinot noir wine barrels and bourbon barrels that had been seasoned with the company's own beer.

Rig Hand Distillery

Nisku, Alberta, founded in 2014

righanddistillery.com

Equipped with a 1,100 litre pot still with columns, a Christian Carl still and a gin still, the distillery produces whisky. vodka, rum and gin with the first whisky appearing in 2017. Bar M was a blended whisky made from wheat, barley and rye. This was followed by the Diamond S single malt, the Rocking R rye and, in autumn 2019, the Lazy B corn whisky.

Sheringham Distillery

Sooke, British Columbia, founded in 2015

sheringhamdistillery.com

Gin, akvavit and vodka were the first to be bottled while the inaugural release of their Red Fife and Woodhaven whiskies came in 2019. The owners work on different mash bills with malted barley, corn, rye and wheat.

Yaletown Distilling

Vancouver, British Columbia, founded in 2013

yaletowndistillingco.com

Distillery, restaurant and bar - the owners produce vodka, gin and the 3 year old single malt Yaletown

Yukon Spirits

Whitehorse, Yukon, founded in 2009

twobrewerswhisky.com

All of the whisky produced is made from malted grains but not only barley but also wheat and rye. The first bottles of the 7 year old Two Brewer's Yukon Single Malt Whisky were released in 2016 and the current portfolio is based on four styles; Classic, Peated, Special Finishes and Innovative.

Australia & New Zealand

Australia

Lark Distillery

Hobart, Tasmania, founded 1992

larkdistillery.com

In 1992, Bill Lark was the first person for 153 years to take out a distillation licence in Tasmania. The success of the distillery forced Bill Lark to bring in investors in the company to generate future growth and since April 2018, Australian Whisky Holdings (AWH) holds a majority of the shares. Late 2019, AWH announced that they would perform a brand transformation of Lark whisky through a three tier price strategy. Including an investment upgrading the production by 350,000 litres, the aim is to turn the whisky from a "local brand to a global hero" with a focus on Asia. In 2020, AWH also changed name to Lark Distilling Co. The whisky is double-distilled in a 1,800 litre wash still and a 600 litre spirit still and then matured in 100 litre "quarter casks". The core products in the whisky range are the Classic Cask at 43% and Cask Strength at 58%. In 2020, Symphony, the first blended malt from the company was launched. Limited releases during 2021 include Rum Cask III, the 19 year old Legacy in honour of Bill Lark, Ruby Pinot Cask Finish, Mizunara Cask, the smoky Chinotto Cask and the fourth edition of Wolf Release where casks that had held smoked porter were used to mature the whisky.

Bakery Hill Distillery

North Balwyn, Victoria, founded 1998

bakeryhill.com

The first spirit at Bakery Hill Distillery, founded by David Baker, was produced in 2000 and the first single malt was launched in autumn 2003. Three different versions are available – Classic and Peated (both matured in ex-bourbon casks) and Double Wood (ex-bourbon and a finish in French Oak). As Classic and Peated are also available as cask strength bottlings, they can be considered two more varieties. Limited releases also occur with one of the latest being Sovereign Smoke – Defiantly Peated and Little French Pete.. After many years of planning, David Baker decided in 2021 to move the distillery to Kensington in the western parts of Melbourne. The new distillery will be operational in late 2021 or early 2022.

Sullivans Cove Distillery

Cambridge, Tasmania, founded 1994

sullivanscove.com

Founded in 1994, Patrick Maguire joined the company five years later as head distiller and co-owner. In 2016, Maguire and the other owners sold the distillery to a company led by Adam Sable who was general manager of Bladnoch distillery for two years. The big break through for the brand came in 2014 when Jim Murray in his Whisky Bible named the French Oak Single Cask the world´s best whisky. The core range from the distillery comprises of American Oak, French Oak (where the barrels have contained tawny) and Double Cask. There is also the Special Cask range where the latest release (in August 2021) was a 12 year old matured in casks that had held the fortified wine Frontignac, Old & Rare with whiskies that are 16 years or older and Limited Edition. In 2021 the owners revealed plans to move the entire operation back to the Hobart waterfront to a site close to where the original distillery was founded.

Hellyers Road Distillery

Burnie, Tasmania, founded 1999

hellyersroaddistillery.com.au

Hellyer´s Road Distillery is one of the larger single malt whisky distilleries in Australia with a capacity of doing 120,000 litres of pure alcohol per year. The distillery is equipped with a 6.5 ton mash tun, a 60,000 litre wash still and a 20,000 litre spirit still. The pots on both stills are made of stainless steel while heads, necks and lyne arms are made of copper. The large stills and a slow distillation call for an unusually long middle-cut, 24 hours. The first whisky was released in 2006 and there are now more than ten different expression in the range, including 10 and 12 year olds, peated as well as unpeated and various finishes. A range of limited releases called Master Series include whiskies up to 17 years old.

Great Southern Distilling Company

Albany, Western Australia, founded 2004

distillery.com.au

The distillery is located at Princess Royal Harbour in Albany. In 2015, the owners opened a second distillery in Margaret River which will is focused on gin production and in autumn 2018 a third distillery, Tiger Snake in Porongurup, started production. The

A huge part of the success of Sullivan´s Cove single malt is due to Patrick Maguire who joined the company in 1999

combined production is 400,000 litres of pure alcohol per year. The first expression of the whisky, called Limeburners, was released in 2008 and the core range now consists of American Oak, Port Cask, Sherry Cask and Peated. Special yet yearly editions include the heavily peated Darkest Winter bottled at 66% and two Director´s Cut – Peated Sherry and Peated Port – both bottled at 61%.

Starward Distillery

Melbourne, Victoria, founded 2008

starward.com.au

The distillery, founded by David Vitale, was moved in 2016 to a bigger site in Port Melbourne. The original stills (an 1,800 litre wash still and a 600 litre spirit still) were complemented in 2020 with a new 7,000 litre wash still while at the same time the old wash still became the new spirit still. The first Starward single malt was released in 2013 and the current range consists of Nova (matured in Australian red wine barrels), Solera (matured in casks that had held apera, the Australian version of sherry), Fortis (fully matured in American oak) and the blended whisky Two-Fold (made from malted barley and wheat). Recent limited expressions include a mesquite smoked single malt, the sixth batch of Ginger Beer Cask and, launched in July 2021, Unexpeated. The latter has been matured in red wine barrels and then finished in ex-Islay casks.

Archie Rose Distilling Company

Rosebery and Botany, New South Wales, founded in 2014

archierose.com.au

What started as a fairly ordinary distillery, both in terms of size and production technique, was completely changed in November 2020 when their new distillery in Botany in south east Sydney was opened. This is now the largest whisky distillery in Australia but what stands out is how the whisky is produced. The mashing is done with a mash filter (the same is used at Teaninich and Inchdairnie in Scotland). The really unique thing though is how they handle their different malts in the process. The whisky from Archie Rose was from the start based on a six-malt mash bill. In the new distillery, each malt variety is handled separately all the way from milling, through brewing, fermentation, distillation and maturation. Only after that is the whisky blended together. This way each malt variety can be handled with regards to its own specific attributes. This technique, which requires lots of fermenters as well as other equipment, has been patented by the company which started a discussion amongst some other distillers in Australia. They fear that the the patent might restrain their own production and, especially, blending.

Apart from producing rye whisky and peated and unpeated single malt, the distillery also makes gin, rum and vodka. In June 2019 Chocolate Rye Malt became their first whisky release and more editions have followed. One was the Ironbark Smoked Rye Malt Whisky in October 2019 where the smoky flavour had been imparted by using water from blocks of ice that had been allowed to melt in a wood-fired oven at a nearby restaurang.

Sawford Distillery

Kingston, Tasmania, founded in 2018

sawforddistillery.com

While Sawford may be a new distillery there is a background that goes back to 2007. In that year Casey Overeem founded the Old Hobart Distillery and eventually he had made a name for himself with his Overeem single malt and was also joined by his daugther Jane. In 2014, Old Hobart distillery was acquired by Lark Distillery and later by Australian Whisky Holdings. In summer 2020, the Overeem trademark and part of the whisky inventory was sold back to Jane (who was married Sawford) and her husband Mark. The equipment was not included and henceforth Overeem whisky is produced at the new Sawford distillery which is equipped with two stills from Knapp Lewer (1,800 and 800 litres respectively).

Other distilleries in Australia

5 Nines Distilling

Uraidla, South Australia, founded in 2017

5ninesdistilling.com.au

The owners built the equipment themselves including a copper pot still and a mash tun. The whisky is made primarily with local barley and the first releases appeared in August 2020 - a vatting of four bourbon casks as well as single barrels such as pinot, sherry, tawny and a special cask strength version.

7K Distillery

Brighton, Tasmania, founded in 2017

7kdistillery.com.au

A wide range of gins were intially released followed by their first single malt in August 2020. This was followed by more bottlings, for instance the Double Barrel in February 2021.

2020 Distillery

Cooroy, Queensland, founded 2020

2020distillery.com.au

While gin has already been launched, the owners are also working on single malt (both unpeated and peated), triple distilled single malt and a 100% rye - all of which have yet to be released.

Adams Distillery

Perth, Tasmania, founded in 2016

adamsdistillery.com.au

After less than two years of production, all the equipment was sold to make way for a huge new distillery which started production in March 2019. Around the same time, the first 2 year old single malt was also released and it was followed by more whisky matured in port, sherry and pinot noir casks. In February 2021, the distillery burned to the ground but the owners have plans to restore it.

Adelaide Hills Distillery

Hay Valley, South Australia, founded in 2018

adelaidehillsdistillery.com.au

With his distillery, Sacha La Forgia is leading the way when it comes to producing whisky from Australian native grains. His trials have been numerous and the first bottling in 2019 couldn´t even be called whisky since wattleseed (which was part of the mash bill) isn´t a cereal grain. The second release though, when weeping grass was used (together with malted barley), found approval in May 2020. In May 2021, 78 Degrees Australian Whiskey was launched. This had been distilled predominantly from unmalted barley together with eleven different specialty malts..

Aisling Distillery, The

Griffith, New South Wales, founded in 2015

theaislingdistillery.com.au

With a focus on malt whisky - gin, vodka and rum is also produced. The first two single malts (matured for 4 years in apera casks and tawny casks respectively) were released in November 2020.

Backwoods Distilling

Yackandandah, Victoria, founded in 2017

backwoodsdistilling.com.au

The distillery is equipped with a 1200 litre copper ot still with an attached column. The first distillation was in January 2018 and the first release of whiskies (a malt and a rye) were in August 2020. One of the most recent appeared in March 2021 with a malt whisky, unusually matured in endemic red gum (eucalyptus) casks.

Baker Williams Distillery

Mudgee, New South Wales, founded in 2012

bakerwilliams.com.au

For the first six years, the owners were focusing on producing gin, vodka and schnapps. The first whisky was Lachlan, released in spring 2018 and made from barley, wheat and rye (all malted). The fourth and latest batch was released in November 2020.

Barossa Distilling Company

Nuriootpa, South Australia, founded in 2016

barossadistilling.com

Located in the historical Old Penfolds Distillery established in 1913, the distillery has focused on gin the first years and have launched a dozen different styles so far. Malt whisky is also produced but is still maturing.

Bellarine Distillery

Drysdale, Victoria, founded in 2017

bellarinedistillery.com.au

Located at the unlikely address Scotchman´s Road, the distillery is equipped with four stills, producing both gin and malt whisky. The first whisky, released in spring 2021, had been matured in charred pinot noir barrels and then married in ex-bourbon casks.

Black Gate Distillery

Mendooran, New South Wales, founded in 2012

blackgatedistillery.com

Apart from malt whisky, the distillery produces vodka and rum. The first single malt was in 2015 when a sherrymatured expression was released. More bottlings have followed, including a 3 year old peated single malt matured in a tawny cask released in early 2021.

Callington Mill Distillery

Oatlands, Tasmania, founded in 2021

callingtonmilldistillery.com.au

In 2017, investor John Ibrahim with interests in Redland and Shene distilleries, bought a property 80 kilometres north of Hobart with the intention of turning it into a major distillery. With an investment of $20m construction started in February 2020 and the distillery started producing in 2021. Equipped with two copper pot stills and eight washbacks, the distillery has a capacity of producing 400,000 litres of pure alcohol

Cape Byron Distillery

McLeods Shoot, New South Wales, founded 2016

capebyrondistillery.com

A family owned distillery situated on a macadamia farm which the founder´s, Eddie Brook, parents bought in 1988. Some 40% of the 96-acre estate is made up of rainforest which was re-generated by the family. When Eddie was working as the brand manager for Bruichladdich and Botanist gin in Australia he met the legendary Jim McEwan and together they decided to build a distillery. The original intention was to do only gin and there are now three varieties in the range. In February 2019, however, they also started producing malt whisky in the 2,000 litre pot still. Although not yet released it is now (2 years old) a whisky by Australian standards.

Castle Glen Distillery

The Summit, Queensland, founded in 2009

castleglenaustralia.com.au

Established as a vineyard in 1990, Castle Glen moved on to open up also a brewery and a distillery in 2009. Apart from wine and beer, a wide range of spirits are produced. The first whisky, Castle Glen Limited Edition, was released as a 2 year old in 2012 while the latest was a 9 year old single malt.

Chief´s Son Distillery

Somerville, Victoria, founded in 2017

chiefsson.com.au

The distillery is equipped with a 4,000 litre copper pot still which makes it larger than most craft distilleries in Australia. The owners focus on malt whisky and the first release appeared in March 2019. They currently have a core range made up of three varieties matured in French oak – the lightly peated 900 Standard, the 900 Sweet Peat and 900 Pure malt – and also the 900 American Oak. Recent limited expressions include The Tanist (autumn 2020) and their second Cask Expression, finished in a combination of ex-porter barrels and ex-Russian imperisl stout barrels (February 2021).

Coburns Distillery

Burrawang, New South Wales, founded in 2017

coburnsdistillery.com.au

Mark Coburn started production in spring 2017 and has so far released several versions of his gin. The single malt turned two years old in July 2019 but has yet to be released. Coburns is one of very few Australian distilleries with its own peat bog for smoking the barley. Plans for the future include having a set of no less than five 5,000 litre pot stills.

Corowa Distilling Co.

Corowa, New South Wales, founded in 2010

corowawhisky.com.au

Situated in a restored flour mill the distillery is focused entirely on single malt whisky using barley from their own estate. Corowa started distilling in 2016 and the inaugural release from their own production was First Drop (aged in port barrels) in August 2018 followed by Bosque Verde (also port) and Quicks Courage (PX sherry). In summer 2020, their first peated whisky was released and March 2021 saw the release of the 4.5 year old Muscat Cask finish.

Corra Linn Distillery

Relbia, Tasmania, founded in 2015

corralinndistillery.com.au

John Wielstra made the first distillation in his hybrid column still in autumn 2016. He is using his own yeast and smokes his barley using dried kelp instead of peat. The first release of single malt was in December 2018 and they are sold as single barrels and bottled at cask strength. A limited edition is called Rueben.

Craft Works Distillery

Capertee, New South Wales, founded 2018

craftworker.com.au

The first releases from the owner, Crafty Fields, were collaborations with other distillers. The first whisky from his own production was I Am..., released in early 2021. This had been matured in a combination of casks that had held shiraz, cabernet sauvignon and vintage port.

Darby-Norris Distillery

Scottsdale, Tasmania, founded in 2018

darbynorrisdistillery.com.au

The distillery recently moved from Kelso to larger premises in Scottsdale. Gin and vodka have been released but the first single malt isn´t expected at least until 2021.

Devil´s Distillery

Moonah, Tasmania, founded in 2015

devilsdistillery.com.au, hobartwhisky.com.au

Malt whisky is the main focus but vodka and various liqueurs were the first bottlings to be launched. The first release of their Hobart

Single Malt was in 2018 with several wood finishes following (pinot noir, rosé, botrytis, stout). A recent limited edition from July 2020, had been matured for 3.5 years in small bourbon casks, then one year in a large rumcask and finally finished for 12 days in an ex-Laphroaig cask.

Edge of the World Distillery

Burnine, Tasmania, founded 2019

edgeoftheworlddistillery.com.au

A family owned distillery with the first spirits distilled in late 2019. Focus is on malt whisky with the first bottlings expected in 2022/2023 but other products, including gin, are also in the plans.

Fannys Bay Distillery

Lulworth, Tasmania, founded in 2015

fannysbaydistillery.com.au

The distillery is equipped with a 400 litre copper pot still and they use a long (7-8 days) fermentation. The first whisky was released in May 2017 and it is now available in three main versions - bourbon, sherry and port. Most of the releases are single barrels and recently they have started to bottle lightly peated versions as well.

Fleurieu Distillery

Goolwa, South Australia, founded in 2016

fleurieudistillery.com.au

A beer brewery was turned into a distillery in 2016 but whisky had been distilled already since 2014. The first single malt appeared in December 2016 and it has been followed by several more with names like Tea in the Sahara, Englishman in New York and From Country to Coast. The latter was a collaboration with Black Gate Distillery and made from whiskies from both distilleries. In May 2021 The Jabberwocky, a marriage of whiskies that did not exhibit the distillery´s typical style, was released.

Furneaux Distillery

Flinders Island, Tasmania, founded in 2018

furneauxdistillery.com.au

Located on Flinders Island in the Bass Strait north east of Tasmania. The fermented wash is brought in from Launceston Distillery and then distilled at Furneaux. The first single malts, peated and matured in bourbon and apera casks, were released in August 2020 and in July 2021 Smoky Wedding Double Oak was launched.

Headlands Distilling Co.

North Wollongong, New South Wales, founded 2018

headlands.com.au

A range of gins and vodka were the first releases from this distillery but in December 2020, the first two single malts were launched, finished in apera and muscat casks respectively. Next up, in 2021, was an Illawarra Plum cask matured whisky..

Hillwood Whisky

Hillwood, Tasmania, founded in 2018

hillwoodwhisky.com.au

The Herron family is focusing entirely on malt whisky with no other spirits produced. The spirit is distilled in a 600 litre copper pot still and maturation takes place in small casks that have previously held either wine or sherry, bourbon and port. The first, small releases (all single barrels) appeared in summer 2020.

Hunnington Distillery

Kettering, Tasmania, founded 2016

hunningtondistillery.com.au

Focusing on gin and vodka, the owners also produce small volumes of triple distilled single malt whisky. The whisky is bottled barrel by barrel and the first release appeared in August 2020.

Iron House Brewery & Distillery

White Sands Resort, Tasmania, founded in 2007

ironhouse.com.au

Established as a brewery it moved to its current location in 2010 and started distilling whisky as well. The first Tasman Whisky (as the brand is called) was released in summer 2019 and the core range currently consists of Port-, Sherry- and Bourbon Cask - all aged for more than 4 years. There is also a peated whisky in the pipeline.

Joadja Distillery

Joadja, New South Wales, founded in 2014

joadjadistillery.com.au

Equipped with just the one still (800 litres), the distillery was expanded in 2015 with a 2,400 litre wash still. The main part of the barley is from their own fields. The first whisky was launched in autumn 2017 with a combined bourbon/oloroso maturation (release 13) in 2021 as their latest bottling.

Jones & Smith Distillery

Spring Hill, New South Wales, founded 2017

jonesandsmithdistillery.com.au

A family owned craft distillery which started producing single malt whisky in August 2018. Their Epoch gin was first released in late 2019 and in 2021 it was time for the inaugural whisky.

Kangaroo Island Spirits

Cygnet River, South Australia, founded in 2006

kispirits.com.au

Focusing on gin for the first decade, Jon (brother of Bill Lark) and Sarah Lark started distilling also malt whisky in 2018. In autumn 2021 the distillery was substantially upgraded with larger stills and the first single malt release is expected in late 2021.

Kilderkin Distillery

Ballarat, Victoria, founded in 2016

kilderkindistillery.com.au

The distillery is equipped with one pair of copper pot stills and have so far released a range of different gins. The first malt whisky release isn´t expected until 2021.

Killara Distillery

Richmond, Tasmania, founded in 2016

killaradistillery.com

Daughter of Bill Lark, Kristy Booth, opened her own distillery in summer 2016 after having worked with her father for 17 years. The succesful Apothecary gin has been on the market for a while and in November 2018 it was time for the first single malt release - a cask strength matured for two years in an ex-tawny port cask. More releases have followed and in April 2021, a 2 year old Killara single malt was one of eight Australian single malts released by the UK independent bottler That Boutique-y Whisky Company. In autumn 2020 the distillery moved from Hobart to a new site in Richmond.

Kinglake Distillery

Kinglake, Victoria, founded in 2018

kinglakedistillery.com.au

Located close to the Yarra Valley, the distillerry is focused on malt whisky produced in a 2,500 litre copper pot still. Unusual features are a mash tun stirred by hand and also the use of chocolate malt in the mash bill. The first whisky was released in March 2021.

Launceston Distillery

Western Junction (near Launceston), Tasmania, founded in 2013

launcestondistillery.com.au

The equipment consists of a 1,100 litre stainless steel mash tun, stainless steel washbacks, a 1,600 litre wash still and a 700 litre spirit still. The newmake is filled into barrels which have previously held bourbon, apera and tawny (Australian port). The first release, matured in Apera casks, appeared in July 2018 and whisky matured in ex-bourbon and ex-tawny, also at cask strength, have followed since. The first peated version appeared in May 2020.

Lawrenny Distilling

Ouse, Tasmania, founded in 2017

lawrenny.com

With a head distiller previously working for Lark and Archie Rose, Joe Dinsmoor, the distillery has initially been releasing vodka and gin. The first distillation of malt whisky was in November 2017 and the first whisky, named Ascension, initially matured in a combination of ex-bourbon and Australian port casks and with a finish in PX sherry butts, was launched in November 2020.

Loch Distillery

Loch, Victoria, founded in 2014

lochbrewery.com.au

A combined brewery and distillery using the wash from their brewery for the whisky production. The first single malt was launched in 2018 and in spring 2021, around 20 different releases had been made including a heavily peated PX sherry cask.

Lower Marsh Distillery

Apsley, Tasmania, founded 2019

lowermarshdistillery.com

With the first distillation in autumn 2019, Steve Knight and Corey Hazelwood are producing malt whisky from barley grown on their own farm. The spirit is matured in a variety of casks (apera, port, Jack Daniels) and the first release is due in 2021

The McLaren Vale Distillery

Blewitt Springs, South Australia, founded in 2014

themclarenvaledistillery.com.au

The distillery was founded by John Rochfort, the previous CEO at Lark Distillery and Jock Harvey of Chalk Hill Wines. In 2020, the two founders split and Harvey is now the sole owner. The distillery

has a capacity to make 50,000 litres and the spirit is matured in Australian ex-wine casks. In 2017, twenty different malt spirits (not yet matured for two years) were launched to showcase different types of maturation and in December 2020, the first two malt whiskies were released - Dutschke Single Cask (ex-tawny port) and Mr Riggs Shiraz Cask with a muscat finish. In autumn 2021 the distillery was expanded with more stills.

Manly Spirits Co. Distillery

Brookvale, Sydney, New South Wales, founded in 2017

manlyspirits.com.au

Equipped with two copper pot stills (1,500 l and 1,000 l), the distillery has already launched gin, vodka and a white dog malt spirit. The first single malt whisky named North Fort is due for release in autumn 2021.

Mt Uncle Distillery

Walkamin, North Queensland, founded in 2001

mtuncle.com

The owners started out by producing gin, rum and vodka - all of which soon became established brands on the market. Their first single malt, The Big Black Cock, was released in April 2014 matured for five years and was then followed by Watkins Whisky.

Nant Distillery

Bothwell, Tasmania, founded in 2007

nant.com.au

The distillery was founded by Keith Batt but was later taken over by Australian Whisky Holdings. The distillery is equipped with a 1,800 litre wash still, a 600 litre spirit still and wooden washbacks. The first bottlings were released in 2010 and the current core range consists of Sherry, Port and Bourbon - all bottled at 43% and 63%.

Noosa Heads Distillery

Noosaville, Queensland, founded in 2018

noosaheadsdistillery.com

Equipped with a 2,000 litre copper pot reflux still, the distillery launched its first products in 2019 – gin, vodka and a white malt. Single malt whisky is maturing but won't be released until 2021.

Launceston Distillery

Old Kempton Distillery

Kempton, Tasmania, founded in 2013

oldkemptondistillery.com.au

Established as Redlands Estate Distillery, the distillery re-located in 2016 to Dysart House in Kempton and later changed the name to Old Kempton Distillery. The distillery is equipped with four stills and the first single malt whisky was launched in 2015. This has been followed by several more releases including Solera Batch 2 and The Old Stables Batch 2 in March 2021.

Otter Craft Distilling

St Peters, New South Wales, founded 2017

ocdistilling.com

This small distillery has launched a wide range of vodkas and in summer 2019 the first single malt whisky was released. Several more have followed, always bottled as a single barrel.

Riverbourne Distillery

Jingera, New South Wales, founded in 2016

riverbournedistillery.com

Located close to Canberra, the distillery produces whisky, rum and vodka. The first two single malts, released in June 2018, were The Riverbourne Identity and The Riverbourne Supremacy followed later by Ultimatum, Enigma and Initiative which is the latest and the first to be rum-finished.

Sandy Gray Distillery

Spreyton, Tasmania, founded 2016

sandygraywhisky.com.au

A micro distillery producing gin and small volumes of single malt that is matured in 25 litre casks. The first whisky was released in September 2019.

Settlers Artisan Spirits

McLaren Vale, South Australia, founded in 2015

settlersspirits.com.au

Until now the distillery has been concentrating on gin but with a new pot still in 2018, whisky distillation has tripled. The only single malt release so far is the port matured Settlers Single Malt.

Shene Distillery

Pontville, Tasmania, founded in 2015

shene.com.au

Damian Mackey started distilling whisky already in 2007. In 2016, with the aid of investor John Ibrahim, the opportunity came for him to move his production to the Shene Estate at Pontville. With four stills and a capacity of 300,000 litres this is one of the largest distilleries in Australia. The whisky is either double or triple distilled and the first release of Mackey single malt was in 2017. In spring 2021, an entire new range was launched; Cognac Release, Elixir of Life, Solera Cask, Mackey Trinity and Mackey Enigma.

Souwester Spirits

Margaret River, Western Australia, founded in 2016

souwesterspirits.com

With a background in the wine business, Danielle Costley decided early on that her spirits (gin and malt whisky) would be matured in ex-wine casks. The first single malt, lightly peated and matured in an ice chardonnay barrique, was released in November 2020.

Spring Bay Distillery

Spring Beach, Tasmania, founded in 2015

springbaydistillery.com.au

A small, family-owned distillery, equipped with a 1200 litre pot still and a 2,500 litre wash still. The first spirit released was a gin

followed in autumn 2017 by the first single malt. More whiskies, matured in port, sherry and bourbon casks, have appeared since.

Stillmaker and Sons Distillery

Montville, Queensland, founded 2019

facebook.com/stillmakerandsonsdistillery/

A family-owned distillery entirely focused on single malt whisky. The first bottled products are expected during 2021.

Tamar Valley Distillery

Hillwood, Tasmania, founded in 2018

hillwoodwhisky.com.au

Equipped with a 600 litre copper pot still this distillery has a pure focus on malt whisky. Maturation takes place in a combination of local casks from Tasmanian vineyards as well as ex-sherry and ex-bourbon. The first releases of Hillwood whisky appeared in June 2020 and the whisky is always bottled as single barrel.

Tara Distillery

Nowra Hill, New South Wales, founded 2019

taradistillery.com

The first spirit from the distillery that was launched was a gin in autumn 2020. The owners also produce an Irish-style single pot still as well as single malt whisky, both of them still maturing.

Taylor & Smith Distilling Co.

Moonah, Tasmania, founded in 2017

taylorandsmith.com.au

Using a self-built, direct-fired 400 litre pot still, the owners produce small volumes of gin and malt whisky. The first 210 bottles of their single malt were released in October 2020 and several more expressions have followed matured in bourbon, sherry or port casks.

Timboon Railway Shed Distillery

Timboon, Victoria, founded in 2007

timboondistillery.com.au

Wash from a local brewery is distilled twice in a 600 litre pot still. The first whisky release (and still a signature expression), matured in port barrels, was made in 2010 and one of the latest bottlings was the limited Governor´s Reserve in February 2021.

Tin Shed Distilling Co.

Welland (Adelaide), South Australia, founded in 2013

iniquity.com.au

The owners opened their first distillery, Southern Coast Distillers, in 2004. Eventually it was closed and the current distillery started in 2013. The first single malt, under the name Iniquity, was launched as a 2 year old in 2015 and the 3 year old batch 20 was released in December 2020. In spring 2021 the heavily peated Flustercluck appeared as part of their Anomaly series.

Tria Prima Distillery

Mount Barker, South Australia, founded 2017

triaprima.com.au

With the distillery, equipped with a 2,200 litre pot still, located in the Adelaide Hills, Paul and Trang Shand are focusing on malt whisky but rum is also on the horizon. The first single malts, the 3 year old Enchantress and Bruxa, were released in August 2021.

Turner Stillhouse

Grindelwald, Tasmania, founded in 2018

turnerstillhouse.com

Founded by ex-Californian Justin Turner, the distillery has so far been focusing on gin. A designated whisky still was installed in summer 2019 and the first single malt release is expected in 2021.

Union Brewery & Distillery (former Geographe Distillery)

Fremantle, Western Australia, founded in 2008

unionfremantle.com.au

Apart from gin and limoncello, malt whisky is also produced. One of the latest releases of Bellwether Single Malt was a 4 year old in November 2018. The distillery moved to Fremantle in January 2020 and was re-named.

White Label Distillery

Huntingfield, Tasmania, founded in 2018

whitelabeldistillery.com.au

This is an unusual distillery in the sense that it is working as a contract brewing and distilling company, producing for other clients. Their customers can either obtain wash for their own distillation or new make spirit distilled to their own specification. The equipment consists of no less than 16 stainless steel washbacks (4,000 litres each) and two pairs of copper pot stills.

Wild River Mountain Distillery

Wondecla, Queensland, founded in 2017

wildrivermountaindistillery.com.au

One of the highest elevated distilleries in Australia, Wild River Mountain released their first single malt, Elevation, in August 2019. Lightly smoked it had been matured in a combination of ex-Tennessee barrels and Australian red wine casks. This was followed by Small Batch, aged in ex-shiraz barrels. More editions of both have followed.

William McHenry and Sons Distillery

Port Arthur, Tasmania, founded in 2011

mchenrydistillery.com.au

The distillery is equipped with a 500 litre copper pot still with a surrounding water jacket to get a lighter spirit. The first whisky was released in 2016 while the latest edition (spring 2021) is a 5 year old, matured in ex-bourbon and finished in a French oak blood tub.

Winding Road Distilling

Tintenbar, New South Wales, founded 2017

windingroaddistilling.com.au

Apart from single malt whisky, both gin and rum is produced. The first whisky was distilled in spring 2019 in a 1,250 litre copper pot still and the first release is planned for 2021

Yack Creek Distillery

Yackandandah, Victoria, founded in 2015

yackcreekdistillery.com.au

Eqyuipped with two stills with columns attached the distillery produces malt whisky, rum, gin and vodka. The first whisky expression, matured in red wine French oak casks and finished in ex-bourbon was released in December 2019 and has been followed by more batches, including lightly peated malt.

New Zealand

Thomson Whisky Distillery

Auckland, North Island, founded in 2014

thomsonwhisky.com

The company started out as an independent bottler but in 2014, the owners opened up a small distillery based at Hallertau Brewery in North West Auckland. The wash for the distillation comes from the brewery. First release was in February 2018 and the current range is made up by Two Tone (rye and barley), Manuka Smoke, South Island Peat and, released in March 2021, the single pinot noir barrel Local Folk & Smoke.

Cardrona Distillery

Cardrona (near Wanaka), South Island, founded in 2015

cardronadistillery.com

The distillery is equipped with 1.4 ton mash tun, six metal washbacks, one 2,000 litre wash still and a 1,300 litre spirit still - both made by Forsyth's in Scotland. Apart from whisky, barrel-aged gin and single malt vodka is also produced. The first 3 year old whisky was released in December 2018 followed by Just Hatched (bourbon and sherry matured). Late 2020 saw the release of the 5 year old Growing Wings (oloroso butt) and in May 2021 Growing Wings Solera and Growing Wings Breckenridge Bourbon appeared.

Other distilleries in New Zealand

1919 Distilling

Auckland, North Island, founded in 2016

1919distilling.com

The owners have a substantial range of gin and in summer 2020 the first single malt was released. Kirikiriroa is 3 year old and was matured in red wine casks. Peated whisky is also produced.

Auld Farm Distillery

Scotts Gap, South Island, founded in 2017

aulddistillery.co.nz

For three generations, the Auld family have been growing grain on their farm and in 2017 Rob and Toni also added distilling. The barley comes from their own land and is malted on site. First distillation was in 2018 and no whisky has yet been released.

Herrick Creek Distillery

Christchurch, South Island, founded in 2020

herrickcreek.co.nz

This micro distillery has already launched gin and although not yet released, three types of whisky are produced - single malt from barley, corn and bourbon style

Lammermoor Distillery

Ranfurly, South Island, founded in 2018

lammermoordistillery.com

Lammermoor is a true "grain-to-glass" distillery or as it´s called in New Zealand "paddock-to-bottle". The Elliots control every step from organically growing and malting the barley through to distilling and maturation. A gin was released early on and the manuka smoked First Edition single malt appeared in 2020 with more bottles following in February 2021.

Reefton Distilling Co.

Reefton, South Island, founded in 2018

reeftondistillingco.com

Starting off by distilling gin, vodka and liqueur, the owners moved to new premises in 2021, added a second still and started producing Moonlight Creek Whisky.

Spirits Workshop Distillery, The

Christchurch, South Island, founded in 2012

thespiritsworkshop.co.nz

For some time now Doug and Anthony Lawry have been making spirits for others in their two copper pot stills including malt whisky for New Zealand Whisky. Recently, however, they have themselves released a single malt under the name Divergence. All are matured in different types of barrels; virgin oak, port, pinot noir and there is also one expression that has been finished in sloe gin barrels.

Asia

China

Laizhou Distillery

Qionglai, Sichuan, founded in 2021

bacchusrio.waimaotong.com

In the city of Qionglai, with a long history of producing baijiu, one of China´s first malt whisky distilleries in modern times has recently been commissioned with a plan to start producing mid October 2021. Laizhou distillery is owned by Shanghai Baccus, the biggest company in China in the ready-to-drink (RTD) segment and a subsidiary of Bairun. Four copper pot stills made by McMillan in Scotland were installed in December 2020 and another four arrived later. They are equipped with condensers made of copper as well as stainless steel. In addition there are also 7 column stills. The distillery will have the capacity to make 5 million litres of malt and 20 million litres of grain yearly.There is also a cooperage on site with nine coopers as well as a custom-made STR-system where wine casks are shaved, toasted and re-charred. The first products to be released will be vodka and gin with whisky coming later. The whisky production will cover both the need for their pre-mixed cocktails but also releases of whisky.

Dong-Ye Distillery

Dong-Ting Lake, Hunan, founded in 2020

www.whiskychina.net

Already in 2014, Weidong Wei started to produce malt whisky in a small 260 litre pot still. When he stopped in 2019 in order to build a new and larger distillery he had filled 120 casks. Some of these will be bottled in 2022 after more than 6 years. In summer 2020 Weidong Wei commissioned his new distillery on the northwest bank of Dong-Ting Lake in the Hunan province. The distillery is equipped with two traditional Scottish-style copper pot stills, designed and built by himself. The wash still is 3,000 litres and spirit still 2,000 litres and the distillery has a capacity of producing 93,000 litres. Chinese barley (two-, four- and six-row) is used and the spirit is filled into mainly ex-bourbon but rye, sherry and STR casks are also used.

India

Amrut Distilleries Ltd.

Bangalore, Karnataka, founded in 1948

amrutdistilleries.com

The family-owned distillery, based in Kumbalgodu outside Bangalore in southern India, started to distil malt whisky in the mid-eighties. The equivalent of 60 million bottles of spirits (including rum, gin and vodka) is manufactured a year, of which 1,5 million bottles is whisky. Most of the whisky goes to blended brands but Amrut single malt was introduced in 2004. It was first launched in Scotland, but can now be found in more than 50 countries. The distillery was expanded with four more stills in 2018 and with a total of two mash tuns and 12 washbacks it now has the capacity of producing one million litres of pure alcohol. The fermentation time for the single malt is 140 hours and the barley is sourced from the north of India, malted in Jaipur and Delhi and finally distilled in Bangalore before the whisky is bottled without chill-filtering or colouring. In May 2019, the owner and chairman of the distillery, Sri. Neelakanta Rao Jagdale, passed away and was succeeded by his son Rakshit and his son-in-law Vikram Nikam.

The Amrut core range consists of unpeated and peated versions bottled at 46% as well as cask strength versions of the two and, finally, Fusion which is based on 25% peated malt from Scotland and 75% unpeated Indian malt. Special releases over the years, often released in new batches, include Two Continents, where maturing casks have been brought from India to Scotland for their final period of maturation, Intermediate Sherry Matured where the new spirit has matured in ex-bourbon or virgin oak, then re-racked to sherry butts and with a third maturation in ex-bourbon casks, Kadhambam which is a peated Amrut matured in ex oloroso butts, ex Bangalore Blue Brandy casks and ex rum casks, Portonova with a maturation in bourbon casks and port pipes, Amalgam comprising of Amrut as well as single malts from Scotland and Asia (with a peated version introduced in late 2018), Spectrum where the fourth edition had been matured in casks made of four varieties of oak, Double Cask, a 5 year old combination of ex-bourbon and port pipes and finally, the 100% malted Amrut Rye Single Malt. Other recent one-off releases include a Madeira Cask Finish and Port Pipe Peated as well as single casks for select markets. In August 2020

Laizhou Distillery

the first triple distilled Indian whisky was released - Amrut Triparva - and in November 2020 the Amrut Fusion X was launched. This was the regular Fusion with a further four years of maturation in PX sherry casks. A special bottling, Neidhal Peated Indian Single Malt, was announced for a release in autumn 2021 where a peated single malt distilled at another distillery had been further matured and bottled by Amrut.

A big surprise in 2013 was the release of Amrut Greedy Angels, an 8 year old and the oldest Amrut so far. That was an astonishing achievement in a country where the hot and humid climate causes major evaporation. In 2015 it was time for an even older expression, 10 years old, and in 2016, a 12 year old was released. Two more releases of the 10 year old (Peated Rum Finish and Peated Sherry Finish) appeared in 2019 and in autumn 2021, 240 bottles of a 12 year old Greedy Angels, matured in an ex-sherry cask and finished in ex-bourbon, were launched.

John Distilleries Jdl

Goa, Konkan and Bangalore, Karnataka, founded in 1992

pauljohnwhisky.com

Paul P John, who today is the chairman of the company, started in 1992 by making a variety of spirits including Indian whisky made from molasses. Their biggest seller today is Original Choice, a blend of extra neutral alcohol distilled from molasses and malt whisky from their own facilities. The brand, which was introduced in 1995/96, sold 152 million bottles in 2019. Another brand is Bangalore Malt, a simpler version of Original Choice, which in recent years has been one of the fastest growing spirits in the world. John Distilleries owns three distilleries and produces its brands from 18 locations in India with its head office in Bangalore and a huge distillery and visitor centre in Goa. The basis for their blended whiskies is distilled in column stills with a capacity of 500 million litres of extra neutral alcohol per year. In 2007 they set up their single malt distillery which was equipped with one pair of traditional copper pot stills and in 2017, another pair of stills were added, doubling the capacity to 1.5 million litres. The large American spirit producer Sazerac owns 43% of the company while the rest is controlled by Paul P John.

The company released their first single malt in autumn 2012 and this was followed by several single casks. Since 2015 the core range consists of three expressions aged 6 years or more; Brilliance - unpeated and bourbon-matured, Edited - bourbon-matured and lightly peated and Bold - heavily peated. In 2019 an entry level bottling named Nirvana, aged for 3 years and bottled at 40%, was also launched. In 2014, two cask strength bottlings were released; Select Cask Classic (55,2%) and Select Cask Peated (55,5%) and since then, more Select expressions have been released, Oloroso and Pedro Ximenez. Part of a special range called Zodiac are Kanya and the recently released Mithuna. The latter, bottled at 58%, was matured in virgin oak and finished in ex-bourbon casks. Limited releases also include the 7 year old Mars Orbiter, a peated whisky matured in American oak and Christmas Edition 2020, lightly peated and matured in a combination of virgin oak, ex-bourbon and ex-oloroso casks.

Other distilleries in India

Imperial Distillers & Vintners

Kundaim Industrial Estate, Ponda, Goa, founded in 2009

thecheersgroup.com

The company, which is part of the Cheers Group founded by Mohan Krishna, is the producer of a variety of different spirits and recently they launched the Three Monkeys Single Malt. Equipped with copper pot stills, the distillery has a capacity of 1 million litres of alcohol per year

Khoday

Bangalore, Karnataka, founded in 1906

khodayindia.com

Khoday is a company working in many areas, including brewing

and distillation. The IMFL whisky Peter Scot was launched by the company already in 1968 and in spring 2019, the Peter Scot Black Single Malt was launched.

McDowell´s Distillery

Ponda, Goa, founded in 1988 (malt whisky)

diageoindia.com

Established in the late 1800s, the distillery produces the best selling whisky in the world, McDowell´s No. 1, with 368 million bottles sold in 2019. Owned by Diageo since 2014, the distillery also produces a very small amount of single malt whisky.

Mohan Meakin

Solan, Himachal Pradesh, founded in 1855

mohanmeakin.com

Founded as a brewery in 1820, possibly by Edward Dyer and incorporated as a company in 1855. It was taken over by H G Meakin in 1887 and finally, Narendra Nath Mohan acquired the business in 1949. Today, the company is making beer, whisky and rum. Their most famous brands are Old Monk rum and Solan No. 1 whisky. Their first general launch of a single malt whisky under the name Solan Gold Single Malt appeared in 2019 and has matured for at least four years.

Piccadily Distillery

Indri, Haryana, founded in 1967, whisky since 1994

piccadily.com

Piccadily Agro Industries was founded in 1952 and started trading in the alcohol business. Piccadily Distillery was registered in 1967 and in 1994 they resumed distilling. The distillery has recently been expanded and the equipment today consists of two mash tuns (4.5 and 6.5 tons respectively), eight washbacks (60,000 litres each), three 25,000 litre wash stills and three 15,000 litre spiri stills - all pot stills stills and made from copper. The total malt capacity is 3,3 million litres of pure alcohol but grain spirit is also produced and on a much larger scale. This makes Piccadily the largest independent malt producing distillery in India. In 2020, in a joint venture with Peak Spirits, they launched their first single malt whisky named Kamet. The master minds behind the whisky is Surrinder Kumar who was the Amrut master blender for many years and Nancy Fraley, a respected blender who has worked with numerous distilleries in the US. Kamet has been matured in a combination of ex bourbon, ex sherry and French oak wine casks. The next expression, soon to be launched, is Indri and this will be an exclusive Piccadily whisky.

Rampur Distillery

Rampur, Uttar Pradesh, founded in 1943

rampursinglemalt.com

This huge distillery, situated east of Delhi, was purchased in 1972 by G. N. Khaitan and is today owned by Radico Khaitan, one of the biggest Indian liquor companies. The capacity is 75 million litres of whisky based on molasses and 30 million litres of grain whisky. They also have a distillery producing whisky from malted barley. An expansion in autumn 2019 increased the capacity of that distillery to 3 million litres per year. A larger mash tun was installed as well as a new wash still (25,000 litres) and a new spirit still (16,000 litres). On top of that, a refurbished and enlarged visitor centre was opened in 2020. They also own another distillery in Maharashtra with a capacity of 52 million litres. The first whisky brand from Radico (in 1997) was 8PM, which sells around 80 million bottles yearly. The first single malt release, the ex-bourbon matured Select, appeared in May 2016 and since then Double Cask matured in a combination of ex-bourbon and European oak sherry casks and PX Sherry (American oak with a PX sherry finish) have been released in the core range. The latest addition was Asava in autumn 2020. Initially matured in ex-bourbon barrels the whisky was then finished in casks that had held cabernet sauvignon wine.

Israel

The Milk & Honey Distillery

Tel-Aviv, founded in 2013

mh-distillery.com

Israel´s first whisky distillery, equipped with a 1 ton stainless steel mash tun, four stainless steel washbacks and two copper stills (with a capacity of 9,000 and 3,500 litres each). The capacity is 800,000 litres of pure alcohol. The first distillation was in March 2015 and the first, limited 3 year old single malt, made before the final equipment was installed, was released in August 2017. A Founder´s Edition appeared in autumn 2019 and in January 2020 their first commonly available and current core expression, Classic, was launched. It is matured in a combination of ex-bourbon and STR wine casks. A series named Elements is based on the Classic ”recipe” but has been matured in other types of casks. Currently there are Sherry (the first whisky in the world matured in kosher sherry casks), Peated (matured in ex-Islay casks) and Red Wine where casks from Israeli wineries have been used. The latest limited range is Apex where the owners have been experimenting with malts being having been fully matured or finished in unusual casks, pomegranate wine for instance. The distillery has a visitor centre with a large variety of tours and workshops.

Other distilleries in Israel

Golani Distillery

Katzrin, founded in 2014

golanispirit.com

Founded by Canadian expat David Zibell, the distillery is equipped with two artisanal copper stills and some of the whisky is matured in wine casks from the nearby Golan Heights Winery. In spring 2020, a new, one ton mash tun as well as two more washbacks were installed and in autumn 2021 another mash tun, two more washbacks and two new 1,000 litre stills were added. The distillery is focusing on single malt from barley and on grain whisky (51% malted barley and 49% wheat). The first 3 year old whisky appeared in late 2017. A number of different single casks have since been launched. Recent releases include the 5 year old Golani Rishon (51% malted barley and 49% wheat), Golani Vino (a single grain matured in wines casks) and Golani Black (single grain matured in new charred oak). There is also a range of single cask single malts named Unicask where the whiskies have matured mainly in casks that have previously held wine or brandy.

Shevet Brewing & Distilling

Pardess Hanna, founded in 2017

shevet.co.il

An impressive brewery founded by Neil Wasserman and Lior Balmas with a distillery attached that is equipped with two traditional copper pot stills. The wash from the brewery is distilled into whisky. A malt whisky by the name Ruach is in the pipeline but has not yet been released.

Yerushalmi Distillery

Jerusalem, founded in 2017

yerushalmidistillery.com

This is David Zibell´s (owner of Golani) second distillery and equipped with a 3,000 litre wash still and a 2,000 litre spirit still it has a capacity of 150,000 litres per year. David´s idea is to concentrate his production of peated whisky to this distillery but also rum and gin is produced. The first whisky distillation was in 2019 and recently they have released the peated single malt (35ppm) Mount Moriah and also four peated single casks in a new range named Solum; Sessile Oak (new French charred oak), Pirate Oak (rum cask), Birra Oak (craft beer cask) and Dessert Oak (white dessert wine cask).

Milk & Honey Distillery

Japan

Yamazaki

Mishima, Osaka, founded in 1923

suntory.com/factory/yamazaki/

In 1923, Shinjiro Torii built the first malt whisky distillery in Japan. Almost a century later, Yamazaki is still at the forefront of Japanese whisky production, in terms of quantity as well as quality. Torii was a pragmatic man, so he decided to build his distillery close to center of commerce at the time, Osaka. The construction of Yamazaki distillery began in late 1922, was completed the following year and the first spirit ran off the stills in November 1924. The distillery started out with two pot stills but has been reconfigured and expanded many times over the years, first in 1957, and most recently in 2013, when four pot stills were added bringing the count to 16. There's plenty of variety in terms of heating method, shape, size, lyne-arm orientation and condenser type, but that's typical of Yamazaki at every stage of production. Since 1988, eight of the washbacks are wooden whereas the other nine are stainless steel. With different peating levels for the barley, different yeast strains and a plethora of cask types, the variety of whisky types created at Yamazaki distillery is quite staggering.

Launched in 1984, The Yamazaki was the first generally available single malt in Japan. These days, 'generally available' applies to the limited editions that Suntory lets out from time to time. In November 2020, a quintet was released under the banner 'Yamazaki 2020 Edition', comprising Puncheon, Bordeaux Wine, Peated Malt, Mizunara and Spanish Oak expressions and towards the end of May 2021, the 'Yamazaki Limited Edition 2021' saw the light of day.

Yoichi

Yoichi, Hokkaido, founded in 1934

nikka.com/eng/distilleries/yoichi/

Masataka Taketsuru set up Yoichi distillery after leaving Kotobukiya (now Suntory) in 1934. He settled on the town of Yoichi, up in Hokkaido, because the locale and climate conditions reminded him of Scotland, where he had studied whisky making. The first spirit ran off the stills in 1936, with the first product launched in 1940. Initially equipped with a single still that doubled as spirit and wash still, the distillery now houses six stills. Coal-heated and featuring straight heads and downward lyne arms, these produce a robust spirit. Although the 'house style' is peaty and heavy, people tend to forget that – like the other big distilleries in Japan – Yoichi is set up to create a wide range of distillates. Between various peating levels, yeast strains, fermentation times, distillation methods and maturation types, it is said that Yoichi is capable of producing 3,000 different types of malt whisky. The big news in 2021 from Yoichi distillery was the construction of Warehouse No.29, with a state-of-the-art racking system and a capacity of around 7,000 casks. The last time a new warehouse was added to the Yoichi complex was 32 years ago, so indications are that quite a bit of stock has been laid down over the past few years.

In September 2015, the entire Yoichi range was axed and replaced with a single option – a new NAS. In September 2021, Nikka released Vol.1 in an ongoing series called "Nikka Discovery". Contrary to expectations, the Yoichi expression was non-peated, whereas the Miyagikyo was peated. Both were limited to the on-trade in Japan.

Mt. Fuji

Gotemba, Shizuoka, founded in 1973

fujiwhisky.com

Mt. Fuji distillery (formerly known as Fuji Gotemba distillery) is nestled at the foot of Mt. Fuji, less than 12km from the peak. The 'mother water' is taken from the aquifer running 100 metres underground. Analysis has shown that the water used today fell on Mt Fuji as snow 50 years ago. The distillery was founded by Kirin Brewery, Seagram & Sons and Chivas Brothers as a comprehensive whisky distillery where all production processes – from malt and grain whisky distilling to blending and bottling – take place on site. Unlike most Japanese distilleries, which followed Scottish whisky-making practice, Mt. Fuji adopted production techniques

Part of the new equipment that was installed at Mt. Fuji Distillery in June 2021

and methodologies from all over the world. After Seagram started selling off its beverage assets worldwide, Kirin became the sole owner of Fuji Gotemba Distillery.

The distillery is well known for its uniquely different styles of grain whiskey making, using column stills, a kettle and a doubler in a modular way. There are also ongoing projects to further diversify the flavor profile of their malt whisky. The distillery has just completed its renovation and two different sets of new pot stills and four wooden washbacks came into use in June 2021. There is also a new aging warehouse and the visitor center and tour program has been renewed too. Under the new flagship brand "FUJI", a NAS single grain expression as well as a 30 year old expression were launched in the spring of 2020. More portfolio innovations – including single malt and one-of-a-kind category products – are planned for release in the near future.

Hakushu

Hokuto, Yamanashi, founded in 1973

suntory.com/factory/hakushu/

Hakushu was built 50 years after the first Suntory malt whisky distillery and is nestled in a vast forest area at the foot of Mt Kaikomagatake in the Southern Alps. It is often referred to as 'the forest distillery': more than 80% of the site owned by Suntory is undeveloped. The original distillery was equipped with 6 pairs of stills. In 1977, capacity was doubled and another 6 pairs of stills added in a building next to 'Hakushu 1'. With its 4 mashtuns, 44 washbacks and 24 stills, Hakushu (1+2) was the biggest distillery in the world at the time. In 1981, Suntory built a new distillery, 'Hakushu 3' or 'Hakushu East' on the site, and decided to phase out production at #1 and #2 in favor of #3. Distilleries 1 and 2 had big stills, but all of the same shape and size, whereas #3 had a variety of stills with different shapes, sizes, lyne-arm orientations, heating methods and condenser types. What they were after was diversity and quality rather than quantity. The distillery as it is operative now is Hakushu 3, albeit with the addition of two pairs of pot stills in 2014, bringing the total to 8 pairs, just like at Yamazaki distillery. It's also worth noting that there is a small grain whisky facility at Hakushu since December 2010.

The Hakushu single malt was introduced in 1994 but spent most of the following decades in the shadow of its bigger brother, Yamazaki. Over the last few years, that has changed. The decision to discontinue The Hakushu 12 in June 2018 was much lamented among whisky enthusiasts, but Suntory recently announced that it would be making its way back, albeit in limited quantities.

Miyagikyo

Sendai, Miyagi, founded in 1969

nikka.com/eng/distilleries/miyagikyo/

Miyagikyo is Nikka's second distillery and legend has it that it took Masataka Taketsuru three years to find the perfect site for it. He settled on the valley that brings the Hirosegawa and Nikkagawa (no relation to the company name) rivers together because of the quality of the water, the suitable humidity and the crisp air. Construction started in 1968 and was completed in May of the following year. Originally known as 'Sendai', the distillery was renamed 'Miyagikyo' when Asahi took control of Nikka in 2001. At present, Miyagikyo is equipped with 22 steel washbacks and 8 huge pot stills of the 'boil ball' type with upward lyne arms, encouraging reflux which – given the slow distillation method (steam-heated) – results in a lighter, cleaner spirit. The site also houses two enormous Coffey stills imported by Taketsuru from Scotland. Moved from Nishinomiya in 1999, these are used to produce grain whisky (Coffey Grain) but, occasionally, are used to distill malted barley (Coffey Malt). Since the summer of 2017, they're also churning out Coffey Gin and Coffey Vodka.

In September 2015, Nikka discontinued the entire Miyagikyo range which included a no-age-statement expression, a 10, 12 and 15 year old because of stock shortages. It was replaced with a new NAS expression, which is the only permanently available Miyagikyo single malt until further notice. In September 2021, Nikka released Vol.1 in an ongoing series called "Nikka Discovery". Contrary to expectations, the Miyagikyo was peated, whereas the Yoichi expression was non-peated. Both were limited to the on-trade in Japan.

Chichibu #1

Chichibu, Saitama, founded in 2007

facebook.com/ChichibuDistillery/

Chichibu distillery was established in 2007 and started producing the year after. The set up is small and compact: a 2,400 litre mashtun (manually stirred with a wooden paddle), eight mizunara washbacks of 3,000 litres each and a pair of 2,000 litre pot stills. Production volume for the 2020-21 season was only 53,000 litres of pure alcohol. The distillery uses mainly local barley and there is an area for floor malting on site. Between Chichibu #1 and Chichibu #2 distillery, there are 7 warehouses: six dunnage style and one racked. The owner, Ichiro Akuto, also has a fully operational cooperage a few minutes down the road from Chichibu #1 distillery.

Washbacks at Hakushu Distillery

Since 2010, the Chichibu team is buying mizunara wood from Hokkaido and a very small number of casks are made out of local Chichibu mizunara.

Supply and demand is Ichiro's biggest headache. There simply isn't enough to go around. The latest 'big' single malt release was The First Ten, which hit the shelves in the fall of 2020. Another release that took people by surprise was Double Distilleries Chichibu x Komagatake 2021. Released in April 2021, this was the result of a secret swap of stock between Ichiro and the team at Mars Shinshu way back in 2015.

Chichibu #2

Chichibu, Saitama, founded in 2019

facebook.com/ChichibuDistillery/

Around 2014, Ichiro Akuto started thinking about setting up a second distillery. Unlike Suntory, Nikka and even Hombo Shuzo, who built their second distilleries in locations that were distinctly different from the environment of their first distilleries, Ichiro wanted to stay in his hometown of Chichibu. His new distillery is just a two-minute drive away from the 'old' one. Construction began in April of 2018 and the first spirit (test production) came off the stills on 9 July 2019. There are many features of the new distillery that are the same as at Chichibu #1, but the new distillery is five times bigger than the first one. Production output for the 2020-21 season was 264,000 litres of alcohol.

At Chichibu #2, two tonnes of malted barley are processed per batch. Whereas Chichibu #1 uses mostly local barley, Chichibu #2 mainly uses malted barley imported from England and Germany. Mashing takes place in a semi-lauter tun. and there are five washbacks made of French oak. The stills are the same shape as at Chichibu #1 but they are much bigger (10,000 litres and 6,500 litres respectively) and both stills are direct-fired. Ichiro expects this to have the biggest impact on the character of the spirit, producing a more robust complex spirit.

Other distilleries in Japan

Akkeshi

Akkeshi, Hokkaido, founded in 2015

akkeshi-distillery.com/en/

Inspired by Islay and its whiskies, and with equipment and methods imported from Scotland, the goal of the team at Akkeshi distillery is to create a whisky that is uniquely shaped by the Akkeshi environment. Production began in the fall of 2016 and relies heavily on peated malt, although non-peated malt is used as well. The distillery has two warehouses on site as well as two near the sea, to explore subtle differences in maturation. The third release ('Boushu') in the distillery's ongoing 24 Solar Terms series was released in May 2021.

Asaka

Koriyama, Fukushima, founded in 2015

sasanokawa.co.jp

Parent company Sasanokawa Shuzo was founded in 1765. Whisky 'making' started in 1946 but don't ask 'how?' because the focus was on the lowest grade of blended whisky. Sake production is the bread-and-butter of the company and that allowed them to ride out some of the tougher periods for whisky in Japan. To mark the 250th anniversary of the company in 2015, a proper malt whisky distillery was set up in a disused warehouse on site. By the end of the year, two small pot stills had been installed. Production officially started in June 2016. The first single malt expression ('Asaka The First') was released in December 2019. A year later, the distillery showed its peated side for the first time with 'Asaka The First Peated', a 3 year old matured entirely in first-fill ex-bourbon barrels.

Eigashima

Akashi, Hyogo, founded in 1919 (whisky since 1984)

ei-sake.jp/en/

This humble producer has been part of the Japanese whisky scene longer than anyone else that is still active today. On paper, it's the oldest whisky producer in Japan – having acquired a distilling license in 1919, four years before Yamazaki. It took them four decades to get their act together, though, and another four decades to release their first single malt (an 8 year old in 2007). The current distillery was built in 1984. Whisky is made during the warmer half of the year. The old spirit and wash still were retired in February 2019 and replaced with brand new stills made by Miyake Industries in Japan. The first distillation in the new stills took place in March that year. All production is matured on site, near the Akashi strait, in old single-story rickety warehouses in a bewildering variety of cask types. For the first time in over a decade, the distillery has been able to release a 12 year old expression again, drawn from a single sherry butt and bottled in late 2020 at 61%.

Ichiro Akuto´s second distillery - Chichibu #2

Hikari

Konosu, Saitama, founded in 2020

no website

Hikari Distillery is the brainchild of Eric Chhoa and is, for the time being, the closest whisky distillery from Tokyo. They are doing their best to stay out of the spotlight for the first few years and focus on creating quality malt whisky, but plans for a visitor center are on the table. The Flemish-style design of the buildings is quite striking. Inside the distillery, all equipment is on skids allowing for easy reconfiguration depending on the task at hand. The distillery got its license in the spring of 2020 and has been making whisky since then, using non-peated malted barley imported from the UK, but there are plans to use local barley in the near future. The distillery is equipped with a one ton mashtun, six stainless steel washbacks (fermentation time 4-5 days), a 3,600 litre wash still and a 5,500 litre spirit still. The owners are not considering releasing anything until at least 2025/26.

Kaikyo

Akashi, Hyogo, founded in 2017

akashisakebrewery.com/the-kaikyo-distillery

Kaikyo Distillery is located on the site of the Akashi Sake Brewery, established by the Yonezawa family, which has been brewing since 1856 and distilling (albeit not whisky) since 1918. To mark their first century of distilling, the company decided to replace their old steel stills with new copper pot stills. A new stillhouse was built to house the new Forsyths stills and the building was named The Kaikyo Distillery after the Akashi-Kaikyo Bridge that lies in front of the distillery. Together with Torabhaig Distillery (on the Isle of Skye), The Borders Distillery and Mossburn Distillers & Blenders, Kaikyo Distillery is part of a family-owned Swedish investment company. There is a close reciprocal relationship between the distilleries in Scotland and the team at Kaikyo in Japan. The aim is to produce a light, fruity spirit that will age well. The first single malt release is slated for 2022. While they're waiting, the distillery is selling a range of blended and 'pure malt' whiskies carrying the Hatozaki brand name.

Kanosuke

Hioki, Kagoshima, founded in 2017

kanosuke.com

Kanosuke distillery is owned by Komasa Jozo, one of the leading shochu makers in Kagoshima prefecture. Their claim to fame is 'Mellowed Kozuru', a barrel-aged shochu launched in 1957. The idea to establish a whisky distillery was born in 2015. Yoshitsugu Komasa, who represents the fourth generation of the family, picked some vacant land next to three warehouses where the company's shochu is matured and had the necessary equipment installed in the summer of 2017: a 6,000 litre mash tun, 5 stainless steel washbacks and 3 pot stills (6,000, 3,000 and 1,600 litres respectively) all with wormtub condensers. The first official single malt whisky, 'Kanosuke 2021 First Edition', was released in June 2021. Made with unpeated malt it was matured mainly in re-charred American white oak casks and ex-shochu casks.

Kurayoshi

Kurayoshi, Tottori, founded in 2017

matsuiwhisky.com/en/distillery/

Kurayoshi first emerged on the Japanese whisky scene in 2015 as a brand rather than a distillery, with age-statement releases of 'Japanese pure malt whisky' at a time when age-statement Japanese whisky had become rare. The fact that Japanese whisky-makers don't swap stock together with the extremely lax regulations governing Japanese whisky made it easy for savvy consumers to figure out that the liquid in the bottles was imported in bulk from abroad. In 2017 they set up an actual distillery, but all of this happened away from the public eye, unbeknownst even to industry-people in Japan. They started with three small Hoga alembic-type stills. In 2018, they added two larger stills and slowly started to let people into their distillery. At the time of writing, whisky was only produced using the large pair of pot stills.

Niseko Distillery is one of the latest to start producing in Japan

Mars Shinshu

Miyada village, Nagano, founded in 1985

hombo.co.jp

Mars Shinshu was built at the peak of whisky consumption in Japan, but 7 years into what would turn out to be a 25-year long decline, the doors were closed. The distillery was mothballed in 1992 and it wasn't until 2011, with whisky sales booming again, that the decision was made to fire up the stills again. Production used to be limited to the winter months, but now it's closer to a typical year-round production schedule with a silent summer season. In 2014, the old pot stills were replaced with brand new ones, built following the original blueprints. In the summer of 2018, 3 Douglas fir washbacks were installed. As part of a massive 1.2 billion yen investment, 2019-2020 saw the construction of a new warehouse, new stainless steel washbacks and mashtun as well as a new visitor centre. In March 2021, locally grown barley was distilled. The most recent limited edition coming out of Mars Shinshu was the Komagatake IPA Finish.

Mars Tsunuki

Minami-Satsuma, Kagoshima, founded in 2016

hombo.co.jp

Towards the end of 2015, Hombo Shuzo started setting up a second distillery in their homebase of Tsunuki in Kagoshima with the first distillation in October. The distillery is the playground of Tatsuro Kusano, the 32-year old head distiller. Kusano learned the ropes at Mars Shinshu under distillery manager Koki Takehira, and some things are the same as there: the season runs roughly parallel with Mars Shinshu, (i.e. late August to early July) and the barley used is the same: non-peated and heavily peated (50ppm). But there are marked differences too not least in the approach to making whisky including the use of specialty malts, various yeast types etc. The first single malt expression, Tsunuki The First, was released in April 2020. The peaty side of the distillery was featured in the follow-up, Tsunuki The Peated which was released in January 2021.

Nagahama

Nagahama, Shiga, founded in 2016

romanbeer.com/nagahama-distillery/

Nagahama Distillery's motto is "one distillation, one barrel" which suits them well, as they are the smallest distillery in Japan at the time of writing. It was set up in a record time of 7 months as an extension of Nagahama Roman Brewery, which was established in 1996 as a brewpub. The distillery officially started production in November 2016. Mashing and fermentation takes place in the equipment used for beer making. For the rest of the process, a small 'still room' with three 1,000 litre Hoga alembic-type stills was created behind the bar counter. The first single malt expressions were released in May 2020. More, limited expressions showcasing the plethora of cask types used have followed.

Niseko

Hokkaido, founded in 2020

niseko-distillery.com

Niseko Distillery is the brainchild of Jiro Nagumo, CEO of Hakkaisan Brewery, a sake producer based in Minamiuonuma city in Niigata prefecture. Nagumo started visiting Niseko over 10 years ago to look for ideas to revitalize his local ski resort (Naeba), which was once the biggest and most famous ski resort in Japan. Little by little, however, he began to see how Niseko might be the perfect place to establish a whisky distillery. Construction started in the spring of 2020 and was completed in December 2020. The equipment includes a Buhler mill from Switzerland, a 1 ton full-lauter mash tun from Slovenia, three Douglas fir washbacks made in Japan and a pair of pot stills from Forsyths in Scotland - one 5,500 litre wash still and a 3,600 litre spirit still. There is also a 600 litre hybrid Holstein still for the production of gin. The first whisky distillation took place on 24 March 2021 and the idea is to

create a "clear whisky that will harmonize a variety of flavors." The distillery's official grand opening was planned for the latter half of 2021.

Nukada

Naka, Ibaraki, founded in 2016

kodawari.cc/en/brewery/nukadabrewry

Nukada distillery was set up by Kiuchi Shuzo in a corner of their new Hitachino Nest brewhouse in 2016. In terms of output, it is the smallest whisky distillery in Japan. The 1,000 litre hybrid still is used to make whisky as well gin. The production volume varies from year to year and is also limited by the fact that the staff is occupied with a multitude of tasks other than making whisky/gin. The distillery is also used to distill beers to make some of the Kiuchi liqueurs.

Okayama

Okayama, Okayama, founded in 2011

whiskyokayama.com/english/

Okayama distillery, owned by Miyashita Shuzo, is undoubtedly the most under-the-radar distillery. The bread and butter of the company is beer and sake, and whisky is a side-gig. Miyashita Shuzo was founded as a sake brewery in 1915. In 1994, they became one of the pioneers of Japanese craft beer. In 2003, the company started distilling some of their hoppy beer in a stainless steel shochu still. Pleased with the way this was developing, they decided to have a go at producing proper malt whisky. They acquired their license in 2011 and started double-distilling batches in their shochu still, but in the summer of 2015, a copper hybrid still was installed, which has been the equipment of choice for whisky making ever since. Production is extremely limited and bottlings are rarely seen.

Saburomaru

Tonami, Toyama, founded in 1990

wakatsuru.co.jp/saburomaru/en/

Wakatsuru Shuzo started making whisky following the end of the Pacific War, but the company has been making sake since 1862. Until 2016, the company's whisky focus was on the bottom shelf, but when current distillery manager Takahiko Inagaki took over the reins, things started to change and the focus is now on quality. In 2018, a new mill and mashtun was installed. In 2019, the distillery started using a new pair of pot stills, the world's first cast copper pot stills also known as Zemon stills. In 2020, a single Douglas fir washback was added to the set-up. This is used after 4 days' fermentation in enamel tanks to encourage late lactic fermentation. In 2021, local Toyama malt was used in the production process, the mashbill being 5% local malt (non-peated) and 95% imported peated malt (47ppm, Islay peat). The 2021 season resulted in about 60,000 litres of pure alcohol which was filled in a variety of casks, including casks made from local Toyama mizunara.

Sakurao Distillery

Hatsukaichi, Hiroshima, founded in 2018

sakuraodistillery.com/en/sakurao/

Sakurao may be a new distillery, but the liquor company behind it is not. Chugoku Jozo was established in 1918 and incorporated in 1938, when it was given its current name. Their liquor portfolio comprises shochu, sake, mirin and various liqueurs. Chugoku Jozo started 'producing' whisky in 1938 and until the liquor-tax change of 1989, their field was 'budget' whisky. In 2003, they launched the Togouchi brand which was made up of whisky imported from abroad. To mark the 100th anniversary of the company, a whisky distillery with a hybrid still to make grain whisky as well as gin was set up. Both peated (20ppm) and unpeated spirit is produced. Casks are matured on site as well as in disused tunnels. July 2021 saw the first release of their own whisky: the Sakurao single malt having been aged on site and the Togouchi single malt in the tunnels.

Following the new standard for Japanese whisky, the company´s intention is to move away from reliance on bulk-import whisky.

Shizuoka
Shizuoka, Shizuoka, founded in 2015

shizuoka-distillery.jp

Inspired by a visit to Kilchoman distillery in 2012, Gaia Flow founder Taiko Nakamura started thinking about setting up a distillery of his own back home. Eventually, Shizuoka distillery was opened in February 2017. The equipment consists of eight wooden washbacks and three pot stills. One of them is from the old Karuizawa distillery while the other two were made by Forsyths. The wash still is directly heated using wood fire while the other two are heated by steam. In December 2020, the first single malt expression was released. This was entirely matured in ex-bourbon barrels and named 'Prologue K' because it was distilled using the ex-Karuizawa still. The follow up, 'Prologue W' (distilled using the wood-fired wash still), was released in June 2021 and was a vatting of malt matured in first-fill bourbon barrels, quarter casks and virgin American oak casks.

Yasato
Ishioka, Ibaraki, founded in 2019

no website

Yasato is Kiuchi Shuzo's second whisky distillery and is located in the Yasato part of Ishioka city. they designed the distillery based on the whisky they wanted to make and what they want to make is a genuinely new type of whisky, using various kind of grains and different types of yeast. There's a four-roller mill, a 5,000 litre cereal cooker for step mashing and rice/buckwheat/corn cooking and a 6,000 litre lauter tun, four 12,000 litre stainless fermenters and four 6,000 litre wooden fermenters. There is also 's a 12,000 litre wash still and an 8,000 litre spirit still. The first distillation took place in early March 2020. The team at Yasato is trying to source casks from small bourbon and rum distilleries and wineries as well as using non-oak barrels.

Yuza
Yuza, Yamagata, founded in 2018

yuza-disty.jp

Kinryu, the owners of the distillery, was founded in 1950 and was a joint venture funded by nine local sake producers, initially to make neutral spirit. Over time, they started making and selling shochu made in a continuous still. Overall consumption of shochu (as well as sake) has been on the decline for decades. To mitigate that, the company decided to start producing whisky and set up a brand new distillery in Yuza city. The first distillation took place in November 2018. The set up and the processes are textbook Scottish and the owners have no intention of releasing whisky any time soon.

Pakistan 

Murree Brewery Ltd.
Rawalpindi, founded in 1860

www.murreebrewery.com

Started as a beer brewery, the assortment was later expanded to include whisky, gin, rum, vodka and brandy. The core range of single malt holds two expressions – Murree´s Classic 8 years old and Murree´s Millenium Reserve 12 years old. There is also a Murree´s Islay Reserve, Vintage Gold.

South Korea 

Three Societies Distillery
Namyangju-si, Gyeonggi Province, founded in 2020

threesocieties.co.kr

With three distilleries having been built in the late 1980s and early 1990s and later closed, this is the first malt whisky distillery in modern times in South Korea. One of the three owners is Andrew Shand who used to work at Speyside distillery in Scotland and later Virginia distillery in USA. Located 40 kilometres east of Seoul, the distillery is equipped with a 5,000 litre wash still and a 3,000 litre spirit still – both from Forsyths and the capacity is one million litres of alcohol. There is also a 700 litre still for making gin, rye, bourbon and experimental spirits. The whisky is maturing in a variety of casks – bourbon, sherry, rye and virgin American oak. With a climate of very hot summers and cold winters, the owners hope to launch their first whisky in 2024.

Two stills made by Forsyths in Rothes for the Three Societies Distillery in South Korea

Taiwan

Kavalan Distillery

Yanshan, Yilan County, founded in 2005
www.kavalanwhisky.com/en

On the 11th of March 2006 at 3.30pm, the first spirit was produced at Kavalan distillery. This was celebrated in a major way a decade later when guests and journalists from all over the world were invited for the 10th anniversary. But it was not just to celebrate 10 years of whisky production but also to witness the recent expansion of the distillery which has made Kavalan one of the ten largest malt whisky distilleries in the world! This rapid development may even have surprised the founder, entrepreneur and business man Tien-Tsai Lee, and his son, the current CEO of the company Yu-Ting Lee. Early on, it was decided that expertise from Scotland was needed to get on the right track from the beginning. Dr. Jim Swan was consulted and he developed a strategy including production as well as the future maturation. Jim Swan passed away in early 2017.

The distillery lies in the north-eastern part of the country, in Yilan County, one hour´s drive from Taipei. Following the expansion in 2016, the distillery is equipped with 5 mash tuns, 40 stainless steel washbacks with a 60-72 hour fermentation time and 10 pairs of lantern-shaped copper stills with descending lye pipes. The capacity of the wash stills is 12,000 litres and of the spirit stills 7,000 litres. Kavalan only uses a very narrow cut from the spirit run, leaving more foreshots and feints to accommodate a complex and rich flavour profile. The spirit vapours are cooled using shell and tube condensers, but because of the hot climate, subcoolers are also used.

On site, there are two five-story high warehouses and the casks are tied together due to the earthquake risk. The climate in this part of Taiwan is hot and humid and on the top floors of the warehouses the temperature can reach 42°C. Hence the angel´s share is dramatic – no less than 10-12% is lost every year. At the moment, Kavalan are doing experiments aiming to reduce the angel's share to below 10%. The distillery has its own cooperage where the preparation of the STR (shave-toast-rechar) casks plays an important part for the final character of the whisky.

Since the first bottling of Kavalan was released in 2008, the range has been expanded and now holds 28 different expressions. In spring 2020, the core range was complemented by two bottlings being priced competitevely to act as an entry level to the rest of the range. One of them was launched already in 2018 and is now called Distillery Select No. 1 while the new expression is Distillery Select No. 2. Apart from them, the core range consists of Classic and an "upgraded" version of that called King Car Conductor. There is also the port finished Concertmaster which was recently supplemented by Concertmaster Sherry. Finally there are Ex Bourbon and Oloroso Sherry, both bottled at 46% and Podium.

The range that first opened the world´s eyes to Kavalan was Solist first introduced in 2009. Matured in different types of casks these are all bottled at cask strength and released in batches. The first two were Bourbon and Oloroso and have been followed by Fino, Vinho Barrique, Brandy, Amontillado, Manzanilla, PX, Moscatel and Port. Another two bottlings are exclusively sold at the distillery visitor centre; Distillery Reserve Rum Cask and Distillery Reserve Peaty Cask. The latter obtains its smoky flavour from maturation in ex-Islay casks. The distillery has produced whisky from peated barley (10ppm) as well and the first time it was released was in autumn 2020 in a single cask, cask strength collection of four named "Kavalan Artists Series". Peated Malt had been matured in STR casks and the other three in the series were Puncheon, Virgin Oak and French Wine Cask. Recent limited releases include two 100 cl bottlings to celebrate the 10th anniversary of the distillery´s first release. Both of them, Sky Gold Wine Cask and Earth Silver Wine Cask, had been matured in ex-Bordeaux wine casks from two different regions. Yet another expression from ex-Bordeaux wine casks appeared in late 2019 to celebrate the 40th anniversary of the foundation of King Car Group and in July 2020, Solist Madeira was released, available only at the distillery. Finally, a limited collection appeared in June 2021 when three bottlings with exotic animals native to Taiwan pictured on the labels were launched.

Whisky is, of course, the main product for Kavalan but production of gin is also carried out. The first release in a series of triple distilled gins appeared in early 2019. In June 2020, the owners launched a "ready-to-drink" range called The Kavalan Bar and since 2018 they are producing beer at a plant in Taoyuan. In May 2019, Kavalan opened their first designated 'Cask Strength Whisky Bar' in the busy Zhongshan District of Taipei. Recreating the inside of the distillery´s warehouse, it was the only bar in the world to carry the full range of Kavalan whisky. Guests can order whiskies straight from the cask and the bar also uses special effects to illustrate the environmental impact on the flavour of the whisky. In July 2020, the owners announced that a second bar was about to be opened at the distillery in Yilan. The Kavalan Garden Bar dominates the second floor of the Spirits Castle. The bar is the first phase of a major revamp of the entire visitor centre.

Kavalan is being exported to more than 60 countries and apart from Taiwan, Europe and the US are the most important markets. There is an impressive visitor centre on site with no less than one million people coming to the distillery every year.

Kavalan Distillery – one of the largest malt whisky distilleries in the world

Other distilleries in Taiwan

Nantou Distillery

Nantou City, Nantou County, founded in 1977
(whisky since 2008)

omarwhisky.com.tw

Located in the central east of Taiwan, Nantou distillery is a part of the state-owned manufacturer and distributor of cigarettes and alcohol in Taiwan – Taiwan Tobacco and Liquor Corporation (TTL). Between 1947 and 1968 it exercised a monopoly over all alcohol and tobacco products sold in Taiwan. It retained the monopolies until Taiwan's entry into the WTO in 2002.

There are seven distilleries and two breweries within the TTL group, but Nantou is the only with malt whisky production. The distillery is equipped with a 2,5 ton full lauter Huppmann mash tun and eight washbacks made of stainless steel with a fermentation time of 60-72 hours. There are two wash stills (9,000 and 5,000 litres) and two spirit stills (5,000 and 2,000 litres). The owners are currently looking to expand the distillery with more stills and warehouses. Malted barley is imported from Scotland and ex-sherry and ex-bourbon casks are used for maturation. Nantou distillery also produces a variety of fruit wines and the casks that have stored lychee wine and plum wine are then used to finish some of their whiskies. Initially the spirit from Nantou was all unpeated but in 2014 trials with peated malt brought in from Scotland were made.

The single malt is sold under the brand name Omar and in 2013, two cask strength single malt whiskies were launched – one from bourbon casks and the other from sherry casks. Three years later Sherry Cask and Bourbon Cask, bottled at 46%, were launched and the two now make up the distillery's core range. Another range is called Liqueur Finish and bottled at cask strength they have all been finished in different wine or liqueur casks; plum, lychee, black queen wine and orange brandy. The Cask Strength range is represented by ex-bourbon, ex-sherry and peated ex-bourbon. Finally there are special editions matured in virgin oak, PX solera sherry cask (10 years old) and ex-bourbon (8 year old). There is also a sub brand named Yushan, mainly for the European market, with one blended malt and three single malts - Sherry Cask, Bourbon Cask and Smoky.

Omar from Nantou Distillery

Africa

South Africa

James Sedgwick Distillery

Wellington, Western Cape, founded in 1886 (whisky since 1990)

threeshipswhisky.co.za, bainswhisky.com

Distell Group Ltd. was formed in 2000 by a merger between Stellenbosch Farmers' Winery and Distillers Corporation, although the James Sedgwick Distillery was already established in 1886. The company produces a huge range of wines and spirits including the popular cream liqueur, Amarula Cream. James Sedgwick Distillery has been the home to South African whisky since 1990. The distillery has undergone a major expansion in the last years and is now equipped with one still with two columns for production of grain whisky, two pot stills for malt whisky and one still with five columns designated for neutral spirit. There are also two mash tuns and 16 washbacks. Grain whisky is distilled for nine months of the year, malt whisky for two months and one month is devoted to maintenance. Three new warehouses have been built and a total of seven warehouses now hold more than 150,000 casks. There is also a highly awarded visitor centre on site. In summer 2021 Distell and Heineken were in negotiations regarding a possible take-over of the company by the Dutch beer brewer.

In Distell's whisky portfolio, it is the Three Ships brand, introduced in 1977, that makes up for most of the sales. The range consists of Select and 5 year old Premium Select, the latter being a blend of South African and Scotch whiskies. Furthermore, there is the 10 year old single malt which was launched for the first time in 2003. A range called the Master's Collection was introduced in 2015 with the idea to annually launch something limited in volume and a South African first. Now into it's 5th year and following on from the 10 year old PX finish, a 15 year old Pinotage cask finish, an 8 year old lightly peated Oloroso cask finish, a 9 year old Fino cask finish came the 11 year old old Shiraz cask finish. Apart from the Three Ships range, the distillery also produces South Africa's first single grain, Bain's Cape Mountain Whisky, where the core version is 5 years old. A limited 15 year old was released in 2019 and in 2020 a 10 year old shiraz finish appeared in travel retail.

The man who tirelessly worked to bring the Three Ships single malt to the market, is Andy Watts. After 25 years as the distillery manager, he has now a role in the company as Head of Whisky. In March 2021 he became the 70th person to be inducted into the Whisky Hall of Fame.

James Sedgwick Distillery

South America

Argentina

La Alazana Distillery

Golondrinas, Patagonia, founded in 2011

laalazanawhisky.com

Located in the Patagonian Andes, this is the first distillery in Argentina concentrating solely on malt whisky production. The distillery is owned and run by Nestor Serenelli and his wife Lila. They are both big fans of Scotch whisky and before they built the distillery, they toured Scotland to visit distilleries and to get inspiration. Eventually, Lila also earned a Master of Science degree in brewing and distilling from Heriot Watt University in Edinburgh. The owners are firm believers in the "terroir" concept where local barley, water and, not least, climate will affect the flavour of the whisky. The distillery is equipped with a lauter mash tun, four stainless steel 1,100 litre washbacks with a fermentation time of 4 to 6 days and two stills and there are now plans to increase capacity. A third warehouse was built in autumn 2020 with space for special warehouse tastings straight from the casks. For the last two years, the owners have been growing their own barley and also do the malting using local peat which means a 100% Patagonia single malt is now maturing in the warehouses. The house style is light and fruity but they have also filled several barrels with peated whisky. The first, limited release was made in 2014 and end of 2019 an 8 year old matured in a combination of ex-sherry and ex-bourbon was launched. The owner´s first 10 year old whisky is due in December 2021.

Other distilleries in Argentina

Emilio Mignone y Cia

Luján, Buenos Aires province, founded in 2015

emyc.com.ar

Owned by brothers Carlos and Santiago Mignone, this became the second whisky distillery in Argentina. The first distillation was in November 2015 and the distillery is equipped with a 300 litre open mash tun, a 250 litre washback with a 72-96 hour fermentation and two stills, directly fired by natural gas. The distillery has two different editions; the EM&C Pampa Single Malt Classic matured in ex-bourbon barrels, which was released in October 2019, and the EM&C Pampa Single Malt Peated matured in PX sherry barrels, launched in 2020. End of 2021 a new Peated edition, that has been matured in ex-whisky casks in a location on the Atlantic coast, will be released. The owners are working on an expansion of the distillery to be completed within the next few years.

Madoc Distillery

Dina Huapi, Rio Negro, founded in 2015

madocwhisky.com

The owner is one of the founders of the first Patagonian distillery, La Alazana. In 2015, he left the company and brought with him some of the equipment, as well as part of the maturing stock to build a new distillery in Dina Huapi. The existing equipment with a lauter mash tun, a washback and a copper pot still was complemented by a wash still and the first distillation took place in September 2016 and a single malt bottled at 40% has been released.

Brazil

Union Distillery

Veranópolis, founded in 1972

maltwhisky.com.br

The company was founded in 1948 as Union of Industries Ltd to produce wine. In 1972 they started to produce malt whisky and two years later the name of the company was changed to Union Distillery Maltwhisky do Brasil. In 1986 a co-operation with Morrison Bowmore Distillers was established in order to develop the technology at Union distillery. Most of the production is sold as bulk whisky but the company also has its own single malt called Union Club Whisky with an 8 year old as the oldest expression.

Muraro Bebidas

Flores da Cunha, founded in 1953

muraro.com.br

This is a company with a wide range of products including wine, vodka, rum and cachaca and the total capacity is 10 million litres. Until recently, the blend Green Valley was the only whisky in the range. In 2014, however, a new brand was introduced. It has the rather misleading name Blend Seven but it appears to be a malt whisky even though it seems that essence of oak is part of the recipe. The main market for the whisky is The Carribean.

The owners of Emilio Mignone y Cia – brothers Santiago (left) and Carlos Mignone

The Year
that was

Including the subsections:
Covid aftermath | The tariff war | The big players
The big brands | New distilleries

It was a year that few of us, if any, had experienced before. It was a year of fear and uncertainty, of social distancing and losing loved ones to a new disease. Of curfews and lockdowns and adapting to new rules and regulations. But it was also a year of supporting each other and coming together, although often in a virtual environment.

The biggest losers in the alcohol business during 2020 were the bars and restaurants. In most countries they were for the better part of the year either closed or allowed to remain open with severe restrictions. Another victim was the global travel retail business. In a world where few people could travel, sales dropped dramatically. For the producers this meant losing two of their most important arenas but it also highlighted the importance of e-commerce where customers in the safety of their homes could order alcoholic beverages. However, this is a route to market that differs a lot from country to country, sometimes due to legislation but often because consumer behaviors are culturally linked.

Global alcohol consumption has been declining for the past few years and according to the IWSR it dropped by 6,2% during 2020. Euromonitor International reports an even worse decrease of 8,5%. Beers and wines suffered the most while spirits managed a little better. All categories bar one lost volumes. It was only tequila/mezcal that managed to grow (+11%). Some of the category's success can probably be attributed to the number of celebrities that have bought into tequila in recent years (George Clooney, Kendall Jenner, P Diddy etc.) but the fact that tequila has been enjoying a momentum makes it more resilient to market turbulence. Rum declined by 11% while both whiskies and brandy/cognac lost 10%. The IWSR believes the global drinks industry wont be back to pre-pandemic levels until 2025 with a growth of 2,9% already during 2021.

Also according to the IWSR, premium brands is the fastest growing segment in the global alcoholic drinks market. They expect the category of spirits that are priced at $200 and up per bottle to increase 9,3% annually until 2025. During the same period, value brands that are priced at $10 per bottle will grow just 0,8% annually. In the last couple of years, several of the producers have started to position themselves in the battle for a piece of the global high-end spirits market which is currently worth $50bn.

The global spirits sales in 2020 in 9-litre cases and broken down into category looks as follows:

CATEGORY	CASES	CHANGE
Other spirits	1.0bn	-9%
White spirit	402m	-2%
Whiskies	365m	-10%
Brandy and Cognac	153m	-10%
Rum	134m	-11%
Liqueurs	110m	-8%
Tequila and Mezcal	39m	+11%
Total	2.3bn	-9%

Source: Euromonitor

The category 'other spirits' is largely made up of Asian spirits such as the Chinese baijiu, the Korean national spirit soju and Japanese shochu. Even though the category lost 9% of its volume during 2020, its dominance in the world spirits market is strikingly clear if you look at a list of the ten most valuable spirits brands in the world compiled by the consultancy company Brand Finance. Not only were the top five brands all baijiu (ahead of brands such as Jack Daniels, Johnnie Walker and Bacardi) but the sum of these five brands' sales in 2020 totalled 86% of the top ten brands. Number one was Moutai with sales of $45,3bn compared to Johnnie Walker with $2,4bn.

Also represented in the 'other spirits' category is the ready-to-drink segment (RTD) which experienced a surge during 2020. With the on-trade market more or less closing down during the pandemic, customers have found a way of enjoying cocktails at home through RTD. The category is definitely not new to the market but while the products were aimed at a younger audience, who were thrilled by flavourful drinks, often highly sweetened, in the 1990s and early millenium the producers are now targeting a new and wider consumer group. Key USP is still convenience but

low-alcohol, sophistication and health-boosting ingredients are equally important.

Let's focus on Scotch whisky for a while. According to the Scotch Whisky Association (SWA), Scotch whisky export is back to the figures of 2010 or as the SWA puts it, the industry has "lost a decade of growth". This is in part true but the reason can not be found just in the pandemic of 2020 nor the tariff war between the US and the EU. For several years the global exports of Scotch declined and it wasn´t until 2016 that the figures were in the black again. This positive trend continued during 2017, 2018 and 2019. If we compare the 2020 figures for total Scotch export they are actually very close to the ones from 2015 - both in terms of value and volumes. The conclusion is that even though the figures for 2020 are alarming, "the lost of a decade of growth" is definitely not due entirely to the unprecedented events of 2020. Other factors have played their part over the years.

Overall, in 2020 exports have fallen in 127 of 179 global markets with the biggest declines being seen in Spain, Japan, Singapore, Germany and the US. The decline in USA alone was 32% in terms of value. which represents around one third of total global losses. Blended Scotch was hit the hardest while single malts, thanks to a strong momentum and in spite of a 25% tariff in the important US market managed better even though values were down by more than 12%. This means that single malts now represent close to 34% of the value of total Scotch exports – by far the highest share ever.

SINGLE MALT SCOTCH - EXPORT 2020

Value:	-12.3% to £1.28bn
Volume:	-6.9% to 128.7m bottles

BLENDED SCOTCH* - EXPORT 2020

Value:	-28.2% to £2.27bn
Volume:	-14.5% to 714m bottles

TOTAL SCOTCH - EXPORT 2020

Value:	-23% to £3.8bn
Volume:	-13% to 1.14bn bottles

* excl. bulk and bottled single and blended grain Scotch whisky.

The European Union

The European Union is still, by far, the biggest export market for Scotch whisky both in terms of volumes and value. The region represents well over a third of the volumes (38,2%) and 33% of the values. If we look just at single malts, the dominance is even greater; volume 45% and value 36%. The region showed red figures for 2020 with volumes down by 6% and values by 15% so the improved market share compared to 2019 is due to the fact that other regions suffered worse, especially North America.

The European Union — Top 3

France	volumes	+2%	values	-13%
Germany	volumes	-14%	values	-25%
Latvia	volumes	+12%	values	+24%

France is still the dominant market for Scotch in the EU and in terms of volumes it is the world's biggest. However, the figures had been slipping for three years in a row so the small increase in 2020 came as a surprise. Values were down by 13% which in a difficult year such as 2020 is modest compared to many other markets. Even though Germany lost 14% in volumes it climbed to second place because Spain lost even more – more than a third of the volumes disappeared. Even worse was Spain's export value dropping by 40% – the biggest decline reported by any of the top 10 markets.

The big surprise is Latvia where both figures were in the black and in fact, if we focus on values it is now the second biggest market in the EU. As always, we have to keep in mind that the majority of the volumes going to Latvia are re-exported to other markets, mainly Russia. Apart from Spain countries such as Italy and The Netherlands were in the double digit reds while Sweden on the other hand went the other way. Values were up by 28% and while this seems surprising, there probably is a good reason. Sales of

alcohol is monopolized by the Swedish government and in a normal year, with no travel restrictions, many Swedes go to Denmark or Germany for their purchase of alcohol due to the lower tax. During the covid 2020 this was obviously more or less impossible.

Asia and Oceania

Asia and Oceania is the second largest region in terms of volumes and, since 2020, also number two in values, overtaking North America. The biggest loss for the region in 2020 was in volumes (-23%) while values declined by "only" 19% when North America lost 30%, mainly due to the 25% tariff imposed on single malts.

Asia and Oceania — Top 3

India	volumes	-28%	values	-38%
Japan	volumes	-26%	values	-22%
Singapore	volumes	-29%	values	-18%

India is still the biggest market in terms of volumes but a huge part of that is blended malt shipped in bulk in order to be blended with Indian-made whisky. In fact blended malt and grain sent in bulk make up more than 50% of the Scotch exports to India. There is a similar story in Japan with 45% of the exports made up by bulk-shipped Scotch whisky. A set of new whisky rules (although voluntary and not enforced by law) regulating what can and what can't be called Japanese whisky was introduced in spring 2021 and it remains to be seen how that will affect bulk exports of

Scotch to Japan in the future. A positive sign though is the UK-Japan free trade deal, the first deal that the UK struck post-Brexit, which was signed in October 2020.

In spite of a significant drop in both volumes and values, Singapore is still in the top 3 in Asia and in terms of value the definite number one with 25% of the totals. In 2020 exports of Scotch single malts were up by 14%. As always when interpreting the numbers for Singapore, it is important to remember that the vast majority of the whisky is re-exported to other markets in the region, not least to ASEAN countries and China and it is also a hub for travel retail

The Taiwanese love of single malts make that market stand out. They have the highest single and blended malt share of total Scotch whisky imports of any country in the world both in terms of volumes (47%) and values (66%). They also have the highest single malt Scotch import per capita in the world (if we disregard Singapore and Latvia which re-export to a large extent).

A potentially much bigger market is of course China where single malts by value were up by 42% in 2020 and by volumes 58%. The development in the last ten years has been incredible and China is now the sixth biggest single malt Scotch market in the world in terms of values. A contributing factor to the success is that import tariffs to China are only 5%.

North America

This is the third largest region in terms of volumes and, since 2020, also in terms of values having been overtaken by Asia & Oceania. In 2020, North America lost 13% in volumes and no less than 30% in values which equally affected both malts and blends.

North America — Top 3

USA	volumes	-12%	values	-32%
Mexico	volumes	-18%	values	-29%
Canada	volumes	+4%	values	-5%

USA is by far the biggest market with 80% of the region's import. It is also the world's most important market for Scotch. In 2019 the values of Scotch whisky shipped to the US was worth £1.07bn. In 2020 that figure had dropped by 32% to £729m. The main reason is of course the tariff war between USA and the EU but in June, the US government dropped the 25% levy on single malts imported from Scotland. You can read more about the Tariff War on page 267.

The second largest market in the region is Mexico but figures declined with double digits in 2020. It is also number 7 in the world in terms of volumes and 15 in values. Mexico is a pronounced blended whisky market where only 2% consists of single malt.

In Canada, on the other hand, 35% of the imports are single or blended malt. The country is the second largest market in the region in terms of values and the decrease in 2020 was significantly less than for the other two countries in this region.

Latin America and Carribean

This region went from double digit growth in 2018, via a smaller increase in 2019 to a year where almost one third (31%) of the values were lost as well as no less than 41% of the volumes. Surprisingly though, single malts were up by 2%. The top 3 markets are responsible for 63% of total volumes and 51% of total values.

Latin America and Carribean — Top 3

Brazil	volumes	+6%	values	-13%
Colombia	volumes	+3%	values	-12%
Chile	volumes	-29%	values	-35%

Brazil, the region's number one market since 2010, showed some resilience with volumes increasing by 6% and even though values dropped by 13%, single malts were strong with values going up by 25%. It is currently the fourth biggest market for Scotch in the world in volumes and number 18 in values.

Colombia in second place reminds of Brazil with a small increase in volumes and a double digit decrease in values. One interesting difference though is that Colombia´s import of single malt is more that 150% larger than that of Brazil. The main market for single malt is still Panama which has 30% of the total imports to the region. Like last year, Chile is in third place but lost substantially more during 2020 than the top 2 countries.

Sub-Saharan Africa

This is a new region since last year when Africa was split into Sub-Saharan and Northern Africa (together with Middle East). For 2020, volumes were down by 12% and values by 22%.

Sub-Saharan Africa — Top 3

South Africa	volumes	-24%	values	-30%
Kenya	volumes	+25%	values	+9%
Angola	volumes	+7%	values	-16%

South Africa is by far the biggest market representing 55% of the values and 59% of the volumes. Its position on the global top list has however weakened in the past few years. It is number 16 in terms of volumes (number 7 in 2017) and 11 in terms of value (9). The drop in 2020 was significant.

Like last year, Kenya is in second place and displayed significant growth in 2020 with volumes up no less than a quarter. This took the country from spot 54 in 2019 to 33 on the global top list. Also Angola managed to climb the global list from place 70 to 42.

Eastern Europe

The third smallest of all regions in terms of volumes and the smallest in terms of value is Eastern Europe. States traditionally included in Eastern Europe but are members of the European Community are not included here. Instead we are talking mainly about Russia and some of the surroun-

Restaurant visitors in London enjoying a world that is slowly opening up albeit with some restrictions still in place

ding countries including the Balkans that are not in the EC. The region was only one of two that managed to increase Scotch imports in terms of volumes during 2020 – up by 12% while values dropped 5%.

Eastern Europe — Top 3

Russia	volumes	+14%	values	-2%
Ukraine	volumes	+39%	values	+58%
Belarus	volumes	+37%	values	+37%

While Russia may be the biggest market in the region no less than 99% of the volumes consist of bulk blend. What is not seen in the official figures for the country are the large volumes that are being re-exported to Russia from Latvia.

Middle East and Northern Africa

Yet another new constellation since last year when entire Africa and the Middle East constituted two separate regions. This region was hit the hardest during 2020 with volumes dropping 38% and values almost cut in half (-49%). The top 3 markets are responsible for 75% av importen.

Middle East and Northern Africa — Top 3

UAE*	volumes	-42%	values	-54%
Israel	volumes	-18%	values	-20%
Oman	volumes	-17%	values	-51%

* United Arab Emirates

The UAE lost more than 50% of the values during 2020. A major part of the imports are destined for duty free sales and with the travel market almost disappearing during covid, the decrease is not surprising. While Israel may have lost 20% of the total values, the part consisting of single malts actually grew by 7%.

Western Europe exc EC

The smallest of the nine regions in terms of volumes and the one that managed the best during 2020. Volumes were up by 35% and values by 11%.

Western Europe exc EC — Top 3

Turkey	volumes	+51%	values	+27%
Switzerland	volumes	+3%	values	-10%
Norway	volumes	+54%	values	+35%

There are only seven markets in the region and Turkey is by far the biggest, responsible for 64% of the total sales. Figures for 2020 were also impressive but Norway came through the pandemic with flying colours as well.

Single malt hot spots

I often get asked the question which countries have a preference for single malt Scotch so let's have a look. In these figures, I have focused on the Top 40 markets and selected the 10 nations with the largest single malt share.

Single malt share of Scotch whisky imports 2020

	Country	Volume	Value
1.	Taiwan	48%	66%
2.	Cyprus	44%	24%
3.	Italy	43%	52%
4.	Canada	34%	57%
5.	China	33%	62%
6.	Singapore	26%	39%
7.	Sweden	23%	58%
8.	Netherlands	22%	58%
9.	USA	20%	36%
10.	Israel	19%	31%

If we instead take into account the number of people living in the respective countries, i. e. volume of single malt Scotch per capita, the ranking looks like this (and again we're talking about the Top 40 markets);

Largest single malt Scotch import per capita in 2020

1. Latvia
2. Cyprus
3. Singapore
4. Taiwan
5. Netherlands
6. France
7. Sweden
8. Italy
9. Australia
10. Canada

It is important to remember that both Singapore and Latvia serve as hubs for re-export to other markets. As for Cyprus, the country´s most important trade partner is the UK and the astonishing increase in single malt imports may have been a sign of stocking up before Brexit came in to force.

Covid aftermath

Writing this in August 2021 when the pandemic is still ongoing, the word aftermath may seem a bit challenging. Still with the speed of vaccination accelerating at least in parts of the world, there is some hope that we have seen the worst. One thing soon became evident in 2020; those producers which relied heavily on sales through travel retail and on-trade (bars and restaurants) were hit harder that others. Another observation was that in markets where on-line sales of alcohol was well developed (for example in USA and China), drops in sales were much lower and sometimes volumes went up compared to 2019. In USA the total beverage alcohol volume was up 2% which was the largest gain since 2002! For the spirits category alone, it was in fact the largest increase since 1990. Consumers who didn't spend money on travels and physical shopping suddenly had the financial means to buy more exclusive spirits on-line.

The large alcohol producers have already shown positive figures compared to the first half of 2020 and as traveling picks up, it looks like the industry may bounce back quicker than many commentators thought in spring 2020. At that time the IWSR presented a report saying it could take until 2024 for global alcohol sales to reach 2019 figures. On the other hand, it is too early to make any decisive predictions. What we are experiencing halfway through 2021 could be a YOLO moment (You Only Live Once) similar to what happened after the great depression in the 1920s. Once you are through a period of severe hardship, you decide to live your life to the full and splash out on things you could not treat yourself to previously. This could be a short-lived effect when things go back to normal. A more lasting effect, and negative to the alcohol business, is that the trend towards sobriety has grown stronger during the pandemic. Many consumers have chosen a healthier lifestyle and sales of alcohol-free drinks of all kinds have accelerated rapidly in the past 18 months. This could prove to be more than just a trend but a change of lifestyle not least amongst young people.

The tariff war

While the covid pandemic has been a major concern for nearly all spirits producers around the world, there has been an even darker cloud looming over Scotch and American whisky. A tariff war that has been going on since 2018. First, let's have a recap of the development.

It all started in 2004 when the USA filed a case with the World Trade Organisation against loans for Airbus, the European aircraft manufacturer. The argument from the US government was that these were illegal state subsidies and was damaging to their own airplane manufacturer, Boeing. In the end, the WTO ruled in favour of USA. When the US government failed to see any compliance to the judgement by the EU, the Trump administration in June 2018 imposed a 25% levy on steel and aluminium imported from the EU. The retaliation from EU came later the same month with a 25% tariff on certain US products including whiskey.

During spring 2019, the US government prepared a list of items receiving new 25% tariffs against EU including single malt Scotch which came into effect in October 2019. In June 2020, the US government threatened to raise the tariff to 100% as well as adding other spirits. One month later Airbus amended their contracts with the French and Spanish governments in an attempt to contribute solving the problem. But the war escalated. The EU imposed 25% tariffs on rum, brandy and vodka while USA added French and German wines to their list.

The first signs of deescalation came in January 2021 when the UK dropped tariffs on US products except for whiskey. And in March 2021, the Biden administration announced a four month suspension on tariffs on both UK and EU products. One month before the suspension was set to expire, USA, EU and the UK agreed a deal where the tariffs would be suspended for five years with one significant exception – the levy on American whiskey exported to Europe remained. This was a significant blow to the producers of bourbon as the EU accounts for half of American whiskey exports and since the tariffs came in place, sales to the EU have dropped by a third.

The US is the world's most valuable spirits market and according to the Scotch Whisky Association the US tariffs on Scotch that have now been suspended, have caused a drop by 35% of value which interprets to more than

£600m. During the trade war some American consumers have shifted their interest from Scotch to American whiskies and that category grew in the US by 8% during 2020. It remains to be seen just how quickly the American market for single malt Scotch will bounce back.

The big players

Diageo

With 27,650 employees, over 200 brands and a presence in more than 180 countries, Diageo is the world's largest spirits company. When they presented their report for the fiscal year ending 30 June 2021, it outperformed the analysts' expectations. Reported net sales increased 8,3% to £12.7bn which means sales are back to the same as the year before the pandemic hit the world. Operating profits also increased (17,7%) to £3.7bn which is 92% of the company's latest pre-covid profit (2018/2019). Diageo's CEO, Ivan Menezes, was pleased but added that he was expecting near-term volatility in some markets. He then continued by saying "However, I remain optimistic about the growth prospects for our industry, with spirits continuing to gain share of total beverage alcohol globally and premiumisation trends remaining strong."

Looking at the company's different geographical regions, North America is by far the most important representing over one-third of their net sales. It was the only region that managed to show growth last year and this year sales increased 20%. Tequila was leading the growth but Scotch blends with Johnnie Walker and Buchanan's were also strong. Single malts on the other hand declined by 13%. Europe and Turkey, second largest, was up by 4% with the UK (+7%), Northern Europe (+22%) and Turkey (+28%) performing well while net sales in Southern Europe only grew by 1%. In Asia Pacific (+14%) China made a strong recovery from last year (+38%) as did Australia (+23%) while India came in a little lower (+13%). In Africa (+20%) most of the countries showed a double digit sales increase, while in Latin America and Caribbean (+30%) it was Brazil, Mexico and Colombia that performed particularly well.

Scotch is the biggest part of Diageo's business with 23% of the net sales followed by beer (15%) and vodka (10%). The majority of the brands are then divided into Global Giants representing 37% of the net sales (Johnnie Walker, Smirnoff, Baileys, Captain Morgan, Tanqueray and Guinness), Reserve representing 25% of sales (for example all Scotch malts, Bulleit and Don Julio) and Local Stars representing 20% of sales (for example Buchanan's, J&B, Windsor, Black & White and Old Parr).

If we look at brands, let's start with Johnnie Walker, the best selling Scotch in the world. The brand's net sales increased by 12% where growth in all regions offset the decline in travel retail. In September 2021 the impressive Johnnie Walker Experience was opened in Edinburgh, part of a major effort which also included new visitor centres at four malt distilleries that are particularly important to

The Johnnie Walker Experience in Princess Street in Edinburgh opened its doors to the public on 6 September 2021

the Johnnie Walker flavour profile. Other blends that did well were Buchanan's (+29%) and Old Parr (+16%). Single malts were up 11% driven by Asia Pacific and Europe and partially offsetting a decline in North America due to the tariff war. The star brand in the Diageo portfolio of spirits in terms of sales growth was however Casamigos, a tequila which Diageo acquired in 2017. Sales were up by no less than 125% and their other tequila, Don Julio, came in at +62%. The figures for some of the other, major brands in the Diageo portfolio were Smirnoff (+5%), Crown Royal (+12%) and Guinness (+-0%).

Two brands in the buoyant gin segment were acquired by Diageo – Aviation American Gin and Chase Distillery – and CEO Ivan Menezes doesn't rule out further investments in other brands. "It's not that easy to find available brands that have a good runway for growth to take off from but you can expect us to be adding more to the business."

Finally, last year we could report on an unusual situation between Diageo and its rival LVMH. For many years Diageo has held a 34% stake in the French company's Moet Hennessy division. When a dividend in the range of €181m wasn't paid to Diageo last year, the company prepared legal proceedings to obtain the money. In January 2021 the matter was settled when LVMH transferred the sum.

Pernod Ricard

Pernod Ricard is the second largest spirits company in the world after Diageo and like its main competitor, the company bounced back from the worrying figures in 2019/2020 when the pandemic took its toll. Unlike Diageo though, total sales did not increase enough to reach the pre-pandemic level. In the full year result per 30th June, reported sales were up by 4,5% to €8.82bn (organic growth was up 9,7%). Profits from recurring operations were up by 7,2% to €2.42bn (organic +18,3%). The company chairman and CEO Alexandre Ricard was pleased; "Thanks to our solid fundamentals, our teams and our brand portfolio, we are emerging from this crisis stronger."

The company has divided their market into three regions where Asia/Rest of the world is the biggest in terms of sales (+11% last year). The growth was first and foremost driven by China (+44%) but also by Korea, Turkey and, to a lesser extent, India. The second largest region is Americas (+14%) and here the growth was on a broad base offsetting declines in Travel Retail. In the third region, Europe (+4%), it was especially Germany, UK and Eastern Europe that contributed to the growth. Global travel retail (not a region in its own right) lost 40% of its sales.

If we look at the figures for specific brands, the growth for almost all of them came in the second half of the report period (January-June 2021). In the first-half fiscal 2021 (July-December 2020) only three of the thirteen Strategic International Brands showed positive figures (Jameson, Malibu and The Glenlivet). For the full year Martell was up by 24% driven by China, Jameson increased by 15% with a strong growth in USA while The Glenlivet did well in all regions increasing sales by 19%. The Scottish blends, Chivas Regal, Ballantine´s and Royal Salute, all increased although by single digits. One brand stands out, namely Aberlour single malt which is part of the company category named Specialty Brands. Sales were up by 32% driven by France and USA. However, the growth for Aberlour should be seen in the light of five years of diminishing sales for the brand.

Edrington

It could have been worse! That pretty much sums up the view from Edrington's management when they commented on the financial year that ended 31 March 2021. Or as CEO Scott McCroskie puts it "...I believe that the relatively modest declines represent a good outcome in the circumstances." The tone was definitely more alarming a year ago when McCroskie four months into the pandemic stated that the company has "...adequate resources to continue to operate for at least 12 months from the date of this annual report."

For 2020/2021 organic sales were down by 15% to £576m while profits before tax decreased by 21% to £178m. Due to closures of bars and restaurants during lockdowns around the world, a global travel retail market contracting and, not least, import tariffs in the USA, the company's flagship brand Macallan saw a significant decline during the year with an exception for China, South-East Asia and Russia. The decrease in sales was shared by the other two single malt brands Highland Park and Glenrothes while Famous Grouse proved to be more resilient. Brugal, the company's premium rum, remained strong not least in its home market, the Dominican Republic. The company has also recently made its entrance into the gin category through a stake purchase in Berry Bros & Rudd's London No. 3 gin.

In March 2020, the company's principal shareholder, The Robertson Trust sold 10% of the shares to Suntory Holdings. The two companies have had a relationship ever since Suntory in the early 1990s bought a 25% stake in the Macallan brand.

Gruppo Campari

With 2020 being an extraordinary year for the entire industry, the net sales for Campari were surprisingly good. They came in at €1.77bn which means the decline stopped at 4,1%. Earnings before interest and tax (EBIT) were down by 20% and reached €322m. Looking at the future, the management team stated that they were cautiously confident in the short-term and optimistic about the long-term business momentum.

The company's main brands are divided into three groups; Global Priorities (56% of the sales) with Aperol and Campari as the top sellers, Regional Priorities (18%) including Glen Grant and Local Priorities (11%) with Wild Turkey. The number one brand by far in the company's portfolio is Aperol which managed to maintain the same sales volumes compared to the previous year while Campari lost 4,5%. Glen Grant had a tougher year losing almost 20% of the sales with travel retail. Italy, USA and South America were especially disappointing while Australia, Germany and France showed positive figures.

In spring 2021 Campari established a new part of the company named the Rare Division with the purpose of growing the super premium portfolio including champagne, cognac, rum and single malt Scotch. The first two brands to benefit from the new strategy are Bisquit & Dubouché cognac and Lallier champagne. A spokesperson explained the reason behind the division by stating "Consumers are drinking less but they're drinking more prestigious spirits."

Beam Suntory

Beam Suntory Inc, a part of Suntory Holdings' alcoholic beverage operations which also includes beer and wine, is the world's third largest drinks group after Diageo and Pernod Ricard. Beam Suntory is responsible for its parent company's non-Japanese spirits operations. For 2020, revenues for the entire division was down by 4.2% to JPY728 billion while operating income decreased 9,2% to JPY130,4bn. Sales increased in markets such as Germany, South Korea and Canada while the figures were in the reds in China, India and Spain.

If we look at the different brands, Jim Beam, the world's most sold bourbon, and Maker's Mark both showed positive sales figures obviously benefitting from the US home market which seems to have mitigated the negative impact of the pandemic on sales of alcohol far better than most other countries in the world. For the first time, Jim Beam succeeded in selling more than 11 million 9-litre cases globally while Maker's Mark came in at 2,4 million cases. There were other brands in the portfolio showing double-digit sales increases including Basil Hayden's bourbon, Roku gin and Hornitos tequila.

Beam Suntory is also the owner of a portfolio of Scotch single malts. Laphroaig takes the lead followed by Islay neighbour Bowmore. The other three are Auchentoshan, Ardmore and Glen Garioch. Also in the Scotch category is the Teacher's blend which sold 18 million bottles in 2020.

In connection with the report Beam Suntory announced a $1 billion investment in new sustainability, diversity and responsible drinking initiatives. This includes reducing water usage and greenhouse gas emissions by half by 2030. CEO Albert Baladi commented: "The environment is shifting around us and we need to be consumer-led in everything we do."

Brown Forman

Already last year the company presented impressive results for the fiscal year ending 30 April 2020. Despite two months of pandemic lockdown affecting results, sales managed to increase by 1% and profits slipped by a mere 1%. One year later Brown Forman again showed resilience. Net sales grew 3% to $3.5bn while operating income increased 7% to $1.2bn.

The main reason for the good result was a solid home market. Alcohol sales in USA grew by 2% during 2020, the largest volume gain in almost two decades. American whiskey also increased substantially due to the tariff war between the EU and USA. While the classic version of Jack Daniels may have lost sales, Woodford Reserve grew and the portfolio of RTD (ready-to-drink) increased even more.

The company also revealed plans for expanding two of their whiskey distilleries – the one in Louisville and the one in Versailles. Both distilleries produce, among other brands, Woodford Reserve bourbon. In spring 2021 Financial Times reported that Pernod Ricard and Brown-Forman may have plans to go through with the spirit industry's only remaining mega-merger. Even if this is only speculation, a merger would mean that Diageo would remain the largest spirits company in the world (19% of the market) while the new constellation would occupy second place (16% of the market). Furthermore, if the two companies would become one it could entail a boost for Pernod Ricard on the important USA market while on the other hand Brown Forman could benefit from Pernod Ricards strong position in Asia and not least in India. The latest mega merger in the spirits business was in 2013 when Suntory and Beam joined forces.

The big brands
Blended Scotch

One would be forgiven to think that all major blended Scotch brands would lose volumes in the year of the pandemic with very little travels and bars and pubs all over the world more or less closed or at least working under restrictions. But that's not the case. Of the Top 20, seven brands increased and if we limit it to the Top 10, three of them showed positive figures. Whether or not you would show resilience depended on the brand's exposure to travel retail and on-trade, the geographical markets and the price category.

The number one, no surprise there, Johnnie Walker came from a 2019 with a 3% decrease of volumes to 2020 where sales went down by a staggering 23%! In terms of bottles that meant 51 million less sold and the brand ended up with 169 million bottles in 2020. Still not bad as it corresponds to the total numbers of 2-4 on the sales list.

Ballantine's, in second place, managed a little better with a slip in volumes of 9% to 84 million bottles. Figures from the brand owner, Pernod Ricard, showed better figures for the second half of the year when sales went down by "only" 5% and in November 2020 a global marketing campaign (Stay True: There's No Wrong Way) was launched.

These brands have been the top two for many years but in place three and four there has been some change. The new number three, despite a 14% drop in volumes, is Grant's which managed to sell 43 million and in place four we have Lawson's which actually reported a one percent growth to 40 million bottles. The biggest loser during 2020 of all 20 top blends comes in at fifth place – Chivas Regal. More than one quarter (-27%) of the volumes vanished which means that they sold 38 million. The unusually high exposure to travel retail sealed the brand's destiny in 2020.

For Black & White in sixth place, the only way is up – no matter what. Sales increased by 2% to 35 million bottles and this was the 11th year in a row with continuous growth for the brand! Only one other blend amongst the Top 30 can boast the same track record, namely Vat 69. Famous Grouse comes in at 7th place with 33 million bottles followed by Label 5 with 31 million. In place 9 we have Bacardi's second top blend, Dewar's with 31 million bottles sold. That meant a 13% drop compared to 2019. Finally, and on the verge of dropping out of the top 10 list, we have J&B which suffered a 22% drop in volumes and landed on

28 million bottles. As late as a decade ago the classic brand sold 58 million bottles.

Single Malt Scotch

Eventhough single malts suffered badly during 2020, both due to covid but also the US tariffs, this is a category which continues to steal market shares from blended Scotch at least in terms of value. Just five years ago the value of Scotch malts was less than a quarter of total exports and in 2020 it is more than a third (34%).

Undoubtedly single malt has become the new cash cow for the Scotch whisky industry with more and more consumers around the world aiming for the next level in their whisky drinking. So, can single malt Scotch become too expensive for the customers? There may be signs pointing in that direction, not least for older expressions which at the moment means anything over 12 years. If we make it very simple and just look at what an average bottle of Scotch single malt is valued at when exported it was £9.94 in 2020 and £8.71 in 2016 – an increase of 14%. The corresponding figures for blended Scotch is £3.18 per bottle in 2020 and £3.32 per bottle in 2016, a decrease of 4%.

For the first time in the history of the Malt Whisky Yearbook we have decided to call it a draw between Glenfiddich and Glenlivet in the battle for the number one spot on the global list of best selling single malts. The figures from different sources are inconclusive and point at different trends. Both brands sold around 14,5 million bottles in 2020 but when Glenlivet only lost 4% of its volumes, Glenfiddich decreased by 21%.

For the rest of the malts on the Top 10 list, there were no sales figures for 2020 available at the time of printing so what follows here is the position and figures from 2019. There may be changes between them in the ranking but, most likely, no new brand has managed to enter the list: Macallan (11.6 million bottles, -1%), The Singleton (6.4 million, +3%), Glenmorangie (6.3 million, +-0%), Balvenie (4.9 million, +9%), Laphroaig (3.9 million, -1%), Cardhu (3.5 million, +14%), Talisker (3.3 million, +8%) and Aberlour (2.8 million, -14%)

Finally, let's take a look at the top whiskies in North America, India and Ireland.

In North America, Jack Daniel's is the undisputed leader and the sixth most sold whisk(e)y in the world with 148 million bottles sold in 2020 which was a decline in volumes of 8%. In second place there is the most sold bourbon in the world, Jim Beam, which managed to grow by 3% selling 128 million bottles. It is followed by the Canadian whisky Crown Royal (97 million, +3%) and two bourbons – Evan Williams (36 million, +7%) and Maker's Mark (29 million, +-0).

In India, we find seven of the ten most sold whiskies in the world even though they cannot be sold in the EU as whisky since they are made from molasses rather than grain. The top 5 are McDowell's No. 1 (308 million bottles,

In 2021 The Macallan and Bentley Motors entered into a global brand partnership

-16%), Imperial Blue (256 million, -19%), Officer's Choice (250 million, -32%), Royal Stag (222 million, -16%) and Original Choice (126 million, -17%).

No brand is as dominant within its category as Jameson. The world's number one Irish whiskey admittedly saw volumes decreasing during 2020 but only by 5% which meant sales of 92 million bottles. Tullamore Dew, number two on the list with 14.4 million bottles, lost 17% of its sales with Bushmills coming in on third place with 8.8 million bottles.

New distilleries

Scotland

This part of the book deals with the embryonic distillery projects – they haven't started producing yet. In some cases their story is more of a plan where neither funds have been secured nor planning permission has been granted.

There has been a virtual explosion of new Scottish whisky distilleries (38 since the new millenium started) with four of them starting production in 2020 or early 2021. You can read more about Brora, Burn O´Bennie, Falkirk and Lochlea in the New Distilleries chapter, page xx-xx.

Another two "new" distilleries that haven't started up yet, are not covered in this section. They are the closed Port Ellen and Rosebank which will hopefully start distilling again in 2022. Read more about them on pages xx-xx.

A third distillery is about to open soon in Edinburgh. Paddy Fletcher and Ian Stirling are building a vertical distillery beside Ocean Terminal Shopping Centre and the Royal Yacht Britannia. Funded by a range of international investors the Port of Leith distillery will cost £12m. The covid pandemic delayed the construction but in November 2020 the foundations were laid and during spring and summer the 40 metre high distillery began to take shape with washbacks being installed in July. The distillery will have a capacity of 400,000 litres of pure alcohol and the owners hope to start distillation some time in 2022. Until the new distillery is ready the owners have been producing gin in a temporary distillery, the Tower Street Stillhouse. They are also conducting a study on different strains of yeast together with Heriot-Watt University. Some of the strains were tried in a test distillation run at Glasgow Distillery

Over on Islay, Elixir Distillers, spearheaded by well-known whisky dealer and collector Sukhinder Singh, finally got the green light on their planning application. The first application was filed in April 2018 but several objections over the years have delayed the process. The clearance from the local council finally arrived in April 2021. Equipped with 16 washbacks and two pairs of stills, the distillery will have the capacity to produce 1 million litres of pure alcohol. There will also be a micro distillery for experimentation and possibly other spirits. On site floor maltings will produce between 60 and 80% of their barley needs. Water is an issue on Islay and while the owners first tried using bore holes and even sea water they have now settled for building a reservoir adjacent to the distillery. The distillery will be situated just outside Port Ellen on the road to Laphroaig, Lagvulin and Ardbeg. In April 2021, it was announced that Georgie Crawford would become the distillery manager. Georgie spent many years managing

Lagvulin and for the past few years she has been supervising the resurrection of Port Ellen distillery.

On the west coast of the Cowal Peninsula, in the west of Scotland (just north of the isle of Bute), the village Polphail was built in the 1970s to house workers on a planned oil rig construction plant nearby. The plans for the oil rig yard were never realized though and the houses that had already been built turned into a ghost town and were finally demolished in 2016. In 2017, Sandy Bulloch, the previous owner of Loch Lomond Distillery, bought the site with the aim to build a distillery named Portavadie. The planning application was approved by Argyll & Bute Council in August 2018 and currently, the site – including planning permission and building warrant approval for a distillery – is offered to the market for £500,000.

Down in the Borders, Mossburn Distillers, owner of Torabhaig distillery on Skye, are involved with two distilleries. One of them, the Reivers Distillery outside Melrose, has already started production. Equipped with pot stills as well as columns, they will be producing mainly rye and mixed grain spirits but genever and other spirits are also talked about. This is a fairly small distillery with a capacity of 100,000 litres. Their other distillery is of a much grander format. It will be built on the site of Jedforest Hotel near Jedburgh and will actually consist of two distilleries – one equipped with three pot stills and a capacity of 1.5 million litres and the other with five columns. The plan is to start with the building of warehouses needed for the company's other operations followed by the distillery. A possible production start will not take place until perhaps in 2025.

Another distillery planned for The Borders has been postponed for the time being. R&B Distillers, which opened their first distillery on Raasay in 2017, are looking to build it in Peebles south of Edinburgh. One of the owners of R&B Distillers is Alasdair Day who launched a blended whisky named The Tweeddale already in 2010.

Remaining in the south, in Moffat in Dumfries and Galloway, the whisky blender Dark Sky Spirits has broken ground on a new distillery which is due to open in 2022. The first building was erected in June 2021 and the owners, Nick and Erin Bullard, are aiming for a small (60,000 litres), traditional distillery with wooden washbacks and a worm tub for cooling the spirits. They will also have a direct wood-fired still in place.

It is not unusual that distillery projects take a lot longer than expected from when the idea is born until a producing facility is in place and Ardgowan in Inverkip 30 miles west of Glasgow is proof of that. Planning permission was received in March 2017 and the owners hoped to start production in 2019. This was later revised to 2021 and the current plan is to have it up and running sometime in 2022/2023. The latest deadline seems to be kept. The founders, Martin McAdam and Alan Baker, have secured a major investment of £7.2m from an Austrian investor, Ronald Grain, who is the founder of the IT company Grain GmbH. Grain is not unused to investment in the spirits business with Cotswolds Distillery being one of the projects he has taken an interest in over the years. In anticipation of whisky from their own production, a range of sourced whiskies called Clydebuilt has been launched with the blended malt Coppersmith as the first release.

Plans to open a combined brewery and whisky distillery

A picture of Gordon & MacPhail´s Cairn Distillery taken in July 2021 with the stills clearly visible in the centre

in Loch Lomond National Park were revealed in spring 2020. The Glen Luss distillery will open up in the village of Luss which is on the A82 on the western shores of Loch Lomond. Planning permission was approved in February 2021 and according to the owners, production should start later in 2021 which probably is a bit too optimistic. Focus will be on malt whisky but gin and rum will also be produced.

The third whisky distillery to open up in Glasgow in modern days is not far away. In July 2017 independent bottler Douglas Laing announced that they had plans to build a distillery named Clutha on the banks of the river Clyde at Pacific Quay, just opposite Clydeside Distillery. The project also includes a bottling complex, a new corporate head office, a visitor centre, a whisky laboratory and an archive. The site for the future distillery had to be moved slightly due to a possible flood risk and then the pandemic delayed the project. Production will now probably start in 2022. The capacity will be 250,000 litres per year and the whisky house style will be robust and sherry driven.

Up in Speyside, The Cabrach Trust plans to build a distillery in the village of Cabrach 15 minutes south of Dufftown. The idea is to convert the old Inverharroch Farm to a distillery and heritage centre including a museum of illicit whisky and smuggling. Planning permission was granted in September 2017 and with £2.1m of the funding in place, the trust applied in 2020 for another £1.4m from the Scottish Government.

Independent bottler Gordon & MacPhail is currently building their second distillery – this time at Craggan, near Grantown-on-Spey in the Cairngorms National Park. Plan-

ning approval was granted in October 2019, construction work started in July 2020 and in June 2021 most of the equipment (a 5 ton mash tun, washbacks and stills) were in place. The Cairn Distillery, with a capacity of around 2 million litres is scheduled to be up and running sometime in spring 2022.

Since Dallas Dhu closed in 1983, the distillery has been preserved as a museum by Historic Environmental Scotland. In 2018 the HES sent out an appeal for interested parties to help redevelop the site and ultimately turn it into a working distillery again. They received more than 70 submissions to that plea and have now made a shortlist of six proposals to see which one they will go forward with.

The chance of Heather Nelson becoming the first woman to found a Scotch whisky distillery vanished in 2017 when Annabel Thomas opened her Nc´nean distillery on the Morvern peninsula. Nelson, who has studied at the Institute of Brewing and Distilling, submitted a planning application to build a distillery on the old World War II airbase at Fearn near Tain in March 2017 and it was later approved in just four weeks. The start of construction and production has been delayed but the project is still ongoing.

A bit further north, just south of Brora, lies Dunrobin Castle which attracts 85,000 visitors each year. Here, Elizabeth Sunderland, a granddaughter of the former head of Clan Sutherland, and her husband Boban Costin have plans to build a single estate distillery housed in an old powerhouse. Planning permission was granted in late 2016 and the owners are now looking for an investor that can pledge the £6m needed.

As far north as you can possibly get on the Scottish mainland lies John O´Groats and here, Derek and Kerry Campbell have received a £198,000 grant from Highland & Islands Enterprise to build the 8 Doors Distillery with a yearly capacity of 60,000 litres. Groundwork, including drilling 60 metre deep boreholes for the water supply, started in November 2020 and the owners are aiming for a production start in late 2021 or during 2022.

Plans for a distillery on Barra has been an ongoing theme for many years now and the story continues. A crowdfunding initiative was launched in early 2019. Yet in spring 2021, they were still looking for funds in the region of £5m.

There are plans for whisky distilleries on a couple of islands in the outer Hebrides. Jonny Ingledew and Kate MacDonald opened a gin distillery on North Uist in April 2019 and in July 2020 they bought the 18th century Nunton Steadings on the island of Benbecula, situated between North and South Uist. The plan is to open a designated whisky distillery within the next couple of years. Businessman Angus A Macmillan and his Uist Distilling Company secured almost £2m in July 2021 from Highlands and Islands Enterprise for yet another distillery named Gramsdale on Benbecula and on South Uist, plans for a community-run whisky distillery were revealed in 2018 and a planning application was submitted in October 2020. The cost for the distillery is estimated at £6.5m and with a 300,000 litre capacity, it will also have its own malting floor using local peat to dry the barley.

In October 2020, it was announced that former Whyte & Mackay chief executive Michael Lunn had plans to set up a new distillery in Stirling. Wolfcraig Distillery, with a construction budget of £15m will have a capacity of 1.5 million litres of alcohol. In June 2021, it was revealed that the original location had been changed to Craigforth Campus in Stirling and the company is still awaiting approval on their planning application. Meanwhile, the legendary master blender Richard Paterson has signed up to be a part of the new distillery while still keeping the main responsibility of blending The Dalmore single malt.

The planning application for a distillery on Hopetoun Estate near Queensferry, 20 kilometres west of Edinburgh, was approved in April 2021. The project is backed by American investors and Julia Mackenzie-Gillanders and Ann Medlock, founders of the bottler Golden Decanters, are behind the project. Ken Robertson, former director of communications at Diageo and former chairman of the Keepers of the Quaich is also involved. The distillery, which will include maltings, will be built near the ruined 16th century Midhope Castle which for Outlander fans is a holy grail. The castle was the setting for Lallybroch in the TV series, the home of Jamie Fraser and his family.

One of the latest projects to be announced (in March 2021) was a distillery in Dunphail south of Forres. Behind it are the owners of the highly regarded Bimber Distillery in London. Still awaiting planning approval, the distillery will have a capacity of 200,000 litres of pure alcohol and also be equipped with floor maltings providing it with 100% of the needs. A production start is planned for 2022.

Speyside Distillers will be building a new distillery before their lease of the current site near Kingussie runs out in 2025. Meanwhile, the blender Glasgow Whisky has acquired Tromie Mills Distillery (as Speyside Distillery is sometimes called) and will eventually use it for a new distillery.

Ireland & Northern Ireland

Few have failed to notice that Irish whiskey has made a magnificent come-back in the recent decades and the speed of opening up new distilleries shows no sign of losing momentum. There are currently 36 distilleries already working (read more about them on in the section Distilleries Around the Globe) and another 17 either being built or seeking funds for starting up. So, let's go through them all.

In Laherdane, Co Mayo, Jude and Paul Davis together with Mark Quick have been tirelessly working on the construction of their Nephin Distillery for quite some time now. A number of delays have occured. The latest, due to the pandemic, stopped Italian engineers from the still manufacturer to fly to Ireland to work on the installment of the stills. The owners are now hoping for a late 2021 or early 2022 start of the distillation. Meanwhile they have a sister company, Nephin Cooperage in Foxford, which has been active for a few years supplying several Irish distilleries with casks.

While still on the west coast, we can report on another project. Sliabh Liag Distillers, in southwest Donegal. It started as a gin distillery with plans to expand into whiskey production as well. That is exactly what James and Moira Doherty still intend to do but instead of distilling whiskey at the present distillery they are building a new one for that, in the historic town of Ardara, 25 km north east of Sliabh Liag and also to move the gin still there. Planning was granted for the new distillery in August 2019. At a cost of €10m Ardara will hold an impressive capacity of 450,000 litres of pure alcohol and production is scheduled to start in late 2021. The idea is to produce triple-distilled whiskey, both single malt and single pot still, and some of it heavily peated as it would have been in the 19th century. Meanwhile, a blended whiskey named Silkie distilled at Great Northern Distillery has been released by the owners.

The island co-op at Cape Clear, six kilometers off the Cork coast, received planning permission in August 2016 to build a €7m distillery on the island. Unfortunately, one of their major investors pulled out along the way and the owners started a Kickstarter campaign in spring 2019 in order to fund parts of the project. A year later a gin distillery was working and they've also obtained planning permission for a separate whiskey distillery to be built.

Gortinore Distillers, based in Waterford, launched their sourced, triple-distilled Natterjack Irish Whiskey in 2019. In late 2020 the owners were granted planning approval to build a whiskey distillery at the site of the Old Mill in Kilmacthomas. Following restoration, the 500,000 litre distillery will be equipped with three copper pot stills.

Further to the west, in Cahersiveen, Co. Kerry, a company is transforming an old sock factory into a distillery called Skellig Six 18. The unusual name was inspired by the number of steps (618) to the top of Skellig Michael, an island situated 10 kilometres off the coast of Iveragh Peninsula. The woman behind the plan is former lawyer June O'Connell and she is hoping they could start the distillation in late 2021 or early 2022.

Killarney in Co Kerry seems to be destined to become

With a possible production start in autumn 2021, Killarney Distillery will become one of the largest in Ireland

a veritable bees nest of distilleries and breweries within the next couple of years. In Fossa, the Killarney Brewing Company are busy completing a distillery of quite some size. Beer production started in 2013 on a site in the centre of Killarney while the new distillery, combined with a brewery, will be situated by Lough Leane on the western outskirts of the town. The distillery will be equipped with two 2,000 litre copper pot stills from Italy and until their first own whiskey is released, sourced whiskey has been released. Once operational, hopefully in the aututumn of 2021, the distillery will employ more than 85 people and aims to attract 100,000 visitors annually. The total investment is worth €24m. Just a stone's throw away, in Aghadoe, Killarney Distillers are planning to build a craft distillery in an old coach house and at the Lakeview Estate Wayward Irish Spirits have built a bonding facility where they blend and mature sourced whiskies under the brand name Wayward. Their plan is to have a single estate grain to glass distillery on the site by 2024.

In County Longford, west of Dublin, Peter Clancy in partnership with his brother and sister, is working on the Lough Ree distillery on the grounds of the old post office in Lanesborough. A gin still is already in place and the Sling Shot Gin has been released. In anticipation of their first own whiskey a sourced whiskey from Great Northern Distillery, matured in a combination of Rioja and brown ale casks, was released in June 2021.

Donegal's first grain distillery in over a century, Baoil-leach, is already up and running but so far owner Michael O'Boyle has focused on gin, rum and poitín. The plan is to start whiskey production in 2022.

In summer 2019, the local council gave the green light to a distillery in the 200 year old Ballykelly Mills near Monasterevin in county Kildare. Behind the project is Je-welfield Ltd with Bono as a shareholder. Monasterevin has a long history of whisky distilling. A distillery was opened already in 1784 and operated until 1934. In the autumn of 2020 construction on the new distillery, to be named Church of Oak, started and one of the consultants is Ian

MacMillan who worked for Burn Stewart for many years.

Further north in Derrylavan, Co. Monaghan and just west of Dundalk, lies Old Carrick Mill Distillery. Gin has already been launched and production of triple distilled whiskey is in the pipeline. The sourced May Loag whiskey is already available.

An old mill in Ahascragh, Co. Galway will be converted into a whiskey and gin distillery by McAllister Distillers. Powered by renewable energy the distillery could be up and running sometime in 2022. In summer 2021 sourced whiskey was released under the brand name Clan Colla.

Finally, in Northern Ireland, there are currently four ongoing projects; Joe McGirr is the mastermind behind Boatyard Distillery in Enniskillen which began distilling in May 2016. The company has had some remarkable success with their gin and vodka and recently they secured £634,000 in funding to grow the business even further, not least in the US. The owners are also planning to launch a whiskey in the near future.

Michael McKeown, founder of Matt D'Arcy & Company, was granted planning permission in summer 2018 for a whiskey distillery in Newry in Co. Down. Around £7m will be invested in the 100,000 litre distillery and a visitor centre. Sourced whiskey from other distilleries including Echlinville was released in spring 2020.

In Garrison Co. Fermanagh, a couple of kilometres from the Irish border, work recently began on a £5m whiskey distillery where the financial backup comes from a group of investors based in London. Scott's distillery takes its name from the original owner of the farm on which the site is based – Hammy Scott. If everything goes according to plans, the distillery could be producing in 2022.

Finally, a new distillery is underway in Lurgan Co. Armagh. Lough Neagh Distillers already operate Spade:Town brewery and are working on building a whiskey distillery as well but the covid pandemic has forced a temporary cessation of it.

Independent
bottlers

The independent bottlers play an important role
in the whisky business. With their innovative bottlings, they increase
diversity. Single malts from distilleries where the owners' themselves
decide not to bottle also get a chance through the independents.
The following are a selection of the major companies.
Tasting notes have been prepared by Gavin D Smith.

Gordon & MacPhail

gordonandmacphail.com

Established in 1895 the company, which is owned by the Urquhart
family, still occupies the same premises in Elgin. Apart from being
an independent bottler, there is also a legendary store in Elgin and,
since 1993, an own distillery, Benromach. At the moment they are
building yet another distillery named Cairn at Craggan, close to
Grantown-on-Spey which will be commissioned in 2022. Gordon
& MacPhail´s part in establishing the interest in single malt Scotch
before the vast majority of producers realised the potential can
not be overrated. The company has an incredible variety of casks
in their warehouses in Elgin and in 2018, they revamped their
portfolio of bottlings. Now there are five distinctive ranges; Connoisseurs Choice is a series well-known to most whisky aficionados
and consists of single malts bottled either at 43% or 46%. Some
of the latest releases include Tormore 1994, Speyburn 2008 and
Glentauchers 1995. Discovery, a new range unveiled in 2018, is
grouped under three flavour profiles – smoky, sherry and bourbon.
Distillery Labels is a relic from a time when Gordon & MacPhail
released more or less official bottlings for several producers. Private
Collection, a new range, features old single malts including bottlings from closed distilleries and recently four Glenlivet from 1975
to 1980 were released. Generations, finally, was first introduced in
2010. This range comprises the oldest and rarest whiskies in stock,
including Mortlach 75 years old which at the time was the oldest
single malt ever bottled. That record was broken in September 2021
when an 80 year old Glenlivet was launched! A total of 250 decanters bottled at 44,9% were released. To celebrate the company´s
125th anniversary, an extraordinary series called ”Last Cask” was
introduced in autumn 2020. The four whiskies (Coleburn, Glenury
Royal, Mosstowie and Glencraig) all came from closed distilleries
or from Lomond stills no longer in use.

Miltonduff 10 year old, 43%
Nose: New leather, toffee, malt, wood
           polish, raisins and ginger.
Palate: Medium-bodied, with sherry,
           cocktail cherries, milk chocolate
           and cinnamon.

The Glenlivet 80 year old, 44,9%
Nose: A fatty, waxy aroma, with
           ginger, white pepper, candied
           orange, milk chocolate and
           maraschino cherries.
Palate: Oily and notably fruity, with figs,
           marzipan and medium-dry
           sherry. Drying to dark choco-
           late. Wonderfully vibrant and
           expressive for its great age.

Berry Bros. & Rudd

bbr.com

The world´s oldest wine and spirit merchant, founded in 1698,
opened a new flagship shop in London in 2017. The famous address
3 St James´s Street, where the company has been since the start,
was returned to its appearance of 30 years ago and is now a space
for consultations. The new store is just around the corner in 63 Pall
Mall. Berry Brothers had been offering their customers private bottlings of malt whisky for years, but it was not until 2002 that they
launched Berry´s Own Selection of single malts. Under the supervision of Doug McIvor, one of the most experienced spirits noses in
the UK, some 30 expressions are on offer every year. A new series
called The Classic Range was released in 2018. It´s made up of four

bottlings of blended malt; Speyside, Islay, Sherry Cask Matured and Peated Cask Matured. In spring 2019, The Perspective Series was launched including four blended Scotch (21, 25, 35 and 40 years old). Early 2020, a new range of seven single malts from 1968 to 1995 was introduced. The whiskies were selected by and named after the company´s longtime brand heritage director Ronnie Cox. In 2021 the company launched a new communication campaign, "Since 1698", and at the same time the spirits range was revamped by way of the first bespoke spirits bottles in the company´s history. The first expressions appeared in summer 2021 and included a Linkwood 2009, a Sutherland 2000 and a Lark Distillery 2016. In autumn 2021 a range of four bottlings from Denmark, Finland, Norway and Sweden was launched as The Nordic Casks #1.

Linkwood 2009, 46%
Nose: Fragrant, with warm, spicy fruitcake, banana and orchard fruits.
Palate: Zesty fruits – tangy and long-lasting, with soft toffee, honey and cocoa powder.

Sutherland 2000, 50,4%
Nose: Slightly earthy, with overt notes of honey and peach, plus polished oak.
Palate: Viscous, nutty, with more honey, caramel, developing tropical fruits and pipe tobacco.

Signatory

Founded in 1988 by Andrew and Brian Symington, Signatory Vintage Scotch Whisky lists at least 50 single malts at any one occasion. The most widely distributed range is Cask Strength Collection which recently featured Fettercairn 1995, Bunnahabhain 2009 and Longmorn 2002. In the same range some staggering single grains also appear from time to time, recently a 36 year old Cameronbridge and a 35 year old Carsebridge. Another range is The Un-chill Filtered Collection bottled at 46%. Some of the latest bottlings released include a Mortlach 2009, a Knockando 2007 and a Linkwood 2008. Andrew Symington bought Edradour Distillery from Pernod Ricard in 2002 and the entire operations, including Signatory, are now concentrated to the distillery in Perthshire.

Ian Macleod Distillers

ianmacleod.com

The company was founded in 1933 and is one of the largest independent family-owned companies within the spirits industry. Gin, rum, vodka and liqueurs, apart from whisky, are found within the range and they also own Glengoyne and Tamdhu distilleries. In autumn 2017 they revealed their plans to resurrect Rosebank Distillery in Falkirk which will be re-opened in 2022. Their single malt range includes The Chieftain´s, which cover a range of whiskies from 10 to 50 years old while Macleod´s Regional Malts are single malts chosen to represent the 5 whisky regions in Scotland. There are two As We Get It single malt expressions – Highland and Islay. The Six Isles blended malt contains whisky from the majority of whisky-producing islands while one of the top sellers is the blended Scotch Isle of Skye available at 8 and 12 years old. Finally, Smokehead, a heavily, peated single malt from Islay introduced in 2006, has become a huge success. The range

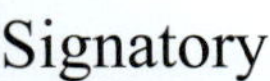

was revamped in 2018 and several new expressions have been released since including Smokehead Rum Rebel. Since July 2021 it is also available as an RTD (ready to drink) mixed with either cola or ginger/lime. In 2016, the company acquired Spencerfield Spirit which included Edinburgh Gin as well as the blended malt Sheep Dip and Pig´s Nose blended Scotch.

The Six Isles Batch Strength, 58%
Nose: Brine and bonfires, mildly medicinal, with strawberries and sweet spices.
Palate: Peaches, peat smoke, prickly pepper and black tea.

Isle of Skye 18 year old, 40%
Nose: Lightly spicy, sweet smokiness, ozone and black pepper.
Palate: Orchard fruits, peat, a suggestion of sherry, oak, dark chocolate and liquorice.

Blackadder International

blackadder.com

Blackadder is owned by Robin Tucek, one of the authors of the classic whisky book, The Malt Whisky File. Apart from Blackadder Raw Cask (bottled straight from the cask without any filtration at all), there are also a number of other ranges – Smoking Islay, Peat Reek, Peat Reek Embers, Statement and special bottlings of Amrut single malt. In recent years, three new brands have become increasingly popular; Black Snake which is a vatting of casks finished in a single sherry butt, Red Snake which are single cask malts, always from first fill ex-bourbon and Sherry Snake from first fill sherry casks. All bottlings from Blackadder are uncoloured and un chill-filtered and most of them are diluted to 43-46% but Raw Cask is always bottled at cask strength.

Murray McDavid

murray-mcdavid.com

The company was founded in 1996 by Mark Reynier, Simon Coughlin and Gordon Wright and in 2000, they also acquired Bruichladdich distillery. In 2013 Murray McDavid was taken over by Aceo Ltd. and a year later they signed a lease for the warehouses at the closed Coleburn distillery for storing their own whiskies as well as stock belonging to clients. The bottlings are divided into six different ranges; Mission Gold (exceptionally rare whiskies bottled at cask strength), Benchmark (mature single malts bottled at 46%), Mystery Malt (single malts where the distillery is not revealed), Select Grain (single grains), The Vatting (vatted malts) and Crafted Blend (blended Scotch from their own blending). The vast majority of the releases are single casks.

Duncan Taylor

duncantaylor.com

Founded in Glasgow in 1938 as a cask broker and trading company. In 2002, the company was acquired by Euan Shand and operations were moved to Huntly. Duncan Taylor´s flagship brand is the blended Scotch Black Bull, a brand with a history going back to 1864. Black Bull was rebranded in 2009 by Duncan Taylor and the range consists of four core releases – Kyloe, an 8 year old, a 12 year old and a 21 year old. There are also limited versions such as 40 year old, 10 year old rum finish and 10 year old sherry finish. The most recent, released in August 2021, is the Peated Edition. The Black Bull brand is complimented by Smokin' which is a blend of peated Speyside, Islay and grain whisky from the Lowlands.

The portfolio also includes The Rarest (single cask, cask strength whiskies of great age from demolished distilleries), Dimensions (a collection of single malts and single grains aged up to 39 years), The Tantalus (a selection of whiskies all aged in their 40s), Battlehill (a range of single malts and single grains) and Rare Auld Grain (a selection of rare grain whiskies bottled at cask strength). The perhaps most popular range in recent years is The Octave. These are single malt whiskies matured for a further period in small, 60-70 litre ex-sherry octave casks. Some of the most recent releases in that range are Laphroaig 2004, Dailuaine 2009 and Dalmunach 2016. In autumn 2019 The Octave Premium with substantially older whiskies, was introduced. Finally, the blended malt category is represented by Big Smoke, a young peated whisky available at 46% and 60%.

Black Bull Peated, 50%

Nose: Bonfire smoke and bubblegum, malt and peaches, slightly medicinal.

Palate: Earthy peat, dark chocolate, toffee, lemon, liquorice dipped in brine.

Octave Glen Grant 30 year old, 55,8%

Nose: Fragrant and full, with sweet sherry, ginger and Christmas pudding notes.

Palate: Full-bodied and initially very sweet, with cocktail cherries and developing dark chocolate. Raisins and plum note in time.

Scotch Malt Whisky Society

smws.com

The Scotch Malt Whisky Society, founded in 1983 and owned by Glenmorangie Co since 2003, has more than 30,000 members worldwide and apart from UK, there is a network of international branches and partner bars in 19 countries around the world. In 2015, Glenmorangie sold the SMWS to a group of private investors and today the SMWS is owned by Artisanal Spirits Company which in 2021 became listed on the London Stock Exchange. The idea from the very beginning was to buy casks of single malts from the producers and bottle them at cask strength without colouring or chill filtration. The Society has played a significant role for the interest in single cask Scotch that has exploded in recent decades. The labels do not reveal the name of the distillery. Instead there is a number but also a short description which will give you a clue to which distillery it is. Around 500 casks are bottled every year. The SMWS operates four venues with bars and member rooms in Edinburgh (Queen Street and Leith), London (Greville Street) and Glasgow (Bath Street) and also works with partner bars around the world. In recent years, the range has been expanded to also include single grain, whiskies from other countries as well as rum, gin, cognac and other spirits.

Compass Box Whisky Co

compassboxwhisky.com

John Glaser, founder and co-owner of the company, has a philosophy which is strongly influenced by meticulous selection of oak for the casks, clearly inspired by his time in the wine business. But he also has a lust for experimenting to test the limits, which was clearly shown when Spice Tree, matured in casks containing extra staves, was launched in 2005. Glaser and Compass Box are also advocating more transparency in the industry where the customer is given as much information as possible about the contents of the bottle. The company divides its ranges into a Signature Range and a Limited Range. Spice Tree (a blended malt), The Peat Monster (a combination of peated Islay whiskies and Highland malts), Oak Cross (American oak casks fitted with heads of French oak), Hedonism (a vatted grain whisky) and The Story of the Spaniard (a blended malt partially matured in Spanish red wine casks) are

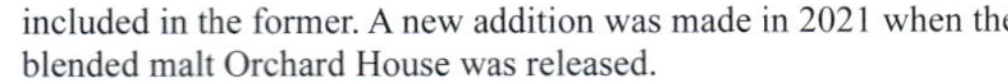

included in the former. A new addition was made in 2021 when the blended malt Orchard House was released.

In the Limited range, whiskies are regularly replaced and at times only to resurface a couple of years later in new variations. Included in the 2020/2021 releases are Canvas where single malt from four distilleries was re-racked for three years into casks that had matured Vino Naranja and Menagerie which is a blend of malt whiskies from Mortlach, Deanston, Glen Elgin and Laphroaig. Furthermore there is Magic Cask where young malt whisky from ten oloroso butts had been vatted together with much older bourbon-matured Imperial single malt. There are also two blended Scotch, Artist´s Blend and Glasgow Blend, with a 50% proportion of malt whisky.

In 2014, Compass Box made a long-term agreement with John Dewar & Sons where the Bacardi-owned company would supply Compass Box with stocks of whisky for future bottlings. In 2015 it was further announced that Bacardi had acquired a minority share of the independent bottler.

Orchard House, 46%

Nose: Floral, with ripe red apples, honey and fudge.

Palate: Supple mouthfeel, lemon and nectarines, tangy oak, drying to black tea.

Canvas, 46%

Nose: Light fruit notes, summer hay meadows and a hint of wood smoke.

Palate: Voluptuous, with ripe cherries, Jaffa orange, chocolate-coated Turkish Delight, pepper and oak.

North Star Spirits

northstarspirits.com

Founded in 2016 by Iain Croucher who used to work for AD Rattray before deciding to go it alone. The latest release in his single cask single malt range in 2021 included a Springbank trilogy, a Mezcal finished Blair Athol and a 5-year-old Glasgow Distilled Single Malt to celebrate 5 years in business. They have developed a Blended Malt range called Supersonic and continue to bottle sherry finished Caol Ila as CHAOS. They have also been recognized by the Scotch Whisky Awards as the Independent Bottler of the Year 2021. I also hear a whisper they may be producing their own Single Malt Scotch Whisky in the not-too-distant future.

Meadowside Blending

meadowsideblending.com

The company may be a newcomer to the family of independent bottlers but the founder certainly isn´t. Donald Hart, a Keeper of the Quaich and co-founder of the well-known bottler Hart Brothers, runs the Glasgow company together with his son, Andrew. There are six sides to the business – blends sold under the name The Royal Thistle, single malts labelled The Maltman, single cask single grains under the label The Grainman, Vintage Cask Reserve featuring ultra rare bottlings, Vital Spark focusing on single malts with "a maritime twist" and, introduced in 2020, The Granary with blended grain whiskies.

Master of Malt

masterofmalt.com

Master of Malt is an online retailer of whiskies, gins, rums, agave spirits, beer, wine and more. As one of the most innovative whisky retailers in the UK, the company also has its own range of single-cask bottlings, everything from old and rare expressions from the likes of The Macallan, Springbank and Littlemill, to world whiskies like the Paul John and Millstone. They have also secured exclusive cask selections from brands like Glenfarclas, The Lakes Distillery, That Boutique-y Whisky Company and Darkness. In addition, Master of Malt stocks Drinks by the Dram 30ml sample-size bottles for nearly every product on the site and customers can entirely customise contents of their own 5x Drinks by the Dram tasting sets. The retailer also offers a "Pour & Sip" whisky subscription service, as well as a Blend Your Own option, personalised whisky and has a pretty impressive gift finder to help with special occassions.

Darkness! Islay 12 year old oloroso finish, 55%

Nose: Sherry-soaked malted barley, spicy sweet peat, and salted caramel.

Palate: Rich in the mouth, earthy, with ginger, sea salt and quite dry lingering peat notes, plus liquorice and Jaffa orange.

Atom Brands

Atom Brands, part of the Atom Group which includes online retailer Master of Malt and the UK Distributor Maverick Drinks, is the producer of several home-grown brands as well as independently bottled whiskies, rums, gins and other spirits from around the world. Included in their portfolio is Drinks by the Dram the creators of the booze-filled Advent calendars, tasting sets and 30ml dram samples, as well as Bathtub Gin, Rumbullion!, That Boutique-y Drinks Company, Character of Islay Whisky Company, Darkness, The Blended Whisky Company, Bitter Bastards, Origin, The 'Hot Enough' Vodka Company and Mr Lyan.

That Boutique-y Whisky Company

thatboutiqueywhiskycompany.com

Established in 2012, this independent bottler is best characterised by its uncompromising approach to flavour and quality with each bottle adorned with graphic novel-style labels hand illustrated by Glasgow-based artist Emily Chappell. The company has worked with over 160 distilleries to date. Creating a range that is a global representation of the whisky category, this past year has seen them launch quarterly "themed" releases (World Series, Rye Series, Australia Series, Home Nations Series and the forthcoming Wine Series) while still releasing casks and small batches from Scotland, both old (Glentauchers 44yo) and new (Nc'Nean 3yo).

Glentauchers 44 year old, 42,1%

Nose: Rich, with fragrant stewed fruits, baked apple, caramel and linseed oil.

Palate: Initially fresh fruits, soon followed by quite tannic oak notes, dark chocolate, cigar boxes and orange marmalade.

The Character of Islay Whisky Company

characterofislay.com

The Character of Islay Whisky Company offers a range of distinctive whiskies with Islay at their heart. A modern, yet romanticised approach to the Islay whisky category, The Character of Islay Company uses fabled characters to create a world at once fictional and factual that aspires to capture all the magic of Islay whisky. The brand's expressions include Aerolite Lyndsay 10 year old, Grace Île 25 year old and The Legend of Fiona Macleod 33 year old. The makers of The Character of Islay Whisky Company, are also behind the Green Isle, as well as the single cask series, Wind & Wave.

Bunnahabhain 2001 19 year old, 56,5%

Nose: Spicy sherry, toffee, malt loaf, chocolate orange and salted peanuts.

Palate: Nutty and peppery, with raisins, prunes, bitter orange, and ultimately very dry sherry.

Seaweed& Aeons& Digging& Fire

The &Whisky range is the brainchild of Atom Brands' innovation arm "Atom Labs", creators of Jaffa Cake gin, Bourbon Bourbon and Burnt Ends (to name just a few). Following the success of S&A&D&F selling thousands of bottles through a single retailer in its first few months, the range widened to include a cask strength version, two sherry-matured versions (one at 40% and one at cask strength) as well as a 10yo bourbon and 30yo single grain Scotch whisky.

Seaweed& Aeons& Digging& Fire 10 year old, 40%

Nose: Sherry, peat embers, lime, rockpools and sea salt.

Palate: Nicely balanced sweet orchard fruits dipped in sherry and ashy peat, with developing liquorice.

The Whisky Agency

whisky-agency.de

The man behind this company is Carsten Ehrlich, to many whisky aficionados known as one of the founders of the annual Whisky Fair in Limburg, Germany. His experience from sourcing casks for limited Whisky Fair bottlings led him to start as an independent bottler under the name The Whisky Agency, a business that celebrated its 10th anniversary in 2018. There are several ranges including The Whisky Agency, The Perfect Dram and Specials with some unusual bottlings.

A Dewar Rattray Ltd

adrattray.com

The company was founded by Andrew Dewar Rattray in 1868. In 2004 the company was revived by Tim Morrison, previously of Morrison Bowmore Distillers and fourth generation descendent of Andrew Dewar, with a view to bottling single cask malts from different regions in Scotland. In 2011, the company opened A Dewar Rattray´s Whisky Experience & Shop in Kirkoswald, South Ayrshire. Apart from having a large choice of whiskies for sale, there is a sample room, as well as a cask room.

One of the company´s best-sellers is a single malt named Stronachie which is actually sourced from Benrinnes. There are currently two expressions, a 10 year old and a 10 year old sherry finish. In 2011 a peated, blended malt, Cask Islay, became the first in a new series called Casks of Scotland where the latest expressions include Cask Islay Sherry Edition and Bourbon Edition as well as Cask Speyside 12 year old Sherry Finish. The AD Rattray´s Cask Collection is a range of single cask whiskies bottled at cask strength and without colouring or chill-filtration. In 2020 a new range of single cask whiskies, The Warehouse Collection, was introduced. Bottled at either cask strength or 46% these are a mixture of full or part casks, 'bin ends' and remnants from casks that have be re-racked. Finally there is the 5 year old blended Scotch Bank Note.

Vintage Cask Collection Invergordon 1988 33 year old, 48,9%
Nose: Quite reticent, with fudge, soft spices and lemon juice.
Palate: Light citrus fruits, notably orange, and wood shavings, followed by almonds, cocoa powder, and lingering citric notes.

Cask Collection Macduff 2002 18 year old, 58,5%
Nose: Slightly herbal initially, with green figs, dates, stewed fruits and faint sweet smoke.
Palate: Sweet in the mouth, buttery texture, spicy, ripe cherries, Turkish Delight and milk chocolate, with raisins and darker chocolate notes in time.

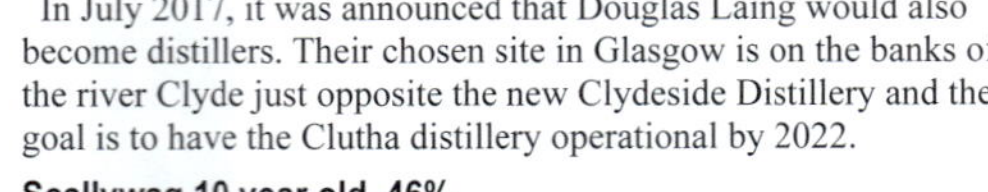

Douglas Laing & Co

douglaslaing.com

Established in 1948 by Douglas Laing, this firm was run for many years by his two sons, Fred and Stewart. In 2013, the brothers decided to go their separate ways. Douglas Laing & Co is now run by Fred Laing and his daughter Cara. Douglas Laing has the following brands in their portfolio; Provenance (single casks bottled at 46%), Premier Barrel (single malts in ceramic decanters) and Old Particular, a range of single malts and grains. The latter has also been expanded with two brand extensions; XOP and XOP "The Black Series". A range named Double Barrel was recently re-branded and consists of expressions where just two single malts have been blended together.

Seven years ago the company started a range that has become highly succesful. The first installment in the series that eventually was given the name Remarkable Regional Malts, was Scallywag – a blended malt influenced by sherried whiskies from Speyside. More versions have followed with Scallywag 10 year old, 12 year old cask strength and Mocha Edition. Regional Malts has been expanded over the years and now also includes Timorous Beastie from the Highlands with no age statement as well as 10, 18, 25 year old and the recent, limited "Meet the Beast". Rock Island is a blended malt combining whiskies from Islay, Arran, Orkney and Jura and can be found without age statement, as a 10 year old and the limited Sherry Edition. The Epicurean represents the Lowlands with a no age statement as well as a 12 year old and two recent limited bottlings - Tawny Port Finish and Ruby Port Finish. The Gauldrons is made from Campbeltown malts and the final regional whisky is Big Peat, a vatting of Islay malts. This was launched several years ago but was later included in the range. The core range is made up of a no age statement bottling and a 12 year old. Recent limited versions include Peatrichor Edition, BBQ Edition and Heroe's Edition.

In July 2017, it was announced that Douglas Laing would also become distillers. Their chosen site in Glasgow is on the banks of the river Clyde just opposite the new Clydeside Distillery and the goal is to have the Clutha distillery operational by 2022.

Scallywag 10 year old, 46%
Nose: Lightly spiced floral notes, ripe pears, fresh leather, shortbread and subtle sherry.
Palate: Polished oak, fudge, allspice, tangy fruits, hazelnuts and black pepper.

Big Peat 12 year old, 46%
Nose: Big aromas of sweet peat and old leather. Ashy, with soot, citrus fruits and brine..
Palate: Sweet orchard fruits, liquorice, roasted peanuts, peppery peat, bonfire smoke.

Malts of Scotland

malts-of-scotland.com

A German bottler founded by Thomas Ewers in 2009. The backbone of the assortment is the Basic Line with three blended malts; Classic (18yo), Sherry (15yo) and Peat (10yo). Apart from other ranges of Scotch single malts, Ewers has also added a range called Malts of Ireland. At the moment he has released more than 100 bottlings and apart from a large number of single casks, there are two special series, Amazing Casks and Angel´s Choice, both dedicated to very special and superior casks.

Hunter Laing & Co

hunterlaing.com

This company was formed after the demerger between Fred and Stewart Laing in 2013 (see Douglas Laing). It is run by Stewart Laing and his two sons, Scott and Andrew. The Hunter Laing portfolio consists of the following ranges and brands; The Old Malt Cask (rare and old malts, bottled at 50%), The Old and Rare Selection (an exclusive range of old malts offered at cask strength), The Sovereign (a range of old and rare grain whiskies), Hepburn´s Choice (younger malts bottled at 46%) and The First Editions. The latter was created by Andrew Laing before Hunter Laing was formed and is now a substantial part of the portfolio. In June 2019, Scarabus, a single malt from an undisclosed Islay distillery, was released as the first in a new range and there are also two small batch blended malts - Islay Journey and Highland Journey. Finally, a remarkable series by the name Eidolon was introduced in late 2020. It consists of three extremely rare Port Ellen single malts and the first was a 36 year old distilled in 1983.

In January 2016, the company announced their intentions of building a distillery on Islay on the northeast coast near Bunnahabhain. Ardnahoe Distillery, with a capacity of making 1 million litres per year, came on stream in November 2018 and was opened to the public in spring 2019. To celebrate their presence on the island, the company has since then released a number of old and rare Islay single malts, often in connection with the Feis Ile, under the name Kinship.

Scarabus Batch Strength, 57%
Nose: Bonfire smoke, orchard fruits, brine and newly-sawn wood.
Palate: Sinewy and mildly medicinal with chilli, honey, toffee and ashy peat.

Scarabus 10 year old, 46%
Nose: Sweet peat, farmyard aromas, new leather, smoked fish and lemon.
Palate: Quite light-bodied, dry peat, treacle, dark chocolate, black pepper.

Wemyss Malts

wemyssmalts.com

Founded in 2005, the family-owned independent bottler opened up their own whisky distillery at Kingsbarns in Fife in 2014. The company is mainly known for its range of blended malts of which there are three core expressions – The Hive, Spice King and Peat Chimney. These are available at 46% un chill-filtered and also in limited edition batch strength. A limited 12 year old Spice King Highland & Islay was also recently released. In autumn 2020 the entire range was rebranded including new packaging. In 2017, the family bottled a new part of their blended malt range called The Family Collection consisting of spirit sourced and fully matured by the family. There were two releases, Vanilla Burst and Treacle Chest and they were followed up in 2019 by Blooming Gorse and Flaming Feast. Two other blended malts are Nectar Grove, released in 2018 and finished in ex-Madeira casks and the oloroso sherry matured Velvet Fig which was relaunched as a 25 year old in 2020 to celebrate the 15th anniversary of the company.

Another side of the business involves single cask single malts. either bottled at 46% or occasionally at cask strength. The names of the whiskies reflect what they taste like although the distillery name is also printed on the label. All whiskies are un chill-filtered and without colouring. In 2019, Wemyss launched a brand new range called the Wemyss Malts Cask Club and in 2021 the range from the owner's own Kingsbarns distillery was revamped and now consists of the 5 year old Balcomie and the new Bell Rock, a vatting of ex-bourbon and ex-oloroso casks.

Kingsbarns Balcomie, 46%
Nose: Fresh and fragrant, with vanilla, peach blossom, pineapple and nutty milk chocolate.
Palate: Orchard fruits, honey, light spices, caramel and dark chocolate, with spicy oak.

Velvet Fig, 46%
Nose: Rich and floral, with vanilla, banana, dates and subtle oak.
Palate: Sweet, with stewed fruits, Christmas pudding, sultanas, ginger and cinnamon, plus milky coffee and more light oak.

Single Cask Nation

singlecasknation.com

In 2011, Jason Johnstone-Yellin and Joshua Hatton, two well-known whisky bloggers, started, in alliance with Seth Klaskin, a new career as independent bottlers. The initial idea with Single Cask Nation somewhat reminds you of Scotch Malt Whisky Society in the sense that you have to become a member (for free) of the nation in order to buy the bottlings on-line. In 2017, the owners decided to develop an alternative way of selling their products and launched a special range of whiskies that could also be found at retailers in a number of states in the USA. This new way of doing business, which they named Single Cask Nation Retail Release, proved succesful and since 2019 their products are available in Europe and Canada as well. The 2nd release for Europe in November 2020 included Invergordon 45 year old, Imperial 24 year old, Clynelish 9 year old, Glen Elgin 10 year old and Aberfeldy 28 year old. Although focusing on Scotch, Single Cask Nation has over the years released bottlings from distilleries in other parts of the world and indeed of other types of spirits.

Elixir Distillers

elixirdistillers.com

The company is owned by Sukhinder and Rajbir Singh, known by most for their three very well-stocked The Whisky Exchange shops in London as well as being the largest on-line retailer of Scotch whisky in the world. In the beginning of October every year, they are hosting the iconic The Whisky Show in London, one of the best whisky festivals in the world and for the last five years they have also been involved in the Old & Rare Show in Glasgow and, most recently, in London. In 2002 they started as independent bottlers of malt whiskies operating under the brand name The Single Malts of Scotland. There are around 50 bottlings on offer at any time, either as single casks or as batches bottled at cask strength or at 46%. In addition there are three subranges; Director's Special which showcases exceptionally old and rare single malts selected by Sukhinder Singh, the accessible Reserve Cask range and the more mature Marriage of Casks.

In 2009 a new range of Islay single malts under the name Port Askaig was introduced. The current range (including limited releases) consists of 100° Proof, 8, 12 Autumn Edition, 25, 28, 34 and 45 year old. Elements of Islay, a series of cask strength single malts in which all Islay distilleries are, or will be, represented was introduced a few years before Port Askaig. The list of the product range is cleverly constructed with periodical tables in mind in which each distillery has a two-letter acronym followed by a batch number. There are blended malts in the range as well (Peat, Peat Full Proof and Peat & Sherry) but the emphasis is on single malts where the most recent bottlings include Ar_{11}, Bw_8, and Oc_4. Sukhinder Singh also has plans to build a whisky distillery on Islay on the outskirts of Port Ellen and in April 2021 the long awaited planning approval finally came through. Equipped with floor maltings and two pairs of stills, the distillery will have the capacity to produce 1 million litres of pure alcohol.

Single Malts of Scotland Speyside 12 year old, 48%
Nose: Old leather, walnuts, dates, raisins, wood polish and Jaffa orange.
Palate: Silky delivery, with spicy sherry, stewed fruits, malt loaf and peppery oak.

Port Askaig 100 Proof, 57,1%
Nose: Lemon juice, ginger, orange, charcuterie and medicinal peat notes.
Palate: Early sweetness gives way to dark berries, with sea salt, savoury smoke, spicy oak and peat smoke.

The Ultimate Whisky Company

ultimatewhisky.com

Founded in 1994 by Han van Wees and his son Maurice, this Dutch independent bottler has until now bottled close to 1,000 single malts. All whiskies are un chill-filtered, without colouring and bottled at either 46% or cask strength. The van Wees family also operate one of the finest spirits shops in Europe - Van Wees Whisky World in Amersfoort - with i.a. more than 1,000 different whiskies including more than 500 single malts.

Svenska Eldvatten

eldvatten.se

Founded in 2011 and since the start, more than 100 single casks, bottled at cask strength, have been released. In their range of spirits they have aged tequila and rum and they have also launched their own rum, WeiRon, as well as gin and aquavit. In 2021 the company celebrated being in business for a decade with a limited 10th anniversary single malt range. Svenska Eldvatten are also importers to Sweden of whisky from Murray McDavid, AD Rattray, North Star Spirits, Sansibar, Hidden Spirits, Claxton´s, Single Cask Nation and, most recently, Spey Whisky.

The Vintage Malt Whisky Company

vintagemaltwhisky.com

Founded in 1992 by Brian Crook, the company today is run by his three children, Andrew, Caroline and Kim, supplying whisky to more than 35 countries. The company also owns and operates a sister company called The Highlands & Islands Scotch Whisky Co. In 2018, they acquired a former factory in Port Ellen on Islay and in 2021 they started transforming it into a rum distillery with the possibility of eventually producing other spirits as well. The most famous brands in the range are two single Islay malts called Finlaggan and The Ileach. The latter comes in two versions, bottled at 40% and 58%. The Finlaggan range consists of Old Reserve, Eilean Mor, Port Finish, Sherry Finish, Cask Strength (58%) and Red Wine Cask Matured. Other expressions in the company´s range are Islay Storm, the blended malts Smokestack and Glenalmond and, not least, a wide range of single cask single malts under the name The Cooper´s Choice. They are bottled at 46% or at cask strength and are all non coloured and non chill-filtered.

Wm Cadenhead & Co

cadenhead.scot

A classic bottler established in 1842. Their core range, Authentic Collection, is made up of single cask cask strength whiskies, exclusively sold in their own shops and on-line. Other collections are World Whiskies (single malts from non Scottish distillers), Closed Distilleries and Small Batch, a range which can be divided into three separate ranges; Single Cask (single casks bottled at cask strength), Small Batch Cask Strength (2-4 casks of whisky from the same vintage, bottled at cask strength) and Small Batch 46% (same as the previous but diluted to 46%). The Creations range consists of small batch blends and blended malts and they also have their own ranges of gin and rum. There are nine dedicated Cadenhead´s Whisky Shops in the UK and Europe.

Adelphi Distillery

adelphidistillery.com

Founded in 1993 by Jamie Walker and named after a distillery which stopped making malt whisky in 1907, the company offers a range of single malts bottled at cask strength with new releases four times a year. There are also two recurrent brands, Fascadale and Liddesdale, where the single malt differs from batch to batch. In 2015, the first two bottlings of a new brand saw the light of day. Together with Fusion Whisky, Adelphi launched The Glover – a unique vatting of single malt from the closed Japanese distillery Hanyu and two Scottish single malts, Longmorn and Glen Garioch. This was followed by The Kincardine and the E&K where Amrut single malt from India was blended with Scotch malt whisky, The Brisbane, a combination of Starward single malt from Australia and Glen Garioch and Glen Grant and The Winter Queen where malt whisky from Zuidam distillery in the Netherlands had been blended with Longmorn and Glenrothes. In 2020, Glover Batch 5 was released which was an exciting blend of two casks from Chichibu

distillery in Japan and two of Ardnamurchan´s (owned by Adelphi) own casks – all four of them ex-bourbon. Since 2014, Adelphi is also making whisky in their own Ardnamurchan Distillery. Since the opening, the owners regularly released malt spirit (less than 3 years old) and in October 2020 the first single malt whisky from the distillery was released.

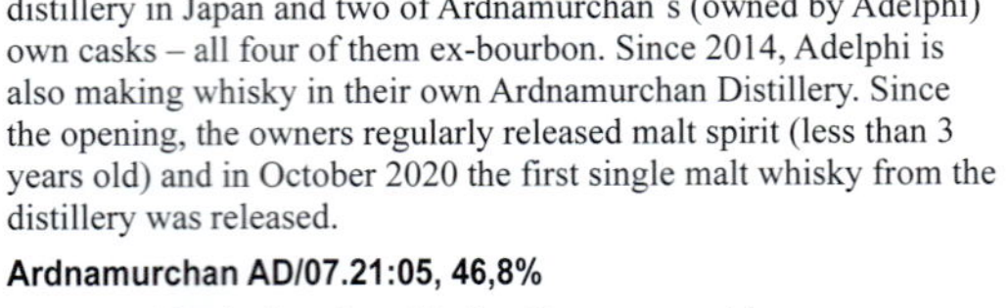

Ardnamurchan AD/07.21:05, 46,8%

Nose:	Fresh, floral and fruity. Oranges and lemons. Nutty, with background honey and toffee.
Palate:	Clean and relatively light. More sweet fruits, soy sauce, a hint of smoke and black pepper.

Breath of the Isles 14 year old, 58,3%

Nose:	Fruity, with brittle toffee, marmalade, salted caramel and a suggestion of chimney soot.
Palate:	Smooth, with soft woodsmoke notes, apricot, white pepper, liquorice and spicy oak

Deerstalker Whisky Co

deerstalkerwhisky.com

The Deerstalker brand, which dates from 1880 was originally owned by J.G. Thomson & Co of Leith and subsequently Tennent Caledonian Breweries. It was purchased by Glasgow based Aberko Ltd in 1994 and is managed by Paul Aston. The Deerstalker range covers single malts as well as blended malt whiskies. Currently there is one core single malt, a 12 year old, and two blended malts - a Peated Edition and a Highland Edition. Limited Deerstalker single malts are released from time to time.

Morrison Distillers

morrisondistillers.com

An independent bottler with plenty of experience in the company. Brian Morrison´s father was the legendary Stanley P Morrison, founder of Morrison Bowmore Distilleries and in the business Brian has been joined by his son Jamie. The company´s most famous range is Carn Mor single malt whiskies. Currently there are three series; Strictly Limited, usually bottled at 47,5%, Celebration of the Cask which are single casks bottled at cask strength and a new series named Family Reserve. Other ranges are Mac-Talla with Islay single malts and Old Perth blended malts.

Edinburgh Whisky Ltd.

edinburghwhisky.com

Founded in 2013 the company is now owned by Gleann Mor Spirits. Single malt single casks are bottled under the name The Library Collection while small batch blended malts are sold under the name New Town. A third range of blended malts called Whisky Row is made up of Smoke and Peat, Rich and Spicy and Smooth and Sweet. The brand was recently revamped.

Sansibar Whisky

sansibar-whisky.com

Started in 2012, this was the brainchild of the current majority owner and CEO Jens Drewitz and Carsten Ehrlich. Their idea was to create a range of high quality single malts from Scotland and to market them in connection with the well known Sansibar restaurant on the island of Sylt in northern Germany. Around 60 bottlings are produced per year and the range also includes rum.

Dramfool

dramfool.com

Bruce Farquhar, a whisky fan and collector for 20 years, decided in 2015 to start as an independent bottler. He sources his whisky from private individuals as well as from brokers and has so far released around 50 different bottlings. In spring 2021 a new range was added - the Jim McEwan Signature Collection where the different styles from Bruichladdich are represented.

Angel´s Nectar

angelsnectar.co.uk

Robert Ransom used to work as the sales and marketing director at Glenfarclas. He left in 2014 and founded Highfern Ltd with the brand name Angel´s Nectar. There are two blended malts, Original (40%) and Rich Peat (46%), as well as two single malts, Speyside (46%) and Islay Edition (47%). Highfern is also the UK importer for Smögen single malt and gin and Langatun Swiss single malt.

The Single Cask Ltd

thesinglecask.co.uk

Ben Curtis was distributor for a number of Scottish distilleries in south-east Asia before he started as an independent bottler in Singapore in 2010. Since then he has moved back to the UK. The business has grown over the years and the brand is now sold in the UK, Europe and Asia. The company also acts as a broker selling casks with both newmake and maturing whisky. A nice feature on their website is a very well written and informative blog.

Selected Malts

selectedmalts.se

A Swedish bottler and blender which started off specialising in fairly young single malts but with a maturation story that stood out from the ordinary. In 2019 they released their own blended malt, Zippin, and later they became distributors for GlenAllachie and James Eadie in Sweden. Recently the company has expanded the business into selling casks to private customers.

The Alistair Walker Whisky Co.

alistairwalkerwhisky.com

Alistair Walker, from the Walker family who used to own BenRiach, GlenDronach and Glenglassaugh, has spent more than twenty years in the whisky business. When the family sold the distilleries in 2016, he decided to start up as an independent bottler. The brand is called Infrequent Flyers and the first releases of single casks appeared in August 2019.The most recent release was in March 2021.

Skene Scotch Whisky

skenewhisky.com

Founded in 2014 and based in Edinburgh. After a few years the company started focusing on buying and selling casks in bond but since 2020 they are again bottling whisky under their own label. One range is called Skene Reserve with single cask single malts aged 20 years or more. Younger single casks are sold under the Cask Classics label and finally there is Black Tartan with a blended malt at its core but also blended-at-birth single cask bottlings.

Watt Whisky

wattwhisky.com

When Mark Watt left Cadenheads he decided to start a company of his own together with his wife Kate who has a background working for both Springbank and Glenfarclas. Their philosphy is to mainly bottle single malt Scotch at cask strength and without colouring or chill filtration. They came off to a tough start bottling their first general release in September 2020 in the midst of the pandemic. Undeterred though, they kept going and until now they have released more than 40 single malts, blended malts, single grains and rums.

The Whisky Baron

thewhiskybaron.co.uk

Jake Sharpe began the business trading casks as an investment but eventually started to sell bottled single cask malt to private customers. One of his biggest sellers was a 23 year old Springbank and recently they have released a Glentauchers 6 year old matured in a sherry hogshead and an unusual Port Charlotte 13 year old matured for the full time in a Vosne Romanee burgundy wine cask. The next step is to present affordable small batch blends in 2022. An interesting feature is the way Sharpe uses AR technicue (augmented reality). Download an app, scan the label with your phone and The Whisky Baron will become "alive" to tell you stories about the particular whisky.

Lady of the Glen

ladyoftheglen.com

Hannah Whisky Merchants was founded by Gregor Hannah in 2012 and is mainly known for their brand Lady of the Glen with bottlings of single malt and single grain Scotch.Around 40 casks are bottled per year and the latest releases include Bowmore 1997, Glen Elgin 2004 and Port Dundas 2000. A new office, bottling hall and warehouses opened in Fife in 2020.

The Islay Boys

islayboys.com

Mackay Smith and Donald MacKenzie are both Islay born and bred and in 2018 they bought the Islay Ales Brewery. Soon after they started as whisky bottlers and at the moment their range consists of Bårelegs single malt (one islay and one Highland) and Flatnöse blended malt and blended Scotch. They are working on moving the brewery to Glenegedale and also integrate a rum- and whisky distillery.

Asta Morris

asta-morris.be

Founded by former Malt Maniac Bert Bruyneel in 2009, the company started with whisky but has later also branched out into rum, cognac and calvados. Typically around 15 single malts are released yearly from young and affordable expressions to old and are bottlings. A special project for Bert is his NOG gin which has been matured in some of his used whisky casks and is bottled in batches.

James Eadie

jameseadie.co.uk

Named after a Scottish brewer and whisky blender in the 1800s, the company was founded by Rupert Patrick who is the great-greatgrandson of James Eadie. With a long background in the Scotch whisky industry Rupert set up as a independent bottler specialising in small batch and single cask Scotch. He also managed to recreate Eadie´s blend from the early days when he launched Trade Mark X which contains 14 of the 16 whiskies that appeared in the original.

Claxton´s Spirits

claxtonsspirits.com

A company with a bonded warehouse on the Dalswinton Estate just north of Dumfries. This facility allows them to have an impressive scheme of re-racking, finishing, blending and bottling - rather unusual for an independent bottler. Focus is on single malt or single grain Scotch bottled at cask strength. Recently they launched a new brand named Claxton´s Exploration Series.

The Perfect Fifth

theperfectfifth.eu

A new, family-owned bottler founded by Karl Schoen and with a focus on rare and old expressions. Initially the brand was available in USA, Singapore and Taiwan only but recently they have expanded to Europe as well. First releases included Springbank 25, Highland Park 31 and Glen Scotia 27 years old. Latest bottlings are Aberlour 30, Cambus 41 and Glenlivet 40 year old.

Whisky
shops

AUSTRALIA
The Odd Whisky Coy
25 Anzac Ridge Road, Bridgewater,
SA, 5155
Phone: +61 (0)417 852 296
www.theoddwhiskycoy.com.au
On-line whisky specialist with an
impressive range. Agents for brands such
as Springbank, Benromach and Berry
Brothers and arrange recurrent seminars.

World of Whisky
Shop G12, Cosmopolitan Centre
2-22 Knox Street, Double Bay NSW 2028
Phone: +61 (0)2 9363 4212
www.worldofwhisky.com.au
A whisky specialist which offers a range
of 400 different expressions, most of them
single malts. The shop is also organising
and hosting regular tastings.

The Whisky Company
162 A Fortescue Av., Seaford, VIC, 3198
Phone: +61 (0)434 438 617
www.thewhiskycompany.com.au
One of the largest on-line retailers of
single malt whisky in Australia with
around 500 products currently in stock.

My Bottle Shop
34D Fitzroy St., Marrickville, NSW, 2204
Phone: +61 (0)2 9516 3816
www.mybottleshop.com.au
More than 2,000 whiskies with some of
them being sourced directly from the
suppliers on demand. On-line only.

The Oak Barrel
152 Elizabeh St, Sydney, NSW, 2000
Phone: +61 (0)2 9264 3022
www.oakbarrel.com.au
They have a nice range of 550 different
Scotch whiskies but it is the range of
Australian whiskies (c 200) that impresses
the most. Wine, beer, cider and other
spirits as well.

AUSTRIA
Potstill
Laudongasse 18, 1080 Wien
Phone: +43 (0)664 118 85 41
www.potstill.org
Austria's premier whisky shop with over
1100 different single malts, including
some real rarities. Shipping within Austria
and to non-EC countries.

Cadenhead Austria
Döblinger Hauptstraße 32, 1190 Wien
Phone: +43 (0)677 622 476 40
www.cadenhead-vienna.at
Focusing on the Cadenhead range but with

a wide range of other whiskies and spirits
as well.

Pinkernells Whisky Market
Alter Markt 1, 5020 Salzburg
Phone: +43 (0)662 84 53 05
www.pinkernells.at
More than 500 whiskies are on offer and
they are also importers of Maltbarn, The
Whisky Chamber and Jack Wiebers.

BELGIUM
Whiskycorner
Kraaistraat 16, 3530 Houthalen
Phone: +32 (0)89 386233
www.whiskycorner.be
A very large selection of single malts,
more than 2000 different. Also other
whiskies, calvados and grappas.

Jurgen´s Whiskyhuis
Gaverland 70, 9620 Zottegem
Phone: +32 (0)9 336 51 06
www.whiskyhuis.be
A huge assortment of more than 2000
different single malts. Also a good range
of grain whiskies and bourbons.

Huis Crombé
Doenaertstraat 20, 8510 Marke
Phone: +32 (0)56 21 19 87
www.crombewines.com
A wine retailer which also covers all kinds
of spirits. A large assortment of Scotch is
supplemented with whiskies from Japan,
the USA and Ireland to mention a few.

We Are Whisky
Avenue Rodolphe Gossia 33
1350 Orp-Jauche
Phone: +32 (0)471 134556
www.wearewhisky.com
On-line retailer with a range of more than
800 different whiskies. They also arrange
3-4 tastings every month.

Dram 242
Rijgerstraat 60, 9310 Moorsel
Phone: +32 (0)477 26 09 93
www.dram242.be
A wide range of whiskies. Apart from
the core official bottlings, they have
focused on rare, old expressions as well as
whiskies from small, independent bottlers.

CANADA
Kensington Wine Market
1257 Kensington Road NW
Calgary, Alberta T2N 3P8
Phone: +1 403 283 8000
www.kensingtonwinemarket.com
The shop has a very large range of

whiskies (more than 1500) as well as other
spirits and wines. More than 80 tastings in
the shop every year. Also the home of the
Scotch Malt Whisky Society in Canada.

World of Whisky
Unit 240, 333 5 Avenue SW
Calgary, Alberta T2P 3B6
Phone: +1 587 956 8511
www.coopwinespiritsbeer.com/stores/
world-of-whisky/
Specialising in whisky from all corners of
the world. Currently there are over 1100
different whiskies in the range including
some extremely rare ones from Scotland.

DENMARK
Juul´s Vin & Spiritus
Værnedamsvej 15
1819 Frederiksberg
Phone: +45 33 31 13 29
www.juuls.dk
A very large range of wines, fortified
wines and spirits with more than 1100
different whiskies (800 single malts).

Cadenhead´s WhiskyShop Denmark
Kongensgade 69 F
5000 Odense C
Phone: +45 66 13 95 05
www.cadenheads.dk
Whisky specialist with a very good range,
not least from Cadenhead's. Nice range
of champagne, cognac and rum. Arranges
whisky and beer tastings. On-line ordering.

Whisky.dk
Vejstruprødvej 15
6093 Sjølund
Phone: +45 5210 6093
www.whisky.dk
Henrik Olsen and Ulrik Bertelsen are
well-known in Denmark for their whisky
shows but they also run an on-line spirits
shop with an emphasis on whisky but also
including an impressive stock of rums.

ENGLAND
The Whisky Exchange
2 Bedford Street, Covent Garden
London WC2E 9HH
Phone: +44 (0)20 7100 0088
90-92 Great Portland Street, Fitzrovia
London W1W 7NT
Phone: +44 (0)20 7100 9888
88 Borough High Street, London Bridge
London SE1 1LL
Phone: +44 (0)20 7631 3888
www.thewhiskyexchange.com
An excellent whisky shop owned by

Sukhinder Singh. Started off as a mail order business, run from a showroom in Hanwell, but later opened up at Vinopolis in downtown London. Moved to a new and bigger location in Covent Garden a couple of years ago and have since then opened two more shops. The assortment is huge with well over 1000 single malts to choose from. Some rarities which can hardly be found anywhere else are offered thanks to Singh's great interest for antique whisky. There are also other types of whisky and cognac, calvados, rum etc. On-line ordering and ships all over the world.

The Whisky Shop
(See also Scotland, The Whisky Shop)
11 Coppergate Walk
York YO1 9NT
Phone: +44 (0)1904 640300

510 Brompton Walk
Lakeside Shopping Centre
Thurrock Grays, Essex RM20 2ZL
Phone: +44 (0)1708 866255

7 Turl Street
Oxford OX1 3DQ
Phone: +44 (0)1865 202279

3 Swan Lane
Norwich NR2 1HZ
Phone: +44 (0)1603 618284

70 Piccadilly
London W1J 8HP
Phone: +44 (0)207 499 6649

Unit 7 Queens Head Passage
Paternoster
London EC4M 7DZ
Phone: +44 (0)207 329 5117

3 Exchange St
Manchester M2 7EE
Phone: +44 (0)161 832 6110

25 Chapel Street
Guildford GU1 3UL
Phone: +44 (0)1483 450900

Unit 9 Great Western Arcade
Birmingham B2 5HU
Phone: +44 (0)121 233 4416

64 East Street
Brighton BN1 1HQ
Phone: +44 (0)1273 327 962

3 Cheapside
Nottingham NG1 2HU
Phone: +44 (0)115 958 7080

9-10 High Street
Bath BA1 5AQ
Phone: +44 (0)1225 423 535

Unit 1/9 Red Mall,
Intu Metro Centre
Gateshead NE11 9YP
Phone: +44 (0)191 460 3777

Unit 201 Trentham Gardens
Stoke on Trent ST4 8AX
Phone: +44 (0)1782 644 483
www.whiskyshop.com
The largest specialist retailer of whiskies in the UK with 20 outlets. A large product range with over 1500 Scotch single malt whiskies as well as other spirits, accessories and books. They also run The W Club, the leading whisky club in the UK where the excellent Whiskeria magazine is one of the member´s benefits. Shipping all over the world.

Berry Bros. & Rudd
63 Pall Mall, London SW1Y 5HZ
Phone: +44 (0)800 280 2440
www.bbr.com/whisky
A legendary company dating back to 1698! One of the world's most reputable wine shops but with an extensive and exclusive selection of malt whiskies, some of them bottled by Berry Bros. themselves. The company is also known as as well respected independent bottler of whiskies and rums.

The Wright Wine & Whisky Company
The Old Smithy, Raikes Road, Skipton, North Yorkshire BD23 1NP
Phone: +44 (0)1756 700886
www.wineandwhisky.co.uk
An eclectic selection of near to 1000 different whiskies. 'Tasting Cupboard' of nearly 100 opened bottles for sampling with regular hosted tasting evenings. Great 'Collector to Collector' selection of old whiskies plus a fantastic choice of 1200+ wines, premium spirits and liqueurs.

Master of Malt
Unit 1, Ton Business Park, 2-8 Morley Rd. Tonbridge, Kent, TN9 1RA
Phone: 0800 5200 474
Phone international: +44 (0)1892 888376
www.masterofmalt.com
Online retailer and independent bottler with a very impressive range of more than 2,500 whiskies, including over 2,000 Scotch whiskies and over 1,500 single malts. In addition to whisky there is an enormous selection of gins, rums, cognacs, armagnacs, tequilas and more. The website contains a wealth of information and news about the distilleries and innovative personalised gift ideas. Drinks by the Dram 30ml samples of more than 3,300 different whiskies are available also they also offer the Dram Club monthly whisky subscription service, as well as a Blend Your Own option, personalised whisky and has a gift finder to help with special occassions.

Whiskys.co.uk
The Square, Stamford Bridge
York YO4 11AG
Phone: +44 (0)1759 371356
www.whiskys.co.uk
Good assortment with more than 600 different whiskies. Also a nice range of armagnac, rum, calvados etc. The owners also have another website, www. whiskymerchants.co.uk with a huge amount of information on just about every whisky distillery in the world.

The Wee Dram
5 Portland Square, Bakewell
Derbyshire DE45 1HA
Phone: +44 (0)1629 812235
www.weedram.co.uk
Large range of Scotch single malts with whiskies from other parts of the world and a good range of whisky books. Run 'The Wee Drammers Whisky Club' with seminars and tastings. In October they arrange the yearly Wee Dram Fest whisky festival.

Hard To Find Whisky
1 Spencer Street, Birmingham B18 6DD
Phone: +44 (0)121 448 84 84
www.htfw.com
As the name says, this family owned shop specialises in rare, collectable and new releases of single malt whisky. The range is astounding - more than 3,000 different bottlings including no less than 480 different Macallan. World wide shipping.

Nickolls & Perks
37 Lower High Street, Stourbridge
West Midlands DY8 1TA
Phone: +44 (0)1384 394518
www.nickollsandperks.co.uk
Mostly known as wine merchants but also has a huge range of whiskies with 1,900 different kinds including 1,300 single malts. They also organize Midlands Whisky Festival, www.whiskyfest.co.uk

Gauntleys of Nottingham
4 High Street, Nottingham NG1 2ET
Phone: +44 (0)115 9110555
www.gauntleys.com
A fine wine merchant established in 1880. The range of wines are among the best in the UK. All kinds of spirits, not least whisky, are taking up more and more space and several rare malts can be found.

Hedonism Wines
3-7 Davies St., London W1K 3LD
Phone: +44 (020) 729 078 70
www.hedonism.co.uk
Located in the heart of London, this is a temple for wine lovers but also with over 1,200 different whisky bottlings from Scotland and the rest of the world.

The Lincoln Whisky Shop
87 Bailgate, Lincoln LN1 3AR
Phone: +44 (0)1522 537834
www.lincolnwhiskyshop.co.uk
Mainly specialising in whisky with more than 300 different whiskies but also 500 spirits and liqueurs. Mailorder worldwide.

Milroys of Soho
3 Greek Street, London W1D 4NX
Phone: +44 (0)207 734 2277
www.milroys.co.uk
A classic whisky shop in Soho with a very good range with over 700 malts and a wide selection of whiskies from around the world. Also a whisky bar within the shop. Recently opened another whisky bar in Spitalfields in East London.

Arkwrights
114 The Dormers
Highworth
Wiltshire SN6 7PE
Phone: +44 (0)1793 765071
www.whiskyandwines.com
A good range of whiskies (over 700 in stock) as well as wine and other spirits. Regular tastings in the shop. On-line ordering with shipping all over the world.

Edencroft Fine Wines
8-10 Hospital Street, Nantwich
Cheshire, CW5 5RJ
Phone: +44 (0)1270 629975
www.edencroft.co.uk
Family owned wine and spirits shop since 1994. Around 250 whiskies and also a

nice range of gin, cognac and other spirits including cigars. Worldwide shipping.

Cadenhead´s Whisky Shop
26 Chiltern Street, London W1U 7QF
Phone: +44 (0)20 7935 6999
www.whiskytastingroom.com
One in a chain of shops owned by independent bottlers Cadenhead. Sells Cadenhead's product range and c. 200 other whiskies. Regular tastings.

Constantine Stores
30 Fore Street, Constantine, Falmouth Cornwall TR11 5AB
Phone: +44 (0)1326 340226
www.drinkfinder.co.uk
A full-range wine and spirits dealer with a good selection of whiskies from the whole world (around 800 different, of which 600 are single malts). Worldwide shipping.

House of Malt
48 Warwick Road, Carlisle CA1 1DN
Phone: +44 (0)1228 658 422
www.houseofmalt.co.uk
A wide selection of whiskies from Scotland and the world as well as other spirits and craft ales. Regular tasting evenings and events.

The Vintage House
42 Old Compton Street
London W1D 4LR
Phone: +44 (0)20 7437 2592
www.vintagehouse.london
A huge range of 1400 kinds of malt whisky, many of them rare. Supplementing this is also a selection of fine wines.

Whisky On-line
Units 1-3 Concorde House, Charnley Road, Blackpool, Lancashire FY1 4PE
Phone: +44 (0)1253 620376
www.whisky-online.com
A good selection of whisky and also cognac, rum, port etc. Specializes in rare whiskies and hold regular auctions.

FRANCE

La Maison du Whisky
20 rue d´Anjou
75008 Paris
Phone: +33 (0)1 42 65 03 16

6 carrefour d l´Odéon
75006 Paris
Phone: +33 (0)1 46 34 70 20

(1 shop outside France)
The Pier at Robertson Quay
80 Mohamed Sultan Road, #01-10
Singapore 239013
Phone: +65 6733 0059
www.whisky.fr
France's largest whisky specialist with over 1200 whiskies and also a number of own-bottled single malts. La Maison du Whisky acts as a EU distributor for many whisky producers around the world. Also run the Golden Promise whisky bar and store in rue Tiquetonne in Paris.

The Whisky Shop
7 Place de la Madeleine, 75008 Paris
Phone: +33 (0)1 45 22 29 77
www.whiskyshop.fr
The large chain of whisky shops in the UK

has now opened up a store in Paris as well.

GERMANY

Celtic Whisk(e)y & Versand
Otto Steudel
Bulmannstrasse 26, 90459 Nürnberg
Phone: +49 (0)911 45097430
www.celtic-whisky.de
A very impressive single malt range with well over 1000 different single malts and a good selection from other parts of the world.

SCOMA
Am Bullhamm 17, 26441 Jever
Phone: +49 (0)4461 912237
www.scoma.de
Very large range of c 750 Scottish malts and many from other countries. Holds regular seminars and tastings. The excellent, monthly whisky newsletter SCOMA News is produced and can be downloaded as a pdf-file from the website.

The Whisky Store
Am Grundwassersee 4, 82402 Seeshaupt
Phone: +49 (0)8801 30 20 000
www.whisky.de
A very large range comprising c 700 kinds of whisky of which 550 are malts. Also sells whisky liqueurs, books and accessories. The website is a goldmine of information, in particular the videos with Horst and Ben Luening which are mainly in German but many English versions are easily found on Youtube.

Cadenhead´s Whisky Market
Luxemburger Strasse 257, 50939 Köln
Phone: +49 (0)221-2831834
www.cadenheads.de
Good range of malt whiskies (c 350 different kinds) with emphasis on Cadenhead's own bottlings. Other products include wine, cognac and rum etc. Arranges recurring tastings and also has an on-line shop.

Pinkernells Whisky Market
Boxhagener Straße 36, 10245 Berlin
Phone: +49 (0)30-308 314 44
www.pinkernells.de
An extensive range of whiskies (more than 700) and they arrange 4-5 tastings monthly. Also work as whisky consultants doing corporate events all over Germany.

Home of Malts
Hosegstieg 11, 22880 Wedel
Phone: +49 (0)4103 965 9695
www.homeofmalts.com
Large assortment with over 800 different single malts as well as whiskies from many other countries. Also a nice selection of cognac, rum etc. On-line ordering.

Reifferscheid
Mainzer Strasse 186, 53179 Bonn
Phone: +49 (0)228 9 53 80 71
www.whisky-bonn.de
A well-stocked shop with a large range of whiskies, wine, spirit, cigars and a delicatessen. They also have a wide range of whiskies bottled especially for the shop. Regular tastings.

Whisky-Doris
Germanenstrasse 38, 14612 Falkensee
Phone: +49 (0)3322-219784
www.whisky-doris.de
Large range of over 300 whiskies and also sells own special bottlings. Orders via email. Shipping also outside Germany.

Finlays Whisky Shop
Hohenzollernstr. 88, 80796 München
Phone: +49 (0)89 3270 979 145
www.finlayswhiskyshop.de
Whisky specialists with a large range of over 1,100 whiskies. Finlays also work as the importer of Douglas Laing, James MacArthur and Wilson & Morgan.

Weinquelle Lühmann
Lübeckerstrasse 145, 22087 Hamburg
Phone: +49 (0)40 300 672 950

Jacobsrade 65, 22962 Siek (showroom)
Phone: +49 (0)4107 908 900
www.weinquelle.com
An impressive selection of both wines and spirits with over 1000 different whiskies of which 850 are malt whiskies. Also an impressive range of rums.

The Whisky-Corner
Reichertsfeld 2, 92278 Illschwang
Phone: +49 (0)9666-951213
www.whisky-corner.de
A small shop but large on mail order. A very large assortment of over 2000 whiskies. Also sells blended and American whiskies. The website is very informative with features on, among others, whisky-making, tasting and independent bottlers.

World Wide Spirits
Hauptstrasse 12, 84576 Teising
Phone: +49 (0)8633 50 87 93
www.worldwidespirits.de
A nice range of more than 1,000 whiskies with some rarities from the twenties. Also large selection of other spirits.

WhiskyKoch
Weinbergstrasse 2, 64285 Darmstadt
Phone: +49 (0)6151 96 96 886
www.whiskykoch.de
A combination of a whisky shop and restaurant. The shop has a nice selection of single malts as well as other Scottish products and the restaurant has specialised in whisky dinners and tastings.

Kierzek
Weitlingstrasse 17, 10317 Berlin
Phone: +49 (0)30 525 11 08
www.kierzek-berlin.de
Over 400 different whiskies in stock. In the product range 50 kinds of rum and 450 wines from all over the world are found among other products. Mail order is available.

HUNGARY

Whisky Shop Budapest
Veres Pálné utca 7., 1053 Budapest
Phone: +36 1 267-1588
www.whiskynet.hu
www.whiskyshop.hu
Largest selection of whisky in Hungary. More than 900 different whiskies from all

over the world. Even Hungarian whisky and a large selection of other fine spirits are available. Most of them can be tasted in the GoodSpirit Whisky & Cocktail Bar which operates in the same venue.

IRELAND
Celtic Whiskey Shop
27-28 Dawson Street, Dublin 2
Phone: +353 (0)1 675 9744
www.celticwhiskeyshop.com
More than 500 kinds of Irish whiskeys but also a good selection of Scotch, wines and other spirits. World wide shipping.

ITALY
Whisky Shop
by Milano Whisky Festival
Via Cavaleri 6, Milano
Phone: +39 (0)2 48753039
www.whiskyshop.it
The team behind the excellent Milano Whisky Festival also have an on-line whiskyshop with almost 500 different single malts including several special festival bottlings.

Whisky Antique S.R.L.
Via Giardini Sud, 41043 Formigine (MO)
Phone: +39 (0)59 574278
www.whiskyantique.com
Long-time whisky enthusiast and collector Massimo Righi owns this shop specialising in rare and collectable spirits – not only whisky but also cognac, rum, armagnac etc. He also acts as an independent bottler with the brand Silver Seal. They are importer for brands like Jack Wiebers, The Whisky Agency and Perfect Dram.

JAPAN
Liquor Mountain Co.,Ltd.
4F Kyoto Kowa Bldg.
82 Tachiurinishi-Machi,
Takakura-Nishiiru,
Shijyo-Dori, Shimogyo-Ku,
Kyoto, 600-8007
Phone: +81 (0)75 213 8880
www.likaman.co.jp
The company has more than 150 shops specialising in spirits, beer and food. Around 20 of them are designated whisky shops under the name Whisky Kingdom (although they have a full range of other spirits) with a range of 500 different whiskies. The three foremost shops are;

Rakzan Sanjyo Onmae
1-8, HigashiGekko-cho, Nishinokyo,
Nakagyo-ku, Kyoto-shi
Kyoto
Phone: +81 (0)75-842-5123

Nagakute
2-105, Ichigahora, Nagakute-shi
Aichi
Phone: +81 (0)561-64-3081

Kabukicho 1chome
1-2-16, Kabuki-cho, Shinjuku-ku
Tokyo
Phone: +81 (0)3-5287-2080

THE NETHERLANDS
Whiskyslijterij De Koning
Hinthamereinde 41
5211 PM 's Hertogenbosch
Phone: +31 (0)73-6143547
www.whiskykoning.nl
An enormous assortment with more than 1400 kinds of whisky including c 800 single malts. Arranges recurring tastings. On-line ordering. Shipping all over the world.

Van Wees - Whiskyworld.nl
Leusderweg 260, 3817 KH Amersfoort
Phone: +31 (0)33-461 53 19
www.whiskyworld.nl
A very large range of 1000 whiskies including over 500 single malts. Also have their own range of bottlings (The Ultimate Whisky Company). On-line ordering.

Wijnhandel van Zuylen
Loosduinse Hoofdplein 201
2553 CP Loosduinen (Den Haag)
Phone: +31 (0)70-397 1400
www.whiskyvanzuylen.nl
Excellent range of whiskies (circa 1100) and wines. Email orders with shipping to some ten European countries.

Wijnwinkel-Slijterij
Ton Overmars, Hoofddorpplein 11
1059 CV Amsterdam
Phone: +31 (0)20-615 71 42
www.tonovermars.nl
A very large assortment of wines, spirits and beer which includes more than 400 single malts. Arranges recurring tastings.

Wijn & Whisky Schuur
Blankendalwei 4, 8629 EH Scharnegoutem
Phone: +31 (0)515-520706
www.wijnwhiskyschuur.nl
Large assortment with 1000 different whiskies and a good range of other spirits as well. Arranges recurring tastings.

Wine and Whisky Specialist van der Boog
Prinses Irenelaan 359-361
2285 GA Rijswijk
Phone: +31 70 - 394 00 85
www.passionforwhisky.com
A very good range of almost 700 malt whiskies (as well as a wide range of other spirits). World wide shipping.

NEW ZEALAND
Whisky Galore
834 Colombo Street, Christchurch 8013
Phone: +64 (0) 800 944 759
www.whiskygalore.co.nz
The best whisky shop in New Zealand with 750 different whiskies, approximately 400 which are single malts. There is also online mail-order with shipping all over the world except USA and Canada. Owned by Michael Fraser Milne who became a Master of the Quaich in 2019.

POLAND
George Ballantine´s
Krucza str 47 A, Warsaw
Phone: +48 22 625 48 32

Pulawska str 22, Warsaw
Phone: +48 22 542 86 22

Marynarska str 15, Warsaw
Phone: +48 22 395 51 60

Zygmunta Vogla str 62, Warsaw
Phone: +48 22 395 51 64
www.sklep-ballantines.pl
A huge range of single malts and apart from whisky there is a full range of spirits and wines from all over the world. Recurrent tastings and organiser of Whisky Live Warsaw.

Dom Whisky
Wejherowska 67, Reda
Phone: +48 691 760 000, shop
Phone: +48 691 930 000, mailorder
www.sklep-domwhisky.pl
On-line retailer with a shop in Reda. A very large range of whiskies and other spirits. Organiser of a whisky festival in Jastrzębia Góra.

RUSSIA
Whisky World Shop
9, Tverskoy Boulevard
123104 Moscow
Phone: +7 495 787 9150
www.whiskyworld.ru
Huge assortment with more than 1,000 different single malts. The range is supplemented with a nice range of cognac, armagnac, calvados, grappa and wines.

SCOTLAND
Gordon & MacPhail
58 - 60 South Street, Elgin
Moray IV30 1JY
Phone: +44 (0)1343 545110
www.gordonandmacphail.com
This legendary shop opened already in 1895 in Elgin. The owners are perhaps the most well-known among independent bottlers. The shop stocks around 1000 single malt whiskies and more than 600 wines and there is also a delicatessen counter with high-quality products. Tastings are arranged in the shop and there are shipping services within the UK and overseas. The shop attracts visitors from all over the world.

Royal Mile Whiskies
379 High Street, The Royal Mile
Edinburgh EH1 1PW
Phone: +44 (0)131 2253383
www.royalmilewhiskies.com
Royal Mile Whiskies is one of the most well-known whisky retailers in the UK. It was established in Edinburgh in 1991. There is also a shop in London since 2002 and a cigar shop close to the Edinburgh shop. The whisky range is outstanding with many difficult to find elsewhere. They have a comprehensive site regarding information on regions, distilleries, production, tasting etc. Royal Mile Whiskies also arranges 'Whisky Fringe' in Edinburgh, a two-day whisky festival which takes place annually in mid August. On-line ordering with worldwide shipping.

The Whisky Shop

(See also England, The Whisky Shop)
Unit L2-02 Buchanan Galleries
220 Buchanan Street
Glasgow G1 2GF
Phone: +44 (0)141 331 0022

17 Bridge Street
Inverness IV1 1HD
Phone: +44 (0)1463 710525

93 High Street
Fort William PH33 6DG
Phone: +44 (0)1397 706164

52 George Street
Oban PA34 5SD
Phone: +44 (0)1631 570896

Unit 23 Waverley Mall
Waverley Bridge
Edinburgh EH1 1BQ
Phone: +44 (0)131 558 7563

28 Victoria Street
Edinburgh EH1 2JW
Phone: +44 (0)131 225 4666
www.whiskyshop.com
The first shop opened in 1992 in
Edinburgh and this is now the United
Kingdom's largest specialist retailer
of whiskies with 20 outlets (plus one
in Paris). A large product range with
over 700 kinds, including 400 malt
whiskies and 140 miniature bottles, as
well as accessories and books. The own
range 'Glenkeir Treasures' is a special
assortment of selected malt whiskies.
The also run The W Club, the leading
whisky club in the UK where the excellent
Whiskeria magazine is one of the
member's benefits. On-line ordering.

The Scotch Malt Whisky Society

(venues)
28 Queen Street, Edinburgh EH2 1JX
Phone: +44 (0)131 625 7484

87 Giles Street, Edinburgh EH6 6BZ
Phone: +44 (0)131 554 3451

38 Bath Street, Glasgow G2 1HG
Phone: +44 (0)141 739 8810

19 Greville Street, London EC1N 8SQ
Phone: +44 (0)20 7831 4447
www.smws.com
A legendary society with more than 20 000
members worldwide, specialised in own
bottlings of single cask Scotch whisky,
releasing between 150 and 200 bottlings
every year. Recently, the Society has also
started bottling whisky from other parts of
the world as well as gin, rum, armagnac
and other spirits. Operates four venues
with bar and restaurant in the UK and
cooperates with partner bars around the
world.

Whiskies of Scotland

36 Gordon Street
Huntly
Aberdeenshire AB54 8EQ
Phone: +44 (0) 1466 795 105
www.thespiritsembassy.com
Owned by independent bottler Duncan
Taylor. In the assortment is of course the
whole Duncan Taylor range but also a
selection of their own single malt bottlings
called Whiskies of Scotland. A total of

almost 700 different expressions. On-line
shop with shipping worldwide.

The Whisky Shop Dufftown

1 Fife Street, Dufftown
Moray AB55 4AL
Phone: +44 (0)1340 821097
www.whiskyshopdufftown.com
Whisky specialist in Dufftown in the heart
of Speyside, wellknown to many of the
Speyside festival visitors. More than 500
single malts as well as other whiskies.
Arranges tastings as well as special events
during the Festivals. On-line ordering.

Cadenhead's Whisky Shop

30-32 Union Street
Campbeltown PA28 6JA
Phone: +44 (0)1586 551710
www.cadenhead.scot
Part of the chain of shops owned by
independent bottlers Cadenhead. Sells
Cadenhead's products and other whiskies
with a good range of Springbank. On-line
ordering.

Cadenhead´s Whisky Shop

172 Canongate, Royal Mile
Edinburgh EH8 8DF
Phone: +44 (0)131 556 5864
www.cadenhead.scot
The oldest shop in the chain owned by
Cadenhead. Sells Cadenhead's product
range and a good selection of other
whiskies and spirits. Recurrent tastings.
On-line ordering.

The Good Spirits Co.

23 Bath Street, Glasgow G2 1HW
Phone: +44 (0)141 258 8427
www.thegoodspiritsco.com
A specialist spirits store selling whisky,
bourbon, rum, vodka, tequila, gin, cognac
and armagnac, liqueurs and other spirits.
They also stock quality champagne,
fortified wines and cigars. There are more
than 300 single malts in the range as well
as plenty of whiskies from the rest of the
world.

A.D. Rattray´s Whisky Experience & Whisky Shop

32 Main Road, Kirkoswald
Ayrshire KA19 8HY
Phone: +44 (0) 1655 760308
www.adrattray.com
Recently revamped, this is a combination
of whisky shop, sample room and educa-
tional center owned by the independent
bottler A D Rattray. A wide range of
whiskies and tasting menus with different
themes are also available.

Loch Fyne Whiskies

Main Street, Inveraray, Argyll PA32 8UD
Phone: +44 (0)149 930 2219

36 Cockburn St
Edinburgh EH1 1PB
Phone: +44 (0)131 226 2134
www.lochfynewhiskies.com
A legendary shop and with a second shop
in Edinburgh since 2018. The range of
malt whiskies is large and they have their
own house blend, the prize-awarded Loch
Fyne, as well as their 'The Loch Fyne
Whisky Liqueur'. There is also a range of
house malts called 'The Inverarity'.

The Carnegie Whisky Cellars

The Carnegie Courthouse, Castle Street
IV25 3SD Dornoch
Phone: +44 (0)1862 811791
www.carnegiewhiskycellars.co.uk
Opened by Michael Hanratty in 2016, this
shop has already become a destination
for whisky enthusiasts from the UK
and abroad. The interior of the shop is
ravishing and the extensive range includes
all the latest releases as well as rare and
collectable bottles. International shipping.

Abbey Whisky

Dunfermline KY11 3BZ
Phone: +44 (0)800 051 7737
www.abbeywhisky.com
Family run online whisky shop specialising in exclusive, rare and old whiskies
from Scotland and the world. Apart from
a wide range of official and independent
bottlings, Abbey Whisky also selects their
own casks and bottle them under the name
'The Rare Casks' and 'The Secret Casks'.

The Scotch Whisky Experience

354 Castlehill, Royal Mile
Edinburgh EH1 2NE
Phone: +44 (0)131 220 0441
www.scotchwhiskyexperience.co.uk
The Scotch Whisky Experience is a must
for whisky devotees visiting Edinburgh
with an interactive visitor centre dedicated
to the history of Scotch whisky. This
five-star visitor attraction has an excellent
whisky shop with almost 300 different
whiskies in stock. Following an extensive
refurbishment, a brand new and interactive
shop has been opened.

Tyndrum Whisky

Tyndrum, Perthshire FK20 8RY
Phone: +44 (0)1301 702 084
www.tyndrumwhisky.com
The new name for Whisky Galore at The
Green Welly Stop. It was established at a
road junction between Glencoe and The
Trossachs 55 years ago and is now run by
the third generation of the family. Well
equipped with a nice range of Scottish
single malts, grains and blends but also
world whiskies and other spirits.

The Whisky Castle

6 Main Street, Tomintoul AB37 9EX
Phone: +44 (0)1807 580 213
www.whiskycastle.com
A legendary shop that has been selling
whisky for more than 100 years. Specialises in single malts (more than 600) and
single casks in particular. Also a range
of whiskies bottled exclusively for The
Whisky Castle.

Whiski Shop

4 North Bank Street
Edinburgh EH1 2LP
Phone: +44 (0)131 225 7224
www.whiskishop.com
www.whiskirooms.co.uk
A new concept located near Edinburgh
Castle, combining a shop and tasting room
combined with a bar and restaurant in 119
High Street. Also regular whisky tastings.
Online mail order.

Robbie's Drams
3 Sandgate, Ayr, South Ayrshire KA7 1BG
Phone: +44 (0)1292 262 135
www.robbieswhiskymerchants.com
An extensive range of whiskies available
both in store and from their on-line shop.
Specialists in single cask bottlings, closed
distillery bottlings, rare malts, limited
edition whisky and a nice range of their
own bottlings. Worldwide shipping.

The Whisky Barrel
Unit 3, Cupar, KY15 5JY
Phone: +44 (0)845 2248 156
www.thewhiskybarrel.com
Online specialist whisky shop based in
Edinburgh. They stock over 3,000 single
malt and blended whiskies including
Scotch, Japanese, Irish, Indian, Swedish
and their own casks.

Drinkmonger
100 Atholl Road, Pitlochry PH16 5BL
Phone: +44 (0)1796 470133

11 Bruntsfield Place
Edinburgh EH10 4HN
Phone: +44 (0)131 229 2205
www.drinkmonger.com
Owned by Royal Mile Whiskies, the idea
is to have a 50:50 split between wine and
specialist spirits with the addition of a
cigar assortment. The whisky range is a
good cross-section with some rarities and a
focus on local distilleries.

Luvian's
93 Bonnygate, Cupar, Fife KY15 4LG
Phone: +44 (0)1334 654 820

66 Market Street, St Andrews
Fife KY16 9NU
Phone: +44 (0)1334 477 752
www.luvians.com
A legendary wine and whisky retailer
owned by the three Luvian brothers with
a very nice selection of more than 1,200
whiskies (600 single malts).

The Stillroom by Deseo
Gleneagles Hotel
Auchterarder, Perthshire PH3 1NF
Phone: +44 (0) 1764 694 188
www.gleneagles.com
Located in the famous hotel, George Bry-
ers has selected a nice range of both rare
and collectible whiskies as well as single
malts from a large number of Scottish
distilleries.

Robertsons of Pitlochry
44-46 Atholl Road, Pitlochry PH16 5BX
Phone: +44 (0) 1796 472011
www.robertsonsofpitlochry.co.uk
With new owner since 2013, the shop has
grown to become one of Scotland's best.
An extensive range of both whisky and gin
is complemented by single malts bottled
under their own label. There's also an
excellent tasting room (The Bothy).

Robert Graham Ltd (3 shops)
194 Rose Street
Edinburgh EH2 4AZ
Phone: +44 (0)131 226 1874

111 West George Street
Glasgow G2 1QX
Phone: +44 (0)141 248 7283

9 Sussex Street, Cambridge CB1 1PA
Phone: +44 (0)1223 354 459
www.robertgraham1874.com
Established in 1874 this company
specialises in Scotch whisky and cigars.
A nice assortment of malt whiskies is
complemented by an impressive range of
cigars. They also bottle whiskies under
their own label.

The Speyside Whisky Shop
110A High Street
Aberlour AB38 9NX
Phone: +44 (0) 1340 871260
www.thespeysidewhisky.com
Opened in 2018, the shop is situated in the
very heart of Speyside, in Aberlour. The
owners specialise in highly collectable
single malts from a variety of distilleries.
Also a wide selection of craft gins.

The Jar
33 Ayr St
Troon KA10 6EB
Phone: +44 (0) 1292 319877
www.thejartroon.com
An extensive range of single malts (over
300) and Scottish gins. Specialises in rare
and collectable releases.

Whisky Please
24 Heather Avenue, Glasgow G61 3JE
Phone: +44 (0)781 806 1010
www.whiskyplease.co.uk
Online retailer of whiskies and other spirits. A nice presentation of each distillery
with a picture and text.

The Islay Whisky Shop
Shore Street, Bowmore, Islay PA43 7LB
Phone: +44 (0)1496 810 684
www.islaywhiskyshop.com
A must for any visitor to Islay, this shop
has an impressive range of Islay whiskies,
some of them very rare and limited.

Aberdeen Whisky Shop
474 Union Street, Aberdeen AB10 1TS
Phone: +44 (0)1224 647 433
www.aberdeenwhiskyshop.co.uk
A nice selection of whiskies but also other
spirits. Free tastings in the shop every
Saturday.

SOUTH AFRICA

WhiskyBrother (2 shops)
Shop 16 D Middle Mall,
Hyde Park Corner Shopping Centre,
Johannesburg
Phone: +27 (0)11 325 6261

Nicolway Mall (top level)
William Nicol Drive, Bryanston,
Johannesburg
Phone: +27 (0)81 081 8832
www.whiskybrother.com
A shop specialising in all things whisky
- apart from 400 different bottlings they
also sell glasses, books etc. Also sell
whiskies bottled exclusively for the shop.
Regular tastings and online shop. Also
run a whisky bar in Johannesburg with
more than 1,000 different whiskies to try.
The owner, Marc Pendlebury, is also the
organiser of The Only Whisky Show in
Johannesburg and Cape Town.

SWITZERLAND

P. Ullrich AG
Schneidergasse 27
4051 Basel
Phone: +41 (0)61 338 90 91
Another two shops in Basel:
Laufenstrasse 16 and Unt. Rebgasse 18,
one in Talacker 30 in Zürich and one in
Kramgasse 45 in Bern.
www.ullrich.ch
A very large range of wines, spirits, beers,
accessories and books. Over 800 kinds of
whisky with almost 600 single malt. On-
line ordering. Recently, they also founded
a whisky club with regular tastings and
offers. (www.whiskysinn.ch).

Eddie's Whiskies
Bahnhofstrasse/Dorfgasse 27
8810 Horgen
Phone: +41 (0)43 244 63 00
www.eddies.ch
A whisky specialist with more than 750
different whiskies in stock with emphasis
on single malts (more than 500 different).
Also arranges tastings.

Angels Share Shop
Unterdorfstrasse 15
5036 Oberentfelden
Phone: +41 (0)62 724 83 74
www.angelsshare.ch
A combined restaurant and whisky shop.
More than 600 different kinds of whisky
as well as a good range of cigars. Scores
extra points for short information and
photos of all distilleries. On-line ordering.

UKRAINE

WINETIME
Mykoly Bazhana 1E
Kyiv 02068
Phone: +38 (0)44 338 08 88
www.winetime.ua
WINETIME is the largest specialized
chain of wine, spirits and food shops in
Ukraine. The company runs 27 stores in
14 regions of Ukraine. An impressive selection of spirits with over 1000 whiskies
of which 600 are malt whiskies. On-line
ordering. Also regular whisky tastings.

USA

Binny's Beverage Depot
5100 W. Dempster (Head Office)
Skokie, IL 60077
Phone:
Internet orders, 888-942-9463 (toll free)
www.binnys.com
A chain of no less than 45 stores in the
Chicago area, covering everything within
wine and spirits. Some of the stores also
have a gourmet grocery, cheese shop
and, for cigar lovers, a walk-in humidor.
Also lots of regular events in the stores.
The range is impressive with more than
2200 whisk(e)y including 600 single malt
Scotch, 500 bourbons, 300 rye and more.
Among other products more than 700
kinds of tequila and mezcal, 600 vodkas,
475 rums and 300 gins.

Statistics

The information on the following pages is based
on figures from Scotch Whisky Association (SWA), Drinks International
and directly from the producers.

The Top 30 Whiskies of the World

Sales figures for 2020 (units in million 9-litre cases)

McDowell´s No. 1 (Diageo/United Spirits), Indian whisky — 25,7
Imperial Blue (Pernod Ricard), Indian whisky — 21,3
Officer´s Choice (Allied Blenders & Distillers), Indian whisky — 20,8
Royal Stag (Pernod Ricard), Indian whisky — 18,5
Johnnie Walker (Diageo), Scotch whisky — 14,1
Jack Daniel´s (Brown-Forman), Tennessee whiskey — 12,3
Jim Beam (Beam Suntory), Bourbon — 10,7
Hayward´s Fine (Diageo/United Spirits), Indian whisky — 9,7
8PM (Radico Khaitan), Indian whisky — 8,4
Crown Royal (Diageo), Canadian whisky — 8,1
Jameson (Pernod Ricard), Irish whiskey — 7,7
Ballantine´s (Pernod Ricard), Scotch whisky — 7,0
Blenders Pride (Pernod Ricard), Indian whisky — 6,6
Bagpiper (Diageo/United Spirits), Indian whisky — 5,3
Kakubin (Suntory), Japanese whisky — 5,1
Old Tavern (Diageo/United Spirits), Indian whisky — 4,5
Royal Challenge (Diageo/United Spirits), Indian whisky — 4,3
Grant´s (Wm Grand & Sons), Scotch whisky — 3,6
Black Nikka Clear (Asahi Breweries), Japanese whisky — 3,3
William Lawson´s (Bacardi), Scotch whisky — 3,3
Chivas Regal (Pernod Ricard), Scotch whisky — 3,2
Director´s Special (Diageo/United Spirits), Indian whisky — 3,1
Black & White (Diageo), Scotch whisky — 2,9
Torys (Beam Suntory), Japanese whisky — 2,9
Sterling Reserve Premium (Allied Blenders & Distillers), Indian whisky — 2,8
Dewar´s (Bacardi), Scotch whisky — 2,6
Famous Grouse (Edrington), Scotch whisky — 2,6
Label 5 (La Martiniquaise), Scotch whisky — 2,6
Royal Green (ADS Spirits), Indian whisky — 2,5
Maker´s Mark (Beam Suntory), Bourbon — 2,4

Source: Drinks International, The Millionaires Club 2021

Global Exports of Scotch by Region 2020

Volume (litres of pure alcohol)

Region	000s of litres	Change
Asia & Oceania	75,733	-22,8
Eastern Europe exc EU	9,785	+12,0
European Union	122,660	-5,8
Latin America & Carribean	34,074	-13,1
Middle East & North Africa	8,182	-37,7
North America	46,835	-12,7
Sub-Saharan Africa	15,061	-15,0
Western Europe exc EU	8,109	+35,6
Total	**320,439**	**-12,6**

Value (£ Sterling)

Region	000s of £	Change
Asia & Oceania	998,003	-19,4
Eastern Europe exc EU	35,357	-4,8
European Union	1,255,605	-15,1
Latin America & Carribean	259,680	-31,3
Middle East & North Africa	120,961	-49,4
North America	904,016	-29,6
Sub-Saharan Africa	137,389	-22,0
Western Europe exc EU	92,691	+11,5
Total	**3,803,704**	**-22,6**

Source: Scotch Whisky Association

Export of Scotch Whisky 2020

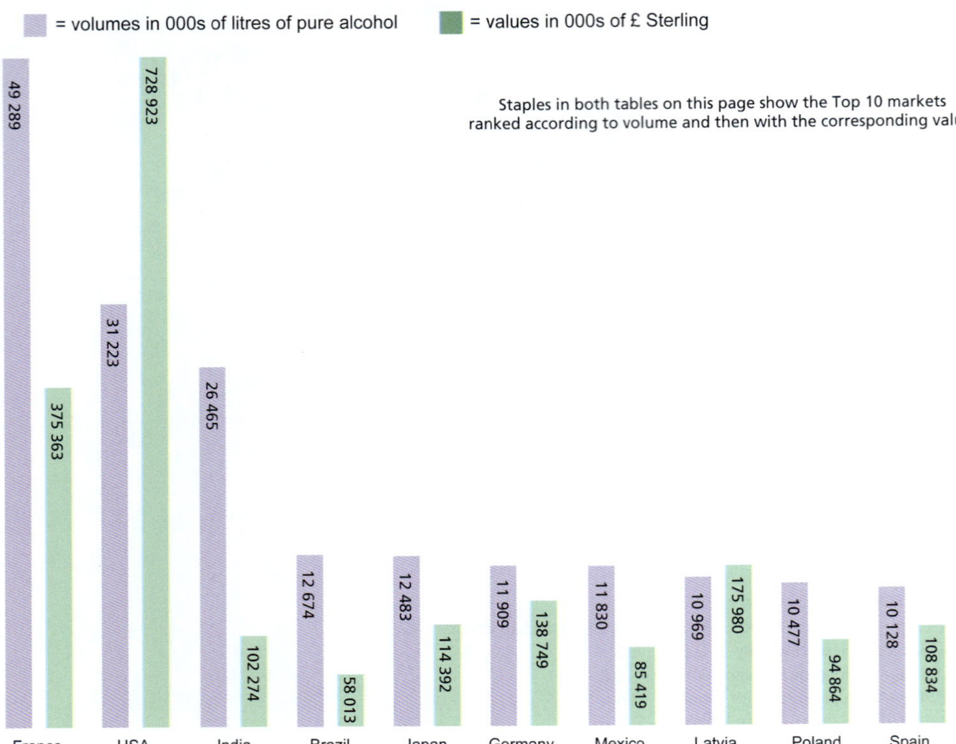

Export of Single Malt Scotch 2020

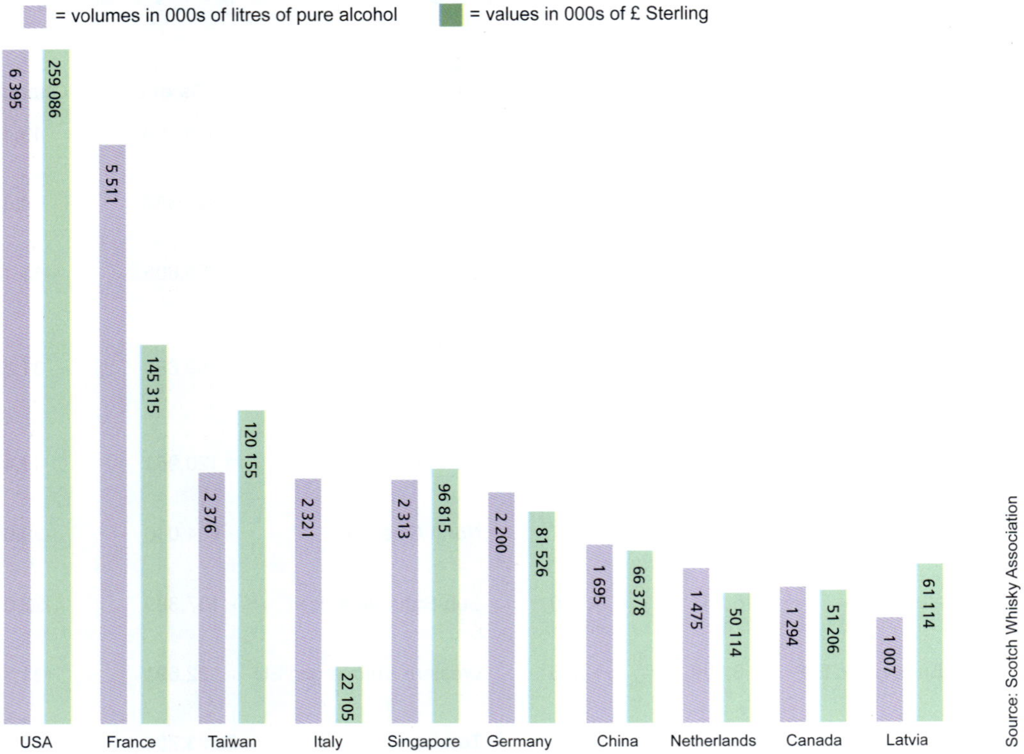

Distillery Capacity

Litres of pure alcohol - Scottish, active distilleries only

Distillery	Litres	Distillery	Litres	Distillery	Litres
Glenlivet	21 000 000	Bowmore	2 150 000	Benromach	700 000
Glenfiddich	21 000 000	Ardbeg	2 100 000	Kilchoman	650 000
Macallan	15 000 000	Ben Nevis	2 000 000	Kingsbarns	600 000
Roseisle	12 500 000	Bruichladdich	2 000 000	Speyside	600 000
Ailsa Bay	12 000 000	Glendronach	2 000 000	Annandale	500 000
Glen Ord	11 000 000	Inchdairnie	2 000 000	Ardnamurchan	500 000
Teaninich	10 200 000	Knockdhu	2 000 000	Bonnington	500 000
Dalmunach	10 000 000	Balblair	1 800 000	The Clydeside	500 000
Balvenie	7 000 000	Pulteney	1 800 000	Royal Lochnagar	500 000
Caol Ila	6 500 000	The Borders	1 600 000	Torabhaig	500 000
Glenmorangie	6 500 000	Bladnoch	1 500 000	Brew Dog	450 000
Glen Grant	6 200 000	Glen Spey	1 500 000	Harris	400 000
Dufftown	6 000 000	Knockando	1 400 000	Glasgow	365 000
Glen Keith	6 000 000	Glen Garioch	1 370 000	Glenturret	340 000
Mannochmore	6 000 000	Glencadam	1 300 000	Edradour	260 000
Auchroisk	5 900 000	Scapa	1 300 000	Holyrood	250 000
Miltonduff	5 800 000	Falkirk	1 200 000	Lindores Abbey	225 000
Glen Moray	5 700 000	Lochranza	1 200 000	Arbikie	200 000
Glenrothes	5 600 000	Glenglassaugh	1 100 000	Isle of Raasay	200 000
Linkwood	5 600 000	Glengoyne	1 100 000	Lochlea	200 000
Dailuaine	5 200 000	Ardnahoe	1 000 000	Burn O´Bennie	180 000
Glendullan	5 000 000	Ardross	1 000 000	Glen Wyvis	140 000
Loch Lomond	5 000 000	Tobermory	1 000 000	Wolfburn	135 000
Tomatin	5 000 000	Oban	870 000	Ballindalloch	100 000
Clynelish	4 800 000	Brora	800 000	Eden Mill	100 000
Kininvie	4 800 000	Glen Scotia	800 000	Ncn´ean	100 000
Tormore	4 800 000	Aberargie	750 000	Daftmill	65 000
Ardmore	4 725 000	Glengyle	750 000	Dornoch	30 000
Longmorn	4 500 000	Lagg	750 000	Strathearn	30 000
Speyburn	4 500 000	Springbank	750 000	Abhainn Dearg	20 000
Dalmore	4 300 000				
Glenburgie	4 250 000				
Royal Brackla	4 240 000				
Allt-a-Bhainne	4 200 000				
Braeval	4 200 000				
Glentauchers	4 200 000				
Tamnavulin	4 200 000				
Craigellachie	4 100 000				
Glenallachie	4 000 000				
Tamdhu	4 000 000				
Aberlour	3 800 000				
Mortlach	3 800 000				
Glenlossie	3 700 000				
Benrinnes	3 500 000				
Glenfarclas	3 500 000				
Aberfeldy	3 400 000				
Cardhu	3 400 000				
Macduff	3 400 000				
Laphroaig	3 300 000				
Talisker	3 300 000				
Tomintoul	3 300 000				
Aultmore	3 200 000				
Inchgower	3 200 000				
Deanston	3 000 000				
Tullibardine	3 000 000				
Balmenach	2 900 000				
Benriach	2 800 000				
Blair Athol	2 800 000				
Bunnahabhain	2 700 000				
Glen Elgin	2 700 000				
Lagavulin	2 600 000				
Strathmill	2 600 000				
Auchentoshan	2 500 000				
Glenkinchie	2 500 000				
Highland Park	2 500 000				
Strathisla	2 450 000				
Jura	2 400 000				
Cragganmore	2 200 000				
Dalwhinnie	2 200 000				
Fettercairn	2 200 000				

Summary of Malt Distillery Capacity by Owner

Owner (number of distilleries)	Litres of alcohol	% of Industry
Diageo (29)	122 340 000	29,5
Pernod Ricard (13)	76 500 000	18,4
William Grant (4)	44 800 000	10,8
Edrington Group (3)	23 100 000	5,6
Bacardi (John Dewar & Sons) (5)	18 340 000	4,4
Beam Suntory (5)	14 045 000	3,4
Emperador Inc (Whyte & Mackay) (4)	13 100 000	3,2
Pacific Spirits (Inver House) (5)	13 000 000	3,1
Moët Hennessy (Glenmorangie) (2)	8 600 000	2,1
Distell (Burn Stewart) (3)	6 700 000	1,6
Campari (Glen Grant) (1)	6 200 000	1,5
Benriach Distillery Co (3)	5 900 000	1,4
Loch Lomond Group (2)	5 800 000	1,4
La Martiniquaise (Glen Moray) (1)	5 700 000	1,4
Ian Macleod Distillers (2)	5 100 000	1,2
Tomatin Distillery Co (1)	5 000 000	1,2
Angus Dundee (2)	4 600 000	1,1
The Glenallachie Consortium (1)	4 000 000	1,0
J & G Grant (Glenfarclas) (1)	3 500 000	0,8
Picard (Tullibardine) (1)	3 000 000	0,7
John Fergus & Co. (Inchdairnie) (1)	2 000 000	0,5
Nikka (Ben Nevis Distillery) (1)	2 000 000	0,5
Rémy Cointreau (Bruichladdich) (1)	2 000 000	0,5
Isle of Arran Distillers (2)	1 950 000	< 0,5
The Three Stills Co. (The Borders) (1)	1 600 000	< 0,5
J & A Mitchell (2)	1 500 000	< 0,5
David Prior (Bladnoch) (1)	1 500 000	< 0,5
Stewart family (Falkirk) (1)	1 200 000	< 0,5
Hunter Laing (Ardnahoe) (1)	1 000 000	< 0,5
Greenwood Distillers (Ardross) (1)	1 000 000	< 0,5
The Perth Distilling Co. (Aberargie) (1)	750 000	< 0,5
Gordon & MacPhail (Benromach) (1)	700 000	< 0,5
Wemyss Malts (Kingsbarns) (1)	600 000	< 0,5
Harvey´s of Edinburgh (Speyside) (1)	600 000	< 0,5
Others (26)	7 890 000	1,9
Total (130)	**414 665 000**	

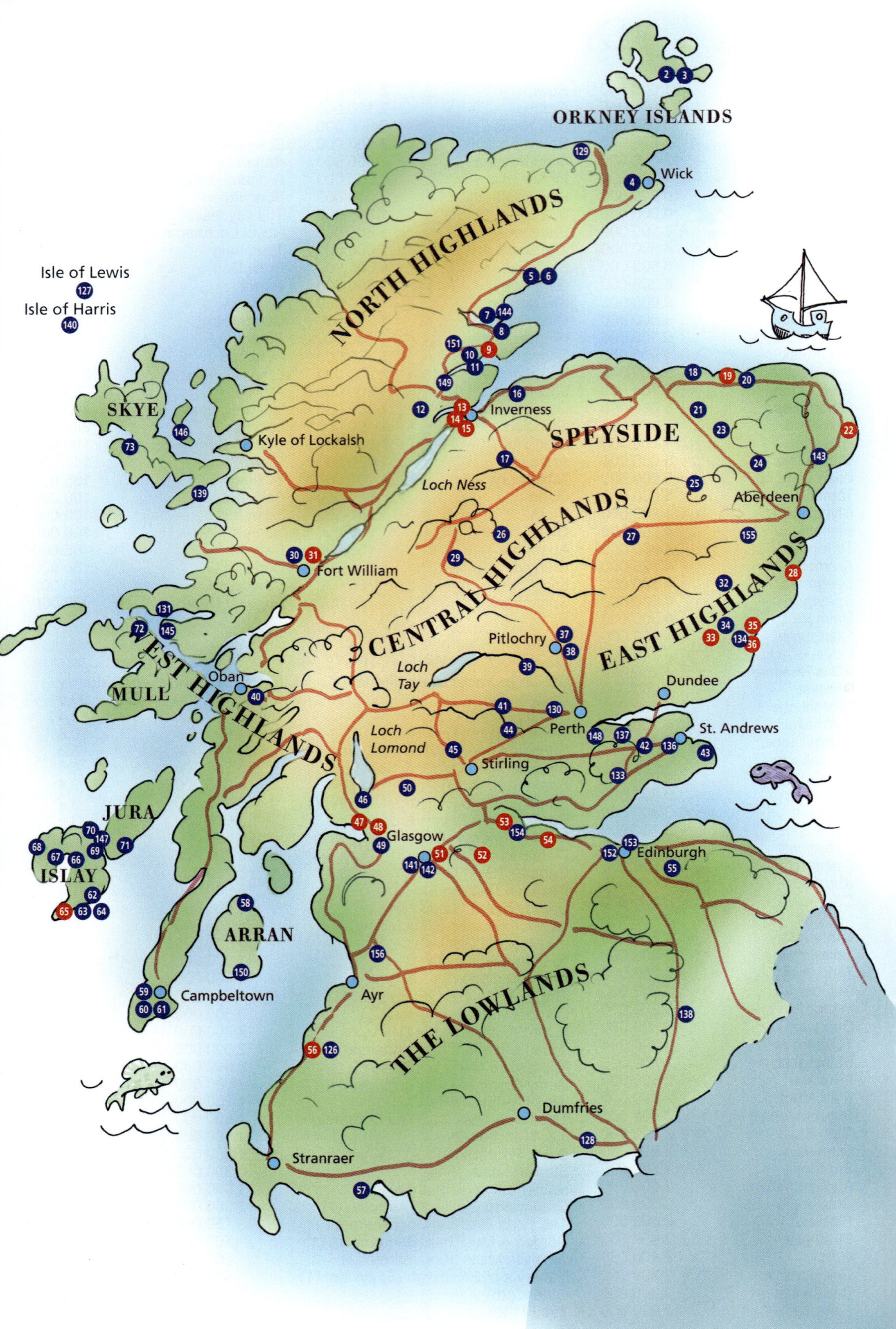

ORKNEY ISLANDS
Wick
NORTH HIGHLANDS
Isle of Lewis
Isle of Harris
SKYE
Kyle of Lockalsh
Inverness
SPEYSIDE
Loch Ness
Aberdeen
CENTRAL HIGHLANDS
Fort William
EAST HIGHLANDS
WEST HIGHLANDS
MULL
Oban
Pitlochry
Loch Tay
Dundee
Perth
St. Andrews
Loch Lomond
Stirling
JURA
Glasgow
ISLAY
Edinburgh
ARRAN
Campbeltown
Ayr
THE LOWLANDS
Dumfries
Stranraer

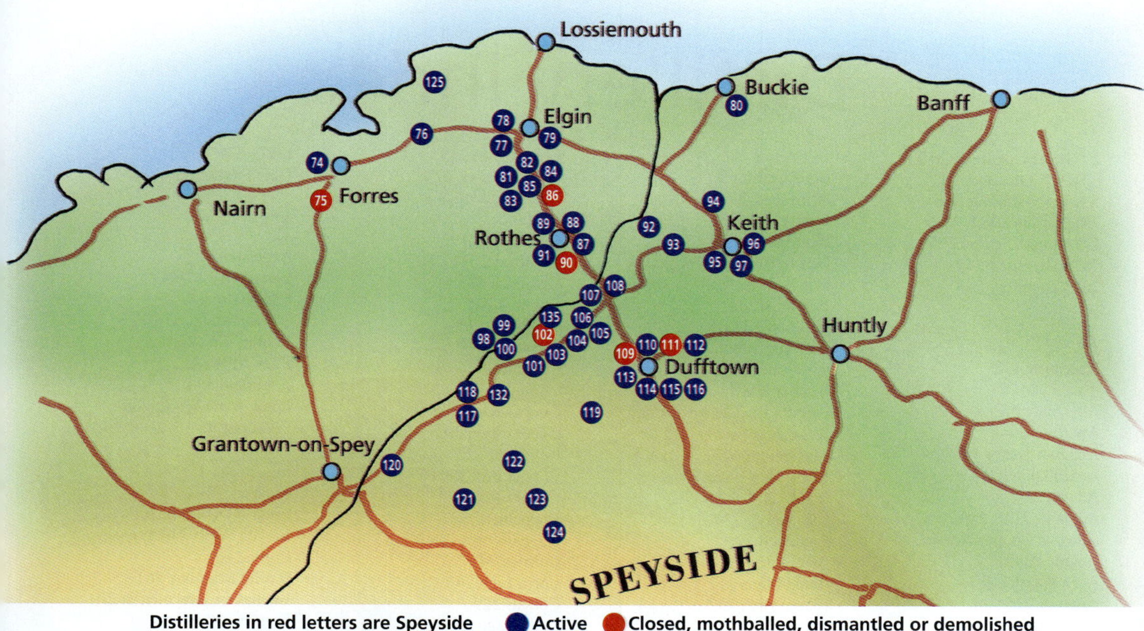

Distilleries in red letters are Speyside ● Active ● Closed, mothballed, dismantled or demolished

c = Closed, m = Mothballed, dm = Dismantled, d = Demolished

148 Aberargie
39 Aberfeldy
106 Aberlour
127 Abhainn Dearg
126 Ailsa Bay
119 Allt-a-Bhainne
128 Annandale
134 Arbikie
62 Ardbeg
25 Ardmore
147 Ardnahoe
131 Ardnamurchan
151 Ardross
58 Arran
49 Auchentoshan
92 Auchroisk
94 Aultmore
7 Balblair
132 Ballindalloch
120 Balmenach
113 Balvenie
19 Banff (d)
30 Ben Nevis
82 Benriach
104 Benrinnes
74 Benromach
9 Ben Wyvis (c)
57 Bladnoch
37 Blair Athol
153 Bonnington
138 Borders
66 Bowmore
124 Braeval
5 Brora
67 Bruichladdich
70 Bunnahabhain
155 Burn O´Bennie
69 Caol Ila
90 Caperdonich (c)
99 Cardhu
142 Clydeside
6 Clynelish
86 Coleburn (dm)
109 Convalmore (dm)
118 Cragganmore
108 Craigellachie
42 Daftmill
103 Dailuaine
75 Dallas Dhu (c)
11 Dalmore
135 Dalmunach
29 Dalwhinnie

45 Deanston
144 Dornoch
110 Dufftown
136 Eden Mill
38 Edradour
154 Falkirk
32 Fettercairn
141 Glasgow
13 Glen Albyn (d)
105 Glenallachie
76 Glenburgie
34 Glencadam
23 Glendronach
116 Glendullan
85 Glen Elgin
35 Glenesk (dm)
101 Glenfarclas
112 Glenfiddich
52 Glen Flagler (d)
24 Glen Garioch
18 Glenglassaugh
50 Glengoyne
87 Glen Grant
60 Glengyle
96 Glen Keith
55 Glenkinchie
122 Glenlivet
31 Glenlochy (d)
83 Glenlossie
14 Glen Mhor (d)
8 Glenmorangie
78 Glen Moray
12 Glen Ord
89 Glenrothes
61 Glen Scotia
91 Glenspey
93 Glentauchers
41 Glenturret
22 Glenugie (dm)
28 Glenury Royal (d)
149 Glen Wyvis
140 Harris
2 Highland Park
152 Holyrood
133 Inchdairnie
102 Imperial (d)
80 Inchgower
47 Inverleven (d)
146 Isle of Raasay
71 Jura
68 Kilchoman
51 Kinclaith (d)

43 Kingsbarns
114 Kininvie
100 Knockando
21 Knockdhu
56 Ladyburn (dm)
63 Lagavulin
150 Lagg
64 Laphroaig
137 Lindores Abbey
79 Linkwood
48 Littlemill (d)
156 Lochlea
46 Loch Lomond
36 Lochside (d)
143 Lone Wolf
84 Longmorn
107 Macallan
20 Macduff
81 Mannochmore
15 Millburn (dm)
77 Miltonduff
115 Mortlach
145 Nc´nean
33 North Port (d)
40 Oban
111 Pittyvaich (d)
65 Port Ellen (dm)
4 Pulteney
53 Rosebank (c)
125 Roseisle
16 Royal Brackla
27 Royal Lochnagar
54 St Magdalene (dm)
3 Scapa
88 Speyburn
26 Speyside
59 Springbank
130 Strathearn
97 Strathisla
95 Strathmill
73 Talisker
98 Tamdhu
123 Tamnavulin
10 Teaninich
72 Tobermory
17 Tomatin
121 Tomintoul
139 Torabhaig
117 Tormore
44 Tullibardine
129 Wolfburn

2 Highland Park
3 Scapa
4 Pulteney
5 Brora
6 Clynelish
7 Balblair
8 Glenmorangie
9 Ben Wyvis (c)
10 Teaninich
11 Dalmore
12 Glen Ord
13 Glen Albyn (d)
14 Glen Mhor (d)
15 Millburn (dm)
16 Royal Brackla
17 Tomatin
18 Glenglassaugh
19 Banff (d)
20 Macduff
21 Knockdhu
22 Glenugie (dm)
23 Glendronach
24 Glen Garioch
25 Ardmore
26 Speyside
27 Royal Lochnagar
28 Glenury Royal (d)
29 Dalwhinnie
30 Ben Nevis
31 Glenlochy (d)
32 Fettercairn
33 North Port (d)
34 Glencadam
35 Glenesk (dm)
36 Lochside (d)
37 Blair Athol
38 Edradour
39 Aberfeldy
40 Oban
41 Glenturret
42 Daftmill
43 Kingsbarns
44 Tullibardine
45 Deanston
46 Loch Lomond
47 Inverleven (d)
48 Littlemill (d)
49 Auchentoshan
50 Glengoyne
51 Kinclaith (d)
52 Glen Flagler (d)
53 Rosebank (c)

54 St Magdalene (dm)
55 Glenkinchie
56 Ladyburn (dm)
57 Bladnoch
58 Arran
59 Springbank
60 Glengyle
61 Glen Scotia
62 Ardbeg
63 Lagavulin
64 Laphroaig
65 Port Ellen (dm)
66 Bowmore
67 Bruichladdich
68 Kilchoman
69 Caol Ila
70 Bunnahabhain
71 Jura
72 Tobermory
73 Talisker
74 Benromach
75 Dallas Dhu (c)
76 Glenburgie
77 Miltonduff
78 Glen Moray
79 Linkwood
80 Inchgower
81 Mannochmore
82 Benriach
83 Glenlossie
84 Longmorn
85 Glen Elgin
86 Coleburn (dm)
87 Glen Grant
88 Speyburn
89 Glenrothes
90 Caperdonich (c)
91 Glenspey
92 Auchroisk
93 Glentauchers
94 Aultmore
95 Strathmill
96 Glen Keith
97 Strathisla
98 Tamdhu
99 Cardhu
100 Knockando
101 Glenfarclas
102 Imperial (d)
103 Dailuaine
104 Benrinnes
105 Glenallachie

106 Aberlour
107 Macallan
108 Craigellachie
109 Convalmore (dm)
110 Dufftown
111 Pittyvaich (d)
112 Glenfiddich
113 Balvenie
114 Kininvie
115 Mortlach
116 Glendullan
117 Tormore
118 Cragganmore
119 Allt-a-Bhainne
120 Balmenach
121 Tomintoul
122 Glenlivet
123 Tamnavulin
124 Braeval
125 Roseisle
126 Ailsa Bay
127 Abhainn Dearg
128 Annandale
129 Wolfburn
130 Strathearn
131 Ardnamurchan
132 Ballindalloch
133 Inchdairnie
134 Arbikie
135 Dalmunach
136 Eden Mill
137 Lindores Abbey
138 Borders
139 Torabhaig
140 Harris
141 Glasgow
142 Clydeside
143 Lone Wolf
144 Dornoch
145 Nc´nean
146 Isle of Raasay
147 Ardnahoe
148 Aberargie
149 Glen Wyvis
150 Lagg
151 Ardross
152 Holyrood
153 Bonnington
154 Falkirk
155 Burn O´Bennie
156 Lochlea

Distillery Index

Distillery Index